For Finlay and Jasper - two future Reds.
I hope.

First published in Great Britain in 2020 by Richard de la Rivière

A CIP catalogue record for this book is available from the British Library
ISBN 978-1-5272-6841-8

Printed by Catford Print Centre

Author
Richard de la Rivière

Production and design
Daniel Spencer

LIVERPOOL F.C.

THE
PREMIER LEAGUE
YEARS

ACKNOWLEDGEMENTS

Various newspapers, magazines and websites have been used in the compilation of this book. They include the phenomenal lfchistory.net, without which the project may have taken twice as long. Match reports I used for reference came mainly from The Guardian and the Liverpool Echo. Player autobiographies and the wonderful fanzine Through the Wind and Rain provided no end of amusing stories or quotes that have gone into the book. The Anfield Wrap website was another vital resource as I tackled the 2010s. Books by Simon Hughes, Brian Reade and Stephen F Kelly also proved most valuable. I'd like to thank Dan Spencer, a fellow Red, for designing the book; Alasdair McKenzie, not only for his proofreading, but for explaining to me what a dangling participle is and removing them all; Matt Collins who, despite supporting Manchester City, gave me some much-needed feedback; and my wife Katy for having the patience to put up with me writing the book in the first place.

Richard de la Rivière

INTRODUCTION

The timing of this book's release couldn't be better, coinciding as it does with Liverpool becoming champions of England for the first time in 30 years. But I got lucky there. I first had the idea in the summer of 2014, after Liverpool had gone so close to winning the Premier League. Writing it during the torturous 2014-15 season and releasing it on the back of a 6-1 defeat at Stoke wouldn't have felt right.

I eventually began the project in January 2019, hoping it would be ready at the end of that season. I soon realised I couldn't finish it in five or six months. It would be a year's work. Publishing it just as Liverpool won their sixth European Cup would have been great, but for it to be released within weeks of Jordan Henderson lifting the Premier League trophy is perfect.

Despite the book's title, its content focuses on all first-team competitions. There's at least one paragraph on each of the 1,492 matches Liverpool have played since the summer of 1992, starting with the Charity Shield, when Graeme Souness unveiled his three centre-back system comprising Nick Tanner, Mark Wright and David Burrows. It goes all the way through to Jurgen Klopp's champions securing their 99th Premier League point at St James' Park in July 2020.

Writing 'Liverpool FC - The Premier League Years' has been a thrilling ride, but not as much as experiencing these moments first time around as a supporter. I can only hope I have done justice to this era of Liverpool FC's history.

Richard de la Rivière

1992-93

"Least said, Souness mended."

I f the 1991-92 campaign had been largely miserable, Liverpool's fortunes were about to plummet further, because the inaugural Premier League season was utterly abject. It was a season of three below-par goalkeepers and atrocious defending. A season when a Liverpool striker entered footballing folklore, guilty of one of the worst misses of all time. A season of nightmares against Chesterfield, Spartak Moscow, Coventry and Bolton. Another season blighted by injuries and another season of Graeme Souness in the manager's chair. In choosing a moment to sum up Liverpool's 1992-93 season, I can do little worse than quote a story from Ronnie Whelan's autobiography, which detailed a post-match dressing-room scene after a heavy defeat at Blackburn, who just happened to be managed by Kenny Dalglish. "Souey went ballistic," Whelan recalled. "[He] started ranting about the older players. He didn't name us but was referring to me, Nicol, Barnes and Rush. He'd raised it as an issue several times in the months before. I was fuming inside because, number one, there was no acknowledgement from him that he might be at fault too. And, number two, it wasn't true. I said to Souey, 'Look it's not as simple as that. You try talking to them [the younger players] and they tell you to fuck off.' That only made him worse. 'Who? Who tells you that?' I just shrugged my shoulders. 'Tell me who they are and I'll back you up.' And I said, 'Just like you're backing me up now?' He flipped after that, and started screaming, 'You tell me!' And I wouldn't reply. It just descended into a shouting match. I snapped back at him, 'Just fuck off and leave me alone!'"

Liverpool made two signings as they geared up for the new Premier League era. They paid Watford £1 million for David James, who was pitched in at the deep end when Bruce Grobbelaar put country before club. He was far from ready to be Liverpool's first-choice keeper. Paul Stewart, who signed for £2.3 million from Spurs, was battling personal demons which eventually came to light in 2016. He had been sexually abused by a football coach for four years from the age of 11. He spent much of his Anfield career at the mercy of alcohol, cocaine and ecstasy and was a shadow of the player who had been man of the match in the 1991 FA Cup Final.

The performances of these two were to be a microcosm of the season ahead. Fault lines ran right through the heart of the club. The 39-year-old Souness was despised by many for selling the story of his heart operation to the reviled Sun newspaper on the third anniversary of the Hillsborough Disaster. The paper has been boycotted on Merseyside ever since the monstrous lies they told about the 1989 tragedy. And, although far less serious, his public congratulating of John Major and the Conservative Party upon winning the 1992 General Election in April went down badly in Britain's most socialist city.

From a footballing viewpoint, Souness had been a failure since his April 1991 appointment. He may have won the FA Cup in 1992, but five of Liverpool's six opponents had been from the lower divisions. Of those, Bristol Rovers, Ipswich Town and Portsmouth had come alarmingly close to eliminating the Reds. A sixth-place finish in Division One was Liverpool's worst since 1965. His transfer strategy can be summed up no better than the fact that he chose not to sign Peter Schmeichel and Eric Cantona. He later claimed he turned down the Frenchman because he was trying to get rid of older, troublesome players, not sign them. His only successful purchase was Rob Jones from Crewe. Most of the Scot's other signings were flops. Not only had the brilliant Peter Beardsley been sold for a measly £1 million, he was replaced by the vastly inferior Dean Saunders, who cost nearly three times more. The Welshman was a number 9, whereas Beardsley played deeper, creating for others. That position wasn't filled until the acquisition of Nigel Clough a year later – and he was even worse than Saunders.

Mark Wright had come to Liverpool to stiffen a defensive line which had lost its impregnability since the days of Alan Hansen and Mark Lawrenson. Although he was quickly named captain, the England international was accident-prone and defended too deep. Any game plan based on the defence maintaining a high line was impossible to implement with Wright. He would later play his best football in a three-man central defence when Roy Evans was in charge. Under Souness, he was regularly one of the worst performers and had the captaincy taken off him during the autumn of 1992. Two more defenders - Torben Piechnik, fresh from winning the European Championship with Denmark, and Stig Inge Bjornebye - would be signed during the season. Souness will remember neither with any fondness, although, like Wright, Bjornebye would go on to flourish under Evans in a different system.

Michael Thomas had replaced Steve McMahon in midfield halfway through 1991-92. He missed most of the rest of Souness's reign with injury but did score a wonderful goal at Wembley. Istvan Kozma was miles off Liverpool standard. Unlike the departing Ray Houghton, Mark Walters was wildly inconsistent but had at least provided Anfield with its two most celebrated moments in the 1991-92 season – the winner against Auxerre in the UEFA Cup and the clincher against Manchester United, which handed the title to Leeds, meaning that United had gone a quarter of a century without winning the league. Perhaps Liverpool supporters overdosed on their rivals' misery on that sunny Sunday afternoon in April 1992. As the Kop gloated mercilessly, who could have guessed that Liverpool would have to wait even longer to land England's biggest prize again?

During the summer of 1992, Souness reassured Grobbelaar that he would be his first-choice goalkeeper ahead of James and Mike Hooper. The unpredictable

Zimbabwean then flew home for a World Cup qualifier, beginning a feud with Souness, which would last for the rest of the season. He would play in just five Premier League matches. The inexperienced James took over and after a bright start, his confidence ebbed away as the error count mounted up. Hooper was little more than third choice. When required to play, he satisfied few.

Grobbelaar was between the posts for the Charity Shield, a 4-3 defeat to champions Leeds, in which Cantona scored three times. Liverpool could only name four substitutes, instead of the permitted five, because nobody else was fit, not the best way to start a season. Steve Nicol, Jan Molby, Steve McManaman, Jones and Thomas were missing from the team which had beaten Sunderland in the FA Cup Final, while Ray Houghton had been sold and Barnes was still injured. Ian Rush and Saunders scored a goal each, but few were convinced that two number 9s could dovetail, despite their Wales partnership. Both pressed with menace, but Rush was coming off the back of his second indifferent season in four years since his return from Juventus, and most of Saunders' goals in his debut season had come against low-level sides, particularly in Europe. Liverpool's third was a comical own goal by Gordon Strachan, who failed to keep out Wright's tame shot. Three days after the Charity Shield, the sides met again in a testimonial for Jim Beglin, who had broken a leg in a cup tie at Goodison in 1987. Rush scored twice. Jamie Redknapp and Saunders also netted in a 4-1 win at Elland Road.

With Grobbelaar departing for Harare in midweek, James was the stand-out player in Liverpool's first-ever Premier League match, as he made several outstanding saves, including three in one fourth-minute attack. But his performance was the only bright spot in a dreadful 1-0 defeat at Nottingham Forest, who would end the season rock bottom in Brian Clough's final year as manager. It was the first league match to be televised by Sky Sports, whose coverage included a two-hour build-up to the 4pm kick-off. It was also the first league match to feature a new rule, forbidding goalkeepers to handle back passes. Liverpool, who donned a hideous green kit, fielded a three-man defence of Nick Tanner, Wright and David Burrows, which failed to deal with the twin threat of Teddy Sheringham and Roy Keane, whose runs from midfield caused havoc. Whelan was the sitting midfielder, with Stewart and Thomas ahead of him. Nicol and Walters were the wide midfielders, offering little defensively. Rush and Saunders were up front. McManaman and Ronny Rosenthal were substitutes, replacing Rush and Walters respectively. Rush went off with a groin injury at the end of an unhappy first half in which he was booked for kicking the ball away – another new rule. The lack of full backs was ruthlessly exposed by Forest. Sheringham scored the only goal in the 29th minute, receiving the ball in oceans of space on the left, before cutting inside Tanner and firing into the top corner. Keane and Stuart Pearce should have been sent off in the first half, but the Reds could have few other complaints. They were totally outplayed and barely threatened. At one point in the second half, a policeman had to calm Souness down when he was berating Wright.

Jones returned for the midweek visit of Sheffield United, Anfield's first Premier League match. Souness switched to an orthodox back four, but it couldn't prevent Brian Deane firing the leaders into a 36th-minute lead. Walters scored Liverpool's first Premier League goal, firing in from outside the box at the Kop end. Stewart crowned his home debut with the winner on 65 minutes. Those who had high hopes for Stewart would have taken heart, but his conversion of Saunders' cross was the high point of his ill-fated Liverpool career.

The Reds featured on Sky Sports again on the second weekend of the season, when Arsenal strolled their way to an easy 2-0 win, with goals coming from Anders Limpar and Ian Wright. With Barnes, Rush, Nicol and Stewart absent, The Times concluded that "the sun is setting on Liverpool's golden era." As with the Forest defeat, Tanner's deficiencies were exposed, but numerous saves from James prevented a thrashing.

Three frustrating draws followed. A fluke by Walters handed the Reds the lead at newly-promoted Ipswich. Chris Kiwomya headed an equaliser. A penalty from Molby, which even Souness admitted shouldn't have been given, restored the lead. Chris Kiwomya made it 2-2 in injury time. The Times concluded that Liverpool didn't even deserve a point, with Ipswich outplaying them for the most part.

It was the same story against Leeds, when a 2-1 lead melted away in the closing stages. A stunning volley by Gary McAllister gave Leeds an early lead, which they threatened to extend on numerous occasions, only for Whelan's impudent curler to level the scores just before half-time. Molby beat John Lukic from the spot with 20 minutes left. Again, Liverpool couldn't hold on. Lee Chapman bundled in a late equaliser and had another goal disallowed for a foul on Steve Harkness. Souness refused to fulfil his post-match media duties. Perhaps he didn't want to be asked why he'd selected four central midfielders with a fifth on the bench, Saunders and Redknapp on the wings with Walters a sub and Stewart up front. A draw at the champions didn't seem a bad result, but Leeds were about to spend the season staving off relegation.

The new £8 million Centenary Stand was opened before a midweek home match with Southampton on 1st September to mark the 100th anniversary of the club's first match at Anfield. On that occasion, Liverpool had beaten Rotherham 7-1. The goals didn't flow so freely this time. Kerry Dixon scored for Saints on 52 minutes. Wright headed in Molby's cross to score his first Liverpool goal. Souness's decision to withdraw the impressive Redknapp was greeted with boos by the crowd. The game ended 1-1. After six matches, Liverpool had made their worst start in 38 years and were languishing in 16th out of 22 teams, just three points clear of the relegation zone. The increase of 4,600 seats took the capacity to 45,000, but the attendance was a mere 30,024.

There was finally a big moment to celebrate when Chelsea came to town. Vinnie Jones bullied Redknapp for 90 minutes, but the young midfielder slid an injury-time winner into the Kop goal. Saunders, in his last match before joining Aston Villa, had opened the scoring with a cute glancing header before high-fiving fans in the Paddock. Eighteen players had been used in seven matches, three more than in the whole of the 1978-79 season.

A quirk of the fixture list pitted the Reds against Sheffield United for the second time in eight Premier League fixtures. An abysmal performance resulted in a 1-0 away defeat, with Adrian Littlejohn scoring after four minutes. "I've got nothing constructive to say," said Stewart, refusing to conduct a radio interview.

The European Cup Winners' Cup provided a welcome distraction, with Stewart scoring the first two goals in a 6-1 win over Cypriot minnows Apollon Limassol. Rush scored the other four, taking his European tally for the club to 19, overtaking Roger Hunt's record of 17.

Back on the domestic front, Liverpool's season was about to hit its nadir. A trip to Villa Park saw Rosenthal produce one of football's all-time worst misses, as he rounded Nigel Spink, straightened up and hit the bar from eight yards. Walters did score a minute later, but Saunders scored the first of two very satisfying goals for himself in a 4-2 win for the eventual runners-up. Nobody could figure why Liverpool hadn't delayed his transfer so he wouldn't be facing the Reds so soon with a point to prove. The game was also an unhappy debut for Piechnik, who was ill at ease all afternoon. Souness later revealed in his 1999 book, The Management Years, that he "was totally depressed and it crossed my mind that I might never again be the strong forceful character that I had been before my operation." Souness wept as he drove up the M6. "Tears came easily on other occasions, apart from the Villa episode, and I feared my personality might be undergoing a massive change," he said. "I was worried and felt vulnerable for the first time in my life."

Anyone who thought Liverpool couldn't be further humiliated didn't reckon on the might of Chesterfield, who would finish the season 12th in the game's fourth tier. The visitors, managed by Lawrie McMenemy's son Chris, were 3-0 up after 48 minutes of the first leg of a second-round League Cup tie in front of 12,533 stunned spectators at Anfield. Rosenthal and Hutchison pulled two back, but Steve Norris broke away to make it 4-2. Walters and Wright got it back to 4-4, with Hutchison hitting the post in the last minute of a crazy game. James, who had remained in goal since that opener at Forest, endured a miserable night, as did Wright. Along with Redknapp, substitute Kozma was one of the few notable performers, helping to turn the game in the second half. James later put his struggles down to the drinking culture at Liverpool. "It was after we drew 4-4 with Chesterfield that I knew I had reached the lowest of the low," he told Shoot magazine. "It was then I knew I had to sort myself out. It had gone too far, and that game just killed me off completely. At Watford I hardly ever went out and didn't drink at all. Then I came to Liverpool and found it a different world. After the Chesterfield game I decided to stop doing all that. I wasn't doing the right things in football and going out was compensating for it. Other people can go out night after night and still play like a legend, but I'm not one of them." Whoever the big drinkers in the squad were, one thing was for certain – nobody was playing like a legend.

Hopes that the comeback might precipitate an upturn in fortunes were dashed, as Wimbledon led 2-0 before 30 minutes were played at Anfield four days later. Burrows was one of many poor performers, but a Molby penalty and a brilliant McManaman volley levelled the scores by the break. Robbie Earle's winner, however, left the Reds in 19th, only clear of the relegation zone on goal difference. Grobbelaar, with his testimonial match against Everton on the horizon, was back in goal. "I am sick and tired of watching people who don't want to die for this club," he said after the fifth league defeat of the campaign. The Reds were 14 points behind leaders Norwich City.

The second leg against Limassol did produce another win, but Liverpool trailed on the hour mark, and Stewart was sent off. Goals by Rush and Hutchison ensured an 8-2 aggregate win. Five substitutes were allowed in Europe and with numerous injuries, James and Hooper took up two of the spots. Souness was also hampered with his European selections by a short-lived rule that limited teams to fielding no more than three foreign players, which included Welsh and Scots.

Liverpool finally managed back-to-back victories, as a lucky Hutchison goal after 80 minutes saw off Sheffield Wednesday at Anfield. Minutes after Carlton Palmer missed a sitter, Hutchison's shot hit the ground before bouncing up and looping over Chris Woods, who had previously looked unbeatable. The win was an enormous relief and took the side to the giddy heights of 15th. It was no coincidence that Wright missed his first game of the season and Liverpool kept their first clean sheet.

There were no further embarrassments against Chesterfield, despite them going 1-0 up in the second leg. Hutchison, Redknapp, Walters and Rush responded. Rush's goal drew him level with Roger Hunt at the top of the Liverpool goalscoring charts.

The next game at Anfield was Grobbelaar's testimonial against Everton, which saw him miss a penalty in a 2-2 draw. Witch doctors armed with spears led him to his place in goal. He later claimed they placed a curse on the club that could only be lifted if he urinated on all the posts. Naturally, he did that many years later, and tried to claim credit for Jurgen Klopp's title win in 2020.

Liverpool went to Old Trafford, chasing a fourth win in a row. United had lost three of their 11, although they would go on to end their 26-year title drought. By half-time, Liverpool were in dreamland, 2-0 up, with Hutchison, Redknapp, Rosenthal and Rush leading the way. Nicol and Piechnik looked solid at the back. Hutchison scored first with the assistance of a Steve Bruce deflection, and Rush turned in Rosenthal's cut back to break Hunt's record with his 287th goal. But it all went wrong late in the game. Mark Hughes scored twice, and Molby was stretchered off after a coming together with Darren Ferguson. Even Ferguson senior admitted United didn't deserve a point. The main factors behind a much-improved Liverpool performance were an effective offside trap, made possible by the exclusion of Wright, and a balanced midfield, with Molby deep and Redknapp and Hutchison providing the mobility.

The positives, though, were outweighed by the Dane's injury and the crushing disappointment of Hughes's injury-time equaliser. This Liverpool team possessed neither the experience nor the resilience to deal with such setbacks, and so it was unsurprising that another chaotic performance was just around the corner. With the Reds level at 2-2 with Spartak Moscow in the first leg of the next round of the Cup Winners' Cup, following strikes from Wright and McManaman, the wheels fell off in spectacular fashion as Grobbelaar was sent off for a professional foul on 84 minutes. Burrows went in goal, failed to save the penalty and then conceded a late fourth. To add to the misery, Rush sustained another injury. An image that summed up the misery of Souness's reign was Grobbelaar being escorted away from the hostile arena by Hooper and James as the hapless Burrows pulled on the gloves.

But there was a pleasant surprise in store at the weekend, as the Reds produced their best display of the season to storm back from an early 1-0 deficit against high-flying Norwich. The goals came from Thomas, Hutchison, Burrows and Walters with a penalty. This scintillating 4-1 win, aided by a Mark Bowen penalty miss, was an unexpected highlight. Liverpool were now 13th, ten points behind Norwich, who trailed Kenny Dalglish's Blackburn on goal difference.

Sheffield United were the opponents for the third time in the season, when the Reds secured a replay with a goalless draw at Bramall Lane in the League Cup. With Wright all at sea once more, Piechnik was the more composed centre half before limping off to be replaced by Tanner. Grobbelaar was also injured, but for some bizarre reason, goalkeeper substitutes weren't permitted in the League Cup, unlike the league, the Charity Shield and European ties. The veteran keeper played on for 15 minutes, and the Blades couldn't find a way past him.

James came back into the side for a trip to White Hart Lane, but was unable to prevent an insipid 2-0 defeat, which included a Nayim wondergoal. The other scorer was future Red Neil Ruddock. Liverpool great Ray Clemence, on the Spurs coaching staff, was sympathetic to the plight of his former side. "Liverpool are still difficult to play against but, like us, they are going through a transitional period." Few fans were as generous. Confidence in the manager had virtually gone. He had won just three of 30 away league matches since his appointment. "Least said, Souness mended," was a very apt fanzine headline at the time.

Some pointed out that minds may have been on the Spartak Moscow second leg four days later. In the previous season's UEFA Cup, Liverpool had lost 2-0 in Auxerre, before winning 3-0 at Anfield. The class of 1992-93, however, embarrassed themselves again, losing 2-0, which meant they went out 6-2 on aggregate. Marsh became the third Liverpool player to be sent off in the competition, whereas previously only Kenny Dalglish and Mark Lawrenson had ever been dismissed in Europe for Liverpool. Souness was absent from the changing room and the dugout, having taken his first-leg protests too far.

Having won just one of the last half-dozen games, Liverpool enjoyed a prosperous November. A Rosenthal brace, including one arrowed into the top corner, and a rare McManaman league goal fired the Reds into a 3-1 half-time lead over Middlesbrough. Rush scored his 200th league goal in injury time. Hooper made his first appearance of the season, with James on the bench.

Four days later, Sheffield United were beaten 3-0 as the Reds made it to the fourth round of the League Cup. McManaman scored two with Marsh, impressing at right midfield, adding a penalty. But the injury curse struck again, with Stewart and Walters hobbling off within two minutes of each other midway through the first half, with only defenders, Jones and Wright, on the bench.

Liverpool enjoyed a 12-day break before a Premier League trip to QPR for a Monday night game televised by Sky Sports. They welcomed back Barnes for his first appearance since April, but his 17th-minute introduction was only necessary because Rush got injured again. Rangers dominated, but Nicol and Marsh remained strong. With Barnes exerting his influence, Liverpool gained a foothold. With two minutes to play, the returning hero released Rosenthal, who shot high into QPR's goal. It was the Reds' first Premier League away win.

A profitable November ended with a satisfying 5-0 dismantling of Crystal Palace at Anfield, which left the Reds in eighth. Two from McManaman and one from the ever-improving Marsh had Liverpool 3-0 up in 19 minutes. Rosenthal and Hutchison landed further blows after the break. Redknapp was excellent again, as was Barnes on his first start, despite being noticeably overweight. Three consecutive clean sheets had been kept, with Nicol and Piechnik at the back.

But all good things must come to an end. Palace were back three days later for a League Cup fourth-round tie. Wiser fans weren't optimistic of another thrashing. And so it proved. This time it was Burrows' turn to fall victim of the first-half injury curse, as he was stretchered off with knee-ligament damage after Gareth Southgate's challenge. Chris Coleman put Palace ahead on 56. Liverpool needed a Marsh penalty, won by Jones, to force a replay.

After Liverpool dominated a goalless first half at Everton, Wright headed the Reds into a 1-0 lead on the hour. The goal scorer had recently lost the armband to Nicol. Mo Johnston equalised for the relegation-threatened Blues. Barnes hit a post. Then came the hammer blow. Former Reds Gary Ablett and Peter Beardsley combined for the latter to score the winner with six minutes left. McManaman was abject. So was Stewart. With Rush injured, Saunders not replaced and Rosenthal substituted, the Reds ended the match with no strikers and no cutting edge.

The only highlight of December came the following Sunday as Kenny Dalglish returned to Anfield for the first time since his 1991 resignation. His Blackburn side started the weekend in second, eight points behind Norwich, but ended in fifth, as a Mark Walters double – one a ferocious shot into the top corner of Tim Flowers' net – earned Liverpool a superb 2-1 win. Nicol and Marsh again impressed. "They were always very generous to me when I was here as a player and as a manager," Dalglish said of the Liverpool fans. "Today, they carried that on."

Liverpool then collapsed into a run of one win in 14 fixtures. Palace knocked them out of the League Cup with a 2-1 win in the Selhurst Park replay. Marsh, now covering at right back with Jones shifted to the left, scored another equalising penalty, but an Andy Thorn goal in extra time, from Nicol's error, put the Londoners into the quarter-finals. Their Liverpool-born manager, Steve Coppell, admitted his men were "lightweight and inexperienced", but a limp and ineffective Liverpool still couldn't beat them.

Scouser Micky Quinn was the scourge of Liverpool in a 5-1 humiliation at Coventry in Bjornebye's debut. The Reds trailed 1-0 at half-time before five goals in 20 minutes, four of them to the hosts, saw Liverpool become a laughing stock. Redknapp had scored a brilliant free kick but was soon sent off. Souness blamed the referee. "We were in command for an hour, but the referee made four strange decisions which totally changed the course of the game," he said.

A phenomenal volley from Rush, as he smashed a right-wing cross into the Anfield Road net, was the highlight of a 1-1 draw with Manchester City. Barnes could have won the match, but his header was poor. Thomas was back in the matchday squad after a long injury, although he remained on the bench. It was the final game of the year and the 32nd of an arduous season. At the end of 1992, the Reds were in 11th, a dozen points behind leaders Norwich.

Thomas started the next game but probably wished he hadn't, as third-tier Bolton Wanderers raced into an early 2-0 lead at a frosty Burnden Park in the third round of the FA Cup. Former Red Mark Seagraves scored the second. With Liverpool's defence abysmal, most notably Hooper and Wright, Barnes admitted it could have been 4-0 at half-time. Souness's half-time motivation included throwing cups of tea around. It sparked a reaction of sorts. A Mark Winstanley own goal, after substitute Rosenthal had hit the post, gave Liverpool a start. A Seagraves error then let in McManaman, and Rush turned in the rebound to save his side from their biggest humiliation since 1959 when Worcester City of the Southern League had knocked them out of the same competition. Rush was in double figures for the season, although half had come against Limassol. "The gaffer was absolutely raging [at half-time]," remembered Nicol. "Using the back of his hand, he sent 20 plastic cups – all filled with hot tea – flying across the dressing-room. The players got soaked. The clothes hanging on the pegs got soaked. Ronnie Moran got soaked. Tea was dripping off the end of his nose, but he stood perfectly still throughout. If we had dared laugh…"

Back in the league, a classy finish from new captain Barnes gave Liverpool a half-time lead against title challengers Aston Villa. It was his first league goal since the opening day of 1991-92, but once more Saunders embarrassed his old club with a second-half winner. Again, he left Piechnik red-faced. The Dane was compared to "[Glenn] Hysen on a bad day with one leg missing," in Through the Wind and Rain. Saunders was forging the sort of partnership with Dalian Atkinson that Souness had envisaged him enjoying with Rush, who missed the match after being injured in training. Jones again struggled at left back, while Thomas was on the wing. Also suffering from a selection process which may as well have involved drawing names from a hat were Bjornebye, deployed at centre half, and Marsh, again at right back – a selection that would backfire four days later. The 2-1 defeat heaped pressure on Souness. One of the enduring images of the afternoon was the young mascot sobbing during his pre-match warm-up with Barnes. A fanzine later used the image, with the skipper threatening to take the boy to away matches as well if he didn't stop crying.

However miserable things were, they could get worse. When Liverpool escaped defeat at Burnden Park, the general feeling was that they would be too strong for the plucky lower-division side on their own turf. Not so. The 1993 FA Cup defeat to Bolton Wanderers remains one of the club's biggest embarrassments. They were ripped apart, lucky to lose only 2-0. David Lee, man of the match, gave Marsh, a torrid time. Souness admitted: "They were better than us in all departments." Thomas, who had only just returned to the team, was now out for the season with an Achilles injury. Only he and Jones played in both this match and the 1992 final. On the bench, although unused, was 17-year-old Robbie Fowler, who was in the matchday squad for the first time, desperate to get onto the pitch. Souness blamed the players, calling them "greedy and gutless". The fans blamed Souness.

The last thing the Reds needed was a trip to Wimbledon six days later. There was little the manager could do with such an injury-ravaged squad, but he did bring in James for Hooper and benched Rosenthal, his only fit forward. As at Everton and Coventry, Liverpool started promisingly, but, with no recognised striker in the 11, they failed to break through. Another first-half injury, this time to Piechnik after he'd conceded a penalty, didn't help. A goal in each half secured a 2-0 win for the Dons, who remained in the relegation zone, despite having done the double over Liverpool. The Reds were down to 12th. They were 8-1 to get relegated with William Hill. Few could believe Souness was still in a job, but chairman David Moores was adamant he was staying.

Exclusion from the FA Cup gave Liverpool a fortnight to prepare for their next match – a daunting trip to Arsenal. They were also struggling in the league but would go on to win both domestic cups. With the infamous Highbury mural in place, a Barnes penalty was the only goal of the game. James had earlier saved a spot kick from Paul Merson. The returning Rush could have had three. Nicol's return led to some defensive stability. Nigel Winterburn was sent off for two fouls on McManaman. It was an impressive victory for Souness.

Again, a promising result couldn't be built upon. Nottingham Forest came to Anfield, firmly embedded in the relegation zone, and forced a 0-0 draw, despite Souness having the luxury of naming an unchanged side for the first time in 13 months. Gary Bannister wasted a late chance and Forest still hadn't won at Anfield for 24 years. They ended up coming last, with Brian Clough retiring.

There was another 0-0 draw four days later at Chelsea, with Barnes missing a late headed chance. Souness was unimpressed with his winger: "He has got a great deal of talent. It is a crime when you don't get involved in the game." With Souness in charge, Barnes was only a fraction of the player he had been under Dalglish. He would re-find his form as a central midfielder for the next boss, Roy Evans.

A 5pm kick-off at the Dell, with the Sky cameras in attendance, saw Liverpool fall short on their travels again. A thumping 25-yarder from Hutchison levelled the scores on the hour mark. It was the team's first goal from open play in five weeks, but Southampton sub Nicky Banger consigned the Reds to their seventh away defeat after Nicol's mistake. Only six points separated the 18-times champions from the bottom three.

A third 0-0 draw in four matches came at home to Ipswich, leaving the Reds in 15th. The newly-promoted Tractor Boys were ten places higher. Barnes, whose every touch for England three days earlier at Wembley against San Marino had been greeted with boos, fared slightly better in club colours. Rush and Stewart were poor. Wright had now been back in the team for six games and had improved noticeably. The game was preceded by a minute's silence for two-year-old James Bulger, whose horrific murder had shocked the nation.

A miserable, winless February came to an end with a hard-fought 1-1 draw at in-form Sheffield Wednesday. Hutchison gave Liverpool a 20th-minute lead, but the 36-year-old Viv Anderson popped up with an equaliser from a corner with eight minutes left. The Reds had failed to beat a side reduced to ten men after Nigel Worthington was sent off. The big news was that Rush had been dropped by Souness and wasn't even named on the bench. It would prove to be a masterstroke.

Liverpool went on to enjoy a more fruitful March, but only after the disappointment of a home defeat to Manchester United. For successive home games, there was a minute's silence, this time for Tony Bland, who had become the 96th victim of Hillsborough, having had his life support turned off on February 22nd. Sadly, a section of United supporters ruined the tribute. In a game not televised, nor covered on Radio 5, United ended the day on top with Liverpool still in 15th, three points ahead of the dreaded 20th spot. Stewart's long pass from near his own line was way off target. He then stood still, playing Mark Hughes onside. His header made it 1-0. It summed up Stewart's season. He went off injured just before half-time. Redknapp, Bjornebye and McManaman also struggled, but Rush, reinstated to the bench, scored a magnificent equaliser at the Anfield Road end early in the second half, swivelling on the corner of the area before volleying over Peter Schmeichel into the far corner. It sparked a great run of form for the master marksman. Five minutes later, James missed a corner, which resulted in Brian McClair scoring the winner. The outstanding Schmeichel had earlier made one of the saves of the season from Hutchison. Burrows, who hadn't played since November, made a welcome return from the bench. A 12-year-old 'Stephen Gerrard', meanwhile, was featured in the matchday programme and was called a 'gem' by Steve Heighway.

Four days later came Liverpool's second win since the middle of December. A 1-0 midweek win over QPR marked the end of a terrible sequences of results.

Rush scored the winner from McManaman's cross with a little under 20 minutes left, but his strike was sandwiched by penalty misses from Marsh and Barnes. The last time the Reds had missed two in a game was in 1973 against Spurs, when Kevin Keegan and Tommy Smith were the culprits. Of more immediate importance was the return of Whelan, who came back into the side for his first appearance since September. His assured protection of the defence and reliable passing game had been sorely missed.

Liverpool earned a third away win in the league at Middlesbrough. Hutchison scored early, but it was quickly cancelled out by an unfortunate own goal from Nicol. The in-form Rush scored the winner in the final ten minutes. Liverpool hadn't played well. Souness claimed that some of his players had been affected by the warmth, a bizarre assertion given it was only mid-March. Four days later, Grobbelaar was loaned to third-tier Stoke City. He would play four matches for Lou Macari's side.

One of the most satisfying wins of the season came in the next game, when Rosenthal's injury-time winner defeated Everton. Both sides had been threatened by relegation, but the Reds' third win in a row took them up to 13th. The Israeli, played onside by Andy Hinchcliffe, took a clever reverse pass from Rush at the Kop end and fired across Neville Southall for the first of several injury-time winners against Everton in the Premier League era. A key figure in the win was Molby, who replaced the injured Wright in the tenth minute. The Dane flourished in the sweeper role, but, typical of Liverpool's luck, he sustained yet another injury and would miss the rest of the season.

A midweek match against Crystal Palace at Selhurst Park, where Liverpool had lost twice already, gave them a chance to move seven places up the ladder, but it ended in a stalemate. With so many injuries, Sammy Lee had even trained for the game, but the legendary midfielder wasn't required to make his first Liverpool appearance since 1986. Rush opened the scoring shortly into the second half with a shot high into the net after being played in by Whelan. The Welshman had another contentiously disallowed three minutes later. Chris Armstrong equalised with 12 minutes left. Souness was ordered from the dugout for abusing a linesman.

Rush's hot streak continued at Ewood Park, but his exceptional goal was the only thing that did go right for them. Kenny Dalglish's Blackburn took the Reds to the cleaners with a brilliant performance as they carved out a 4-1 win. "In a season of feeble displays, this must take some sort of prize," concluded Through the Wind and Rain. This was the performance that led to the infamous post-match dust-up between Souness and Whelan. The Irishman was on form, and was a major reason for Liverpool's improvement in March.

For most of his career, Rush had specialised in bread-and-butter goals, but this season was proving to be an exception. Having already scored stunning goals against both Manchester clubs, Rush hammered the ball with his left foot from outside the area into the top corner of relegation-threatened Oldham's net as the Reds ground out a 1-0 victory.

Two days later, on Easter Monday, he scored again as the Reds picked up a point at Maine Road. Burrows drove into the area, and Rush tapped in his low cross at the far post for his seventh goal in eight games since being dropped against Sheffield Wednesday.

Given his form, the odds on him scoring Liverpool's first Premier League hat trick must have been short, but that honour befell Walters against Coventry. The 4-0 win was also retribution for the 5-1 thrashing dished out by the Sky Blues before Christmas. Walters volleyed in Hutchison's cross for the first, before a perfect chip caught out Jonathan Gould. His treble was completed from the penalty spot after Stewart had been brought down. Burrows completed the rout with a 30-yard screamer.

Four days later, Barnes and Walters were in great form when champions Leeds came to town, boasting an even worse away record than Liverpool's. Each of the veteran wingers netted in a 2-0 win. Incredibly, the Reds were now in fifth.

Norwich could no longer win the league when Liverpool visited on the first day of May, but the third-placed Canaries had enjoyed a magnificent season. They beat the Reds courtesy of a bizarre incident involving James. The 22-year-old was holding onto the ball when he kicked out at John Polston. He was dismissed by David Elleray. David Phillips beat substitute Mike Hooper with the penalty.

James remained in goal for the trip to Oldham, which had originally been postponed on Boxing Day, as his ban didn't kick in for another game. His final game of the season saw him score an own goal and concede three times. It was a microcosm of an error-strewn season for the former Watford keeper. This time it was Hutchison who was red-carded – the sixth of the season. Rush scored twice for the Reds – the first an exquisite lob from outside the box and the second a precise header from Barnes' cross. Liverpool's away form had been appalling all season. They had won three, drawn seven and lost 11.

Media reports suggested that Souness would soon be relieved from the manager's job, if not before the final game of the season then very soon after it. It was suggested that lawyers and financial advisors were trying to come up with an amicable settlement for Souness, who had three years left on his contract, which was reportedly worth £350,000 per year. "I am being portrayed as a mercenary, someone who is holding the club to ransom, but that is not true," said Souness. "All I want to do is see out the next three years at Liverpool Football Club. I feel we are still a good side and that we are only two or three players short of being able to challenge for the championship." Kenny Dalglish, Kevin Keegan, Ron Atkinson, Steve Heighway, Peter Reid, John Toshack and Steve Coppell were linked to the job.

The season ended on a high in the most bizarre circumstances. Souness was absent from Anfield for the final game of the season, apparently scouting a player at Coventry. His programme notes had been replaced with a rallying cry from the chairman. Joyous fans assumed he was about to be sacked. A flag day had been arranged for the Kop, and the carnival atmosphere contributed to Liverpool hammering Spurs 6-2 to end the season in sixth place. Rush and Barnes rolled back the years with a brace apiece, as did the recalled Grobbelaar with a penalty save from Teddy Sheringham, whose goal for Nottingham Forest had beaten Liverpool in their opening match of the season. Stuart Nethercott turned Steve Harkness's cross into his own net, and Walters added a penalty for Liverpool's other goals.

The fans' delight lasted barely 24 hours. A press conference on Sunday May 9th announced that Souness would be staying on as manager, with Roy Evans becoming his assistant. It was a crushing blow to the optimism generated by the Spurs victory, and it proved to be a monumental error of judgment by Moores. All he did was prolong the agony for another half-season.

1993-94

"Some of the players were sorry to see him go. The rest weren't."

Graeme Souness again went for a couple of marquee signings as Liverpool prepared for the new campaign. Mark Wright and Dean Saunders hadn't lived up to expectations in his first season, Paul Stewart and David James had failed in his second and, although they made promising starts, the new boys for 1993-94, Nigel Clough and Neil Ruddock, also proved to be expensive mistakes. None of the team's other glaring problems had been dealt with, so it was little surprise that Liverpool again had nothing to play for by the end of January. To everybody's relief, Souness finally departed, replaced by his assistant Roy Evans.

Souness has since defended his record by pointing to the ageing squad he inherited from Kenny Dalglish in 1991, but according to the lfchistory.net website, the manager actually increased the average age of the side throughout his reign. For his first match in charge, against Norwich in 1991, the average age of the 11 was 28.01. For the Sheffield Wednesday match, which kicked off the new season in August 1993, it had risen to 28.97. There were half a dozen players over the age of 30 selected that day: Bruce Grobbelaar, Steve Nicol, Mark Wright, Ronnie Whelan, Jan Molby and Ian Rush. John Barnes would have made it seven, had he been fit. Mark Walters was 29. It was a curious strategy, since many of these experienced players had consistently let him down. It also meant limited game time for Jamie Redknapp and Don Hutchison, two of the better performers in 1992-93.

The Scot had also wanted to improve the squad's fitness and questionable dietary habits, having seen how far ahead Serie A was during his time at Sampdoria. But many players suffered injuries as a result of his tougher training sessions. Having tried, and failed, to address fitness and lifestyle issues, he seemingly abandoned the plan in the summer of 1993, signing the overweight Ruddock and Julian Dicks. Several others looked unfit and sluggish. The team started well but quickly ran out of steam.

One pre-season surprise was the appointment of Rush as captain. He had never appeared captaincy material and didn't get on with Souness. He often reacted petulantly to being substituted or dropped. His form had deserted him for long spells, apart from that exceptional spell in the spring of 1993, and like many other senior players, he was regularly cursed by injuries. Souness admitted in his book The Management Years that his decision was essentially an olive branch, as he hoped to fix their relationship and get the best out of him. It seemed the wrong reason to make somebody captain, especially coming from Souness, arguably Liverpool's greatest skipper. Istvan Kozma was the only player to depart during the summer. David Burrows, Mike Marsh and Mike Hooper left a month into the season.

Things clicked nicely into place on day one against Sheffield Wednesday. Grobbelaar kept goal. Rob Jones and Stig Inge Bjornebye were the full backs. Ruddock and Wright were the centre backs. Whelan and Molby were in midfield, flanked by Walters and Nicol. Clough and Rush were up front. On a dream debut, Clough scored either side of half-time, arrowing in a shot via the crossbar, before a predatory six-yard-box strike sealed a 2-0 win. Ruddock impressed too – certainly an upgrade on Torben Piechnik. A couple of days earlier, the big centre-back had scored the only goal, conceded a penalty and broken Peter Beardsley's cheekbone in Whelan's testimonial against Newcastle – a performance somewhat typical of his time at Anfield. Wednesday's Carlton Palmer was dismissed on 13 minutes. The Reds dominated and could have had a hatful. Few were getting carried away, but the sound of the whole Kop singing Clough's name was hugely uplifting. The Times described the new pair as "the heart and the brains lacking for much of last season." That may have appeared the case on day one, but it would soon become apparent that Clough lacked the former and Ruddock had absolutely none of the latter.

With Liverpool's away record so abject for two seasons, it was satisfying to see the Reds win two in a row on their travels. Queens Park Rangers were beaten 3-1 with first-half goals from Ian Rush, Steve Nicol (his last for the club) and Clough. The latter drew comparisons to Kenny Dalglish as his deft flick of Nicol's cutback went in off the post. Ray Wilkins scored a sensational goal for QPR.

Liverpool went top for the first and only time under Souness when they thrashed newly promoted Swindon Town 5-0. Ruddock got his first for the club. Steve McManaman added two. Whelan and Marsh scored a couple of outstanding goals. Wright was thriving without Piechnik. Whelan and Molby were dominating in midfield. "I'm absolutely delighted to have some of the best players in English football and, if they desire it and want it, we have a chance in every competition," said Souness. "We can only get better and, if we do, we can start frightening a few teams." Ten goals in three games – his optimism was understandable.

Predictably, though, it began to unravel. Tottenham came to Anfield for a midweek match and when Clough scored his fourth goal in four games after McManaman had bamboozled Dean Austin, everything was still rosy. But a dose of reality was delivered by Teddy Sheringham, whose brace put Spurs ahead by the interval. Time was still on Liverpool's side, as was most of the possession, but they barely threatened an equaliser. "I can't believe we've lost to a five-a-side team," remarked an irritated Souness.

Liverpool hit back with a commanding performance against Leeds. Rush scored his 200th league goal as the ball reared up and hit him in the face before nestling in the bottom corner. Molby beat John Lukic from the penalty spot after Rob Jones was fouled. The young full back had enjoyed a superb start to the season.

If August had been promising, Spurs apart, September was horrendous, yielding not a single league goal. It started with an abysmal performance at Highfield Road in a 1-0 defeat to Coventry. Future Red Phil Babb scored the goal and had no problems keeping Clough quiet. Jones was sent off for the first time in his career after for two yellows. David Rennie terrorised Molby and Whelan. Grobbelaar was at fault for the goal. "Old age is catching up with Liverpool," concluded The Times.

It was certainly catching up with Barnes, who was yet to feature. The day after the Coventry setback, news emerged he was facing a lengthy spell on the sidelines. He would go on to miss the first 14 league matches. Twelve months earlier, he had been absent from the start for 15 games. In Souness's first full season, he played in the first two, then sat out the next 21. He had been Liverpool's best player by a distance under Kenny Dalglish. Throughout the Souness era, when he wasn't injured, he was overweight, slow and not a shadow of the player that had the world at his feet from 1987 to 1991.

Liverpool were certainly on the ropes after the visit of Kenny Dalglish's Blackburn in mid-September. Mike Newell scored the only goal of the game, but the Reds' lack of discipline was disgraceful. Molby clattered into Kevin Gallacher and in the ensuing melee, Wright pushed Newell and Ruddock punched him. Ruddock also escaped punishment for a follow through which could have broken one of the goalscorer's ankles. Jones, already booked, might have been sent off again after lunging at Paul Warhurst. Rush departed on 80 minutes with a groin strain to cap off a miserable afternoon.

Souness responded to his team's disciplinary woes by signing the West Ham left back Julian Dicks, in a swap deal with Burrows and Marsh, who didn't really deserve to be booted out. Dicks was a talented footballer, but, like Ruddock, Molby, Nicol and Barnes, he was unfit and overweight, and, like Ruddock, he wasn't scared to get stuck in, and had the disciplinary record to show for it. He debuted against Everton with his parents unaware he had even made the move. They returned from holiday, switched on the radio and were stunned to hear him playing in a Merseyside derby, in which Liverpool were comprehensively outplayed, outrun and outfought. "We were second to everything," lamented Souness. This time the indiscipline was between teammates, as Grobbelaar and McManaman came to blows after Mark Ward's goal. The goalkeeper's behaviour was appalling. The Reds hadn't scored an equaliser all season and didn't threaten one here. Tony Cottee doubled the lead in the second half and, predictably, Liverpool had no answer. "Souness must stay!" chanted Everton supporters. Those early-season wins seemed a lifetime ago. This old and unfit team didn't have any answers. Souness responded by booting Whelan out of the side. The Irishman didn't play again until Souness had gone.

Respite came in the League Cup at Fulham. September 1993 may have been utterly miserable, but it did see the debut of one Robert Bernard Fowler, a remarkably confident young striker, who scored in a 3-1 win, along with Rush and Clough. The 18-year-old was destined for greatness.

Liverpool's slide down the league was alarming, going from first to second, then third, fifth and ninth. By the time Chelsea made it four defeats in a row, the Reds were 13th. Fowler and McManaman missed chances. Two worthwhile penalty appeals against player-manager Glenn Hoddle were ignored. Dennis Wise should have been sent off for poleaxing Clough. When Neil Shipperley scored on 49 minutes, it was no surprise that Chelsea saw it out. Nothing had changed since Souness's early-summer reprieve. In fact, considering the end-of-season form in 1993, things had got a whole lot worse.

The Premier League losing streak eventually ended with the visit of Arsenal. Rush and Fowler laboured with no service, as the Reds' Premier League impotency stretched to five games. As at Chelsea, Clough operated in the hole at the expense of any width. But Liverpool held firm at the other end, at least. It was a welcome clean sheet.

After the Arsenal game, Souness had said of Fowler: "He will prove himself every bit as clinical as Rush." In the second leg against Fulham, the teenage sensation scored all five of Liverpool's goals to equal the club record of goals in a match, held by John Miller, Andy McGuigan, John Evans and Rush. Even when the Reds had beaten the same opposition 10-0 in 1986, no one had scored five. It was an incredible personal achievement. Many spoke highly of the young players during the Souness years. Some flattered to deceive. Fowler was the real deal.

The Toxteth Terrier scored his first league goal – and Liverpool's first in seven painful weeks – in a 2-1 home win over Joe Royle's Oldham. The Reds trailed for much of an awful game. With supporters streaming away and Ruddock playing as an emergency striker, Fowler scored the first equaliser of the season on 87 minutes. Then came the double whammy for Oldham as Graham Barlow scored an injury-time own goal. It wasn't exactly convincing, and it might have kept the manager in his post for a while longer, but it was three much-needed points. "Please don't ask me any more questions," said Souness, struggling to explain why his side had been so poor for the majority of the game. "Can I go and get drunk now?"

With Dominic Matteo making his first-team debut, Liverpool needed another late goal to get something from their trip to Maine Road. Trailing 1-0 to a David White goal, his fifth against the Reds in little over two years, Rush popped up with an 89th-minute equaliser to secure a barely deserved point. The goalscorer spoke of closing the gap on Manchester United. It was now at 14 points after just a dozen matches.

With Liverpool chasing hard for the signature of the Southampton and England goalkeeper Tim Flowers, Grobbelaar reminded everybody why such a deal was deemed necessary when his clearance from Ruddock's back pass hit the onrushing Ian Marshall and flew into his net in the 22nd minute of a League Cup tie at home to Ipswich. Fortunately, Liverpool were already 2-0 up by then, with both goals coming from Rush. The Welshman completed his hat-trick in the second minutes before a late Ipswich penalty, after Wright had handled, ensured a nervy ending. It had been a tough season, but Rush had racked up seven goals. As for Flowers, he chose to join Blackburn instead. James and Hutchison may have been relieved, as they had been lined up to be part of a swap deal.

Rush scored again in a 4-2 win over relegation-threatened Southampton, who still had Flowers in goal. Grobbelaar, bizarrely, placed a bunch of flowers in the net and told his opposite number they would be the only flowers coming to Liverpool. Saints also boasted the magnificent Matt Le Tissier, who scored two tremendous goals, but the headlines were hogged by Fowler for bagging his first league hat trick. His feats meant that new signing Clough was already on the bench. It was a handy win for Liverpool, but little success was going to be attained with a Harkness-Nicol-Stewart-Matteo midfield.

Another routine home win, this time over West Ham, saw the Reds move into fifth. Burrows and Marsh were welcomed back to Anfield, although Dicks missed the reunion with injury. Liverpool were frustrated for over an hour before a clinical finish by the recalled Clough was followed by an own goal by the veteran Alvin Martin. Jones got injured, and Stewart was badly out of sorts again. Further evidence that all was not well at the club emerged the next day with Souness preventing Academy coach Steve Heighway from appearing on Sky Sports. The former winger was ordered to leave the studios just before filming began.

After an international break which saw England and Wales fail to qualify for the World Cup in the USA, Liverpool produced a dismal performance at Newcastle in a match which would later make headlines for wholly unique reasons. The Reds were shambolic, with Andy Cole notching a hat-trick inside half an hour. Thankfully, that was as bad as it got, and it remained 3-0. Piechnik made his first appearance of the season, replacing the injured Wright. It turned out to be his last game for the club. He was replaced by the returning Barnes at half-time, as Souness tried to salvage something from the wreckage. Kevin Keegan's team had only just been promoted and were already superior to Liverpool, although Souness pointed out that the 14 players in the matchday squad were the only fit players. A year later, Grobbelaar would be accused of letting in the goals on purpose in exchange for cash, with the ensuing investigation and trials rumbling on for years.

Next up were Aston Villa, who had thus far failed to replicate their form of the previous season, although they were still above Liverpool. Barnes got his first start of the season, with Molby back after a two-month layoff. Fowler opened the scoring on the stroke of half-time with a clever back-header from Matteo's cross. Dalian Atkinson equalised. But Redknapp, sent through on goal by Fowler, smashed in the winner at the Kop end on the hour mark. Grobbelaar made brilliant saves from Dean Saunders and Dalian Atkinson. It was an impressive result, but Villa had been the better side, prompting Souness to complain that the referee's shirt clashed with the Villa kit.

Quite possibly the dullest match of the season came next as Wimbledon secured a 1-1 draw in the third round of the League Cup at Anfield. Molby's early penalty, the team's only shot on target, preceded a late strike from Robbie Earle. The Reds were woeful and remained in the competition because of Wimbledon's profligacy and excellent defending from Wright. "I am dumbfounded," admitted Souness. "I cannot understand how we can play so well against Villa and then play so badly three days later."

One poor performance often led to another, and that's what happened when Liverpool travelled to Sheffield Wednesday three days later. Wednesday's three goals comprised an own goal from Ruddock, an own goal from Wright and a walk-in for Mark Bright with Grobbelaar stranded somewhere near the halfway line. Fowler, with his 12th in 13 games, scored the only normal goal of a hideous 3-1 defeat. As he had been the season before, Rush was dropped for this fixture. Souness promised to recall him immediately.

He was back with a goal for the midweek visit of Queens Park Rangers on December 8th. Les Ferdinand fired Rangers ahead on ten minutes, following a Grobbelaar mistake. Barnes equalised but later limped off. Rush's goal put Liverpool 2-1 up at the break. Simon Barker levelled the scores in the first minute of the second half. But a Molby penalty, won by Redknapp with ten minutes remaining, sealed a much-needed victory. Both QPR scorers were dismissed – Barker, for his reaction to the awarding of the penalty, and Ferdinand, who got a second booking for kicking the ball away. Skipper Ray Wilkins and manager Gerry Francis had to persuade Ferdinand to leave the field.

Again, good was followed by bad as Liverpool could only scrape a draw against Swindon Town, the Premier League's worst team. There was no score for an hour until John Moncur scored. Barnes equalised. Keith Scott restored Swindon's lead. The Reds needed a header from Wright on 86 to take a point. It was another embarrassing performance and result.

Things got even worse three days later as Liverpool lost a penalty shootout at Wimbledon in the League Cup. Those who questioned whether Rush was captaincy material would have noted he wasn't among the penalty takers. Liverpool again needed two equalisers: Ruddock with a 20-yarder seven minutes before half-time and an own goal from Hans Segers, who somehow punched the ball into his own net at the end of normal time. Walters won a penalty in extra-time, but Barnes couldn't convert. In the shootout, Ruddock scored, Redknapp missed, Barnes scored, Walters missed and Fowler scored. Only Vinnie Jones missed for the Dons, who won 4-3. To cap a miserable night, Wright and Molby succumbed to first-half injuries. The Dane's ripped calf muscle sidelined him for the season. The Reds had played well in defeat, but that was little consolation. It was the club's first-ever loss on penalties in competitive matches.

Liverpool were back in the capital at the weekend to play Tottenham. Preceded by a minute's silence for the great Danny Blanchflower, it was a thrilling game and further evidence of Fowler's ability. With his side a goal down at the break, the young striker scored two in six minutes, with Redknapp landing a free kick in between, only for Spurs to score twice in the final quarter to force a 3-3 draw. Barnes was substituted injured at half-time, with his replacement Clough setting up Fowler's first.

A goalless draw at Bramall Lane followed, only really notable for Rush's angry reaction to being substituted for Walters with ten minutes left. He refused to watch the remainder of the game from the Liverpool bench, choosing instead to stand several yards away. Liverpool, wearing a gold and black third kit, were poor again. The defence was "porous and pedestrian", according to The Times. Dicks, making his first appearance since the win over Oldham in mid-October, was notably off the pace. The Guardian believed they should have been four behind at the break.

As 1993 came to an end, Liverpool drew a fifth-consecutive match, this time against Wimbledon at Anfield. An own goal by future Red John Scales put the home side ahead after a bright start, but it was cancelled out by John Fashanu five minutes before half-time. The only thing memorable from a tedious second half was the Kop baiting Vinnie Jones about his recent skirmish with Wolfie on ITV's Gladiators. Liverpool hadn't beaten The Dons in seven attempts under this manager. Souness's men ended the year in eighth on 33 points, 20 shy of leaders Manchester United. Progress had been non-existent. After the same number of games (22), the Reds had been on 29 points a year earlier.

Liverpool actually enjoyed a decent January in the league, Souness's final month with the club. It began with a New Year's Day victory at Ipswich, the first away win since Swindon in August. Ruddock's opener was cancelled out by Ian Marshall, but up popped Rush with an 88th-minute winner. Worryingly, though, Marshall and Chris Kiwomya's pace had exposed Wright and Ruddock all afternoon. According to Through the Wind and Rain, Ruddock had "arrived looking like Ron Yeats and now looks like Eddie Yeats." In The Management Years, Souness told of a senior player telling a journalist that "maybe it won't be such a bad thing if we lose all of them," referring to a run of three matches, including Bristol City in the FA Cup, that could decide the manager's future. Souness didn't name the culprit, but said he had played in the side beaten by the lower-division club. "I hope he can look me in the eye if we meet again," said Souness. Coincidentally or not, Barnes was made to apologise to him via the matchday programme later in the month for comments in the Sunday Express.

Manchester United strutted into town 21 points ahead of Liverpool on January 4th. Souness's reign had been miserable enough, but it went hand in hand with United winning the first two Premier League titles. A second flag day was organised on the Kop, and it led to one of the most memorable Anfield atmospheres. "Once the Kop has become all-seater, I doubt whether we will ever witness such passion and commitment from a crowd again," noted the

Manchester Evening News. Some left in disgust when United went 3-0 up in 23 minutes. Fowler had blazed a first-minute sitter into the Kop before goals from Steve Bruce, Ryan Giggs and Denis Irwin left Anfield depressed at the yawning chasm that existed between the teams. Suddenly, from nothing, Clough smashed a magnificent 30-yarder into Peter Schmeichel's net via the bottom of the post. When he added a second on 38 minutes, fans were lighting flares on the Kop. The noise was deafening. The second half was like a five-a-side match. Incredibly, it contained just one goal, as Ruddock's clever touch played in substitute Bjornebye down the left. The centre-back rose masterfully to bullet the Norwegian's cross past Schmeichel. Anfield erupted. It was witnessing a classic. The last ten minutes were anti-climactic, with neither side wanting to surrender a point, but for 80 minutes, this was football at its most breathtaking.

Four days later, it was back down to earth with a bump. After 65 minutes of an FA Cup tie at Ashton Gate, Liverpool were being held at 1-1 by Bristol City. Rush had scored the Reds' goal – his 40th in the competition, leaving him one short of Denis Law's record. Then the lights went out and the match was abandoned. Records of the game, including Rush's goal, were expunged.

Oldham Athletic were rolled aside with a superb second-half performance at Boundary Park. Dicks scored a scorching goal, his only one for the club from open play, before Fowler and Redknapp clinched an impressive 3-0 win. Michael Thomas came on as an 86th-minute substitute for his first game in 12 months, after snapping his Achilles in the Cup defeat at home to Bolton in 1993.

Rush did move to within one of Law when the Bristol City tie was re-staged. Again, he scored first. Again, Wayne Allison equalised. Anyone believing the job was done, with the replay to be played at Anfield, had clearly forgotten the events of 12 months earlier. Far worse than the failure to win was a fractured ankle sustained by Fowler, whose 16 goals in 19 appearances represented an astonishing introduction to senior football. He wouldn't be seen again until the middle of March.

Another handy league result was a welcome distraction for Liverpool. Liverpool's home game with Manchester City followed a minute's silence for Sir Matt Busby, who had captained both clubs before managing Manchester United to wonderful success in spite of the Munich air crash, which killed many of his team. A few City supporters ruined the tribute. Their team scored early, but Rush compensated for the absence of Fowler by equalising and then heading an injury-time winner. It was a deserved win against a struggling side now in the bottom three. Tony Coton had saved City from a thrashing. Liverpool were fifth.

"You could touch the wintry discontent pouring from the stands and terraces," was Through the Wind and Rain's description of Anfield as Liverpool were humiliated in another FA Cup replay. A Brian Tinnion stunner saw the Reds dumped out of the Cup by Bristol City. The manager had overheard the team talk of his counterpart, Russell Osman, who pointed out the Reds' many weaknesses. Souness conceded that every one of them was true. "I knew that night I was wasting my time trying to produce the Liverpool team that the fans craved," he wrote. In his 33 months as boss, there had been defeats to Peterborough, Bolton and now Bristol City, with significant scares against Stoke City, Port Vale, Bristol Rovers, Ipswich Town, Portsmouth and Chesterfield. There were no more excuses. To the relief of many, he resigned from the job, giving his successor half a season to begin the rebuilding process. "Some of the players were sorry to see him go," said Barnes in his autobiography. "The rest weren't." His final act was to sell Ronny Rosenthal to Spurs for £250,000. The Israeli had made just three substitute appearances all season, after providing some memorable moments in 1992-93.

Former captain Alan Hansen was the early favourite to take over, but quickly distanced himself from the role, which soon went to the 45-year-old Roy Evans. His appointment prompted headlines like 'Back to Basics'. He was the steady hand who would reintroduce the 'Liverpool Way' that Souness had veered away from. He was less impulsive. Approachable and warm, players wouldn't have to walk on eggshells around him. Having served under Shankly, Paisley, Fagan and Dalglish, he had an abundance of coaching experience and tactical nous. But he was dealt a tough hand in the remaining three and a half months of the season, with trips to several of the top sides on the horizon. It would be eight months before any tangible improvement appeared.

A recall for Whelan, whom Souness had discarded, marked Evans' first game in charge – a 2-2 draw at Norwich. Chris Sutton twice gave the Canaries the lead, only for an Ian Culverhouse own goal and Barnes to haul them back. Norwich keeper Bryan Gunn was sent off for a late handball just outside the area, which denied Liverpool a winner. "The spirit was tremendous," said the new manager. "I thought my players were absolutely magnificent." Whelan was outstanding, as was McManaman on the right. Too often under Souness, the young winger had been on the periphery of games.

Nine days later, Liverpool produced a performance as bad as anything served up under Souness. After 49 minutes at The Dell, they trailed Southampton 4-0, with Matt Le Tissier having scored a hat trick. His first was thumped in on 26 seconds. Dicks responded with a penalty. Another shot from the left back was parried by Dave Beasant, with Rush knocking in the rebound. Southampton had started the evening in the relegation zone. The average of the Liverpool side was 29.23. Evans had a significant rebuilding job to do – much more so than the one that confronted Souness in 1991.

Things got worse for Evans with a 2-0 defeat at Leeds. Future Red Gary McAllister scored the second a couple of minutes before Grobbelaar, who had been at fault for Leeds' opener, limped off. It was his final appearance for the club. He was replaced by James, who would remain between the posts for 213 consecutive matches. Speculation that Rush might leave, with Manchester City interested, was quashed by both player and manager. Clough was an unused substitute.

Evans' first home match as manager came against Coventry City. Rush fired the Reds into an early 1-0 lead, and that was how the match ended up. Liverpool sat back and invited pressure from the Sky Blues, who were managed by Reds legend Phil Neal. Barnes was poor, and Clough wasn't required again. James kept a clean sheet on his first full game of the season. "[He] was tested only by troubles of his own making, showing he is truly of the Grobbelaar mould," reported The Guardian with incontrovertible accuracy.

Another away defeat came at Dalglish's Blackburn, who had closed the gap to Manchester United to four points. Rovers weren't at their best, with Dalglish ruing the decision to play Alan Shearer up front on his own. They were still too good for Liverpool, for whom Barnes was disappointing again. Rovers won 2-0.

Fowler made a welcome return to the side and, as champion players tend to do, he landed a crucial goal on the big stage. Former Red Dave Watson opened the scoring in the 150th league derby, but with Sky Sports still showing action replays of his goal, Rush equalised from Dicks's long ball. It was his 25th goal against the Blues. Fowler then beat both the offside trap before shooting past Neville Southall for the winner at the Kop end. James made a big save from Peter Beagrie in injury time as the Reds clung on.

The new manager enjoyed successive wins for the first time when Chelsea were beaten 2-1 at Anfield. Ian Rush and a Craig Burley own goal had the Reds two up inside 19 minutes before Burley scored at the right end just after half-time. Liverpool held on, again thanks to James. McManaman was outstanding, hitting the woodwork, as did Jones.

A dull game at Arsenal saw the Reds beaten 1-0, with a Paul Merson goal just after the break. Wright left the field injured just before the half hour. The Gunners had their minds on a Cup Winners' Cup semi-final in Paris three days later. Liverpool looked like they were counting down the days till the end of the season.

Another tough away game resulted in the same score. With Dalglish needing a favour from his old club, Liverpool were unable to oblige at Old Trafford. But they gave it a damn good go. Fowler was benched, with Liverpool fielding a five-man midfield and only ill-fortune denied them a point. They were trailing to a Paul Ince header when Michael Thomas was awarded a penalty by Keith Hackett after he was scythed down by Andrei Kanchelskis. But after a brief consultation with a linesman, Hackett reversed the decision. Evans was bewildered. No satisfactory explanation was forthcoming.

When Rush fired an early goal past Sheffield United, it seemed the floodgates would open against a relegation-threatened team without an away win all season. But this was Liverpool, and they capitulated in style. They'd missed several opportunities to extend the lead, and Nicol's lack of pace and fitness were ruthlessly exposed by Adrian Littlejohn, with Jostein Flo scoring from a rebound. The same player scored the winner with a header. "I sometimes think I'm managing two different teams," said Evans of this team's inconsistency. Of the experienced players, only Rush had done well. There were only three games left in front of the old Kop.

Evans looked on course for his first away win when Liverpool led Wimbledon with a minute to go at Selhurst Park, following Redknapp's stunning 25-yarder.

Fowler had gone close several times while McManaman and Redknapp missed chances to double the lead. The Reds were duly punished with an injury-time equaliser by Gary Elkins.

In a morning kick-off on Grand National day, Liverpool beat struggling Ipswich 1-0. It was a low-key match, but the goal, scored by Dicks from the spot after Hutchison was fouled, was to be the last scored by the Reds in front of the famous terrace.

The club commemorated the fifth anniversary of the Hillsborough Disaster, which had fallen 24 hours earlier, before a 2-0 defeat to Newcastle. The gates were shut early, with many unable to gain entry. Rob Lee and Andy Cole scored early in each half, with Liverpool offering little in return. The brilliant Peter Beardsley nearly scored with a spectacular volley late in the game. How Liverpool had missed him over the last three years. He and Barry Venison left the field to a rapturous reception from all four sides of the ground. The Reds were down to seventh, with the Magpies in third. "We preach the passing game here but in the end, you can pass yourself to sleep," said Evans.

A win on their travels finally came as Liverpool beat West Ham United 2-1, despite Martin Allen's first-minute goal. Fowler equalised from a Barnes pass before Rush landed the winner with two minutes remaining, capitalising on Tony Gale's ill-advised back pass. It was to be his last goal of the season – just his 13th in 41 league matches. It was his fourth late goal of the campaign. Those strikes against Man City twice, Ipswich and West Ham were worth seven points. The new captain had also played a key role in the development of Fowler.

The big day for the Kopites finally arrived on April 30th, as they would stand for the last time to watch their team. Billy Liddell, Albert Stubbins, Ian Callaghan, Tommy Smith, Steve Heighway, David Johnson, David Fairclough, Phil Thompson, Kenny Dalglish and Craig Johnston were introduced to the crowd before kick-off. Then, quite poignantly, the treble-winning manager Joe Fagan strolled into the spring sunshine, flanked by Nessie Shankly, widow of Bill, and Jessie Paisley, wife of Bob, who was too ill to attend. The honour of scoring the final goal in front of the Spion Kop went to Jeremy Goss of Norwich City, who won 1-0. Playing towards the Kop in the second half, Liverpool could have played until midnight and not scored. To a man, they were awful, unlike the 16,000 Kopites.

The season ended with a meaningless game at Villa Park. Fowler scored first, set up by Rush, and with Everton seemingly doomed to relegation, losing 2-0 to Wimbledon, the travelling fans were buoyant. But Villa won 2-1 which left Liverpool in eighth, and the Blues came back to win 3-2 and remain in the Premier League. It summed up a miserable season. The ball was now in the court of Roy Evans to do whatever he could to turn around this disheartening state of affairs. Many of his players looked like they should have been playing for sides at the bottom of the league. Many were the wrong side of 30. Many were injury prone, overweight, or both. The scale of the rebuild can't be underestimated. In the summer of 1994, Liverpool found themselves on a precipice. How quickly could Evans undo the damage done by Souness?

1994-95

"Whereas Mr Souness did everything wrong,
Mr Evans has done everything right."

There have been few Liverpool summers with more heightened gloom than that of 1994. Roy Evans had been in charge for three and a half months, in which time the team had slid from fifth to eighth. Little had changed tactically. Performances were as limp as they had been under Graeme Souness. The old Kop was farewelled with defeat to Norwich. Julian Dicks, Mark Wright and Don Hutchison were punished for disciplinary issues. Dicks and Hutchison wouldn't play for the club again. Bruce Grobbelaar, Torben Piechnik and Ronnie Whelan also left. There was a 4-1 defeat in a friendly at Bolton. Nobody had been signed by the time the new season kicked off. And the first game of the new season was going to be against Crystal Palace at Selhurst Park, Liverpool's bogey ground.

The changes that Evans would make, however, were subtler than Souness's. He was an astute tactician. He may have bought two expensive players in September, but he improved the squad by improving the players. He made tactical alterations that one suspects Souness would not have considered. A few weeks into the season, he would change the formation of the side more markedly than ever before in Liverpool's modern history with a wing-back system. A couple of key players flourished in new roles. He showed that talented players had been at the club all along, but some of them just hadn't been used properly. Fitness improved significantly, resulting in fewer injuries. The football was breathtaking at times. Liverpool were a joy to watch for the most part under Evans. With expectations low, he landed the League Cup and although they were never quite in the title race, they spent a lot of the season in third. Fans were smiling again and that hadn't happened for a long time.

To the surprise of everybody, Liverpool obliterated Palace on the opening day, beating them 6-1, and it proved to be no flash in the pan. It was obvious at 5pm that day that this was going to be a much-improved season. David James kept goal all season. In a 4-4-2 formation, Rob Jones and Stig Inge Bjornebye were the full backs. Evans had been turned down by Bolton centre back Alan Stubbs and was still trying to sign Coventry's Phil Babb when the season began, so Neil Ruddock was partnered at centre half by Steve Nicol, who had finished the previous season dreadfully. Jamie Redknapp played alongside Jan Molby in midfield. Steve McManaman and John Barnes filled the wide roles. With Molby and Barnes, skipper Ian Rush made it a trio of over-30s who had much to prove after injuries and indifferent form under Souness. The prodigious Robbie Fowler partnered the Welshman. Molby looked fit and his passing was as deadly as ever. Ruddock was dominant. The full backs were up and down the touchlines all day. McManaman and Barnes weren't consigned to the wings, where they had struggled under Souness. They relished their freer roles. Molby scored first, from the spot, after Jones was brought down. McManaman ran 80 metres before finding the top corner with a sumptuous finish. It was his first goal for nearly a year. Fowler punished sloppy defending to score from outside the box. Rush scored twice, sandwiching McManaman's second. Palace had left Liverpool so much space, and the Reds countered with devastating results.

It was a promising start, but sterner tests lay ahead. Surely Arsenal wouldn't be so generous. But Liverpool, or rather Fowler, destroyed them in a stunning first half at Anfield. In the space of just four and a half minutes, he scored three goals to blow the Gunners away. He fired in a loose ball from close range for his first. Then he found the bottom corner from the edge of the box for number two. For his hat trick, he ran onto a pass from Barnes and scored at the second attempt. There was disbelief in the stands. How much better could this teenager get? It looked like a record that would stand for years, but it was broken by Southampton's Sadio Mane, who scored three goals in two minutes and 56 seconds against Aston Villa in 2015.

And Liverpool matched their start to the 1993-94 season by making it three wins in a row when they beat Southampton 2-0 at The Dell, with Fowler and Barnes firing past Bruce Grobbelaar, who had left Anfield in the summer. The Zimbabwean had been replaced on the Anfield bench by the Dane Michael Stensgaard, whose name is now firmly embedded in footballing folklore on account of an infamous ironing-board injury he sustained a year into his Liverpool career.

The signing of centre half Babb, who had impressed during the World Cup with Ireland, was confirmed on the first day of September. He cost a club record £3.6 million. Then, to everybody's surprise, John Scales, a quick, aggressive, ball-playing centre back, whom Souness had chased, was recruited the following day from Wimbledon for £3.5 million. It was most intriguing. How would Evans fit them in, along with Ruddock? Wright's days looked numbered. Few were bothered after he had complained to The Sun when Evans disciplined him in the summer. He was now in the reserves.

Scales, who went on to enjoy a stellar season, made his debut in a flat back four, with Babb an unused sub, in a frustrating 0-0 draw at home to West Ham. Even with Tony Cottee sent off on 54 minutes for lunging in on Jones, the Reds couldn't break through. Molby, after a promising start to the season, was off the pace. Barnes and Fowler hit the woodwork. Bjornebye forced a couple of saves from Ludek Miklosko.

Three more points went begging on an agonising afternoon at Old Trafford. A much-improved Liverpool outplayed Manchester United for nearly an hour, with McManaman on song, but they failed to break through. Redknapp hit the bar. Babb came on for Molby for his debut on 70 minutes. Within a minute, United went ahead when Scales' misplaced header was seized upon by Andrei Kanchelskis. A couple of minutes later, Brian McClair made it two. It was a harsh lesson for the Reds, who lay in fifth.

First Division Burnley came to Anfield for the first leg of a second-round League Cup tie. Scales headed the opening goal from Redknapp's cross just before half-time. It later emerged that various players had backed him at odds of 33-1. Former Evertonians Adrian Heath and Alan Harper came close to equalising. Fowler wrapped up a 2-0 win late in the game.

The Reds ended Newcastle's 100% record with a 1-1 draw at St James' Park. Rush cancelled out Rob Lee's opener when his long-distance shot was fluffed by Pavel Srnicek. Philippe Albert was red-carded on 82 minutes, but the Reds couldn't capitalise. It was a landmark day, with Evans unveiling his three-man centre-back system of Scales, Ruddock and Babb, which would be the hallmark of his managerial era. Jones and Bjornebye pushed forward as wing backs. Barnes and Molby formed a skilful yet immobile centre-midfield pairing, with McManaman operating in a free role ahead of them. Rush and Fowler were the strikers. Evans had barely changed the squad, but numerous tactical changes would transform the team's fortunes as the season progressed.

McManaman's hat-trick saw off Sheffield Wednesday a week later at Anfield. 1-0 down to an Ian Nolan goal after the visitors dominated the first half, Liverpool turned on the style. Rush scored first, with McManaman's three coming between the 54th and 86th minutes, although one was heavily deflected off Des Walker. His first was outstanding, as he arrowed his shot into the far corner, following a lengthy dribble from the left. They were his first goals at Anfield in nearly two years. His free role saw him pop up all over the field. Wednesday couldn't handle him.

Burnley were brushed aside 4-1 at Turf Moor in the League Cup second leg with run-outs for Nicol, Redknapp - who scored twice - and Clough, who was also on target. Fowler got the other goal. Lee Jones, a Souness signing from Wrexham, came on for his debut. When they had played in the reserves together, he appeared to have the same potential as Fowler.

Villa were next up for Evans' in-form side, and they were beaten 3-2 at Anfield. Ruddock powered in a close-range indirect free-kick before a double from Fowler - the first a wonderful finish - sealed the points. But question marks were beginning to arise over the new defensive system. Five goals had been conceded in four games since the switch to three at the back. After Villa's second, a late consolation, James held an imaginary gun to his head.

Three more were shipped in at Ewood Park when Liverpool lost 3-2 to Blackburn but they did produce one of their greatest Premier League goals. A deflected Fowler shot saw the Reds lead at the break, only for Mark Atkins to equalise. It was a sweet moment for Atkins, as it had been his injury-time own goal which rescued Liverpool in the third round of the FA Cup in 1991. Chris

Sutton put Rovers 2-1 up, but Barnes responded with one of the finest goals of his career, as he met Bjornebye's cross with a jaw-dropping scissor kick which flew into the bottom corner. But Sutton's winner sent the visitors home with nothing.

The back three kept their first clean sheet when Wimbledon visited on October 22nd. McManaman, Fowler and Barnes – his first at home for ten months – scored the goals as Liverpool beat the Dons for the first time since the days of Kenny Dalglish. Those on the roofless Kop got drenched, but their team was finally making them proud again. The difference in McManaman was astounding. He looked a completely different player now. His 20-yard curler into the top corner was stunning. Barnes was transformed in his new role. "McManaman was the main beneficiary of my passing," said Barnes in his 1999 autobiography. "I gained a lot of satisfaction from seeing Steve do what I used to do, knowing that I had given him a good ball in the right area of the field. From an attacking perspective, Steve's position was the most important in the Liverpool side. The relationship between him and me was similar to that between Rivaldo and Dunga for Brazil at France '98. He needed to receive the ball early. I would tell Jamie and Rob Jones to release the ball quickly, before defenders or midfielders could pick up Steve. Delaying the moment would cut off McManaman's legs." It was a far cry from them being stranded on the wing under Souness.

The third round of the League Cup brought Stoke City to Anfield. Rush scored two, with Paul Peschisolido scoring in between for the Division One team. It wasn't convincing, though. Unused sub Clough, now seemingly out of favour, received a supportive reception from the crowd, despite his father, a couple of days earlier, regurgitating lies about the Hillsborough Disaster in a television interview to hawk his new book. He would later apologise for this in a column with Four Four Two magazine, but Liverpool fans never forgave him.

Back in the league, Ipswich were beaten 3-1 at Portman Road with a screamer from Barnes followed by a brace from Fowler, whose goals were created respectively by McManaman and Bjornebye's brilliance. Rob Jones, who had never scored for the club, hit the post. After 11 Premier League matches, Liverpool were fifth, six points behind leaders Newcastle, but with a game in hand. Fowler was on the verge of signing a four-year contract. The future looked bright.

But there was no room for complacency, as Queens Park Rangers proved two days later on Sky's Monday Night Football. Barnes scored a well-worked equaliser with 25 minutes remaining, but when McManaman, who had come close to putting Liverpool ahead, lost possession with six minutes left, Liverpool were punished by a Les Ferdinand winner. It was a frustrating defeat against a relegation-threatened team. It was the first disappointing performance of a season which was 10 weeks old. Babb had a night to forget. His strength was as a man-marker in a flat back four, and he was still adapting to the new season.

The Reds picked up a valuable win against newly promoted Nottingham

Forest, who were enjoying a superb season. Forest were missing their star striker, Stan Collymore, but Liverpool had theirs. Fowler, in his 50th game, diverted Redknapp's shot into the Kop goal to give his side an early 1-0 lead which remained intact. Babb responded with an excellent performance.

The day of the next match, at home to Chelsea, was dominated by Bruce Grobbelaar, now at Southampton, being accused of match-fixing when he had played for the Reds. The games in question were the 3-0 defeat to Newcastle in November 1993 when Andy Cole had scored a hat-trick, the thrilling 3-3 draw at home to Manchester United two months later, when he made a couple of fine saves, and Evans' first match as manager – the 2-2 draw at Carrow Road in February 1994. Grobbelaar strenuously denied the allegations. He was eventually cleared and went on to sue The Sun. He won the libel case too, but the paper appealed, and his damages were reduced to a token £1, leaving him to pay the newspaper's legal fees. Chelsea stunned Liverpool fans further with a third-minute goal, but two classy finishes from Fowler and a Ruddock header from a corner gave the home side a 3-1 win. In Southampton's first match after the allegations were aired, Arsenal fans threw wallets at Grobbelaar, but he kept a clean sheet in a 1-0 win.

For the third season in a row, Liverpool embarrassed themselves at Goodison Park. The Reds went into the match in third, while Everton were rooted to the bottom with just one win in 14. But they benefited from the new manager bounce, with old boy Joe Royle coming in to rescue the club after Mike Walker's sacking. As at QPR, Liverpool failed to deal with route-one football. Defensive vulnerabilities were too easily exposed. Duncan Ferguson, on a two-month loan from Glasgow Rangers, headed in a corner on 57 minutes, 24 hours after being taken into police custody and breathalysed. Paul Rideout sealed the win in the dying moments. Fowler and Rush were isolated. Molby tore a hamstring.

Ruddock scored an own goal against his former club Spurs in a 1-1 draw at Anfield. Fowler scored a penalty six minutes before half-time after Sol Campbell fouled McManaman. The young defender, playing at left back, made amends by sending in the cross which cannoned off Ruddock and past James. Fowler and Spurs' Jurgen Klinsmann missed late chances. Questions were still being asked of the defence, with only two clean sheets kept in a dozen matches since the switch to three centre backs. "Evans is clinging to his three central defenders like a drowning man ... let's get back to 4-4-2 pronto," wrote fanzine editor Steven Kelly.

The performance of the season, individually and collectively, came at Ewood Park in the fourth round of the League Cup on the last day of November. It was the club's 150th match in the competition, which was introduced in 1960. Up against the in-form strike force of Shearer and Sutton, and partnering the prolific Fowler, Rush, on his 600th Liverpool appearance, was the striker least likely to steal the show. But his thunderous opener was followed by two goals more typical of Liverpool's all-time leading scorer. Sutton pulled one back in the last minute as his side lost 3-1.

Unfortunately, it was followed by another frustrating league performance. Rush scored early against Coventry, as he had done in February in Evans' first home match as manager, but this time the Reds couldn't hold on. Sean Flynn equalised 12 minutes into the second half. Liverpool hadn't won at Highfield Road since November 1990. Rush scored again three days later in his testimonial against Celtic – a 6-0 win. Kenny Dalglish, at 43, was a second-half substitute.

Back at Anfield a week later, Liverpool drew a blank against Crystal Palace in front of the Sky cameras. The Reds had rifled six past Palace on the opening day of the season but couldn't deal with McManaman's absence. Clough was given a rare chance but didn't take it as the game petered out to a 0-0 draw.

Chelsea also kept Liverpool at bay at Stamford Bridge, to take the run of Premier League games without a win to five. Again, there was no creativity without the injured McManaman. It would have been worse had James not touched Dennis Wise's shot onto a post, while Scales played superbly. "Our problem is we can't seem to score," said Evans. The Reds trailed Blackburn by 10 points. They had dropped 11 in the last five games. Rush, in his 2008 autobiography, said of the 1994-95 season: "Deep down I knew we lacked the hard, steely edge and single-mindedness you need to win titles. On our day we could beat any team and we did. Some of the youngsters got carried away, thinking we could turn on the style every match when some called for the rolling-up of sleeves and a battle. The hallmark of a truly successful team is achieving those single-goal victories when you're not on the top of your game."

McManaman returned to the side for the 11:30 am Boxing Day trip to second-bottom Leicester City and Liverpool returned to winning ways. A Fowler penalty and a well-worked goal from Rush sealed the points. James saved a penalty, given away by Barnes, when it was 0-0. The Foxes lost Simon Grayson to a late red card but still pulled one back courtesy of an error from James, who then redeemed himself with a fabulous injury-time save. Given the recent run, the result was all that mattered.

Manchester City came to Anfield two days later and frustrated Liverpool for 55 minutes until Terry Phelan headed into his own goal. With the Reds keen to wrap the game up, McManaman was at the top of his game, forcing a couple of saves from Andy Dibble. Redknapp also went close. Dibble then upended Rush, but the subdued Fowler failed from the penalty spot. He had had a poor game. But then, two minutes later, he made amends in stunning fashion, unleashing a left-foot rocket into the Kop goal to seal the points. The Reds were up to third.

The final game of 1994 came on New Year's Eve as the Reds won 2-0 at Elland Road. Redknapp scored a superb free-kick from 25 yards - his first league goal of the campaign. Fowler got the second. Few were unhappy with the start Evans had made to his first full season. The new system was paying dividends and there was cohesion between the attacking players. James, Ruddock, Bjornebye, McManaman, Barnes and Rush had improved significantly from their form under the previous manager. Liverpool were third at the turn of the year, seven points from Blackburn and four from Manchester United, with both sides still to visit Anfield. One downside, however, was a palpable lack of depth. McManaman's December absence had been costly. Steve Harkness had been used at right back. Substitutes were often unused, with Evans having little faith in Clough, Thomas and Walters. Wright was still in the reserves. Dicks and Hutchison had been moved on. But the manager had far fewer injuries to deal with than his predecessor. Assessing the state of play at the halfway stage, Anfield legend Tommy Smith said: "Whereas Mr Souness did everything wrong, Mr Evans has done everything right."

The winning streak continued with a 4-0 demolition of Norwich. Scales headed in Bjornebye's corner. Fowler added two, the second after a magnificent piece of control following James's clearance. Rush made it four with a glancing header. The Kop, perhaps unrealistically, sang "We're gonna win the league!" It was the first time it had been sung for a long time. A day later came the terrible news that recent reserve-team player Ian Frodsham, who was seen as a genuine talent, had passed away after a battle with cancer. He had just turned 19.

An FA Cup third-round match against a lower-division side beginning with 'B' was enough to send shivers down the spine of any Liverpool supporter still recovering from the Souness days. The Reds returned from Birmingham still in the competition with a 0-0 draw, but that had also been the case after trips to Bolton and Bristol City. Barry Fry's side were unlucky not to win.

Four days later, Liverpool progressed to the semi-finals of the League Cup with a 1-0 defeat of Arsenal, thanks to a ingenious free-kick routine which saw Rush slide the winner past David Seaman. "I have no complaints," said the beaten manager George Graham. "This reminded me of the Liverpool of old – top quality." After a tricky transition to the new defensive system, Liverpool had now conceded just one goal in eight games.

Unfortunately, the worst home performance of the season punctured the optimism. Second-bottom Ipswich, with former Red John Wark in their ranks, went 1-0 up after half an hour, and Liverpool were unable to respond. Despite dominating possession, they couldn't break down Ipswich's low block, which often saw nine men behind the ball. Barnes missed out with a thigh injury. McManaman was Liverpool's best, and he forced Craig Forrest into several fine saves. Nicol was an unused sub – the last time he would be involved in the matchday squad. The Reds were still third, but it was the first of three league matches without a win.

The visit of Birmingham for the Cup replay proved to be another tough game. Redknapp, who had played poorly against Ipswich, scored a first-half goal which was cancelled out by Ricky Otto's strike. Extra time and penalties followed. City missed all four of their penalties. Redknapp and Bjornebye scored after Ruddock's was saved. Liverpool won the shootout 2-0 – their first win in the competition since 1992.

Liverpool's league match at Wimbledon was called off three days before the Anfield derby. A dull match finished goalless with Everton's physicality, particularly involving McManaman, upsetting Evans. The Blues were winning their battle with relegation and were now up to 16th. Twenty-four hours later, Manchester United's Eric Cantona kung-fu-kicked a racist Crystal Palace fan and would be banned until October. United were seven points ahead of Liverpool in second.

A tricky FA Cup tie, this time at Burnley, finished 0-0, with Liverpool lucky to still be in the hat. A couple of days later came the sad news that former chairman Sir John Smith had died, having suffered from cancer.

Another game, another draw, as Evans' men travelled to Nottingham Forest on February 4th. Stan Collymore tapped in at the far post to make it 1-0 after James had been beaten to a through ball by Brian Roy. Fowler equalised in injury time, despite the harsh 52nd-minute dismissal of Babb for a professional foul on Steve Stone. The red card sparked the visitors into life, with Mark Crossley twice denying Fowler before he eventually took advantage of good work from Thomas and McManaman. The goal, Fowler's first in over a month, kept Liverpool a point ahead of Forest. Collymore spent most of the season linked with the Reds and Manchester United. He was desperate for the latter but United had signed Andy Cole in January, opening the door for Liverpool to pursue Collymore at the end of the season.

A Barnes header from a Bjornebye corner just before half-time saw off Burnley in the FA Cup replay. Ruddock was sent off for a professional foul after his slip almost sent in Liam Robinson, who had played in the Bristol City side of 1994 that had conquered Anfield. Burnley sub Ted McMinn, who had played for Souness at Rangers, was dismissed after the final whistle for swearing at a linesman.

Back in the league, Liverpool tossed away two more points with a 1-1 draw with Queens Park Rangers at a saturated Anfield. Scales equalised after Walters had sent Rush to the byline. Kevin Gallen, Fowler's old England Under-18 striking partner, had scored a sixth-minute opener which had been gifted by James. It was a wretched performance. Any lingering title hopes were now gone. Had Liverpool been able to win home games against West Ham, Spurs, Palace, Ipswich, Everton and QPR, all of whom had been in the bottom half of the table when visiting Anfield, the Reds would be a point clear of Manchester United at the top, with a game in hand.

Another disjointed Anfield display was rescued by an injury-time winner from Fowler against Crystal Palace in the first leg of the League Cup semi-final. It was his 24th of the season. But would it be enough to take to Selhurst Park? On the same night, an Ireland-England international was abandoned due to crowd trouble.

A third cup tie in four games saw another underwhelming Anfield performance as Wimbledon earned a replay with a 1-1 draw. The Dons hit the post in the last minute. Fowler equalised on 33 minutes after an early goal from Andy Clarke. Vinnie Jones missed the match after biting a Daily Mirror journalist's nose in Dublin. Liverpool would now have to overcome two crucial cup ties at Selhurst Park.

41

A first league win since the second day of January came in the final week of February at Hillsborough, Liverpool's first win there since the 1989 tragedy. Chris Bart-Williams scored for Wednesday. Barnes equalised just before half-time. McManaman curled the winner into the corner of Kevin Pressman's net on the hour. James was in excellent form, despite having to continue with a leg injury. Evans was facing a goalkeeping crisis with reserve keeper Stensgaard injured. Tony Warner was one of several goalkeepers to warm the bench in 1994-95, but Evans didn't want to use him at Hillsborough.

Liverpool moved into the quarter-finals of the FA Cup with a convincing 2-0 win at Wimbledon in the replay. Barnes and Rush scored first-half goals, with the 33-year-old Welshman equalling Denis Law's record of 41 in the competition. Five of them had come in finals. Redknapp and McManaman were exceptional.

The perfect week was completed when the Reds beat Newcastle United at Anfield. Fowler, after a rasping Walters shot was parried, and Rush, following a defensive lapse, scored the goals in a seven-minute spell in the second half. "It's back to how it was here," said Peter Beardsley, with a hat tip to his former side. His old partner in crime, Barnes, was in great form. A stunning performance from Pavel Srnicek kept the score down.

The good run continued as Liverpool booked an early-April visit to Wembley by winning the second leg of their semi-final against Crystal Palace. It was their second cup win at Selhurst Park in eight days. Fowler scored the only goal just before the half-hour mark with a clinical finish. The goal killed the tie and Liverpool were on easy street thereafter. Souness had had a terrible record against Palace and Wimbledon. Evans had just won two crucial cup ties at Selhurst Park. There was more to this team than pretty football.

The four-game winning run ended at the worst possible time. When Fowler headed in Walters' cross to put Liverpool 1-0 up at Anfield in their FA Cup quarter-final against Spurs, they seemed a shrewd bet to emulate Arsenal's double cup achievement of 1993. But Teddy Sheringham levelled the scores on the stroke of half-time and Jurgen Klinsmann broke Kopite hearts with a last-minute winner. They still gave the German a sporting reception. But with veteran defender Gary Mabbutt shackling Rush, Liverpool had little to offer. Spurs, with Ronny Rosenthal and Nick Barmby in their line-up, were worthy winners.

For the first time in the season, Liverpool lost successive games when Ron Atkinson's Coventry City came to Anfield and won 3-2 in front of just 27,183 spectators. Peter Ndlovu bagged a hat-trick. He scored two in the first half, including a penalty won by former Red Mike Marsh. The returning Molby converted a penalty of his own on 76 minutes. Ndlovu completed his trio. David Burrows diverted Molby's free kick into his own goal in the last minute. It proved to be the Dane's final appearance for the club. The one-goal margin flattered an abysmal Liverpool. Wright made the matchday squad for the first time after being banished to the reserves all season, but his services weren't required on the night.

Five days later, Liverpool responded in magnificent style against Manchester

United. Redknapp scored a superb opener, firing into the bottom corner of Peter Schmeichel's net from the edge of the area. Thomas created the second, crossing for McManaman, whose sliced shot was turned into his own goal by Steve Bruce. The returning Wright produced an outstanding display against Mark Hughes. United were awful without the talismanic Cantona, often relying on long balls. The result kept Kenny Dalglish's Blackburn six points clear at the top. The Kop chanted his name.

A midweek trip to Spurs saw Ruddock captain the team in the absence of Rush and Barnes. Wright was back on the bench. The highlight of a scoreless match was James saving a Klinsmann penalty, which had been conceded by the stand-in skipper with 18 minutes remaining. "He was looking for a penalty and he got one," remarked Evans. "That was the Jurgen of old."

The Reds had an 11-day break before their next game, which was the League Cup Final against Division One's Bolton. The line-up was James; Scales, Ruddock, Babb; Jones, Barnes, Redknapp, Bjornebye; McManaman; Rush, Fowler. Thomas, Walters and goalkeeper Alec Chamberlain were unused substitutes, with the latter winning a medal without ever playing for the club. Wanderers boasted former Red Mark Seagraves, and Jason McAteer, who would soon team up with Evans' squad, as well as David Lee and John McGinlay, who had tormented Liverpool in 1993. McManaman, who had scored once in five months, plundered two wonderful goals, which saw him collect the man-of-the-match award from Sir Stanley Matthews. His first came in the 37th minute, as he took Barnes's pass, and evaded Alan Stubbs and Scott Green before beating keeper Keith Branaghan. His second saw him get the better of Green, McAteer and Seagraves. He then curled a low shot past Branaghan. Alan Thompson pulled one back with a ferocious strike, but Wanderers couldn't find an equaliser. Rush lifted his first and only trophy as Liverpool captain.

Bruce Grobbelaar returned to Anfield for the first time since the match-fixing allegations. The Kop afforded him a rapturous reception and the 37-year-old blew kisses back. He watched his Southampton team take an early lead, but Rush levelled the scores with a close-range header, before firing Liverpool into the lead shortly after the break with an inch-perfect 25-yarder. Fowler secured the points with a 70th-minute penalty. The bad news was a broken leg sustained by Bjornebye, who had impressed many throughout the season in the demanding wing-back role.

Young winger Mark Kennedy, a £2 million signing from Millwall, made his debut at home to Leeds. Evans had made him the most expensive teenager in Britain. The 19-year-old Irishman hit the crossbar as his side lost 1-0, but that was the highlight of his time at the club. Liverpool were terrible and could have no complaints with the result. A day later, there was some pleasing news as Jones was named in the PFA team of the year, and Fowler was crowned Young Player of the Year.

Fowler celebrated his award with an injury-time winner at Highbury following McManaman's brilliance, to secure a third win of the season against Arsenal.

It wasn't the best of performances, and Thomas ended the game at right back after injuries to Jones and Scales. Kennedy played well again, but his Liverpool career would soon fizzle out. He was primarily a winger and they weren't required in a wing-back system.

Fewer than 48 hours later, on Good Friday, Liverpool lost 2-1 at Maine Road with another insipid performance. McManaman, one of the few to impress, produced a scintillating finish, with City scoring either side of it. Rush missed a couple of chances. With the League Cup and subsequent UEFA Cup place secured, it was clear the Reds were easing up.

The players made amends on Easter Monday with a 2-0 home win over Leicester, who were reduced to ten men on 70 minutes. Fowler, from outside the box, and Rush scored the goals. It was Fowler's 25th in the Premier League and 31st overall. The three points were welcome, but it was another uninspiring performance.

Nearly a year to the day after Norwich ruined the Kop's party, Rush's late goal pushed the Canaries to the brink of relegation. Four teams were due to be relegated to reduce the Premier League to 20 teams. Harkness, recently on loan at Southend, scored Liverpool's first.

A goalless draw at Wimbledon followed, a match in which little happened other than Ruddock sustaining a hamstring injury, which ended his season. It was the team's fourth game of the season at Selhurst Park and the only one they hadn't won.

Another shoddy performance led to a 2-0 defeat at Aston Villa. Dwight Yorke scored a couple of headers in the first half, with the second set up by former Red Dean Saunders. Injuries meant Thomas and Walters started in the wing back positions. Only McManaman deserved to escape criticism. It was the first away defeat since November. "It was a deckchair day for us and not acceptable," said Evans. Perhaps the manager was becoming too lax with the players. He allowed the singer Robbie Williams, a mate of Jones, to travel with the players on the team bus. Stan Collymore met up with the players in London later that evening. He walked through one open hotel-bedroom door to find a scantily-clad future teammate sampling the delights of two young ladies. "Welcome to the Premiership," he thought to himself as he hastily departed. With celebrity girlfriends and nights out in London after games, it wouldn't be long before the squad would find the 'Spice Boys' tag hard to shrug off.

The team was now in free fall, as Don Hutchison scored twice for West Ham as the Reds lost their final away game 3-0. Fowler, Clough and McManaman missed chances. Progress had certainly been made but it was a shame the season was fizzling out with nothing to play for. Third place had now gone. The result secured the Hammers' Premier League status.

The season finished with Liverpool in the spotlight. The title race came down to the final day, with Blackburn two points ahead of Manchester United, who had the better goal difference. Rovers needed to win at Anfield. Should they fail, they needed United to drop points at West Ham. With many Liverpool fans openly supporting Kenny Dalglish's Blackburn, Shearer put them ahead. Barnes equalised in the second half with such a calm finish. There was no question of the Liverpool players being anything other than totally professional. United were drawing 1-1 at Upton Park, with Andy Cole missing chance after chance. Fowler was denied a stonewall penalty after a clumsy challenge by David Batty. Chris Sutton and Alan Shearer missed late sitters in front of the Kop as a nervous Blackburn knew a United winner at Upton Park would cost them the title. Liverpool resolutely denied Rovers the winner they craved. United kept firing blanks in East London, so when Redknapp fired in a sensational free kick to win the game for Liverpool, it made no difference to the title race. Within ten seconds, the final whistle at West Ham confirmed that Dalglish had won his fourth championship as a manager. Ronnie Moran hugged him before he went onto the pitch to celebrate with his players. Rovers lifted the trophy as both sets of supporters revelled in Manchester United's misery.

Liverpool finished fourth, 15 points behind the champions. They had frittered away 30 against the bottom eight. But they could be delighted with a huge improvement on the previous three seasons. It was fun watching the Reds again. Hope and optimism were quickly returning. Roy Evans was doing a fine job.

1995-96

"Win, draw or lose - first on the booze."

Liverpool's resurgence under Roy Evans may have continued during the 1995-96 season, but by the end of a thrilling season, there were questions to be answered about the culture of the club and the professionalism of its players. On the one hand, Liverpool supporters witnessed some of most scintillating football since the great Barnes-Beardsley-Aldridge team of 1987-88. On the other, there were suggestions of underachievement which would plague Evans for the rest of his time as manager. The Reds had been many people's favourites to win the league at the start of the season, but they spent much of the campaign on the periphery of the title race and finished third, 11 points off the top.

The only new player on day one was Stan Collymore, who joined from Nottingham Forest in a British record transfer of £8.5 million. Casually flitting between brilliance and anonymity, his fortunes in red would ultimately mirror that of the entire team. "Discipline was slack when I joined Liverpool," he noted in his 2004 autobiography. "The club was clinging to its links with past glories through players like Ian Rush and John 'Digger' Barnes. The truth was they weren't worth their place in the team anymore, but Rushie and Digger were untouchable." It was a harsh assessment of Barnes, who was still making the team tick. As for Collymore, it took him three months to settle in. He was magnificent for the next four. Then he went missing for the final month and delivered one of the worst individual performances in living memory in the FA Cup Final.

Another key addition came in September with the £4.5 million arrival from Bolton Wanderers of Jason McAteer, who had been on the verge of joining Blackburn. He was primarily a central midfielder, but for Liverpool he would slot in seamlessly at right wing back, with his speed, stamina and crossing ability making him perfect for the offensive side of that role. But he too was inconsistent and unreliable, and he struggled in subsequent seasons to replicate his 1995-96 form. He left the club, like Collymore, having failed to fulfil his potential.

The week that summed up Evans's Liverpool came in April. The famous 4-3 win over Newcastle was followed by a miserable 1-0 defeat at Coventry, which ended any hopes of the title. There was also the 'White Suits' Cup Final against Manchester United, when the culture of the entire club was subjected to national ridicule. Suggestions of unprofessionalism and poor off-field behaviour began to surface throughout the season. Collymore vented his frustrations in a magazine article. Neil Ruddock floored Robbie Fowler at an airport. The drinking culture was as strong as ever. "Win, draw or lose – first on the booze," could have been the mantra of the squad, soon to be universally known as the 'Spice Boys'.

As in 1993, the season began with a home match against Sheffield Wednesday. David James was in goal. Rob Jones and Steve Harkness were the wing backs. Ruddock and John Scales were injured, so Dominic Matteo played as the left-sided centre back, alongside Mark Wright and Phil Babb. Barnes partnered Jamie Redknapp in midfield, with Steve McManaman in his usual free role. In a strange decision, Rush got the nod over Fowler to partner Collymore up front. With Fowler's bleached hair and knockabout approach to life, he would have to earn his recall to the 11, which he inevitably did. But Evans had taken the easy option in excluding the youngster and early-season problems could have been avoided had he just partnered Fowler with Collymore from the off. Michael Thomas was the other outfield sub. Just as in the 1993 opener, it was the newcomer who grabbed the glory against Wednesday, as Collymore curled in a stunning 25-yarder on the hour mark. The star of that fixture from two years prior, Nigel Clough, was still at the club, but barely getting a look in. Other big names out of favour were Paul Stewart, Mark Walters and Jan Molby.

Another wonder goal settled the next match, against Leeds United at Elland Road. This time it came from the boot of Tony Yeboah as his thunderous shot struck the underside of James's crossbar and crossed the line. It would be voted the BBC's goal of the season. Evans fielded the same line-up, although Collymore departed injured, replaced by Fowler. Evans claimed his record signing should have had a penalty before he exited. Jones hit the post late in the game with a shot that deflected off Barnes.

A trip to Spurs meant Liverpool's tough start had pitted them against the teams ranked third, fifth and seventh at the end of the 1994-95 season. Fowler replaced the injured Collymore. Ruddock made his first start of the season, coming in for Matteo. Barnes was the star, scoring twice in the first half to take his tally for the club to 100. Fowler's 50th made it 3-0. A Barnes own goal, with two minutes remaining, left the final score an impressive 3-1 to Liverpool.

An unconvincing 1-0 win over Queens Park Rangers at Anfield saw the Reds move into third. Collymore and Scales were still missing. Ruddock scored the only goal of a scrappy game from Rush's knock down and then enacted an offensive celebration in which he and a few others lay on the turf, pretending to be dead. At least Liverpool had won, having picked up just one point from Rangers the season before.

The Reds were also disjointed when they lost 1-0 at Selhurst Park against the ten men of Wimbledon. Perennial bad guy Vinnie Jones was harshly dismissed on 22 minutes after a set-to with a frustrated Collymore. Mick Harford put the ten men ahead on the half-hour mark. Liverpool turned the screw but were unable to draw level. Paul Heald made crucial saves from Fowler, Collymore and

McManaman. Five points dropped in five games represented a mediocre start.

A 1000% rise in ticket prices didn't prevent a sell-out crowd of 33,500 in Vladikavkaz for Liverpool's first European match in nearly three years. Of that number, only 45 were supporting Liverpool. The public address system played the Beatles hit 'Help' before kick-off, with the announcer declaring, "You will need it, friends from Liverpool!" Redknapp scored a phenomenal winner, after Spartak Vladikavkaz, who were about to be crowned Russian champions, had taken the lead. A howler from James allowed Mirdzhalol Kasimov's free kick go straight in. McManaman rounded the keeper and equalised with a shot from the tightest of angles, before Redknapp picked out the top corner from 30 yards. It was a stupendous goal. At Speke airport after the flight home, Ruddock and Fowler came to blows. "It was after a European game ... in some godforsaken Eastern European shit-hole," wrote Fowler in his autobiography, doing his bit for Anglo-Russian relations. "It was so bad you couldn't even sleep in the beds in the hotel, they were so full of fleas. You had to have the lights on too, so the cockroaches didn't come out." On the flight home, Fowler discovered two pairs of shoes had been cut to pieces and narrowed down the culprit to Scales, Harkness or Ruddock. He exacted his revenge on the latter first. "He was going through a bit of a marriage crisis at the time," said Fowler. "[His wife] made a gesture by buying him these really nice, dead expensive Italian leather shoes, so I cut them into tiny little pieces. He was really aggressive and was going on about me having to buy him a new pair. 'Fuck off,' I said. He turned round and twatted me in the mouth. I had a cut nose and lip and blood was pouring off me. There was a trail going from the tarmac right into the baggage reclaim. That was used as yet another stone to throw at Roy Evans, which was a big regret for all of us."

Despite the long journey home, Liverpool tore the champions Blackburn apart with a sensational first-half performance at Anfield three days later. Rovers had also played Russian opposition, losing 1-0 at home to Spartak Moscow in their Champions League group. Redknapp arrowed in a superb opener before Fowler weighed in with a diving header. Collymore, on the half hour, then curled an unbelievable shot into Tim Flowers' top corner from nearly 30 yards. The Reds were magnificent. Blackburn were floundering, only above the relegation zone on goal difference. Dalglish was no longer manager, having moved into a director-of-football role. McAteer came on for his Liverpool debut in the 82nd minute.

He made his first start against Sunderland in the League Cup second-round first-leg match at Anfield, which the Reds won 2-0. The new boy played in midfield, with Jones and Harkness still the wing backs. "It was an indescribable moment of magic when I pulled the shirt on and then ran on to Anfield with the team," he said. Ruddock skippered the side, which won 2-0 with goals from McManaman and substitute Thomas. The latter had wanted to leave the club and had been linked with Atalanta over the summer. James saved a penalty from Michael Gray.

The improved form continued as Bolton were swept aside 5-2 at Anfield. With Rush now on the bench, the star was Fowler, who had scored four goals by the 67th minute. Wanderers pulled two back before Harkness rifled in a beauty from more than 25 yards. Fowler ranked the achievement above scoring five in the League Cup against lower-division Fulham in 1993. The downside was the performance of Collymore, who had done little in a red shirt aside from those brilliant goals against Wednesday and Rovers.

An uneventful and uninspiring 0-0 draw at home to Vladikavkaz followed, which saw the Reds move into the next round of the UEFA Cup. Ruddock was booked in both legs and would be suspended from the next game.

After Eric Cantona kung-fu kicked a Crystal Palace fan in February 1995, he was suspended until the beginning of October. Liverpool's fixture at Old Trafford had been scheduled for Saturday September 30th. Not surprisingly, Sky Sports requested it be moved to the Sunday, thereby allowing the Frenchman to play. It took him just 67 seconds to set up the first goal of a titanic match, with Nicky Butt the beneficiary. With Old Trafford being redeveloped, there were no away fans to spur them on, but Liverpool grew into the game, enjoying much of the possession. Fowler equalised, capitalising on both Gary Neville being out of position and Peter Schmeichel's near-post weakness, by lashing the ball into the top corner. Seven minutes after the break, he scored again, running on to Thomas's pass, shouldering Neville off the ball before lifting his shot above a stranded Schmeichel. Liverpool had penalty appeals turned down after fouls on McManaman and Fowler but the weakest shout for a penalty won over David Elleray after Redknapp and Giggs had come together. Cantona made it 2-2, keeping United a point ahead of Liverpool in third. For the fourth time in a row, Liverpool left Old Trafford with less than they deserved. They had completely outplayed United.

The Reds failed to kick on, producing three indifferent displays. Sunderland were beaten 1-0 in the second leg of the League Cup, with Jones dismissed. The wing back would now sit out three domestic matches. Fowler lobbed Alec Chamberlain for the goal. Collymore, still on the fringes of Evans' side, came off the bench and had a goal ruled out for offside.

Liverpool then chucked away two points with a goalless draw at home to Coventry – the sort of result that had prevented a title bid in 1994-95. Collymore was misfiring again. Substitute Rush had a goal ruled offside. Unhappy with the prospect of spending much of the season on the bench, the veteran was linked with a move away from the club.

Another 0-0 occurred in Denmark against Brondby, with Rush hitting the bar. James and Wright kept Liverpool in the tie. It seemed a decent result, but the lack of an away goal would prove costly. One disappointed player was Molby, who failed to make the 21-man squad following a loan spell at Barnsley. When the midfielder queried his omission, Evans was honest enough to say he had simply forgotten about him. The big Dane was soon on his way.

An impressive Sunday afternoon win at The Dell started with another early goal conceded. But the Reds were superb for the next hour, with McManaman scoring twice. Redknapp wrapped up the win. Matt Le Tissier, who had scored five times against Liverpool in the 1993-94 season, was sent off for two yellow cards.

Two games against Manchester City, the first in the League Cup, saw the Reds rack up ten goals. Scales, Fowler, Rush and Harkness scored as Liverpool moved into the fourth round of the competition they were defending. The only difference between the sides, according to City manager Alan Ball, was the quality of the finishing.

Three days later, the Reds moved into third place with a 6-0 blitz of a side which would end the season relegated. "I had to sit back and admire them," admitted Ball. Rush and Redknapp scored inside five minutes. Fowler and Ruddock doubled the lead. The centre forwards each bagged a second. Liverpool were four points behind Newcastle, who had a game in hand. The only negative at the club was Collymore. His struggle to fit in at Liverpool was about to become a major issue.

The ensuing 30 days cast a huge shadow over Liverpool's season. From Hallowe'en to the last game in November, the Reds went out of two competitions and their title ambitions were severely hampered. The nightmare run began with a 1-0 home defeat to Brondby in the second leg of their UEFA Cup tie. Rush had a goal ruled out in the first minute. The Danes' deep defending forced the Reds to shoot from distance. Dan Eggen put the visitors ahead with 12 minutes left when Scales lost him from a corner. Because of the away goals rule, Liverpool needed two. They hadn't looked like scoring one.

Liverpool's game at St James' Park was the most frustrating of the season. Les Ferdinand and Rush exchanged early goals. The Reds dominated thereafter, missing chance after chance, with Fowler squandering the most. "What's it like to be outclassed?" sang the visiting fans, but then came the late sucker punch as James couldn't hold Rob Lee's shot and Steve Watson followed it in. "They have given us a lesson in football and deserved something out of the game," admitted Kevin Keegan, the Newcastle manager. For an hour, Liverpool had played their best football under Evans.

Collymore's future at the club came under scrutiny in mid-November when an interview with FourFourTwo magazine was deeply critical of club and manager. "If I felt now that I would be stuck at Liverpool for the next two years and just be average – and just go through the motions – I would give up football tomorrow without a doubt," he said. "I don't know of any other industry that would lay out £8.5 million on anything and then not have some plan from day one of how they are going to use it. So many clubs – I've got to be careful here – are a shambles. You go there thinking they are going to be centres of excellence and they are far from it." He had a point, but his own form was so dire he was now in the reserves. After a 2-0 defeat to Bolton in the second string, Ronnie Moran, Evans's right-hand man, said to Collymore: "You'll never get back into the first team playing like that." According to Moran's son, Paul, who co-wrote his life story, "Of all the players in my dad's time at the club, Collymore is the only one I can remember him saying he never liked. Dad thought Stan was a disruptive influence who felt he was better than everyone else." Liverpool's handling of the episode was far from professional however, with Evans reduced to reading out the player's apology.

The manager's mood would hardly have been helped by Redknapp injuring a hamstring in England's 3-1 win over Switzerland. Back on the field, a new low was reached with a derby defeat at Anfield. Andrei Kanchelskis scored a quick-fire double in the first 20 minutes of the second half, the second of which should have been kept out by James. The Reds could only muster a last-minute goal from Fowler and were now down to seventh. Collymore wasn't even on the bench. Rush had an early goal disallowed for offside, as he had against Brondby, and was critical of Liverpool's lack of a Plan B.

Rush now needed a cartilage operation, which meant a recall for Collymore for the trip to Upton Park. It was the only game Liverpool didn't lose in this miserable month. This free-flowing game was wide open, but nobody managed a breakthrough. Collymore and Fowler missed a couple of chances each. The 0-0 draw took the team up to sixth.

Another visit to the north east ended in a 2-1 defeat. This time the performance was woeful. Middlesbrough scored after two minutes. Ruddock headed in McAteer's cross to level the scores. Within a minute, future Red Nick Barmby scored the winner. Liverpool were in crisis.

The defence of the League Cup ended in round four when Newcastle visited Anfield. Steve Watson scored another late winner, this time chipping James from the edge of the box with glorious precision. Ruddock was substituted with a groin injury. "November has been a nightmare," said a fed-up Evans. "It's not through any lack of effort because we work really hard."

The turning point came on the second day of December as Collymore rifled an equaliser into the roof of Southampton's net. It was another game without a win and a shocking first-half display, but the scenes that greeted the goal represented a sea change in everybody's spirits, not least Collymore's. Fowler nearly beat Dave Beasant with an incredible 50-yard chip. "You cheeky bastard!" shouted the keeper. The Southampton match would be the first of 20 unbeaten, as Liverpool were about to turn their season around in spectacular style.

The first win of that sequence came at Bolton's Burnden Park. Collymore scored the winner just after the hour mark. "I am still looking for more from him," said Evans of the goalscorer, "but at least we are now putting the balls into his feet." It was the Reds' first win in eight matches, despite the absence of Redknapp, Rush, Thomas, McAteer and Ruddock. Phil Charnock, last seen in the 4-4 draw with Chesterfield in the miserable autumn of 1992, was on the bench, although unused. Clough made his last appearance for the club.

Next came one of the highlights of the season, as two goals from Fowler sent Manchester United back along the East Lancs Road seven points adrift of leaders Newcastle. The Reds had closed to within four of United. Liverpool dominated the match and could have racked up half a dozen goals as Collymore missed several one-on-ones with Schmeichel. Luckily, Fowler had brought his shooting boots. His impudent free kick on the stroke of half-time left the angry Dane rooted to the spot. Instead of accepting the blame, he chose to scream at his teammates. The second half was as one-sided an event as Anfield had seen in months, but it wasn't until the 87th minute that the points were sealed. McManaman broke downfield and fed Fowler, who cut inside and lifted the ball over Schmeichel. It was a magnificent performance, with Thomas bossing the midfield. United's tactics were found wanting as Liverpool's wing backs, McAteer and Jones, enjoyed far too much freedom.

Fowler followed that up with another brilliant display of finishing as he scored another treble against Arsenal at Anfield. Ian Wright scored an eighth-minute penalty after Mark Wright brought him down, but Fowler, courtesy of three Collymore assists, brought Liverpool their third consecutive win. His first was a beauty, as he picked out David Seaman's top corner from 20 yards. It was his second Anfield hat-trick against Arsenal in two seasons, although this one took 48 minutes, not four and a half.

After a Boxing Day date at Villa Park was postponed, Liverpool's final game of the calendar year came at Stamford Bridge, where two McManaman goals gave the Reds a point. John Spencer scored twice for Chelsea. McManaman lashed a half-volley into the corner of the net from the edge of the box for the first equaliser. The 23-year-old's next goal was also from outside the box. He wasn't a regular scorer, but when they did come, they had a habit of arriving in twos. James made a crucial late save from Dutch legend Ruud Gullit. Liverpool were third at the turn of the year, ten points behind Newcastle.

The New Year's Day fixture with Nottingham Forest saw Collymore booed and abused relentlessly by the away fans, especially when Forest raced into a 2-0 lead by the 18th minute. When he crossed for Fowler to halve the deficit with a close-range header, the atmosphere totally changed. The noise reached fever pitch as Liverpool surged forward, looking for an equaliser. "At 1-2 there was a howling, roaring scream that must have put the fear of God into Forest and made our boys feel like supermen," reported Through the Wind and Rain. When it came, on 41 minutes, it was almost identical to the first, as Collymore's inch-perfect left-wing cross was headed home by Fowler. And then in the second half came the moment the Forest supporters dreaded. Having already gone close with an audacious half-volley from 30 yards, Collymore capitalised on a dreadful mix-up between Steve Chettle and goalkeeper Mark Crossley to score the goal which put Liverpool 3-2 up. In the closing stages, he gained his third assist, for the second time in a matter of weeks, to cap an incredible individual display, when Colin Cooper turned his cross into his own net. It was the perfect start to 1996.

A fit-again Rush also enjoyed a dream start to 1996. Having been named in the New Year's Day Honours list with an MBE, he scored in the 7-0 shellacking of Rochdale in the FA Cup third round, a goal which took him above Denis Law as the highest scorer in the competition's history, with 42. His first had come in 1979 for Chester City against Workington. Collymore scored his first Liverpool hat trick with Fowler, McAteer and a Peter Valentine own goal completing the rout.

The unbeaten run was maintained at Sheffield Wednesday, but only just, thanks to an 87th-minute equaliser by Rush. Steve Nicol, who had nearly drowned over the Christmas period while rescuing his dog, was in the Wednesday side. Jones had earlier hit a post as Liverpool dominated much of the play.

Another impressive win followed against Leeds. Trailing 1-0 to Ruddock's header, Leeds were reduced to ten men just after the hour after Gary Kelly's professional foul on Jones. Fowler converted the penalty – Liverpool's first in 40 games – before adding a second six minutes later. Collymore powered in a fourth in the last minute of normal time before Ruddock smashed in his second in time added on. Liverpool were now in second, a dozen points behind Newcastle.

After the fourth-round FA Cup tie at Shrewsbury was postponed, Villa presented a much sterner challenge than Leeds, starting the game three points behind the Reds, with a game in hand. The first half was goalless, with Villa keeper Mark Bosnich producing a save from Collymore that The Times compared to Gordon Banks' against Pele in 1970. But Collymore did convert a free kick after an hour before Fowler sealed Liverpool's first league win at Villa Park in a dozen attempts. Collymore's frustrations were now behind him. He and Fowler were forming a lethal partnership. Although his behaviour had left something to be desired in the autumn, some of his claims had been true. His transition into the squad had been mismanaged.

After Evans was presented with the Manager of the Month award for the second time in a row, Liverpool's progress was punctured slightly by Tottenham, who emerged from their trip to Anfield with a goalless draw. It was the first blank the Reds had drawn in 11 matches. Barnes made his 500th league appearance, but the match was something of a damp squib.

Collymore was again on top form as Liverpool won 2-1 at Loftus Road. His early 25-yarder hit the bar before Wright put the Reds ahead with his first goal of the season. Fowler doubled the lead on the half-hour, steering Collymore's through ball past Juergen Sommer. QPR pulled one back, but Liverpool held on, despite an unconvincing second half. Redknapp came off the bench for his first appearance since November. His return gave Evans a dilemma, with Thomas and Barnes having forged such a balanced partnership. For the time being, the manager kept faith in his two experienced midfielders.

On Valentine's Day came the sad news that English football's greatest manager, Bob Paisley, had died after a lengthy battle with Alzheimer's. In an astonishing nine-year reign from 1974 to 1983, Paisley landed six league titles and three European Cups, among many other triumphs. He signed some of the club's finest players – Phil Neal, Terry McDermott, Kenny Dalglish, Graeme

Souness, Alan Hansen, Ian Rush, Mark Lawrenson, Ronnie Whelan and Steve Nicol. Many of his European Cup winners came from lower-division clubs. His funeral was a private affair, with a public memorial service arranged for Liverpool's Anglican Cathedral in April.

Another lower-division team were hammered in the FA Cup, the only domestic trophy to elude Paisley, as the Reds beat Shrewsbury Town 4-0 in a morning kick-off on the third Sunday of February. Collymore opened the scoring with a scuffed shot, but Town held their own for much of the game. An own goal from Dave Walton with 20 minutes left was followed by goals from Fowler and McAteer.

Back in the league, Liverpool completed the double over champions Blackburn, surviving a late siege. Collymore scored an early brace – one of them with a tame shot that hit a divot and comically flew over Tim Flowers' shoulder. His second was a free kick. Jason Wilcox pulled one back before the break. The goal that eventually decided the game came from Thomas's deflected shot, after Fowler's good work. Tim Sherwood reduced the deficit with seven minutes left. Liverpool were left clinging on. It was the first Blackburn home game of the season that Alan Shearer had failed to score in.

A minute's silence for Paisley preceded the fifth-round FA Cup tie with Charlton Athletic. Fowler scored early. Collymore doubled the lead on the hour. Fowler had 27 for the season and Collymore 14, although he was becoming as much a creator as scorer now. Kim Grant pulled a late goal back, but the Reds had done enough and were unbeaten in 15 matches. Twenty-four hours before the game, it was announced that Rush would leave at the end of the season.

The run continued in style at home to Villa, when an incredible onslaught saw Liverpool lead 3-0 after just eight minutes. McManaman scored a brilliant volley on the turn, arrowing Barnes' flick into the bottom corner in the first minute. Then it was the Robbie Fowler show. On three minutes, he turned former Red Steve Staunton with breathtaking cockiness and fired the ball just inside Mark Bosnich's post from 25 yards. It was one of the goals of the season. Five minutes later, he was released down the left and his shot squirmed through Bosnich. The game petered out subsequently, but those eight minutes were a warning that Liverpool were a major force. "We're gonna win the league!" sang the Kop.

A thoroughly boring 0-0 draw at Leeds in the sixth round of the Cup may have been frustrating, but at least the Reds on an off day had enough character to get a replay. Still scarred by January's 5-0, Howard Wilkinson fielded a five-man defence, which Liverpool failed to break down. Fowler and Collymore were reduced to 25-yard potshots. McManaman hit the side netting. "Rarely has a match promised so much and delivered so little," concluded Henry Winter in the Telegraph.

Liverpool were then involved in one of the most compelling matches of the season at home to Wimbledon. McManaman scored his eighth of the season before the break. But two goals in six minutes put the visitors ahead with half an hour to play. The Reds bombarded the Kop goal, and had three goals disallowed, including a belter from Thomas. They eventually earned a point with Collymore's equaliser. It was a poor result in terms of the title race, but with three goals chalked off, it was hard to be critical. Evans had fielded the same starting line-up for eight matches in a row. McAteer and Jones were settled in the wing-back roles. Wright, Scales and Babb were the centre-back trio. In Redknapp's absence, Thomas had formed a more balanced midfield partnership with Barnes. McManaman, Collymore and Fowler were terrorising defences.

Harkness replaced the injured Babb in a routine win over Chelsea three days later. After a frustrating first half, in which Collymore hit the bar, Wright made the breakthrough on 53 minutes, heading in Barnes's cross. Fowler, in his 100th league appearance, added his 62nd goal in that time, glancing McAteer's cross past Kevin Hitchcock.

The unbeaten run stretched to 20 when Liverpool progressed into the FA Cup semi-finals for the 19th time. In the quarter-final replay, Leeds were swept aside by a magnificent second-half performance, with the imperious McManaman scoring another brace to move into double figures for the campaign. Fowler made it 3-0 with a free kick John Lukic should have saved. Ruddock was back in the side for his first game since January.

The first defeat since November came at the City Ground as Collymore endured an unhappy return. Forest's Steve Stone scored the only goal three minutes before half-time following a mistake by James. The record signing, who received a police escort into the ground, was jeered as he was substituted with 20 minutes left, having earlier been booked. Forest had been beaten 5-1 at home by Bayern Munich four days earlier but had no problems keeping Liverpool out.

The team responded superbly at Old Trafford by beating League Cup winners Aston Villa 3-0 in the FA Cup semi-final. Ticket prices of £38 kept the crowd to just 39,072, but they saw Fowler score a brilliant diving header from the recalled Redknapp's free kick, and then a wonderful dipping left-footed volley. He had made his England debut four days earlier. A jubilant McAteer rounded off the scoring with a late tap-in – his third goal in the competition. Liverpool had beaten an impressive Villa side three times in two months, racking up eight goals and conceding none. Before the three games, Villa had conceded just 16 in 22 games. Ruddock kissed James on the forehead after one save. Liverpool would be playing Manchester United at Wembley.

"Collymore closing in ... Liverpool lead in stoppage time! Kevin Keegan hangs his head. He's devastated!" Euphoria rained down from the Kop when Liverpool went 4-3 up against Newcastle in injury time in the most talked-about game in Premier League history. "The noise was unbelievable," said Collymore. "A great roar that went right through me. I thought my head was going to explode." While Collymore's goal became one of the Premier League's most iconic moments, the quality of Liverpool's other goals is often forgotten. Redknapp played a sumptuous second-minute ball which Jones cushioned adeptly for Collymore. He got to the line and swung in an inch-perfect cross for Fowler to nod home.

Goals from Les Ferdinand and David Ginola, with James and McAteer at fault, put the Geordies ahead at the break. James then rolled the ball to McAteer, who played a long pass up the right wing to McManaman. The playmaker drove into the Newcastle box and squared it to Fowler, whose first-time left-footed shot flew past Pavel Srnicek. Within a minute, the Magpies led again. With lovely vision, Peter Beardsley opened up the Liverpool midfield. Rob Lee sent Faustino Asprilla clear. The Colombian was played onside by Scales and shot past the advancing James with the outside of his foot. The keeper tried to stop the low shot with his head, as he was out of his box. The Reds hit back. McAteer sent in a peach of a cross for Collymore to turn in. 3-3. James made a crucial late save from Ferdinand. And then came the killer moment. Scales, Barnes and Rush, who had come on for Jones, played a series of short passes between then, which took the Reds into the Newcastle area. Man of the match McManaman was screaming for Rush to find him on the right. Instead, Barnes took over, looked up and saw Collymore in oceans of space on the left. The record signing took one touch to steady himself and then rifled a swerving shot inside Srnicek's near post to send the supporters crazy. It was a truly amazing moment. The win was deserved, as Liverpool had two-thirds of the possession and 29 shots to Newcastle's 12. It was all the sweeter after November's injustice at St James' Park. The Reds trailed leaders Manchester United by five points after 32 matches.

The next result summed up Evans' Liverpool as much as the 4-3. Having given themselves something of a footing in the title race again, the Reds lost 1-0 at Ron Atkinson's second-from-bottom Coventry City three days later with an underwhelming performance. "We might not have scored if we had played until midnight," admitted Evans, who then went on to bemoan that not enough injury time had been played. Noel Whelan scored after 18 minutes. Ex-Red Steve Ogrizovic saved well from Fowler, who also hit the woodwork twice. Liverpool offered little else. Harkness broke a leg in a challenge with John Salako. "It was a shambolic display," said Scales, "one extreme to the exact opposite. It was terrible. I was terrible. Roy can't take the blame for that. Individually, we all made errors."

Two days later, on Easter Monday, Liverpool bounced back with a comfortable 2-0 win at home to West Ham. A weakened team featured Bjornebye and Matteo, with Thomas one of the centre backs and Mark Kennedy on the bench. Collymore and Barnes scored first-half goals in a dull game.

As had been the case in 1995, Liverpool slackened up in April, and the league season fizzled out. Fowler rescued a point at Goodison with an 87th-minute equaliser from Collymore's superb cross. Kanchelskis had again scored for Everton. Liverpool dominated the second half, and Collymore hit the bar with a stunning 30-yarder before Fowler struck. A week later, Fowler came third in the Football Writers' Association Footballer of the Year behind Cantona and Gullit. He had already been named best young player by his peers.

Rush played at Anfield for the final time when he replaced Fowler in the 60th minute of Middlesbrough's visit at the end of April. But he couldn't give the crowd the goal they craved, with Collymore scoring the only goal of a lifeless game. Rush threw his shirt into the Kop after the game, as he had done against Watford in 1987 before his move to Juventus.

The penultimate league game was a scoreless draw at Arsenal, with Liverpool grateful to James for making a string of excellent saves. "He has been exceptional this season," said Evans.

The last league match saw the Reds draw 2-2 at Maine Road, a result which sent Manchester City down. Steve Lomas turned McManaman's cross into his own net before Rush scored his 346th and final goal for the club. Clough was in the City team, having moved there for £1.5 million in January. He was substituted on 68 minutes. Within ten minutes, City restored parity but mistakenly believed that a draw would rescue them.

Liverpool didn't just have the FA Cup Final to look forward to. Their kids had also booked a place in the FA Youth Cup Final, which would take place over two legs against West Ham, who had beaten the Tommy Smith-captained Reds in the 1963 decider. Along the way, the Reds had beaten Bradford, Luton, Sheffield United, Manchester United and Crystal Palace. The squad included Jamie Carragher, Michael Owen, David Thompson and Jon Newby. The captain was the defender Phil Brazier. Owen had scored two hat-tricks including one against United in a 3-2 win in which Liverpool had been totally outplayed. Carragher had played in midfield throughout the competition but moved into defence for the final, replacing the suspended Eddie Turkington. Rio Ferdinand and Redknapp's cousin Frank Lampard were in the Hammers' side. The young Reds won the first leg of the final 2-0 at Upton Park, with Owen away on England Under-16 duty. Newby and David Larmour got the goals. Owen returned for the Anfield leg and headed Liverpool's first goal after Lampard had opened the scoring. Stuart Quinn got the winner, giving the Reds a 4-1 win on aggregate in front of a crowd of 25,000.

Six days after the final league game, Liverpool's players were wandering around Wembley in their white Armani suits before their FA Cup Final with Manchester United. "It was the biggest fucking mistake we made," said Redknapp, admitting the players looked "a bunch of idiots." Defeat to United was bad enough, but the pre-match attire would come to define the Roy Evans years. As for the match itself, Ruddock was dropped by Evans, admitting he was reduced to tears by the decision. Babb would offer more mobility in the left centre-back position. The game made for an awful spectacle. Liverpool's attacking flair had been on display all season, but teams were finding it easier to neutralise it. Collymore had a stinker, reduced to pointless long-rangers. He hadn't slept and had even knocked back a brandy with supporters in the early hours. United had been unable to deal with Liverpool's wing-back system when played at such devastating pace earlier in the season, but this time, they shackled McManaman, Barnes, McAteer and Jones. Going forward, they were almost as bad as Liverpool, but they won a painfully bad game with a late goal when James's weak punch fell to Eric Cantona, who volleyed goalwards. Rush, Jones and McAteer failed to get anything on it and the League and Cup double was United's.

While the final is remembered for the white suits, there were several other examples of Liverpool's rank unprofessionalism that day. Players and staff partied long into the night at a prime Soho venue, the Emporium, whose logo was even emblazoned on the Liverpool team bus that day. Redknapp apologised to the players for persuading Collymore to come to Liverpool. Evans told some of the players the record signing would be gone by the start of the next season because he was so bad for morale. Collymore, meanwhile, revealed in his book that he slept with the manager's 18-year-old daughter that night. Scales had earlier rowed furiously on the team bus with coaches Doug Livermore and Sammy Lee about the lack of professionalism at the club.

This most promising of seasons had ended in such disappointment. They had the talent to recover but they would never shake off the 'Spice Boys' tag and the unfair perception that they cared more about their social lives than they did about winning trophies.

1996-97

"Beyond Merseyside, no one knew the truth about what happened at Hillsborough. People had swallowed the lies that the right-wing press told, together with what the government and the police put out there."

When the pain of the FA Cup Final had worn off, there were plenty of reasons to be optimistic heading into the new campaign. No one expected Liverpool to win the league in 1996, but they had got themselves into the race on the back of four months of thrilling football in the winter and spring. If that could be repeated, and with a few tweaks here and there, the Reds would surely challenge for the title again, or even win it.

Roy Evans had failed on his promise to the players to get rid of Stan Collymore, but all the fans knew at that stage was that he was an exceptional footballer who had more than played his part in the 1995-96 season. Robbie Fowler and Steve McManaman had proven to be two of the best homegrown talents anyone could remember. With plenty of other talent in the squad, now was the time to land some major silverware. But when the Premier League title was in Liverpool's hands in April 1997, they blew it. They lost their bottle and, most damningly of all, nobody was really surprised. The 1996-97 season will always be remembered at Anfield for Liverpool coming fourth in a two-horse race. A very mediocre Manchester United clinched the 1997 title with just 75 points, the lowest points tally of any Premier League winner. The faults that were so apparent in the summer of 1996 hadn't been addressed.

The 'Spice Boys' tag has never gone down well with the players it was aimed at. Some of the criticism was certainly deserved. Some of it wasn't. Fowler and McManaman couldn't keep compensating for the faults of others. Fowler wrote in his 2005 autobiography: "Two little words that's all, and yet what were incredible times at Anfield – successful, exciting, breathless seasons when I played probably the best football of my life – are dismissed with contempt by those two tiny words." He had a point when it came to criticism of him. He deserved none. He was one of the best strikers in the world between 1994 and 1997.

The only new signing was Patrik Berger, one of the stars of the Czech Republic's impressive march to the final of Euro 96. He joined from Borussia Dortmund for £2.25 million. He spoke later of how basic Melwood was. "I was a little bit shocked Liverpool should have it like this," he said. "Everything was old. The only thing that was up to date was the grass, which they cut every day." Berger started spectacularly, but his transition into the side on a regular basis was mishandled. He seemed to be rated by everybody but Evans.

There were no significant calls in the summer of 1996 for Liverpool to sign new defenders or a goalkeeper. They had conceded fewer goals than the champions in successive seasons. Despite occasional erratic moments, David James was then viewed as a safe pair of hands, capable of world-class saves. Jason McAteer had enjoyed a tremendous first season at right wing back. There were concerns over the fitness of Rob Jones on the left, but Stig Inge Bjornebye would go on to have an excellent season. There was no shortage of centre backs. Mark Wright and John Scales were two of the best around. Dominic Matteo looked promising. Neil Ruddock and Phil Babb were still around. Steve Harkness was recovering from his broken leg.

The biggest concern, perhaps, was the midfield, where John Barnes and Jamie Redknapp were too similar. Neither were mobile or physical or scored many goals. Barnes could keep things ticking over, but it was becoming harder to spot the strengths of the injury-prone Redknapp. The midfield had possessed more bite and purpose with Michael Thomas next to Barnes in 1995-96. When Redknapp replaced Thomas in the spring, the team lost its drive. A top-class midfielder should have been on Evans' radar in the summer of 1996. Few had concerns over the Collymore-Fowler partnership, but Ian Rush had gone, so there was no longer a natural back-up, other than young kids Lee Jones, who Evans didn't seem to rate, and Michael Owen, who didn't emerge until April.

The opening match at Middlesbrough was one of those games that summed up the Roy Evans era. Three times Liverpool took the lead in their new ecru away kit. Three times Fabrizio Ravanelli equalised. It was a fabulous match and Liverpool's attack looked as fluent as ever, but it was two points dropped against a side who would eventually be relegated. James was in goal. McAteer and Bjornebye were the wing backs. Wright, Babb and Matteo were the centre backs – Scales's pre-season had been disrupted by laryngitis and the stress of his wedding being called off. Barnes and Thomas were in central midfield, with Redknapp injured during England's Euro 96 campaign. McManaman roamed behind Collymore and Fowler. For the first time, five substitutes could be named in the Premier League. Liverpool's squad looked sparse as Evans chose Tony Warner, Ruddock, David Thompson, Lee Jones and Jamie Carragher. The latter three had been part of the team which had won the 1996 FA Youth Cup. Bjornebye scored the first Premier League goal of the season with a low left-footed shot, followed by a strange celebration. It was his first goal for Liverpool. The Norwegian's career was back on track after his 1995 leg break. McAteer conceded a penalty which Ravanelli converted. Barnes restored Liverpool's lead, chesting down McAteer's cross and half-volleying into the corner. The Italian cancelled it out seven minutes later. Fowler stabbed Bjornebye's cross into the roof of Alan Miller's net. Again, Liverpool couldn't hold on. The £7 million man's hat-trick goal made it 3-3 with nine minutes remaining. Barnes, Wright and Bjornebye all caught the eye.

Two days later, on Sky's Monday Night Football, the first time the programme had been broadcast from Anfield, two late McManaman goals against Arsenal gave Liverpool their first win of the season. His first deflected in off Steve Bould. The second was a follow-up to David Seaman blocking Barnes' shot. The same line-up and bench were chosen. Jones and Thompson came on for Collymore and Fowler for the final four minutes.

James saved Liverpool from an embarrassing defeat at home to Sunderland in game three. The keeper, recently called up by England, saved twice from Niall Quinn against the newly promoted side. Ex-Red Paul Stewart had a strong shot blocked by Thomas. At the other end, Barnes hit the bar with a header from Bjornebye's corner. McManaman, closely man-marked all game, and Fowler both went close, but more points were dropped against a team that would be relegated.

Babb was the unlikely scorer when Liverpool travelled to Highfield Road to beat his former team. McAteer swung in a dangerous ball, and the defender side-footed his first goal for the club. Coincidentally, he had scored the only goal of the same fixture almost three years to the day earlier for Coventry. McManaman and Collymore spurned chances to double the lead, but it was a handy three points against a team that had been a thorn in Evans' side. The game was the first of a winning streak of seven in all competitions.

Liverpool were unconvincing in their 2-1 defeat of Southampton, needing a last-minute Steve McManaman goal. Graeme Souness was back at Anfield for the first time since his 1994 resignation and received a warm reception. He set up his side to frustrate Liverpool. Collymore scored his first of the season six minutes before the break. Former Red Jim Magilton equalised. Towards the end, an error from Neil Heaney put McManaman clear and he rounded Dave Beasant to win the match. Matteo continued his excellent start to the season. Redknapp made his first appearance. Berger came on for his Liverpool debut.

The first game in the European Cup Winners' Cup, which Liverpool entered as FA Cup runners-up because Manchester United were in the Champions League, took place in Finland. The Reds beat MyPa-47 1-0. Bjornebye continued his impressive start to the season with the only goal of the game, hammering in a left-footed shot from just inside the box.

Berger, complete with Alice band to keep his hair in place, enjoyed a dream Sunday afternoon at Filbert Street when his brace of second-half scorchers put Leicester City to the sword, having replaced Collymore at half-time. "I've never seen a ball move so fast in my life," said the Foxes' keeper Kasey Keller. "It's a good job I didn't get in the way of either shot or I'd have been back in the net with them!" Thomas scored in between as the Reds won 3-0 to go top.

On his first start, at the expense of Collymore, Berger scored two more in a wonderful 5-1 victory at home to Chelsea. Fowler's header from Bjornebye's perfect cross was the first goal. Matteo strolled through the Chelsea midfield to release Berger, who rounded Kevin Hitchcock to score. On the stroke of half-time, an Andy Myers own goal, from another Bjornebye cross, made it 3-0.

61

Berger side-footed in at the Kop end after a Chelsea error and then a volley from Barnes deflected in off Dennis Wise. Chelsea pulled one back as Liverpool eased off, but it was a dream performance against a star-studded side. Berger was the Premier League player of the month for September.

Another superlative goal by the Czech helped see off MyPa-47 in the second leg of the Cup Winners' Cup. He nutmegged a defender before finding the corner with an unerring finish. Collymore and Barnes added second-half goals, as the Reds triumphed 3-1 (4-1 on aggregate). Fowler missed the match with an ankle injury, and Wright sustained a depressed fracture of the cheekbone, which would sideline him for six weeks.

A classy early goal by Collymore sent Liverpool on their way as they negotiated a tricky game at West Ham to remain top of the league. A disgruntled Hammers fan threw a drink at him as he celebrated. Slaven Bilic profited from non-existent marking from a corner to equalise, before Collymore departed injured. Evans replaced him with midfielder Redknapp, later admitting he should have introduced young Lee Jones. With Fowler still absent, Berger finished the game up front with McManaman. Ten minutes into the second half, Thomas blasted the winning goal into the bottom corner. West Ham's Julian Dicks hit the bar against his old club, while James denied Tony Cottee and Iain Dowie. McAteer clipped the crossbar in the closing stages. Liverpool were three points clear of Arsenal after eight matches.

For the fifth season in a row, Liverpool got less than they deserved at Manchester United. Still without Fowler, the Reds dominated but couldn't find a way past man of the match Peter Schmeichel. McManaman wasted the most chances. He fired "with all the accuracy of a blunderbuss," according to the Sunday Times. Liverpool's profligacy was ruthlessly punished by David Beckham, who found the corner of James's net from the edge of the box in the first half. "We created so many chances," complained Evans. "And I'm not talking about half chances, I'm on about clear headers from five yards. If we could have put one away, I think we'd have scored three of four." It would prove to be a costly defeat. Victory would have put Liverpool seven points clear of United. Instead of cursing the bad luck that seemed to accompany them to Old Trafford every year, perhaps Liverpool lacked United's big-game mentality.

The Cup Winners' Cup took Liverpool to Switzerland, where they beat FC Sion 2-1. An error from Matteo let in the hosts to score first, but Fowler, back in the team after four games, levelled the scores after Berger's shot had been pushed onto a post. Barnes scored the winner in the second half, heading in Bjornebye's corner.

Anfield's Merseyside Derby was postponed due to a waterlogged pitch, on the same day Newcastle beat Man United 5-0. In their next game, Liverpool drew 1-1 at Charlton in the third round of the League Cup. Evans picked his strongest team against the second-bottom side in Division One. Fowler cancelled out David Whyte's goal. Charlton had plenty of chances to win. The Reds were lucky to still be in the competition.

Back in the league, two Fowler goals accounted for Derby County in front of the Sky cameras. Liverpool made life tough for themselves by conceding a late goal. With a game in hand, the Reds were a point behind Arsenal and Newcastle. The game had been preceded by a minute's silence for the victims of the Guatemala City Stadium disaster, in which 83 fans died, as well as for the Chelsea vice-chairman Matthew Harding, victim of a helicopter crash.

Four days later, Anfield staged an incredible game as the hosts recovered from an early 2-0 deficit to defeat Sion 6-3. The aggregate score was 8-4. With the team two down in 23 minutes, the outstanding McManaman levelled the aggregate score before half-time. Bjornebye then scored his second European goal of the season before Sion scored another to hold the advantage, courtesy of the away-goals rule. A backheel from Barnes, similar to the one he scored at Crewe in 1992, and a quick-fire double from Fowler sealed the tie, before Berger scored in the last minute to end a crazy night. "McManaman and Patrik Berger are their two best players," said Sion's coach, Michel Decastel. "The rest of the team play for them and off them." The Reds were into the quarter-finals, which would be played in March.

The month of November had ruined the 1995-96 season, so it didn't bode well when Liverpool were hammered at Ewood Park in the first match of the month. It was another defensive shambles as Blackburn won 3-0. A clean sheet hadn't been kept since the thrashing of Leicester in mid-September. The defence hadn't settled all season, with injuries to Ruddock, Wright and Scales causing problems for the manager. Bjornebye, who was enjoying an excellent season, came off injured in the first half. Collymore, who had been an unused sub for four straight matches, replaced Berger on the hour. To add to Liverpool's misery, it was Rovers' first win of the season, as they had struggled to deal with the departure of Alan Shearer. They remained rooted to the foot of the table, having been champions just 18 months earlier.

With the first team out of action for ten days, Collymore caused a stir by refusing to play in a reserve-team game at Tranmere, in which Ruddock and Scales played. Amid rumours he could be kicked out, he was fined £20,000 by the club – the largest ever imposed on a Liverpool player. He was selected to play another second-string game against Sheffield Wednesday, alongside Redknapp, Michael Owen and Paul Dalglish, with Kenny in attendance. This time he turned up. But he caused more controversy by making an offensive gesture and shouting at journalists in the press box when he scored the first of his two goals. The club looked into this latest indiscretion but took no action. He was linked with a move to Aston Villa and that's where he went at the end of the season.

The Reds responded by beating Charlton 4-1 in the League Cup replay. Wright and Redknapp scored early before two second-half goals from Fowler eased Liverpool into the quarter-finals. Evans was still unsure of his best formation and starting line-up, with both Berger and Collymore now on the bench, with three midfielders - Barnes, Thomas and Redknapp - starting.

A shut-out was finally kept at Elland Road as Liverpool turned over Leeds United, for whom Ian Rush was playing. He hadn't scored in 13 Leeds appearances, although he was being played on the right wing by George Graham. After bad misses by McManaman and Fowler, the returning Ruddock scored after Gary Kelly failed to clear a corner. Liverpool spurned several more chances but sealed the game in injury time when Nigel Martyn miscontrolled the ball near the halfway line. McManaman slid it past him and walked it into the net before the joyous visiting fans.

Having got back on the horse in the Premier League, the Reds were then held to two frustrating draws at Anfield. Both games saw a pedestrian Liverpool squander a lead. In the rearranged Merseyside Derby, an injured McManaman left the field after 17 minutes, but the in-form Fowler headed the Reds into the lead on the half hour. But Joe Royle's Everton kept at Liverpool, and the introduction of Duncan Ferguson disrupted the Reds' rhythm. They were rewarded with an equaliser from Gary Speed on 82 minutes. Everton fans sang the name of Eric Cantona, who had scored the winner in May's FA Cup Final. The Blues were unbeaten in five derbies, and Liverpool were denied top spot.

Three days later, Collymore scored after just 33 seconds against Wimbledon, but the Reds failed to build upon it. They performed dreadfully, allowing the Londoners back into the game. An unsettled crowd got on the players' backs, and the players were eventually booed off after an equaliser from future Red Oyvind Leonhardsen. Evans and McAteer criticised the supporters. Matteo was stretchered off in the first half after a clash of heads. Liverpool regularly struggled against well-organised, aggressive sides, and here was another example. They were a point behind Newcastle but still five ahead of eventual champions Manchester United.

The side responded with two excellent wins over the North London teams, starting with Arsenal in the League Cup. Liverpool won 4-2 with the Gunners scoring two penalties. Fowler continued his great form with two goals, one from the spot and the other from McAteer's cross. McManaman and Berger also scored. Arsenal's Steve Bould was sent off on 56 minutes for a second yellow card. "Liverpool are the best side we have played since I joined Arsenal," said the Gunners' new boss, Arsene Wenger.

On Sky's Monday Night Football, two goals in four minutes of play, either side of the break, earned the Reds a comfortable 2-0 win at White Hart Lane. Thomas scored just before the break with a finish similar to his goal at Upton Park. Then McManaman's pea roller jumped off a divot and flew over the shoulder of Spurs keeper Ian Walker, who had crouched down to collect the ball. It was identical to Collymore's goal at Ewood Park the season before. McManaman, the game's best player, joked that Liverpool had brought with them 'the portable divot'.

Three days after the Spurs game, on December 5th, Jimmy McGovern's drama-documentary about the Hillsborough Disaster was broadcast on ITV, telling the story of the Hicks, Glover and Spearritt families between 1989 and 1991. "'Hillsborough' is the most important piece of work I've ever done and ever will do," said Christopher Eccleston, who played Trevor Hicks, father of teenagers Sarah and Victoria, who passed away in the tragedy. "Beyond Merseyside, no one knew the truth about what happened at Hillsborough. People had swallowed the lies that the right-wing press told, together with what the government and the police put out there. Jimmy wrote it to correct those lies and, most importantly, to allow the families to grieve – because the lies devastated and destroyed the grieving process." Although the cover-up would continue for years to come, the film is seen as one of the turning points in a fight for justice that was still ongoing more than 30 years after the disaster.

Back on the field, and typical of the 1996-97 team, those wins over Arsenal and Spurs were followed by an embarrassment as mid-table Sheffield Wednesday, who included Steve Nicol four days shy of his 35th birthday, won 1-0 at Anfield. McAteer's surrendering of possession led to Peter Atherton's goal on 21 minutes. The goal scorer shackled a subdued McManaman for much of the match. It was becoming an effective tactic to tie down Liverpool's playmaker. A heroic display by Kevin Pressman kept Liverpool at bay but there could be no excuses. Wednesday even had chances for a second. It was a dreadful result. "I'd hate to think we are nothing more than a McManaman team," said Evans. A couple of days later, Scales was sold to Tottenham for £2.6 million. He had barely put a foot wrong in his time at the club.

The Reds bounced back with two more impressive performances, starting with a 5-1 thrashing of Middlesbrough, in which Fowler scored his 100th Liverpool in 165 matches, one fewer game than it had taken Rush. He scored the first after just 29 seconds, beating Collymore's goal against Wimbledon by four seconds. His next was the milestone goal, before Bjornebye scored his fourth of the season. Fowler scored two more in the second half. Back in the side, Collymore registered a hat-trick of assists, as he had done twice in the previous season. But he was trailing the Norwegian wing-back for goals.

Collymore was back to his best for the visit of Nottingham Forest in mid-December, as an unchanged Liverpool won 4-2. His season was mirroring his first campaign – a slow start had seen him dropped in the autumn before he hit form in the winter. He scored twice against his old club, with Fowler and a Des Lyttle own goal completing the scoring. Stuart Pearce scored one of Forest's goals with a stunning free kick. The result took the Reds top for the first time since September and left Forest bottom, facing a second relegation in five seasons. At half-time, there was a period of applause to raise awareness of the fight for justice for the 96.

Liverpool travelled to the north east for their last game before Christmas, emerging from St James' Park with a 1-1 draw. Fowler and Collymore almost conjured up an incredible start from the opening kick-off, with the latter dribbling deep into the Magpies' half, before playing in Fowler, whose goal-bound header was cleared off the line by Darren Peacock. Shearer scored first after James tipped Les Ferdinand's header onto the bar. Fowler equalised just before half-time, slamming in McManaman's pullback. James saved brilliantly from Ferdinand, and Thomas cleared another effort off the line. On the surface, it seemed a decent result, but it was a patchy performance against a side which had picked up just four points from a possible 18. Barnes completed 51 from 52 passes, according to the statistics used by Sky Sports, but none were regarded as 'key' passes. Peter Beardsley was one of Newcastle's best, six and a half years after Souness sold him for a measly £1 million. Berger remained an unused sub; the glorious start he had made to his Liverpool career hadn't been built upon, with Evans struggling to utilise him in the 3-5-2 system.

The Reds remained top after a frustrating draw with Leicester on Boxing Day, the club's first home match on December 26th since 1989. Steve Claridge put the Foxes ahead with 14 minutes to play, but Collymore restored parity four minutes later with a clinical finish after playing a one-two with Wright who had a superb game. Fowler missed out with an ankle injury, with Berger taking his place. He missed a late chance to win the game. Evans clearly didn't rate Lee Jones, a more natural number nine, who barely featured during the season, despite often being named substitute.

Barnes scored a sublime goal in Liverpool's final match of 1996, to cement their lead at the top of the table. With Dave Beasant scrambling back into his goal from the corner flag, Barnes calmly sent the ball goalwards from 40 yards. After an agonising few seconds, it was clear it was going to cross the line with the veteran keeper still stranded. Few could have produced such a moment of magic, and it came on 76 minutes, as Liverpool had looked set for another irritating draw. Graeme Souness's side were second bottom. Liverpool had lost just six matches in all competitions in 1996, but there had been too many draws. In the second half of the year, the defence looked porous and the midfield lacked bite. The Reds were five points clear at the top, although Manchester United and Arsenal each had a game in hand. They had also reached two quarter-finals, but Evans would have to find a significant improvement if Liverpool were to win their first title in seven years.

1997 began with a terribly disappointing defeat at Stamford Bridge as Thomas's blind pass was seized upon by Roberto di Matteo, who scored the only goal of the game. Substitute Berger caused Chelsea problems, especially with Liverpool switching to a flat back four, but the performance was a far cry from the 5-1 win in September. "We were just too negative in possession," said Evans.

Liverpool had nearly all the ball in their next game against Burnley in the FA Cup but could only manage a 1-0 win against a team whose manager, Adrian Heath, only seemed concerned with keeping the score down. Collymore produced the only goal from Bjornebye's squared pass a dozen minutes into the game and nearly added another with an incredible over-the-shoulder volley from fully 70 yards late in the game.

The Reds' League Cup hopes came to an end in the quarter-final at Middlesbrough. The hosts were two up in 27 minutes, with lifelong Red Craig Hignett one of the scorers. McManaman got one back with 25 minutes remaining, but Liverpool couldn't force an equaliser. The headline "Evans Slams Sloppy Liverpool", was becoming the story of the season as they were pressed into error after error. After Chelsea, Boro were another team to turn the tables on the Reds after losing 5-1 at Anfield. They were in the Premier League's bottom three. There were two pieces of good news for Liverpool, however. Rob Jones made his first start since the FA Cup Final, and Jamie Carragher made his first-team debut in midfield, replacing Jones in the 75th minute. It was the first of 737 appearances he would make before his 2013 retirement. But the biggest story of the day was Kevin Keegan's resignation as Newcastle United manager. He would be succeeded by Kenny Dalglish.

Three days later in the Premier League, Liverpool were unable to break down West Ham at Anfield. Injuries to Babb and Ruddock disrupted the team. A sick Wright was already missing but they still had the troops to beat the division's 17th-best team at home. Barnes, Fowler and Berger each hit the woodwork in the first half, but the Hammers were the better side after the break. Liverpool were still top, but only because they had played more games than Arsenal, United and Wimbledon.

Wright returned to ease the defensive crisis for the visit of Aston Villa, but Evans still had to bring in the Norwegian Bjorn Tore Kvarme, whose clearance came through in the nick of time. He went straight into the side, with Matteo the third centre back. Carragher made his first start, in the middle of midfield, and marked it by flattening Gareth Southgate after 20 seconds. And then he scored the opening goal in the 50th minute, heading in Bjornebye's corner at the Kop end. It was a Roy of the Rovers debut. Collymore scored eight minutes later, also with his head, before Fowler scored the third in 13 minutes. It would be the last time Liverpool would be top in 1997. By the time they played again, United had won their game in hand.

The impressive form was taken into the FA Cup fourth-round tie at Stamford Bridge when goals from Fowler and Collymore had the Reds 2-0 up at the break. McManaman missed a sitter to make it three. But the disgraceful second-half collapse, precipitated by Mark Hughes coming on at the break, was all too typical of this side. Hughes pulled one back. Gianfranco Zola equalised. Gianluca Vialli scored twice. The four goals had come in 26 painful minutes, with Liverpool embarrassed on national television. "We could sense the fear in them," said Hughes, whose goal had beaten Liverpool in the 1985 semi-final. "It looked as if they didn't fancy it," added player-manager Ruud Gullit. Few could disagree. It was the first time since 1964 that Liverpool had lost after being two up. After the game, a furious Sammy Lee urged Carragher, who hadn't played, not to follow in the footsteps of some of the "bottlers" in the team.

The last thing Liverpool needed was a six-a-side competition in Amsterdam, but they had agreed to enter the 1997 Euro Sixes, along with Ajax, AC Milan and Glasgow Rangers. Each club received £120,000. The first game took place the day after the Chelsea humiliation, with Liverpool hammered 5-0 by Milan. Roberto Baggio even hit the bar from his own half. The starting line-up was

Warner, Harkness, Babb, Redknapp, Fowler and Thomas. They then lost 7-3 to Rangers, with Matteo (two) and Barnes scoring, and 8-1 to Ajax. Carragher was also in the squad. The huge defeats were an embarrassment, but at least no one got injured, unlike Rangers' Paul Gascoigne, who had to miss England's next game. The competition was never repeated.

The Reds bounced back by winning at 10-man Derby County, with a clinical 75th-minute goal from Collymore. Darryl Powell had been dismissed just after half-time for going studs-in on Kvarme, leaving Derby manager Jim Smith incandescent.

There was an 18-day gap until the next game, which Liverpool appeared to have used well. They obliterated Leeds at Anfield with an outstanding first-half performance. Lucas Radebe was tasked with man-marking McManaman but picked up a yellow card after 39 seconds. Fowler scored first from Collymore's cross. A 60-second brace from Collymore put Liverpool 3-0 up at the break. Redknapp scored his first league goal of the season three minutes from time. Rush made his first appearance at Anfield since leaving, coming on to a rapturous reception in the 73rd minute.

Liverpool hadn't strung together three straight wins since September, and so it was little surprise that they threw away two more points at home to Blackburn Rovers. Fowler hit the post twice and missed numerous other sitters. Matteo hit the bar in injury time from Bjornebye's cross. Liverpool's luck was out but it was their home record letting them down. Fifteen points had been dropped at Anfield, with more to come.

Another defeat came when Ian Taylor's 83rd-minute goal was enough to beat a lacklustre Liverpool at Villa Park on the second day of March. Seven minutes earlier, Fowler had been guilty of an incredible miss, blazing a volley over the bar from three yards. Manchester United's lead was now four points, with ten games remaining.

The Reds were back in Europe four days later, against the Norwegians Brann Bergen. Fowler marked the occasion by scoring one of the best goals of his career. Bjornebye headed the ball infield. Fowler flicked the ball over both his own head and that of his marker with the outside of his left foot. He waited for the ball to descend and smashed a half-volley past the helpless Vidar Bahus. It was a sensational goal, but Liverpool couldn't build on it. Geir Hasund equalised three minutes into the second half, and it finished 1-1. Collymore was dropped for Berger, while Harkness made his first start of the season.

For the second year in a row, the Reds beat Newcastle 4-3 at home. Nobody could quite believe it. Again, the winning goal came in injury time at the Kop end, but the similarities ended there. Both teams had plenty to be embarrassed about, with the Magpies pitiful for 70 minutes before Liverpool caved in, conceding a three-goal lead and, with it, seemingly, their title hopes. But Barnes found Bjornebye, and the wing back provided yet another assist in an impressive personal season when Fowler headed his cross home, sparking bedlam in the stands. The hero from a year ago, Collymore, again an unused sub, barely cracked a smile. "The truth is that, yes, I was gutted," he later revealed. "A year earlier, that had been me. A year earlier, I had been the hero, and now I was being made an outcast." Liverpool had been magnificent in the first half, surging into a big lead courtesy of McManaman, Fowler and Berger. But a James error gifted Keith Gillespie a goal with 19 minutes left before goals from Faustino Asprilla and Warren Barton tied the score with two minutes left. The three points were most welcome, but the cracks in this Liverpool side couldn't be covered up. Still, they had closed the gap to one point on Manchester United, who still had to visit Anfield.

Liverpool again followed up a 4-3 win over Newcastle by dropping points, this time against bottom-three side Nottingham Forest. Fowler scored on three minutes from McAteer's cross. The same player should have scored again but missed his kick. Former Red Dean Saunders missed a gilt-edged chance. Ian Woan equalised on the half hour. Worryingly, the hosts were more threatening in the second half, with McAteer clearing off the line from Steve Chettle and James having to deny Saunders and Pierre van Hooijdonk.

A comfortable second-leg win over Brann put Liverpool in their first European semi-final since Panathinaikos in 1985. Berger missed two early chances before Fowler won a penalty, which he converted himself. With so many one-goal leads squandered in the season, the home fans became frustrated early in the second half, especially when Berger needlessly strayed offside. He was replaced by Collymore, whose impact was extraordinary. He set about the Norwegians, immediately winning a corner. A minute later, he went right through the heart of the defence. Although his finish was slightly fortuitous, the goal was superb, and his no-nonsense approach was exactly what was needed. Fowler wrapped up the tie by placing Bjornebye's cutback into the corner before proudly displaying a T-shirt in support of the striking Liverpool dockers. Along with McManaman, he did the same at the final whistle and both players sent funds to the cause, although they were fined by UEFA for their actions. "Robbie Fowler, football genius and Grade A man," noted Through the Wind and Rain.

The striker was back in the news the following Monday when, with Liverpool 1-0 up at Highbury, he was awarded a penalty. Incredibly, he tried to convince referee Gerald Ashby that he hadn't been fouled. It was a remarkable act of sportsmanship, especially with the title on the line. Ashby didn't reverse his decision. Fowler's weak penalty was saved by David Seaman, who had conceded the penalty, but McAteer followed in the rebound to score his first league goal for the club. Collymore had scored the first, his 14th of the season. Ian Wright pulled one back with 11 minutes left, but the Reds held on to maintain Evans' impressive record against the Gunners, which was seven wins and a draw in three seasons in all competitions.

A great win, unfortunately, was followed by two season-defining defeats. With United losing at home to Derby the day before, Liverpool needed to beat Coventry at Anfield to return to the top on goal difference with the same number of games played. Fowler volleyed emphatically past Steve Ogrizovic early in the second half. But Liverpool caved in. Two Gary McAllister corners led to Coventry goals – the second after an appalling injury-time error from James. It was a horrible collapse and spoke volumes about Liverpool's character. Coventry, after all, had been bottom of the league at kick-off. For the second time in 12 months, the Sky Blues had dealt Liverpool's title hopes a vicious hammer blow.

The Reds embarrassed themselves in the French capital four days later in the first leg of the Cup Winners' Cup semi-final. The season was turning into a humiliation. The hapless James had another stinker as Liverpool were pummelled 3-0 by Paris St Germain. He fluffed an 11th-minute cross which led to Leonardo scoring. Just before half-time he could only parry a cross-shot, and Benoit Cauet bundled in the loose ball. Late in the game, Jerome Leroy added a third to complete a shocking night for the Reds. McManaman had a goal wrongly disallowed for offside, which would prove crucial. A booking for Harkness meant he would miss the second leg. "We didn't defend, and we didn't attack," said Evans. "Ca c'est Parfait" and "L'incroyable Paris" were two local headlines. In truth, they had beaten a poor team.

A much-needed win was ground out at Peter Reid's Sunderland which kept Liverpool within three points of United. Fowler scored his 30th of the season with a header. He then turned provider for McManaman to double the score. Ex-Red Paul Stewart headed in Chris Waddle's corner to set up a nervy final half hour, but the Reds hung on, grateful to Steve Howey for missing a sitter. Michael Owen was one of five unused substitutes.

The only positive to be taken from the midweek Merseyside Derby, the day after the eighth Hillsborough anniversary, was that Liverpool didn't lose. Another lead was squandered. Worse, perhaps, was the sending-off of Fowler which would see him miss the last three league games. It was hard to see where enough goals would come from without him. Liverpool went ahead with an own goal from Claus Thomsen, which was originally credited to Redknapp. Fowler hit the bar. Neville Southall saved brilliantly from Redknapp. Duncan Ferguson equalised with 25 minutes left, before Fowler was red-carded with David Unsworth on 82. Everton fans rejoiced in costing the Reds two points. Alex Ferguson was back-slapped in the stand. Liverpool still hadn't won at Goodison in the Premier League era.

United didn't actually win the league at Anfield three days later, but everyone knew it was done and dusted after James and Liverpool embarrassed themselves yet again. Berger and Collymore were on the bench; Evans had failed to get anywhere near the best out of either of them over the course of the season. United's defenders easily got the better of an isolated Fowler. Terrible marking from corners allowed Gary Pallister, of all people, to score two headers. In between, Barnes, in what would be his last Liverpool start, equalised with his fourth goal of the season, heading in McAteer's cross after a short corner. Andy Cole had missed an open goal after a horrendous mix-up between Kvarme and James. Fowler spurned a promising chance before Pallister's second, which came from James completely missing Beckham's corner. United's third was presented to them by probably the worst mistake of the 26-year-old goalkeeper's horrendous run of form. He got nowhere near Gary Neville's high, hopeful cross, allowing Cole an easy header. The performance summed up the 1997 Liverpool to a tee. In the dressing-room, Ferguson quietened his players so they could listen gleefully to Evans shouting at his.

The manager's selection for the second leg against PSG represented the end of an era in two ways. First, Barnes was dropped, not even on the bench. Second, the three centre-back formation was scrapped for a more traditional 4-4-2. Although 3-5-2 would occasionally feature again under Evans, it was the end of it being a regular thing. Wright and Ruddock were in the middle, with McAteer and Bjornebye the full backs. Redknapp and Thomas were the central midfielders, with Berger and McManaman wide. Fowler and Collymore were the strikers. The four attacking players were finally on the field together. Unlike the league campaign, at least Europe was to end on a high with some pride restored. Amid a magnificent atmosphere, reminiscent of the famous European nights of yesteryear, Fowler put the Reds ahead on 11 minutes with his 31st goal of the season. The Kop became standing-room only for the night, but despite the incessant pressure, PSG held out until half-time. Liverpool didn't score another until 79 minutes, when new captain Wright powered in a header. The Reds bombarded the Parisians' goal but were unable to force extra-time. James even went forward for a corner and headed over the bar. "The last ten minutes of the game were the longest and most difficult of my life," said Ricardo, the PSG coach. It was also the last time that Fowler and Collymore played together. They had the makings of one of the great Liverpool strike partnerships, but after an inconsistent season for the latter, Evans called time on his Anfield career. "I didn't understand him," said Fowler, "and by the end I realized that his attitude was doing terrible damage to the team. He needed to go." He cited Collymore not turning up to training, offering various excuses, not mixing with the other players and even being jealous of Fowler. "I always sensed that he resented my success," he continued, "and gradually he stopped passing to me."

The last home game of the season saw Tottenham beaten at Anfield for the first time in four years. With rugby league pitch markings still visible after a Super League match between St Helens and Castleford the previous Sunday, the Reds signed off at home with a win, although it was hardly convincing. Fowler began his suspension, so Collymore and Berger were paired in attack and they each scored after Darren Anderton had put Spurs ahead. Teddy Sheringham, linked with Liverpool, spurned a clear-cut chance to double the lead. The crowd gave the players an enthusiastic ovation during their post-match lap of honour.

Mathematical title hopes were finally gone when the Reds lost 2-1 against Wimbledon on the first Tuesday of May. Jason Euell and Dean Holdsworth had the Dons two up with 35 minutes to go. Evans threw on Owen for his senior debut three minutes later, and he marked the occasion by latching onto Bjornebye's through ball and slotting it past Neil Sullivan. He became the club's youngest goal scorer at 17 years and 144 days. It was the start of a great Anfield career, but the end of Liverpool's championship bid. "Michael's emergence sealed my fate," said Collymore.

There was still one more thing for Liverpool to screw up. For the first time, a place in the Champions League would be awarded to the runners-up. But failure to beat Sheffield Wednesday, who used three different goalkeepers, saw the Reds come fourth, behind Manchester United, Newcastle and Arsenal. With Barnes on as sub, Liverpool dominated the second half, only for Wednesday to catch them on the counter with the opening goal on 75 minutes. The hosts' substitute goalkeeper, debutant Matt Clarke, who had replaced the injured Kevin Pressman, was then sent off for handling outside the box. With seven minutes remaining, Redknapp curled the resultant free-kick past stand-in keeper Andy Booth, who had started the game up front. Liverpool dominated the rest of the game, but Owen and McManaman missed late chances.

Such a frustrating season could not have ended more appropriately. The Reds had come fourth in a two-horse race and had been denied a Champions League spot by a centre forward playing in goal. In hindsight, this should have been the end of Roy Evans as Liverpool manager.

1997-98

"Awful, disorganised, cowardly rubbish served up by arrogant wasters led by a jellyfish with the tactical ability of an amoeba's fingernail."

O f all the Liverpool signings that have been described as the "final piece of the jigsaw", Paul Ince was the biggest disappointment. He was immediately handed the captaincy; but the self-styled 'Guvnor' turned out to be no leader. He was bought to replace John Barnes and form a more balanced partnership with Jamie Redknapp, but it soon became apparent that Ince possessed none of Barnes's skill and guile. He was bought to add steel to a lightweight midfield, but he proved to be far from the enforcer that had helped Manchester United win the first two Premier League titles. He would be the man to end the 'Spice Boys' culture; but he was the biggest Spice Boy of the lot. Alex Ferguson was memorably captured on camera labelling Ince "a big-time Charlie", a humiliation which weighed heavily on the midfielder. There were reasons United hadn't missed him. Further down the line, Gerard Houllier would quickly identify him as the bad egg in a dysfunctional dressing room. Nobody other than Ince himself objected when the Frenchman turfed him out.

Ince was one of four newcomers. After long, drawn-out negotiations, Evans signed him from Inter Milan for £4.2 million. Other signings included fellow midfielders Oyvind Leonhardsen from Wimbledon for £3.5 million and Danny Murphy from Crewe for £1.5 million. And, in what looked an shrewd piece of business, Karl-Heinz Riedle was signed for £1.8 million from Borussia Dortmund, fresh from his two goals in the Champions League Final win over Juventus. The Danish keeper Jorgen Nielsen signed for £400,000. But Evans missed out on Teddy Sheringham, who went to Manchester United, and Marcel Desailly, who joined Chelsea a year later.

Leaving the club were Stan Collymore, who went to Aston Villa for £7 million, and Lee Jones, an unused substitute for much of the previous campaign, was signed by Tranmere Rovers for £100,000. John Barnes left on a free after the first game. Michael Stensgaard, now recovered from his ironing mishap, returned to Denmark.

As was the case after the White Suits final, Roy Evans neglected to fix many of the problems at the club. The Reds would finish a flattering third in 1997-98 but were never in the title race. A decent performance was invariably followed up by an indifferent one. For all of Ince's talk that his partnership with Redknapp was the best in Europe, they were nowhere near that level. Robbie Fowler was never quite the same from this season onwards with fitness issues always a worry. Perhaps he also missed Collymore – he never found another partner who complemented his game so well. Steve McManaman was eyeing up a departure. Patrik Berger still wasn't trusted by Evans. The components that had made the manager's reign so enjoyable were breaking up, but the glaring problems were multiplying.

A tough opener on a baking-hot day at Wimbledon ended 1-1. David James was in goal. Rob Jones replaced Jason McAteer at right wing back after his injury-plagued 1996-97 season. Stig Inge Bjornebye remained on the left. Mark Wright, Neil Ruddock and Phil Babb made up the three centre halves, although Evans would mainly go for 4-4-2 in 1997-98. Michael Thomas and new skipper Ince combined in midfield. McManaman had the free role. The wonderfully impressive Michael Owen and Riedle were up front after Fowler had sustained a pre-season knee injury. After Vinnie Jones fouled Riedle, the 17-year-old Owen equalised with a penalty with 19 minutes left, following his debut goal there in April. He and Murphy argued over who should take the spot-kick. Given their respective records from 12 yards throughout their Liverpool careers – Owen missed ten, Murphy none – it's a shame the midfielder didn't win the argument. Murphy then missed a late chance to secure the three points. Leonhardsen, Bjorn Tore Kvarme, Berger and Redknapp also missed the start of the season with injury, while Ruddock injured a knee in the game. Barnes was an unused sub in what would be his last involvement with the club. He left on a free transfer to Kenny Dalglish's Newcastle United, who had also signed Ian Rush from Leeds United.

Ince led the side out at Anfield for the first time and responded positively to the Kop when his name was chanted. But it was followed by the sort of defeat that had become all-too-familiar in recent seasons. Leicester defender Matt Elliott scored after 72 seconds, beating the dawdling Babb to Emile Heskey's cross. Liverpool huffed and puffed for over 80 minutes before Graham Fenton made it 2-0 after James had parried Heskey's shot. Many spectators were leaving when Ince pulled one back with an outstanding 25-yarder. Fans streamed back onto the Kop and were met with a brief "Kopites are gobshites" chant from the Lower Centenary. The Anfield Road end was temporarily out of action with a second tier being added.

More points were dropped at Ewood Park, which left Liverpool hovering above the relegation zone. After a goalless first half, Owen seized on an error, tore into the Blackburn half and scored with a low shot. Martin Dahlin equalised on 84 minutes. Rovers, managed by Roy Hodgson, were top of the league.

A much-needed win, and a very impressive one, came in game four as a couple of aesthetically-pleasing goals gave Liverpool a 2-0 win at Elland Road. McManaman, who had just seen a £12.5 million move to Barcelona collapse, placed a superb shot into the bottom corner after dribbling in from the right wing. Riedle wrapped up the points with a sumptuous chip over Nigel Martyn after he had bamboozled Robert Molenaar. James made a string of saves, keeping his first Premier League clean sheet since February.

LIVERPOOL F.C. THE PREMIER LEAGUE YEARS

The death of Diana, Princess of Wales resulted in the postponement of Liverpool's home game with Newcastle on the last day of August. They had to wait a fortnight before their next game, against Sheffield Wednesday Anfield. Thomas, Bjornebye and Riedle all forced saves from Kevin Pressman in a scoreless first half. Just after the break, Ince put the Reds one up and Thomas doubled the lead with a brilliant goal from distance. Wednesday benefited from non-existent marking to pulled one back, but Liverpool held on.

Three days later, Liverpool took part in a pulsating UEFA Cup match at Celtic. After a rousing rendition of 'You'll Never Walk Alone', Owen kept his composure to land an early goal, but the Hoops turned the tie on its head with goals from Jackie McNamara and Simon Donnelly – the latter a hotly disputed penalty. But with time ebbing away, McManaman scored a truly stunning goal. He knocked the ball past a Celtic player deep in his own half, ran around him to retrieve it, dribbled through the midfield and unleashed a tremendous curling shot from outside the box, which went in off the post. Liverpool had two away goals to take back to Anfield.

Another draw came at Southampton as Riedle's headed opener from Bjornebye's pinpoint cross was cancelled out by Kevin Davies. Fowler made his first appearance of the season from the bench after his pre-season injury in Scandinavia. The game would be Wright's last for the club. He had been voted the club's player of the year in 1996-97.

The visit of Aston Villa was all about the return of Collymore. After an ill-advised tabloid interview, he received an angry reception from Liverpool fans and cried after the match. He had scored just once in nine games for Villa and made no impact on this game. Owen won a 55th-minute penalty, which Fowler converted. McManaman, captain for the night, added a mesmeric second. It was reminiscent of his fabulous strike in Glasgow, starting from deep, before eating up the ground and firing low past Mark Bosnich from the edge of the box. A slaloming Owen fed substitute Riedle the clinching goal in the last minute. The young striker still hadn't scored at Anfield, despite making a most promising start to his senior career.

The inconsistency continued at Upton Park where the Reds were beaten 2-1. John Hartson gave West Ham the lead against the run of play in the 15th minute. At the other end, Fowler missed a couple of gilt-edged chances but made amends by crashing home a magnificent 20-yard volley. He later hit the bar with a chip and had a penalty appeal turned down. But the winning goal came at the wrong end, as Eyal Berkovic steered home from the edge of the box. Liverpool had 25 minutes to hit back but couldn't. Riedle, again a substitute, came closest. The Reds were ninth after eight games, seven points off top-placed Arsenal.

The second leg of the Celtic tie was something of an anti-climax, compared to the events of Parkhead, but that was just what Liverpool wanted. Desperate for a goal, Celtic forced the pace and won the plaudits, but they were unable to break through. Liverpool rode their luck at times, with James producing another wobbly performance, but they got the 0-0 they needed, despite a lengthy injury list.

The best performance of the season took Liverpool into sixth as they demolished Chelsea 4-2 at Anfield in early October. Berger was the hero, scoring a classy hat trick, with Fowler adding the fourth. The Czech lobbed Ed de Goey for the first, slammed home Bjornebye's cutback for his second and completed his trio in the second half by rounding the keeper and slotting home at the Kop end. Fans were desperate to see more of Berger. Whether the manager trusted him was another matter. Chelsea's Bernard Lambourde was sent off, which prompted player-manager Ruud Gullit to bring himself on at the expense of Gianfranco Zola, who had just scored the visitors' equaliser. "He didn't warm up, just took his gear off and went straight on into midfield," recalled Carragher, who played in the holding-midfield role for the Reds. "He was absolutely unbelievable."

With a Labour government now in power, an inquiry into new evidence concerning the Hillsborough Disaster was ordered by Home Secretary Jack Straw. But it got off to a dreadful start when retired judge Lord Justice Stuart-Smith visited Liverpool and immediately insulted the club's fans upon meeting the bereaved. The 69-year-old had been appointed to re-examine the 1990 Taylor Report and decide whether there should be a new inquest. When he met Phil Hammond, father of 14-year-old Phillip, one of the youngest victims of the tragedy, he asked: "Have you got a few of your people or are they like the Liverpool fans [and] turn up at the last minute?" Hammond later said: "I just walked away. I still can't believe that remark. This is supposed to be neutral." Amid more accusations of a cover-up, Stuart-Smith concluded in 1998 that there was no new evidence and so a new inquest wasn't necessary. His handling of the issue would be described as "a debacle" by Phil Scraton in October 2012, when the Hillsborough Independent Panel concluded that 41 of the 96 victims could have been saved. Straw later expressed his regret at Stuart-Smith's findings.

The League Cup took Liverpool to the Hawthorns where they beat West Brom 2-0. Berger and Fowler scored second-half goals. Leonhardsen made his debut which had been delayed by injury.

There then followed an appalling four days, which underlined the frailties that Evans had failed to address. It started with another nightmare at Goodison as crisis-torn Everton, now managed for the third time by Howard Kendall, produced a dominant performance that was entirely out of sync with their season. Their task was made easier by Liverpool's centre-half pairing of Ruddock and Kvarme, which must rank as one of the worst Liverpool have ever fielded in a derby. Fowler seemed certain to score but Craig Short got in a timely block. James made a point-blank save from Graham Stuart. The hopelessly sluggish Ruddock headed an own goal on the stroke of half-time. He'd been at the club for at least a year too long. Perhaps Evans should have sold him when he dropped him from the 1996 FA Cup Final. Both sides had chances. Earl Barrett cleared an Ince header off the line with his hands, but it went unspotted. The game hinged on that decision. Not long later, Kvarme lost the ball to 18-year-old Danny Cadamarteri, who turned Ruddock inside out and fired past James. "Everton went to war and Liverpool could not cope," reported one scribe. The Reds hadn't won at Goodison since 1990.

There was worse to come in Europe, courtesy of an abysmal 3-0 capitulation at the hands of Strasbourg, who were struggling near the foot of their domestic league. Evans switched back to the wing-back system, with Harkness joining Saturday's pairing. It didn't work. Redknapp came in for his first start since his Euro 96 injury. David Zitelli scored a brilliant first-half opener with a 20-yard volley. He hit a post early in the second half. Liverpool threatened with Redknapp and Fowler before Zitelli beat Kvarme to a cross in the 63rd minute. 2-0. Denni Conteh's shot beat James at the near post to make it three. Ruddock, now totally off the pace, was hauled off for Owen. He wouldn't play for the club again. McManaman and Owen forced late saves from Alexander Vencel. Liverpool had still never scored on French soil against a French team. They had been humiliated by the most average of teams.

With Evans' job hanging by a thread, the Reds hit back with a 4-0 win over Derby, which saw Fowler, on his 100th first-team appearance, score twice and miss a penalty. Leonhardsen scored his first Liverpool goal before McManaman, now on the wing rather than a free role, rounded off the scoring in the last minute with a rare header. A four-goal win was handy, but it couldn't undo the damage of the Everton and Strasbourg defeats.

When Fowler scored inside a minute at Bolton, who fielded 36-year-old Peter Beardsley, it appeared another big score could be on the cards. But Liverpool couldn't build on their lead and Fowler was sent off on 75 minutes when he floored Per Frandsen. He would miss three games, as would Ince, who picked up another booking. Nathan Blake capitalised on Bolton's numerical advantage by equalising with six minutes left, leaving Liverpool frustrated. "If kamikaze pilots formed a union, Liverpool's players would be putting themselves forward as leaders," mused the Liverpool Echo.

The second leg against Strasbourg saw a repeat of April's Paris St Germain tie, as Liverpool fell just short of a heroic comeback. The first half was goalless, and it wasn't until the introduction of Berger and the excellent Riedle in the second half that Liverpool sparked into life. The German won a penalty on 63 minutes, which Fowler converted. One down, two to go. Riedle headed the second with six minutes to go, but the Reds ran out of time. In the 4,500th match in their history, Liverpool had salvaged some pride, as they had against Paris St Germain in April, but there was less sympathy for them this time. The general consensus was that the writing was on the wall for Evans.

Back in the league, Liverpool moved up to sixth with a clinical second-half dismantling of Tottenham at Anfield. McManaman tapped in a rebound on 47 minutes. Leonhardsen and Redknapp added two more before Owen completed the rout. It was the teenager's first goal at Anfield. Redknapp played superbly, as he had done against Strasbourg.

For the first time in the calendar year of 1997, Liverpool had won three consecutive games when they brushed aside Grimsby Town in the League Cup. Evans fielded a strong team and the headlines were grabbed by Owen, who scored three more Anfield goals. He followed in a rebound for the first, then he converted a penalty before unleashing an outstanding curler into the top corner at the Kop end.

The winning run came to an excruciating end when the Reds lost to bottom side Barnsley in the Premier League. An unfit Ince had been risked against Grimsby, causing him to miss this match. Fowler was also absent. McManaman took the armband again. Barnsley had conceded 16 goals in their last three away matches, but kept a clean sheet at Anfield, and won the game with a 35th-minute goal by Ashley Ward. Riedle missed two promising first-half chances. Owen, Leonhardsen, McAteer and Riedle all went close in the second half but there was no denying the Yorkshiremen.

To show just how Jekyll and Hyde this Liverpool side was, they went to Highbury and beat the champions-elect Arsenal 1-0, thanks to a sublime McManaman volley from Bjornebye's throw-in. Owen and Riedle missed further chances, but Liverpool had secured an impressive result. It was only the Reds' second away win in the league from eight attempts. It was Arsenal's first home defeat of the season, and they would lose only one more game before making certain of winning the title.

Liverpool were nine points behind leaders Manchester United when they met at Anfield in early December. A win was a must. A defeat would see the Reds too far adrift. After a goalless first half, Andy Cole scored six minutes into the second half, following another error by Kvarme. Fowler equalised from the spot after Owen was upended. Parity lasted until the 70th minute when David Beckham curled in a free kick. Cole's second killed off Liverpool's hopes in both the game and the title race. 3-1 was the same score from April's game. United fans taunted Anfield, chanting, "Evans must stay" and "It's just like watching Barnsley!"

The Reds bounced back with four Premier League wins on the spin, starting with a 3-0 win at Selhurst Park. Not even Crystal Palace's surprise signing from Juventus, Attilio Lombardo, could make a difference. McManaman steered in McAteer's deflected corner. Owen's burst of pace saw him race past Andy Linighan before he flicked the ball over Kevin Miller. Leonhardsen scored from ten yards to seal the points. The only change to the side was Harkness coming in at left back for Bjornebye. The Norwegian was a shadow of the player who had made the PFA team of the year in 1997. He was a much better wing back than full back, so the move away from 3-5-2 didn't suit him.

Brad Friedel signed for the Reds from Columbus Crew a week before Christmas for £1 million and would eventually take his place on the bench before coming into the team later in the season. In their next game, Liverpool beat Coventry 1-0, a fortnight before the sides would play in the third round of the FA Cup. Owen scored the only goal of an uneventful game, sliding in McManaman's cross on 14 minutes. Liverpool were left clinging on but managed to keep a clean sheet.

The first goal against Leeds on Boxing Day was Liverpool's 4000th league goal at Anfield. It was scored with aplomb from just inside the box by Owen, who was now strongly linked with an England call-up. Fowler scored a late brace, while Ince returned to the side. It was a superb performance which saw Liverpool overtake Leeds into fourth.

On something of a roll now, the Reds overturned a 1-0 deficit to win at Kenny Dalglish's Newcastle. Steve Watson, Liverpool's nemesis from the autumn of 1995, put the Geordies ahead on 17 minutes but McManaman's brilliant double turned things around before the break. He chested down Fowler's pass before unleashing an unstoppable volley from 20 yards. He then swept Owen's cross with unerring accuracy into the corner of the net for his ninth goal of the season, many of which had been breathtaking individual goals. Leonhardsen also caught the eye. Fowler clipped the bar with a second-half free kick. John Barnes was playing against Liverpool for the first time since 1987 and forced a great save from James. Ian Rush was an unused sub. At the end of 1997, Liverpool were fourth, nine points behind Manchester United but with a game in hand.

Not for the first time, a promising run was halted in embarrassing fashion as Coventry came to Anfield and dumped Liverpool out of the FA Cup with contemptuous ease. Redknapp's free kick put the Reds ahead early, but Gordon Strachan's men dominated thereafter. Owen missed out with flu. City denied Fowler and McManaman any space. Goals from Darren Huckerby, Dion Dublin and Paul Telfer sealed Liverpool's fate.

Liverpool faced another tricky cup tie four days later when they went to Newcastle for a League Cup quarter-final. The game went to extra time, with 36-year-old Rush and 34-year-old Barnes both playing the full two hours. Three days earlier, Barnes had set up Rush's FA Cup winner at Goodison, much to the amusement of Liverpool fans. The deadlock was finally broken by Owen five minutes into extra time, with Fowler later making it 2-0.

A fifth straight Premier League win was secured by two Redknapp goals against Wimbledon at Anfield. Newly crowned player of the month McManaman set up the first on 71 minutes for Redknapp to shoot across goal and into the far corner. The midfielder then swerved a magnificent shot past Neil Sullivan with the outside of his right foot and into the top corner to secure the points. The Reds were in fourth, nine points behind leaders Manchester United with a game in hand.

That game in hand was at Filbert Street, and Liverpool could only draw 0-0. One-time target Matt Elliott, who had scored in August at Anfield, was in commanding form at the back for Leicester, ensuring that goalkeeper Kasey Keller had little to do. The Reds were terrible, with Leonhardsen toiling to little avail, and Berger still only getting ten minutes off the bench, at a ground where he had so spectacularly announced his arrival in 1996.

The rearranged Newcastle game meant the sides were meeting for the third time in just over three weeks. Owen's clinical finish, over Hislop and into the

Kop goal via the crossbar, meant the Reds had won all three. "He had no right to score a goal like that," said Dalglish. It had been a below-par performance, with too many players struggling to find any rhythm, but Liverpool were at least able to field a settled side. The erratic James was still in goal. McAteer had played most of the season at right back, with Harkness recently replacing Bjornebye on the left. Matteo had been a regular at the back, partnered now by Babb but for most of the campaign by Kvarme. Redknapp and Ince were in centre midfield, which forced Leonhardsen out of position onto the left, where he rarely looked comfortable. McManaman was more restricted in a four-four-two formation, often playing on the right, with Fowler and Owen up front. After a promising start, Riedle was out of favour. Even with a hat trick against Chelsea, Berger got little game time.

The Reds played host to Middlesbrough in the first leg of the League Cup semi-final. Boro's Paul Merson made it 1-0 just before the half-hour mark, but Redknapp quickly equalised with a superb 25-yarder. Fowler scored the winner on 82 minutes but endured a difficult night in the face of criticism for his wage demands of £50,000 per week. He was having a poor season and hadn't scored in six games before hammering in Owen's cutback at the Kop end. In-form Redknapp got injured and would miss four games.

Having won 19 points from 21, Evans believed Liverpool were back in the title race, but the wheels fell off. His side drew three and lost three of their next six matches in league and cup. First up were high-flying Blackburn when a win would have cut United's lead to just two points. Colin Hendry and future Red Stephane Henchoz produced a centre-half masterclass in a 0-0 draw. McManaman departed injured at half-time. McAteer broke his leg in the second half. Fowler had another stinker. Leonhardsen hit the bar. Owen went close. Evans described it as "a good day at the office," bearing in mind United had lost. It really wasn't.

Just as everybody accepted that Liverpool were back in the title race, they were inevitably beaten at home by Southampton, who had won just one game in 28 at Anfield. James conceded an early penalty, which David Hirst converted. Owen smashed in a close-range equaliser to celebrate his recent England call-up. Liverpool pushed for a winner, but Saints keeper Paul Jones was in outstanding form. Liverpool collapsed with six minutes remaining, conceding twice on the counterattack through Egil Ostenstad and Hirst. Owen pulled one back, but his side had been embarrassed. "It's nice for a bluenose to come here and win. I'm going to have a pint now and a gloat," remarked the Southampton manager David Jones, who used to play for Everton.

It had looked like Liverpool had tightened their defence, conceding just one goal in six games before Southampton. But they shipped in the same number of goals at Sheffield Wednesday with Kvarme back in the side. In fact, they would go on to concede 24 in a dozen games, stretching into April. Benito Carbone scored for Wednesday. Owen equalised. It remained 1-1 until just past the hour mark, when Paolo Di Canio and Andy Hinchcliffe rattled in a quick double. Evans sent on Berger and Riedle for Kvarme and Jones, and the former Borussia Dortmund pair elicited something of a response. Owen pulled one back after Fowler had hit a post, and then equalised from Ince's precise through ball to complete a stunning hat trick. The teenager nearly won the game with a brilliant chip, but Kevin Pressman got a hand to it. He was outshining Fowler with ease. After four sensational seasons, Fowler hadn't been himself following the pre-season knee injury sustained in Norway. Stan Collymore believed the emergence of Owen affected Fowler in that he was no longer the boy wonder. They were too alike to make a successful partnership. Perhaps Evans would have been better off choosing between them, with Riedle coming back into the side, but it would have taken a brave manager to ditch Fowler.

On the day of Liverpool's second-leg trip to Middlesbrough in the League Cup semi-final, news broke of the Home Secretary Jack Straw's appalling decision to deny the Hillsborough families a new inquest. So much for the tide turning under a Labour government. After Stuart-Smith's comments back in October, few were surprised. Years later, Andy Burnham said that Rupert Murdoch's influence over Tony Blair prevented it from happening. On the field, the players surrendered their League Cup hopes with a disgraceful performance. After just four minutes, the Reds were 2-0 down and 3-2 behind on aggregate. Carragher, standing in for Redknapp in midfield, scythed down Mikkel Beck for a penalty after 83 seconds, which Merson converted. Two minutes later, Fowler lost possession and Merson's long ball sent in new signing Marco Branca, who fired under James. Fowler immediately forced a save from Mark Schwarzer but Liverpool, in their all-yellow kit, were beaten by the lower-division side.

The Reds welcomed the Blues for the second derby of the season, which finished 1-1. Duncan Ferguson scored after the break, only for Ince to equalise at the Anfield Road end. Owen and Fowler had spurned three early opportunities as Liverpool threatened to run riot, but they failed to sustain the tempo. Fowler was substituted late in the game, with a knee injury which would end his disappointing season. At full time, Evans told Friedel to get ready for the next game. He was as fed up with James as everybody else. Victory would have taken Liverpool into second. As it was, they were nine points behind the leaders again. Once again, Everton fans celebrated a derby draw like they'd won a cup. In a season when they avoided relegation by the skin of their teeth, Liverpool took just a point off them. The Reds hadn't won a derby for four years.

On an afternoon of bitterness and controversy, a Stan Collymore brace helped Aston Villa beat Liverpool 2-1 at the end of February. Owen's seventh-minute penalty, won by Leonhardsen, put the Reds ahead but Collymore equalised within four minutes with a low shot which deflected in off Jones. He then fired the winner midway through the second half after Ian Taylor had hit the post. He was later substituted to avoid a red card. Collymore accused Harkness of racist abuse during the match. The Cumbrian defender denied the allegation, threatening to sue the striker. Collymore later tried to punch him outside the changing rooms. In his book, Fowler put the initial bad blood down to a time

Harkness deposited faeces in Collymore's washbag, something he did to other players as a practical joke. Friedel made his debut. The American revealed in his book that James never spoke to him in his time at the club. James described losing his place as "one of the most profound moments of my career. I couldn't get over it." He admitted he dreaded seeing Friedel before a match and how childish the situation was. United had won just four points in the last 15, but Liverpool had picked up only three. Had they beaten Blackburn, Southampton, Wednesday, Everton and Villa, they would be joint top. Instead, they were 12 points adrift.

The Reds finally managed a win when they overturned an early deficit to beat second-bottom Bolton at Anfield. Alan Thompson hammered in a 25-yarder on seven minutes. He then hit the bar from the same range. Matteo saved Liverpool when Arnar Gunnlaugsson seemed certain to make it two. Riedle was lost to a first-half injury, replaced by the long-forgotten Mark Kennedy, who had recently been on loan at QPR. Ince, from a corner, and Owen, sent through by the captain, scored the second-half goals that turned the game around. Kennedy played well in his only appearance of the season and his last for the club.

Three times Liverpool trailed at White Hart Lane but three times they equalised. In his second spell at the club, Jurgen Klinsmann headed Spurs into the lead. McManaman levelled from Owen's pass. David Ginola scored a wonderful goal. Ince responded with a close-range overhead kick. Ramon Vega restored Spurs' lead on 80 minutes. McManaman had the last word with a minute left, scoring a goal which left him writhing in pain after Owen had hit the post. It was a pulsating game, but it further highlighted Liverpool's defensive frailties. Harkness was partnering Matteo at centre back, with Jones and Bjornebye the full backs. Carragher was flitting between defence and midfield, although he was picked on the right wing at Tottenham. Babb was on the bench. The careers of Wright and Ruddock seemed over.

One of the craziest games of Liverpool's Premier League years came at Oakwell at the end of March 1998 as they beat eight-men Barnsley with an injury-time winner from McManaman. The bare facts don't do the game justice. Referee Gary Willard had to be led from the field for his own protection on two occasions. Neil Redfearn's opener was outweighed by Riedle's double. Darren Barnard was the first to be sent off just after half-time for tripping Owen. Twelve minutes later, Chris Morgan followed him with Owen left clutching his face. Home fans ran onto the pitch to remonstrate with the referee. The game was stopped for at least five minutes after a steward led Willard to safety. A goal and two men up, Liverpool almost threw the match away. Willard turned one penalty appeal down before Babb tripped Georgi Hristov. Redfearn dispatched the penalty with the Reds facing the embarrassment of drawing the most winnable of games. But McManaman popped up with a winner which prompted a mini pitch invasion. On the bench, Fowler's crutches were in the air in celebration. There was still time for Barnsley skipper Darren Sheridan to be dismissed for taking his protestations too far, or possibly for a head-butt on Ince in the build-up to the goal. It was that sort of afternoon. Barnsley fans invaded the pitch again. Ince executed a perfect rugby tackle on one of the culprits, as did a Barnsley player. The almost-relegated Tykes would face an FA inquiry for the events on and off the field.

The next away game, at 5pm on Good Friday, was also memorable as Liverpool made the short journey to Old Trafford. Barnsley and Manchester United had provided Anfield with its worst afternoons in the 1997-98 season, so it was satisfying for the Liverpool fans to take such enjoyment from both away trips. United had been humbled again in Europe, this time by lowly Monaco, and their league title was fast slipping away to Arsenal – Betfred had stupidly paid out on United winning the title in March. They needed to beat Liverpool, but for once the Reds came away from Old Trafford with something resembling a just result. Murphy played in the number-10 role behind Owen, and the former Crewe man was outstanding. Ronny Johnsen headed in David Beckham's first-half corner. Ince, McManaman and Owen all went close to an equaliser. The latter was booked for lunging in on Peter Schmeichel. Then on 40 minutes, he scorched past Pallister and steered the ball past the Dane. Three minutes later, he went in recklessly on Johnsen and was sent off. The ten men dealt with the anticipated second-half bombardment and fought for every inch. Redknapp outplayed Beckham, and Liverpool could even have won the game, with Leonhardsen forcing a save. It ended 1-1. United were seven points clear of Arsenal, having played four more games. The Reds were third, 12 behind the leaders with two games in hand. For the second away game in a row, Liverpool fans were attacked after the match.

After a minute's silence to mark the ninth anniversary of Hillsborough, the Reds saw off Crystal Palace at Anfield on Easter Monday. Substitute David Thompson bagged the winner five minutes from time with his first for the club. Leonhardsen scored in the first half before Marcus Bent levelled on 72 minutes. The game was played on the tenth anniversary of Liverpool's greatest performance of the modern era – the 5-0 win over Forest in 1988, which prompted Tom Finney to describe the display as the best he had ever seen. Liverpool had fallen a long way in 120 months.

A brilliant Owen goal was the only standout moment of a dull game at Highfield Road as the Reds drew 1-1 with Coventry. Liverpool were poor. Redknapp picked up a season-ending injury.

With yet another Evans season petering out, Liverpool were thrashed at Stamford Bridge after a contemptible display from several players. Riedle scored the only goal as the Reds were thrashed 4-1. "Awful, disorganised, cowardly rubbish served up by arrogant wasters led by a jellyfish with the tactical ability of an amoeba's fingernail," was the rather cruel assessment in Through the Wind and Rain, a fanzine which was now at the end of its tether with the manager. The only plus was the return of McAteer after his broken leg. Chelsea were now above Liverpool in third.

A blistering first half saw Liverpool four up at half-time against Harry

Redknapp's West Ham in their penultimate game at Anfield. Owen scored on four minutes, before McAteer added a quick-fire double midway through the half - the first after woeful defending from Rio Ferdinand. Leonhardsen added the fourth just before the break. Ince, still despised by Hammers fans, scored the only goal of the second half on the hour mark from nearly 30 yards to make it 5-0. Liverpool were now assured of a place in next season's UEFA Cup.

Another visit from a London club saw Liverpool mete out another thrashing, as Liverpool beat the newly crowned champions Arsenal 4-0. The Gunners had clinched the title three days earlier and may have enjoyed a drink or ten in between. Both sides were without a similar number of key personnel. The Reds set about Arsenal from the kick-off and scored three times in a 12-minute burst shortly before the break. Ince fired in two, with Owen adding a spectacular third to take him to the top of the Premiership scoring charts with 18. The newly anointed Young Footballer of the Year would eventually finish level with Chris Sutton and Dion Dublin – not bad for a player described by England manager Glenn Hoddle as "not a natural goal scorer". Arsene Wenger sent on Patrick Vieira to stem the tide, but Carragher soon went through him. Owen missed a penalty. Leonhardsen added a late fourth. Thomas came on as a substitute against his former club, having spent ten games on loan at Middlesbrough earlier in the year.

A disappointing season ended with a 1-0 defeat at Pride Park, with Paolo Wanchope scoring the only goal for Derby midway through the second half. It was their first win over Liverpool since a 4-2 win in March 1978. Owen and Carragher played well. No one else was worthy of the shirt. It was the sort of ending that an inconsistent and frustrating season like this perhaps merited.

With three fewer points than in 1996-97, a finish of third place was deeply flattering. Significant changes were needed at Anfield, but nobody could have anticipated what was on the horizon. On 16th July 1998, a bespectacled Frenchman by the name of Gerard Houllier walked into the club to share the managerial duties with Evans. How could such a set-up work?

1998-99

"Abraham Lincoln's prospects were brighter when he went to collect his theatre tickets. And he was assassinated before he finished his popcorn."

Of all the unfathomable decisions Liverpool FC has ever made, 1998's joint-manager debacle ranks among the very worst. What on earth possessed the club to pair together two men who had never met each other is anybody's guess. All too predictably, this shotgun marriage ended in a quick divorce, and the season was a subsequent write off.

After another trophyless season, It wasn't unreasonable to suggest that Liverpool should add to their backroom staff in the summer of 1998, especially with the retirement of the great Ronnie Moran, one of the most influential coaches in the Reds' history. Reports of indiscipline running through the squad hadn't disappeared. Whether they were true or not, Liverpool needed to tackle the perception that they were a club living in the past, on and off the field. Even so, the arrival of the 50-year-old Gerard Houllier, who had been heavily linked to Celtic and Sheffield Wednesday, was a head-scratcher. Liverpool secretary Peter Robinson had known Houllier for years and even considered him as a possible successor to Kenny Dalglish in 1991. It was he who persuaded both Houllier and the board that it would work. Patrice Bergues was also appointed, taking over from Moran. He would prove to be a talented coach and a popular appointment. Doug Livermore was still on the staff but would leave with Evans in November.

Joint managers were rare. Few believed it could be a success. There were so many questions. "How would it work?" being the most obvious. Why Houllier, the man who had failed to get France to the World Cup in 1994 and then so crassly and ridiculously blamed it on David Ginola? If the board wanted a change, many wondered, why didn't they just sack Roy Evans? "We weren't stupid," Robbie Fowler wrote in his 2005 autobiography. "We knew what Houllier was there for and it wasn't to help the gaffer … except maybe find the exit. No one knew who made the decisions, who was in charge. I don't think either of them knew. Things happened like the gaffer would announce what time the bus was leaving for an away game, and then Houllier would change it by 15 minutes. How daft was that?" Dominic Matteo called it "one of the most ridiculous decisions of all time." Des Kelly, the Mirror columnist, was another doubter. "Abraham Lincoln's prospects were brighter when he went to collect his theatre tickets," he wrote. "And he was assassinated before he finished his popcorn. How anyone thinks that two men can assume joint control of a football club like Liverpool beggars belief. The split might not come in a week, perhaps not in a month. But it will come."

Looking at the squad that greeted Houllier when he arrived, David James and Brad Friedel were vying for the goalkeeping jersey. The often-calamitous James should have been shipped out at least a year earlier. Friedel was nothing like the great goalkeeper he would become at Blackburn and Aston Villa. Houllier and Evans agreed that an upgrade was needed but agreements couldn't be reached with Frenchman Fabien Barthez and Paraguayan Jose Luis Chilavert. Rob Jones's fitness could no longer be relied upon. Jason McAteer and Stig Inge Bjornebye were less assured as full backs than wing backs. Steve Harkness had been unable to discover his pre-broken leg form. At centre back, Bjorn Tore Kvarme and Matteo had played the most games in 1997-98, but were too error prone.

In midfield, Paul Ince had done reasonably well in his debut season, but no more than that. He would return from the World Cup injured, and his second season failed to ignite. Jamie Redknapp continued to frustrate with inconsistency and injury but would go on to enjoy a much-improved season. Oyvind Leonhardsen scored a few goals but was out of position on the left. The progress of Jamie Carragher, Danny Murphy and David Thompson was most welcome and there was another youngster waiting in the wings by the name of Steven Gerrard.

Up front, Robbie Fowler had been below par before his season-ending injury in February. Patrik Berger and Karl-Heinz Riedle were given too few chances by an increasingly negative Evans. Steve McManaman had enjoyed an stellar season after the club had tried to sell him to Barcelona, although he was less effective on the wing in a 4-4-2 formation than he had been in his mid-1990s free role. He was also running down his contract, eyeing a move out of the club within the year. Michael Owen had the world at his feet. Could Liverpool help him become the world star he had the potential to be? Stan Collymore may have had his drawbacks, to put it mildly, but he still hadn't been replaced. Fowler wasn't the same player without him and would continue to struggle.

Joining the club were Steve Staunton and Vegard Heggem, who were signed to fill the full-back positions. It was Staunton's second spell at Anfield, having played for Liverpool between 1988 and 1991. They were joined by striker Sean Dundee in an underwhelming summer's business. Evans later told lfchistory. net: "One player I do regret signing was Sean Dundee. He was terrible on and off the pitch. He didn't take any notice of me, did what he wanted and lacked discipline. He certainly shouldn't have joined Liverpool."

Moving on were Neil Ruddock and Michael Thomas. One story that summed up Ruddock's time at the club involved a player having a pound coin in his sock and passing it to a teammate at a set piece they were defending. The player stuck with the coin at the end of the match would have to buy a round of drinks. "There was one game when we were lining up to defend a free kick and it was being passed along the wall," Ruddock told Sky's Soccer AM in 2003. "We lost that one 2-1." Few fans mourned his £400,000 departure to West Ham. He should have been moved on at least a couple of years earlier. Mark Wright, who had got better as he got older, had also played his last game for the club, with a back injury forcing him to retire in September.

The season began with a promising 2-1 win at Southampton. Friedel began the season in goal. Heggem and Staunton were the full backs. Babb partnered Carragher in the heart of defence. McAteer played on the right of midfield with McManaman on the left. Ince and Berger were in the centre. Owen and Riedle were up front. James, Kvarme, Harkness, Leonhardsen and Thompson were substitutes. Egil Ostenstad put the hosts ahead. Riedle quickly equalised and Owen won the match for the Reds with 17 minutes left, volleying in on the turn. Owen, Carragher and Heggem were the best players. It was a handy start for the managers.

A 0-0 draw at home to champions Arsenal wasn't the worst of results. Redknapp played his first game in five months, from the bench. It was a compelling game, despite the lack of goals. Owen, whose new five-year deal was announced ten minutes before kick-off, played well, but Liverpool created few chances. Friedel, Babb and Carragher were excellent in keeping Marc Overmars, Dennis Bergkamp and Nicolas Anelka at bay.

A genuine sit-up-and-take-note performance came at St James' Park, where the Reds thrashed Newcastle 4-1. Ruud Gullit had just taken over from Kenny Dalglish, but his promise of 'sexy football' went unfulfilled. The Geordies, for whom Paul Dalglish was an unused sub, lost Didi Hamann to injury on 12 minutes. Owen scored twice in the next six minutes. Newcastle pulled one back after Babb's error, but Owen soon skinned two defenders and flicked the ball over Given. "That's ridiculous," said Sky's Andy Gray. "You can't do anything but applaud." Berger added a magnificent fourth, rifling into the bottom corner on the stroke of half-time. It was a tremendous performance from Owen and Liverpool. They looked like a team who could challenge for anything. They were top after three games. More good news was to follow, with Fowler making his comeback in the reserves.

They stayed top with a 2-0 midweek victory over Coventry at Anfield. Berger scored first, side-footing Ince's pass into the bottom corner. McManaman created the second for Redknapp. Riedle and Redknapp went close to a third. Owen had a goal disallowed in each half. Evans and Houllier could do no wrong.

The first cracks appeared at struggling West Ham, where a bafflingly negative team selection resulted in a 2-1 loss. Harkness came into a three-man midfield. Riedle was sacrificed. Owen was up front on his own. The unnecessary tinkering backfired as Liverpool found themselves 2-0 down. Ince had a poor game against his old club. Riedle came on for Harkness and headed in McAteer's inch-perfect cross. It was the sort of defeat, like Spurs in August 1993, that suggested that a promising start might have been misleading.

A trip to Slovakia saw Liverpool begin their 27th European campaign with a stroll-in-the-park 3-0 win in the UEFA Cup against Kosice. McManaman was captain in Ince's absence. Carragher played in midfield. The big story was the return of Fowler, who set up the third for Owen with a wonderful piece of chest control and an inch-perfect through ball. Berger fired in a long-range free kick, and Riedle scored from McManaman's cross.

Fowler was back among the goals in a crazy 3-3 draw at home to Charlton. Twice Liverpool went behind, twice they equalised. Then it looked like they'd won it, only to be denied. Ince was again absent. With Liverpool choosing Harkness ahead of McAteer, Murphy or Thompson, Charlton dominated the midfield. At the back, Staunton and Babb weren't up to the challenge. Fowler scored the first equaliser. Berger got the second with a sensational 25-yarder. Fowler scrambled in a fortuitous goal on 82 minutes, but Steve Jones made it 3-3 a minute later after Liverpool failed to clear.

A Thursday-night visit to Old Trafford saw the Reds exposed as no more than pretenders. An extraordinary pre-match outburst from Alex Ferguson had been televised in which he called Ince "a big-time Charlie." The skipper was abject. Friedel had a wretched game and flapped at a cross, which led to McAteer handling. Denis Irwin converted the penalty. Riedle thought he had equalised but was offside. Paul Scholes scored the second. Berger missed a chance. United were now a place ahead of Liverpool in third. Aston Villa and Derby were the top two.

Kosice were seen off with a 5-0 thumping at Anfield. Redknapp scored two superb goals from distance. Fowler also bagged two and missed a penalty. Ince scored the other. James was back in goal. The visitors were reduced to ten men when Marek Spilar was sent off for a "desperate lunge on a flying Owen." Spilar took his own life in 2013, aged 38.

The next game is remembered for Babb sliding into a post testicles first as he tried to clear Pierluigi Casiraghi's goal-bound shot, which gave Chelsea the lead at Anfield on Evans' 50th birthday. Babb tried to play through the pain barrier but eventually left the field. It was revealed that two vertebrae in his lower back had been pushed to one side and he would miss six games. Redknapp equalised with an 84th-minute free-kick. Houllier had set the midfielder a target of 15 goals for the season. It had taken him seven years to score 26.

After a promising start, Liverpool were dropping like a stone. The signing of Dundee had become an embarrassment. He hadn't played a single minute of first-team action. Murphy was nowhere to be seen either, which was curious after his promising display at Old Trafford in April. Neither goalkeeper was up to the job and the defence was as leaky as ever. Ince and McManaman had played through injuries because the squad was so threadbare. Ince had been embarrassed by Ferguson's comments, with many Liverpool fans suspecting it to be true. McManaman's future was in doubt. Well into the final year of his contract, there seemed every chance he would leave for nothing at the end of the season.

A trip to Goodison, where the inexperienced Carragher and veteran Staunton

- a curious centre-back pairing - would be marking Duncan Ferguson, was hardly ideal. But they got the better of Everton's attackers, helping Liverpool earn a rare clean sheet in a 0-0 draw. Kvarme and Matteo could only make the bench, showing how far down the pecking order they had fallen. Fowler missed a host of chances. Redknapp lasted only half the match. Liverpool were in seventh, having topped the table five weeks ago.

Another 0-0 draw came at home to Valencia in the UEFA Cup. Owen was rested. James, McManaman, Carragher and Heggem acquitted themselves well, but no one else did. That an away goal hadn't been conceded was one of the few other positives to take from the night. The crowd was just 26,004.

Liverpool responded with an avalanche of goals against Nottingham Forest, a team who were on their way to their third bottom-placed finish in seven seasons. Owen, who had scored just twice in 11 games, landed four goals, having replaced Fowler. It was his fourth hat trick for the club and his first four-goal haul, which took his tally to 33 in 59 matches for Liverpool. The highlight was the opener, as he opened his body and curled the ball into Dave Beasant's top corner. McManaman scored the other in a resounding 5-1 win. It was his first goal of the season, although he barely cracked a smile.

Next up were Fulham in the third round of the League Cup. In front of thousands of empty seats, the first goal came courtesy of Simon Morgan putting through his own net in the 53rd minute, as he deflected in Thompson's shot. Paul Peschisolido equalised with a brilliant curling shot from the right angle of the penalty area. But a penalty from Fowler, won by Owen, and Ince's glancing header put the Reds into the next round. The £2 million Dundee came on as a late sub for his Liverpool debut. At the same time, Peter Beardsley was sent on by Kevin Keegan. Beardsley had been signed 11 years before Dundee – the contrast between the two could hardly have been sharper. It was a measure of Liverpool's decline. The little magician would never play at Anfield again and received a rapturous reception.

No one knew it at the time, but Evans had won his last game as a Liverpool employee. A poor run of results, starting with defeat at Leicester in the Premier League, saw him fired. Tony Cottee scored the only goal at Filbert Street, with 13 minutes left, shortly after Emile Heskey had come close. McAteer was dismissed for a foul on Muzzy Izzet. Staunton was still an emergency centre back. Fowler struggled in a ten-minute cameo. Despite dropping 15 points out of 21, Liverpool were somehow fourth, just six points from the summit.

An incredible game in Spain saw Liverpool progress to the third round of the UEFA Cup. The Reds drew 2-2 with Valencia and progressed on away goals. The Spaniards, managed by Claudio Ranieri, went 1-0 up before the break, after Fowler missed a clear-cut chance. Liverpool knew one goal would be enough, and after an inspiring team talk from Evans, they gradually gained a footing in the game. Fowler missed another chance. Owen was through on goal a couple of minutes later but could only hit the goalkeeper. Dundee came on for Heggem. The big moment came in the 81st minute when Owen hit the byline and crossed for McManaman to head in an away goal that would take Liverpool through. Valencia pushed hard for a winner, but Liverpool stood firm, and when they brought the ball away, Berger fired in a trademark left-footed thunderbolt low into Jose Canizares' net on 86 minutes. Valencia needed two in. There was still time for three red cards and another goal in eight crazy minutes of injury time. The veteran Italian Amedeo Carboni got involved with McManaman, which an already-booked Ince couldn't resist wading in to. All three were sent off - McManaman harshly, Ince deservedly. The otherwise excellent James scored an unfortunate own goal. Despite the chaos of the closing stages, Liverpool were through.

It was after this game that an incident occurred that amplified the growing wedge between the managers. Liverpool were incensed by the performance of the French referee Gilles Veissiere, but Houllier wanted to take him some shirts as a souvenir. Evans chastised Houllier in front of the players. The players sided with the English manager. Houllier, according to Fowler, angrily threw down the shirts and stormed out. Fortunately, Veissiere didn't hold it against Liverpool, as he later refereed the 2001 UEFA Cup final. Fowler also claimed that Evans decided to leave that night, knowing he could no longer work with his new colleague. According to McAteer's book, Evans broke the news to him before the game that he was dropped and then confided in him that he could no longer stomach the arguments with Houllier.

Evans lasted two more games. Derby, with five first-teamers missing, came to Anfield and won 2-1, leaving Liverpool in eighth. With the Reds two down in 27 minutes after a couple of counterattacks, only McManaman looked like getting any change from the Derby defence. Redknapp scored a late goal.

Then it was Tottenham's turn to embarrass the Reds at Anfield, this time in the League Cup. They were 3-0 up just after the hour mark, with John Scales one of the scorers. Friedel was at fault for the first two. Owen pulled one back with nine minutes left, but the Reds had no more to give. It was another appalling performance. "Bye bye Evans!" taunted the Spurs fans and "Are you Tranmere in disguise?" He resigned the next day, tearfully relaying the news to the players. Lifelong Red Brian Reade wrote: "Word emerged from Melwood that a couple of senior players had mimicked his tearful farewell, with others creasing up with laughter at the impressions." The consensus was that Evans had given his players too much leeway and they had walked all over him.

Evans's time as Liverpool boss has perhaps become unfairly tarnished with the 'Spice Boys' image. Many of the stories were probably true, but there were just as many myths. What is certain is that he was responsible for rescuing the club after the Graeme Souness era and for producing some of the best football Liverpool had played in years. His average league position of 3.5 is better than any Liverpool manager of the Premier League years until Jurgen Klopp. Anyone trying to work out why Manchester United ended up with the trophies in the mid-90s, need only examine the respective line-ups. Using the 1997 title race as an example, only Fowler would have been certain of making a combined team.

However good McManaman was, few rated him higher than David Beckham or Ryan Giggs. Peter Schmeichel was in a different league to James - likewise Gary Neville, Denis Irwin, Roy Keane, Paul Scholes and Eric Cantona, compared to McAteer, Bjornebye, Redknapp, an ageing Barnes and Collymore. Various players have been quick to point the finger at Evans, possibly looking for someone else to blame for their lack of success.

One person to benefit from the 'Spice Boys' tag was Houllier, as it played into his negative portrayal of both the team's lack of quality and the unhealthy culture of the club. He certainly had a big job ahead of him, but his talk of a five-year plan was just buying himself time. Evans's last term had been and would be far superior to the final seasons of Liverpool's other Premier League managers, from Souness to Brendan Rodgers. They did finish third, after all. Indeed, Houllier's last two seasons would be as bad as anything Souness served up. Fowler certainly saw the spin doctor at work in the Frenchman. "What really started to annoy me after Roy left was how Houllier suddenly started to rubbish a lot of what had happened before his arrival," he said. "The way he started talking to the press, you could have been forgiven for thinking Liverpool had been fighting relegation for the last few years and that he had been brought in to save us. It was designed to make Roy look bad and Houllier look like some sort of hero who had ridden into the city to rescue Liverpool Football Club." McAteer expressed similar sentiments. But Houllier does deserve credit for ridding the club of some of its negative influences and, in time, he would rebuild the squad in his own mould. His wonderful 2001 successes was entirely of his own making. But firstly, the 1998-99 season had to be played out, and it would continue to be an atrocious campaign. He couldn't do much wheeling and dealing until the summer, so the board had wasted a whole season with their joint-manager fudge.

Things got worse before they got better with another abysmal home defeat, this time to Leeds, in Houllier's first match in sole charge, alongside his new assistant Phil Thompson. Fowler had a terrible game but did manage to convert a penalty on 68 minutes after Riedle had been clobbered by Nigel Martyn. But a late collapse led to a 3-1 defeat. Harry Kewell had a hand in two of the goals. The first had come as Liverpool appealed for another penalty. Leeds tore downfield and young Alan Smith scored with his first touch in senior football. The Reds were now 11th. "I now have a psychological job and a footballing job on my hands," said the manager. One player he would shortly clash with was Ince. As one writer noted: "In the centre circle, for that is now his exclusive domain, Paul Ince moaned and whinged his way through the entire afternoon without once threatening to make a meaningful contribution."

Houllier's first away game was at unbeaten leaders Aston Villa where the Reds ripped up the form book. From Berger's corner, Ince gave Liverpool a lead on two minutes. Fowler made it 2-0 on seven. Collymore executed a disgraceful tackle on Harkness, who was stretchered off. The bad blood from last season's race row still lingered. Collymore was only booked, admitting in his autobiography he had gone after Harkness, who thought his leg had been broken again. It was stretched ligaments. Berger and Owen could have scored before Dion Dublin pulled one back. Three goals in eight minutes midway through the second half decided the game. Fowler got the first of them. Dublin scored again from Collymore's cross. Fowler then completed his hat trick on 66 minutes. Moments later, Owen dived in two-footed on Collymore, who retaliated by grabbing the teenager's neck. The former Liverpool striker was sent off. Finally, James denied Dublin a third goal by saving his penalty. The game was even crazier than the one in Valencia.

Unfortunately, a great performance was followed by a shambles in Spain as Celta Vigo took control of their UEFA Cup third-round tie. Owen gave the Reds a half-time lead, but he and Fowler spent most of the game isolated with the midfield too slow to support them. Profiting from abysmal defending, the Spaniards roared back to win 3-1. One of the scorers was Valeri Karpin, who had beaten Liverpool with Spartak Moscow in 1992.

Steven Gerrard had been named on the bench for the first time for the trip to Spain, although he didn't get onto the field. He was now training with the first-team squad along with Stephen Wright, as Redknapp remembered years later. "[He] just turned and hit this pass, and the flight of the ball, I was like 'wow, did I just hear that right?' It was like a different noise! And then about five minutes later, [he] went flying into Paul Ince and smashed him up in the air and I was like 'we've got a special one here!' I remember Gerard Houllier coming up to me and saying, 'What do you think about Stephen Wright?' I was like 'yeah, yeah good player ... but the other kid's the one. He is going to be different class.'"

Gerrard, in the number 28 jersey, got his first taste of the action when he came on in injury time for Heggem against bottom-placed Blackburn at Anfield. A brilliant 25-yarder from Ince and a lucky goal by Owen saw the Reds avoid a fourth successive home defeat. It was also a first clean sheet in ten matches. A day earlier, Houllier had made his first signing as sole manager, bringing in Jean-Michel Ferri, a 29-year-old defensive midfielder from Istanbulspor for £1.5 million. He had previously won the French title with Nantes. He would play just twice for the Reds, amid rumours that Houllier had signed him to be a dressing-room mole.

Liverpool then lost three on the bounce, starting with defeat at White Hart Lane. With Redknapp suspended and McManaman injured, Gerrard started the match but couldn't prevent Spurs going 2-0 up. Playing in a wide role, he was run ragged by David Ginola before being replaced by David Thompson on 55 minutes. "The new lad looked a bit out of his depth," noted Through the Wind and Rain. The second Spurs goal came from the unfortunate Carragher. Berger got one back with an outstanding free kick. Owen went close, but the Reds couldn't force an equaliser.

Gerrard played the full 90 for the first time in the second leg against Celta, but the Reds went out of Europe with a 1-0 defeat, 4-1 on aggregate, thanks to a classic counterattack goal just before the hour. "They sent boys out to do a man's job against a talented Celta Vigo side, and the result was all too painfully predictable," lamented the journalist David Maddock. Ince, Redknapp and McManaman were suspended – that incident in Valencia had proven costly. Fowler skippered the side.

A third successive defeat came with a 1-0 defeat at Wimbledon. Played onside by Bjornebye, Robbie Earle scored his fifth goal against the Reds since 1992. Neil Sullivan was the hero, making several saves including an Owen penalty. A booking for Ince led to another suspension. After a solid debut season, the skipper struggled in 1998-99. Now in 12th, Liverpool were on their worst run in 44 years and were just nine points clear of the relegation zone. Good news came later in the day with Owen crowned BBC Sports Personality of the Year, although it was principally for his World Cup exploits. The last time the club had been acknowledged by the programme was in 1986 with the Team of the Year award and player-manager Kenny Dalglish coming third in the main prize.

A four-match winning streak was most welcome, and it started with a routine 2-0 home win over Sheffield Wednesday. "It was efficient," said the impressive Redknapp. "That's what we need right now." Berger and Owen scored the goals in the first half. With Evans gone, the Czech was having a fine season. Carragher was excellent again, but the second half was poor, with Babb, Bjornebye and Fowler labouring.

Boxing Day brought about a rare win at the Riverside, which was capped off by a remarkable individual goal by Heggem, his first for the club. In fact, not only was Liverpool's record at Middlesbrough's new stadium a wretched one, but nobody had beaten Bryan Robson's men there for 14 months. Owen got a touch on Carragher's shot to score the opener. It was cancelled out by Brian Deane, who profited from James missing Paul Gascoigne's free kick. Redknapp, again the best player, restored Liverpool's lead ten minutes before half-time, smashing in an indirect free-kick from 12 yards. Heggem sealed the points by dribbling past three defenders before flicking the ball over Mark Schwarzer. McManaman made his comeback from injury in the last 15 minutes, while Houllier later insisted that Fowler wasn't for sale. He only had 18 months left on his contract and there were worries he would follow McManaman's example by running it down.

On the way back from Middlesbrough, Carragher was texted by a mate to say he was going to be on the front page of the following day's News of the World. He'd been snapped having sex with a stripper at the team's Christmas party, dressed as the Hunchback of Notre Dame. "It wasn't much of a story when you broke it down," Carragher recalled. "A 21-year-old Scouser gets bladdered on a festive work night out and ends up getting caught in a compromising position with a stripper." He was summoned to see a laughing Houllier and Thompson, and the latter said: "Don't worry, son, I've been there." The manager told him he was one of six players who would definitely be at the club next season. "You, Michael, Gerrard, Berger, Heggem and Redknapp will stay. If you're going to be with me, you've got to be more careful." Carragher would go on to win the club's

Player of the Year award, following an outstanding season at centre back.

Back on the field, Liverpool overturned a two-goal deficit to beat Newcastle 4-2. Didi Hamann, who had left the field injured when Liverpool won 4-1 at St James' Park, was this time sent off after half an hour for two bookings. His first offence saw McManaman substituted with an ankle injury, replaced by Gerrard. Nobby Solano and Andreas Andersson scored the Magpies' goals. Three quarters of the game had gone when Owen finally got Liverpool on the board, steering Carragher's shot past Shay Given. Riedle equalised on 71 from Heggem's cross. Owen slotted home a rebound to put the Reds ahead with ten minutes left. The German sealed a thrilling game four minutes later by beating the last defender and rounding the keeper. Heggem was one of the keys to Liverpool's recovery, enjoying oceans of space on the right. Berger was excellent too. It was the final game of a torrid year. Liverpool were seventh, eight points off leaders Villa.

The new year started with an FA Cup win at First Division Port Vale. Redknapp and Berger dominated the midfield as the away side built up a 2-0 interval lead with a penalty from Owen, whose father Terry had played for Vale. Ince added another, nodding in Babb's header. Substitute Fowler made it three in injury time with a rasping left-footer from Owen's pass.

Another 0-0 with champions Arsenal underlined the gradual defensive improvements that had been made over the winter. The defenders had the luxury of playing behind a strong midfield, but the form of Staunton at centre half had been a revelation. Where to play the Irishman was one of the major disagreements of the joint managers, but Houllier would have eventually felt vindicated in seeing him as a stopgap for the problems in the middle of the defence. He had partnered Carragher or Babb for much of the season. Bjornebye hadn't had the best of seasons. Heggem had proven to be a shrewd signing on the right. Carragher flitted between defence and midfield and was having a tremendous campaign. The Gunners were challenging strongly for the title, but Liverpool's simple game plan earned them a point.

The Reds crashed seven past Southampton a week later. When the Saints had won 3-2 at Anfield a year earlier, their manager Dave Jones quipped that he was "off for a pint and a gloat." How he had those words rammed down his throat as Houllier's men rattled in the goals. Fowler scored his second hat-trick of the season as his tally of league goals went past the century mark. Owen scored his customary goal from Babb's cross, although he could have had four in the first ten minutes. Even Matteo, Carragher and Thompson got on the score sheet in an incredible 7-1 win.

From one of the high points of the season to one of the lows. Liverpool were superb for much of their fourth-round FA Cup tie at Manchester United. Owen gave them an early lead with a header from Heggem's cross after a scintillating counterattack. Liverpool, with three centre halves, stood firm as United piled on the pressure. Ince cleared off the line. Fowler went close with an audacious curler from miles out. Roy Keane hit a post in the second half. Carragher charged down Ryan Giggs on the rebound. Ince retired injured, replaced by McAteer, which left Houllier later accusing his captain of cowardice. It would be McAteer's last appearance for the club. Yorke equalised on 88 minutes, tapping in Cole's header. Heartbreak. And then came the cruellest of blows as Ole Gunnar Solskjaer scored the winner in injury time after Liverpool failed to deal with a long ball. It was an agonising defeat but a performance the new manager could build upon. It was the beginning of the end for Ince at Liverpool. "When my Liverpool team is 1-0 up at Old Trafford in a cup tie, I don't expect my captain to limp off with an injury," Houllier told him in front of the squad. "If he has to come off the pitch, I expect it to be on a stretcher because he needs to go to hospital in an ambulance." Owen and Carragher were in awe of the manager's takedown of the captain. "What a manager we've got here," Owen observed.

The defeat was McAteer's last game for the club. He was sold to Blackburn for £4 million, a move which left him devastated. In truth, he had only really played well in the now redundant wing back role and not as a central midfielder, where he had played for Bolton. Liverpool bought two defenders in January 1999 – the Norwegian Frode Kippe from Lillestrom for £700,000 and Cameroonian Rigobert Song from Salernitana for £2.6 million. Kippe would play just twice for the Reds. Another signing was that of Fowler, who penned a new long-term deal.

The crushing disappointment of Old Trafford sent the Reds on a dismal run of just one win in six matches. Houllier kept the three centre-back system. Perhaps the system had its merits against United, but in much more winnable matches, it unbalanced the side. Song made his debut in a 2-1 defeat at Coventry, with the returning McManaman scoring Liverpool's only goal in the closing moments. The winger's future had now been settled – he would be leaving on a free transfer to Real Madrid in the summer. James was erratic again. Houllier blamed the pitch.

Another 3-1 win over Middlesbrough was a relief for the manager, especially after they roared into a 3-0 interval lead. Owen scored an early goal before Heggem volleyed in his second of the season; like his compatriot Bjornebye in 1996-97, his only league goals came home and away against Boro. Ince made it three just before the break, shortly after he'd been booked, this time for a foul on Gascoigne, which would result in yet another ban. The second half saw a red card for Matteo and a late goal for Phil Stamp. The Reds were up to fifth.

A terrible afternoon at Charlton Athletic saw a 1-0 defeat and another red card, this time for Carragher for use of an elbow. Keith Jones scored moments later, following Staunton's howler. McManaman and Fowler missed chances. Ince was booked again. John Barnes came on as a second-half sub for Charlton, in what would be his final involvement in a match featuring the Reds. Houllier was scathing in his assessment of referee Mike Reid. "When my players get the teamsheet and see Mr Reid's name, they think they are playing against 12 men."

A home game with West Ham saw the Reds drop two more points. Song, who had made a solid start, Staunton and Babb were the centre halves, with Heggem and Bjornebye wing backs. Carragher partnered skipper Redknapp in midfield while Ince was banned. McManaman roamed behind Owen and Fowler. It wasn't the most balanced of teams. Fowler put Liverpool ahead, only for Frank Lampard to equalise. Owen restored the lead just before half-time, with his shot deflecting in off Liverpool target Rio Ferdinand. The only goal of the second half came from sub Marc Keller. McManaman had a poor game, and his withdrawal for Berger was cheered by the crowd. Phil Thompson claimed in his 2005 book, 'Stand Up Pinocchio', that Ian Wright, a non-playing member of the West Ham squad, had spent the afternoon throwing chewing gum at his back while the assistant coach was bawling instructions from the touchline. According to witnesses, Wright was encouraged by Ince, while the Liverpool substitutes Harkness, Berger and Ferri laughed. "[Ince] was going to be a problem," wrote Thompson. "We knew that from day one. He was all-powerful in the dressing-room. Everyone knew about the 'Guv'nor' hype. He was a strong character. If we were to move on, he needed to move on."

The next game at Stamford Bridge is best known for a bizarre incident involving Fowler and Chelsea's Graeme Le Saux. It was incorrectly rumoured in footballing circles that the Channel Islander was gay, and he was taunted for it regularly. Fowler went further than most, bending over as Le Saux lined up a free-kick, pointing his backside at the defender and shouting homophobic insults. Fowler initially refused to apologise, but in 2014, upon publication of Le Saux's autobiography, he said: "I am genuinely sorry. It was used as a wind-up but looking back I shouldn't have done it. It is embarrassing." Owen scored Liverpool's only goal, when they were already two down. Ferri made his debut, coming on for Ince just after half-time. The reporter at The Times was critical of the Ince-Redknapp partnership, which Ince had called the 'best in Europe'. "Houllier is building around foundations that are just not strong enough. Both Liverpool and England are suffering because the partnership of Ince and Redknapp in midfield is considered a perfect combination of guile and guts. Well, it ought to be, and on occasion it has been, but their fine performances do not outweigh their disappointing ones." Liverpool again started with three centre backs and struggled to adapt to 4-4-2 in the ninth minute when Heggem was injured.

Four days after Harkness joined Graeme Souness's Benfica for £350,000, Liverpool were again humiliated on the road, this time at Pride Park. Fowler's penalty, won by Owen, cancelled out a soft Derby goal from a corner. Paolo Wanchope's brace put the game beyond the Reds, although Fowler scored again to make it 3-2 from Matteo's cross. James was a nervous wreck. Sixth-placed County, managed by Jim Smith, had done the double over Liverpool. Staunton and Owen sustained injuries. Houllier, for reasons known only to himself, was still experimenting with three centre backs. All of Derby's goals came from set pieces, and they should have scored more. With a three-week gap until the next game, Liverpool travelled to France and were beaten 2-1 by Fourth Division

Boulogne, with Berger scoring the Reds' only goal. As far as mid-season breaks go, it was almost as embarrassing as the Euro Sixes in 1997.

Liverpool finally scraped a win at the start of April, when Everton visited Anfield. The Reds hadn't beaten the Blues for five years but Houllier would enjoy a much better derby record than his predecessor. The players marked the tenth anniversary of Hillsborough before the game. Once more, Fowler grabbed the headlines, as he celebrated his first goal by pretending to snort cocaine – a response to Evertonian insults. Houllier was rewarded for reverting to 4-4-2, although the Reds had fallen behind to a wonder goal by Olivier Dacourt inside 40 seconds. Ince won a penalty on the quarter-hour mark, which Fowler steered home before dropping to his knees before Everton's fans and putting a finger to one nostril before sniffing the white line in front of him. He got up, clenched his fists in front of them and did it again. It was an apt retort to the lies that had spread around the city and something he still had no regrets over, according to his 2019 book. Four minutes later, McManaman, in his last derby, flicked on a corner, and Fowler gleefully headed past Thomas Myrhe. Marco Materazzi hit the post with a free kick. Owen was denied by Myrhe. David Weir blasted over. Fowler nearly completed a hat trick, but Berger did eventually secure a two-goal cushion with a precise 20-yarder. Francis Jeffers pulled one back, and Gerrard had to clear two goal-bound shots off the line to preserve the three points. In victory, Houllier still managed to embarrass himself by claiming that Fowler's celebration was an African routine, inspired by Song, whereby the players would 'eat the grass' in celebration. Houllier was ridiculed by the media for the excuse and, according to Fowler, later confided in a journalist that he regretted it. "I was made to look ridiculous because of Fowler, and I defended him," he allegedly said. "I tell you, I will never make that mistake again." Fowler said: "I don't think he ever forgave me for that."

On top of the Le Saux affair, Fowler now faced a further FA charge and ended up being banned for six matches for the incidents – two for the homophobic taunts and four for the celebration – a damning indictment of the FA's values. He was also fined £32,000 by the club. "The club deeply regrets what happened and made it very clear that they would not allow any player, or other persons, to damage the club's reputation without taking a firm response," said chairman David Moores. "The club, however, recognises that for far too long Robbie has been the subject of totally unjustified allegations and rumours about drugs and other personal matters which can only be described as a pack of lies."

As this nightmare season limped on, the Reds dropped two more points at Ron Atkinson's Nottingham Forest on Easter Monday. Redknapp scored first with a ferocious 25-yard free kick. Forest levelled on the hour. Owen made it 2-1, but a superb injury-time equaliser by Pierre van Hooijdonk denied the Reds. Three times in the early Premier League years, the twice European champions came last. Liverpool beat them just twice in those six matches.

A goalless draw at fourth-placed Leeds saw Riedle miss Liverpool's best chances. Gerrard was excellent, but the game is best remembered for Owen tearing a hamstring in the 25th minute. It would affect him for the rest of his career. His season was over, which, on top of Fowler's ban, was a blow. With Houllier desperate to get him back as quickly as possible in the early part of the 1999-2000 season, Liverpool mismanaged the injury, meaning that when he did return, he had lost acceleration, which he never recovered. For the rest of his career, the hamstring in question was only supported by two tendons, rather than three. That led to an imbalance, which resulted in not just further hamstring issues, but other injuries too.

Fowler played his last game before his ban kicked in, against Aston Villa at home. Just as in 1997, the only goal was scored by Ian Taylor. Fowler headed a good chance wide as Liverpool badly missed Owen. Even Dundee got a four-minute run out. That night, Fowler had his nose broken, a tooth chipped, and his eye blackened in a bar by an Everton fan, who was jailed for the attack.

As treble-chasing Manchester United were winning 3-2 against Juventus in the Champions League semi-final, Liverpool were beaten 1-0 at home by Leicester City, with former Evertonian Ian Marshall scoring in injury time. Picking the ball out of the Kop goal was James's final act as a Liverpool player. Riedle was the only striker until Dundee came on at the end. The players were booed off for the second time in four days. McManaman, Ince and Leonhardsen could have scored. Like Derby, the Foxes had now beaten Liverpool twice. It was hard to imagine things getting much worse. Nearly every season in the 1990s had tailed off and ended disappointingly.

Liverpool did make something of a response by winning three and drawing one of their last five matches. Friedel replaced James for the rest of the season. Three goals in nine first-half minutes, from McManaman, Redknapp and Leonhardsen, sealed the points against Blackburn, who fielded McAteer and the soon-to-be-Red Stephane Henchoz.

A commanding second-half performance saw Liverpool overturn a 2-0 half-time deficit at home to Spurs. Carragher scored his second goal of the season for Spurs – more than he had scored for his own team. Stefan Iverson headed in a second. Mauricio Taricco was dismissed for two yellows. Gerrard replaced Kvarme at the break, and Liverpool were transformed. Redknapp got one back from the penalty spot after Riedle was brought down. Ince equalised on 77 minutes, set up by Redknapp. Two minutes later, McManaman won the match from Song's cross. It was his last goal for the club.

Four days later, Anfield witnessed another comeback as Liverpool tried to derail Manchester United's title challenge – as they had done in 1992 and 1998. Goals from Dwight Yorke and Denis Irwin, with a penalty conceded by Carragher, put the Red Devils two up. Berger replaced Song with Liverpool reverting to a flat back four, before Redknapp started another comeback with a penalty. Jesper Blomqvist should have been sent off for a professional foul on Leonhardsen, but only the penalty was awarded. Irwin correctly received a second yellow card for kicking the ball away with 15 minutes left. Liverpool piled men forward, including Ince, who bundled in the equaliser with four minutes left. He celebrated with the Kop - a sweet moment for him following Ferguson's 'big-time Charlie' jibe. Sniffing victory, Liverpool went long and Carragher got to the ball ahead of Schmeichel, but his header floated agonisingly wide. The title was now in Arsenal's hands. United chairman Martin Edwards preposterously claimed a championship medal be struck for the referee David Elleray, who received death threats from United fans.

Numerous fans boycotted the side's final away fixture of the season at Hillsborough, in protest at Sheffield Wednesday's attitude to the 1989 disaster. They were still refusing to erect a memorial. Liverpool people couldn't take in flowers to lay at the Leppings Lane end. Instead, they had to place them on a table outside. Fewer than 1,200 Liverpool fans saw the Reds beaten 1-0. Richard Cresswell scored with three minutes left. "Liverpool didn't seem to care whether they won or lost," reported The Observer, an attitude Thompson sensed after the game. Friedel hit back at the assistant manager. "All you ever do is shout, scream and moan," he said. "You never give us any encouragement."

A miserable season ended with a home defeat of Wimbledon, whose manager Joe Kinnear had suffered a heart attack in March. McManaman was given a positive reception by the Kop to mark his last game. Ince set up Berger for the first. McManaman found Riedle, who made it 2-0. Ince scored the final goal to give the Reds a 3-0 win.

Liverpool finished in the flattering position of seventh, 25 points behind the champions Manchester United. They had been just eight adrift on New Year's Day. With McManaman going, Owen injured and Fowler's best days behind him, Houllier and his staff had a huge rebuilding job ahead of them.

1999-2000

"The way you're playing, I'm surprised you're happy to be seen out in public. You shouldn't be in the team."

Gerard Houllier hadn't got much right so far. It wasn't his fault that the club had put him in the invidious joint-manager position, but the Reds had been abject even after the dismissal of Roy Evans. The second half of the 1998-99 season had been gruelling fare. His signings – Jean-Michel Ferri, Frode Kippe, Rigobert Song and Djimi Traore – represented some of the worst business the club had ever done. His 5-3-2 system was too negative and left the team unbalanced. Robbie Fowler's ban, Michael Owen's injury and Steve McManaman's exit weren't his fault, but they added to a very pessimistic summer in 1999. To make matters worse, Manchester United had just won their treble and weren't shy in gloating about it.

Like Roy Evans in 1994-95, Houllier improved things quicker than expected. Unlike Evans, and more like Graeme Souness, the Frenchman adopted a revolutionary approach, but with more success than the Scot. Out went David James, Paul Ince and Oyvind Leonhardsen, while the club managed to get most of its money back on Ferri and Sean Dundee. The injury-cursed Rob Jones also departed, on a free to West Ham. Bjorn Tore Kvarme and Karl-Heinz Riedle left after the season began.

Ince took his departure badly, telling a tabloid: "I just wanted to punch Houllier in the face. If I was younger, I would have. He would have deserved it. All Thommo does is shout his mouth off, he doesn't coach. Yes, he was once a great player for the club but now he's meant to be a coach. He should realise that coaching is not about swearing at players and that's all he does." Former Red Steve McMahon sided with Houllier and Thompson: "It is players like Ince who have got Liverpool into trouble in the first place."

Whereas the 1998-99 recruitment had been among the worst in the club's history, Houllier got it right this time, fixing the fragility of the spine. In came centre halves Sami Hyypia from Willem II for £2.5 million and Stephane Henchoz from Blackburn for £3.5 million. They were joined by holding midfielder Dietmar Hamann from Newcastle for £8 million after Houllier had initially targeted West Ham's Marc-Vivien Foe. Goalkeeper Sander Westerveld came on board from Vitesse Arnhem for £4 million. Houllier's attacking signings weren't so hot though, and with Fowler and Owen struggling with injury, fitness, and form during 1999-2000, it proved costly. Playmaker Vladimir Smicer signed from Lens for £3.75 million. Titi Camara joined from Marseille for £2.6 million. Erik Meijer arrived on a free from Bayer Leverkusen. They varied from average to poor, but the quality of the defensive triumvirate provided the manager with a formidable foundation for the rest of his time in charge.

The good and bad of the recruitment can be seen when the 1999-2000 league table is compared to the previous season's. The Reds would ship just 30 goals, easily the lowest number in the Premier League and 19 fewer than in 1998-99. Westerveld was an upgrade on James and Brad Friedel. Hyypia, Henchoz and Hamann transformed the defensive side of the team. But only 51 goals were scored, compared to 68 in Houllier's first season. Smicer was a decent player, but he wasn't in McManaman's league. Meijer was nowhere near Liverpool standard. Camara scored some spectacular goals, but Houllier clearly had little time for him. Owen and Fowler got far fewer than usual, but the Reds did collect an extra 13 points and challenged until the final day for a Champions League spot.

The ins and outs didn't just represent on-field changes. The summer's transfer business marked the beginning of a more professional outlook at the club. Moving into the 2000s, there was a game-wide recognition that diet and lifestyle had to change, particularly in relation to alcohol. "Houllier's first summer in sole charge was when he really started to stamp his own mark on the team," acknowledged Dominic Matteo. "The thinking behind bringing in so many signings from abroad as the homegrown lads left was that the manager wanted to change the culture at the club. He wanted us to stop going out and to eat better, which I admit was the right thing to do."

The season began in Sheffield where, for the third time in seven seasons, Liverpool beat Wednesday on the opening day. Westerveld kept goal. Vegard Heggem, Hyypia, Jamie Carragher and Matteo were in defence, with Henchoz injured. Hamann and skipper Jamie Redknapp formed the centre of midfield. Smicer and his compatriot Patrik Berger played wide. Fowler and Camara were the strikers, with Owen's hamstring keeping him sidelined, despite Houllier's attempts to rush him back in pre-season. David Thompson, Steve Staunton and Meijer came off the bench, with goalkeeper Jorge Nielsen and Rigobert Song not called upon. A superb finish from Fowler, the new vice-captain, and a clinical follow-up from Camara put the Reds in the driving seat, with a brilliant Benito Carbone strike halving the lead with two minutes left. "A Camara with no negatives," mused Gary Lineker on Match of the Day. The downside was Hamann injuring his ankle ligaments, but Redknapp's impressive performance made up for his absence, with one reporter writing: "Redknapp chased and snapped like a wide-jawed Alsatian attempting to lure Liverpool out of slumbers."

Steven Gerrard replaced Hamann for the first home game of the season, against Watford, on an afternoon when everything went wrong. Graham Taylor claimed Watford were fired up by the Liverpool bus getting a police escort straight past their coach, which was stuck in traffic. Tommy Mooney scored the only goal after Liverpool had four goes at clearing a free kick. "From the early stages, I did not recognise my team," said Houllier.

Another defeat came at the Riverside where Brian Deane scored the only goal. Ince lined up for Middlesbrough, who lost Paul Gascoigne on 19 minutes. Houllier returned to his ill-fated back three with Staunton, Hyypia and Carragher the centre halves and Heggem and Matteo the wing backs. Gerrard played well, as did Heggem and Camara, although the Guinean missed a couple of chances.

Liverpool went to Elland Road in game four, as they had done in 1997, desperate for a win after a dodgy start. Again, they defied the odds. Playing 4-4-2, Liverpool went behind to an unfortunate own goal by Song. Camara equalised with a magnificent curler, which went in off the crossbar. The winner came from another own goal as Lucas Radebe got to Berger's cross ahead of Fowler, with the ball flying into the bottom corner. It was a commendable result, given Henchoz, Hamann and Owen were still to return.

Another big team were brushed aside as Arsenal were beaten 2-0 at Anfield. Fowler fired in an absolute beauty in the eighth minute, as his 25-yarder crashed in off the bar. Redknapp and Fowler each had a couple of chances to add to the lead. Berger also went close. The Reds continued to dominate and were rewarded when Berger's free kick was deflected into the Kop goal. Westerveld saved an injury-time penalty from Davor Suker. On Match of the Day that night, Reds legend Alan Hansen called it the best Liverpool performance since his days. Owen made his first appearance of the season, replacing Camara with three minutes remaining. In hindsight, he was returning far too soon, and his hamstring would never be right again. Houllier and physio Mark Leather had fallen out over whether Owen should do strengthening work on the muscle or whether he should join in five-a-sides, which Houllier demanded. Leather left the club in the middle of pre-season, leaving Owen without a physio to consult at a critical time in his recovery.

Next came a game that will be etched into Carragher's memory. Liverpool were so unlucky to lose 3-2 at home to Manchester United, with Carragher scoring two first-half own goals. Matteo gave David Beckham far too much space. After the first own goal, Hyypia made it 1-1 with a diving header after new United goalkeeper Massimo Taibi missed Redknapp's free kick. Taibi was otherwise magnificent and won the man-of-the-match award on his only decent appearance for United. Mikael Silvestre was another United debutant, having just chosen United over Liverpool. He was booed all day, but the Reds put him under little pressure. 3-1 down at the break, the Reds dominated the second half, aided by the sending-off of Andy Cole, who had scored United's other goal. A switch to an attack-minded wing-back system helped, especially with the marauding Gerrard on the right. But they could only find one more goal – a neat side-footed finish from Berger. Owen caused problems as a second-half sub. Smicer missed a one on one. But United just about held on. In his autobiography, Carragher told how he was attacked for his performance by none other than Westerveld's wife. "'You're a disgrace,' she said to me. 'The way you're playing I'm surprised you're happy to be seen out in public. You shouldn't be in the team.'" Carragher was probably more worried with Houllier's assessment of his performance than Mrs Westerveld's. "Any faith Houllier had in me as a centre back was gone for good," he wrote. "I still find the haste with which Houllier changed his mind about my best position puzzling. My contribution the previous season seemed to be written off on the basis of one nightmare half. I'd won rave reviews at centre back throughout 1998-99, despite having to cope alongside numerous defensive partners." Carragher would spend the rest of the Houllier era at right back or left back, an indictment on the manager's judgment.

Houllier fielded some fringe players in the League Cup second-round first-leg tie at Hull City, something which Evans rarely did. Three of them scored the goals. Murphy and Meijer bagged a brace apiece - their first goals for the club, with Staunton adding a late fifth as the Reds won 5-1. Traore made his debut. Owen made his first start of the season. Smicer picked up an injury.

Back in the Premier League, two more points were dropped at bogey side Leicester City. The Foxes scored early - with Tony Cottee capitalising on a howler from Matteo - and late. Owen fired a brace in between – the first from the penalty spot after a foul on Berger and the second from Matteo's pass after Camara had stormed into Leicester's half. With Frank Sinclair sent off on 51 minutes, Liverpool should have been able to hold on to their 2-1 lead, but they became sloppy and complacent. Few were surprised when Muzzy Izzet equalised with five minutes left. Thompson was red-carded in injury time for a second yellow, demonstrating a lack of discipline that would eventually curtail his time at the club. Matt Elliott elbowed Owen and was banned for one match.

The second leg of the League Cup saw Hull beaten 4-2 at Anfield. Henchoz made his first appearance of the season. Friedel enjoyed a rare start, as did young Welshman Layton Maxwell, who marked his only Liverpool appearance with a second-half goal after Murphy had scored the opener. 2-0 down, Hull were soon level, but Riedle added a late double in his last game for the club. Kippe and Jon Newby came off the bench.

After the next three games, Liverpool's season was on the brink of ruin. First up was Everton at home, a game which saw two Liverpool red cards. Kevin Campbell scored the only goal on four minutes. Liverpool barely threatened an equaliser. Westerveld and Francis Jeffers were sent off for a fight – in the loosest possible sense of the word – before Gerrard was despatched for a horror tackle on the goal scorer in injury time. Owen could have been sent off for lunging at David Weir. Staunton ended up in goal and made a spectacular save from future Red Abel Xavier, tipping over the bar. Hamann made a welcome return from his opening-day injury, lasting 64 minutes. The Reds were now 12th. Worse news was Fowler's ankle injury which would see him miss the next nine games. Riedle was sold to First Division Fulham for £250,000, leaving Liverpool light up front.

A 0-0 draw at Villa wasn't a bad result, especially with Staunton sent off for two yellows on the half-hour mark against the club Liverpool had re-signed him from. The second was for breaking from a defensive wall too quickly. The red card was later rescinded but it was Liverpool's fourth in three league games, in which just two points were gained. Houllier preferred Meijer to Camara, but the

103

Dutchman fired another league blank. Along with Smicer, Owen and Redknapp, he did go close, but as the game wore on, Villa pushed Liverpool back.

The Reds then went out of the League Cup, losing 2-1 to Southampton. Houllier fielded his strongest available side, albeit with Friedel replacing Westerveld, but they failed to hold on to a second-half lead. Owen scored Liverpool's goal on 53 – his 50th in 93 appearances for the club – but he was guilty of missing several chances to put the tie to bed. Dean Richards, whose error had let in Owen, equalised, and Trond Egil Soltvedt scored an injury-time winner. Houllier was under pressure.

Liverpool finally got back to winning ways when they beat Chelsea at a rainy Anfield, a result which was something of a turning point in the season. Thompson scrambled in an early second-half winner from Staunton's free kick. Owen missed a penalty with 16 minutes left. It was his third failure from the spot in a Liverpool shirt. After a poor run of form, Meijer was axed. Murphy was the most forward player in a five-man midfield. He justified his selection with an excellent performance and won the penalty which saw Marcel Desailly dismissed. At the back, Hyypia continued to impress, dominating Chris Sutton. Chelsea ended the match with nine men, with Dennis Wise sent off in injury time for lashing out at Smicer. Chelsea had beaten Manchester United 5-0 in their previous game, so this was a decent result, however unspectacular it may have been.

Two days later, the players were in Northern Ireland, playing Omagh Town to raise money for those affected by the bombing in the town a year earlier. Liverpool won 7-1, with the goals coming from Camara (two), Meijer (two), Smicer, Berger and Redknapp.

The Reds then returned to the scene of their League Cup embarrassment and gained a 1-1 draw, but they missed a bucketload of chances again. Soltvedt scored again for Southampton. Camara equalised with aplomb on 81 minutes after Redknapp's shot was blocked. Owen was rested in favour of a Meijer-Camara partnership but, following his introduction in the 58th minute, he left the field with another hamstring injury. When he departed, three subs had already been made, so Liverpool finished with ten men. Saints missed a couple of late chances. After 11 games, the Reds were in 11th, ten points behind leaders Leeds.

A much-needed upturn in form followed, with the Reds winning four successive league matches. West Ham were the first victims, with Camara scoring the only goal from Song's pass. His emotional celebration left fans puzzled. It later emerged that his father had died earlier in the day. He had another disallowed. It was a handy win over a Hammers team which included future stars Rio Ferdinand, Joe Cole and Frank Lampard, as well as ex-Red Neil Ruddock, who spent most of the game kicking Camara and Meijer.

Bradford City were next at Anfield. Liverpool were convincing winners after Dean Windass put City 1-0 up. According to Houllier, the Reds had been "too soft and gentle" in the early stages, but another goal from man of the match Camara changed the game. He took Staunton's pass, left a defender for dead and fired into the corner from 20 yards. The Guinean was a popular figure on the Kop. His five goals thus far comprised three equalisers and two winners, but Houllier seemed far from convinced. It was like Evans with Berger again. Redknapp gave Liverpool the lead from the spot after Berger was fouled. Heggem wrapped up the points two minutes after coming off the bench with a similar goal to the one at the Riverside a year earlier. The Norwegian was popular for his attacking abilities, but with doubts over his defending, he had lost his place in the side. As well as Camara, Berger enjoyed an impressive game.

A 2-0 win over Derby County lifted Liverpool to fifth. The fixture came almost a year to the day since the same side humiliated the Reds in the final days of the joint managership. Owen returned but didn't look right. Camara, Carragher and Redknapp missed first-half chances. Murphy scored his first league goal for the club on 65 minutes, although it went past Russell Hoult with the aid of a deflection. Redknapp scored the second four minutes later after a horrendous error from the Derby keeper. With Houllier approaching a year in charge, most observers concluded that he was doing a fine job. Hyypia and Henchoz drew comparisons to Alan Hansen and Mark Lawrenson in the Liverpool Daily Post. There was little flair on show, but a solid and resilient Reds side were grinding out results.

There was a fortnight between games because of internationals, and in this time came a truly bizarre piece of transfer speculation. The News of the World reported that Liverpool were interested in the French Under-21 international left back Didier Baptiste, who played for Monaco. They could, it was reported, pick him up for £3.5 million, writing, "We think Didier Baptiste would be an ideal addition to Liverpool's back four. He's a really attractive player, and you will be seeing a lot more of him in the News of the World." The Times, The Guardian and even Liverpool's own premium-rate ClubCall service ran with the story over the next couple of days. The only problem was that Baptiste was a fictional character in Sky One's football soap opera Dream Team. The character had mentioned he was on the verge of moving to a big club who were managed by a Frenchman. An Arsenal fan posted it on a message board, where it is believed it was seen by a news agency, who passed it onto the News of the World, who clearly weren't bothered whether what they printed was true or not.

A brilliant goal from Owen at the Stadium of Light helped Liverpool on their way to three points against high-flying Sunderland. Still a teenager, Owen had been heavily criticised following recent England games against Scotland, but he chased a long pass from the superb Hyypia, held off Jody Craddock and cleverly lifted the ball over Thomas Sorensen. Berger put the game to bed with five minutes left with a rare right-footed goal, following Thompson's trickery on the right wing. Thompson was enjoying a fabulous season, but he would soon fall out of favour. Carragher was dropped after a fan contacted the club to say he had been drinking in town. Redknapp was about to miss four months with a knee injury. Liverpool were six points behind leaders Manchester United.

Owen's fortunes came crashing down to earth when the Reds were beaten at Upton Park. Barracked by the home fans, criticised by the media and mocked by Hammers' manager Harry Redknapp, Owen didn't enjoy the best of afternoons. He had a goal disallowed, missed a good chance and was booked for diving. He struggled up front on his own and was substituted. Despite his goal at Sunderland, he hadn't looked fit since his hurried return from injury and perhaps shouldn't have been on England duty. Owen had been a national hero in 1998. Within 18 months, he was, with no justification, now the national scapegoat.

Bottom side Sheffield Wednesday were blown away after taking the lead in an early December fixture at Anfield. Hyypia, recently named the Premier League's player of the month, scored with a bullet header from Thompson's corner. Murphy made it 2-1 with a left-footed volley after Kevin Pressman had parried Thompson's fierce shot. In front of the Sky Sports cameras, Gerrard then scored his maiden Liverpool goal on 69 minutes, dribbling through the heart of the Wednesday defence and firing into the corner. The excellent Thompson made it four with a left-footed curler. Fowler made his first appearance since the derby, replacing Owen in the last ten minutes.

Unusually, the FA Cup began for top-flight teams in December and Liverpool were competent enough to avoid embarrassment at Steve Bruce's Huddersfield, who were top of Division One and unbeaten at home. Houllier fielded a strong team, although Fowler's ankle injury had flared up again, meaning he missed out. Goals from Camara and substitute Matteo ensured Liverpool won 2-0. Gerrard played right back instead of Song. Carragher was in midfield. Every Owen touch was booed by Huddersfield fans for no obvious reason.

Anfield celebrated the 40th anniversary of Bill Shankly's managerial appointment before their 2-0 win over Coventry City. A mosaic of cards held up by supporters on the Kop spelled out 'SHANKS', with two images of his face either side of the St Andrew's cross. Pipers played 'Amazing Grace' to which the Kop sang his name. Legends including Ian St John and Kevin Keegan joined in the pre-match 'You'll Never Walk Alone'. Three days before his 20th birthday, Owen spun away from Gary Breen to open the scoring on the stroke of half-time. Camara struck a wonderful goal from 25 yards on 74 minutes. The team were fifth at Christmas and with just 14 goals conceded in 18 games, they boasted the meanest defence. Hyypia had made a huge difference. Carragher and Henchoz had made very adept partners. It was a significant upgrade on last season's Staunton-Matteo partnership.

A Boxing Day trip to Newcastle saw the Reds gain another point after a thrilling game. Alan Shearer glanced in Gary Speed's free kick. Camara, Berger and Murphy missed chances before Owen took Camara's pass and squeezed his shot into the corner. He then seized on a terrible back pass to give Liverpool a 2-1 lead, but Duncan Ferguson equalised midway through the second half.

The Reds' final match of a disappointing decade came at home to Wimbledon, whom they saw off with a commanding second-half performance. The Liverpool goals were all Wimbledon-like, coming from a corner, a free kick and a long ball. Gerrard and Carragher dominated the midfield. Hyypia was dominant at the back. Owen side-footed home Murphy's corner. Marcus Gayle equalised. Berger soon curled home a 20-yard free kick. Fowler came on to rapturous cheers and headed a third. 1999 had been a difficult year, but on the back of a significant improvement in November and December, the Reds could look ahead to the new millennium with some optimism. Houllier was named manager of the month for December. Liverpool were still fifth, trailing leaders Leeds by seven points.

The new millennium got off to an ominous start as Liverpool lost 1-0 at Spurs. Chris Armstrong scored the only goal. Owen and Fowler were absent again, leaving the Reds with little cutting edge, although Camara and Smicer did force saves from Ian Walker.

A week later, the Reds were dumped out of the FA Cup by second-tier Blackburn at Anfield. Another season would end trophyless. Houllier picked Gerrard at right back and Carragher in central midfield. Fowler and Owen were still missing. Nathan Blake fired the winner on 84 minutes. Liverpool were woeful. "We ran out of ideas," admitted Houllier. Rovers were deserving winners. It was the third Anfield defeat to lower-division opposition in eight years.

Liverpool then embarked upon a 13-match unbeaten run that did much to strengthen Houllier's reputation. The first match of the sequence came at Watford, where Liverpool won a five-goal classic. Carragher and Gerrard swapped positions, and a much-improved performance saw the outstanding Berger and Thompson give the Reds a 2-0 lead. But the Hornets scored a minute before half-time and a minute after it to make it 2-2. The winning goal came from Smicer, his first for the club, on 71 minutes as he took Owen's pass and found the bottom corner. The Czech had endured a tough start to English football and hadn't played more than three games in a row. More good news followed on the Monday when the signing of Markus Babbel was announced for next season on a Bosman. The Bayern Munich defender would be a world-class addition.

With Fowler and Camara missing, the last thing Houllier needed to see was Michael Owen clutching his hamstring and limping out of a 0-0 draw at home to Middlesbrough. Liverpool strikers either couldn't stay fit or couldn't find the back of the net. The Reds ended the match with Meijer and Jon Newby leading the attack. It could have been far worse, as Boro's best chance fell to their skipper Ince, but when clean through, he stopped to check he was onside and Westerveld tackled him, to the delight of the crowd. One of the few pluses was the imperious Gerrard in midfield.

With Owen and Fowler injured, Liverpool needed goals from midfield and three players responded with stunning strikes at home to second-placed Leeds. Gerrard was top notch again, but the goals came from Hamann, Berger and Murphy. The German's first for the club came on 19 minutes as his free-kick flew into Nigel Martyn's net after taking a slight deflection off Jonathan

Woodgate. Martyn was keeping Leeds in the game and when Bowyer headed past Westerveld, the Reds were left to curse their wastefulness. Berger restored the advantage, smashing a sensational 25-yarder into Martyn's net. The goal, bizarrely, was celebrated by referee Mike Reed with a brief fist pump and a cry of 'Yes!'. He later explained he was congratulating himself for correctly playing an advantage. Westerveld saved from Kewell, but the final word was Liverpool's as Murphy scored their third goal from outside the box, hammering the ball into the top corner.

Eight days later, the Reds emerged from Highbury with a 1-0 win to complete a league double over Arsenal. Playing a mere 33 minutes, the star was Gerrard. He played a stupendous through ball for Camara to score the only goal on 18 minutes. He then prevented an equaliser with a magnificent block on Freddie Ljungberg. Arsenal hadn't beaten Liverpool in six years and couldn't capitalise when Gerrard went off injured. It was Houllier's first win in London. The three points took the Reds into third, the last of the Champions League places.

With a big gap until the next league game, Liverpool travelled to the south coast to take on Bournemouth in a friendly to celebrate their centenary. They won 4-0, with the young Irish winger Richie Partridge, Berger, Murphy and Camara scoring.

The next Premier League match came at Old Trafford against leaders Manchester United. The Reds produced another credible, battling performance and came away with a 1-1 draw. Berger scored a screamer of a free-kick from 30 yards on 27 minutes. United only equalised when Hyypia was off the field receiving treatment after a foul by Ole Gunnar Solksjaer. To rub salt into the wound, it was the Norwegian who stabbed in the goal on the stroke of half-time. Having dominated the first half, Smicer and Owen missed chances after the break. Carragher made a stunning clearance to deny Teddy Sheringham in injury time. Liverpool had been superb, and Ferguson's comment that "only we tried to win" was absurd. The result left the Reds in fourth, ten points behind United with a game in hand. A win would have had them back in the title race with a dozen games left.

The following week's big news was the signing of Emile Heskey from Leicester for £11 million, a new club record. It was a considerable sum for a player whose goal record was just one in four. Bearing in mind Owen and Fowler's injury records and Meijer's form, Houllier perhaps felt he had little choice. The 22-year-old debuted the next day at home to Sunderland and made a dream start, driving into the box in the second minute and winning a penalty. Berger smashed it past Thomas Sorensen in his 100th league game for Liverpool. Meijer, still searching for his first league goal, put Heskey's cross over the bar and had a goal ruled out for offside. Owen made little impact as a late sub. Kevin Phillips levelled the scores from the spot with 13 minutes to play after he was fouled by Westerveld.

Two more points were dropped at home to Aston Villa on the Ides of March. Yet another missed penalty from Owen cost Liverpool. Berger was fouled by Gareth Southgate to win the penalty, but Owen hit the underside of the bar. The sight of record signing Heskey moving to the wing to accommodate substitute Meijer didn't please many on the Kop. One of the few bright spots of the night was the return from injury, after four months, of Redknapp, who replaced Gerrard as a late substitute. The Reds had lost just two in 19 and were third in the league, now 11 points from United. The next day saw the long-serving Peter Robinson leave the club. One of football's great administrators, he had been club secretary between 1965 and 1992, after which he became chief executive.

Liverpool were back in the winners' circle when they returned from Derby's Pride Park, something of a recent bogey ground, with a 2-0 win. Houllier received a rapturous reception from the travelling Kop after the game, praising him for his work in transforming the fortunes of the side. The big screens showed highlights of Liverpool's dreadful defeats at Derby in the last two seasons, which served to remind how far they had come. "Last year we were absolutely hopeless," said Houllier of his last game at Derby. "I left the ground ashamed of myself and of my team." Owen scored first on 17 minutes, his first goal of the new millennium, executing a master finish into the corner of Mart Poom's net. In a sharp performance, he could have scored several more before his second-half withdrawal. Camara added the all-important second, cutting inside Steve Elliott and sliding the ball into the corner.

Thompson had a first-minute goal disallowed for a push against Newcastle. Camara eventually opened the scoring, sweeping Gerrard's cross into Given's net at the Anfield Road end. Now Liverpool's top scorer with ten, one could only wonder how many he would have had if Houllier rated him as highly as the fans did. The Reds were in complete control, only for Alan Shearer to equalise in a rare Newcastle attack. But Redknapp, a 78th-minute substitute, rose above Duncan Ferguson to head home Murphy's corner. "I ran as fast as I could towards the manager, my own manager, Gerard Houllier," Redknapp recalled. "I screamed every expletive imaginable in his direction. It was an explosion of emotion. The injustice [of not being selected] overcomes you." Quite why Redknapp thought he was worthy of selection ahead of Hamann or Gerrard was anyone's guess.

An Owen brace set Liverpool on their way to a 3-0 win over Coventry, but the big news was Heskey scoring his first for the club in his fifth appearance. Liverpool dominated the game and should have had a hatful. Owen had now scored 12 in 19 starts but only completed six of those games. Heskey headed in Berger's free kick to complete the scoring. Gerrard and Hamann caught the eye. Redknapp was again absent, having got injured in the reserves. Steve Ogrizovic, the Sky Blues' 42-year-old keeper, who had won a European Cup medal with Liverpool in 1981, made the last of his 25 appearances against the Reds. It was also Gary McAllister's final appearance against Liverpool, but for different reasons. The 35-year-old playmaker would join Houllier's revolution in the summer on a free transfer.

Back at Anfield, another spectacular 25-yarder by Berger opened the scoring against mid-table Spurs. Owen made it two after exchanging passes with Heskey, who was in great form. The partnership was looking promising. The

Reds moved into second spot behind United, who were almost home and dry in defending their title. Liverpool were favourites to secure one of the other two Champions League spots.

Heskey weighed in with two more at Selhurst Park against Wimbledon on a terrible pitch. The Dons pulled one back, but the Reds hung on to remain second.

Amazingly, Heskey's second against Wimbledon was Liverpool's last goal of the season. Having lost just one league match since November, the Reds collapsed at the worst time possible and missed out on the Champions League. A horror run of three defeats in five games, with no goals, began with a 0-0 at Goodison Park. The controversial moment came right at the end as Graham Poll blew for time as the ball was heading into Westerveld's goal off ex-Red Don Hutchison. He hadn't been ten yards away from the goalkeeper's free kick in any case, but the Blues took the decision badly. Owen, Hamann and Berger could have won it for Liverpool, the veteran Mark Hughes likewise for Everton. Fowler replaced the injured Heskey at the break for his first appearance of the calendar year.

The Reds were two down in 14 minutes at Chelsea, with former World Footballer of the Year George Weah and Roberto di Matteo scoring. Hyypia had a rare off day, pulled all over the field by Weah. Berger was denied a penalty after Frank Leboeuf pulled him back, and Jody Morris escaped a second yellow for what resembled a rugby tackle on a marauding Gerrard. But they could have few other complaints, as Ed de Goey barely had a save to make.

A year earlier, Leicester had embarrassed Liverpool at Anfield in the low point of the 1998-99 season. This time they beat the Reds 2-0. Berger volleyed against the bar from 30 yards in the second half. Pegguy Arphexad saved impressively from Fowler (twice), Berger and Redknapp. He obviously caught Houllier's eye, as he signed him during the off-season. Only weeks earlier, the manager had insisted nothing had yet been achieved, despite a season of very tangible progress. His words were being proven prophetic. With two games left, the Reds were two points behind the vital third position. United were champions, with Arsenal likely to take second.

Houllier switched to a 4-3-3 formation, leaving Liverpool unbalanced at home to Southampton in the penultimate fixture of the season. Henchoz's header hit the top of the bar. Hamann was the sacrificed midfielder, which left the Reds all at sea. Perhaps harshly, some booed the Reds at the final whistle. Fowler, in his first start since injury, couldn't get into the game. Camara and Heskey, either side of him, weren't much better. Fowler was substituted. "I went off down the tunnel boiling, unable to speak," he wrote in his book. "I got showered, still livid, still feeling cheated, and as soon as the match was over I left the dressing room and went into one of the lounges." When Thompson told him Houllier demanded his return, Fowler told him to pass on the message to "fuck right off." Liverpool were losing an entire season's momentum at just the wrong time. Two points gained from a possible 12 left Liverpool having to beat Bradford City on the final day to stand a chance of making third. City needed a win to have a chance of staying up.

Leeds drew 0-0 at Upton Park on the final day, meaning that Liverpool needed three points from Valley Parade to move above them into third. But they couldn't stop the rot. They couldn't even manage a draw, losing 1-0 to a David Wetherall header as Bradford escaped relegation. Liverpool had to settle for fourth. Managed by former Red Paul Jewell, the Yorkshiremen were worth their win. Liverpool were lifeless – downright terrible, in fact. Fowler was left behind in Liverpool and could have few complaints in terms of form or having just told the manager where to go. But no forward looked likely to break down the Terriers' defence. The sad truth was that Bradford had beaten Liverpool with Lee Sharpe, Stuart McCall, Peter Beagrie, Dean Windass and Dean Saunders in their side. "It is a sad way for us to finish our season," said Houllier. That was an understatement. From back in Liverpool, Fowler left Houllier a voicemail after the game. "I'm gutted you cost me the Champions League," he said. "I hope you're fucking satisfied in leaving me out now."

Six months' good work had been undone in just five games. The Roy Evans seasons had a habit of fizzling out, but not like this. Houllier made excuse after excuse in that woeful last month, but his selections and tactics left plenty to be desired. Due to injury and poor form, Liverpool's attack hadn't been right all season, but few could have expected them to go five matches without a goal with a Champions League spot up for grabs. The Reds were still the Premier League's chokers, while Manchester United walked off with yet another title.

2000-01

"Go out there and make yourselves fucking legends!"

"We have the sketch, now is the time to colour it in," wrote Steven Kelly, the editor of Through the Wind and Rain. It was an apt analogy of where Gerard Houllier and his players stood on the eve of the new season. And colour it in they did, as the Reds landed an unprecedented cup treble over a marathon 63-match season, 20 more than the previous campaign. In an extraordinary season, they also secured Champions League football with a top-three finish.

In summarising the squad in the summer of 2000, the defence had just conceded the fewest number of goals for a decade. Sander Westerveld was an improvement on his predecessors but was far from the best around. Sami Hyypia was many people's choice for player of the year in 1999-00. The understated Stephane Henchoz was excellent after his autumn debut. Jamie Carragher excelled at both right back and centre half. Dominic Matteo had played left back for most of the season, but Houllier clearly wasn't keen. Rigobert Song was a wholehearted but limited player.

Holding midfielder Dietmar Hamann had endured an inconsistent and injury-hit season but did show some signs of the dominant player he would become. Steven Gerrard had a stellar campaign and clearly had a wonderful future. Vladimir Smicer struggled for form and fitness. Danny Murphy still wasn't getting the minutes he deserved. David Thompson did well centrally and on the right but could be too easily baited by opponents. Patrik Berger was continuing to enjoy life at a post-Roy Evans Liverpool. Injuries had taken their toll on Jamie Redknapp and he wouldn't feature in the treble-winning campaign.

The worries centred around the strikers. Robbie Fowler hadn't been at his best since 1997 and had a terrible relationship with Houllier, although they did at least temporarily patch up their differences in pre-season, with Fowler keeping the vice-captaincy. But a pre-season injury sustained in Glentoran saw him miss the start of the season. Michael Owen had struggled to put together any significant run of fitness since his hamstring went at Leeds in April 1999. Emile Heskey had impressed few in his dozen games. Houllier clearly wasn't keen on fans' favourite Titi Camara. Erik Meijer wasn't up to it. No strikers were signed over the summer.

The free transfers of Markus Babbel and Gary McAllister had been announced well in advance. Joining them would be Bernard Diomede, a French winger from Auxerre, for £3 million, Leicester goalkeeper Pegguy Arphexad on another free and Nicky Barmby, who crossed Stanley Park for £6 million. Everton fans were apoplectic, but Ian Rush questioned whether he would even make the Liverpool team. He had a point. Houllier was also trying to sign German left back Christian Ziege from Middlesbrough, although it wouldn't be finalised until after the season began. He would eventually cost £5.5 million, but the Reds were later charged with tapping him up. He wasn't worth the hassle. Hamann told Matteo, "Listen Dom, don't go because you'll do a better job than Ziege." If only Houllier had confided in Hamann. Matteo would join Leeds for £4.75 million on the eve of the new season, and Houllier regretted selling him, according to Carragher.

Also leaving the club were Stig Inge Bjornebye and Phil Babb. Neither defender had played a game in 1999-2000. The 29-year-old Babb went on a free, having cost £3.6 million in 1994. Thompson headed to Coventry for £2.75 million. Houllier still hadn't got over him brawling with a Leeds player in a reserves match in January 2000. Houllier's attitude towards academy graduates appeared to be to cash in on them as soon as someone made a decent offer.

Liverpool were given an immediate opportunity to exact revenge upon Bradford City. Westerveld was in goal. Babbel, Henchoz, Hyypia and Djimi Traore were in front of him. Hamann and Gerrard were the centre midfield, with Smicer and Barmby wide of them. Heskey and Owen were up front. McAllister, Carragher and Berger came off the bench. Arphexad and Murphy weren't required. Liverpool fans weren't quite convinced with Heskey and his habit of drifting onto the wings. He was having a poor game until he took Hamann's pass on 67 minutes, turned Ian Nolan, sprinted into the box and hammered the ball into the top corner. Hamann and Smicer were among Liverpool's best players, but it wasn't a convincing performance.

Two days later, the Reds lost 2-0 at Arsenal in a crazy Monday night fixture. There were three red cards. Lauren put the Gunners ahead on eight minutes, after Westerveld failed to deal with a corner. McAllister was sent off on his full debut for a foul on Patrick Vieira, who was later dismissed himself. Hamann was the third player to be sent off, for two bookings, although the referee later asked the FA to rescind the second yellow card. Thierry Henry doubled the lead in stoppage time. Even without the red cards, Liverpool lacked fluency, with Houllier choosing to bench Owen in favour of a five-man midfield.

The Reds were involved in an even more bizarre game five days later at the Dell. No one was sent off this time, but Liverpool, in their new gold alternative kit, managed to spurn a 3-0 lead in the final 17 minutes, courtesy of some appalling defending. The manager reverted to 4-4-2, with Smicer supporting Owen up front. Carragher partnered Hamann in midfield. Owen scored his first goals of the season, both with his left foot, with Hyypia scoring in between. Smicer provided all three assists. But Liverpool collapsed, failing to deal with three crosses, all of which led to goals. Babbel told a newspaper of his frustration of having to play right back and not centre half. "Respect your teammates when you talk to journalists," Houllier told him in front of the squad. "How do you think Sami Hyypia and Stephane Henchoz felt reading this rubbish?"

Owen took his form into a midweek home game against Aston Villa, bagging a stunning hat trick inside 33 minutes. Five goals in two games was the perfect response to him being benched at Highbury. He'd also been overlooked by England in favour of Andy Cole. His first was set up by Heskey, who pounced on a loose pass from Gareth Southgate and cut back for Owen. David James was responsible for the next two goals, with the sort of errors that blighted his Liverpool career. He wandered out to meet Smicer's corner, changed his mind and allowed Owen a simple header into the unguarded net. The next was even worse. Traore put Owen through on goal. The goalkeeper rushed out and missed the ball, and Owen completed his treble. Steve Stone pulled one back on 83 minutes, but the Reds held on this time.

The entertainment showed no sign of abating as the Reds edged out long-ball merchants Manchester City in a five-goal thriller three days later. Carragher captained the side in the absence of Hyypia, one of eight absentees. Owen ran onto Heskey's through ball to steer the ball past Nicky Weaver for the first. Hamann chested the ball down on the edge of the box and volleyed into the top corner. But the defence proved to be the Achilles heel again as two City goals, with substitute George Weah the inspiration, tied the scores late on. Liverpool responded immediately when a long throw from debutant Ziege led to Hamann smashing in a half-volley to win the match. The midfielder scored just eight league goals for the Reds in seven years, so this brace was as unexpected as it was invaluable. Liverpool were fourth after five games, a point behind joint leaders Manchester United and Leicester City, but the concession of eight goals in the last four games was a worry.

A clean sheet was kept in the next game – a 1-0 win at Rapid Bucharest in the first UEFA Cup game. Barmby scored after some trickery from Owen. Song had earlier prevented a Bucharest goal with a vital block. Diomede made his debut. Ziege was awarded his first start. Fowler made his first appearance of the season, coming off the bench with ten minutes left.

Gerrard put the Reds one up at West Ham, firing Murphy's left-wing cross into the roof of the net, but the bottom side escaped with a 1-1 draw after Paolo di Canio's equaliser from the spot. Owen missed out with a back injury sustained in Romania. Fowler made another appearance off the bench.

A day after the club signed the young French left back Gregory Vignal from Montpellier for £500,000, two more points were tossed away at home to Sunderland, just as they had been in March. Liverpool lost Heskey to an early injury and to compound their woes, Kevin Phillips scored a stunning 25-yarder. A fit-again Owen headed in his seventh of the season from Ziege's free-kick after Diomede was fouled. The French winger was enjoying his best Liverpool game, and his spectacular scissor kick from Ziege's cross was the closest the Reds came to a winner.

Hyypia and Berger were back in the side for the visit of Rapid Bucharest in the second leg of their UEFA Cup tie. Fowler made his first start of the season. Houllier was at pains to point out the only thing that mattered was the result as a 0-0 draw was enough to see his team progress, but it was turgid stuff.

The nadir of an inconsistent season thus far was reached at Stamford Bridge on the first day of October. After ten minutes, Westerveld punched a Chelsea corner into his own net. Jimmy Floyd Hasselbaink doubled the lead a minute later after the Liverpool defence was cut to pieces. Eidur Gudjohnsen pounced on a careless back pass from Henchoz to score his first Chelsea goal in the second half. Gerrard and Owen were the only two to perform to any reasonable level.

There was a fortnight in between games because of World Cup qualifiers, with Hamann scoring the last-ever goal at the old Wembley with a long-range free kick as Germany beat England 1-0. Liverpool obviously used the time off to good effect, as they hammered Derby 4-0. Heskey finally netted again, scoring a superb hat trick. The first was a header from the in-form McAllister's corner. His next was rifled into the top corner from nearly 25 yards. He then slid Barmby's low cross into the net for his first treble in senior football. A superlative goal from Berger finished off an incredible passing movement with a rasping 20-yarder into Mart Poom's bottom corner. Owen was concussed after an accidental knee to the head and would miss five games. Having been stretchered off, he tried to convince the physio and doctor he was okay to go back on, only to collapse in the dressing room. An ambulance was called to take him to hospital before he was taken back to the ground. Such was the trauma to his brain, he wept all the way home. "I was later told that the impact of the knee had disturbed the area of my brain that controls emotions," he wrote in his book. "I was bawling, telling all the lads that I could have been dead." Heggem was another early injury victim. The Reds were fourth. Derby were bottom. "I'm very pleased for him," said Houllier of Heskey. "The boy has tremendous qualities - pace and power and at times he is more capable than he thinks. He has to believe in himself a bit more."

The hat trick triggered a great run of form for Heskey. His old club Leicester were next in town, and he scored the only goal of the game, steering Babbel's long pass between the posts in front of the Kop. Twenty-four shots produced just that one goal. Westerveld protected the points by making a late save from Muzzy Izzet. Liverpool moved above the Foxes into third.

The Reds weren't quite as impressive at home to Slovan Liberec in the second round of the UEFA Cup, winning by just a goal to nil. Fowler, up all night at the birth of his daughter, blazed a penalty into the Kop eight minutes into the second half, following a foul on Hamann. Still without a goal since December, Fowler missed other chances too. But with three minutes remaining, Heskey swivelled and smashed Barmby's deflected shot into the roof of the net. According to Fowler, "One of the papers said at least I had an excuse for playing shit, but what about the other ten players, because we did have a shocking night. Houllier went ballistic again. He rang the reporter, coated him, and said he was just trying to get Fowler in the side. I was gobsmacked."

With Everton fans arriving at Anfield intent on hurling as much abuse at Barmby as possible, it was fitting that he should open the scoring in the Merseyside derby. The Reds were easily the better side and deserved their 3-1 victory. The Paul Gascoigne-inspired Blues made the better start, but Barmby headed home in the 11th minute. Westerveld's error allowed Campbell to equalise, but Liverpool took control in the second half. Barmby's header found Heskey 25 yards out, and his bullet of a shot made it 2-1. Westerveld then released Smicer, who was fouled in the area by Thomas Gravesen. The red card was brandished. Berger converted the penalty. The man of the match was Gerrard, playing at right back. Babbel was back in the centre of defence, covering for the injured Henchoz.

Fowler scored his first goal in 11 months, as his 104th-minute winner knocked Chelsea out of the League Cup at Anfield. Murphy and Gianfranco Zola exchanged first-half goals. Hasselbaink and Fowler went close to breaking the deadlock before the latter took Berger's pass and squeezed the ball past Ed de Goey from the edge of the box. Heskey was sent off in the last minute for a second yellow card.

Houllier reverted to 4-5-1 for the trip to Leeds. Carragher was at centre back in the continued absence of Henchoz. Heskey was up front on his own. After 17 minutes, headers from Hyypia and Ziege had the Reds in pole position at 2-0 up. But an error from the German left back – it was fast becoming obvious he couldn't defend – allowed Mark Viduka to halve the Leeds deficit. The same player equalised two minutes into the second half. Smicer restored Liverpool's lead just past the hour, touching Berger's cross past the last defender and firing into the corner. Viduka levelled again on 73 minutes, turning Berger and finding the corner. The Czech winger was left with a long-term knee injury. Two minutes later, the Australian lifted the ball over Westerveld to cap a tremendous personal performance. The Reds had been beaten 4-3 in a tumultuous game. Talking on Sky in 2020, Carragher said the game was the end of Ziege as a left back at Liverpool. He also said the German defender was "possibly the highest-paid player in the Premier League," which was something of an indictment of the club's transfer strategy.

Liverpool survived another goal fest to progress into the third round of the UEFA Cup. A Jiri Stajner header put Liberec 1-0 up, but Ziege's free-kick saw Barmby score a carbon-copy goal. Ziege was otherwise terrible, his confidence now eroded. Heskey continued his recent run of goals with a clever flick of Smicer's cross. Owen sealed the tie with the aid of a deflection from the edge of the box. David Breda fired in a brilliant 20-yarder, but the Reds were through with a 3-2 win, although they didn't look like a team who would be lifting silverware any time soon.

Coventry were the victims of a superb Liverpool performance at Anfield three days later. McAllister scored against his old club, swooping on a loose ball on the edge of the box, beating a defender and firing in with deadly accuracy. Smicer had a goal disallowed for offside, but Gerrard opened up a two-goal cushion, heading in McAllister's free kick. David Thompson scored a sensational long-range goal on his return to Anfield and shouted, "Fuck off!" to Houllier for good measure. The last ten minutes belonged to Heskey. He headed in Babbel's flick from close range before controlling a clearance and lobbing future Red Chris Kirkland for an exquisite goal from 20 yards.

When Fowler put Liverpool one up at White Hart Lane, things continued to look rosy, but the Reds caved in, conceding first-half goals to Les Ferdinand and Tim Sherwood. Hyypia forced a reflex save from a corner but Liverpool were unable to find an equaliser. One player conspicuous by his absence so far was Camara, who Houllier was having regular potshots at via the media. He wouldn't figure for the club again.

The first leg of the UEFA Cup third round sent Liverpool to Greece to play Olympiacos, who rarely lost at home in Europe. Barmby continued his excellent record in the competition, side-footing Heskey's flick into the roof of the net. He hit the bar in the second half. Alekos Alexandris made it 1-1 with a spectacular scissor kick. Gerrard restored the Reds' lead from Barmby's corner. Smicer hit a post but the Greeks came strong late in the game, and Alexandris scored his second in injury time.

Another tough away game in the league resulted in another defeat. This time, the Reds were two down to Newcastle and managed only a goal from Heskey in response. A weak tackle from Carragher, filling in at left back, allowed Nobby Solano to score first. Fowler forced Shay Given into a splendid save. Hyypia headed onto the bar and had another cleared off the line. With 20 minutes left, Keiron Dyer skipped past Hyypia and beat Westerveld to double the Magpies' lead. Heskey lobbed Given for his ninth goal in nine games to get one back, but Liverpool failed to further trouble the goalkeeper. Few could understand how a defence boasting Babbel, Henchoz, Hyypia and Carragher could be so unreliable. Successive defeats left Liverpool in fifth after five defeats in eight away games.

An 8-0 win is always a handy way to bounce back, and that's what Liverpool produced in the fourth round of the League Cup at Stoke. Fowler led the way with three goals and three assists. Arphexad started. Stephen Wright and Richie Partridge were handed debuts. Stoke should have gone ahead after four minutes when Arphexad's howler let in Peter Thorne, but he hit the post. Ziege opened the scoring moments later. Smicer made it two. Babbel turned in Fowler's clever overhead kick. Fowler nodded in Hyypia's flick-on to put his side four up at the break. The Finn became the third defender to score when he slid in Murphy's cross. Fowler unselfishly set up Murphy for the sixth and completed his hat trick with the last two goals. The game was a huge deal in Iceland, with almost the entire nation watching due to Stoke being owned by an Icelandic consortium.

The Reds then eased past Charlton Athletic in the Premier League at Anfield. Mark Fish turned Ziege's cross into his own net to score a fifth-minute own goal. It took 73 minutes for the next goal, and it came when Heskey headed in Smicer's cross. Babbel rounded off the scoring with a three-yard header following a short corner. Heskey was lucky not to be sent off for a couple of bad fouls, which led to a post-game spat between Houllier and Alan Curbishley. The Guardian concluded that the managers' disagreement was more entertaining "than an antiseptic game, the scoreline of which hugely flattered Liverpool."

Olympiacos were finally seen off in the second leg at Anfield, with lone front-man Heskey getting another key goal. Barmby put him through on goal on 28 minutes, and he steered the ball under the keeper. Barmby then latched onto Murphy's pass, rounded the goalkeeper and found the net via the near post. Smicer missed a late chance to increase the margin of victory, but the Reds were through, 4-2 on aggregate. The competition would begin again in February with a daunting trip to AS Roma.

For the fourth time, a European match was followed by a disappointing Premier League result, as a Marcus Stewart goal on the stroke of half-time gave Ipswich Town a 1-0 win. Heskey was excluded by Houllier, to the surprise of many. "We couldn't believe it when we saw that Heskey wasn't on their team-sheet," said Stewart. "That's when we knew we had a real chance." New signing Igor Biscan, who had joined from Dynamo Zagreb for £5.5 million, made his debut as a substitute.

Fulham were next up at Anfield, in the fifth round of the League Cup. The Cottagers managed to force extra-time after a goalless 90 minutes, but the Reds were too strong after that. Murphy hit the bar and the post with free-kicks, and Fowler forced a fine save but was otherwise poor. Smicer went around the keeper but could only find the side netting. Owen, on his 21st birthday, broke the deadlock in the 105th minute, turning in a rebound from his own header. Smicer then side-footed in a square pass from Barmby, who then rounded off a 3-0 win in the final minute.

Liverpool chose the perfect place to turn around their scratchy away form when Murphy's splendid free kick saw them win 1-0 at Old Trafford. Heskey had a header cleared off the line, but the key moment came two minutes before the break. Gary Neville, inexplicably, met Gerrard's long ball with his forearms, volleyball-style. Murphy curled a beauty into the corner of the net from 20 yards. Gerrard and Biscan got the better of Roy Keane and Nicky Butt in midfield. Carragher didn't give Beckham an inch. Owen hit the bar in the second half from Babbel's pass as Liverpool threatened to extend the lead. They didn't manage to do that, but as Smicer raced through on goal with ten minutes remaining, Luke Chadwick was sent off for hauling him down. It was United's first home defeat since December 1998 and Liverpool's first triumph there since John Barnes scored twice in March 1990. They were now ten points adrift of United.

Within days of the success at Old Trafford, Fowler, an unused sub, was scolded by the manager for not joining in the on-pitch celebrations. He then discovered from his agent that the club had agreed to sell him to Chelsea for £12 million. Houllier denied it to the player but said he could leave if he wanted to. The press got wind of the story, forcing Houllier to deny Fowler was going anywhere. But the manager's deteriorating relationship with his stand-in skipper certainly wasn't affecting the team as Liverpool thrashed Arsenal at Anfield with a magnificent performance. Gerrard, fast becoming an absolute star, smashed in a belter of a volley from the edge of the box to get the Reds on their way. Owen followed up Heskey's shot to double the lead on the hour mark. Barmby scored ten minutes later. Fowler came on to a hero's reception and finished off the Gunners in injury time, beating Alex Manninger with a left-footed shot. He would later receive calls from Kenny Dalglish, Ian Rush and John Aldridge, urging him not to let Houllier get him down.

However impressive those triumphs were, they were bookended by defeats to Ipswich and Middlesbrough, and that's why Liverpool weren't challenging for the title. The Boxing Day reverse at the Riverside was most disappointing, with Gerrard one of the few players to look anything like his usual self. Westerveld was at fault for the goal, parrying a shot which was tapped in by Christian Karembeu. Houllier blamed ice on the ball. The Reds ended the year in sixth, 13 points behind leaders Manchester United.

The first game of 2001 produced three points against Southampton, but only just. Gerrard scored a quite unbelievable goal in the 12th minute, smashing the ball past Paul Jones from 35 yards via the underside of the bar. Trond Egil Soltvedt squeezed the ball inside Westerveld's near post following an uncleared corner. Just as it seemed a draw was inevitable, Babbel headed in the winner from close range. It came on 86 minutes. The German defender had stayed on despite an injury, with all three substitutions having been made.

The third round of the FA Cup reverted to its usual January slot and the Reds earned a routine win over Rotherham United. Heskey scored first with a diving header. Biscan was sent off on the hour for a second yellow. The win was wrapped up with two goals in two minutes, from Hamann and Heskey, both created by Murphy. Vignal made his debut as a second-hand substitute. Another new signing, Finnish striker Jari Litmanen, watched from the stands. The 29-year-old had been transferred from Barcelona on a free transfer. Fowler was another onlooker, having been dropped for two games for his part in a late-night skirmish in town. He denied any wrongdoing, claiming he was the victim of an unprovoked assault by a couple of doormen and that the bar's CCTV "just happened to go missing".

Litmanen's debut wasn't the happiest but he did create a goal. Having not played competitive football for eight months, he came off the bench at Crystal Palace in the first leg of the League Cup semi-final. Owen missed several chances. Heskey and Barmby also should have scored, but the Reds found themselves trailing 2-0. Litmanen set up Smicer to pull one back but it ended 2-1. Palace striker Morrison said of Owen's performance, "I would have put at least two away." He would regret those words.

The Reds responded by winning 3-0 at mid-table Aston Villa. Murphy hit the post with an angled shot from 25 yards but hammered in the rebound from 20. Gerrard's goal was even better, as he ran onto Murphy's clever flick and smashed it past David James from outside the box. Murphy scored the third via a deflection. Litmanen was magnificent on his first start. Staunton was in the Villa team, having moved back on a free transfer in December. Brad Friedel, Camara, Song and Meijer also departed.

Once again, Liverpool stumbled against Middlesbrough and had now failed to beat them in all four games since Ince's transfer. The Reds were woeful in the first half and although they improved, it ended 0-0.

When Crystal Palace came to Anfield for the second leg of the League Cup semi-final, they were hit by a red tide that swept them away. Buoyed by Morrison's comments, the Kop cranked up the volume as the Reds attacked that end in the first half. It was 3-0 after 18 minutes. Smicer scored first, having been played in by Fowler. The next goal was a work of art. The ever-improving Murphy watched Litmanen's cross all the way onto his right foot and volleyed it inside the near post from 15 yards. Biscan slid the ball into the bottom corner after running onto Fowler's impudent backheel. After three goals in six minutes, Liverpool were 4-2 up on aggregate. McAllister hammered a post from 25 yards. Murphy scored his second six minutes into the second half, before Morrison's air kick in front of a gaping goal led to the biggest cheer of the night. Palace keeper Aleksandrs Kolinko was sent off for a professional foul on Fowler, who later made it 5-0 from Murphy's pass. It was a magnificent response to the disappointment of the first leg.

With games coming thick and fast, the Reds went to Leeds for a midday kick-off in the fourth round of the FA Cup. Barmby broke the deadlock on 87 minutes from a tight angle after Fowler hit a post. Heskey made sure of the win in injury time after Fowler's breathtaking skill on the left touchline. After a flat November and an inconsistent December, there was now justified talk of a cup treble. Fowler's return to form was also a talking point, especially following rumours of a strained relationship with the manager. "I've always said that we want four quality strikers at Liverpool," said Houllier. "I don't want Robbie Fowler to leave the club."

A return to Premier League action saw a 1-1 draw at bottom-three side Manchester City. Heskey scored two minutes before half-time. Danny Tiatto equalised just into the second half. It was the first goal conceded by Westerveld in 420 minutes. Babbel and Smicer missed chances from McAllister corners.

Camara and Song were back at Anfield at the beginning of February as Liverpool beat West Ham 3-0. Smicer fired in first with a brilliant 25-yarder to keep up his recent run of form. Fowler scored from outside the box to make it 2-0 at half-time. He soon made it three and had a hat-trick goal disallowed. It was a commanding win, but the title was long gone, with the Reds 18 points behind Manchester United.

There was controversy galore in the Reds' next game. Don Hutchison put Sunderland ahead, but Litmanen opened his account from the spot with 11 minutes left. McAllister had been fouled outside the box. Sunderland fumed at the decision, as did the entire media, but Fowler had a winning goal wrongly ruled out for offside which barely got a mention. The home side were having an outstanding season, sitting one place behind the Reds in fourth.

Starting in Rome, Liverpool then had four cup games in a row, a sequence of matches that would help define the season. At the Serie A leaders, Fowler and Owen were partnered in attack with Barmby on the wing. Owen, in his first start in eight games, seized upon a defensive error, stepped inside the last defender and shot across Francesco Antonioli and into the bottom corner just into the second half. And it got better, as Ziege's right-wing cross was glanced into the net by Owen. Roma, managed by Fabio Capello, never had a sniff. It was a phenomenal performance to rank alongside some of Liverpool's famous European nights, but fans were attacked after the game, just as they had been by Roma supporters in 1984.

Houllier shuffled his pack for the visit of Manchester City in the fifth round of the FA Cup. Biscan and Smicer replaced McAllister and Barmby in midfield. Heskey and Litmanen took over from Fowler and Owen. A foul on Smicer allowed Litmanen to score from the spot. The Finn was in a class of his own. Heskey scored from Litmanen's exquisite pass. City got one back before half-time, but Smicer won another penalty early in the second half and converted it himself, with Litmanen now off the field. Babbel glanced in Ziege's free kick. Shaun Goater pulled one back late in the game.

Liverpool, for once, were on the right end of an astonishing refereeing decision when Roma came to Anfield, seeking to overturn their two-goal deficit. It was going well for the Italians after Owen had a weak penalty saved. Guigou opened the scoring from distance. Referee Jose Maria Garcia-Aranda then pointed to the spot after Babbel's handball. He then changed his mind and awarded a corner before handing out numerous yellow cards for dissent. He completely lost control. One of those players, Damiano Tommasi, was later booked again and dismissed. The Reds had survived a massive scare and were into the quarter-finals.

The first trophy of the season was collected at Cardiff's Millennium Stadium three days later, after Birmingham City were beaten in a penalty shootout. Owen was left out. The team was: Westerveld; Babbel, Henchoz, Hyypia, Carragher; Gerrard, Hamann, Biscan, Smicer; Heskey, Fowler. Skipper Fowler, the only survivor of the 1995 triumph, scored a brilliant 20-yard volley from Heskey's knockdown on the half hour to put Liverpool in the ascendancy. "Even as Emo jumped, I could see that the keeper had strayed off his line a little and the ball bounced up at the perfect height for me to get a proper contact to smash it over his head," he wrote. Fowler ran to the bench, sidestepped Houllier, and celebrated with club captain Redknapp, who hadn't played all season. But the Reds couldn't finish off the plucky Division One side. Henchoz scythed down Martin O'Connor. Darren Purse equalised from the spot. Henchoz could have conceded another in extra time but was adjudged not to have fouled Andy Johnson. Hamann hit the post from 25 yards. Neither side found a winner. The German missed a penalty in the shootout but McAllister, Barmby, Ziege, Fowler and Carragher found the target. Westerveld saved from Martin Grainger and Andy Johnson to leave City manager Trevor Francis in tears. "Gerard Houllier told us to remember how winning felt and urged us to use it as an inspiration," remembered Carragher, whose penalty was one of the highlights of the day. Fowler lifted the Worthington Cup and the Alan Hardaker Trophy for man of the match.

Premier League inconsistency continued to dog Liverpool as they went down 2-0 at fourth-placed Leicester City. The Reds had ridden their luck in the last two games but were dismal here. Westerveld, hero of Cardiff, "gave a performance of astonishing cowardice," according to Through the Wind and Rain, which also concluded, "we can still only play against teams who allow us to do so." The Guardian compared Houllier's side to "a flickering lightbulb, only this time the filament failed altogether." Ade Akinbiyi and Muzzy Izzet scored the goals.

A humdrum 0-0 draw in Portugal in the first leg of the UEFA Cup quarter-final wasn't a result to be sniffed at. In fact, it was classic Houllier as Liverpool stifled Porto in a game of few chances. It was the first of three successive cup games.

Back on Merseyside, the Reds reached the FA Cup semi-finals by winning 4-2 at John Aldridge's Tranmere Rovers. They had beaten Everton 3-0 at Goodison in the fourth round and then Southampton 4-3 after being 3-0 down, although Houllier bizarrely asserted they were "capable of playing Champions League football." Murphy quietened the crowd on 13 minutes by heading in a cross from Owen, who then doubled the lead with his first goal on English soil since Christmas. Steve Yates nodded Tranmere back into the game early in the second half. Gerrard quickly restored a two-goal lead, heading in McAllister's corner. Wayne Allison halved the deficit for a second time after Fowler's back pass hit Babbel and fell perfectly into his path. A nervy 24 minutes ensued until they were awarded a penalty on 82 when McAllister was fouled. Fowler fired past John Achterberg, Liverpool's future goalkeeping coach, to end the scoring. After the game, the Reds avoided Arsenal and Tottenham in the semi-final draw, instead landing Wycombe Wanderers.

The second leg of the Porto tie was much more comfortable than many had anticipated. Gerrard played on the right, with Smicer behind a front two of Owen and Fowler. Murphy controlled Gerrard's long cross, possibly with the use of a hand, and hit the ball across the goalkeeper towards the far post. His shot seemed too weak, but in it crept. Liverpool struck again with another strange goal. Owen rose to meet Gerrard's cross 12 yards out with a strong, downwards header. It pinged off the turf and into the top corner of Pedro Espinha's goal. Porto never looked like getting even one back. Owen describes his performance that night as the best of his career. The Reds would play Barcelona in the semi-final.

The hit-and-miss form continued with a 1-1 draw at home to Derby County. "Liverpool were so wretched before the interval that it was a little surprising they eventually emerged with anything tangible," The Guardian concluded. Deon Burton scored in the ninth minute. Owen equalised on 51 after exchanging passes with Litmanen. He later put three chances wide. The game marked 300 appearances for Fowler in his Liverpool career. The Reds had taken just seven points from a possible 18.

International matches meant Liverpool had two weeks until their next game. It was worth the wait, as the Reds destroyed champions Manchester United with a dominant first-half performance at Anfield to complete their first league double over them since 1979. Gerrard's opener was sensational, as he found the top corner of Fabien Barthez's goal from 30 yards. Fowler then found himself in space in the United box and drove the ball into the roof of the net. Murphy was sent off midway through the second half for two bookings, prompting an immediate double substitution from Houllier, as he sought to see the game out. Heskey hit a post late on. According to The Guardian, Liverpool had "bludgeoned United into realms of mediocrity," but had to settle for just 2-0. On the injury front, Litmanen had broken his wrist playing for Finland against England at Anfield, but Berger was on his way back, scoring on his comeback for the reserves.

Very little happened in the first leg of the UEFA Cup semi-final as Liverpool, in their 50th match of an arduous campaign, successfully parked the bus before the phrase had even been coined. The Nou Camp kick-off was delayed so viewers of EastEnders could discover who had shot Phil Mitchell. They may have offered little up front, but Liverpool delivered a defensive masterclass that meant Marc Overmars, Rivaldo and Patrick Kluivert didn't get a sniff. Barca fielded future managers Pep Guardiola and Luis Enrique, as well as Pepe Reina and Bolo Zenden, who would sign for the Reds in 2005.

From Barcelona to Wycombe Wanderers, in a match just as important as Liverpool travelled to Villa Park for the FA Cup semi-final. Wycombe's manager Lawrie Sanchez had scored Wimbledon's winner against Liverpool at Wembley in 1988. Embarrassment was avoided this time but Wycombe, 18th in the third tier, performed with distinction. Two late goals ensured the Reds' passage to the final. Substitute Gerrard fizzed in a 78th-minute cross, which Heskey headed in from close range. Five minutes later, Fowler floated a delightful free kick into the top corner from 20 yards. Wanderers pulled one back when Keith Ryan lobbed Westerveld from eight yards, but they didn't come close to finding another. The Reds were heading back to Cardiff.

Five dropped points in two Premier League matches against fellow Champions League chasers Ipswich Town and Leeds was hardly ideal. At Ipswich, just two days after Wycombe, Heskey accelerated into the box and beat Richard Wright just 15 seconds into the second half. But Liverpool conceded an equaliser on 77 minutes, which left Ipswich in third.

A morning kick-off on Good Friday pitted fifth-placed Liverpool against fourth-placed Leeds. Three points separated them, although the Reds had two games in hand. Fowler and Owen had been restored to the starting line-up but failed to provide any spark. First-half goals by Rio Ferdinand and Lee Bowyer, who had spent the last ten weeks in court following a city-centre fracas, put Leeds in the driving seat. McAllister and Smicer replaced Murphy and Berger.

Gerrard pulled one back nine minutes after half-time but was sent off on 70 minutes for two yellows. The game ended 2-1. Leeds would soon play in the semi-finals of the Champions League but the Bowyer case, which also involved Jonathan Woodgate, would have severe repercussions for them.

When David Unsworth buried an 83rd-minute penalty to level up the Easter Monday Merseyside Derby at Goodison against 10-man Liverpool, something special was needed to end the mini-slump. Anything less than a win would leave Houllier's men as outsiders in the Champions League race. Substitute Vignal then surged into the Blues' half and was brought down. McAllister lined up the free kick. He had pinched a few yards, but nobody considered he was close enough to shoot. Everton expected him to float the ball into the box, as he had done minutes earlier when Hyypia forced a great save from Paul Gerrard. But the Scot took everybody by surprise by curling the ball over the two-man wall and into the corner of the net. It was a goal fit to win any derby. Heskey had earlier opened the scoring. Duncan Ferguson scored his fourth derby goal to equalise. Babbel then restored the Reds' advantage with a stunning breakaway goal. Fowler missed a penalty. Biscan was sent off. Unsworth made it 2-2. McAllister's intervention proved to be a major turning point not just in this wonderful derby, but in the season as well.

Barcelona were McAllister's next victims as his first-half penalty took Liverpool into the UEFA Cup Final on one of Anfield's great nights. The lack of an away goal in the Nou Camp meant a score draw would suit Barca, so the second half was a backs-to-the-wall job for the players and a stomach-churner for the fans. Owen and Hyypia missed first-half chances before McAllister's corner was inexplicably handled by Kluivert. The 36-year-old's penalty found the top corner of the Anfield Road goal, giving Pepe Reina no chance. Heskey or Gerrard could have increased the lead, but the Reds were left clinging on at the end. Alan Hansen, on BBC duties, had to change his shirt, as he was sweating so much. But, amid a raucous atmosphere and nerves aplenty, Liverpool kept Barcelona at bay, with Hyypia and Henchoz leading the way. The Reds would play the Spaniards Alaves in the final.

The games continued to come thick and fast, with Houllier continuing to rotate. Spurs at home was the eighth game in 23 days. An early goal by Heskey, from Berger's pass, settled some nerves, but when Willem Korsten equalised from Oyvind Leonhardsen's cross, they were jangling again. Enjoying a wonderful Indian summer, it was McAllister who broke the deadlock, with another penalty following a handball deep into the game. Fowler headed in Babbel's cross to make it 3-1.

Liverpool had the rare luxury of six whole days to prepare for their next game. They used the break well as they virtually consigned Coventry City to relegation. It was long overdue payback for those painful April defeats in 1996 and 1997. Gordon Strachan's players did hold out for 83 minutes, before Hyypia headed in McAllister's corner. The Scot sealed the game with a superb free kick. He looked like he'd lost a winning lottery ticket, aware as he was of his old team's fate. Owen may not have scored, but he was coming into form at just the right time.

Another 2-0 win and another McAllister free kick came two days later at Bradford City. Owen squeezed the opener into the near post. He then won the free kick which McAllister dinked into the net off the underside of the bar midway through the second half.

One of the key days in the race for third came on Saturday May 5th. Owen's hat trick put Newcastle to the sword, while Leeds lost 2-1 to Arsenal. Babbel created the first, with his pass splitting two defenders, allowing Owen to beat Shay Given. The young marksman scored two more to secure a comfortable 3-0 victory. Hamann was outstanding against his former club. Liverpool were in third, three points clear of Leeds and Ipswich after 36 games each.

The 60th match of a crazy season could have seen the Reds strengthen their grip on third by beating Chelsea, but two Jimmy Floyd Hasselbaink equalisers left them frustrated. Owen maintained his hot streak to score his 20th of the season on eight minutes, when he clipped the ball over Carlo Cudicini. Hasselbaink beat Westerveld from 35 yards to cancel it out. The 21-year-old restored Liverpool's lead with a close-range volley. But Chelsea's Dutch striker punished them again with a low drive into the bottom corner. Liverpool now had to win at Charlton, three days after the UEFA Cup Final in Dortmund, to secure the all-important third place.

The second final of the season was against Arsenal at the Millennium Stadium in the FA Cup. Liverpool had lost to the Gunners in the 1950 and 1971 FA Cup Finals, as well as the 1987 League Cup Final and the 1989 title decider at Anfield. Houllier selected the following players: Westerveld; Babbel, Henchoz, Hyypia, Carragher; Smicer, Hamann, Gerrard, Murphy; Heskey, Owen. Fowler looked livid at his exclusion during the pre-match amble on the pitch. In the searing Cardiff heat, Liverpool failed to get to grips with Arsenal, particularly in midfield, where Patrick Vieira outshone Gerrard. Thierry Henry was played into the clear on 17 minutes. He went around Westerveld and straightened up, but Henchoz turned the ball around the post with his elbow. No penalty. When Freddie Ljungberg went around the Dutch goalkeeper on 72 minutes, he did manage to find the net, putting Arsenal a goal up.

A lifeless Liverpool looked doomed in the Cardiff heat. As they pressed forward, Arsenal broke. Henry got the better of Henchoz, who seemed to handle again. His shot was saved by Westerveld, and his weak follow-up was cleared by Hyypia. Somehow, Liverpool were still alive. McAllister, Berger and Fowler had replaced Hamann, Murphy and Smicer. And then the match turned. With seven minutes remaining, substitute McAllister sent in a left-wing free kick. Arsenal failed to deal with it. Babbel nodded into the pathway of Owen, who volleyed superbly into the corner from close range as he fell to the ground. As the game restarted, Owen checked the clock to see if he had time to finish Arsenal off in normal time. He did. Five minutes later, an Arsenal attack broke down, and Berger brought the ball clear from Liverpool's box. He looked up and played a long left-footed pass over the top of Arsenal's defence. Now in overdrive, Owen outpaced Lee Dixon and beat Tony Adams, before firing a shot with his left foot across David Seaman and into the far corner. In five magical minutes, he had won the FA Cup all on his own. This was a world-class centre forward at his very peak. "If I could bottle one day and experience it again, that afternoon in Cardiff would be in," said Owen. "It was like poetry. I wish the moment somehow lasted forever." Redknapp, in his shirt and tie, and Fowler lifted the cup, which was perhaps hard on Hyypia, captain for the day, and, as ever, a colossus. It was Liverpool's sixth FA Cup triumph. Two trophies were in the bag, with another still to play for.

The trophy hunt moved on to Germany where Liverpool faced Spaniards Alaves in the UEFA Cup Final in Borussia Dortmund's Westfalenstadion. Alaves had finished tenth in La Liga, 31 points behind champions Real Madrid, so Liverpool were clear favourites, but with so many weary players, nobody was taking anything for granted. The line-up was: Westerveld; Babbel, Henchoz, Hyypia, Carragher; Gerrard, Hamann, McAllister, Murphy; Heskey, Owen. "Go out there and make yourselves fucking legends!" Thompson instructed the players before the match. The Reds made a dream start when, in just the third minute, Babbel headed in McAllister's free kick. Westerveld tipped a long-range free kick around the post. Owen got between the lines to play in Gerrard, who drilled the ball past Martin Herrera to make it 2-0. Alan Hansen in the BBC studio mimicked smoking a cigar to the Liverpool fans behind the other goal. But the notion that the rest of the final would be a cakewalk was quickly scotched by substitute Ivan Alonso heading in Cosmin Contra's right-wing cross. Liverpool absorbed the disappointment and set about restoring the two-goal advantage. Hamann slid a perfect ball through to Owen from his own half. The striker rounded Herrera and was brought down just inside the box. Penalty, but no red card. McAllister sent the penalty into the bottom corner. 3-1 at half-time.

The cup treble seemed a formality, but within six minutes of the restart, Westerveld had been beaten twice, and it was 3-3. Both goals were scored by the centre forward Javi Moreno, with a header and a daisy-cutter free kick, which embarrassed the wall. Back to the drawing board. Inexplicably, Moreno was taken off. Reds fans were relieved to see the back of him. Smicer and Fowler replaced Henchoz and Heskey. Fowler had endured a tough few years under Houllier, but in the 73rd minute he shifted the ball past two defenders on the edge of the box and fired with unerring accuracy into the bottom corner for a goal described as "boys' own stuff" by the BBC's Barry Davies. It was fit to win any final, but as in the League Cup decider, Fowler was denied the winning goal in the last minute. Alaves lined up a corner. Westerveld got nowhere near it, and the former Manchester United winger Jordi Cruyff headed in to make it 4-4. "I wanted to go over to Sander and shake him by the throat," Fowler recalled. Liverpool had to face golden-goal extra-time. Fowler had a goal disallowed for offside, before the Spaniards' discipline deserted them. Magno Mocellin and Antonio Karmona were sent off for second yellow cards. When McAllister sent over the free kick from the latter's offence, it was glanced into his own net by Delfi Geli to make it 5-4. A penalty shootout had been just three minutes away. Liverpool had won their third UEFA Cup and had completed their cup treble. Hyypia and Fowler lifted the trophy in front of 30,000 rapturous Liverpool supporters. The game was described as the greatest of all European finals.

Even with three cups won, there was still another game to play. It was dubbed the 'fourth cup final'. Liverpool had to beat mid-table Charlton Athletic at the Valley on Saturday May 19th to secure a Champions League place. Henchoz was injured. Vignal came in. Fowler replaced Heskey. Berger and Barmby started. With the nightmare at Bradford a year earlier still vivid, the Reds were leggy and unconvincing in the first half. Only Westerveld kept it goalless. Eventually, things clicked into place. The breakthrough came from Fowler. Sasa Ilic's punch was weak, but nobody could have legislated for Fowler's back-to-goal, over-the-shoulder lob which dropped under the crossbar for the goal which broke the dam. With the burden of pressure lifted from their shoulders, Liverpool destroyed Charlton in the final third of the game. Murphy cut infield from the right and sent a left-footed shot into the bottom corner from the edge of the box. McAllister went close with a 20-yard free kick. Fowler sent a rasping shot from the inside-left channel into the far post. Owen sealed the win by scoring the team's 71st league goal and their 127th in all competitions. Another crack at the European Cup beckoned.

Amid extraordinary scenes, half a million fans greeted the team's open-top bus parade around Liverpool. In a sea of red, the League Cup, the FA Cup and the UEFA Cup were shown off to the adoring masses. It had been a truly remarkable season.

2001-02

"Ten games from greatness."

With three cups on the sideboard and Liverpool back in the Champions League, Gerard Houllier's stock couldn't have been higher. The players had bought into his ethics. The fans loved him. The focus now shifted to Liverpool becoming champions of England or champions of Europe - or even both, in a perfect world. In the end, Liverpool won neither the Premier League nor the Champions League in 2002, nor did they defend the domestic cups. Everyone was just relieved at the end of a traumatic season that Houllier was still alive.

There was little transfer activity during pre-season. Norwegian left back John Arne Riise, who had been on the verge of signing for Fulham, joined from Monaco for £4 million, replacing the disappointing Christian Ziege, who joined Spurs for the same fee. The 20-year-old, who even bought Ziege's house, wasn't a regular in the team at Monaco, who had just finished 11th in Ligue 1. Czech striker Milan Baros joined from Banik Ostrava for £3.2 million, although he had to endure a lengthy wait to secure a work permit and would barely feature in 2001-02. The Reds were keen to sign the Blackburn winger Damien Duff, but couldn't meet Rovers' hefty price tag. Someone else who left the club was assistant manager Patrice Bergues, who went to Lens. He would later sell El-Hadji Diouf to Houllier. He was replaced by Jacques Crevoisier. "Bergues was a top coach," wrote Jamie Carragher, "but his replacements Jacques Crevoisier and Christian Damiano [in 2003-04], never commanded the same respect."

The triumphs of 2001 ensured fans were at their most optimistic for years. Marcus Babbel, Sami Hyypia, Dietmar Hamann, Steven Gerrard and Michael Owen belonged in the top bracket of players. Stephane Henchoz might have looked like the weak link in the three finals, but he'd had an excellent season. Jamie Carragher was getting better and better, but the signing of Riise suggested he might struggle to keep his place. Danny Murphy had enjoyed some great moments too.

There were still areas that needed addressing. Sander Westerveld's next mistake rarely seemed far away. Gary McAllister had defied all expectations but at 36, he wouldn't be a regular, and without him, there might not be enough creativity from midfield. There was a lack of quality on the wings, where Houllier preferred to use central midfielders like Murphy or Gerrard. Patrik Berger's season had been disrupted by the knee injury at Leeds. Vladimir Smicer flitted between brilliance and anonymity. Nick Barmby scored freely in the cups but looked less convincing in the rough and tumble of the Premier League. Robbie Fowler had had his best season since 1997, scoring 17 goals in 48 appearances, but his relationship with Houllier was never far from collapsing. Jari Litmanen, the fourth-choice striker, oozed class but the manager wasn't convinced. More injuries for Owen would see Liverpool struggle for goals.

Despite a thrilling Champions League run and Liverpool gaining their highest Premier League points tally, the story of the season was the health of the manager. He had looked traumatised in the closing stages of the UEFA Cup Final, according to witnesses close by. He had no break over the summer, choosing to attend the Confederations Cup in Korea, where he had trouble sleeping. With the season starting early and with trips into Europe to tie up deals for Anthony Le Tallec, Florent Sinama-Pongolle and Baros, Houllier was unable to come off the treadmill.

Having finished third in 2001, the Reds experienced the dubious honour of the Champions League qualifying stage for the first time. They were drawn against the Finnish side FC Haka, who were managed by Keith Armstrong. He had once scored for another Finnish side, Oulu Palloseura, against Liverpool in a 10-1 defeat. Pegguy Arphexad played in goal, with Westerveld injured. Babbel, Henchoz, Hyypia and Carragher made up the defence again. Hamann, Gerrard and Berger were in midfield. Litmanen played behind Heskey and Owen. McAllister, Murphy and Fowler appeared off the bench. Jorge Nielsen, Riise, Traore and Barmby were unused. Finns Litmanen and Hyypia received a standing ovation from the locals. Heskey scored the first goal of the new season with a close-range diving header from Gerrard's cross. Owen rattled in a second-half hat-trick. Hyypia got the other goal in a convincing 5-0 win.

Four days later, Liverpool played champions Manchester United in the Charity Shield at Millennium Stadium under a closed roof. Riise made his debut. Westerveld was back in goal. The Reds made a dream start when McAllister converted a second-minute penalty following Roy Keane's trip on Murphy. Heskey then flicked on Westerveld's long kick, allowing Owen to turn Gary Neville and beat Fabien Barthez to make it 2-0 inside 15 minutes. Ruud van Nistelrooy scored for United, who had most of the ball, but they were unable to equalise, as Liverpool won a fourth trophy of 2001, which Hyypia collected.

Fowler wasn't even on the bench. It soon transpired he had been involved in a training-ground spat with Phil Thompson. The striker claimed he was practising his shooting. Thompson was behind the goal and claimed the net had billowed out and nearly hit him. "It couldn't have hit him because there was a net in the way," Fowler wrote. "I would have had to have a radioactive shot to burn the net away to actually get the ball through to him." A slanging match erupted, in which Thompson reportedly told Fowler he had been at the club too long. The vice-captain wouldn't play again until he apologised.

Owen was the hero as the Reds got their league campaign underway with an unconvincing home win over West Ham. After a minute's silence to remember

Liverpool legends Joe Fagan, Billy Liddell and Tom Saunders, who had passed away during the summer months, Owen produced two classic finishes. Arphexad was in goal. Biscan came into the side. Litmanen and Owen were up front. Owen latched onto McAllister's backheel for his first, escaping the clutches of Rigobert Song and firing past Shaka Hislop into the corner. Paolo di Canio equalised with a beautifully executed Panenka penalty following a foul by Henchoz. Owen bamboozled Christian Dailly and fired a blistering shot into the corner from 15 yards for the winner. Worryingly, Babbel was withdrawn at half-time, citing immense fatigue. He was replaced by Riise on his league debut. Redknapp came off the bench for his first appearance in over a year. Fowler watched the game from the Main Stand, having still not apologised to Thompson.

The Reds confirmed their place in the Champions League group stage by beating FC Haka 4-1. Rare starts were handed to Redknapp, Bernard Diomede, Stephen Wright and Gregory Vignal. A contrite Fowler was back and scored first from Redknapp's corner. Traore's error allowed Haka to equalise. Redknapp and Heskey scored early second-half goals, before an own goal by former Manchester United trainee David Wilson gave Liverpool a 9-1 aggregate win.

Winning the UEFA Cup meant Liverpool had a crack at European champions Bayern Munich in the Super Cup in Monaco. The Reds were sensational. Having signed from Monaco, it was apt that Riise opened the scoring, turning in Owen's low cross. Heskey then stormed past Robert Kovac and Thomas Linke and beat Oliver Kahn to double the lead. Thirteen seconds into the second half, man of the match Owen seized on an error and slotted past Kahn. Hasan Salihamidzic and Carsten Jancker got a couple back for Munich, but it wasn't enough to stop Hyypia, Fowler and Redknapp lifting Liverpool's fifth trophy of 2001. At the team hotel, Houllier knew he was unwell. "I like swimming, but I didn't feel like using the pool," he told Steven F Kelly for the book 'Gerard Houllier – the Red Revolution' "Physically, I felt something was wrong, but I did not show that to my players. If you show you are weak, the team will be weak."

A trip to Bolton was Liverpool's sixth game in 19 days. It became an evening to forget for many reasons. It was the end for Westerveld at Liverpool and it was Babbel's last game for over a year. Fowler was booked for diving, played terribly and was substituted. Bolton sat back, and Liverpool couldn't open them up. In their first game against a Sam Allardyce-managed team, the Reds went behind to Michael Ricketts' header. Heskey equalised immediately from McAllister's pass and almost scored again eight minutes later. The final word went to Dean Holdsworth. His speculative 20-yarder was inexplicably fumbled by Westerveld before it trickled over the line. Houllier discovered Westerveld hadn't apologised to his teammates after the game and took that as a further sign of Westerveld's arrogance. On the team bus, the goalkeeper knew he had played his last game for Liverpool.

Houllier's response was incredible. On the final day of August, four days later, he signed two goalkeepers – the Pole Jerzy Dudek from Feyenoord for £4.85

million and young Chris Kirkland from Coventry for £6 million. Westerveld couldn't have been told any more emphatically that he was surplus to requirements and eventually joining Real Sociedad in December for £3.75 million. Arphexad, who had won five medals without playing in a final, joined Portsmouth on loan. Kirkland had always been a Liverpool fan. He had a ticket for the Leppings Lane End at Hillsborough in 1989, but his mother wouldn't let him go. She took him to watch his aunt sing in a musical in Leicester instead. Houllier flew to France with Rick Parry to complete the Le Tallec and Sinama-Pongolle transfers. "When I got back from France, I was absolutely exhausted," Houllier told Kelly. "Usually, I would be tired the following day and recover, but this time it took a week." With no domestic football due to internationals, Houllier had a three-day break in France and visited a doctor in Paris. An ECG and a blood-pressure test showed no abnormalities.

Houllier wasn't the only one with health problems. Babbel had been withdrawn at half-time in the Bolton game, complaining of flu-like symptoms. He was initially ruled out for a month, but was later diagnosed with Guillain-Barre syndrome, an inflammatory disorder of the peripheral nerves which attacks both the nervous and respiratory systems. Ten percent of sufferers die from it. He was treated in Germany but wouldn't feature again in the Liverpool team for a year. When he did recover, he told The Guardian of his ordeal. "I couldn't run, I couldn't even breathe," he said of the Bolton match. "I just told the boss: 'I really don't know what's wrong with me, but this is unbearable.' I'd noticed it before. After the Charity Shield, I'd felt unusually tired, but I thought it was something to do with the roof being closed and the air not being too good in the Millennium Stadium." Two or three months after being diagnosed with the Epstein-Barr virus, which causes glandular fever, Babbel returned to Liverpool to train but lost the feeling in his toes, feet and lower legs. He was then diagnosed with Guillain-Barre. "If my respiratory muscles had stopped working and I had not had a respirator available, I could have died." He spent most of December in a wheelchair, struggling to speak. As much as it was devastating for the player, it was also bad news for the team, as he had been magnificent in his debut season.

On top of all that, many Reds had to contend with international fixtures, the highlight of which was England winning 5-1 in Germany. All their goals came from Liverpool players – an Owen hat-trick, Gerrard and Heskey. With so much going on, it wasn't a surprise that Liverpool weren't entirely focused on their next fixture. On Babbel's 29th birthday, his teammates produced an appalling display in a 3-1 home defeat to Aston Villa. Six points dropped in the first three games was hardly ideal, as the Reds had been tipped to challenge for the title. Riise came in at left back, with Carragher switching to the right to replace Babbel. Owen was benched and only played for half an hour. Dudek made his debut, but couldn't prevent Dion Dublin heading in Paul Merson's free kick. Gerrard nodded McAllister's corner past Peter Schmeichel. Villa struck next when Dublin totally missed his kick and it fell to Lee Hendrie, who couldn't miss from seven yards. Gerrard was back on the right where he hated playing. Late in the game, he nearly cut George Boateng in half with a knee-high tackle. Up went the red card. Darius Vassell put Liverpool out of their misery with a late clincher.

The Champions League group stage got underway on September 11th, ten hours after the appalling terrorist attacks on the USA. Liverpool entertained Portugal's Boavista amid an understandably subdued atmosphere. The Portuguese took a third-minute lead, with the Liverpool defence flummoxed by a long ball. Owen equalised on the half hour with a clinical finish from Heskey's pass. In a dour game, Liverpool were unable to find a winner. Few were in the mood for football.

Another long ball undid the Reds as Kevin Campbell scored early in the Goodison derby. Gerrard soon equalised by smashing the ball into the far top corner when everyone expected a cross. Owen then slotted home his 13th goal of the season with a penalty following David Unsworth's foul on Heskey. The third goal was a gem. Riise, who, along with Vignal, had an excellent game on the left, ran 50 yards, turned a defender inside out and smashed the ball past Paul Gerrard.

In their next Champions League game, Liverpool travelled back to Dortmund, scene of May's incredible UEFA Cup win. This game was totally different - a 0-0 draw. Hyypia had a header cleared off the line. Owen could have had a penalty. That was as exciting as it got for the 500 travelling Reds.

A piece of Litmanen magic lit up the home game with Spurs in the Premier League. Twelve minutes into the second half, the 30-year-old received the ball in the inside-left channel, 12 yards from the area. He cut infield and unleashed a ferocious shot, which curled away from Neil Sullivan and in off the far post. Unfortunately, Owen sustained another hamstring injury. Two and a half years on from the original Elland Road injury, he was still plagued by the issue. The Reds were in fifth, three points behind leaders Bolton but with two games in hand.

The Finn was again the only goalscorer as the Reds won their first Champions League match. In the 23rd minute of their home game with Dynamo Kiev, he followed up Gerrard's 30-yard free kick, which had rebounded off the post, and scored via the underside of the bar. He had already had a goal disallowed for offside.

An early goal and a late goal saw Newcastle off at St James' Park. Riise took advantage of Robert Lee's error to score on three minutes, smashing the ball into the roof of the net. The impressive Fowler had a goal disallowed before Murphy sewed up the points by scoring from the edge of the box. Having sidelined him all season, Houllier finally gave Fowler a full game but refused to discuss his performance after the game. "Nice try," he said to a journalist. "I'm not talking about Robbie. Hard luck." Newcastle boss Bobby Robson did at least say, "Robbie Fowler is one of the best strikers in the country."

After an international break which saw England qualify for the World Cup with a 2-2 draw with Greece, the Reds were embarrassed by a 2-1 home defeat to Grimsby Town in the third round of the League Cup. Kirkland made his debut and kept a clean sheet over the 90 minutes, during which Barmby, Litmanen and Heskey missed chances. McAllister opened the scoring in the first period of extra time with a penalty given for handball. Marlon Broomes equalised on 113 minutes. With penalties less than a minute away, boyhood Liverpool fan Phil Jevons won the match with an outrageous shot from 30 yards in front of the jubilant Grimsby fans. Vignal, who had made an impressive start to the season, fractured a foot and wouldn't play again for over a year. He was replaced by Frode Kippe, who made the last of his second Liverpool appearances. He was still playing in Norway's top flight at the age of 41.

October 13th 2001 was a dark day for Liverpool FC. In a quite unremarkable game, Leeds led a leggy-looking Liverpool 1-0 at the break. Houllier put his morning chest pains down to indigestion. He delivered a much shorter than usual address to his players at the break, before retiring to the physio's room, where Heskey was being treated. Thompson took over the team talk. None of the players gave the manager a second thought, apart from Heskey, who could see he was in distress. Heskey was about to be substituted for Litmanen. Dr Mark Waller and physio Dave Galley examined Houllier and called an ambulance. Houllier wanted to carry on. They overruled him - and saved his life in doing so. Galley told a stunned Thompson they believed Houllier had suffered a heart attack. The players went back onto the pitch none the wiser. His wife Isabelle accompanied him in the ambulance. An oxygen mask was fitted. He arrived at Broadgreen Hospital, still annoyed he wasn't at Anfield, overseeing the second half. Houllier was told he hadn't had a heart attack, but that he had a dissection in his aorta, which was leaking blood. He was prepared for an operation and told there was a 30 percent chance he could die. Asked if he wished to speak to anybody, he wanted a moment alone with Isabelle. He understood the implications of the question. Thankfully, he came through the 11-hour procedure. Two of the reasons he survived were that the streets around Anfield were deserted at half-time, so the ambulance could get in and out quickly, and the world-renowned surgeon, Abbas Rashid, had chosen, for the first time in months, to stay in the city for the weekend, rather than travel away to see his daughter. He was called into the hospital to conduct the operation.

The 54-year-old remained away from managerial duties until March, with Thompson taking over. His first job was to oversee the second half, where Murphy equalised after Fowler's exquisite chip had come off the bar. On ITV, Terry Venables put Liverpool's second-half improvement down to Litmanen replacing Heskey at the break. Thompson told his stunned players about the manager after the game, before going to see him. "Gerard came past on his bed, going to theatre," wrote Thompson in his 2005 autobiography. "He had drips everywhere and he was sitting up slightly. Isabelle was with him. I went over and got hold of his hand and said, 'Don't worry, you are going to be alright. You are in good hands. You can rely on the staff and me.' I was so emotional it was untrue."

Thompson and his players convened at Speke Airport the next day for the four-hour flight to Ukraine to play Dynamo Kiev in the Champions League. They knew Houllier had come through a marathon operation, but they didn't know much else. With Thompson urging them to "do it for the boss", Liverpool emerged with a 2-1 win. Murphy scored first. Tiberiu Ghioane equalised. Smicer then headed Berger's cross back to Gerrard, who smashed a left-footed shot into the bottom corner. Heskey was spat at by a Kiev defender as he came off the field, with the culprit receiving a four-match ban. It was an important win, which Thompson dedicated to Houllier.

Liverpool were at Leicester four days later, and the day belonged to Fowler. He and Hyypia scored in the first ten minutes, both from McAllister crosses. Fowler scored again just before the break. Dennis Wise pulled one back, but the stand-in skipper completed his hat trick with a clinical right-foot volley just inside the box, from Smicer's cross. They would be the last Liverpool goals of his first spell at the club.

Victory at Boavista would have taken Liverpool into the next group stage of the Champions League but, in the club's 200th European match, they could only manage a draw. McAllister forced a save in the first minute and then had a goal disallowed. Hyypia surrendered to a sixth-minute hamstring tweak. Murphy continued his run of form, curling in a 20-yard free-kick after Fowler was fouled. The hosts hit the bar before equalising in the second half from a corner. There was still half an hour left, but neither side could force a winner. Heskey was racially abused from the stands throughout the match.

A trip to the Valley saw Owen mark his comeback with a goal in a routine 2-0 win. Charlton could have had an early lead had Paul Konchesky not miskicked, but then Redknapp volleyed in Gerrard's flick-on. It was his first league goal in more than 18 months. Owen sealed the points by latching onto Hamann's through ball and lifting the ball over Dean Kiely. Stephen Wright was sent off with two minutes to play for a second yellow card.

The 21-year-old defender more than made up for his misdemeanour when he helped keep alive Liverpool's Champions League dreams. With the Reds needing at least a draw in the final group game against Borussia Dortmund, Wright's header late in the game secured qualification. Smicer opened the scoring after 15 minutes, smashing Heskey's header past Jens Lehmann. Owen, still far from 100 percent, was replaced by Fowler on 75 minutes. Wright made sure of qualification by nodding in Berger's cross with eight minutes remaining. Dortmund's Lars Ricken hit the bar, but the Germans hadn't offered enough going forward. Liverpool topped Group B, with Boavista in second, and were drawn with Barcelona, Roma and Galatasaray in the next pool. Dortmund were eliminated but would end the season as Bundesliga champions. Hamann would miss the first match of the next stage, having collected a third yellow card.

Thompson continued his impressive run as acting manager with a 3-1 victory over champions Manchester United. The morning newspapers carried his glowing tribute to Houllier. "He is up there with the best, the Shanklys and the

Paisleys," he said. And the Kop joined in with a tribute of their own – a mosaic of cards with the manager's initials and the French tricolour. Owen scored first with a carbon copy of his Boavista goal on 31 minutes, hitting the same part of the net from virtually the same blade of grass. Riise then scored a goal that will never be forgotten by anyone lucky enough to witness it. Hamann touched an indirect free kick to him, and he smashed the ball into the Anfield Road goal via the underside of the crossbar. It's hard to think of a better struck free kick in Liverpool's history. David Beckham pulled a goal back, but Owen restored the two-goal cushion, heading into an unguarded net after Fabien Barthez had been beaten to a long throw-in by Heskey. Liverpool were second, a point behind Leeds with a game in hand. United, looking for their fourth successive title, were sixth.

An away game at Ewood Park saw Graeme Souness in the opposing dugout. He and Thompson were sworn enemies for two reasons. The Scot had replaced the Scouser as captain in 1981, a decision which left Thompson devastated. Eleven years later, Souness sacked Thompson from his coaching staff. Souness broke the ice with a pre-match handshake that appeared to take Thompson by surprise. Former Reds Brad Friedel and Stig Inge Bjornebye were in the Blackburn team. Owen leapt above Henning Berg to open the scoring with a great header from Gerrard's cross, but Matt Jansen frustrated them with an equaliser seven minutes after half-time. Murphy missed a chance in injury time, but an unambitious Liverpool didn't deserve more. They went top and stayed there when Leeds lost to Sunderland 24 hours later.

Thompson suffered his first defeat when the Reds were humbled at home by Barcelona in the first game of the second Champions League phase. Hamann's suspension would prove crucial. Heskey missed a couple of chances. Owen was played through by Smicer and beat Roberto Bonano with an expert clip into the far corner. Phillip Cocu cleared off the line from Heskey. Barcelona were simply incredible for the rest of the game, passing Liverpool off the park. Patrick Kluivert equalised from Rivaldo's chipped pass. Dudek saved from Marc Overmars as Barca finished the half on top. Owen could have restored the lead but couldn't manage to scramble the ball in. At the other end, substitute Fabio Rochemback finished wonderfully from 20 yards, bending the ball inside the post with precision. Marc Overmars put Liverpool out of their misery, rounding Dudek to score. Two of Barca's goals were offside, but Liverpool could have no complaints on the balance of play. They had been comprehensively outplayed.

Liverpool stayed top of the Premiership after a strange home game with Sunderland, which turned out to be Fowler's last before he was sold to Leeds. Heskey ended a 20-game goal drought, heading in Murphy's free-kick. Hamann was sent off a minute before the break for a two-footed lunge on Bernt Haas. "Trudging to the dressing room for the interval, I knew exactly what was coming next," Fowler wrote in his book. "Sure enough, Thompson starts blathering on about changing the style, strengthening the midfield, showing resilience ... and of course taking me off to bring on an extra midfielder. So my epitaph at Anfield was to be sacrificed at half-time to strengthen the midfield and go all defensive. Kind of sums up my time under Houllier." The Reds hung on to their 1-0 lead against a Sunderland team which included Jason McAteer.

Fowler's £12 million transfer to Elland Road went through on November 29th, four days after the Sunderland game. He was still the supporters' favourite player but had failed to find any consistent form since 1997, blighted by injuries, Houllier's rotation policy, a tempestuous relationship with the management and an increasingly direct style of play, which was more suited to Owen's pace and Heskey's build. But from 1993 to 1997, there hadn't been a better striker in Britain. Fowler's first autobiography was scathing of Houllier, whom he believed had always plotted to get rid of him. It should be noted, though, that the Frenchman made him vice-captain, then captain, and picked him ahead of a fully-fit Owen for the 2001 Worthington Cup Final. The truth, perhaps, was that Owen had taken Fowler's mantle as Liverpool's chief goalscorer and Heskey looked the more natural partner, rather than having two out-and-out number 9s playing together. Fowler was never really suited to Houllier, in terms of playing style or discipline. But the manager was guilty of allowing the ill-feeling and paranoia on both sides to fester for too long by not making a tough decision sooner. "Houllier used the local paper, the Liverpool Echo, to feed stuff to the fans, questioning my form and ability," wrote Fowler in 2005. "From the start of the 2000-01 season, there was a concerted campaign against me conducted by Houllier ... They used to give marks for each player in the paper, and if ever Chris [Bascombe] marked me up then Houllier was on, asking why he'd given me that rating." The Liverpool fans hadn't seen the last of Fowler, but it was sad to see a bona-fide Liverpool legend depart in such circumstances.

A sixth-minute goal from Owen earned Liverpool all three points at Derby. Man of the match Dudek saved a penalty from 33-year-old Fabrizio Ravanelli on 86 minutes after Heskey had handled. "He's been outstanding for us all season," Thompson said. Owen had now scored 19 goals in 19 games. This one came after Mart Poom had carelessly spilled Berger's tame 20-yarder. Thompson and Murphy won the monthly Premier League awards for best manager and player.

As the Reds waited for their plane to Rome to take off, a mischievous member of the cabin crew announced, "We appear to be one person short on the passenger list. Mr Fowler, please make yourself known to the crew." There were stony faces among the staff. The Reds frustrated the Italians, grinding their way to a 0-0 draw. Hyypia and Henchoz were magnificent, helping their team earn their first point in the group. Smicer and Heskey spurned Liverpool's best chances. For the third game in a row, Liverpool had kept things tight. People were starting to call them boring.

Liverpool consolidated top spot by beating Middlesbrough 2-0 at Anfield. Owen struck yet again, the 99th of his astonishing Liverpool career. His goal was a screamer, similar to Litmanen's against Spurs. Berger then rifled one in from over 20 yards. The second half was goalless. With Litmanen playing instead of Heskey, Liverpool were easier on the eye. Thompson had won six league matches from seven to take Liverpool six points clear of Arsenal, having played 14 games each. A first league title in 12 years was becoming a distinct possibility. The next evening, Houllier joined Thompson and the players as they were presented with the Team of the Year award on the BBC's Sports Review of the Year programme. Thompson looked distinctly uncomfortable being ribbed by host Gary Lineker about the sale of Fowler. A day later, Houllier addressed the club's Annual General Meeting and left the room in tears after delivering his speech.

They say that the Manager of the Month award is often a jinx, but the Reds' latest award proved to be even worse. After being recognised by the BBC, Liverpool's season took a significant downturn, with Owen drying up just one goal short of his ton. By the time he scored his hundredth goal, the Reds had dropped ten points. When you consider that they ended up losing out in the title race by seven points, it was a costly blip. Fulham came to Anfield with a young Steve Finnan at right back and ground out a 0-0 draw. Owen missed three opportunities in the first half alone.

Once again, the Reds endured a nightmare at Stamford Bridge, as they were stuffed 4-0 by Chelsea. They hadn't won at the Bridge since 1990. Owen was injured and with Fowler gone, the attacking options on the bench were Bernard Diomede and Richie Partridge. It was the third blank in five games following Fowler's exit. Graeme Le Saux scored an early goal. Hyypia, Gerrard and Biscan were denied equalisers. Jimmy Floyd Hasselbaink doubled the lead with a lovely chip over Dudek. McAllister had a penalty saved by Carlo Cudicini after Riise had been fouled. The keeper made further saves from McAllister and Riise. Sam Dalla Bona put the game beyond Liverpool with a third. Eidur Gudjohnsen rubbed salt into the gaping wound in injury time. A four-goal defeat was thoroughly underserved on the balance of play, but Liverpool had to take it on the chin. They were still three points clear of Arsenal and Newcastle. Twenty-four hours later, Owen was named the winner of the prestigious Ballon d'Or, as the best player in Europe. He finished ahead of Real Madrid's Raul and Bayern Munich goalkeeper Oliver Kahn.

Arsenal came to Anfield just before Christmas and had too much for a spluttering Liverpool side. A year to the day earlier, the Reds had hammered Arsenal 4-0 at Anfield but, with a 2-1 win, the Gunners gained their first triumph at Liverpool in nine years. To add to Liverpool's misery, Arsenal outplayed them with ten men after the sending-off of Giovanni van Bronckhorst. Owen had a shot cleared off the line by Ashley Cole. In first-half stoppage time, Freddie Ljungberg won a penalty, which Thierry Henry slotted low to Dudek's right. Litmanen and Smicer were introduced but the Reds soon found themselves two down. Gerrard, who had a poor game, saw his pass intercepted. He was then beaten by Robert Pires and Ljungberg turned in the Frenchman's low cross. Litmanen got one back with a far-post header from Owen's mishit shot. Liverpool deserved no more.

Three days before the Arsenal game, the Reds pulled off a stunning transfer coup in signing Nicolas Anelka on loan from Paris St Germain. The media didn't get a whiff of any possible deal. He was unveiled at the same time as Baros, whose visa had finally come through. Finally, Liverpool had a much-needed injection of firepower. With Fowler gone, and Heskey nowhere near the form of a year ago, much would be expected of the Frenchman. He made his debut as a 69th-minute sub for Litmanen at Villa Park in a must-win game. Peter Schmeichel gifted the Reds their opener in the most bizarre way, as his throw struck the referee, Andy D'Urso, and rebounded to Litmanen, who found the unguarded net from 25 yards. Lee Hendrie turned in a rebound after Dudek had parried Juan Pablo Angel's shot. Litmanen then hit a post with a penalty when Gerrard was fouled. The only goal of the second half saw Berger's lofted pass chested down by Smicer, who found the corner of the net.

With the team having finally won again, four dropped points in the next two games was hugely damaging. Owen, at least, did finally get back on the scoresheet with an 88th-minute equaliser at Upton Park. Anelka got his first start and forced David James into three saves, but West Ham went ahead with a Trevor Sinclair goal from outside the penalty area. Litmanen replaced Smicer with 15 minutes left, and Liverpool stepped up a gear. His cross was met by Heskey, who held the ball up perfectly for substitute Owen to smash past the blond-haired James. It was his hundredth goal for Liverpool, who were fourth at the end of the year. At the end of the year, the Reds were behind Arsenal, Newcastle and Leeds in fourth place. They were just two points off the summit, with a game in hand.

New Year's Day brought Bolton Wanderers to Anfield, where Sam Allardyce's men frustrated the Reds again. Gerrard scored first on 50 minutes, knocking the ball forward for himself, surging into the area and clipping the ball over Jussi Jaaskelainen. The Reds again fell into the trap of trying to hold on to the lead instead of killing the game off and Scouser Kevin Nolan punished Liverpool's inability to clear a long throw-in by equalising with 12 minutes left.

The FA Cup offered a welcome distraction from the Premier League blip. Their defence of the competition began with a 3-0 home win over a Birmingham City side which included David Burrows, now 33. Owen curled in the opener from 20 yards. He made it 2-0 with a goal created by Anelka and hit the bar in the second half. Anelka sealed the win by scoring his first goal for the club with a well-taken 20-yarder that nestled in the corner.

The Premier League woes continued at Southampton when a Riise own goal sealed an agonising 2-0 defeat. Owen was missing with an ankle injury and without him Liverpool were toothless. Litmanen created one chance for Anelka, whose shot was tipped over by Paul Jones. Southampton turned up the pressure in the second half. Hyypia fouled substitute Matt Oakley in the box. James Beattie converted from the spot. Riise entered the fray on 68 minutes. Moments later, the left back headed over Dudek for Southampton's second. Thompson held his head in his hands on the touchline. The winter nightmare was showing no signs of ending. Murphy and Smicer were two players who were struggling badly. Despite the avalanche of recently dropped points, Liverpool were still just three points shy of leaders Leeds, but with every passing game, they were looking less and less like potential champions.

Anyone looking for the best assist in Liverpool's Premier League history might nominate Gerrard's sublime through ball to Riise to earn the Reds a point at Highbury. Ljungberg scored a third goal against Liverpool in eight months on 62 minutes, when he converted Pires' cutback. The Gunners' advantage lasted four minutes, as Gerrard hit a 50-yard first-time pass with the outside of his right foot, into the vast open space in Arsenal's half. The pass was so perfect that Riise didn't even need a touch to set himself before calmly slotting past Stuart Taylor.

Six days later, Liverpool could only draw at home to Southampton. A blistering start saw Owen score after Hamann's shot was parried – one of three openings in the first eight minutes. But Liverpool failed to build on their lead. Gerrard departed with a back injury. Kevin Davies equalised. The Reds had no answer. Indeed, it was Southampton who hit the post late in the game. Carragher and Murphy received some catcalls from frustrated supporters. Houllier phoned both to lift their spirits. "Some Liverpool supporters cheered when I was substituted," Murphy said in Simon Hughes' Ring of Fire in 2016. "It was only a few of them. But hearing that negativity – god, it was probably the lowest moment of my career. It was like a dagger through the heart. I felt like crying." The Telegraph headline, "Liverpool fading away without Houllier at helm," seemed harsh on Thompson, but only eight points had been gained from a possible 27. Title hopes were fast vanishing.

There was no better place for Liverpool to turn around their fortunes than at the leaders Manchester United. Wright did a great job at right back against Ryan Giggs. Carragher reverted to the left with Riise playing ahead of him. Liverpool were solid, compact and defended heroically before scoring a late winner. Just weeks after his miracle assist at Highbury, Gerrard was at it again. Receiving the ball 35 yards out, just to the right, he lofted a defence-splitting pass into the area, which Murphy lobbed over Fabien Barthez. It was his second winner at the ground in successive seasons. "Initially there was joy," said Murphy. "Then there was a bit of relief. Then the feeling of 'fuck you' came along, if I'm being honest. A 'fuck you' to the doubters." Dudek made a late save from Giggs and the points were Liverpool's, who moved into third.

Arsenal were the opponents for the third time in five weeks, this time in the FA Cup. Liverpool again failed to beat them. Their defence of the game's oldest competition ended in controversial scenes as three players were sent off in four crazy second-half minutes. Dennis Bergkamp opened the scoring in a relatively tranquil first half. Keown was first to go, for a professional foul on Owen on 67 minutes. Three minutes later, Bergkamp joined him for an over-the-top tackle on Carragher. But the defender then hurled a coin back into the crowd, after it had been thrown at him, and he too was dismissed. The Reds couldn't make the most of a man advantage for the second time against the Gunners. It was the second time in two seasons that three players had been sent off in this fixture.

Back in the Premier League, the Reds saw off Leicester City in a dull midweek match at Anfield, with Heskey taking Hamann's pass before clipping the ball over the keeper to break the deadlock. One interested observer was Abel Xavier, who had joined the club in a surprising move from Everton for £750,000, a move that didn't go down well with everybody, as it led to the departure of Wright, who had just earned no end of plaudits at Old Trafford. "I can understand why that annoyed the Academy staff," wrote Carragher. "Wrighty would give you that extra 10 percent commitment, and with the right coaching and quality players around him, he could have stayed at Liverpool for a lot longer. Replacing him with Xavier was nonsense from both a football and business point of view."

Fowler faced Liverpool for the first time since his November transfer when the Reds travelled to Elland Road for a Sunday-afternoon fixture. He had settled in quickly at his new club, scoring seven goals, including a brace against Everton, in sharp contrast to Heskey, who had scored just once in the same time frame. But it was the Reds' striker who stole the show with a brace in a 4-0 win. Rio Ferdinand sliced Murphy's free-kick into his own net for the opener. Heskey scored two well-taken goals in two minutes just after the hour mark. Owen then headed his 21st goal of the season. Having kept Giggs quiet at Old Trafford, Wright barely gave Harry Kewell a kick. The Liverpool fans chanted Fowler's name for much of the afternoon. "That loyalty and love from them made me think – for the first time since the move, really – that I might have made a terrible mistake," he wrote in 2019.

Next up was 6-0 thrashing of Ipswich. From looking utterly toothless, Liverpool had just rattled in ten away goals. The first goal took everybody by surprise, for it came from the right back Xavier, 15 minutes into his debut. Heskey doubled the lead. Liverpool ran riot in the second half. Hyypia headed in Murphy's corner. The injured Dudek had to be replaced by Arphexad. Owen grabbed a couple. Heskey made it a half-dozen in injury time. The win took Liverpool back to the summit of the Premier League but Newcastle, Manchester United and Arsenal had games in hand.

A tough night in the Champions League saw Liverpool unable to break down a stubborn Galatasaray side at Anfield. With the team having picked up one point from six, a 0-0 draw with the Turks was far from ideal, especially as Gerrard was stretchered off with a groin injury. Long-range free kicks from Hamann, Riise, Hyypia and Heskey all went close, but it wasn't to be.

Anelka scored his first league goal for Liverpool in Anfield's Merseyside Derby, but the Reds dropped more points. Tomasz Radzinski put the Blues ahead with a mishit shot that dribbled in off a post, but Anelka's goal, after Heskey's exquisite dummy, earned a point. Liverpool were down to third.

Another 1-1 draw, this time in Istanbul, saw Liverpool's Champions League hopes hanging by a thread. What went in their favour was that most of the other group results had been draws. Heskey's 79th-minute equaliser was priceless. It was created by the sparsely used Litmanen, who had only been on the field five minutes. His drag back and flick fooled the Turkish defence, allowing Heskey to fire home. The Reds were bottom of the group.

Despite his impact in Turkey, Litmanen got just ten more minutes at Fulham but sealed the three points with a last-minute goal. Thompson's refusal to give him the time his talent deserved was one of the reasons Liverpool would eventually come up empty-handed. Anelka scored on 13 minutes, firing into the far corner from 18 yards. Thereafter, the Reds sat back, deciding to hold on to what they had got. Henchoz, in particular, was magnificent. The Finn sealed the game, nodding Xavier's long ball past Edwin van der Sar and finishing from a tight angle.

Next up was one of the performances of the season as the Reds tore apart Bobby Robson's Newcastle, with Murphy and Anelka imperious. That morning, Houllier had been smuggled into Anfield to deliver a rousing talk to the players, which convinced Hamann they were going to win the league. Floodlight failure delayed the kick-off by half an hour, one of several such incidents in the 2001-02 Premiership. When play got underway, there was no stopping Liverpool. Anelka drove from halfway down the right wing and played in a low centre which Murphy steered into the near corner. The ex-Crewe man then beat Shay Given from 14 yards, before Hamann rounded off the scoring against his old club with a classy side-footer from 20 yards. It was a superb team performance. Thompson was deservedly receiving plenty of plaudits for the job he was doing, stepping into the manager's shoes in such difficult circumstances. "Thommo changed immensely when he took over the reins from Gerard," Murphy told Simon Hughes. "Six months before, maybe he wouldn't have been capable of being so subtle, knowing how to deliver a boost, knowing exactly what was needed … Suddenly, Gerard became ill and a Zen-like quality took over Thommo. He wasn't shouting and screeching in training any more. Sammy Lee became the enforcer. Thommo became the observer. Bob Paisley had to change when he got the job from Bill Shankly in unexpected circumstances, didn't he? I think he would have been a bloody good manager if he'd tried elsewhere."

For the second year in a row, Liverpool secured a handy goalless draw in Barcelona's Nou Camp. Hyypia and Henchoz, as usual, were outstanding. At the other end, Litmanen looked sharp against his former club. Gerrard missed a couple of chances. Javier Saviola hit an upright late in the game. Philip Cocu fluffed the rebound. Baros made his debut as a 74th-minute sub for Heskey - his only appearance of the season. The Reds were still alive, although a yellow card for Hamann would rule him out of the Roma game.

Before the Barca game, Liverpool were found guilty of making an illegal approach for Christian Ziege 18 months earlier and were fined £20,000. It wasn't an eye-watering sum, but Middlesbrough still intended to pursue the matter in the High Court. Coincidentally, the Reds' next game was at Boro, and a 2-1 win was much-needed, but it was dour stuff again. Without Gerrard, the Reds were outplayed in midfield for significant portions of the game. Frank Queudrue missed two chances for Boro. Heskey's first-half opener followed beautiful approach play from the superb Anelka. Riise doubled the lead with seven minutes left with an inch-perfect drive from 20 yards for his sixth of the season. Gareth Southgate pulled one back. It was Liverpool's 11th away win in 17 matches.

And then came a night no one will forget. Gerard Houllier's unexpected return to the dugout three days later for the must-win Champions League match with Roma was the moment of the season. With no-one anticipating his presence, photographers were suddenly spotted huddling around the entrance to the pitch from the changing rooms. Out he strode to a wonderful reception. Houllier hugged the Roma manager, Fabio Capello. It set the tone for what lay ahead. Gerrard replaced the suspended Hamann – a holding midfielder wasn't a priority in a game Liverpool needed to win 2-0 – but they would have to do without the injured Owen and the ineligible Anelka. Second-choice goalkeeper Chris Kirkland had knocked himself unconscious in a steam room 24 hours earlier, so Arphexad took his place on the bench. It was astonishing that the Reds had failed to win any of the five group games, scoring a mere two goals, but qualification was still in their hands. Amid a crackling atmosphere, the home side started emphatically, attacking the Anfield Road end. A 30-yard scorcher from Smicer was tipped over. From the corner, Murphy was caught by Marcos Assuncao. With only five minutes played, Liverpool had a penalty. Litmanen, the Reds' best attacking player in this competition, sent Francesco Antonioli the wrong way. Roma searched for an equaliser, but Hyypia and Henchoz were imperious against Gabriel Batistuta and Francesco Totti. The key goal came in the 63rd minute. Litmanen was fouled. Murphy lofted in a free kick from 35 yards. Heskey headed brilliantly into the Kop goal. Bedlam. The noise was deafening. Liverpool had done what they had set out to do. "I've never seen Liverpool play like this," Capello lamented. The quarter-finals of the European Cup awaited them for the first time in 17 years. Houllier was back.

In hindsight, Houllier returned too soon, as he later acknowledged. "I can tell you I made a mistake going back when I did," he told the journalist Chris Bascombe in 2019. "My surgeon was not happy about it. I did not even tell Rick [Parry] and David Moores until three hours before kick-off. It was a great night, but I paid for it." Over the remainder of the season and the off-season, Houllier made a number of costly misjudgements.

As the Reds' home game with Chelsea headed into injury-time, any realistic hopes of landing the title appeared to be fading. Litmanen, who had only been sent onto the field in the 84th minute, released Heskey down the left. He powered to the by-line and sent in a deep cross to Smicer, standing on the far side of the penalty spot. The Czech watched the ball onto his right foot perfectly and hammered it emphatically past Carlo Cudicini to score the only goal of the game. Smicer had also been a sub, replacing the injured Gerrard on 28 minutes. It sent Liverpool top, a point clear of Manchester United, with each side having played 32 games. But Arsenal had two matches in hand and were just two behind the Reds. They were the clear favourites, but Liverpool were well in the race.

Owen was back with a goal six days later as Liverpool earned a routine 2-0 home win over Charlton Athletic. Smicer put the Reds a goal up, heading in Murphy's free kick. The Czech, who had come off the bench for the injured Heskey, had a hand in the second when he diverted Anelka's pass into the path of Owen, who stretched out to turn the ball into the net.

"Ten games from greatness," was Houllier's assessment ahead of Liverpool's Champions League quarter-final at home to Bayer Leverkusen. There were five league games left and, if all went to plan, the same number in Europe. The team was in good shape. Dudek had enjoyed an outstanding debut season. The defence looked as mean as ever. Gerrard and Carragher were on their way to becoming two of the club's finest local talents. Anelka was making up for the loss of Fowler. Owen was back from his latest injury. Leverkusen were favourites to win the Bundesliga, so Liverpool's 1-0 first-leg win was a handy result. The goal, just before half-time, was a tap-in from Hyypia, following a corner. The Reds were criticised for being too defensive and not trying to take a bigger lead to Germany. "Other teams can keep the ball," said Houllier dismissively. "I would rather keep the result."

There was no league game before the second leg, which came six days later. Xavier replaced Smicer. Carragher switched to left back. Riise was ahead of him. The game was a classic, the sort of high-scoring, to-and-fro affair one would associate with the Roy Evans era, not Houllier's. Liverpool simply lost control in the Bay Arena, before and after Litmanen's stunning 78th-minute goal, which briefly put them in the ascendancy. Owen's finishing and defensive solidity were the two things Liverpool had long relied on. Both let them down in a wretched second leg. Michael Ballack cancelled out the first-leg score with a thumping long ranger. Xavier equalised from Murphy's corner just before half-time – a valuable away goal. But the Reds collapsed in the most heartbreaking manner. Owen missed two chances on the counterattack. The turning point came on the hour mark when Houllier made a dreadful error. He withdrew his holding midfielder Hamann, just when he was most needed, replacing him with the lightweight Smicer. Within two minutes, Ballack scored again. Five minutes after that, Dimitar Berbatov put the Germans 3-2 ahead on aggregate. Liverpool had crumbled in the most un-Liverpool-like manner. Litmanen, though, a first-half sub for Heskey, scored a stunning goal to put his side ahead on away goals. They couldn't hold out. With six minutes left, their soft centre was exposed again when Lucio shot through Dudek's legs to send Liverpool crashing out. Had they progressed they would have played Manchester United in the semi-final, a team they had beaten five times in a row. Leverkusen also beat United but lost to Real Madrid in the final.

Houllier's "ten games from greatness" statement looked distinctly foolish now, particularly as it was his substitution that had precipitated the collapse. It was hard to criticise the manager after all he had been through, but hindsight shows he returned too early and made too many mistakes. "He was sunk by a sub," concluded Chris Bascombe in the Liverpool Echo in 2004, when Houllier was eventually sacked. "The dip began. It became a blip, turned into a plateau and eventually led the club into a black hole." Hamann couldn't believe the substitution either. When leaving the ground, he told inquisitive fans that he wasn't injured. Houllier chastised him for being critical and asked why he had underperformed. The manager cited him being out of position for Ballack's first goal. "Gerard was never prone to moments of madness, but in his terms, I think he had one in 2002," Hamann argued in his 2012 autobiography. "He made an error of judgement that cost us the opportunity of being European champions."

In between the Leverkusen games, Arsenal beat Spurs 2-1 with a late penalty. The North London derby was earmarked by optimistic Reds as a game where the Gunners might stumble. Liverpool's next game took them to the Stadium of Light, where Owen's goal saw them win 1-0. Anelka hit a post. The Reds were second, a point behind Arsenal, who had an extra game to play.

Liverpool did hit top spot a week later, but only because they played 24 hours before Arsenal. They beat Derby County 2-0 at Anfield, with Owen grabbing both goals in the week he also scored at Anfield for England as skipper. The result relegated Derby. Played in by Smicer, Owen enjoyed some luck as the ball fell perfectly for him to scoop it over Andy Oakes in the 15th minute. He later rounded the keeper and slid the ball home from a tight angle.

By the time Liverpool went to White Hart Lane, Redknapp had become a Tottenham player, joining them on a free transfer in mid-April. Hyypia replaced him as club captain. Redknapp watched from the stands as his new side drove a stake through the heart of Liverpool's title challenge. Gustavo Poyet scored the only goal on 41 minutes. The Reds were unable to respond. Hyypia and Riise went close with headers but as was too often the case, when the Reds went a goal down, they had no answer. Arsenal needed to win one of their remaining three games and the title was theirs. They were crowned champions two days later when they beat Bolton 2-0.

With second place up for grabs, Liverpool beat Blackburn 4-3 in a crazy game on the same night Manchester United lost 1-0 at home to the champions. Murphy squeezed one into the corner of the Kop goal despite being on the ground for the opener. Blackburn's best player, Damien Duff, who Liverpool had chased in the summer, equalised superbly. Anelka restored Liverpool's lead with a clinical finish after a mazy run. Andy Cole made it 2-2. Hyypia headed in the game's fifth goal. Matt Jansen scored the third equaliser for Graeme Souness's team. With five minutes left, Heskey turned brilliantly on the edge of the box, got outside the last defender and fired a shot across the keeper and into the far corner.

Liverpool's final opponents of a 59-game season were Ipswich Town, who needed to beat the Reds 11-0 and hope that Sunderland lost in order to escape relegation. It didn't quite happen. The Reds required a win to finish above Manchester United for the first time since 1991. Riise provided two emphatic finishes to put Liverpool in control. Owen lobbed Andy Marshall just after half-time to make it 3-0. Smicer skipped through two tackles and beat Marshall.

McAllister replaced Murphy on 82 minutes for his final Liverpool appearance. "What a waste of money!" chanted the Kop to one of the best free transfers in the club's history. Anelka made it five with three minutes left. Carragher made his 53rd appearance of the season, despite carrying an agonising knee injury for months. "He had a knee problem for virtually a full season and couldn't face missing one game," said Owen. "Every single minute of the day, he was doing things to get rid of this pain. He couldn't even walk, and he was playing every single game." A post-season operation ruled him out of the World Cup.

Liverpool had been unable to add a major prize to the Charity Shield and Super Cup, but there were more reasons for optimism than pessimism in the summer of 2002. They had ended the season as runners-up with 80 points, their best tally since 1988. Houllier had come through his operation and was back in charge. The consensus was that with the right signings, the Reds would be well placed to end their title drought in 2003.

2002-03

"Sadly the message on his tombstone will read, 'Here lies the man who bought Salif Diao, Bruno Cheyrou and El-Hadji Diouf'."

THE summer of 2002 was a fiasco.

In one transfer window, Gerard Houllier took Liverpool as far backwards as they had been during his first season as he made mistake after mistake after mistake. He later admitted he wasn't back to full health. He had returned to the post too soon. The Reds were about to embark upon two wretched seasons that were as bad as anything Graeme Souness served up.

His first signings, Jean-Michel Ferri and Frode Kippe, were abject, but they didn't impact negatively on the progress of the club because they barely played. But the 2002 signings of Bruno Cheyrou (£3.7 million), El-Hadji Diouf (£10 million) and Salif Diao (£4.7 million) were calamitous. The chance to take that final step from second to first in the Premier League was well and truly blown. Houllier had also tried to sign Lee Bowyer from Leeds United. The move looked certain to happen before it hit a couple of snags and collapsed. It was a damaging episode for the club, given the player's recent highly-publicised court case involving an Asian student. Bowyer had been cleared of grievous bodily harm and affray but later paid a large settlement after a civil case. Houllier also missed out on Newcastle-bound Hugo Viana. Jamie Carragher was distraught with Houllier's signings, writing "Sadly the message on his tombstone will read, 'Here lies the man who bought Salif Diao, Bruno Cheyrou and El-Hadji Diouf'." Houllier also signed the defensive midfielder Alou Diarra, whom he likened to Patrick Vieira. But he spent his entire time as a Liverpool player on loan to other clubs before being sold to Lens in 2005. He played in the 2006 World Cup Final, one of 44 French caps he won. Houllier's approach with him was utterly bizarre.

To compound the summer debacle, the manager elected not to turn the Nicolas Anelka loan deal into a permanent one, which was a staggering misjudgement. Anelka continued to score and create in the Premier League long after Houllier had left Anfield. But Houllier preferred Diouf and was also trying to prise Djibril Cisse from Auxerre, although he would have to wait for that deal. He also allowed Jari Litmanen to leave on a free. That wasn't a surprise given how little game time he had given the Finn, but it was symbolic of Houllier's approach. The target man Emile Heskey was always going to be preferred to the skilful Litmanen. Nick Barmby and Stephen Wright left for fees of £3.75 million and £3 million. Barmby had done little at Anfield and was sold for just over half what he was bought for. Wright was another promising academy player bombed out by Houllier. Gary McAllister went back to Coventry City on a free, leaving as a bona-fide Liverpool legend for his contribution to the treble-winning season.

The Reds had boasted the best defence in the Premier League in 2001-02, despite losing the world-class Markus Babbel for most of the season. But they had scored 20 fewer goals than third-place Manchester United. It was clear where the problem lay. Too often, they would be unable to breakdown a well-organised defence. When they did score first, they sought to protect their advantage rather than double it. When they went a goal down, they rarely came back to win. The losses of Anelka and Litmanen, on top of Robbie Fowler's departure seven months earlier, were too big to overcome. Michael Owen had endured three injury-hit campaigns and had just played in the World Cup. Heskey had failed to build on his 2001 form.

Liverpool did win silverware in 2002-03, beating Manchester United in the League Cup Final in Cardiff, but it was a rare highlight in a miserable season. They collapsed after a promising start in the league and were humiliated in the FA Cup at Anfield by lower-division opposition for the fourth time in 11 seasons. They were also embarrassed in both European competitions. The new signings were atrocious. Steven Gerrard's form deserted him in the autumn. Jerzy Dudek endured an even more alarming slump. Heskey had a shocking campaign. There was little depth in any position. It was the season Houllier lost control.

Game one came at Cardiff as Liverpool failed to defend their Community Shield against Arsenal. The Gunners had won the league and FA Cup, so the Reds were invited along as Premier League runners-up. They were beaten by World Cup winner Gilberto Silva's 68th-minute goal. Dudek retained his place in goal. Abel Xavier and Djimi Traore were the full backs, with the ever-dependable Sami Hyypia and Stephane Henchoz between them. John Arne Riise, Gerrard and Dietmar Hamann made up a narrow three-man midfield, with Diouf, Heskey and Owen completing the 4-3-3 formation. Babbel made a welcome return to competitive action from the bench, following his lengthy lay-off. Danny Murphy, Milan Baros, Vladimir Smicer and Cheyrou were also sent on. Chris Kirkland and Carragher were unused. Neither side were convincing, but Arsenal always seemed more likely to score. Two days later, a Liverpool XI, including Kirkland, Babbel, Carragher, Smicer and Patrik Berger lost 1-0 to Chester City.

The Premier League campaign began with a promising 1-0 win at Villa Park. Heskey was dropped to the bench. Murphy came in to stiffen the midfield in a more conventional 4-4-2. Carragher was still on the bench after knee surgery over the summer, although he was back much quicker than expected. Future Red Peter Crouch was in the Villa side while Steve Staunton, who hit the crossbar, featured for the final time in a game involving the Reds. Riise scored two minutes after the break with a low drive, set up by the outstanding Murphy. Owen missed a late penalty, which had been won by Gerrard.

After a minute's silence to remember Nessie Shankly, Diouf enjoyed a dream home debut against Southampton, scoring after three minutes and then again on 51. His performance was accompanied by the cringeworthy chant from the Kop, "Diouf, Diouf, Diouf's on Fire!" Heskey powered in a cross from the left, which the Senegalese turned in at the back post with his chest. His second was also created by Heskey as he headed in from close range. Another new boy, Cheyrou, won a late penalty, which was converted by Murphy.

There then followed a remarkable run of 2-2 draws, with Liverpool conceding a late equaliser in each game. At Ewood Park, they fell behind to a David Dunn goal. Murphy equalised with a brilliant right-footed finish from Xavier's cross. It was one of Xavier's few positive contributions, as he was turned inside out all night by Damian Duff, who had been a summer target for the Reds. With 13 minutes remaining, substitute Smicer sent over a cross and Riise scored a header that looped over the former Reds keeper Brad Friedel. But Blackburn's Corrado Grabbi scored with a bullet header a minute after coming on.

The second 2-2 was a travesty. Liverpool dominated Newcastle for 80 minutes and could have been five up. Instead it was just two, following a well-placed shot from Hamann and a penalty from Owen after Hyypia had been fouled. Owen spurned several gilt-edged chances. Craig Bellamy then set up an 80th-minute goal for Gary Speed before Alan Shearer scored a stunning header with two minutes left.

Birmingham did exactly the same as Newcastle nine days later when Clinton Morrison, a one-time laughing stock at Anfield, scored twice to cancel out the Reds' 2-0 lead. Owen missed numerous first-half chances, but Murphy scored a wonderful free kick. When Diouf played in Gerrard four minutes after the restart, the points seemed secure. Houllier toyed with the idea of hooking Owen but decided to bring on Berger for Diouf. Defensive wobbles surfaced again, exacerbated by the half-time withdrawal of Henchoz with injury. He would miss the next two games. After an error by Traore, Stern John squared to Morrison for Birmingham's first on 61 minutes. The same player headed the equaliser in the last minute. Six points had been frittered away from winning positions. Houllier was hammered on the local phone-ins.

Quite unbelievably, Bolton also scored a late goal to make it 2-2 at the Reebok Stadium, but this time there was a late winner for the Reds. Owen was an unused sub. The star of the show was Baros, who marked his full debut with a couple of blistering goals, having earlier hit the post. Bolton had scored in between Baros's goals, and Ivan Campo scored their second on 87 minutes. But Heskey grabbed the Reds a much-needed victory. Liverpool's shakiness was partly due to Diao playing in defence.

For the first time, Liverpool FC came across a man called Rafael Benitez, the manager of Valencia, where the Reds played their first Champions League match. Houllier spoke of Liverpool adopting a more offensive approach but with the Argentine Pablo Aimar running the show, Valencia dominated the Reds. Aimar's opener involved the most exquisite passing. Ruben Baraja made it 2-0.

Diao and Diouf were hooked at the break after woeful performances, replaced by Cheyrou and Owen. Houllier had spent all season chopping and changing his front men, to little effect. Liverpool had conceded ten goals in five games. Hamann, who was sent off for two yellows, labelled Valencia the best team he had ever played against. They had won La Liga the season before and would win it again in 2003-04.

Owen's poor start to the season continued as he missed another penalty, this time at home to West Brom. Murphy sent him clear. Russell Hoult rugby-tackled him and was sent off. His replacement, Joe Murphy, had just signed from Tranmere and was making his Premier League debut. With family members in the ground supporting Liverpool, the Irish Under-21 goalkeeper dived to his right and saved Owen's weak penalty. Albion should have had a penalty of their own three minutes later. It took Liverpool another 20 minutes to break down the ten men, and it was the in-form Baros who scored, heading in Gerrard's cross with expert precision. Riise made sure of the win, smashing Owen's lay-off into the net via the far post. The Reds were second after seven games, two points behind Arsenal.

Anfield's 100th European match saw the Reds dominate the Swiss side Basel, only to end up with a frustrating 1-1 draw. Owen had another shocker and was withdrawn on 79 minutes. Riise could have had three in the first seven minutes. Baros scored again with a first-time shot from Heskey's square pass. The Reds failed to add another and were punished just before half-time when Carragher's missed header let Julio Rossi in. Liverpool went on to miss several chances and were booed off at the end. The directors were beginning to mull over the financial implications of an early Champions League exit. Morale was low. Several players were unhappy with their lack of game time, which was an unfortunate by-product of having such a large squad.

Typically, when Owen's form returned, the results were spectacular. Up against Kevin Keegan's Manchester City, which included Anelka and one-time Liverpool target Marc-Vivien Foe, Owen struck early and went on to complete a stunning hat trick. They were his first goals of the season from open play. His third goal came in injury time with a thunderous shot going in off the post.

A 5-0 win over Spartak Moscow, conquerors of Liverpool in 1992, provided the first Champions League win of the campaign. Heskey scored early and late, with Cheyrou, Hyypia and Diao scoring in between.

For the second time in sixth months, the Reds beat Chelsea 1-0 at Anfield with a last-gasp goal. Henchoz's calf flared up again, which would keep him out for a sustained period. Traore replaced him at half-time. The visitors had just been knocked out of the UEFA Cup by Viking Stavanger. Hyypia had a volley tipped over by Carlo Cudicini. Gerrard rattled the bar from long range. The breakthrough came in the 89th minute. Diao sent Heskey through and his dink over the goalkeeper rebounded off the post. Owen joyously smashed the ball home from a yard. The three points kept the Reds on Arsenal's heels.

149

The Reds enjoyed a similar outcome two weekends later at Elland Road. Diao, Cheyrou, Baros and Diouf all started, and it was the Senegalese midfielder who turned in the winning goal, from his compatriot's pass halfway through the second half. The Reds created little else. Terry Venables' Leeds missed several chances, with Dudek in top form. A 2-1 defeat for Arsenal at Everton, courtesy of a last-minute wonder goal from 16-year-old Wayne Rooney, meant Liverpool were a point clear after each side had played ten games.

The winning run continued in the Russian capital as Owen's ninth Liverpool hat-trick saw off Spartak Moscow. Aleksandr Danishevksy fired the hosts ahead. Owen made it 1-1, heading in his first European goal for a year. His next came as he prodded home from centimetres out after Hyypia had hit the bar. Murphy put the hat trick on a plate for him as he tapped in from close range. Heskey left the field with a groin injury, replaced by Gregory Vignal, who was making his first appearance for a year. Unfortunately, he was shortly subbed, with Houllier believing he needed more height. After four games, Liverpool were second in Group B with seven points.

The Reds maintained top spot, beating third-place Spurs 2-1 at home. Murphy curled in a 20-yarder on 71 minutes. Dean Richards equalised. Just as it seemed two points would be dropped, Owen, who had a first-half goal disallowed, won a penalty, which he side-footed into the corner. The Reds were undefeated in the league since they were beaten at White Hart Lane in April. Redknapp made his first appearance against Liverpool and was given a great reception. The Reds were four points clear. Things were looking rosy for Houllier, a year on from his operation.

Another game with Benitez's Valencia brought another footballing lesson. The difference in approach was stark - hit it long to Heskey against the sort of pass and move much of Liverpool's historic success had been built upon. The Spaniards won 1-0 at Anfield with a deflected first-half goal from Francisco Rufete. Aimar controlled the match again. Liverpool couldn't get a foothold. Hamann remembered the encounter with his future manager. "I couldn't help but admire this team and the way they had been set up," he wrote in his book. "As we walked off the pitch downhearted and defeated, I looked over to the celebrating bench of the Valencia team. A big huddle had formed as they bounced up and down, wrapped up in their celebratory joy. As the huddle unfolded and the players ran over to applaud their fans, there stood a man who had been in the centre of the group. He was small and smiling, with a receding hairline. He was taking in the atmosphere with the air of a man who felt he had a right to stand proudly in such a famous arena. His name was Rafael Benitez. At that time not many had heard of him, yet I think on that night a few people that mattered in the higher echelons of Liverpool Football Club had noticed him."

"I am the greatest!" proclaimed Diouf on the front cover of November's Four Four Two magazine. But at the start of the month, he was becoming a regular on the bench as Liverpool's runaway Premier League form continued with a 2-0 home win over West Ham, before which Houllier was presented with the

Manager of the Month award. After a dozen games, they had won nine and drawn three. Owen scored both goals, aided by Smicer playing behind him with Murphy and Heskey on the wings. Still struggling with a hip injury, Gerrard was on the bench, coming on for Smicer. Diouf, now out of favour, remained unused. He was even last pick in the Melwood five-a-sides. Houllier had been had by his old mate Bergues.

The manager shuffled his pack for the visit of Southampton in the third round of the League Cup. Kirkland kept goal magnificently. Young full back Jon Otsemobor made his debut and didn't put a foot wrong in what would be his only appearance of the campaign. Babbel and Vignal made rare starts after long absences. Biscan played centre half, where he would feature again for Houllier. Even Bernard Diomede made the bench. Gerrard was named captain. Berger scored a wickedly deflected free kick, the last of his 28 goals for the club. Southampton equalised, but Diouf tapped in from three yards to restore the lead. Baros slid in Berger's cross for the third.

Not for the first or last time, the Reds would choke in the Middlesbrough smog. But this one was costly. Liverpool's defeat at The Riverside wasn't just three points lost, it was a significant turning point in Houllier's reign. It precipitated the most miserable three months imaginable. November 1995 and the winter of 2001-02 were bad, but they were mere blips in comparison to what lay ahead now. Seven points clear on the morning of the Boro game, the Reds were about to embark on a 11-match streak without a Premier League win. They went over four months without a league win at Anfield. All the flaws in Houllier's squad were laid bare. Heskey was now a left winger. Henchoz was missed, with Houllier refusing to consider Carragher at centre back because he was too small. There was never a Plan B in the difficult times. In nearly three years, Liverpool had won just one game in which they went behind. They were playing the ugliest football imaginable, and they created nothing at Middlesbrough. Murphy played in the hole behind Owen in a negative 4-4-1-1 formation. Gareth Southgate scored the only goal, with eight minutes remaining, from Dudek's error. "Had we drawn 0-0, I'd have been livid, but I'm convinced Houllier would have been celebrating the [unbeaten] record," Carragher wrote in his book. "That mattered more to him than the three points."

Liverpool were dumped out of Europe three days later in the most humiliating fashion. Needing to beat Basel, the Reds went 3-0 down in half an hour. Houllier responded by withdrawing Gerrard on half-time. He was replaced by Diao. "That made my subbing even more shaming," Gerrard said. "Even if I was playing on a four out of ten, I could have done what Diao did!" But it was Diao's vision that sparked the attack which resulted in Murphy pulling one back. The impressive Smicer got another back. "Hallo, hallo!" screamed Clive Tyldsley on commentary duties, a phrase he would memorably use in another match two and a half years later. Owen equalised with five minutes left, turning in the rebound to his own penalty miss. But there was to be no winning goal. Houllier blamed ill-fortune. "You can have the best game plan in the world but when you concede a goal after 90 seconds, it counts for nothing," he said. That didn't say much for his game plans. For the second season in a row, Liverpool exited the Champions League after an uncharacteristic six-goal thriller. They would now enter the UEFA Cup. Houllier laid the blame squarely on the shoulders of Gerrard, with the following appearing on the club website: "Once a player starts to think 'I am king of the world' then there is difficulty and danger. I am frustrated with him. I have given him my trust and my faith, but talent without work is frustrating."

A home match against Sunderland seemed the ideal chance to gain a morale-boosting win. Houllier handed a first league start of the season to Babbel. But up against a defence which included Phil Babb and a team managed by Howard Wilkinson, the Reds were unable to break through, despite having 21 shots on goal to zero. Gerrard was an unused sub, much to the Kop's frustration. Babbel missed a chance. Murphy hit the bar. Owen's header was saved by Jurgen Macho. McCartney cleared off the line as Diouf looked likely to pounce. Many more chances were missed. It was written off as "one of those days." There were plenty more of them to come.

Hamann scored Liverpool's best goal of the season in a 3-2 defeat to Fulham at Craven Cottage. Facundo Sava got the first of a brace after just five minutes, after Dudek fumbled a long-range shot. The Reds wasted several attacks before Sean Davis made it 2-0. Hamann thundered in a sensational indirect free kick on 62 minutes, which was still rising as it hit the top corner. Sava scored again with another goal from outside the box. Fulham's Alain Goma was dismissed on 70 minutes. Baros pulled one back on 86, but it was too little, too late. A once-dependable defence was now vulnerable, with Henchoz missing ten games. Babbel looked a fraction of the player he had been in 2001 and was subbed at half-time.

Liverpool finally won a match when they beat Vitesse Arnhem 1-0 in the first leg of the UEFA Cup third round. With Henchoz fit again, the Reds turned in a competent away performance, although it was far from pretty. Owen found the net on 27 minutes. They should have scored more, but with the home leg still to come, they were in pole position to progress.

A run of five straight wins over Manchester United was ended in the most embarrassing fashion at Anfield on the first day of December. Chinks in Dudek's armour had been evident in recent weeks but he came up with the biggest clanger possible at the worst possible time, allowing the tamest of back-headers from Carragher to trickle through his legs. It was an error that would have made a child blush. Diego Forlan could hardly believe his luck as he tapped the ball into the empty net. Three minutes later, the Uruguayan beat Dudek at his near post for his second. It was another error by the Pole. Hyypia got one back on 82 minutes, with a left-footed half-volley from 16 yards. And then Hamann hit a rocket which, somehow, Fabien Barthez touched to safety. The game was a tale of two goalkeepers, although Gerrard was poor again. The Reds were now four points adrift of Arsenal.

Joe Royle's Ipswich were up next, in the League Cup. Dudek received a supportive reception from the Kop. Xavier won a rare outing, while there were debuts for young striker Neil Mellor and midfielder John Welsh, the latter coming off the bench. Once more, Liverpool were below par and needed Diouf's penalty after Mellor was tripped to cancel out Tommy Miller's early opener, which had been gifted by Babbel. The German was taken off at the break. It was fast becoming clear he had little future at the club. Mellor missed a couple of chances before the game went to penalties. Nine of the ten penalties were converted, with Ipswich's Jamie Clapham missing. Gerrard, Baros, Riise, Carragher and Diouf scored their penalties.

Another Premier League catastrophe awaited Liverpool at the Valley as they lost 2-0 to Charlton. Kirkland couldn't prevent goals from Jason Euell and Paul Konchesky, of all people. Henchoz and Hyypia looked far from the impregnable pairing they had been for three years. The Reds were fourth and dropping like a stone.

The second leg with Vitesse Arnhem was negotiated with little fuss, as another 1-0 win saw Liverpool progress to the fourth round. After some early chances for the Dutch side, including an absolute sitter, Owen was put through on goal by Murphy in the 20th minute and scored at the second attempt.

Another league game, another defeat. It was now four in a row. This time it was at Sunderland, a team that hadn't scored for eight and a half hours. But along came a Liverpool team missing Hyypia, and Gavin McCann dinked the ball over Kirkland after the Reds had been carved open. Carragher was harshly adjudged to have handled, but Kirkland saved McCann's penalty low to his left. Baros equalised, having been played in by Murphy, but Michael Proctor won the game with a low shot following Gerrard's inability to clear. As in the home game, Liverpool created plenty, but Jurgen Macho made numerous saves, as he had done in December. It was Sunderland's first home win over Liverpool since 1958.

Houllier kept saying a good team doesn't lose two in a row. The only thing that helped Liverpool avoid such an ignominy was regular cup games. A trip to Villa Park was next, in the quarter-finals of the League Cup. It was an exhilarating game. Traore tripped Lee Hendrie, allowing Darius Vassell to beat Kirkland from the spot. Murphy scored a superb free kick after Oyvind Leonhardsen fouled Baros. Riise found Baros, who scored from the edge of the box. Gerrard sprinted ahead of the Czech striker to fire home. 3-1. Back came Villa, with Thomas Hitzlsperger scoring from 30 yards. Henchoz deflected Dion Dublin's shot past Kirkland to make it 3-3. Murphy then fired home the winner in injury time after Gerrard had found room to cross. Sadly, Babbel was withdrawn on 39 minutes. His comeback hadn't gone well, and he wouldn't play for Liverpool again. It was a desperate shame.

The Anfield derby ended goalless, with the most noteworthy moment being a horrendous two-footed challenge by Gerrard on Everton's Gary Naysmith. Heskey missed with a header. Rooney hit the crossbar in the second half. "To hear the celebrations in the Everton dressing-room," said Houllier, "they were very happy with the draw."

Boxing Day produced another home draw, as Andy Cole frustrated Liverpool with a late equaliser for Blackburn. Riise scored on 17 minutes but, characteristic of Houllier's sides, Liverpool sat back. Rovers came forward, and Cole's leveller was sublime, as his dipping volley from 30 yards left Kirkland with no chance. It was now Liverpool's worst league run for nearly 50 years. Elsewhere, 16-year-old James Milner became the Premier League's youngest goal scorer, netting for Leeds in a 2-1 win at Sunderland.

On the day Reds legend Albert Stubbins passed away, Liverpool produced a much better performance at Highbury. Murphy converted a 69th-minute penalty following Sol Campbell's foul on Baros. Franny Jeffers then spun away from Riise and dived. Jeff Winter pointed to the spot and booked the nonplussed Riise. Thierry Henry sent Kirkland the wrong way. Hyypia and Henchoz were assured at the back. In midfield, Cheyrou and Diao looked lost. Owen departed on 38 minutes with another hamstring concern. Having been comfortably clear in November, Liverpool were sixth at the turn of the year, nine points behind the Gunners. Few believed Houllier would recover from this.

The slump was a full-on crisis by the time Liverpool travelled to St James' Park on New Year's Day. Laurent Robert, who had recently been accused of attacking a journalist, scored with an early free kick. With Diao, Biscan, Cheyrou and Diouf starting, such results weren't altogether surprising. Murphy was suspended. Owen, Heskey and Hamann were injured. Diao was sent off halfway through the second half for a second booking.

There was brief respite from the Premier League misery when the Reds went to Maine Road in the FA Cup. Mellor and Traore started. Seconds after Diouf was denied an early second-half penalty, Smicer sent in a cross which was handled by Marc-Vivien Foe. Murphy's penalty was as convincing as ever, sending Peter Schmeichel the wrong way. Shaun Goater missed a late header for City. Diouf almost lobbed Schmeichel from 45 yards in the last minute.

The first leg of the League Cup semi-final took Liverpool to Bramall Lane to play Neil Warnock's Sheffield United. Mellor kept his place and scored his first Liverpool goal in the 34th minute, turning in Hyypia's flick-on from close range. But the Blades roared back with two late goals from Michael Tonge. It was another pitiful Liverpool performance. "This is a poor team, basic, confused, relying on physical presence and defensive solidarity and the odd bit of creativity," was Through the Wind and Rain's analysis. "Substitutions were made for the sake of it."

The winless league run stretched to 11 against Villa at Anfield. Owen smashed in a loose ball from a tight angle. Dion Dublin's penalty, after Hyypia had fouled Gareth Barry, made it 1-1. Thirteenth-placed Villa were the better side. Liverpool were now in seventh, 11 points behind leaders Arsenal, who had a game in hand. Twenty-eight points had been dropped in this painful sequence of matches. Houllier had blamed everyone and everything but himself. This is when his reign should have ended.

The nightmare league run finally came to an end at St Mary's, as Heskey's 14th-minute header from Riise's free kick saw off Southampton. Liverpool started like caged lions, getting into the opposition from the first whistle. In his programme notes, Gordon Strachan had called the match a six-pointer for a UEFA Cup place, a measure of Liverpool's decline, but his players offered very little. It was a thoroughly merited and much-needed three points. Gerrard praised Heskey after the game, suggesting he needed to play like that more often.

Liverpool needed extra time to get past Sheffield United and into the final of the League Cup. Diouf, now on the right wing, fired in a brilliant 20-yarder to level the aggregate score. It was the only goal of the 90 minutes. The away-goal rule didn't apply after normal time, so another half hour was played in which the Blades knew they had to score. Owen, whose alleged gambling habits had been seized upon by the press, scored the deciding goal two minutes into the second period of extra-time. There was an ugly incident after the game, when Sheffield United manager Neil Warnock claimed that Henchoz had spat on the floor near him. "He was the only one," said Warnock. "All the other Liverpool players were magnanimous. All of them. But then, he's not English, is he, so you expect one or two things like that."

The Reds went to Selhurst Park in the fourth round of the FA Cup. The game finished goalless. Kirkland was stretchered off after 25 minutes, having collided with Dele Adebola. Heskey's primary contributions were in his own box. Owen was shackled by Hayden Mullins. Crystal Palace posed the greater threat, with Liverpool settling for a draw against a lower-division team. Their fans mocked Liverpool's tactics, shouting "Hoof!" with every long ball. It wasn't just them; it was becoming a regular response to Houllier's tactics.

For the first time in ages, Anfield enjoyed a moment of genuine euphoria when Heskey's last-minute header rescued a point against title-chasing Arsenal. Robert Pires ensured the dominant Gunners led at the break. Riise fired in gloriously from the edge of the box on 52 minutes. Dennis Bergkamp restored Arsenal's lead on 63, when his shot deflected past the otherwise excellent Dudek. Diao set up the injury-time equaliser with an inch-perfect cross for Heskey to power into the Kop net.

Two early goals at Upton Park set the tone for a Sunday-afternoon stroll in the park against West Ham. Baros headed in Riise's corner on seven minutes. Another corner from the Norwegian wasn't cleared two minutes later, and Gerrard fired in a superb 25-yarder. Midway through the second half, Riise sent over another in-swinger, which Hyypia headed back for Heskey to nod in. The only West Ham player to perform was their young right back Glen Johnson.

With Gerrard now belatedly banned for three matches for his derby-day challenge on Gary Naysmith, Cheyrou took his place for the FA Cup replay against Crystal Palace. It was another humiliation. Palace were even down to ten men when they scored the killer second. Hopes of emulating the 2001 treble were left in tatters. Liverpool dominated the first half but couldn't score. Julian Gray rifled past Dudek on 55 minutes. Heskey ran 70 yards unchallenged from a Palace corner but shot meekly at Cedric Berthelin. Anfield groaned. Dougie Freedman was sent off for elbowing Henchoz, but the Reds failed to capitalise, and the Swiss defender turned Gray's cross past his own goalkeeper with ten minutes remaining. "Mentally, they just sank," admitted Houllier of the team after Heskey's miss. It said much of his players. As Through the Wind and Rain summed up: "Faith can move mountains, but we're asking Gerard Houllier: not to have a major 'blip' in the middle of a season, not to send a team out to bore the living daylights out of people, not to put Emile Heskey's considerations before the good of the club (Camara, Fowler, Litmanen, Anelka – Baros and Mellor to follow?), not to squander yet more transfer money on cheap, useless imports, not to continue the deterioration of the squad since the treble, not to talk incessant bullshit that makes the club and its fans a laughing stock."

Houllier missed the home game with Middlesbrough with gastroenteritis - "at least it was pouring out of the right end for once," noted the same fanzine. With or without him, the Reds still couldn't win a league match on their own turf. Geremi scored a wonderful free kick, after which Liverpool huffed and puffed, looking entirely unconvincing. Eventually, Owen produced a face-saving equaliser with 12 minutes left.

The UEFA Cup started up again at the end of February, with Liverpool crossing the Channel to play Auxerre. Owen, who had scored just once in 15 games, was denied by goalkeeper Fabien Cool. Dudek made a couple of key saves at the other end. Hyypia scored the only goal, steering his left-footed shot into the bottom corner.

Stephen Clemence, son of the Reds finest goalkeeper Ray, headed Birmingham into a 1-0 lead against Liverpool at St Andrews. Houllier withdrew Carragher just after the hour mark, and Clinton Morrison took advantage to score his third of the season against the Reds. Owen pulled one back from Murphy's long pass, but Liverpool failed to get another as Birmingham earned their first win since before Christmas. Cheyrou was completely outplayed by Robbie Savage.

The Reds wrapped up the Auxerre tie with a 2-0 win at Anfield. Murphy's clever flick sent Owen clean through and he dinked the ball over Cool. Six minutes later, Cool's howler allowed Murphy's 30-yarder to creep in. Djibril Cisse played for the beaten French side. The BBC's Barry Glendenning described it as "one of the most turgid football matches I've ever seen."

Next up were Manchester United in the final of the League Cup. Alex Ferguson's side were in great form, having just beaten Juventus home and away in the Champions League. They were also on a run which would see them overhaul Arsenal for the league title. In Cardiff, they came up against a Liverpool side which was able, somehow, to shrug off four months of atrocious form in one afternoon. Houllier selected the following side: Dudek; Carragher, Henchoz,

Hyypia, Riise; Murphy, Hamann, Gerrard, Heskey; Diouf, Owen. Baros, Biscan and Smicer came off the bench, although Baros himself was subbed, and cried in the dressing room after the game. The Reds enjoyed some luck along the way, but after going ahead on 39 minutes when Gerrard's long-ranger was deflected over Barthez's head by David Beckham, they defended manfully. Henchoz made a wonderful goal-line clearance, this time without using his hands, as Paul Scholes seemed certain to score. The game was reminiscent of the Old Trafford cup tie in 1999, but this time Liverpool killed United off. With the Reds under pressure, they countered superbly. Hamann released Owen, and he outpaced Roy Keane to finish with aplomb. "Manchester United have been found wanting in nearly every department today," reported The Guardian website. Dudek was the man of the match after a string of outstanding saves as he exorcised December's demons. Each defender excelled, with The Guardian picking Riise as Liverpool's best outfield player. They had some choice words for Diouf, though - "as maladroit as a Rochdale reserve" - and Heskey - "lots of aimless running, complaining to the referee and generally flattering to deceive." Hyypia lifted the trophy. It was a pleasing moment in what had become a terrible season.

On March 6th, Liverpool won a Premier League match at Anfield for the first time since November 2nd when they beat Bolton 2-0. Henchoz was missing, ruled out for six weeks, his second lengthy absence of the season. After fantastic approach play by Owen, Diouf headed in the first from no more than a couple of inches. The two then reversed roles, as the Senegalese set up Owen in the second half. The three points were welcome but playing one up front and deploying a containing, counter-attacking game against the team in 17th wasn't the way to win over fans.

The much-anticipated Battle of Britain saw Liverpool earn a 1-1 draw at Celtic Park in the first leg of the UEFA Cup quarter-final, but they were engulfed in controversy, as Diouf spat in the face of a local supporter. The prolific Swede Henrik Larsson scored in just 100 seconds, but Heskey took Riise's pass to fire low into the bottom corner on 16 minutes. There was no further scoring. Towards the end of the game, Diouf lost his footing on the track around the pitch, encouraging attention from Celtic fans. One rubbed his head. Diouf turned and spat into the crowd. West Ham fans had recently accused him of doing the same. Diouf apologised and was fined two weeks' wages by Liverpool – around £60,000. He was charged and banned for two European matches by UEFA, who deemed he had been provoked. Celtic were fined £2,300 for the conduct of two of their supporters. A couple of weeks later, Diouf said of the fan, "If he had done that in the street, I'd have knocked him out." Diouf had recently been named African Footballer of the Year for the second time in a row.

The disgraced forward began the next match, at Spurs, as Liverpool won 3-2 at White Hart Lane. Dudek's error allowed Mauricio Tarrico's 25-yarder to squirm over the line on 49 minutes. Houllier later accused the Argentine of trying to get Diouf sent off. For once, the Reds responded positively to going behind. Owen tapped in Gerrard's perfect low cross. Heskey headed in Gerrard's cross from close range. Man of the match Gerrard capped a great second half by taking Murphy's pass on the counter and firing it past Kasey Keller from 20 yards. Teddy Sheringham pulled one back after Liverpool couldn't clear a corner, but the Reds had done enough. The Reds were two points behind fourth-placed Chelsea and one adrift of Everton in the race for the last Champions League spot.

Back at Anfield for the second leg against Martin O'Neill's Celtic, Liverpool were appalling, losing 2-0 on the night and 3-1 on aggregate. It was a third exit from a European competition in under 12 months. Heskey went close midway through the first half. Henrik Larsson and John Hartson nearly scored. Celtic did eventually go ahead with Alan Thompson's free kick at the end of the first half. In the second half, Carragher denied Larsson. Gerrard missed when clean through. Dudek tipped over from Larsson. Hartson eventually sealed the game on 81 minutes with another goal from outside the box. The defeat was entirely consistent with Liverpool's post-November form. Celtic moved into the last four, where they beat Boavista. They lost the final in extra-time to Porto.

With eight Premier League matches left, the Reds defeated Leeds 3-1 at Anfield. Leeds had endured a far worse season than Liverpool, amid terrible financial difficulties. Several players had been sold including Robbie Fowler, who was now at Manchester City. Terry Venables had just been dismissed. Relegation was a possibility. The Reds were two up in 20 minutes. Diouf's cross was deflected to Owen, who finished emphatically. Murphy then scored one of the goals of the season. Riise was injured on the left wing in a challenge with Danny Mills. Leeds didn't put the ball out of play. Nor did Liverpool and when it came to Murphy on the angle of the penalty area, he unleashed a fabulous curling shot into the far top corner of the Kop goal. Mark Viduka got one back, but Gerrard side footed into the corner to seal the points. Each of the goal scorers played magnificently.

Manchester United exacted some revenge for the League Cup Final by hammering Liverpool 4-0 at Old Trafford, although the score was extremely flattering. Owen was absent, injured on England duty. Hyypia was sent off for a professional foul on Ruud van Nistelrooy after four minutes. There had been a slight tug of the arm, enough for a penalty. The Dutchman converted the penalty. Houllier immediately withdrew Baros and sent on Biscan to replace the Finn at centre back. It took United an hour to get another, and it came from the spot again, with Biscan clattering into Scholes. With the ten men exhausted, Ryan Giggs and Ole Gunnar Solksjaer added further goals.

A routine 2-0 home win over Fulham saw the Reds keep up the pressure on Chelsea and Everton for fourth. Murphy injured his neck in the warm-up and was replaced by Smicer, who had a superb game. Heskey hooked in his ninth of the season. Owen, having missed a sitter 30 seconds earlier, sealed the points in the second half. Steve Finnan, heavily linked with a move to Liverpool, was in the Fulham side. "I haven't felt much worse than I did with a home game with

Fulham in April 2003," Carragher wrote in his book. "I'd asked Houllier if the rumours we were signing Finnan were true, and he fobbed me off by denying it. The fans obviously didn't believe him because Finnan was given a warm reception ... From my perspective, however, it was a personal slight. I'd been determined to outshine Finnan that day, and I was named man of the match. I wanted to hear supporters saying we don't need another right back because we've got Carra, but the enthusiasm for Finnan suggested no one was worried about my future at the club."

The Reds moved above the Blues into fifth, winning 2-1 at Goodison on Easter Saturday. Houllier often told his players before derbies, "Keep 11 men on the pitch and you will win." He was proven right again, as Everton finished the match with nine men. Hyypia and Henchoz missed out through suspension and injury. Traore and Biscan were the centre backs, but the latter lasted just eight minutes. Diao came on at right back, with Carragher moved to the centre. Owen scored first, cutting in from the left and firing a low shot past Richard Wright. Carragher rashly conceded a penalty 12 minutes into the second half, which David Unsworth blasted past Dudek. But Murphy won the game with a goal similar to the one he scored against Spurs in October, curling the ball beautifully into the top corner from 25 yards. David Weir and Gary Naysmith were sent off in the final nine minutes for second bookings.

When all seemed lost, two late goals secured a 2-1 home win over Charlton Athletic. The Londoners had won just one point in six matches but took the lead on 47 minutes after a horrendous error by Traore. With Liverpool fans coming to terms with yet another disappointment, Hyypia got on the end of a Gerrard flick from Riise's corner and prodded the ball home in the 86th minute. And then in injury time, Gerrard engineered a way into the area from the left wing and found the bottom corner with Dean Kiely at fault. It was as undeserved a win as you could get, but it kept alive Liverpool's top-four hopes. Murphy, who had been substituted, hurled a plastic bottle at Phil Thompson and later apologised.

An incredible second half saw the Reds coast to a 6-0 victory at already-relegated West Brom. Owen got four and Baros two. Five of the goals came in the second half. None of the goals were particularly spectacular. The Reds were level on points with Chelsea. The two were due to play each other on the final day of the season with fourth place up for grabs.

Robbie Fowler was back at Anfield in Manchester City colours on what proved to be a costly afternoon for the Reds. Baros opened the scoring with a clinical top-corner finish past Peter Schmeichel. After the Dane saved spectacularly from Diouf, Nicolas Anelka hit a late double, underlining what a mistake Houllier had made in letting him go. Chelsea had been beaten at West Ham, and so a win at Stamford Bridge would see the Reds take the all-important fourth spot.

Things looked rosy at the Bridge when Hyypia headed in Murphy's free kick in the 11th minute, but Marcel Desailly levelled within minutes. Jesper Gronkjaer scored the winner on 27 minutes. Liverpool barely threatened an equaliser, other than a Baros goal which was disallowed for a handball. Gerrard was sent off for a second yellow card in the closing minutes after a shocking challenge on Graeme Le Saux. Chelsea were about to be taken over by Roman Abramovich and his Russian billions. They were heading in a very different direction to Houllier's Liverpool.

"I wouldn't say it was a disappointing season," said the manager. He wasn't kidding anyone, apart from the board, who elected to keep him in his job.

2003-04

*"I had a hollow feeling inside. I knew the manager had to go.
This wasn't the Houllier I knew."*

They say you make your own luck. Liverpool had none in 2003-04, nor did they deserve any. The football was pitiful. They were miles off the top. The cups brought even more embarrassments. Gerard Houllier was clinging onto a job he should have lost in the summer, trotting out excuse after excuse. Supporter morale was at rock bottom. Everyone knew his time was up. The last person to cotton on was David Moores.

There was little transfer activity to suggest any improvements were on the horizon. Out went Patrik Berger, Bernard Diomede, Vegard Heggem and Pegguy Arphexad, all on free transfers. Markus Babbel, with whom Houllier had fallen out, joined Blackburn on a season-long loan as he continued his recovery from Guillain-Barre syndrome. In came Harry Kewell for £5 million from Leeds, Steve Finnan from Fulham for £3.5 million and the young French cousins Anthony Le Tallec and Florent Sinama-Pongolle for £1.5 million apiece from Le Havre. They had been signed in 2001 but remained at the French club on loan. They were now 18. Two years after missing out on Blackburn's Damien Duff, Houllier went back in for the Irish winger but couldn't complete with big-spending Chelsea. Christian Damiano replaced Jacques Crevoisier on the coaching staff.

The signing of Kewell would apparently precipitate a new attacking approach. That certainly didn't materialise. The Australian had his moments in a Liverpool shirt, but they were few and far between. The same could be said for the young Frenchmen. Houllier had repeatedly told the world and his wife that he had beaten numerous top clubs to these two 'gems'. Neither lived up to expectations, although the manager had set the bar too high with his hyperbole, as he tended to do. Their signings also led to the club passing up the opportunity to sign Cristiano Ronaldo. According to Phil Thompson's autobiography, the 18-year-old Portuguese sensation was offered to the Reds, but they baulked at his wage demands and were reluctant to tie up more than half the summer's transfer budget on a trio of young players from overseas. Liverpool also missed out on the 33-year-old Alan Shearer, who eventually re-signed with Newcastle. At one point, Houllier was convinced Liverpool would land him. Through the Wind and Rain joked he'd have probably played him at left back.

Finnan's arrival was the least heralded, and there was someone at Anfield less than thrilled to see the full back at the club. "The closest I came to leaving was in 2003 when Steve Finnan joined the club," wrote Jamie Carragher. "The list of full backs Houllier brought in as direct competition was endless. I'd seen off Song, Babbel and Christian Ziege, but still the manager was looking for an alternative. John Arne Riise signed from Monaco with a reputation for goals. Houllier even bought Abel Xavier from Everton. For a very brief spell, I wondered if I could be bothered to prove myself anymore. It became tiresome heading into every new season with the same cloud hanging over me, fighting a constant battle for security. Finnan, who later proved a shrewd signing for us even if I didn't welcome him at the time, nearly broke my resolve by doing nothing more than just walking into Melwood. On the day Finnan signed, it seemed even Houllier was putting the boot in. 'In the modern game, it's important for a full back to be able to attack,' he said at the press conference. 'You cheeky bastard!' I shouted at the television." The manager still wouldn't consider Carragher as a centre back, instead preferring Stephane Henchoz, Djimi Traore or Igor Biscan to partner Sami Hyypia.

The season started against moneybags Chelsea, who were beginning a new era of being able to buy whomever they wished. Fielding numerous new players, they faced a largely unchanged Liverpool side. Jerzy Dudek was still in goal. Henchoz was fit again to partner the skipper Hyypia. Carragher and Riise were the full backs with Danny Murphy and Kewell ahead of them. Biscan and Bruno Cheyrou made a very unconvincing central-midfield pairing with Steven Gerrard suspended and Dietmar Hamman injured. Owen and Heskey were up front. The latter had scored just six league goals in 2002-03. Liverpool needed much more from him. Owen had two years left on his contract and was in no hurry to sign another. Murphy and Owen forced saves from Carlo Cudicini. Dudek was in similar form at the other end. Juan Sebastian Veron opened the scoring on 25 minutes following Henchoz's slip. Houllier sent on El Hadji Diouf, Finnan and Milan Baros, and it was the Senegalese who won a penalty with 11 minutes left. Owen dragged his weak shot wide of the post but earned a reprieve when a linesman spotted that Cudicini had moved too early. Owen smashed his second attempt into the roof of the net. But Chelsea walked away with the points when Jimmy Floyd Hasselbaink was played in by Frank Lampard, and he drove emphatically past Dudek. "I remember being at the side and could see Finnan warming up," Carragher recalled. "I was right back and was having a pretty good game. I looked at Phil Thompson and said, 'He's not bringing me off, is he?' He said, 'Don't you want to come off?' I said, 'I'm not coming off!' So he put me to centre back!" It's hard to imagine Houllier being so indecisive in his early days at Liverpool.

Gerrard and Diouf came into the side for the trip to Aston Villa, which ended goalless. Diouf, Murphy, Riise, Kewell and Owen all went close to a winner. The Australian was mainly used on the right, to the surprise of many.

The visit of Spurs resulted in another 0-0. Gerrard and Smicer missed chances. Owen had a goal disallowed for a push. Finnan came in for his first start, with Carragher moving to left back. Biscan partnered Hyypia at the back

The out-of-form Riise was now on the bench. "I didn't play well that autumn," he wrote in his book. "The confidence was gone. I no longer understood what Houllier wanted me to do. I was unclear when he wanted me to attack and when he wanted me to defend, and I lost the assuredness in my play, doubt seeped in, and I was caught out of position more and more often."

The Reds finally got their season moving with a convincing Saturday-lunchtime victory at Goodison Park. With Everton fans singing about Liverpool's relegation prospects, Owen scored first, assisted by Kewell. Baros then fought his way into the area before laying it off to Owen to score from 16 yards. The Australian later opened his Liverpool account smashing Owen's cross into an unguarded net. Carragher played magnificently. Houllier had won four in a row at Goodison.

After an international break, the Reds won 3-1 at Blackburn, but in the first 17 minutes, Baros fractured an ankle and Carragher broke a leg. The scorers were the same as in the derby, and in the same order. Baros's injury came inside two minutes after a legal challenge by Babbel, one of three ex-Liverpool players facing them. Matt Jansen scored superbly for Graeme Souness's side. Owen beat Brad Friedel from the spot after Diouf was fouled. To conclude an explosive opening to the match, Lucas Neill was sent off for the horror challenge that broke Carragher's leg. Kewell, Owen and Gerrard went close before Smicer got the better of Babbel and set up a goal for Owen. Kewell wrapped up the win with the third goal. Carragher later told the story that some friends saw Neill in the Trafford Centre and phoned him, offering to mete out some revenge. The only problem was David Thompson, the other ex-Liverpool player at Rovers, was there, and Carragher didn't want him to become a witness to an assault. The defender would return to action in January, Baros a month later.

The Reds won a third consecutive game when they beat Leicester 2-1 at Anfield. Owen scored another penalty when Smicer was fouled. Liverpool made heavy weather of sealing the win, but Heskey made sure on 74 minutes with his first of the season, flicking the ball into the far corner from six yards. Marcus Bent pulled one back in the last minute.

Liverpool's European campaign began in Slovenia with a 1-1 draw against the might of Olimpija Ljubljana. Skipper Anton Zlogar put the hosts ahead on 66 minutes. Owen soon equalised with a goal that made him the club's top European scorer with 21.

They may have avoided humiliation in Europe, but not in London. A 3-2 defeat at Charlton punctured Liverpool's mini-revival in the Premier League. Kewell got Smicer away with a superb through ball, and the Czech flicked it past Dean Kiely. But the Reds were hit by a Kevin Lisbie hat-trick. Owen got Liverpool's other goal with another penalty. Without Henchoz and Carragher, the defence just wasn't strong enough. Hyypia and Riise had made poor starts to the season.

Houllier described the next game, against Arsenal, as "make or break". Unfortunately, his team lost 2-1. It proved to be the last match that Hyypia enjoyed as club captain before he was replaced by Gerrard. Kewell brilliantly fired Liverpool into a 14th-minute lead with a left-footed half-volley against a team which wouldn't lose a game in the entire Premier League season. The Reds were superb in the first half hour but Hyypia put through his own net from a wide free kick. The winning goal was magnificent, as Pires fired superbly into the top corner of Dudek's net from 25 yards. Owen departed with a shin injury towards the end after trying to block a clearance from Ashley Cole. After eight games, Liverpool were in eighth, nine points behind the Gunners. The weekend ended on a strange note as young right back Jon Otsemobor, an innocent bystander, was shot in the buttocks in a city-centre nightclub. He didn't last long at the club and later claimed the incident saw him unfairly tarnished. "People started saying I was involved in gangs – you know, a young, black Scouse lad, so anybody who didn't know me would automatically believe what was being said," he said in a 2019 interview.

Gerrard's first game as official captain was the second leg with Ljubljana. The Reds won 3-0. Le Tallec scored the first goal under the new skipper on his first Anfield start. Heskey and Kewell added the others. It was the big striker's 50th for the club in 185 games. Diouf missed a late penalty, following a foul on Finnan. Liverpool progressed 4-1 on aggregate.

Defeat at Portsmouth was Liverpool's third league defeat on the bounce. Owen was injured. Liverpool's four outfield subs were Le Tallec, Pongolle, Traore and young midfielder John Welsh. Heskey hit a post after three minutes. Patrik Berger scored a minute later. Pompey should have had more. Sinama-Pongolle missed two late chances. Biscan was anonymous. Diouf was taken off before he was sent off. The Reds were in for a long, tough season.

Relegation-threatened Leeds, now managed by Peter Reid, were next up at Anfield. Owen was back with a goal. Alan Smith equalised. Murphy restored Liverpool's lead with a free kick. Sinama-Pongolle made it 3-1 with his first goal for the club. Leeds were heading for relegation. "Florent Sinama-Pongolle and Anthony Le Tallec will be gems for the future," said Houllier. "They are not ready yet."

A crazy League Cup win against Blackburn had everything. David Thompson set up Dwight Yorke to nod in the game's first goal on 35 minutes. Shortly after, Lucas Neill was red-carded again for a professional foul on Sinama-Pongolle. Murphy's emphatic penalty tied the scores. Heskey put the Reds 3-1 up with a couple of headers. He then fluffed a hat-trick by missing a penalty. Kewell made it 4-1. Diouf had a hat-trick of assists. Barry Ferguson and Yorke each got a late goal.

The Reds came away from Fulham with a barely deserved 2-1 win. Heskey turned in Finnan's cross. Louis Saha equalised before half-time. In the last minute, the ever-improving Sinama-Pongolle drew a penalty from Zat Knight, which Murphy converted. There was still time for Luis Boa Morte to be dismissed for a horrendous challenge on Sinama-Pongolle. The big talking point, however, was Owen, who still hadn't signed a new deal.

A trip to Romania in the second round of the UEFA Cup saw the Reds emerge with a 1-1 draw with Steaua Bucharest. In the pouring rain, Traore scored a beauty, coming in from the left and stroking the ball into the far corner from outside the box. The Reds conceded a second-half equaliser and needed a great save from Dudek to avoid defeat.

For the second season in a row, Manchester United came to Anfield, profited from Dudek's errors and won 2-1. With Owen absent again, promising possession wasn't turned into goals. A dull game remained goalless for an hour until Ryan Giggs' cross eluded Dudek and went straight in. He scored again with the Polish keeper at fault. Kewell pulled one back from Sinama-Pongolle's cross and the young Frenchman was denied a late penalty after a challenge from Rio Ferdinand. Heskey missed a late sitter. The Reds had now lost at home to the top three sides. Babbel, meanwhile, scored for Blackburn against Everton. "Scoring against Everton is special," he said after the game. I'm a Liverpudlian. I'm only here on loan." With the Reds regularly fielding Diao, Biscan and Traore, few could work out why he wasn't still around.

With Liverpool in crisis, a trip to the Riverside, where they had an awful record, wasn't going to lift anybody's spirits. A draw saw them slide further down the table. Kirkland replaced Dudek and kept a clean sheet but Heskey, Diouf and Owen drew a blank at the other end. There wasn't a single shot on target in a miserable game.

At least the Reds were able to progress in the UEFA Cup with a second-leg 1-0 win over Steaua Bucharest. Biscan was fortunate not to concede a penalty, but victory was secured by Kewell's towering header from Gerrard's cross on 48 minutes. The Steaua president had promised to build a new church in Bucharest if his team won.

Liverpool's sixth Premier League win in 14 matches came at the hands of Birmingham at Anfield. Mikael Forssell bundled in Robbie Savage's free kick. Gerrard converted a penalty for his first goal of the season after Sinama-Pongolle was fouled. Kewell scored another classy header, this time from Riise's cross. Heskey sealed the win by chesting down Diao's cross and finishing with a magnificent scissor kick. Liverpool were 14 points off the top after 14 games.

The club's League Cup defence ended in another high-scoring match, with Bolton Wanderers winning 3-2 at Anfield. Otsemobor looked promising. Bolton led for much of the game before Murphy headed in Diao's long cross midway through the second half. Jay-Jay Okocha made it 2-1 when his free kick left Dudek stranded. Smicer scored a sensational equaliser on 88 minutes, curling the ball in from 20 yards. In injury-time, Diao went in rashly on Kevin Davies and Youri Djorkaeff's penalty went in off the post. Kewell picked up an injury and would miss two games.

The most Liverpool could realistically hope for in the league was a top-four finish. Their rivals for fourth would be Newcastle United where the Reds picked up a point in early December. Otsemobor kept his place. Murphy scored after Newcastle failed to deal with a long ball from Riise. But Kirkland felled Laurent

165

Robert, allowing Shearer to score from the spot. It was a decent result on paper, but Houllier was again a victim of his own negativity. All too often, Liverpool would sit back at 1-0.

Having left St James' Park in fifth, the Reds were down to ninth after a shocking 2-1 home defeat against Southampton. With an Otsemobor-Biscan-Hyypia-Riise defence, the result wasn't entirely surprising. It took just 73 seconds for Brett Ormerod to race into the clear, evade Hamann and slot past Kirkland. Michael Svensson made it two with a header from a corner. Heskey got one back when he tapped in after Antti Niemi had parried Gerrard's shot. For the third year in a row, Liverpool were enduring a nightmare December. "We were terrible," remembers Riise. "Houllier was singled out by the bookies to be the first manager sacked in the Premier League. That poison in sport called doubt spread through the team. It seeped into everything. It seemed like Houllier began to doubt his own system and what he stood for. In the end hardly anything seemed to work."

Revenge over Bolton was gained on Boxing Day. Kewell was back but didn't look fit. Hyypia crashed in a header from Murphy's corner on the half hour. Sinama-Pongolle headed in Riise's cross 64 seconds into the second half. Smicer scored a third header from Murphy's free kick. Kirkland would miss a month after breaking a finger. Otsemobor delivered an excellent performance, as he had done against Southampton.

The Reds encountered several old boys when they played at the City of Manchester Stadium, drawing 2-2 with City. Managed by Kevin Keegan, City's attack comprised Steve McManaman, now back from Madrid, Robbie Fowler and Nicolas Anelka. The latter opened the scoring from the spot after Riise had tangled with Fowler at a corner. A stadium power cut meant only the furthest-away camera picked up Smicer's equaliser from Murphy's corner. With ten minutes remaining, Hamann lashed a brilliant half-volley past David Seaman from 25 yards. But up popped Fowler in injury-time to equalise. Otsemobor was substituted for tactical reasons in the first half and wouldn't play for the club again. He was soon loaned to Bolton, which led to a further strain in the relationship between Houllier, who believed the club wasn't producing youngsters of the right quality, and Steve Heighway, the Academy's head honcho, who believed Houllier wasn't giving them a chance. The year ended with Liverpool in sixth, a massive 20 points behind leaders Manchester United.

Yeovil Town were Liverpool's first FA Cup opponents at Huish Park. The game was televised by the BBC, probably in anticipation of an upset. The Reds did at least avoid that, but it took them 70 minutes to find a way past the Division Three side. With Liverpool heavily linked with Auxerre's Djibril Cisse, Heskey was under pressure to deliver and he latched onto Murphy's diagonal pass and found the far corner. Murphy doubled the lead with a penalty, following an outrageous dive by Kewell. The midfielder embarrassed himself by shushing the Yeovil fans after scoring.

Next came one of the surprises of the season as the Reds turned over Chelsea at Stamford Bridge. The winning goal came after 33 minutes and was quite astonishing, as Heskey and Cheyrou carved open the Chelsea defence. The French midfielder finished Heskey's cross emphatically. Houllier had once called him "the new Zidane", and after 18 months he had finally done something noteworthy in a Liverpool jersey. A groin injury sustained by Dudek saw Patrice Luzi make his only appearance for the first team in the final 13 minutes. Diouf was sent off in the closing minutes, although his second yellow card was rescinded. Hyypia, Hamann and Heskey were all magnificent. It was Liverpool's first league win at Stamford Bridge since 1990.

With Dudek and Kirkland injured, Liverpool managed to make an emergency loan signing of Southampton's Paul Jones in time for the visit of Aston Villa. The 36-year-old became the club's oldest debutant since the war. The bench was made up entirely of Frenchmen – Luzi, Traore, Le Tallec, Cheyrou and Sinama-Pongolle. Having been an unused sub at the Bridge, Owen returned to the line-up and managed to hit the bar from less than a yard. The only goal of the game was a complete fluke as Kewell's cross hit Mark Delaney and wrong-footed Thomas Sorensen. Jones made a great save from Darius Vassell. Diouf was outstanding, running Jlloyd Samuel ragged. He would soon be off to the African Cup of Nations, along with Diao, which would test the depth of Houllier's squad further.

The Reds were unable to make it three league wins on the bounce, losing 2-1 at White Hart Lane. Owen hit a post. Biscan conceded a penalty, which Robbie Keane converted. The Croat later misjudged a long ball and Helder Postiga shot past Jones. Kewell pulled one back, cutting in from the left and firing inside the near post. Owen had a late penalty shout for handball turned down, but Liverpool hadn't done enough. Houllier remained under big pressure. One name repeatedly linked to the job was Celtic's Martin O'Neill, much to Houllier's ire. The manager claimed O'Neill must have friends in the media and a good agent. An incandescent O'Neill phoned Houllier to put him straight. He didn't even have an agent.

Cheyrou was back on the scoresheet as Liverpool drew 1-1 at Molineux against lowly Wolves. Houllier persevered with Biscan at centre back, despite substituting him at Spurs. Henchoz was on the bench. The French midfielder scored on 42 minutes, courtesy of Finnan's clever pass. Liverpool again sat back and conceded a 90th-minute equaliser to Kenny Miller, set up by Paul Ince of all people. Carragher made his comeback after missing 23 matches. He played the full 90 minutes. "I was never appreciated more by the supporters and the management than when I wasn't available," he wrote. "The fans began to see how much I added to the defence ... John Arne Riise said he felt undermined hearing how the defenders weren't coping without me."

One of the highlights of the season came in the fourth round of the FA Cup as the Reds beat Newcastle 2-1 at Anfield. A Finnan-Henchoz-Hyypia-Carragher defence was far stronger than Liverpool had been able to call upon all season.

Incredibly, Cheyrou scored twice more. His first came after Heskey's shot was blocked. Laurent Robert cancelled it out with a wicked, long-range free kick. Cheyrou's winner came just after the hour; a bullet header from Gerrard's inch-perfect cross. He now had four goals in five games, but this would be as good as it got for him. Dudek made a superb save from Shearer in injury time.

Sadly, Liverpool didn't have a goal in them a week later, as struggling Everton ground out a 0-0 draw at Anfield in the 170th Merseyside derby. Gerrard went close four times. Le Tallec had a header cleared off the line. Everton, now five points from safety, had plenty of chances too. Carragher was lucky not to concede a penalty for handball.

Despite not scoring since October, Owen was up front on his own again for the trip to Bolton. Liverpool drew 2-2. With the team trailing 1-0 at half-time, Hyypia headed in Gerrard's free kick. Youri Djorkaeff restored Wanderers' lead only for man of the match Gerrard to score a second equaliser, with a close-range volley after great work from Pongolle and Le Tallec. Owen came close to a winner but could only divert Gerrard's pullback wide. Otsemobor was an unused sub for Bolton, as was Javi Moreno, scorer of two goals in the 2001 UEFA Cup Final.

Owen finally broke his duck when he ran onto Hamann's pass, skinned Richard Dunne and clipped the ball over David James three minutes into Manchester City's visit to Anfield. McManaman, who was booed by the home fans, set up a 50th-minute equaliser for Shaun Wright-Phillips. A minute later, Gerrard fired the Reds ahead again, tapping in after a fumble from James. When Houllier brought on Biscan for Cheyrou, he was jeered by fans. Liverpool were fourth, ahead of Newcastle on goal difference. They were 17 points behind Chelsea in third and 23 behind unbeaten leaders Arsenal.

Owen scored his 150th Liverpool goal after 69 seconds of the fifth-round FA Cup tie at home to Portsmouth but it was dismal fare thereafter. Once more, the Kop chanted "Attack! Attack! Attack!" Pompey, missing Teddy Sheringham and Patrik Berger, grew into the game, and there was a depressing inevitability about Matt Taylor's equaliser.

Kirkland and Baros returned for the replay, but it was to no avail. Owen missed yet another penalty, as his weak effort was easily saved by Shaka Hislop. Richard Hughes scored the winner with 18 minutes left, hammering a left-footed drive into the bottom corner. Liverpool couldn't find an equaliser. Owen was devastated at training the following day but to Carragher's dismay, Diouf, who hadn't played, seemed to be taking the defeat rather better. "I've never met a player who seemed to care less about winning or losing," the defender wrote in his book. "Diouf drove in with his rave music blaring out of his car, then danced his way across the car park into the building. You'd think we'd won the cup the way he carried on. His attitude disgusted me."

Liverpool's last chance of silverware came in the UEFA Cup where they faced Levski Sofia in the third round. The Reds took control of the tie in the first leg at Anfield with two goals in four minutes, midway through the second half. Gerrard scored first with a vicious low volley from the edge of the box. Kewell then curled in a magnificent shot from the right wing to give Liverpool a cushion. Baros impressed on his first start since his injury. Owen missed several chances and, with his contract situation never out of the media, wasn't having a happy season. Robbie Fowler wrote in his first book that Owen was now getting the treatment he once suffered. "[Houllier] couldn't just bomb him out because of the fans, so he started questioning him, started trying to undermine him, and attempted to disrupt his relationship with the fans, just like he did with me." he wrote. "Chris [Bascombe] wouldn't have it by then and stuck up to him. Every time he gave Michael a decent write-up, Houllier would go mad and have a go. One day, when Chris had supported Michael again, there was a row, and Houllier blurted out, 'If Michael pissed on your hands, you'd say it was Lucozade.'"

Back in the league, the Reds played out a thrilling 2-2 draw at Elland Road with all the goals coming in the first half. Bottom side Leeds, now managed by club legend Eddie Gray, were only a couple of points from safety. Kewell, a target for the boo-boys, scored a rasping opener, similar to his goal against Sofia. Erik Bakke equalised from close range, following a poor header from Henchoz. Mark Viduka lobbed Kirkland to put Leeds 2-1 up. Baros then broke through a couple of defenders and fired superbly past Paul Robinson to level the scores. Liverpool looked more likely to score a second-half winner but had to settle for a point.

The second leg in Bulgaria saw a feast of goals as the Reds progressed with ease. Gerrard rounded the keeper and scored from a tight angle. Owen beat the offside trap to tuck away Kewell's pass. Levski were soon back on terms through Georgi Ivanov and Sasa Simonovic. Hamann nodded in Gerrard's corner to restore the lead. On his 250th Liverpool appearance, Hyypia headed home Gerrard's corner to extend the lead to 4-2 and 6-2 on aggregate.

The Reds were in European action again a week later, but a draw at home to Marseille wasn't the desired result. After a turgid first half, Baros put Liverpool ahead after Gerrard touched Owen's through ball past Fabien Barthez. Didier Drogba, whom Liverpool would see much more of in future, scored a crucial away goal with 12 minutes left. The second leg was a fortnight away, in which time Liverpool had three Premier League games to negotiate.

The first, a dismal defeat at Southampton, left the Reds in eighth. James Beattie scored a breakaway goal on 51 minutes after Biscan's error. Owen missed yet another penalty on 73 – why he was still taking them was anyone's guess. It was his tenth miss in Liverpool colours – 11 if you count the opening-day penalty against Chelsea which he was able to retake. Kevin Phillips wrapped up the points with a long ranger that deflected over the restored Dudek via the foot of Riise. The Pole was back in goal because the luckless Kirkland had broken a wrist in training, saving a shot from Kewell. It summed up his Liverpool career.

Hamann scored Liverpool's goal of the season in a midweek home game with Portsmouth. In the sixth minute, Owen floated a ball back, and the German crashed in a 20-yard swerving volley into the top corner. It was an unbelievable strike. The outstanding Owen then chested down Carragher's cross and slotted the ball past Shaka Hislop. Pompey hit the bar, before Owen sealed the game by glancing in Gerrard's corner. It was Liverpool's only win in four games against Portsmouth, who were now third-bottom. The Reds were up to fifth, a point behind fourth-placed Charlton and ahead of Newcastle on goal difference. Birmingham, Aston Villa and Fulham were also in contention.

An afternoon of utter boredom was served up to those who attended the visit of second-bottom Wolves. Liverpool had most of the ball but could do nothing with it until Hyypia bulleted a header from Gerrard's injury-time corner past Paul Jones. The mood was a mixture of relief and embarrassment as Liverpool continued to limp towards fourth spot.

Any chance of Liverpool landing a trophy rested on a result in France against Marseille on March 25th. Houllier kept faith with Biscan at centre back. Henchoz was on the bench. Heskey was preferred up front to Baros, Diouf and Pongolle, each of whom were benched, as was Cheyrou after his burst of goals in January. Liverpool made a dream start when Heskey blasted the ball past Barthez from Gerrard's through ball. Murphy went close to doubling the lead but an incident in the 36th minute was to decide the tie. Steve Marlet, the former Fulham striker, was played in on goal and shot wide but his arm had been tugged by Biscan, who was sent off. Gerrard called the Croat a 'tit' in his book for getting red-carded. Drogba nailed the resultant penalty. Houllier was livid and spent most of the half-time break checking the footage on a monitor rather than talking to his players. A second Liverpool goal would have meant Marseille needed two, but the Reds failed to threaten. Owen suffered another hamstring injury on the hour mark and couldn't continue. Marseille dominated the second half and won the tie with a header by Abdullah Meite. Liverpool were out. According to the Spanish journalist Guillem Balague, "[It was] the first time Rafa Benitez's name was mentioned in Liverpool FC's upper echelons. The strong rumour was that if Gerard Houllier didn't improve things rapidly, then Benitez was top of the list to replace him." Porto's Jose Mourinho was also a candidate, according to newspapers.

A goalless draw at Leicester was hardly the result to reinvigorate the fans. At least Newcastle's defeat at Bolton kept the Reds in fourth. Diouf and Sinama-Pongolle were benched again. Both had enjoyed purple matches earlier in the season but were out of favour and behind Heskey and Baros in the pecking order. Hamann, in his 200th Liverpool game, went close with a volley. Cheyrou hit a post, but there was little else to get excited about.

The Reds bounced back with an emphatic 4-0 drubbing of Blackburn Rovers. Lucas Neill wasn't selected by Graeme Souness, so Rovers did at least finish the match with 11 men. Heskey set up an early goal for Owen, whose shot squirmed past Brad Friedel and into the corner. The recalled Diouf bamboozled two defenders before his cross was turned into his own net by Andy Todd. Owen hammered the ball past Brad Friedel for his second and Liverpool's third. Baros replaced Owen late in the game and set up a fourth for Heskey.

A midday Good Friday assignment at Highbury against unbeaten leaders Arsenal was never going to be easy, but the Reds found themselves 2-1 up at half-time. Hyypia headed Liverpool ahead on five minutes. Thierry Henry equalised. Owen restored the lead, slotting in Gerrard's magnificent through ball. The Gunners were superb in the second half, with Pires making it 2-2 before Henry scored two more. Hamann had an awful game.

Defeat at Highbury was excusable, but a 1-0 home defeat to Charlton wasn't. Carragher was finally moved into the middle of defence instead of Biscan. Thompson admitted in his book it was one of the few things he and Houllier had disagreed on, with the manager preferring the Croat, unable to forget Carragher's own goals against Manchester United way back in 1999. The game was decided by Shaun Bartlett's headed goal from a corner. Dean Kiely made an amazing save from Smicer. Despite two Easter defeats, Liverpool were still fourth. Charlton were still in the running for fourth, two points behind the Reds with a game in hand.

A 0-0 draw at home to Fulham was enough to test anyone's patience. Fortunately, Newcastle and Charlton would each win just one of their last half-dozen matches. It's incredible to think that if either side, or Aston Villa, had finished the season strongly, Istanbul in 2005 wouldn't have happened. Gerrard missed a penalty in front of the Kop after a handball. Kewell and Heskey each hit an upright.

An untelevised trip to Manchester United was where Liverpool got their battle for fourth spot back on track. There were four games left, and the Reds managed to get four positive results. Since Carragher's move to centre back, the Reds were tighter and didn't defend so deep. For the third time in four seasons, Murphy scored the only goal at Old Trafford. Owen and Gerrard were no longer on spot-kick duties after recent misses, but the former Crewe midfielder had a 100% record for Liverpool. United hadn't conceded a league penalty for over ten years but Murphy emphatically hit Tim Howard's top corner to give Liverpool three valuable points. Again, he shushed the crowd. At least it wasn't Yeovil this time. Despite the result, it was on this afternoon that Carragher knew Houllier's days were numbered. "By this stage, the Gerard Houllier in front of me was a pale imitation of the man who'd strolled into Melwood and taken on the most powerful player in the club [Paul Ince]," he wrote. "He'd seek the opinions of Stevie and Michael to reassure him his team selections were right. He told them his team included Cheyrou and Baros rather than Murphy and Heskey. Stevie and Michael ... didn't agree. Houllier changed his mind. I had a hollow feeling inside. I knew the manager had to go. This wasn't the Houllier I knew. In 1999 he'd never have put the opinion of any player above his own."

A 2-0 win over Middlesbrough kept the Reds in fourth. Newcastle's defeat at Manchester City the day before was a real fillip. Murphy scored another crucial penalty after Owen had been fouled. Heskey extended the lead three minutes after that, set up by Owen's flick.

The penultimate game of the season was a resounding 3-0 win over at Birmingham. Owen scored again from Heskey's precise pass. Heskey, heavily linked with a move to Birmingham, grabbed a goal of his own, turning in Gerrard's square pass. He did eventually move to St Andrews, for £6.25 million. Kenny Cunningham was sent off for a foul on a marauding Gerrard. Late in the game, Murphy released Gerrard and the inspirational captain, easily Liverpool's player of the season, slid the ball into the corner. Another win; another clean sheet. Villa and Newcastle drew their games that weekend. Champions League qualification was now firmly in Liverpool's hands. Off the field, there was much talk of either Thailand's prime minister Thaksin Shinawatra, "whose human rights record," according to the Telegraph, "rivals that of General Pinochet," or local property tycoon Steve Morgan, a Tory party donor, buying a stake in the club. In the end, neither man was successful.

Newcastle's inability to win at Southampton in midweek knocked them out of the top-four race ahead of their trip to Anfield on the final weekend of the season. Villa, meanwhile, started the day three points behind but with an inferior goal difference of 12. So, barring the most astonishing of miracles, the Reds were going to clinch fourth, even if they lost to the Magpies. Before the game, Houllier angered fans by saying, "I was asked to qualify for the Champions League only every three years and we have done more than that." It was either an admittance that Liverpool standards had plummeted on his watch (Roy Evans achieved a top-four finish in each of his four full seasons) or he was being economical with the truth to save his job. The game finished 1-1. Shola Ameobi produced a clinical finish for the opener. Gerrard's wonderful, curling through ball was touched home by Owen midway through the second half. At the end of such a trying season, there was a note of poignancy. One of Liverpool's unused subs on that final day was goalkeeper Paul Harrison, whose father Gary and uncle Stephen had been killed at Hillsborough.

Nine days after the last game, the club took the decision they should have taken at least a year earlier. Houllier, along with his assistant Thompson, was fired. Two years of puerile football and woeful signings had pushed the board too far. "I think it was a sensible decision," said Riise. "My emotions were mixed," wrote Carragher. "I was personally sorry for Houllier, but I knew it was the right decision. The club needed a fresh start. The supporters now perceived Houllier as a manager who bought poor players and talked rubbish. Their view of him had been contaminated by his final two seasons. For me, he'll always be the boss who did everything except win the title at Anfield."

An exciting new era was about to dawn, but would Owen and Gerrard be part of it?

2004-05

"The time has come for Liverpool to play in yet another European Cup Final."

From a shortlist that included Jose Mourinho, Alan Curbishley, Gordon Strachan and Martin O'Neill, the new manager was Rafael Benitez. He would go on to become one of the most adored figures in the club's history. That wasn't just down to the remarkable Champions League success in Istanbul, the greatest night in Liverpool's history. There was a bond between Benitez and the Liverpool fans, the sort of relationship the Kop had enjoyed with Shankly and Dalglish.

Mourinho was considered 'not a Liverpool manager' after his infamous touchline celebration at Old Trafford as Porto knocked Manchester United out of the Champions League. "One of our core values was respect and that includes treating other clubs and people with respect," chief executive Rick Parry reflected in 2016 with the author Simon Hughes.

Bearing in mid the club's desperation to win the Premier League, Benitez was clearly a more attractive proposition than Curbishley, Strachan and O'Neill. The Spaniard managed the Valencia team which ran rings around Gerard Houllier's Liverpool in 2002. The 44-year-old had broken the Real Madrid-Barcelona stranglehold on La Liga in 2002 and 2004 with a fraction of their resources. Liverpool needed a manager who could do exactly that. His relationship with the Valencia board had collapsed and he departed with a year remaining on his contract.

Benitez brought with him Pako Ayesteran as his assistant. Sammy Lee chose not to stay on. What the new manager thought of the squad was anyone's guess. Steven Gerrard was blunt with him when they first met. "I'm not sure you appreciate how bad we are," said the wantaway skipper. The strength of the spine did at least give him something to work with, but there was much deadwood to clear out. There was no reliable goalkeeper - Jerzy Dudek made too many mistakes and Chris Kirkland was injury-prone. Right back Steve Finnan had a decent first season. John Arne Riise was better going forward than he was defending. Gregory Vignal hadn't been seen for ages. Djimi Traore mainly played in the middle and hadn't been convincing, although Benitez did persuade him to reject Everton's overtures. At centre back, nobody wanted to see Igor Biscan again. Stephane Henchoz was declining. Sami Hyypia had dipped slightly from his early-Houllier form but was an obvious pick. Houllier had finally relented and picked Carragher alongside the Finn, and Benitez would leave him there. Their partnership would thrive.

Gerrard was now one of the best players in the world but had spent the summer considering his future to the extent it affected his Euro 2004 performances. He seemed certain to leave for Chelsea but announced his intention to stay in late June. The same soap opera would be played out the following summer. Having watched him closely before he moved to Liverpool, Benitez told Gerrard he moved around too much for a central midfielder and unbalanced the side. Didi Hamann was an adept holding midfielder but hadn't been at his best for some time. Danny Murphy struggled in Houllier's last season, failing to replicate his 2002-03 form. His best football had been as a left midfielder, tucking inside to protect the full back. The inconsistent and lightweight Vladimir Smicer could occasionally prise open a defence but was hit and miss and often injured. Harry Kewell scored some spectacular goals but was also inconsistent and picked up too many injuries. Bruno Cheyrou was out of his depth. He was soon off to Marseille on loan. Salif Diao hadn't improved. Anthony Le Tallec was far from the gem that Houllier hoped he would be and went on loan to St Etienne before the season started, despite scoring a brace in a 2-1 friendly win over Wrexham.

Up front, Emile Heskey had departed before Benitez arrived. Owen was still around, but no one knew how long for. His form had been patchy in 2003-04, and his fitness was still an issue, although he was one of the few top-drawer players Benitez inherited. Florent Sinama-Pongolle looked promising but seemed better off the bench. Milan Baros was top scorer in the 2004 European Championships, but Houllier hadn't rated him. El-Hadji Diouf went to Bolton on loan, never to play for Liverpool again. Nobody mourned his departure.

According to Guillem Balague in his book, Season on the Brink, "Rafa soon realised he had a much bigger job than he had imagined. In some cases, the squad lacked basic knowledge and, more worryingly, even the enthusiasm to learn." Nor did he have an unlimited budget like Mourinho at Chelsea. Houllier had already signed Auxerre's Djibril Cisse for £14.5 million. Benitez didn't want him, but it was too late. The new manager's first capture was Malaga's right back Josemi for £2 million. Shortly after the season began, Real Sociedad midfielder Xabi Alonso signed for £10.7 million. Luis Garcia cost £6 million from Barcelona. The Spaniards would play a big part in the Champions League success.

As well as Heskey, out went Babbel on a free to Stuttgart and Murphy to Charlton Athletic for £2.5 million. The latter admitted he should have fought for his place. Perhaps Benitez had been too quick to try and break up the influential English clique of Gerrard, Carragher, Owen and Murphy. It wouldn't be long before another of them went.

The season began in some farce, as photographers at Liverpool's opening Champions League qualifier against Grazer AK were more concerned with one of the substitutes rather than any of the first 11. Owen was one of seven on the bench, but with speculation of a move to Real Madrid, an appearance would see him cup tied. Dudek was in goal. The back four was Josemi, Hyypia, Carragher and Riise. Gerrard and Hamann were in midfield, with Finnan and Kewell wide.

Baros and Cisse were up front. In front of 15,000 spectators at the Arnold Schwarzenegger Stadium, Liverpool won 2-0, with Gerrard producing two clinical finishes. The second followed Benitez moving him into the number-10 position, which would become a feature of the season. Kewell had a hand in both. Gerrard had a third disallowed. Riise could already see that Liverpool were playing differently. "Already Benitez's brand of football could be seen in our play," he wrote. "There were fewer long passes and the classic passing game of Liverpool was back." Full back Stephen Warnock and midfielder Darren Potter came off the bench for their debuts, but Owen remained on his backside. He was soon heading to Real Madrid for a paltry £8 million. His true market value was far higher, but he was running his contract down, and it was the most Liverpool could get. Antonio Nunez came the other way for £1.5 million, but after injuring a knee in his first training session, the 25-year-old winger wouldn't make his debut until November. It was an awful deal for the Reds, but Benitez needed what he could get for Owen to help fund the signings of Alonso and Garcia, knowing he could leave for nothing a year later. Owen may have been just 24 but, in hindsight, his best days were behind him. Liverpool had mismanaged his injuries over the years, and at no future club was he a fraction of the player he had been in his early seasons at Anfield. Even so, the fans would never forgive him for running down his contract.

The league campaign began with a Saturday lunchtime fixture at Spurs, who were captained by Jamie Redknapp. Benitez kept the same 11 and was rewarded with a half-time lead, as Cisse turned in Carragher's flick. Liverpool had been the better side, but Spurs took over and Jermaine Defoe equalised. Carragher could have headed a late winner. A goal on his league debut was a dream start for Cisse, but his Liverpool career failed to match the lofty expectations that greeted his arrival. "Djibril was exactly the same as Milan Baros," wrote Carragher, "likely to impress in one game but disappoint in the next."

The new manager's first home game was a 2-1 win over Manchester City. "Where is Pinocchio?" enquired the City fans, noting the lack of an animated Phil Thompson on the touchline. He had departed with Houllier. Nicolas Anelka put City one up after mistakes from Carragher and Dudek. Liverpool were soon level when Baros clipped the ball over David James. The winner came when man of the match Gerrard followed up a shot from Baros. City's Richard Dunne was dismissed for two yellows. For the third game in a row, Warnock was impressive as a second-half substitute. The Carragher-Hyypia partnership was ever improving. Josemi had made a promising start, although it wouldn't last. Riise had kept Shaun Wright-Phillips quiet. The win took Liverpool into third, but it would be the only time all season they would be in the top four.

A decent start was followed by two disappointing defeats. Grazer came to Anfield and although they failed to overturn their two-goal deficit, they did win 1-0. Henchoz, Potter and Diao started but the pitiful Reds fell behind to a 54th-minute scorcher from Mario Tokic and never looked like equalising. The final whistle confirmed Liverpool's progress to the Champions League group stages, but few would have backed them to make a mark in the competition. On the same day, Liverpool were a whisker away from being sold to lifelong fan Steve Morgan, owner of Redrow Homes. He and Moores had shaken hands on a deal but when Morgan tried to lower the price, the chairman called the deal off.

Alonso and Garcia went straight into the 11 for Liverpool's Premier League match at Bolton. It was a forgettable debut for both. Hyypia had his nose broken in a challenge with Kevin Davies, who then scored the winning goal. Garcia had a late goal wrongly disallowed for offside. Cisse missed a clear-cut chance to equalise.

A 3-0 home win over West Brom was just what Benitez needed. Alonso was benched, while Finnan got another go on the right of midfield. The imperious Gerrard scored his fourth of the season after exchanging passes with Garcia. Finnan then scored his only goal for the club after cutting inside and rifling just inside the near post. Garcia also notched his first for Liverpool.

The first significant win for Benitez came in the Champions League when the 2004 beaten finalists, AS Monaco, lost 2-0 at Anfield. Alonso's passing was sublime. Garcia continued to impress behind the lone striker, Cisse. And it was those players who were involved in the first goal, as the French striker fired past Flavio Roma. Garcia had chances, but it was Baros, on for Cisse, who settled the match. He controlled Josemi's long pass, beat a couple of defenders and clipped the ball past the keeper.

Sky's Monday night fixture was Liverpool's trip to Old Trafford, where they had won on three of their last four visits. The broadcaster was obsessed with Liverpool's zonal marking, which was still in its infancy. Vox popping Reds fans outside the ground, Sky did persuade a few to agree with their pundit Andy Gray that "a zone can't score a goal," but this was a defensive system which would soon see Liverpool almost impregnable against some of Europe's finest. On the night, however, the Reds came up short with United's Mikael Silvestre scoring twice. To Gray's delight, both were headers from set pieces. John O'Shea scored an own goal in between. Rio Ferdinand was playing his first game for eight months after missing a drug test. He needed the trainer to bring him a biscuit halfway through the second half. Worse than the defeat was the news that Gerrard had broken a metatarsal in his left foot. He would be absent for two months.

Without their captain, the Reds dismantled Norwich City. Hamann and Warnock came in for the injured Gerrard and Kewell. Alonso controlled the midfield. Garcia hit a post. Cisse missed a couple of chances. The opener came when Baros fired past Robert Green from the edge of the area. Garcia beat two defenders and scored with the aid of a deflection. The third came from a clever free kick, as Cisse fired low into the corner from 20 yards.

The inconsistency continued when the Reds were downed by Olympiacos in their tenth game of the season. Cisse was sacrificed for an extra midfielder, as Josemi played right back with Finnan moving forward. Liverpool had no answer to Ieroklis Stoltidis' goal on 17 minutes when he got above Hyypia to nod in

Rivaldo's free-kick. The home side were reduced to ten men, but lacklustre Liverpool couldn't capitalise.

Porto's Champions League-winning manager, Jose Mourinho, had been linked with Liverpool. He went to Chelsea instead. With Benitez's Valencia winning the UEFA Cup, they would have met in the Super Cup had they stayed put. Instead, they faced each other in a league match at Stamford Bridge, which Liverpool lost 1-0. Kirkland and Traore made their first starts of the season and helped keep Chelsea at bay for over an hour. Carragher was Liverpool's best player. The defining moment came when substitute Joe Cole touched in Lampard's low free kick. Chelsea had conceded just one goal in eight matches and were behind only Arsenal. Liverpool were down in 11th. The league season was shaping up to be another race for fourth. An international break meant Liverpool had a fortnight off before their next game.

In October 2004, the Hillsborough families had to endure an appalling article in The Spectator, a right-wing political magazine, edited then by Boris Johnson, the Conservatives' arts spokesman – a job he would later be sacked from for lying to party leader Michael Howard. Written by Simon Heffer, the article referred to "drunken fans at the back of the crowd who mindlessly tried to fight their way into the ground," and Liverpool people seeing "themselves whenever possible as victims." Heffer and Johnson didn't even know how many had died and couldn't be bothered to google it, referring to "the deaths of more than 50" fans. Howard sent Johnson to Liverpool to show his contrition, but his presence did little to calm feelings.

Another trip to the capital saw Liverpool play Fulham in the Reds' 4000th league match. After half an hour, mistakes by Diao and Garcia had led to two Luis Boa Morte goals, but Liverpool stirred themselves into a wonderful comeback, one which Benitez would refer to at half-time in Istanbul. Alonso replaced the abysmal Diao. The deficit was halved with a Zat Knight own goal. Baros equalised with 19 minutes remaining. Josemi was sent off for a second booking, but the numerical disadvantage didn't stop Liverpool. Alonso lined up a 20-yard free kick and, with the aid of a deflection, scored his first Reds goal to make it 3-2. Finally, substitute Biscan found the top corner from a similar range. It was Benitez's first domestic away win. Johnny Cash's 'Ring of Fire' boomed out of the away end. It would soon become the season's anthem. Liverpool were seventh and if they won their game in hand, they would be fourth.

A 0-0 draw at home to 2003 semi-finalists Deportivo La Coruna was painfully dull. Baros went around the keeper on 28 minutes but was unduly hesitant. It was one of several first-half chances. The Reds moved the ball around nicely and had 15 goal attempts, but few were threatening. At the other end, Riise headed off the line.

Liverpool's 2000th league game at Anfield produced a 2-0 win over Charlton Athletic, which took them up to fifth. Danny Murphy was in Alan Curbishley's side and received a warm reception. His replacement Alonso was outstanding again. After several missed chances, Riise scored his first goal for 20 months when he crashed a 20-yarder into the bottom corner. The Norwegian was now playing on the left of midfield, with Traore behind him. Garcia found the top corner with a curling effort from 25 yards to seal the points.

Benitez made ten changes for the League Cup tie at Millwall towards the end of October. The returning Dudek skippered the side. Henchoz, debutant Zak Whitbread, Diao, Potter, Sinama-Pongolle and Neil Mellor received rare starts. The game was played amid an unpleasant atmosphere with some home fans singing about Hillsborough. Phil Hammond, chairman of Hillsborough Family Support Group, said the abuse was "sickening - I'm not surprised the Millwall fans were doing that. I wouldn't expect anything else from the likes of them". Diao scored first with the outside of his right foot when Warnock's corner wasn't cleared. Baros scored a late brace to secure a 3-0 win; the first from Warnock's pass, the second from Potter's.

The only positive of the last game of October was that Liverpool avoided defeat. A 2-2 draw against second-bottom Blackburn Rovers represented two dropped points but, far worse, Cisse suffered an appalling double fracture of the left leg, which would sideline him for most of the season. Riise scored on seven minutes when he put Alonso's raking pass away with a fierce left-foot drive. Jay Bothroyd equalised nine minutes later. Cisse's injury came shortly before half-time. Brett Emerton handed Rovers the lead in first-half stoppage time after Hyypia and Carragher failed to clear. Ten minutes into the second half, Garcia played in Baros, who held off the last defender and found the corner. Everyone's thoughts were with Cisse after the game. It looked a horrific injury.

Liverpool responded by winning at Deportivo La Coruna. Baros could have scored after 30 seconds, but the game's only goal came on 14 minutes, when Jorge Andrade turned Riise's cross into his own net. The Norwegian had a shot cleared off the line. Garcia missed a late chance. Kirkland received a blow to the head in the second half, courtesy of Biscan, who, along with Traore, was outstanding. Carragher and Hyypia were dominant. It was an excellent result, which went a long way to helping the side progress from the group stage.

Next came one of the worst results of the season, as Steve Bruce's Birmingham left Anfield with a 1-0 win. Garcia missed a sitter, among several chances for Liverpool. Birmingham's only attack of note saw Darren Anderton score the winner on 76 minutes. Full backs Josemi and Traore were the weak links. Garcia and Kewell were also poor. Up front, Sinama-Pongolle made his first league start under Benitez but did little to catch the eye.

The day after the death of former skipper Emlyn Hughes, who had lifted the European Cup in 1977 and 1978, the visit of holders Middlesbrough in the League Cup prompted the manager to include several fringe players again, including Irish winger Richie Partridge, who made his first appearance in nearly three years. One absentee was Kewell, who was undergoing an intensive personal training programme, in the hope it would spark some sort of form. In front of 28,176 fans, the game remained goalless until Mellor's brace in the final seven minutes. Partridge and Potter created the goals.

Baros was the hero as Liverpool scraped past Crystal Palace. He won a penalty, which he converted, but Tony Popovic got the better of Josemi and equalised. Just before half-time, Baros tapped in his second, set up by Kewell. Josemi was again at fault when Michael Hughes made it 2-2. More dropped points looked likely until Baros won and converted another penalty in injury time. The goals themselves may have been unspectacular, but he did win both penalties. With a shortage of experienced strikers, Liverpool needed him in form.

But after tearing a hamstring in a World Cup qualifier, he missed a trip to Middlesbrough, Liverpool's bogey ground. The Reds fielded no genuine strikers. Kewell and Garcia, who had a goal disallowed, played furthest forward, although Sinama-Pongolle and Mellor were on the bench. Gerrard was also a sub, making his comeback from injury. Chris Riggott and Bolo Zenden scored the Boro goals.

The Reds lost again when they went to Monaco in the Champions League. Garcia lasted three minutes before succumbing to a hamstring injury. His replacement, Josemi, needed 20 stitches to the head and was substituted in the second half. Baros was still absent. Mellor was up front on his own. A handball led to Javier Saviola's goal on 54 minutes. Gerrard missed Liverpool's best chance. The Reds would now need to win their final group match against Olympiacos 1-0 or by two goals. A booking for Hamann meant he would be suspended.

Even in a European Cup-winning season, there were few moments that made Anfield explode like Mellor's last-minute winner against champions Arsenal. Gerrard was deployed in the number-10 role behind the young forward, a role he would become familiar with as the season wore on. Sinama-Pongolle played on the right, before making way for debutant Nunez. Kewell disappointed again, this time on the left. Gerrard should have had a penalty. Mellor hit the bar after being wrongly flagged offside. Kewell missed with a header. Finnan played a long, diagonal pass to Kewell, who, running backwards, cushioned it into the path of his captain and from Gerrard's clever pass, the Spaniard hit a stunning 20-yarder which smashed into Jens Lehmann's top corner. As Anfield erupted, Benitez gave his players a thumbs-up. Alonso's goal is often forgotten because of the quality of Mellor's strike. Patrick Vieira finished off an exquisite team move to make it 1-1. In injury time, Hamann won a free kick near his own penalty area with a comical dive. The ball was launched forward and flicked on, and Mellor hit a swerving shot from 25 yards which beat Lehmann all ends up. It was a fabulous moment which gave the Reds their first win over the Gunners since the 2001 Cup Final.

Another League Cup game saw another weakened line-up, although this was at White Hart Lane. There was a debut for the young full back David Raven and also winger Mark Smyth off the bench. Liverpool were outplayed by Spurs, but the hosts failed to break through until Jermain Defoe scored three minutes into the second period of extra-time. Sinama-Pongolle levelled from the spot following a handball on 117 minutes. The Reds won the subsequent penalty shootout 4-3, with goals from Henchoz, Partridge, Welsh and Sinama-Pongolle. Potter missed. For Henchoz and Partridge, it was their final touch of a ball for the club, shades of Graeme Souness in 1984 and Smicer to come. Frederic Kanoute and Michael Brown failed to score for Spurs. It was a remarkable result for such a young team.

Kewell scored his first goal in ten months in a 1-1 draw at Villa Park. The Reds dominated the first half. Mellor and Gerrard should have added a second. At the other end, Carragher was harshly adjudged to have fouled Gavin McCann. Nobby Solano fired in the free kick. Gerrard was taken off, with an eye on the Champions League group decider against Olympiacos. Traore ended up on the left wing.

With his future at the club still in the air, Gerrard spoke before the game of not wanting "to wake up on Thursday morning in the UEFA Cup ... If we don't qualify for next season, I'll have to consider my future." From here on, the season seemed to be more about Gerrard than anyone else. "There's more than one player at this football club," an exasperated Carragher felt like shouting at journalists who talked about little else. But the attention the skipper received was understandable after Olympiacos. When his team needed him most, Gerrard produced one of the great Anfield moments. Hamann's absence gave Liverpool more of an attacking edge, similar to the crucial group-stage win over Roma in 2002, from which he was also suspended. Kewell played in the hole behind Baros. Rivaldo fired in a 26th-minute free kick, meaning Liverpool needed three. Gerrard kicked the ball away in anger and was booked. He would miss Liverpool's next European match. After an insipid first half, Benitez switched the formation to 3-5-2. Sinama-Pongolle replaced Traore and made an immediate impression, equalising after skilful play on the left wing by Kewell. Gerrard had a goal disallowed for a push by Baros. With ten minutes to go, another sub, Mellor, scored from close range. With Anfield bouncing, Carragher dribbled forward, executed a Cruyff turn and lofted a ball infield to Mellor. "Set it! Set it!" Gerrard shouted. And the young forward's cushioned header bounced perfectly for his skipper, whose vicious half-volley swerved away from Antonis Nikopolidis and into the corner of the net. The scenes on the Kop hadn't been seen for years. A steward hugged Benitez, who barely smiled. The Reds were in the last 16 of the Champions League again. It was the goal that ignited the Benitez reign. Liverpool were a force again, in Europe at least.

After the joy of Olympiacos, the Reds had to go to Goodison a couple of days later. Inexplicably, Diao came in for Alonso. Benitez maintained his five-man midfield away from home, with Sinama-Pongolle on the right. Mellor was the lone attacker. In the 200th Merseyside derby, Mellor and Diao missed chances before Lee Carsley scored the only goal, leaving the Reds a dozen points behind the Blues, albeit with a game in hand. It was Liverpool's first defeat at Goodison since 1997.

Further Premier League frustration followed as Liverpool frittered away a couple of points at Anfield against Portsmouth. Gerrard scored a sublime free-kick on 70 minutes, but an injury-time equaliser from Lomana LuaLua was frustrating. The recalled Dudek was at fault but Benitez had to take some blame for making a defensive change just before the equaliser.

Having moved from Blackburn, Graeme Souness was now managing Newcastle. Their visit to Anfield a week before Christmas was the tenth occasion he had managed against the club he'd captained with such distinction. A convincing 3-1 win for Liverpool meant he still hadn't won any of those matches. Patrick Kluivert put the Geordies ahead. An own goal by Titus Bramble, under pressure from Hyypia, restored parity. Mellor's neat side-footed finish, following a pass by Baros, made it 2-1. The Czech then latched onto a great ball by Kewell, rounded Shay Given and made it 3-1. Lee Bowyer was sent off for a high challenge on Sinama-Pongolle. Baros nearly scored another with an audacious overhead kick from Finnan's cross.

Riise scored a couple of screamers in a 5-0 win on Boxing Day at bottom side West Bromwich Albion. Liverpool enjoyed total domination, although it was only 1-0 at half-time, thanks to the Norwegian smashing in Gerrard's pass. Cosmin Contra, who'd played for Alaves in the 2001 UEFA Cup Final, was sent off for deliberate handball, as he stopped Nunez from scoring his first Liverpool goal. Baros missed the penalty. Sinama-Pongolle, Gerrard, Riise and Garcia all found the target in the second half.

The entertainment didn't flow quite so easily two days later as the Reds hosted Southampton in their final match of 2004. Sinama-Pongolle scored the only goal from Alonso's precise pass. Despite winning three games in a row, the Reds were still sixth, half a dozen points behind Everton in fourth. Leaders Chelsea were 15 points away.

New Year's Day saw a titanic clash at Anfield between Liverpool and Chelsea. The Reds raised their game and matched the champions-elect, only to lose 1-0 to a late Joe Cole shot that deflected in off Carragher. The Reds had a penalty turned down when Tiago handled. Alonso had his ankle broken in a challenge with Frank Lampard. Liverpool's best chance fell to Traore. It was that sort of day. Benitez had enjoyed precious little luck so far.

Liverpool then got away with a handball in a 2-1 win at Carrow Road two days later. Carragher was the culprit early in the second half, but it wasn't seen. Soon after, Garcia chased Riise's long pass and lofted the ball over Robert Green. The Norwegian added the second after Green had saved from Sinama-Pongolle. Norwich pulled one back, but it wasn't enough. The win would be Liverpool's only points in a traumatic January.

The semi-final of the League Cup saw Benitez field a much stronger side than in previous rounds. Second-tier Watford did their fans proud, but Gerrard scored the only goal of the first leg at Anfield, created by substitute Baros.

Liverpool made three signings in January 2005. Veteran defender Mauricio Pellegrino joined from Valencia on a free transfer. Fernando Morientes signed from Real Madrid for £6.3 million. Benitez had wanted Bayer Leverkusen's Dimitar Berbatov but with the two sides due to meet in the Champions League, that wasn't going to be possible. Neither Pellegrino nor Morientes would be eligible for Champions League ties. The young Cumbrian goalkeeper Scott Carson came from Leeds for £1 million. Henchoz left for Celtic on a free and had a pop at Benitez on his way out. Nevertheless, fans wouldn't forget his contribution under Houllier, especially in 2001.

Three consecutive defeats was the last thing Benitez needed. The first, a home defeat to Manchester United, saw Morientes and Pellegrino endure disappointing debuts. Wayne Rooney scored the only goal, which Dudek fumbled into his own net. It was another gaffe against United by the Pole. A Kopite threw his phone at Rooney as he celebrated. Wes Brown was dismissed on 65 minutes, but Liverpool still created little.

The next defeat was one of the low points of the season, although given the line-up he fielded, one suspected Benitez wasn't too bothered that Liverpool had gone out of the FA Cup to lower-division Burnley. In a rearranged match at Turf Moor, Traore's comical own goal was the difference, but the bigger story was the manager selecting the likes of Warnock, Raven, Whitbread, Welsh and Potter. Hyypia, one of the few players with any experience was as bad as anyone else. The backlash was unrelenting. Picking such a weak team in the FA Cup hadn't been seen before at Liverpool. Critics hammered the manager, but his thin squad would have struggled with a fixture pile-up. Who knows if Istanbul would have been possible on the back of an FA Cup run?

Alan Hansen warned Liverpool were in danger of becoming a relic when they lost at Southampton. David Prutton put the Saints ahead on five minutes. Peter Crouch doubled the lead. Hansen said: "It always used to be 'first is first and the rest is nowhere' ... We're certainly not a relic yet, but we're nearer to it now than we were 15 years ago." The Reds were vulnerable at the back as injuries to Finnan and Josemi saw Carragher switch to right back. The unconvincing Pellegrino came into the middle. Hamann was another who was struggling. Liverpool didn't look like getting one back, let alone two. The absence of Alonso was hurting.

A third appearance in the League Cup final in five years was secured when Liverpool won the second leg of the semi-final at Watford. Again, the only goal came from Gerrard. Benitez reverted to a five-man midfield, and the extra man suffocated the Hornets. Finnan and Carragher were outstanding. As the game wore on, Liverpool looked more likely to break the deadlock, and the skipper did just that with 13 minutes remaining as he shot across Paul Jones and into the far corner. Yet another injury was sustained when Sinama-Pongolle, an 85th-minute substitute, suffered an anterior cruciate ligament injury. It would be the end of his season.

A much-needed league win came at the Valley on the first of February. Trailing to a Shaun Bartlett goal, the Reds burst into life midway through the second half and won the game with brilliant goals from Morientes, his first for the club,

182

and Riise, who was now hitting top form. Inter Milan had approached him in January, but he knocked them back. Smicer came off the bench to make his first appearance of the season.

One feature of the Charlton win was the promising Baros-Morientes partnership, which further blossomed in a 3-1 home win over Fulham. The Spaniard's superb glancing header from Garcia's cross on nine minutes was quickly cancelled out by Andy Cole. The Reds took control in the second half as Hyypia nodded in Gerrard's free kick. Baros added the third.

Birmingham completed a league double over the Reds with a 2-0 win at St Andrews. Hyypia, in his 300th Liverpool match, fouled Emile Heskey. Walter Pandiani converted the penalty. On the stroke of half-time, Julian Gray made it two. Liverpool switched to 4-4-2 in the second half but created little. Everton had lost to Chelsea the day before, meaning a win would have closed the gap on fourth to just two points. Benitez was incandescent. "We told the team that Everton had already lost and that we could close the gap, but they didn't react," he told Guillem Balague. After the game, Benitez suggested to Carragher that he start fights in the showers with "teammates who weren't doing their job," as that's what the Argentinian players did at Valencia. Carragher declined.

A welcome break from the fight for fourth came with two season-defining matches. First up was Bayer Leverkusen in the Champions League, the team that had so painfully eliminated the Reds in 2002. The suspended Gerrard was replaced by Biscan. Morientes couldn't play, so Baros ploughed a lone furrow up front. It took the Reds 15 minutes to break through and it was the much-maligned Biscan who beat two men in midfield before presenting Garcia with a slide-rule through ball. The Spaniard made no mistake to send Anfield into raptures. Twenty minutes later, Riise curled in a 20-yard free kick. Dudek saved spectacularly from Bernd Schneider in the second half. As the game was petering out, Hamann lined up a free kick, and as the Kop chanted his name, he stroked the ball over the wall and past Hans-Jorg Butt. There was a sting in the tail, however. Dimitar Berbatov sent in a harmless shot from miles out. Dudek could only parry into the path of Franco, who steered the ball home. The manager glared at his goalkeeper. Liverpool won 3-1, but a 2-0 win for the Germans in the second leg would take them through, and they'd convincingly beaten Real Madrid and Roma at home in their group.

Next up was the League Cup Final in Cardiff against Chelsea. Outside the stadium, a huge, gold-framed portrait of the new manager was held aloft. "I felt like the Ayatollah," said Benitez, who plumped for Morientes as the only recognised striker, with Garcia playing in the hole. The team was: Dudek; Finnan, Carragher, Hyypia, Traore; Kewell, Hamann, Gerrard, Riise; Garcia, Morientes. Chelsea had just lost 2-1 to Barcelona and had to make do without Arjen Robben. Liverpool made the perfect start as Morientes set up a goal within 45 seconds for Riise, who volleyed home emphatically. It was now a backs-to-the-wall job and, with Hamann immense, even though Gerrard was below par, Liverpool frustrated their star-studded opponents. With little over ten minutes left, Chelsea floated a harmless free kick from halfway, which Gerrard glanced into his own net via the post. It was a heartbreaking moment, especially with the skipper now odds on to join Chelsea in the summer. Mourinho taunted the Liverpool supporters and was ordered away from the dug-out. Dudek saved well from Duff to ensure extra-time. "Gerrard urged us on," said Riise, "but I could see that he was really bothered by his own goal." Chelsea enjoyed even more luck in the added period. After Biscan, who along with Nunez and Baros, had come off the bench, missed an inviting chance, Didier Drogba bundled in Glen Johnson's long throw on 107 minutes. Mateja Kezman scored another scrappy goal. Nunez pulled one back with a short-range header a minute later, but the Reds were unable to force an equaliser. The defeat hurt, but the experience of going toe-to-toe with Chelsea would serve Benitez and his players well later in the season. For Gerrard, the scars would take longer to heal after hearing his mum had been sitting near Liverpool fans dishing out abuse to the captain and his partner after his own goal. "She was sitting there all proud, and then she had to listen to that poison," he wrote in his first book. "They are cowards. They would never repeat their jibes to my face ... Being labelled a traitor and having my mum on the phone in buckets of tears, I didn't deserve."

Dudek, Traore, Kewell, Hamann and Mellor were now added to a lengthy injury list before the trip to Newcastle. Carson made his debut. Smicer enjoyed his first start of the season. Le Tallec came off the bench for his first league appearance under Benitez, but Liverpool lost 1-0 as Laurent Robert scored his third goal against the Reds since 2003. Souness finally had a win on the board against his former employers. Away form in the league continued to be terrible. Through the Wind and Rain summed it up perfectly: "If Amundsen and Scott had travelled to the Antarctic in the knowledge that a Liverpool away game lay in wait, they'd have thought 'fuck it' and stayed at home."

But there were no such problems on the continent. Twenty-four hours after Benitez had been photographed enjoying a beer with supporters in Cologne, his side produced a fabulous performance in the Bay Arena to move into the last eight of the Champions League. Before the game, the manager had countered Gerrard's quotes that Liverpool couldn't make the final by saying, "I prefer the players to say, 'Why is it not possible for us to get there?' If Porto won the Champions League last year, then why can't it be us this time? I don't want to hear any member of my squad saying that it can't happen." Garcia was the hero, scoring twice in four first-half minutes to put Liverpool in complete control. Baros added another midway through the half, five minutes after Benitez had withdrawn Hamann for Smicer – the same substitution had been made so disastrously by Houllier in the same stadium three years earlier. The other subs were Welsh and Nunez, with Carson, Raven, Le Tallec and Potter not called upon. It was hardly the bench of champions, but Benitez was working wonders with such a threadbare squad. Leverkusen pulled one back, but a 6-2 aggregate win set up an intriguing quarter-final with Juventus, nearly 20 years on from the horrors of Heysel.

The side's inconsistency bit again a week later in a dull, goalless game at Anfield against Blackburn. The Reds were seven points behind Everton in fourth, with nine games to play.

The Blues were next up at Anfield and Liverpool were fantastic, tearing into their neighbours from the first whistle. A free kick was rolled into Gerrard's path in front of the Kop. Instead of blasting it, as he had done against Portsmouth in December, he calmly rolled it into the corner from 20 yards. Morientes soon hit the crossbar with a wonderful dipping volley from nearly 40 yards. Garcia pounced to nod in the rebound. The Reds were flying, but injuries to Warnock, Hamann, Morientes and Garcia would hamper them. The first three went off before half-time. The latter hobbled through the match. Baros was sent off on 77 minutes. Tim Cahill pulled one back five minutes later, but the Reds, with nine fit men and a limping Spaniard, held on to win an enthralling derby. With Everton having taken just 11 points from 11 games in 2005, the gap was down to four points.

Gerrard finally addressed rumours of his move to Chelsea, calling them "absolute rubbish," although he followed that up with "I haven't made up my mind." Other transfer rumours centred around a possible return for Owen, who had predictably spent much of the season on Madrid's bench. Back on the field after a fortnight's gap, an injury-hit side scraped past Bolton 1-0 with a late Biscan header. Amid numerous injuries and caution ahead of the Juventus game, there were no strikers in the starting line-up. Biscan and John Welsh were the midfield. Given the circumstances, it was a commendable result against the side in sixth.

Three days later came the big one. Juventus at home in the quarter-final of the Champions League – a stage few could have deemed possible in August. The clubs remembered the 39 victims of Heysel with an impeccable tribute, led by Phil Neal, Ian Rush and Michel Platini, who had all played on that fateful night in 1985, although Neal had embarrassed himself by refusing to talk about Heysel with a Guardian journalist, who promptly filed the cringeworthy dialogue of him haggling for a fee, amid several other poignant contributions from those involved. A wreath was laid in front of the travelling supporters. The Kop help aloft a mosaic of cards, which read "Amicizia" – friendship. It was appreciated by some Juve fans, but others turned their backs. Buoyed by an incredible atmosphere, Liverpool started magnificently, even with the inexperienced Carson, Traore, Le Tallec and Biscan being up against Gianluigi Buffon, Lilian Thuram, Alessandro del Piero, Zlatan Ibrahimovic and Pavel Nedved. The latter had unwisely said that Liverpool "had no hope of winning". The Reds were two up in 25 minutes. Hyypia, angered at having been benched for the last three games, volleyed in from close range from a corner. Garcia then beat Buffon, the world's best keeper, from outside the box with a sensational dipping volley. Le Tallec was superb in his only meaningful contribution to Liverpool. An error from Carson allowed Fabio Cannavaro an away goal, which made Juventus favourites to progress. It was the only blot on a brilliant Liverpool performance. Benitez was working wonders with the barest of ingredients.

LIVERPOOL F.C. **THE PREMIER LEAGUE YEARS**

Liverpool's 500th Premier League match was a thoroughly drab affair as they went down to a late goal at Manchester City, for whom Robbie Fowler was playing on his 30th birthday. With only eight days in between the two Juventus legs, it was understandable that Liverpool's intensity was lacking. Dudek, Hyypia, Hamann and Baros didn't play. A point would have taken the Reds into fourth, although Everton had a game in hand, but Kiki Musampa's injury-time goal left Liverpool in fifth.

The second leg at the Stadio delle Alpi couldn't have gone better. Despite suggestions that the 3,000 travelling Liverpool fans could be in danger, they returned unscathed. And the team ground out a 0-0 draw, which secured a semi-final with Chelsea. Gerrard missed out with a thigh strain and watched the game at home with friends, leaving the room whenever Juventus had the ball in a threatening position. Alonso played his first game since New Year's Day and looked like he'd never been away. Dudek was back in goal. Cisse came off the bench for his first action since his leg-break. Ever the tactical genius, Benitez ordered his players to kid the Italians by playing for the first two minutes in a 4-2-3-1 formation, before reverting to a compact 3-5-2. Ibrahimovic missed a sitter just minutes into the game. Cannavaro hit a post in the second half. Juventus barely threatened otherwise. The low block which had denied Chelsea for much of the League Cup Final, kept Juventus at bay with Hyypia and Carragher at their commanding best. When the final whistle went, Liverpool's heroes celebrated. So did Chelsea's players, assembled in a West London bar. They had avoided Juventus and would only have to beat this mediocre Liverpool team to make the final.

Tottenham came to Anfield three days later, and a 2-2 draw left Liverpool's top-four hopes looking very slim. Erik Edman scored with an outrageous shot from about 40 yards. Garcia equalised just before half-time with a shot on the turn from 20 yards. Robbie Keane restored the lead, but Hyypia volleyed a wonderful equaliser from outside the box. Gerrard missed a penalty and hit a post. He claimed after the game he was finished with penalties.

A rare win on the south coast came next as the Reds prevailed in a midweek match at Fratton Park. Morientes scored his third goal for the club after four minutes. Portsmouth levelled. Garcia gave Liverpool a 2-1 lead before the break. Riise made both goals. The second half was scoreless. Benitez maintained the 3-5-2 formation. Gerrard was on the bench. Everton beat Manchester United for the first time in a decade. Realistically, fourth was gone, but the Reds had their eyes on a much bigger prize.

With the first leg of the semi-final three days away, Liverpool were below-par at Selhurst Park. It was hardly unexpected, especially with Pellegrino, Le Tallec and Welsh in the side and Potter the first to come off the bench. Traore was used as a wing back. Gerrard was subdued. Morientes was poor again. Baros left the field needing stitches. Andy Johnson scored the only goal on 34 minutes, to which Liverpool barely looked like countering. An irate Benitez responded to every question on Sky Sports by saying, "Let's think of the next match."

The atmosphere at Stamford Bridge in the first leg of the Champions League semi-final resembled that of a library. Chelsea had been lucky to win both league matches. They had been incredibly fortuitous to win the League Cup. Maybe their luck would now run out. "Everything it was possible for a club to do wrong ahead of a semi-final, Chelsea did in 2005," wrote Carragher. "Every cocky interview they gave, every idle boast, worked in our favour." The rivalry between Liverpool and Chelsea cut far deeper than anyone could have imagined. Everything about the clubs was different, and Reds fans hadn't forgiven Mourinho for Cardiff or for so openly pursuing their captain. Benitez sent his team out to play for a goalless draw, and they got it, having reverted to four at the back. The only downside was a booking for Alonso, after a dive by Eidur Gudjohnsen, or Eimur Good-diver, as he was soon nicknamed. He would miss the second leg. Gerrard had endured dental surgery on the day of the game to remove an abscess and failed to make an impact, although he did provide a sublime cross from which Baros tested Petr Cech with a glancing header from the edge of the box. Carragher could have been awarded a penalty when he was dragged to the ground at a free kick. The hosts dominated the final stages, but the Reds kept their shape, and their goal remained intact. "99.99% of Liverpool fans are now sure they are going through," observed Mourinho. "Jose is wrong," remarked Phil Thompson on Sky Sports. "100% of Liverpool fans think they're through now."

With five players rested, the Reds again failed to win in the league straight after a European clash, but not too many fans were bothered as the Reds drew 1-1 at home to Middlesbrough. As they were trailing to an early goal, Gerrard equalised with a spectacular volley from over 30 yards, as he hammered the ball into the corner of the Kop goal past future Red Brad Jones. The abysmal Pellegrino was hooked at half-time, with Riise moving to centre back. Hamann made a welcome return from injury as a late sub. With Alonso suspended, the German would be needed against Chelsea, despite a lack of match fitness.

Tuesday May 3rd, 2005 takes some beating as Anfield's greatest night. Maybe Barcelona in 2019 edged it. Perhaps Inter Milan or St Etienne still top the pile. In the away dressing room, Mourinho wrote '33' on the whiteboard, reminding his players of their Premier League lead over Liverpool. They were still favourites to progress, despite the goalless first leg, but with the Anfield decibels off the scale, the Reds made the perfect start. With consummate skill, Gerrard flicked Riise's pass into the path of Baros, who lifted the ball over Petr Cech. The keeper ploughed into him. Garcia poked it goalward. William Gallas hooked it away from under the crossbar. Lubos Michel was about to award the penalty and dismiss Cech when he saw linesman Roman Slysko make a signal. Goal! The Kop became a red sea of flailing limbs. Replays showed the ball hadn't quite crossed the line, but a goal was the better outcome for Chelsea than facing a penalty with ten men. They only needed a score draw. The Reds had 86 minutes to protect their lead, with Finnan, Carragher and Hamann a booking away from missing the final. But Liverpool's experience in Cardiff stood them in good stead. They knew the game plan worked. Only a freak own goal had stopped them that day. This time they had the Anfield crowd behind them and, sure enough, Chelsea froze in this most intimidating of atmospheres. All they could offer was hoofing the ball up to Robert Huth in the closing stages. As the minutes ticked down, their only effort on target in either leg had been a Frank Lampard free kick. John Terry glanced at the clock. Eighty-eight minutes. His eyes filled with tears. His magnificent team had dominated the Premier League, but they couldn't free themselves from the shackles of Benitez's game plan. Liverpool were nearly there. There was still time for one heart-stopping moment. Dudek missed a punch. The ball fell to Gudjohnsen. With the goal gaping, he was about to break Anfield hearts as Michael Thomas had in 1989. This might have been worse – league titles came along regularly back then. Who knew when Liverpool would be on a stage like this again? But the Icelandic striker was punished by the footballing gods for cheating Alonso out of a place in the match. Carragher deflected his shot wide, and a goal kick was given. Justice. The six added minutes were soon over. The time had come, as commentator Clive Tyldesley put it, for Liverpool to play in yet another European Cup Final. Mourinho, the self-anointed "Special One" would moan about the 'ghost goal' for years, but he knew the decision was the lesser of two evils for Chelsea. He also knew he had been second best in the tactical battle with Benitez. "The best team lost," he moaned. Riise recalled: "We laughed at how furious Mourinho had been on the touchline." The crowd celebrated wildly, with 'The Fields of Anfield Road' never sung more heartily. "You can spend millions on the best players and invest in one of the world's top coaches, but the one thing you can never buy is fans," said Carragher, the real hero of this European campaign. He had dominated the Chelsea forwards in both legs. Benitez drank coke until 2am in an Albert Dock bar. The Kop adored their new manager. The Reds would play AC Milan, the club that had so fascinated a young Benitez in the late 1980s, in Turkey on May 25th.

A 3-1 defeat at Highbury meant Liverpool had failed to win 12 of the 14 matches that followed a European tie. But no one cared. The Reds were in their seventh European Cup Final – seven more than Arsenal. In his 200th league game, Gerrard scored Liverpool's goal from distance, but the defeat meant fourth spot was Everton's. David Moyes called them the best team on Merseyside. Arsenal beat Everton 7-0 three days later.

The league season ended with a 2-1 home win over Aston Villa. Cisse got both the goals, the first since his terrible injury. An angry Smicer was omitted from the squad, believing he would also miss out on the Champions League Final. The Reds came fifth and were given a rapturous reception in the customary end-of-season lap of honour, as they were cheered off to Istanbul by the supporters.

As I write this 15 years later, it is still hard to find the words to do justice to the 2005 Champions League Final played at Istanbul's Ataturk Stadium. Quality oozed from the Milan team sheet – Dida; Cafu, Maldini, Stam, Nesta; Gattuso, Pirlo, Seedorf, Kaka; Crespo, Shevchenko. They ran rings round Liverpool in the first half but, somehow, against all odds, Gerrard was hoisting aloft that beautiful silver trophy shortly after midnight local time. Liverpool's line-up was: Dudek; Finnan, Carragher, Hyypia, Traore; Garcia, Alonso, Gerrard, Riise; Kewell; Baros. In what proved to be a cataclysmic error, Benitez benched Hamann, selecting an Alonso-Gerrard axis, which was overrun in the first half. Another baffling selection was that of Kewell, who played in the number-10 role behind Baros before submitting to a groin injury on 18 minutes. Traore gave the ball away after six seconds. He conceded a free kick after 22 seconds. Andrea Pirlo whipped in an inviting ball and with Liverpool's second zonal-marking line of Riise, Alonso and Finnan too deep, skipper Paolo Maldini volleyed home from 12 yards after 50 seconds. Nightmare. "Our whole idea had been to press Milan high up the pitch and try to take advantage of their lack of pace at the back," said Benitez. "That early goal forced us into a total change of tactics." There were no further goals for 38 minutes, during which time Liverpool created little but should have had a penalty for handball by Alessandro Nesta. With the Reds still protesting, Milan broke at the speed of light. Andriy Shevchenko set up Hernan Crespo, who couldn't miss. A minute before half-time, the same player scored again with a sumptuous flick over Dudek. 3-0. "Game over," according to Andy Gray. Kaka was running riot. Liverpool faced humiliation. Gerrard noticed Gennaro Gattuso smirking and waving to fans as they left the field.

Having to deliver the most important talk of his life in a language he was still learning, Benitez momentarily lost control in the dressing room. "Shower," he said to Traore, wanting to replace him with Hamann, to gain a footing in midfield. The physio then told Benitez that Finnan might not last the game. The angry right back denied this, but the manager got Traore to put his boots back on and replaced the Irishman instead. He explained to his players that he wanted to revert to 3-5-2 but had 12 men on his whiteboard, as he had also wanted to bring Cisse on. There was no Churchillian speech, but Benitez got his tactical tweaks through to the players. Hamann would play alongside Alonso, with Gerrard pushed forward into the number-10 role. "The boss was brilliant, truly brilliant, at half-time," wrote Gerrard in 2006. The players returned to the strains of 'You'll Never Walk Alone' from defiant Liverpool supporters. In the stands, Diego Maradona remarked he had never seen support like it.

There were few tangible signs of anything changing early in the second half. Traore still looked out of his depth. Dudek saved a rasping Shevchenko free kick. But Alonso had noticed something. "Milan sat back and suddenly they weren't tight on us," he told Simon Hughes. "In the first half they'd chased the game but after the break they stopped. That allowed us space and time on the ball." Riise's left-wing cross was blocked. He had another go, and Gerrard used his neck muscles to plant a perfect header past Dida. Out of nowhere, Liverpool had a goal. Some pride was restored. Gerrard demanded more noise from the supporters. Two minutes later, with no other option, Smicer shot from 20 yards and scored his first goal of the season, with Baros getting out of the way in the nick of time. The European Cup Final was alive again. The Italians were still dazed when Baros played in Gerrard. Gattuso brought him down. Surely a red card and a penalty. Only the latter. Carragher remonstrated wildly with Mejuto Gonzalez, but Gattuso remained on the pitch. There was a brief debate over who would take the penalty. Gerrard had given up penalties after missing against Spurs - and he'd been fouled. Garcia picked up the ball. "Fuck off, Luis!" snapped Carragher. He remembered Benitez's designated choice was Alonso, who had never taken a penalty as a professional player. He was clearly nervous. Dida saved low to his right. Despair. The Spaniard smashed the rebound into the roof of the net. Joy. An explosion of unconfined joy. Liverpool had breached the world's best defence three times in six minutes. No one had seen anything like it, especially on a stage like this.

It was 3-3, and there was still half an hour to play. An hour, should it go to extra time. Riise stung Dida's palms with a crack from distance. Neither side wanted to risk much. Traore cleared off the line from Shevchenko. Carragher produced a sensational tackle on Kaka. Cisse replaced Baros. Carragher came up with another last-ditch tackle on Shevchenko. The players were exhausted. Extra-time. Gerrard moved to right back, his third position of the match, to mark the troublesome Brazilian substitute Serginho, and nullified his threat. Liverpool were shattered. There was little chance of them scoring. It was just a case of clinging on for penalties. Carragher cramped up after two heroic blocks. And then the much-maligned Dudek produced the greatest-ever piece of Liverpool goalkeeping - an astonishing double save to deny Shevchenko, with penalties just minutes away. The second was a quite unbelievable reaction save. The Pole calmly got up and nodded. "That was the save that won the Champions League," said Benitez.

As Dudek tried to focus on the impending shootout, Carragher got in his face, shouting and waving his arms, telling him to put the opposition off, Grobbelaar-style. Benitez calmly chose the kickers. Eight players wanted to take one. He discounted Alonso, Garcia and Carragher. Gerrard would be number five. Milan went first, as Liverpool had in 1984. And just like Steve Nicol in Rome, Serginho started the penalties by blazing wildly over the bar. Liverpool's advantage was cemented when, with a broken toe, Hamann drove the ball just inside Dida's right-hand post. Pirlo, the great Andrea Pirlo, had his weak shot saved by Dudek, whose antics may have distracted him. When Cisse netted, Liverpool were in dreamland at 2-0. Former Newcastle striker Jon-Dahl Tomasson pulled one back. Dida saved from Riise, who surprisingly chose to place rather than blast. Kaka scored. Suddenly it was 2-2. But Liverpool had a kick in hand. Smicer, with his last strike of a football for the club, sent Dida the wrong way. Carragher berated him for celebrating. Match point Liverpool. With the weight of the world on his shoulders, Shevchenko ran a hand through his hair. He adjusted his shirt. He went for a Panenka. Dudek wasn't fooled. He got a hand to it and pushed it back towards the devastated striker. Bedlam. Liverpool had won their fifth European Cup. The trophy was theirs to keep forever. Benitez had turned water into the finest red wine on the grandest of stages. Nothing would ever top this.

2005-06

As the celebrations went long into the summer, two issues needed to be resolved; namely Steven Gerrard's future, and whether Liverpool would be allowed to defend the trophy they had won in such sensational circumstances.

No one seemed to know for certain whether a team finishing fifth could enter the tournament as holders. It was an oversight on UEFA's part that when they extended qualification to England's top four, they hadn't factored in that the winners might finish outside that number. Liverpool had twice before qualified as holders and not via league position, in 1978 and 1981, so common sense prevailed, and the Reds were entered into the qualifying stages, although at the first round, not the third.

As for Gerrard, he had delighted Liverpool fans by saying, "How could I leave after that?" on the Ataturk pitch when asked about his future. But the club dawdled, and an offer to him hadn't been made by 1st July. Such amateurism wasn't hardly a surprise - after all, the club shop was closed the day after the final, when every item could have been sold five times over. Suddenly and unthinkably, Gerrard put in a transfer request. A young supporter burned an old 'Gerrard 17' shirt for the Sky Sports News cameras. Chelsea made an offer of £32 million. Liverpool turned it down. Gerrard believed Benitez didn't want him. Liverpool thought he wanted to leave. It was an misunderstanding borne out of poor communication, the club's lack of professionalism and the captain's relationship with the manager. Then came the transfer request. And then the U-turn. After talking it over with his father and brother, Gerrard couldn't walk away. A new offer was made, and it was signed on the day Jamie Carragher agreed his extension. The release clause was removed. Gerrard didn't want to consider leaving Liverpool again. He admitted in a podcast with Carragher in 2020 that he had regrets. "I have to accept the part that I played and the flirtation with Chelsea, and the ego and coldness between me and Rafa. Maybe with a bit of maturity or experience we could have avoided some of the shit that got out, or how far it did get. There is relief there but at the same time I probably needed to do that with Liverpool to make them realise what they've got." Gerrard offered to relinquish the captaincy. Benitez insisted he kept it.

While Gerrard stayed, others left, namely Vladimir Smicer, Mauricio Pellegrino, Igor Biscan, Antonio Nunez and Milan Baros, along with several young players who had been on the fringe of the first team under Benitez or Houllier, including

Jon Otsemobor, Richie Partridge and Gregory Vignal. Baros did feature in August before leaving for Aston Villa. El-Hadji Diouf's loan deal with Bolton was made permanent. In came Bolo Zenden on a free from Middlesbrough and Pepe Reina from Villareal for £6 million - "the best goalkeeper in Spain," according to Benitez. Mohamed Sissoko, who had played for Benitez at Valencia, signed up for £5.6 million from under the noses of Everton. He was soon followed by Southampton striker Peter Crouch for £7 million. Younger players Antonio Barragan, Miki Roque, Jack Hobbs and Besian Idrizaj also joined. Benitez was interested in Chilean winger Mark Gonzalez from Albacete but would have to wait a year for his permit. Although an improved and more consistent season lay ahead, it wasn't the recruitment of European champions. Only Reina went on to make a significant mark at the club. Benitez missed out on Nemanja Vidic, Dirk Kuyt, Simao Sabrosa and the great Luis Figo. Figo was desperate to join but Liverpool hoped to get him for nothing. Real Madrid wanted £1 million, so he went to Inter Milan, where he won four Serie A titles in four years. Portuguese winger Simao was about to fly to England to complete a £10 million move to Anfield when the Benfica president blocked the move, fearing a backlash from angry fans. It was a big loss, as he went on to knock the Reds out of the Champions League.

What wasn't in doubt was that for the first time in the Premier League era, Liverpool had a world-class manager. Benitez had arrived with a top-class reputation and enhanced it beyond anybody's wildest expectation with the events in Istanbul. Valencia plummeted without him and for a long time, fans mourned his departure. Four days after Istanbul, text messages swept among their supporters. "Sunday, match against Osasuna, homage to Benitez. Pass it on."

The season began at Anfield as early as 13th July with the first leg of the first qualifying round of the Champions League. Gerrard's hat trick saw off the Welsh champions, Total Network Solutions, who later changed their name to The New Saints FC. They were the only goals of the game. Reina was the only debutant in the 11. Steve Finnan, Jamie Carragher, Sami Hyypia and Stephen Warnock made up the defence. Darren Potter, Xabi Alonso, Gerrard and John Arne Riise were in midfield, with Anthony Le Tallec operating behind Fernando Morientes. Zenden and Djibril Cisse came off the bench.

After a 3-0 friendly win at Bayer Leverkusen, a similarly strong team got the same result at the Racecourse Ground a week later. Cisse opened the scoring. A foul on Potter gave Liverpool a penalty, but Dietmar Hamann, the man who had beaten Dida from 12 yards in Istanbul with a broken toe, failed to get his weak shot past Gerard Doherty. Gerrard, off the bench, added two more in the closing stages. Benitez praised Doherty for keeping the score down in both legs. The Reds were through 6-0 on aggregate.

Sissoko and Crouch debuted in Lithuania as the Reds beat FBK Kaunas 3-1 in the next qualifier. Cisse scored again to equalise Giedrius Barevicius's opener. Carragher's header was his first Liverpool goal for six and a half years. Gerrard knocked in a second-half penalty.

Scott Carson and Zak Whitbread started the second leg a week later. It took 77 minutes for the Reds to score, but further goals from Gerrard and Cisse wrapped up the tie. Liverpool won 5-1 on aggregate.

With so many injuries, Liverpool could only name six subs for the trip to CSKA Sofia in the third round. Cisse and Morientes had the Reds 2-0 up in half an hour. CSKA pulled one back before the Spaniard completed a 3-1 win. With the club constantly linked with a return for Michael Owen, the two scorers would have been satisfied with their recent form. Gerrard had set all three up. Full back Barragan made what would be his only Liverpool appearance as a late sub.

In the first league match, at Middlesbrough, Morientes started with Cisse and Baros on the bench. It was the latter's last involvement for the club. Florent Sinama-Pongolle was still recovering from the ACL injury picked up at Watford in January. Benitez was keen to sign Owen. They were held to a 0-0 draw, despite a red card for Boro's Ugo Ehiogu on 75 minutes. Despite seven goals in the five qualifiers so far, and numerous assists, Gerrard missed several chances at the Riverside.

Alonso netted the winner with an outstanding first-half free kick against Sunderland in the first league game at Anfield on an otherwise uninspiring afternoon. In both games, Morientes was up front on his own again and cut an isolated figure. With Baros on his way out, Crouch injured, and the Owen transfer difficult to get over the line, options up front could be thin for another season, although Cisse did have a goal wrongly disallowed. Defensively, the side looked more compact and organised. Sissoko had started promisingly in his defensive midfield role.

Just as they had done a year earlier, the Reds lost their last qualifying game at Anfield, but they had done enough to progress on aggregate. CSKA's Valentin Iliev scored the only goal on 14 minutes. Sinama-Pongolle made a welcome return after seven months injured as a late substitute. Everton were beaten over two legs by Villareal in their qualifier. After all the arguing over a five-way split over the TV money, there would be just four English teams in the Champions League group stage.

The seventh European fixture before the end of August saw the Reds win the Super Cup against CSKA Moscow. Liverpool fans sang Owen's name in the belief that he was on the verge of signing, but it was Cisse who was the match-winner. With Liverpool trailing for much of the match, he popped up with an 82nd-minute equaliser. He scored again, 13 minutes into extra-time. Then he turned provider to help Garcia clinch the game on 109 minutes. With Gerrard injured, Carragher lifted the silverware.

Owen eventually signed for Newcastle for £16 million, twice what the Reds had received from Madrid in 2004. Benitez had been keen to pair him with Crouch but wouldn't go higher than £12. Owen wasn't keen on Newcastle but was desperate for regular football in a World Cup year. He insisted on a get-out clause in his Newcastle deal should the Reds want him in the future. But even though Liverpool were light up front, with just Morientes, Crouch and Cisse, hindsight proved it was a bullet dodged. Despite being just 25, Owen's peak fitness and his best football were behind him.

Benitez reverted to two strikers - Cisse and Crouch - for the trip to Spurs, but they still failed to register a goal. A goalless draw at White Hart Lane wasn't the worst result, and with Crouch having a goal disallowed and Riise hitting the underside of the bar with a sensational volley, it could have been different. After three league games, the Reds had scored one goal and conceded none.

In his first game of the season, Florent Sinama-Pongolle scored in Liverpool's first Champions League group game. Real Betis were the opposition, and the Reds beat them 2-1 at Anfield. The young Frenchman cleverly chipped the keeper from the edge of the box inside 90 seconds. When Zenden set up Garcia for a second on 13 minutes, the Reds were flying. Sissoko was maintaining his excellent start to the season. Betis pulled one back but couldn't find another.

The low-scoring league campaign continued with the visit of Manchester United in mid-September. This turgid, goalless bore fest is best remembered for Garcia breaking Roy Keane's foot. Keane never played for United again. Liverpool were marginally the better side.

Finally some excitement in the Premier League arrived in Birmingham as the Reds drew 2-2 at St Andrews. Characteristic of the previous four league games, the game was scoreless for over an hour before Garcia placed Gerrard's pass into the bottom corner. Birmingham responded with a quick-fire double, including an own goal from Warnock. Carragher looked to have rescued a draw, but after his header hit the underside of the crossbar, it was cleared away by the hand of Neil Kilkenny, who was sent off. Cisse's penalty earned a point.

Having come through the qualifiers, Liverpool weren't protected from meeting fellow Premier League sides and, sure enough, they were grouped with Chelsea. Twenty-one weeks after that titanic semi-final, they met again at Anfield, where the Reds played out their fourth 0-0 draw in six weeks.

It was a different story when the same side came back four days later. Gerrard hammered in the equaliser in the first half, but Chelsea ran away with the points, winning 4-1 – the club's worst home league defeat since Manchester United had beaten them by the same score in 1969. Hyypia endured a rare off-day. In 13th place, Liverpool were 17 points behind Chelsea, who had played two extra games. That would eventually be cut to nine. If only Liverpool had started the campaign better.

Ten-men Blackburn were holding Liverpool to another 0-0 until the final 15 minutes of the next game at Anfield, when Cisse broke the deadlock with a free kick, nearly a year to the day since his broken leg against the same opposition. He had also drawn the professional foul which resulted in a red card for Blackburn's Zurab Khizanishvili on 33 minutes. Otherwise, he struggled, and there was little chemistry with his strike partner Crouch, who was yet to score a Liverpool goal. Morientes was faring little better and missed a sitter.

Another 1-0 win came away to Anderlecht in the Champions League. Benitez persisted with the 4-5-1 formation he had used for much of the season. Hamann, Sissoko and Alonso made a formidable midfield trio, while Cisse bagged himself another winner with a thunderous volley. It was a positive follow-up to his public complaints of a lack of opportunities.

The manager's terrible away league record surfaced again, as the Reds were sunk 2-0 at Craven Cottage. Collins John scored after half an hour. Tony Warner, Liverpool's one-time back-up goalkeeper, replaced the injured Mark Crossley and made saves from Morientes, Garcia, Hyypia and Cisse. Luis Boa Morte wrapped up the win in the closing stages. Gerrard hadn't played since the Chelsea game. Kewell started for the first time since Istanbul. The Reds were 12th, just four points above the drop zone. Benitez's away record in the Premier League now stood at five wins from 23 matches.

He lost on his travels again when Liverpool were eliminated from the League Cup at the first hurdle. They were beaten 2-1 by lower-division Crystal Palace. Scott Carson, David Raven, Zak Whitbread and Darren Potter all started. The returning Gerrard scored a 40th-minute equaliser. Marco Reich won the game for Palace halfway through the second half. With so many European games having been squeezed into the campaign already and a trip to Japan to come, Benitez probably didn't lose much sleep over the defeat. He didn't believe either performance in London merited a defeat.

Happily, the Reds were about to embark on the first of two long winning streaks in the league. This particular sequence began at home to West Ham. Benitez had by now reverted to selecting two strikers but on this occasion Cisse and Morientes drew blanks. Alonso scored a brilliant opener, albeit with the aid of a deflection. Hyypia hit an upright. Garcia had a 20-yarder tipped around the post. Zenden made it two with his first for the club, cutting in from the left and hammering it into the far corner. Gerrard played on the right, where he would figure for much of the season, with considerable success.

Anderlecht were beaten again in Europe, this time 3-0 at Anfield. Morientes, Garcia and Cisse bagged the goals which virtually secured qualification to the knockout stages. Garcia's goal was a phenomenal header at the Kop end from Finnan's cross. Crouch's barren run continued. An Anderlecht player was sent off for racially abusing Sissoko and was banned for three games.

The Reds needed two late goals to win a Saturday lunchtime kick-off at Villa Park. Future Red James Milner almost got former Red Milan Baros through on goal, but Carragher made one of his trademark tackles. Substitute Crouch won a penalty on 84 minutes, which was converted by Gerrard on his 300th Liverpool appearance. Alonso made it 2-0 in the last minute with a thumping shot from the edge of the box.

A 3-0 win over Portsmouth saw Liverpool move into the top half of the table for the first time since August. There was a moment of tragicomedy for Crouch who, despite the presence of Gerrard and Cisse, took a 23rd-minute penalty to rid himself of the albatross around his neck. The kick was saved, Zenden scored from the rebound and a devastated Crouch was obliged to look happy and join in the celebrations. Cisse added a fluke when a right-wing cross sailed into the top corner. Morientes wrapped up an easy win with ten minutes left.

Qualification to the Champions League last 16 was secured with a 0-0 draw at home to Betis. Hyypia and Carragher were commanding at the back. Crouch played well but still couldn't score. A knee injury ended Zenden's season.

A 1-0 win away to Manchester City took the ever-improving Reds into seventh. Nine clean sheets in 12 league matches was a new club record. The goal came from Riise on his 150th league appearance after a one-two with Gerrard. Liverpool were 15 points from the summit, albeit with two games in hand. They were just two away from Manchester United in fourth.

Liverpool moved ahead of Bolton, Tottenham and Wigan and into the top four by winning a midweek game at Sunderland. An exquisite volleyed through ball on the turn by Alonso set up Garcia for the first. Gerrard made it two from another stunning assist by the Spanish playmaker. Although Sissoko was red-carded midway through the second half, Sunderland had little to offer. Riise hit the bar after a great run. Benitez's 4-4-2, with Gerrard on the right, was starting to pay off. All that was missing was a goal for Crouch.

The big moment finally came in his 19th game and there was still an element of comedy about it. At 1,229 goalless minutes, Crouch had beaten Arthur Rowley's record of 1,019 from 1954 for how long it took a Liverpool striker to get off the mark. He drove at the Wigan defence and let fly from 20 yards. The ball hit a defender and looped over Mike Pollitt, who tried to tip it over the bar and only managed to help it into the net. Crouch celebrated like he'd won the Champions League, but would it go down as his goal? No one knew at the time, but it eventually did. Twenty-three minutes later, he bagged another with a clever side-footed lob. Garcia made it 3-0.

With Benitez reverting to 4-5-1, Liverpool drew another Champions League match with Chelsea 0-0. Michael Essien was fortunate to stay on the pitch after a horror tackle on Hamann, who called it "the worst tackle I have ever received." Neither side created much. Liverpool finished top of the group. Chelsea came second.

Back in the league, a couple of late Morientes goals at home to Middlesbrough moved the Reds into second, 12 points behind Chelsea with a game in hand. The Reds had now gone ten games without conceding a goal.

The next stop was Japan for the Club World Cup. A club-record 11th clean sheet was achieved against Deportivo Saprissa in Yokohama as the Reds won through to the final of the competition. Crouch scored two impressive goals in a routine 3-0 win over the Costa Ricans, showed live on the BBC. Gerrard scored the other with a fierce volley.

After 1,041 minutes, Reina finally conceded a goal. It came against Sao Paulo in the final, and it was enough for the Brazilians to win the trophy. It was the club's third appearance in the final, after defeats to Flamengo in 1981 and Independiente three years later. Liverpool dominated the final, having 21 shots, 17 corners, three disallowed goals, two attempts that came back off the bar and a penalty appeal turned down. The last-minute disallowing of Sinama-Pongolle's goal for an apparent offside against Garcia was a very tight call. Two days before the final, Benitez's father, Francisco, had died. With funerals in Spain taking place so quickly after death, Benitez decided to remain in Japan with the team. The players enjoyed a night out after the final. Hamann and Carragher were arrested. Carragher managed to get away after Liverpool fans created a diversion. Hamann spent the night in police custody.

While Liverpool were in Japan, Robert Kraft, the owner of New England Patriots, withdrew his interest in buying the club. Moores and Parry had been very keen to deal with him. Moores was still keen to sell, so Liverpool could compete at the top end of the transfer market and either redevelop Anfield or move elsewhere.

Worries that the 6,000-mile trip could destabilise the Reds were immediately dispelled with a routine home win over Newcastle. Michael Owen made his first appearance against the Reds and endured such taunts as "Where were you in Istanbul?" and "You should have signed for a big club!" Gerrard and Crouch scored in the first half. Lee Bowyer was sent off in the second half for a poor challenge on Alonso. Owen didn't get into the game all afternoon. "I've never felt as low in my life, sitting in the players' lounge afterwards, with my family and my mum in tears," he told Simon Hughes. Gerrard and Carragher criticised the fans' behaviour.

The Reds were magnificent at Goodison two days later. It was true that Everton were struggling, but form has rarely counted for much in such games. Crouch and Gerrard scored a couple of fabulous goals in the first 18 minutes. James Beattie got one back just before half-time, but Cisse wrapped up the win two minutes into the second half, curling the ball into the far corner. The Blues ended up with nine men after Phil Neville and Mikel Arteta were sent off.

A momentous year ended with a convincing performance over Bryan Robson's West Brom at Anfield. Having come so close so many times in the first half, Crouch scored the only goal on 51 minutes, heading in Kewell's inch-perfect cross. The gifted Australian was afforded a rare standing ovation when he was substituted. Liverpool battered Albion but Tomasz Kuszczak was in great form. It was the tenth league win in a row, leaving the Reds in third, four points behind Manchester United and 15 behind Chelsea. The Reds had two games in hand over both.

The winning run came to an end at Bolton when mistakes from Reina and Hyypia handed the hosts an early gift. Gerrard won a penalty and converted it himself on 67 minutes. But El-Hadji Diouf, of all people, restored the advantage for Bolton, with the ball going in off his shoulder. Garcia scored a brilliant equaliser on 82. Cisse was just wide with a late header as Liverpool had to settle for a 2-2 draw.

A quite amazing game at Luton was the beginning of a journey that would take the club to their seventh FA Cup success. When Gerrard put the Reds one up with a sumptuous curler on 15 minutes, a routine win seemed likely. He didn't even celebrate. But incredibly, Luton were 3-1 up by the 53rd minute, with Cisse having missed a penalty. Liverpool had exited the competition on this ground in 1987, and the same outcome was looking increasingly likely here. But Sinama-Pongolle narrowed the deficit and Alonso scored from over 35 yards. Sinama-Pongolle headed the Reds into the lead with 17 minutes left before Alonso put the icing on the cake in injury time by scoring from at least 60 yards with his weaker foot to take the final score to 5-3. Liverpool fan Adrian Hayward won £25,000, having staked £200 at 125-1 that the Spaniard would score from his own half during the 2005-06 season.

After Liverpool had conceded five goals to Bolton and Luton, things returned to normal with a 1-0 win over Spurs. And it was Kewell who maintained his recent form with a stupendous volley in front of the Kop for his first goal in over a year. He watched Finnan's deep cross onto his left foot and smashed it inside Paul Robinson's near post. Reina made a crucial late save from Mido to preserve the points.

Liverpool went to Old Trafford on a high, just a point behind United with two games in hand. Their opponents had just lost the Manchester derby 3-1 with Robbie Fowler scoring the last goal of the game for City. "You'll lose again next week!" he shouted at United's players. Alas, it didn't happen. Benitez's men were the better side, but when Cisse blazed over from three yards with Edwin van der Sar stranded, a goalless draw looked likely. Even that was denied to Liverpool when Rio Ferdinand scored a thumping injury-time header from a set piece. Gary Neville ran the length of the pitch to goad the Liverpool fans.

In the new transfer window, Benitez signed defenders Jan Kromkamp and Daniel Agger, as well as youngsters Paul Anderson and David Martin. The most exciting of the quartet was Agger, who cost £5.8 million. Then, out of the blue, on the 27th of the month, the Reds announced that Robbie Fowler would be returning to the club on a free transfer from Manchester City. He was certainly no longer the player who had scored so freely between 1993 and 1997, but he would be a welcome addition to Benitez's striker options, signing for the rest of the season. "To get the call to come back, you can imagine how happy I was," said Fowler, who had been in Istanbul as a fan. Out went John Welsh and Josemi.

The fourth round of the FA Cup took the Reds to Fratton Park, where they beat Portsmouth 2-1. Kromkamp went straight into Finnan's right-back position but Fowler was cup-tied. A penalty for handball was put away by Gerrard. Riise added a brilliant second before half-time. Pompey got one back, but the Reds held on.

Fowler received a raucous welcome when he came on for his second Liverpool debut as a 64th-minute sub at home to Birmingham. Gerrard had just put the Reds a goal up from Morientes' pullback. The roof almost came off the Kop when Fowler replaced Crouch, but the evening would end in disappointment.

Alonso scored a late own goal, and a late overhead winner from the returning hero was disallowed for offside. Agger also made his debut, with Carragher on the bench.

A trip to the champions saw more league points dropped. Goals from William Gallas and Hernan Crespo sealed a 2-0 win for Chelsea before Reina was sent off for pushing Arjen Robben in the face. The winger's play-acting angered Benitez, who pledged to visit him in hospital. Liverpool were 21 points adrift, albeit with two games in hand.

A three-match suspension for Reina meant a return for Istanbul hero Dudek, but he conceded twice just before the break in a 0-2 defeat at Charlton. With Gerrard absent, Liverpool were woeful and had no answer. Fowler made his second appearance, as a substitute for Crouch. The Reds had wobbled since Ferdinand's goal at Old Trafford, picking up just one point from 12.

Fowler made his first start at Wigan, where the Reds got back to winning ways. Hyypia scored the only goal on the half-hour mark, with the assist coming from his centre-half partner Carragher. A great save from Dudek prevented an own goal by the Finn. Managed by former Red Paul Jewell, newly promoted Wigan were in seventh and were enjoying a superb season.

Valentine's Night produced an exciting game against Arsenal and a thoroughly deserved 1-0 victory. Gerrard had a penalty saved, but the Reds kept up the pressure, and when substitute Hamann shot from distance, the otherwise outstanding Jens Lehmann could only parry. Garcia bundled in an 87th-minute winner. He had only been on the field for three minutes. Eighteen months on from their unbeaten champion season in 2004, the Gunners weren't quite the same force. The Reds were ten points clear of them.

A third 1-0 win in a row produced one of the highlights of the season. Just weeks after his ignominious celebration at Old Trafford, Gary Neville would have to face the Anfield crowd in the fifth round of the FA Cup. Kewell barged him off the field in the opening minutes to set the tone. In Alonso's absence, Hamann produced another big-game performance. Finnan, too, was excellent. The Reds took the lead with an 18th-minute Crouch header that went in via both posts. It was the first goal from one of the club's centre forwards since New Year's Eve. Liverpool failed to add to the lead but getting into the quarter-finals was all that mattered. It also gave Benitez his first win over United after four straight losses. The game, however, is best remembered for Alan Smith having his leg broken when charging down a thunderous free kick from Riise in the closing stages. Reds fans were accused of trying to push over Smith's ambulance as they left the stadium, but the local ambulance service denied any knowledge of this, as did Smith in a subsequent interview with FourFourTwo magazine.

A trip to Portugal in the last 16 of the Champions League produced a disappointing 1-0 defeat at Benfica. Surprisingly, Benitez went with a 4-4-2 formation, with an unwell Gerrard benched along with Hamann. Sissoko partnered Alonso, with Morientes and Fowler up front. The Portuguese were nothing special, but the Reds were below par and went down to a late header from Luisao. It was a costly defeat. Sissoko sustained an eye injury which appeared to threaten his whole career at one point.

Kewell scored the only goal in a home win over Manchester City, with Reina making a spectacular save from Trevor Sinclair to safeguard the points. Crouch hit the bar late in the game. Joey Barton was sent off on 52 minutes for two yellow cards, but the Reds couldn't get another. He was the ninth player of the season to be sent off against Liverpool.

More dropped points against Charlton followed, with a 0-0 draw at Anfield. This time Benitez picked Cisse on the wing, with Fowler partnering Crouch, but according to Through the Wind and Rain, the performance "carried on the current trend of all-out attack, feeble finishing and inspired opposition goalkeepers." Fowler had a goal wrongly disallowed for offside.

The Reds bowed out of the Champions League, as Benfica won 2-0 at Anfield in the second leg of the last-16 tie. Liverpool were weakened by the absence of Hyypia, who had played every minute of 57 consecutive European games, dating back to 2001. He was replaced by Traore. Benitez again dropped Hamann and went with two strikers - Crouch and the struggling Morientes. Garcia blazed over a big chance to level up the aggregate score. The killer goal, which left Liverpool needing three, came from summer target Simao Sabrosa in the 36th minute as he beat Reina brilliantly from 25 yards. Crouch's header came back off the post. Gerrard slid a late chance wide, and the Portuguese wrapped up a 3-0 aggregate win in the last minute. But the disappointed home fans gave the players a standing ovation, recognising the mark they had made in Europe over the last 18 months. Alonso described it as his favourite Liverpool memory. "The game was over, but we stayed on the pitch for a long time," he said. "The fans gave us an impressive round of applause and we almost cried when they sang 'You'll Never Walk Alone'. My heart was breaking because we couldn't repay all those people for their love."

The final defeat of the season came in mid-March at Arsenal. Benitez had now lost all six of his league visits to Old Trafford, Stamford Bridge and Highbury. Thierry Henry scored a sublime opener. Alonso went close with a swerving shot from distance. Garcia headed in a rebound from Gerrard's long shot on 75 minutes. But the Reds shot themselves in the foot. Alonso was sent off, and Gerrard played a terrible back pass straight to Henry who rounded Reina to score with seven minutes left. The Reds were now five points off United in second, having played a game more.

Fowler finally got off the mark, with a close-range header in a 5-1 rout of Fulham at Anfield. His first-ever Liverpool goal had come against the same opposition in 1993. Fulham equalised, but a Michael Brown own goal from Kewell's cross restored the lead. Morientes made it 3-1 on 70 minutes, turning in a rebound from close range. The last two goals came right at the end, with Crouch cleverly flicking in from close range and Warnock slamming home a rebound from Finnan's shot for his only Liverpool goal. He'd only been on the pitch for two minutes. The best news for Liverpool was Benitez agreeing a new four-year deal with the club, eliminating rumours he may go to Real Madrid, who were reportedly willing to double his wage.

The Spaniard experimented with three centre halves – Hyypia, Carragher and Agger - for the trip to Newcastle, for whom Michael Owen was absent with injury. Kromkamp and Warnock were the wing backs. Gerrard was in the middle, partnering Hamann, with Alonso benched. The Spanish playmaker hadn't quite hit the heights of his debut season. Sissoko was still absent with his eye injury. Crouch scored on ten minutes from Kromkamp's cross and then assisted Gerrard, who finished clinically after a one-two. The Geordies pulled one back, but a professional foul on Crouch led to a red card for Jean-Alain Boumsong. Cisse's penalty made it 3-1. The Frenchman was enduring an up-and-down season. He had scored 11 goals by the end of November but had fallen down the pecking order.

After eight goals in two games, the Reds scored nearly as many in 90 minutes as they reached the FA Cup semi-final in style. They were two up in five minutes at St Andrews against a hopelessly outclassed Birmingham, against whom Benitez hadn't won in four league matches. Liverpool went on to win 7-0. Hyypia headed home inside a minute. Crouch added two more in the first half. The goals after the break came from Morientes, Riise, Cisse and an own goal from Olivier Tebily. It was comfortably Benitez's biggest win as manager, and there was a welcome return for Sissoko, who wore protective glasses.

The superb form continued as Liverpool beat Everton 3-1, despite the early sending-off of Gerrard for two bookings. Wearing '08' on his back to promote the 2008 European Capital of Culture initiative, he booted the ball into the crowd on 17 minutes, frustrated at Everton being awarded a free kick. Then, from that set piece, he stupidly ploughed into Kevin Kilbane and his derby was over. "He needs to learn for the future," said Benitez. "He is very disappointed at letting the team down." Everton fans celebrated his exit like a winning goal, but their players lost their bottle, unable to handle becoming favourites to win. Having lost their shape, they gifted the Reds an opener when Phil Neville headed into his own goal on the stroke of half-time. One hundred seconds into the second half, Garcia doubled the lead with a brilliant lob over Richard Wright. Cahill got in front of Crouch to get one back, as he had done in the Anfield derby a year earlier. Carragher shoved Crouch and called him an idiot. Crouch believed Sissoko was at fault. An Alonso free kick hit the bar. Andy van der Meyde was then sent for an early bath for elbowing the outstanding Alonso in the face. David Moyes held his head in his hands, knowing Everton were done for. Kewell sealed the match with a sensational 25-yarder which fizzed into the far corner. Gerrard hogged the headlines, but Liverpool's domination despite a numerical disadvantage was wonderfully impressive. The Liverpool v Everton fixture had now seen 14 Premier League red cards, four ahead of Aston Villa v Newcastle.

Another game, another win, as the Reds won 2-0 at West Brom. From Cisse's pass, Fowler scored his 173rd Liverpool goal to move ahead of Kenny Dalglish into fifth place in the club's goalscoring list. Ian Rush, Roger Hunt, Gordon

Hodgson and Billy Liddell remained ahead of him. Cisse got the second before half-time from Alonso's 60-yard pass.

Fowler was on the mark a week later when the Reds downed Bolton 1-0 at Anfield. Just before half-time, he found the bottom corner of the Anfield Road goal to give Liverpool their fifth league win in a row.

A week later, the day after the 17th anniversary of Hillsborough, Fowler notched again as Blackburn were beaten by the same score at Ewood Park. In something of a rarity for this fixture, Blackburn didn't have anyone sent off, although Cisse, who hit the woodwork twice, was the victim of an ugly challenge from Lucas Neill. Successive winners went a long way to ensure Benitez handed Fowler another year. Carragher was a rock at the back again.

For the second year in a row, Liverpool beat Mourinho's Chelsea in a major semi-final, this time in the FA Cup at Old Trafford. The Londoners failed to deal with the presence of Kewell, who had a magnificent day – their narrow diamond formation was easily exploited by Liverpool's width. Riise scored on 21 minutes with a low free kick. Garcia made it two by breaking away and shooting early to surprise Petr Cech. This one definitely crossed the line. Didier Drogba's goal from Riise's error on 70 minutes led to a nervy end, especially when Joe Cole blasted over, but Liverpool held on to book a final date with West Ham in Cardiff. Liverpool couldn't beat Chelsea or United in the league but had beaten both in the cup. "We can compete with Chelsea for one game but not for nine months," said Benitez. "If we have two or three new players, maybe we can be contenders." Mourinho blanked Benitez after the game, failing to acknowledge him or congratulate him on reaching the final. Twenty-four hours later, Gerrard was named the PFA Player of the Year. He and Carragher were voted into the Premier League Team of the Season.

The Reds met Alan Pardew's Hammers four days later in a league game where a red card for Garcia, just a minute after he came onto the field, ruled him out of the final. West Ham's Hayden Mullins befell the same fate, with the same consequence, both for violent conduct. From the left wing, Cisse scored both goals in a 2-1 win. Benitez had the luxury of making eight changes from the semi-final.

Aston Villa were Liverpool's next victims as they found themselves 1-0 down at Anfield inside four minutes. Alonso slid a perfect through ball to Morientes, who turned Gary Cahill inside out and found the corner of the net. It was a shame Morientes wasn't able to produce more of that in his 18 months at the club. Gareth Barry tapped in an equaliser in the second half, but his goal only served as a cue for Gerrard to win the game with a rapid brace, the second of which, from 25 yards, was one of the goals of the season. He had now hit 20, not bad for a player who had spent much of his time on the right of midfield. Benitez spoke of his captain establishing himself "as the best midfield player in the world" during the forthcoming World Cup. Twenty-year-old James Milner stood out for Villa with some inch-perfect crosses.

LIVERPOOL F.C. **THE PREMIER LEAGUE YEARS**

Liverpool won their last league game of the season 3-1 at Portsmouth, as they ended up in third place on 82 points, one behind Manchester United and nine behind Chelsea. It had been a 37-point gap in 2005. The indifferent start had cost Benitez a shot at the title. Alonso was stretchered off on 41 minutes with an ankle injury. The goals came in the second half, with Fowler opening the scoring, turning in Morientes' pass. Crouch scored the team's 100th goal of the season after Cisse's low cross was parried by Dean Kiely. Pompey pulled one back, before Cisse wrapped up the league campaign after beating the offside trap. This 11th win on the bounce equalled a club record set between February and April 1989.

Ten years on from winning their first FA Youth Cup, Liverpool were in the final again, against Manchester City, having overcome Cardiff, Ipswich, Burnley, Carlisle and Southampton. The Reds won the first leg of the final 3-0, with Robbie Threlfall, Ryan Flynn and Miki Roque getting on the scoresheet. Two goals from Daniel Sturridge made it a nervy second leg, but they won the cup 3-2 on aggregate. Stephen Darby and Jay Spearing were also in the Liverpool squad.

With shades of Istanbul, Liverpool came back from the brink to win a wonderful, madcap 125th FA Cup Final. The skipper played the match of his life, scoring two fantastic goals, with many naming the match "The Gerrard Final". Sissoko was also superb. The quality of Cisse's strike is often forgotten, but his magnificent volley, from Gerrard's exquisite cross-field ball, got Liverpool on the board when they were desperate. There were other parallels with Istanbul – Kewell went off injured, Hamann came off the bench to stiffen the midfield and extra time saw an astonishing late save from a Liverpool goalkeeper before the Reds triumphed on penalties.

Benitez's line-up was: Reina; Finnan, Carragher, Hyypia, Riise; Gerrard, Sissoko, Alonso, Kewell; Cisse, Crouch. According to Guillem Balague's book, Season on the Brink, Benitez and his staff knew before the game that some of the players were not in the right frame of mind. "A key member of the Liverpool backroom staff cast a worrying look over the players and confided to a colleague that some of the assembled squad were about to fail the team," wrote Balague. "He reeled off the names one by one: 'His mindset is not right; neither is his, or his, or his. They are scared. We are going to struggle.'" It was a surprising observation given the team had just amassed 82 league points, but he was obviously correct, as the Reds found themselves 2-0 down before half an hour had been played. Reina, Finnan, Hyypia, Riise, Alonso and Kewell were all below their best. Alonso, hampered by his ankle injury, conceded possession to Yossi Benayoun in the 20th minute, and a quick Hammers transition ended with a Carragher own goal. Seven minutes later, Reina fumbled Matthew Etherington's tame shot from the edge of the area. Dean Ashton followed it in. West Ham had too much pace for Liverpool. Benayoun was playing magnificently. Benitez reverted to 4-5-1, switching Cisse to the left. Crouch had a goal wrongly disallowed for offside on the half hour, but Cisse's tremendous volley a minute later from Gerrard's beautifully flighted 30-yard pass halved the deficit. It was the French striker's last Liverpool game.

Reina made a crucial double save from Marlon Harewood and Benayoun in the first minute of the second half. Morientes replaced Kewell. Liverpool were soon back on terms. Alonso floated a ball into the box, and Crouch's nod down was smashed into the top of the net by Gerrard from 13 yards in the 54th minute. He had now scored in the finals of the UEFA Cup, the League Cup, the Champions League and the FA Cup. Incredibly, West Ham came back and went 3-2 up ten minutes later with another hugely fortuitous goal as Paul Konchesky's misdirected cross flew over Reina and into the net. Alonso was replaced by Kromkamp, with Gerrard playing centrally. Hamann came on for Crouch, giving the skipper the freedom to roam forward, but he cramped up on 84 minutes and could barely walk. Exhausted, he skewed a late 30-yard free kick high and wide to the jeers of the Cockney fans, who thought their heroes were home and dry. The 40-year-old Teddy Sheringham came on to help close the game out. As the game entered four minutes of injury time, Cisse collapsed with cramp. West Ham cleared from their right-back area. Riise sent a high diagonal ball into the area. It came back out to Gerrard, a footballing genius at the peak of his powers. Riddled with cramp and barely able to walk, he let fly from 35 yards and scored one of the greatest cup-final goals in living memory. A wide-eyed Riise ran to him shouting, "I can't believe it!" West Ham manager Alan Pardew, who'd scored the winner against the Reds for Crystal Palace in the 1990 FA Cup semi-final, was stunned. 3-3. Extra-time.

With energy levels barely above zero, extra time was played at testimonial pace, sometimes with cramp-ridden bodies strewn across the pitch, awaiting treatment. Finnan and Sissoko were badly affected. Gerrard and Cisse were still struggling. Carragher went down too. Physically, West Ham looked to be in better shape. Benayoun was running around as though the game was only ten minutes old. Having kicked off in mid-July, Liverpool's season was in its 11th month, and it was showing. Riise was a whisker away with a 30-yard piledriver. Cisse miscontrolled Morientes' header when he was almost certain to score. Hyypia almost scored a goal that would have been better than Gerrard's. Anton Ferdinand, brother of Rio, cut out a cross when Morientes was inches away from making it 4-3. But it was West Ham's only attack of the added period that came closest to winning the game. Nigel Reo-Coker's header was acrobatically touched onto the post by Reina. Hyypia tried to clear the rebound but missed his kick. The ball fell invitingly to Harewood, who had been unable to walk minutes earlier. The unguarded goal was five yards away, with Reina stranded. He cocked his left foot, ready to win West Ham's first FA Cup in 26 years. He miskicked hopelessly, and that was that. Alan Wiley's whistle signalled penalties.

Hamann went first in the penalty shootout, and with his last kick of a ball for the club, he found the net. Reina saved brilliantly from Bobby Zamora. Hyypia's unconvincing side-footer was saved by Shaka Hislop. Teddy Sheringham levelled the scores. Gerrard's penalty was perfectly placed. Reina saved from Konchesky. Still scarred by his miss a year earlier, Riise smashed his penalty straight down the middle. Liverpool were almost home and dry. Ferdinand was the third player to have his kick saved by Reina, and the cup was Liverpool's, for the seventh time. "We knew with Reina in goal we had a fantastic chance of winning it," said Gerrard, who received English football's most famous trophy from a sombre-looking Prince William.

The players' celebrations were nothing like they had been in Istanbul. They had been slightly lucky to beat West Ham, but it was just reward for an excellent season. Two years in, and Benitez was doing a great job.

2006-07

"John Arne Riise has just come to my room to say you attacked him with a golf club."

Rafa Benitez had improved Liverpool beyond recognition from Gerard Houllier's last couple of seasons, but it was more to do with tactical tweaks than the quality of his signings. Using Jamie Carragher at centre back rather than full back, where Houllier had played him, was a masterstroke. Using Steven Gerrard further up the pitch, with two central midfielders behind him, paid similar dividends. Benitez's zonal marking and rotation raised eyebrows among tactically inept former players in the media, but Liverpool supporters very quickly had complete faith in the former Valencia boss.

In two years, Benitez had recruited shrewdly in Xabi Alonso, Pepe Reina and Daniel Agger, but his attacking signings hadn't been the best. If Liverpool were going to challenge for the 2006-07 title, he needed to bring in some top-drawer attacking talent. But he failed. He chose Jermaine Pennant over Dani Alves, so he would have enough money left to sign a striker - a calamitous misjudgement. Dirk Kuyt would prove to be a popular player, but largely for his work ethic rather than his ability to prise open mean defences. Craig Bellamy only lasted a season. Young wingers Mark Gonzalez, whose work permit had finally come through, and Nabil El Zhar didn't come up to scratch. Signings from the previous season like Peter Crouch, Bolo Zenden and an ageing Robbie Fowler were nowhere near title-winning standard.

Other new signings included Brazilian left back Fabio Aurelio, who had been at Valencia with Benitez, on a free, and the young Argentinian centre back Gabriel Paletta. Liverpool would later be linked with Blackburn right back Lucas Neill, Carragher's bête noire, but he plumped for West Ham. Out went Fernando Morientes, Didi Hamann, Djimi Traore, Neil Mellor, Jan Kromkamp, Bruno Cheyrou, and a handful of young players. Djibril Cisse went to Marseille on loan and didn't play for Liverpool again.

The most significant story of the season would be David Moores selling the club to Tom Hicks and George Gillette. The Americans mortgaged the club to the hilt and their ownership so nearly ended in administration. Chaos and civil war would dominate the next few years.

Pre-season saw Pepe Reina appear in midfield in the closing stages of a 3-2 defeat to Kaiserslautern. A full-strength Liverpool was then subjected to a 5-0 hammering at the hands of German side Mainz, who were managed by a certain

Jurgen Klopp. The real action began with the visit of Israeli side Maccabi Haifa in the first leg of the third qualifying round of the Champions League. In front of Reina was a back four of Steve Finnan, Hyypia, Carragher and John Arne Riise. Momo Sissoko and Alonso were in midfield, with Pennant and Zenden on the wings. Gerrard played behind the lone striker Bellamy. With so much cash riding on Champions League qualification, it was alarming to see the Reds fall behind to a Gustavo Boccoli goal on the half hour. Bellamy quickly equalised after Sissoko's shot had been parried. It took them until the 88th minute to find a winner and it came from the Chilean Gonzalez, who had spent six months of 2005-06 on loan at Real Sociedad, awaiting his permit. He'd only been on the pitch for two minutes when he finished off Alonso's deep pass at the far post.

Benitez benched Gerrard, Alonso, Bellamy and Hyypia for the Community Shield against Chelsea. They still managed to beat the champions, who fielded new signings Michael Ballack and Andriy Shevchenko. Riise scored an incredible goal on nine minutes, running over 60 yards before firing in from distance. Shevchenko equalised before half-time, but Liverpool gained a deserved victory when Crouch headed in Bellamy's cross with ten minutes to go. The outstanding Sissoko dominated Chelsea's midfield of Ballack, Essien and Lampard. Debutant Aurelio was one of five substitutes who were introduced in the second half. Carragher and Gerrard lifted the shield together.

Disappointingly, the first league game of the season yielded only a draw at newly promoted Sheffield United. It set the tone for a season when Liverpool didn't win on the road until December. By then a shot at the title was long gone. Benitez operated a 4-4-2, with Gerrard in midfield alongside Sissoko in the absence of Alonso. Gerrard took several months to get going in the 2006-07 season. Riise and Carragher succumbed to first-half injuries. United's Rob Hulse scored straight after the break following terrible marking at a free kick. Hyypia hit a post. Gerrard then stormed into the penalty area after a one-two with Fowler. He had to take evasive action to avoid Chris Morgan's rash tackle, lost his footing and was awarded a penalty, which Fowler converted. The post-match interviews were dominated by Neil Warnock's predictably irascible reaction to the decision, but he failed to acknowledge that Morgan, who had already been booked, got nowhere near the ball and should have received at least a second yellow.

The second leg of the Maccabi tie was played in Kiev because of the political situation in Israel. For a third consecutive year, Liverpool were made to sweat at this stage of the competition. Pennant set up a close-range header for Crouch. Maccabi soon equalised. Another goal would force extra-time, but the score remained 1-1. The Reds were through 3-2 on aggregate.

The Kop celebrated its 100th birthday as the Reds beat West Ham 2-1. Bobby Zamora scored first, smashing the ball towards goal from the wing. Reina could only parry it into the net. Aurelio had been caught out in the build-up. Agger equalised with an incredible shot. Receiving the ball in the centre circle, he took a few steps and unleashed a rocket into the top corner. The Cup Final pattern was continuing – West Ham scoring flukes, Liverpool scoring gems. And then, on the stroke of half-time, Crouch showed his nimbleness in rounding Roy Carroll and slotting home the winner. Debutant Kuyt displayed an abundance of energy as a second-half sub, not least when he took a free kick to himself and dribbled at a bemused West Ham defence.

It hadn't been the worst start to the season, but the next game provided a huge wake-up call. In a third consecutive lunchtime kick-off in the league, Liverpool suffered their worst defeat to Everton since 1964. The 3-0 score didn't reflect how the game had gone, but the returning Carragher was off the pace, and Reina made a comical error at the end. The out-of-form keeper was tempted to return to Spain with Valencia until Benitez talked him around. Riise made his comeback as a sub, but then twisted his ankle again. Everton were so delighted to win a derby, they released a DVD of the game.

Having signed for PSV Eindhoven, Kromkamp lined up against the Reds in a 0-0 draw in the first Champions League group game. Eindhoven hit the bar after an error from Sissoko. Kuyt and Gerrard hit the post.

The blip continued at Stamford Bridge, where Benitez suffered his fifth successive league defeat to Mourinho. Ballack was sent off for imposing his studs on Sissoko's thigh. The Reds created several chances, but Gerrard, Crouch and Kuyt spurned the best of them. Didier Drogba's brilliant shot on the turn from 20 yards was the only goal of a niggly game. Liverpool were 15th, nine points behind surprise leaders Portsmouth, albeit with a game in hand. For the third year in a row under Benitez, they were miles off the pace after a slow start.

The Reds enjoyed their first win in nearly a month when two goals, memorable for different reasons, saw off Newcastle. Michael Owen missed another Liverpool reunion after a World Cup injury. Kuyt got off the mark when he slid home a right-wing cross from Finnan. Garcia hit a post in his 100th game for the club. Kuyt spurned an easy header, but none of that mattered when Alonso won a tackle 60 yards out, looked up, and chipped the goalkeeper Steve Harper. It was an astonishing goal.

In a game of two terrible misses, it took an hour for Liverpool to break down struggling Spurs at Anfield. Kuyt hit a post in the first half. After an hour, Jermaine Jenas somehow failed to convert an open goal from five yards. A minute later, Gerrard prised open up the Spurs defence. Bellamy hit the post from two yards with the goal gaping, but Gonzalez slammed in the rebound. The impressive Kuyt made it two with a fierce drive. The returning Riise scored a magnificent third from 35 yards in the last minute. Spurs, with Danny Murphy, were just a point clear of the relegation zone. The Reds were up to sixth.

Three more Anfield goals were scored against Galatasaray in the Champions League. Crouch got two of them – the second a stunning scissor kick – which prompted Through the Wind and Rain to note "he looked like a daddy longlegs on fire." Garcia scored in between. Kuyt hit the post again. But the Reds eased off, with second-half sub Umit Karan scoring twice with a quarter of the game still to play. With the Turks in the ascendency and creating havoc on the wings, Liverpool were relieved to hear the final whistle.

The winning run came to a shuddering halt with a 2-0 defeat at Bolton - a third defeat in seven league games. As poor as Liverpool were, the first goal was unlucky, as the assistant referee believed Reina had carried the ball out of his area before kicking downfield. He was wrong. Gary Speed knocked in the free kick. The Reds lost another goal after the break. For the seventh match in a row, someone hit the woodwork – this time it was Alonso from 20 yards. The hard-luck stories were mounting up. Benitez was facing mounting criticism for his rotation policy, with four changes for this game and Gerrard out of position on the left. He had made at least one change to his starting line-up for 94 consecutive matches.

Another disappointing result came at home to Blackburn after an international break. Crouch had a shot cleared off the line. Benny McCarthy put Rovers 1-0 up on 17 minutes after inept defending from Finnan and the out-of-form Reina. Craig Bellamy headed his first league goal for the Reds just after the hour. He had endured a frustrating time since his debut goal against Maccabi. There was no winner to follow. The Reds were tenth, eight points behind leaders Chelsea.

Crouch scored the only goal from Bellamy's corner as the Reds won in south-west France against Bordeaux. Warnock missed a late chance to seal the win. It was a dreadful performance, but Liverpool were in a strong position in the group.

Any chance of winning title number 19 was surely gone when a tame performance saw the Reds lose 2-0 at Old Trafford. Only a point had separated the teams in May 2006, but it was clear it would be the Red Devils challenging Chelsea's supremacy, not Benitez and his players. Gonzalez was out of his depth on the wing, lasting 52 minutes. It was the day Reds fans knew he wasn't up to scratch. He was replaced by Pennant, who wasn't good enough either. It was the fourth away defeat in the league on the spin. Paul Scholes and Rio Ferdinand got the United goals.

Five wins on the bounce were most welcome. First up was Reading at home in the League Cup. Benitez made eight changes. There were four debutants - Gabriel Paletta and Lee Peltier, with James Smith and Danny Guthrie on the bench. After an abject 43 minutes, a clearly overweight Fowler, who hadn't made the bench in recent weeks, opened the scoring with a beautiful dink over the advancing keeper. Riise scored a minute later from the edge of the box. Paletta headed in a third from a corner. The visitors pulled one back from a set piece. Crouch immediately restored Liverpool's three-goal cushion after a one-two with Fowler. Pennant had a hand in all four goals. Reading got two back to expose Liverpool's shortcomings at the back and set up a nervy last five minutes. The Reds managed to hang on. Two days after the game, one director anonymously told The Mirror: "We have paid too many inflated prices and inflated wages for players who are not doing the job. We have too many players of poor quality. When the manager decides they are not doing the job, we cannot get rid of them because nobody wants them for the sort of money we want back. It means we're losing money we can't afford to lose. Normally, by the time you get to October, you'd expect the manager to know his best team and stick with it but there are no signs of that happening. I don't think he could tell you what his best team is."

A 3-1 league win over Martin O'Neill's unbeaten Aston Villa was more like it. Kuyt hammered in Hyypia's knock down. Man of the match Crouch side-footed home a cross from Finnan. Garcia slid the ball under Thomas Sorensen just before half-time. Gerrard hit a post. Gabriel Agbonlahor got one back. Reina made a spectacular save from a Chris Sutton header. This was the 99th successive game that Benitez had changed his starting line-up.

Just as he was expected to complete a unique century, the wily Spaniard selected an unchanged side for the home game with Bordeaux in the Champions League. It was the first time he had done so since February 2005. "He named the side an hour before kick-off and the lads were looking around in astonishment," said Gerrard. Garcia volleyed home the captain's right-wing cross halfway through the first half. Fernando Menegazzo was sent off for head-butting Riise. The skipper made it two with 20 minutes left after Zenden had put him through. Garcia scored again to make it 3-0. With two games left, the Reds had qualified for the last 16. Benitez commented on the resignation of director and former chairman Noel White, one of the five founding architects of the Premier League, who owned up to the post-United criticism. "The most important thing at the end is the club," Benitez said. "These things don't normally happen here, and I didn't have a bad relationship with him, but this is a big club and we have a way of doing things."

Kuyt put Liverpool 1-0 up against Reading from Crouch's knockdown in a win that took Liverpool into seventh. Carragher and Hyypia went close from distance. Kuyt wrapped up the points from a yard out after Marcus Hahnemann had parried from Crouch. The Dutchman had made a solid start to life at Liverpool, not just with goals but an immense work rate. One impressed onlooker was the Manchester United manager, Alex Ferguson. In an otherwise bizarre chapter about Liverpool in his 2013 autobiography, he did at least praise the former Feyenoord striker. "Dirk Kuyt was as honest a player as you could meet," he said. "I'm sure he was 6 feet 2 inches when he arrived and ended up 5 feet 8 inches because he ran his legs into stumps."

Liverpool moved into the quarter-finals in the League Cup when they won at lower-division Birmingham. Dudek, Paletta, Gonzalez, Peltier and Fowler saw more action. Agger scored the only goal, hammering in from close range on the stroke of half-time. Gonzalez won a penalty, but Bellamy's weak effort was saved. He was later fined for taking the penalty ahead of Benitez's designated taker, Fowler. Steve Bruce could at least take comfort in keeping Liverpool to just one goal, rather than the seven last time they'd met. But the win came at a price, as Sissoko dislocated his shoulder. With Hamann's departure in the summer, it would be a costly injury. Benitez had recently described the Malian as the team's battery, and with Gerrard and Alonso not always convincing as a two-man partnership, it was indeed a blow for the Spaniard. Sissoko wouldn't play again until February, by which time Benitez was on the verge of signing a world-class replacement.

Another tough away assignment produced another woeful performance, as Liverpool's first trip to The Emirates ended in a 3-0 defeat. For most of the season, Benitez had fielded a 4-4-2, with two weak and unproductive wingers and two strikers, neither of whom were natural goalscorers. This time, he bucked the trend by playing Gerrard on the right and, quite incredibly, Zenden in central midfield. Sissoko was missed. Robin van Persie punched the ball past Reina in the second minute, but the referee spotted it. The Dutchman still looked surprised. Mathieu Flamini scored towards the end of the first half. Even Kolo Toure was able to race through a yawning chasm between Hyypia and Carragher to side-foot past Reina. Gerrard failed to mark William Gallas at a corner and then blamed Riise when the Frenchman nodded in from close range – a microcosm of an abysmal second-half performance. A late Bellamy header was ruled offside. The Reds now had one point from six league games on the road, with no goals from open play.

A chance to finally score an away goal was spurned at Middlesbrough in the club's 5000th match. Gerrard was back in the middle next to Alonso. The breakthrough wouldn't come. Kuyt fired wide. Crouch header's was cleared off the line by Jonathan Woodgate. Yakubu missed an open goal for Boro. Not for the last time, Mark Schwarzer would keep Liverpool at bay, as they drew a blank at the Riverside for the fifth season in a row. Benitez was under pressure. Sections of the media hammered him when he was successful, so they relished barren periods like this. With Liverpool in ninth, 16 points off leaders Manchester United, the barrage of criticism was relentless.

A 2-0 win over PSV Eindhoven secured top spot with a game to spare in the Champions League, but Alonso succumbed to a 21st-minute hip injury. Gonzalez and Pennant were also injured to leave Benitez's midfield and wing options severely depleted. But at least Eindhoven were seen off with goals from Gerrard and Crouch.

Benitez plumped for 3-5-2 for the visit of Manchester City. Hyypia, Carragher and Agger were the centre halves, with Finnan and Riise the wing backs. The game was scrappy, but Gerrard took advantage of Joey Barton's error midway through the second half and fired in from 20 yards.

With the team having won 11 from 12 at Anfield in all competitions, a goalless stalemate at home to Portsmouth was a disappointment. With Zenden absent, Carragher played in midfield, alongside Gerrard. Bellamy was in a Cardiff court, accused of assault. The young Moroccan El Zhar made his debut as a substitute. Other subs included Paletta and Guthrie. In a game of few chances, Gerrard's diving header went just wide in the closing moments. The Reds would have moved into fourth with a win but were still in seventh. Pompey, who included David James and David Thompson, remained in third.

At a lunch for businessmen in Newcastle, the former editor of The Sun, Kelvin MacKenzie, said of his paper's appalling Hillsborough coverage: "I only apologised on World At One because Rupert Murdoch told me to. I wasn't sorry then and I'm not sorry now." The Kop would respond in its own unique way a month later during an FA Cup match with Arsenal.

With one goal in four league games, the Reds found their goalscoring touch at Wigan, as they finally won on the road. Chris Kirkland and Emile Heskey were in the opposition ranks, but they found themselves 4-0 down at the break after a Kuyt and Bellamy-inspired blitzkrieg. The Welshman fired into the top corner on nine minutes after some terrible defending. It was the first away goal from open play in 10 hours and 19 minutes. The same player scored again when Gerrard put him in on goal. Bellamy then showed his unselfishness by squaring to Kuyt to tap in when he could have had a hat trick. It was the Dutchman's first goal in eight matches. There was still time for Lee McCulloch to turn Gerrard's free kick into his own net before half-time. Perhaps the upturn in Bellamy's performance was a result of being found not guilty of two counts of assault in Cardiff Magistrates Court the previous Wednesday. Little happened in the second half, other than Heskey hitting the post.

The match at Galatasaray was effectively a dead rubber, so Benitez fielded Dudek, Paletta, Guthrie, Peltier and Fowler, with the young Spaniard Miki Roque coming off the bench. It was to be his only appearance for the Reds. He was loaned out three times before leaving for Real Betis in 2009. His career ended when he was diagnosed with pelvic cancer in 2011. He died the following year, aged 23. At the Ataturk, scene of Liverpool's most incredible triumph, Fowler scored first, turning in Bellamy's cross but the Reds found themselves 3-1 down after some awful defending. Fowler scored again after skilful wing play by Pennant, but Galatasaray won 3-2. Liverpool still topped the group, but with Real Madrid, Barcelona, Inter Milan and Roma having come second in their respective groups, further progress would be tricky.

Liverpool continued their Premier League improvement with a 4-0 hammering of Fulham at Anfield, racking up 32 goal attempts to six. Even Carragher scored. Such was the Reds' inconsistency, the first 53 minutes yielded no goals, but when the dam burst, they were most impressive. Gerrard knocked in the rebound from his own penalty miss. Carragher scored at the far post from Agger's flick-on six minutes later. It was his first goal since 1999. Garcia scored next, with a brilliant flicked header from the edge of the box. And then in the last minute, Gonzalez stroked in a left-footed free kick. It was Reina's 28th clean sheet in 50 league games – a club record. Ray Clemence, Bruce Grobbelaar and Dudek had each managed 25. The Reds were up to fourth, but in terms of points, they were nearer to the relegation zone (14) than they were to the leaders (16). Despite all the criticism he had received recently, Benitez had got to 50 league wins in England quicker than Bob Paisley and Alex Ferguson. Off the field, rumours of a takeover were doing wonders for supporter morale, with Dubai International Capital the frontrunners to buy the club.

Another convincing win came at Charlton. Istanbul hero Djimi Traore conceded an early penalty for kicking Pennant in the head. Alonso swept it home. The accident-prone left back did make some amends by clearing Pennant's shot off the line. The second goal took its time in coming. After Kuyt hit a post, Bellamy scored from Finnan's long pass. Gerrard made it 3-0 with an exquisitely-placed shot into the far corner from Crouch's knockdown. It was a satisfying afternoon for him against a side managed by Les Reed, who had been on the England coaching staff during Euro 2000. "I have no respect for Reed or [fellow coach Derek] Fazackerley," wrote Gerrard in his first autobiography. "I was a young lad who had never been away from home to play football before. They didn't seem to understand that not everyone can board a plane, settle in a strange hotel far from the family they love, and find it easy. In fact, they made me feel like shit. My homesickness worsened whenever I was forced to be in their company. I felt they could have shown more care and sympathy. They were always pushing me, always telling me to buck up my ideas." Charlton were in 19th and heading out of the division. After such inconsistency, Liverpool were now third, and with the toughest away games behind them, there was much to be positive about. But the Champions League draw had just pitted them against holders Barcelona in the last 16.

There was only one side worse than Charlton, and that was Watford, who visited Anfield two days before Christmas. A goalless first half may have triggered some more doubts in the stands, but man of the match Bellamy broke the deadlock on 47 minutes. Crouch hit the woodwork before Alonso sealed the win near the end, curling in a 25-yarder.

Just as things were looking up, the Reds were awful at Ewood Park on Boxing Day. Bellamy and Crouch fluffed first-half chances and were made to pay when Benny McCarthy netted. A run of seven clean sheets in the league was over. Kuyt missed a chance to equalise and Alonso twice went close from long range. Former Red Brad Friedel was unbeatable in the Rovers goal.

Spurs had improved markedly since the teams had last met, but they couldn't prevent the Reds from winning at White Hart Lane on 30th December. Garcia scored a scrappy goal in first-half stoppage time. In torrential second-half rain, Finnan headed onto his own bar, but Spurs created little. It was an impressive, although slightly fortuitous, result. Liverpool were being linked with the Argentinian midfielder Javier Mascherano, who had signed for West Ham in the summer. The year ended with the Reds in fourth, 16 points off the top and two behind Bolton in third.

"We are prepared to fight first and then play our football," wrote Benitez in his programme notes on New Year's Day before the Reds entertained Bolton. It was to prove an accurate assessment of what would unfold, as Liverpool turned on the style in the final 30 minutes. The highlight was Crouch repeating his goal against Galatasaray. Finnan hit the bar in a goalless first half. But after Crouch acrobatically scissor-kicked Pennant's cross into the Kop-end goal, Liverpool strolled to victory. Gerrard, awarded an MBE in the New Year's honours list, made it two with a cool side-footed finish into the top corner. Kuyt added a late third from Garcia's pass.

Two crazy games in four days against Arsenal at Anfield saw Liverpool score four, concede nine, and exit both domestic competitions. The FA Cup third-round game saw a six-minute protest from the kick-off about the BBC's decision to allow the odious Kelvin MacKenzie back onto their screens. After a rousing rendition of 'You'll Never Walk Alone', the Kop help aloft a mosaic of cards, reading "The Truth", which had been MacKenzie's disgraceful headline in 1989. For the first half-dozen minutes, the length of time that was played at Hillsborough before it was abandoned, the Kop chanted "Justice for the 96!" Before a large BBC audience, Tomas Rosicky scored two excellent goals in the closing stages of the first half. Kuyt pulled one back on 71 minutes with a close-range header, but Thierry Henry settled the match with six minutes left after an error from Carragher.

Much weaker sides were fielded in the League Cup fifth-round tie three days later, which produced nine goals. The game had everything. Gonzalez broke his leg after four minutes. Jeremie Aliadiere sprung the offside trap to score first. Fowler equalised with a clever flick from Garcia's pass. Julio Baptista, a Brazilian on loan from Real Madrid, fired in a long-range free kick on 40 minutes. Song and Baptista both scored in a lengthy period of first-half stoppage time. 4-1. Dudek saved a Baptista penalty, conceded by Hyypia, but the striker did complete his hat trick two minutes later. Garcia departed injured with a cruciate ligament injury in his right knee. Sadly, it would be his last game for the club. A stunner by Gerrard and a header from Hyypia made it 5-3, but Baptista crowned an astonishing personal display with his fourth goal on 84 minutes.

Back in the league, Liverpool remained in third with a comfortable win at Vicarage Road. Goals from Bellamy and Crouch (two) came in 14 minutes either side of half-time. Like a lot of strikers on a hat trick in the Benitez years, he was then substituted, a tactic of the manager to keep a player hungry. With takeover talks hotting up, the manager shot down rumours that David Beckham would be coming in on loan.

Benitez finally ended his Premier League losing streak against Chelsea with an easy 2-0 win. The game was the 100th in the competition for both he and Jose Mourinho. With three Chelsea centre halves absent, Kuyt profited from a defensive mix-up to fire past Petr Cech. Pennant then scored one of the goals of the season, with an outrageous dipping volley from the right angle of the penalty area. It was his first for the club. Mourinho sent on the misfiring Andriy Shevchenko, allowing the home fans to remind him of Istanbul. Riise hit the bar from 40 yards. Crouch was unable to head in the rebound. Just five points now separated the sides. Unfortunately for both, Manchester United looked set to win their first title in four years.

There was a ten-day gap until the next game, away at West Ham. Eight months after coming so close to beating Liverpool in the cup final, the Hammers were now in the bottom three. After a scoreless first half in which Reina made a couple of wonderful saves, Kuyt took just ten seconds to score the first goal, rifling in off the bar from 25 yards. Birthday boy Crouch scored an equally scintillating second, side-footing Riise's cutback into the net from the edge of the box. Bellamy and Kuyt could have scored, before debutant Kepa Blanco scored for the hosts, but they didn't have another goal in them. A day later, the Reds signed full back Alvaro Arbeloa from Deportivo La Coruna for £2.5m. Stephen Warnock, Darren Potter and Salif Diao all left for pastures new.

Liverpool were now on the verge of being sold. The American tycoon Robert Kraft had previously shown an interest but hadn't made a bid. The Prime Minister of Thailand, Thaksin Shinawatra, was keen, but the board refused to sell to him "for honourable reasons." When he bought Manchester City later in the year, he was called "a human rights abuser of the worst kind" by a leading human rights group. Dubai International Capital, the investment arm of the Dubai Royal Family, had been favourites for months to buy the club, but their lack of urgency frustrated Liverpool. American businessman George Gillett was also in the frame, but he didn't have the funds to go it alone.

DIC suddenly offered a take-it-or-leave-it ultimatum with a strict time frame, which angered Moores. He plumped for Gillett, who by now had found a business partner in billionaire Tom Hicks. It proved to be a ruinous decision that would set the club back years. They paid £174 million for the existing shares. They paid off the club's debt of £44.8 million and pledged £215 million for the new stadium, promising "a spade in the ground in 60 days." That quote of Gillett's would come back to haunt them. They didn't invest a dime of their own. It all came via a one-year loan from The Royal Bank of Scotland.

Gillett had gone from billionaire to bankruptcy by 1992, suffering the indignity of having to buy back his clothes and his dogs. He built himself up again, owning ski resorts and North American sports clubs. He had invited Moores and Parry to Canada, where nobody had a bad word to say about him. "We had looked into George Gillett's affairs in detail, and he came up to scratch," said Moores in 2010. "To a great extent, we took Tom Hicks on trust, on George's say-so." That was the fatal error. Hicks, who was in George W Bush's inner circle, was an expert in leveraged buyouts, buying companies, loading them with debt and selling them for a huge profit. With his business partner, he purchased Dr Pepper and 7Up in the 1980s for $646 million and sold up for $2.5 billion. He bought sports clubs, but fans of Brazilian football club Corinthians, the Texas Rangers and the Dallas Stars held the same low opinion of him as Liverpool fans would. It was pointed out to Moores in 2010 that a Google search would have told him everything he needed to know about Hicks, but he took him on Gillett's word. Whereas Moores hadn't investigated Hicks, Hicks had certainly done his research on Liverpool. "The more I looked, the more I became convinced it was an opportunity to buy a crown jewel of sports at a modest price," he later revealed.

"Gillett and Hicks produced a substantial offer document containing all the key assurances re: debt, the stadium, investment in the squad and respect for Liverpool FC's unique culture, traditions and legacy," Moores continued. "It was impressive stuff - and it did the trick. For the motion to be carried, we needed around 90 per cent in favour. Over 1,700 shareholders voted, and the result was 100 per cent in favour of accepting the offer. Ultimately, the deal we signed up to was laid out in unambiguous terms in the share offer document. It is a matter of fact that the document pledged there would be no debt placed on the club, and significant funds would be made available for investment in the squad and the new stadium. I signed up for that - not money." The Guardian's Paul Hayward wrote at the time that Liverpool had "rebuffed a suitor wealthier than Roman Abramovich to foxtrot with George Gillett and a partner who showed up later than a mystery man in a Hollywood thriller."

Back on the field, the five-match winning run in the league ended with a goalless Merseyside Derby at Anfield, despite the Reds having 25 attempts on goal to Everton's six. Bellamy had a goal chalked off. Reina saved from Andy Johnson. The Blues defended manfully but were outraged when Benitez said: "Everton put eight or nine men behind the ball and defended deep, but that's what small clubs do. When a team comes to Anfield and only want a point what else can you call them but a small club?" Everton responded with an article on their website denying they were a small club. The fallout lasted for days, with angry Blues calling radio stations and writing to the local press.

Sissoko made a welcome return to action, but that was the only silver lining, as the Reds lost at Newcastle. Bellamy needed just six minutes to open the scoring after a defensive calamity, but it proved to be the first time in 15 matches that the Reds scored first and didn't win. Twenty minutes later, Reina's clearance hit Obafemi Martins, who couldn't believe his luck as he walked the ball into an empty net. With 20 left, Nobby Solano beat Reina with a penalty, conceded by Riise, who told Gerrard to fuck off when he chastised him for the error. The Norwegian apologised to his captain in the changing room.

The Champions League recommenced in February, and Liverpool's 2-1 win over Barcelona in the Nou Camp was one of the most eye-catching in the club's illustrious European history. Riise and Bellamy came to blows at a Portuguese hotel in the week before the game, with the Welshman attacking the Norwegian with a golf club after a drinking session. Benitez opted for an Alonso-Sissoko midfield, with Gerrard on the right and Riise on the left. Bellamy partnered Kuyt up front. Incredibly, the two men in the headlines got on the scoresheet after Deco had given the holders a 14th-minute lead. Bellamy got free at the back post to head Liverpool level. Naturally, he celebrated with a golf swing. Kuyt missed an easy header in the second half. Reina saved from Javier Saviola. Lionel Messi blazed over an easy chance under pressure from Arbeloa, who marked him superbly in both games. Finnan kept Ronaldinho quiet on the other side. Bellamy set up the winning goal for Riise, who dispatched the ball into the roof of the net for the only right-footed goal of his professional career. The golf club story was huge, and it cemented Bellamy's bad-boy reputation. In his book, he explained he tried to persuade Riise to sing a song at a karaoke event. Riise refused, snapping at Bellamy before retiring to bed. Bellamy stewed over the snub, claiming the Norwegian had previously been rude to him in training.

Despite Finnan trying to stop him, he took a 7-iron from his room, found Riise asleep and hit him across the backside and the legs. "You ever speak to me like that in front of people again, I will wrap this round your head," he told his teammate. On the same night, Dudek was arrested and held in police custody for refusing to leave a bar. Benitez had to go and take him back to the hotel in the small hours. When he returned, Bellamy was ordered to see him. "John Arne Riise has just come to my room to say you attacked him with a golf club," said the manager. Bellamy gave his side of the story and apologised to Riise the next morning. He admitted in his book it was bullying behaviour. Riise's version isn't too different, although he claimed the only reason he didn't beat Bellamy up was to preserve team morale.

Despite playing such a prominent role at the Nou Camp, the Welshman knew his Liverpool days were numbered, not because of the golf club incident, but because he was left out of the matchday squad for the next game with Sheffield United. "When the teamsheet went up on the Friday, I looked at it with a degree of confidence for the first time. My name wasn't on it. Not even among the subs. I thought, 'I don't think I can do this again next year, being on the bench, not knowing when you're starting, not knowing if you're in the squad.' It didn't motivate me. It deflated me." Benitez did release the Welshman at the end of the year, and he went on to play a prominent role in the early days of Manchester City's mega-money era, before returning to Liverpool under Kenny Dalglish.

Without Bellamy, the Reds hammered Sheffield United 4-0. Despite his temporary incarceration in that Portuguese police cell, Dudek kept goal. Javier Mascherano's protracted move had finally gone through and he made his debut alongside Gerrard, with Pennant and Gonzalez on the wings. Fowler and Crouch were up front, although the latter lasted just 23 minutes before he had his nose broken by a kick in the face. He was replaced by Kuyt. Two Fowler penalties for fouls on Gerrard had the Reds in a great position by the 25-minute mark. They were the last of his 183 Liverpool goals. Hyypia and man of the match Gerrard added two more in a four-minute second-half spell.

In this form, Benitez must have fancied a first league win over Manchester United, but it was the same old story, as the leaders took the spoils with a late goal. Riise fizzed a free kick just wide. Carragher did brilliantly to slide-tackle Ronaldo and then Rooney in a matter of seconds as they were about to shoot. Edwin van der Sar saved from Bellamy, who then had a goal disallowed for offside. Riise's piledriver whistled over the crossbar. Paul Scholes was sent off. Crouch had a close-range shot saved. The Reds had been easily the better side, but John O'Shea scrambled in a 90th-minute winner at the Kop end to extend United's lead to nine points – 19 over Liverpool.

A 0-1 home defeat to United was hard to take, but the same result against Barcelona sent the Reds into dreamland. Arbeloa marked Messi expertly again, despite being more of a right back than a left back. Riise fired wide and then hit the bar with a dipping volley. Victor Valdes made a double save from Bellamy and Kuyt. Carlos Puyol blocked Riise's effort from the rebound on the line. Sissoko hit the bar from 40 yards with Valdes nowhere. This was all in the first half, but the Reds' inability to convert their dominance gave Barca hope. Ronaldinho hit the woodwork. With 15 minutes left, Eidur Gudjohnsen rounded Reina and halved the aggregate deficit. Ronaldinho shot tamely at Reina. Crouch could have sealed it, but he fired Pennant's cross into the Kop. The final whistle went. Liverpool were through on away goals. Anfield exploded with joy. "Tactically, the first 30 minutes were among the best I ever saw Liverpool play," wrote Benitez in his 2012 book, Champions League Dreams. PSV Eindhoven awaited the Reds in the last eight. The Reds would be huge favourites to win that.

In a slightly less intense occasion, Kuyt and Fowler came closest to breaking the deadlock in the league at Villa Park. Villa had a penalty shout turned down, but this feeble game remained goalless. The Reds were fourth, a point behind Arsenal, who had played a game fewer.

A Crouch hat-trick ensured the Reds moved above the Gunners when they met at Anfield at the end of March. Arbeloa and Pennant exchanged backheels before Crouch turned in the Spaniard's low cross on four minutes. He then headed in Aurelio's deep cross. Agger glanced in Aurelio's free kick on the hour mark. William Gallas scored Arsenal's 13th goal of the season against the Reds – in fact, Benitez had put the scores of their previous three meetings, 0-3, 1-3 and 3-6, up on the wall of the dressing room to motivate his players. Crouch had the last word by finishing brilliantly with his left foot in front of the Kop. He had the perfect hat trick – one with each foot and one with his head. "He was superb," said Wenger. "Everything he did was intelligent. He has the size of a basketball player but the skill of a real football player."

A 3-0 win in Eindhoven as good as put Liverpool into the semi-finals of the Champions League. Carragher made a club record 58th European appearance for Liverpool, now ahead of Phil Neal. Gerrard's 15th European Cup goal – a bullet header into the bottom corner midway through the first half – took him ahead of Ian Rush. Alonso missed two chances in the first minute of the second half, but Riise soon doubled the lead, blasting the ball into the top corner from 30 yards. Crouch's header just after the hour was the icing on the cake. Kuyt picked up an injury-time booking, possibly on purpose, as, although it would see him banned from the second leg, it meant the slate would be wiped clean for the semi-final. After the team had made such an unconvincing start, this was turning into a promising season, but Aurelio ruptured his Achilles and would miss the rest of the campaign. It was a costly injury, given what was to unfold in the semi-final.

Arbeloa scored his first Liverpool goal 15 minutes into the away game at Reading when he raced from his own box, played a one-two with Crouch and found the bottom corner. Brynjar Gunnarsson equalised, and Crouch's defensive header hit his own crossbar. Reading were favourites, but they failed to deal with Pennant's clever cross, and Kuyt headed the winner with five minutes left.

The second leg against Eindhoven was a stroll. The score was only 1-0, but there was never a danger of the Dutchmen mounting a comeback. Benitez benched Gerrard and Carragher but otherwise fielded his strongest side. Dirk Marcellis was sent off for a foul on Zenden. Set up by Fowler, Crouch scored the only goal. With a 4-0 aggregate win, Liverpool would play Mourinho's Chelsea again in the semi-final.

A bore draw at Manchester City was next, but with the top four virtually guaranteed, few were too concerned. Alonso went for goal from inside his own half, but it went a yard over. Carragher and Kuyt could have scored. The vice-captain got away with a penalty shout against him for handball.

After Anfield paid its respects to the 96, the Reds got stuck into Middlesbrough. Mascherano hit the bar with a header before Gerrard struck magnificently into the bottom corner from nearly 30 yards. Crouch was fouled as he tried to meet a Pennant cross. Gerrard sent Mark Schwarzer the wrong way from the spot.

Champions League qualification was assured when a brace from Kuyt did for Wigan on the penultimate weekend of April. His first was a header from Pennant's left-wing cross. He swivelled and shot into the bottom corner for his second, following Bellamy's approach play. Gonzalez put a late header wide. On his 100th game for the club, Reina made a point-blank save from a header.

The first leg of the Champions League semi-final saw Chelsea attempt to improve on the Stamford Bridge atmosphere from 2005. Each of their fans was given a little flag by the club. Liverpool were flat but at least restricted Chelsea to just one goal. Joe Cole scored it just before the half hour after great work by Didier Drogba. Gerrard was close to equalising in the second half. Lampard could have made it two. Chelsea deserved their win. Despite the tie being on a knife edge, Benitez later spoke of his anger. "I was angry with myself, my staff and my players because we had not performed," he said. "I cannot analyse the future of a player in one or two games, but some players must realise that they are playing for a European Cup final and for their futures. Things can change quickly and decisions over whether you stay with a top side or leave do depend on these next weeks." Benitez didn't elaborate on which players he was referring to, but Bellamy and Alonso were substituted at Stamford Bridge and neither would start the second leg.

With a top-four position in the bag, the league season petered out as Benitez sent another weakened team to Portsmouth. There was a debut for Argentinian left back Emiliano Insua and runouts for Dudek, Paletta, Gonzalez and Fowler. El Zhar came off the bench. Alonso and Bellamy played, after their midweek withdrawals. Pompey scored two in five first-half minutes after awful defending. Zenden hit the bar. Skipper for the day Hyypia headed in Fowler's corner just before the hour, but the Reds had no more goals in them.

For the third season in a row, Benitez tactically outclassed Mourinho in a major semi-final, despite his side being clear underdogs. In a totally one-sided second leg, the Reds won 1-0, hit the woodwork and had a goal disallowed before winning a penalty shoot-out to get to their seventh European Cup Final. "I have never witnessed an atmosphere like the one that greeted us in the stadium that night," Bellamy recalled. The shapeless Blues couldn't get any footing in the game. Zenden and Pennant prevented the Chelsea full backs, Paulo Ferreira and Ashley Cole from getting forward. An ingenious free kick routine, which Benitez hadn't used since his Valencia days, saw Gerrard square the ball to Agger, who calmly side-footed into the corner of Petr Cech's net from just inside the box. Twenty-two minutes had been played. Reina denied Drogba early in the second half, but the Reds were easily the better side. Cech saved well from Crouch. Kuyt planted Riise's cross against the bar. In extra-time, Kuyt had a goal disallowed for offside. The Dutchman then had a fierce shot saved in the second period. Full time. Penalties – at the Anfield Road end of the ground. Zenden scored with aplomb as Benitez sat cross-legged on the touchline, not just exuding an aura of calm, but ensuring those at the front of the Paddock could see. Reina saved magnificently from Robben. Alonso scored, as did Lampard. Gerrard maintained Liverpool's advantage. Geremi could only fire at Reina. If Kuyt scored, the Reds were through. He found the bottom right-hand corner of Cech's net. Liverpool were in their seventh European Cup Final. Kuyt and Reina shared a moment of euphoria milliseconds before the rest of the squad swamped them. "You are a fucking genius," an elated Bellamy told the manager. "Ultimately Liverpool's fans and players just wanted it more," wrote local journalist Chris Bascombe. "The brutal truth for [Peter] Kenyon, Abramovich and Mourinho is this: they always will." The players and staff celebrated long into the night. Gerrard hitched a ride home on a milk float. Twenty-four hours later, it was confirmed that once more, the Reds would meet AC Milan in the final, this time in Athens, after the Italians had dumped out Manchester United.

Benitez opted to rest numerous first-teamers again for the trip to Fulham, Liverpool's penultimate league game. Only Reina and Pennant from the second-leg 11 started. Kewell played his first game for a year. Clint Dempsey scored the only goal halfway through the second half for the Cottagers, who had Papa Bouba Diop send off in the last minute. The result went a long way toward seeing Fulham stay up, ultimately at the expense of Sheffield United, whose manager Neil Warnock was enraged with Benitez's selection. The Reds ended their away campaign with 18 goals in 19 games, with just six wins.

A stronger side took to the field for the last league game, against relegated Charlton at Anfield, although there was a debut for Italian goalkeeper Daniele Padelli. Fowler was captain on his last appearance for the club. Matt Holland scored early after Mascherano's error. Alonso equalised in the second half. Darren Bent put Athletic 2-1 up. Fowler left the field to a standing ovation on 88 minutes but was cursing his luck when Liverpool were awarded a penalty seconds later in front of the Kop. It would have been an apt way to sign off. Kewell, who had earlier hit the crossbar, made it 2-2. "Maybe my players were thinking about the final," was the manager's summary of a poor performance. The Reds finished third, 21 points behind champions Manchester United.

Liverpool successfully defended their FA Youth Cup in 2007, beating Manchester United in the final on penalties. Having seen off West Brom,

Chelsea, Reading, Sheffield United and Newcastle, the Reds lost 2-1 at Anfield in the first leg of the final, with Craig Lindfield getting the Liverpool goal. But Robbie Threlfall scored the only goal of the Old Trafford leg to force extra time and penalties. Liverpool keeper David Roberts saved the first kick from Magnus Wolff Eikrem. Ray Putterill, Lindfield, Ryan Flynn and Threlfall were all successful for the Reds before Sam Hewson's miss was decisive.

Ten days later, Liverpool would contest their second Champions League Final in three seasons. This time the training camp was in Spain. Nobody was assaulted with a golf club, but Crouch came within a whisker of running over Kuyt in a go-karting incident. "I went flying into him," Crouch recalled. "He jumped up, I went under him and I went straight into the fence. The go-kart burst into flames. Rafa was fuming. He wouldn't even look at me. I said to him 'I promise you it wasn't my fault, the brakes just failed' and a fella went out and took it out for a lap and said 'Yep the brakes have gone'."

With much of the build-up centring around the incredible Istanbul final, this was a more sterile affair. The team was: Reina; Finnan, Carragher, Agger, Riise; Pennant, Mascherano, Alonso, Zenden; Gerrard; Kuyt. 'The best midfield in the world' didn't really perform, other than Mascherano stifling Kaka. Gerrard played number 10 but was a shadow of his best. Kuyt was the lone striker, a role which would have gone to Crouch if he'd hit him with the kart. The Reds lined up in a 4-4-1-1 formation, which is what they should have done from the start in Istanbul, whereas here, it would have perhaps been wiser to play 4-4-2 with Gerrard on the right instead of Pennant, and Bellamy or Crouch partnering Kuyt – how the Reds had lined up against Barcelona.

Liverpool played to a typical Benitez game plan. Pennant had a shot saved. Alonso was a whisker away with a 25-yarder. Nesta got in a timely block on Kuyt. But on the stoke of half-time, Andrea Pirlo's free kick hit Pippo Inzaghi on the bicep and wrong-footed Reina. It was a complete fluke and should have been disallowed for handball. The Reds hadn't exactly dominated but they had been the better side. They didn't recover. Gerrard got free in the box down the inside left but chose to hit it with his right, and his shot was tame. It summed up his performance. Kewell replaced the ineffective Zenden after an hour but wasn't much better himself. Benitez gambled by taking off Mascherano for Crouch, but it backfired when Kaka finally found some space and played in Inzaghi, who rounded Reina and rolled the ball in with eight minutes left. Benitez brought on Arbeloa for Finnan, electing not to introduce a frustrated Bellamy. Dida tipped over Crouch's shot from 20 yards. Kuyt headed in Pennant's corner after Agger's flick-on, but the sands of time beat Liverpool, and AC Milan were European champions again.

Benitez was devasted at the result. An administrative cock-up meant he and chief scout Eduardo Macia didn't even have a hotel room. Angry with the evasive owners for cancelling a post-match meeting about the summer's transfer business and flying home, Benitez and Macia wandered the rainy streets of Athens in the small hours, pondering how to change things. The manager was also frustrated with chief executive Parry, whom he felt never acted quickly enough with the players he wanted. They returned at 7am before Benitez conducted a press conference, urging the new owners to loosen the purse strings. "If we don't change things, we will not be contenders," he argued. Hicks and Gillett were livid, particularly Hicks. "His instinct was to throw on his Stetson," wrote Brian Reade, "pull a Colt .45 out of his holster and pump Rafa full of lead." Privately, the owners agreed to sack him as soon as his position weakened. Anfield's civil war was underway.

Parry was also in the firing line for his handling of the Athens ticket fiasco, which had seen 7,200 tickets of Liverpool's measly allocation of 16,779 go to former shareholders as a sweetener for selling their shares to the Americans. Only 9,579 of the club's actual fanbase qualified for a ticket. This led to the first fan protests of the Americans' reign, which would soon become commonplace.

Liverpool had ended the season strongly, but it was Benitez's first trophyless campaign, not counting the Super Cup. After Athens, one fan on The Guardian website noted, "This loss is down to the lack of a real 20-goal per season striker." In his three seasons, Benitez had worked wonders without a world-class goalscorer like Ian Rush, Robbie Fowler or Michael Owen. However, a marksman of similar pedigree would soon be heading to Anfield.

2007-08

"You lying bastard, get out of our pub!"

Fernando Torres may not have won a trophy with Liverpool but of all the post-1990 players judged to be 'the final piece of the jigsaw', he was the one who lived up to expectations. Watching the young Spaniard in full flight, with the Kop performing the 'Torres Bounce', was a joy to behold. He took to English football magnificently, and his link-up with Steven Gerrard was reminiscent of some of the great Liverpool attacking partnerships down the years.

Rafa Benitez had phoned him soon after Athens, persuading him and his girlfriend to fly to Liverpool. Having housed them for 48 hours in a luxury city-centre apartment, which they were told they couldn't leave in order to keep the deal a secret, Benitez plied them with local cuisine and DVDs of Liverpool legends. It did the trick. The 23-year-old signed for a club record £20 million from his boyhood club Atletico Madrid. Perhaps Tom Hicks and George Gillett were hoping to disprove what Benitez had said after Athens. The owners had also unveiled their new-stadium plans – a 70,000 seat, £300 million futuristic wonderment, with an 18,000-seat Kop. They weren't hated at this stage, although it wouldn't be long before the fans' fury was vented upon them.

Lucas Leiva, Andriy Voronin, Yossi Benayoun and Ryan Babel were other newcomers among a raft of young, unproven players. Voronin wouldn't go on to score regularly for Liverpool, but he had been prolific for Mainz under the managership of Jurgen Klopp. Benayoun and Babel enjoyed promising first seasons. Departing were Bolo Zenden, Jerzy Dudek, Robbie Fowler, Luis Garcia, Craig Bellamy, Mark Gonzalez and Gabriel Paletta, while Djibril Cisse's exit was made permanent.

Two players Benitez missed out on were Manchester United left back Gabriel Heinze and Lyon winger Florent Malouda. Heinze was keen to cross the great divide, but Alex Ferguson refused to sell to the Reds. Benitez took it to a tribunal and lost, without having an alternative in place. His faith in John Arne Riise was eroding, while the fitness of Fabio Aurelio couldn't be trusted. Benitez had managed him in Spain, and it was the same story there. Heinze went to Real Madrid. Malouda was another example of the manager being angered by what saw as the chief executive's incompetence, as he would later explain to Brian Reade. "I wanted Florent Malouda but [Rick] Parry wouldn't pay the signing-on fee, so he went to Chelsea. He brought in Ryan Babel and paid £2 million more than we wanted to. He paid too much for Jermaine Pennant and Yossi Benayoun and he made a big mistake with Javier Mascherano's contract because he allowed him a get-out clause, which ended up costing the club more money." Benitez was still frustrated at his comparative lack of spending power. "Here is the truth: I am driving an old BMW while Ferguson and Mourinho are driving Ferraris. I have to swerve and cheat to beat them, and I can do that, but I need the money and the back-up to beat the Ferraris."

Liverpool's first game was at Villa Park in the Premier League. Benitez, sporting a new goatee, handed a debut to Torres, with Voronin and Babel making their first appearances as substitutes. Pepe Reina was in goal again. Steve Finnan, Daniel Agger, Jamie Carragher and Alvaro Arbeloa were the back four. Steven Gerrard and Xabi Alonso made up the central midfield, with Jermaine Pennant and Riise the wide pair. Torres partnered Dirk Kuyt up front. The first Liverpool goal of the season was an own goal from Martin Laursen, who got to Kuyt's pullback ahead of Torres. The Reds were punished for their inability to find a second when Gareth Barry scored an 86th-minute penalty, after Carragher handled under no pressure. But Gerrard curled in a sublime free kick, just inside the right angle of post and bar for Liverpool's first opening-day win since their win at the same ground in 2002. "There is no question that they are a fine team who can maintain a challenge to Manchester United, Chelsea and Arsenal," said the Villa manager, Martin O'Neill.

The third qualifying round of the Champions League took the Reds to Toulouse, where Voronin scored the only goal just before half-time. Torres was rested ahead of Sunday's home game with Chelsea. Gerrard played for only 65 minutes before fracturing a toe. In sweltering conditions, the game had no more intensity than a pre-season friendly. Toulouse lacked ambition, and Liverpool were unable to open them up. The game was only lit up by the Ukrainian's brilliant 25-yarder. One of Liverpool's opponents was 17-year-old substitute Moussa Sissoko, who would play against them again in the 2019 final.

Torres announced his arrival in wonderful style against Chelsea. Taking Gerrard's pass in the inside-left channel, he slowed down and then burned away from Tal Ben Haim before slotting the ball past Petr Cech at the Anfield Road end. It was a stunning goal which encapsulated all of his qualities. But just past the hour, referee Rob Styles gave Chelsea a penalty, for which he would later apologise, when Malouda and Finnan collided. Lampard beat Reina from 12 yards. Riise, Kuyt and Babel went close to a winner, but it ended 1-1. Benitez fumed at the penalty decision. The Reds had comfortably been the better side. It was the last time Benitez and Mourinho would face each other in this fixture. The Portuguese would soon find himself booted out by Roman Abramovich.

In a new black third kit, Momo Sissoko scored his only Liverpool goal at Sunderland, in a lunchtime kick-off in late August with a low, rasping 25-yarder - the Reds' 7000th league goal. The Malian was replacing Gerrard, whose toe injury had flared up again. Voronin made the points safe at the end. Torres was imperious. Craig Gordon kept the score down with a catalogue of outstanding saves. Sami Hyypia breaking his nose was Liverpool's only concern.

Sebastian Leto and Lucas made their debuts in the return leg against Toulouse. The Argentinian Leto played 75 minutes before giving way to Babel. The Brazilian Lucas came on for the final 22 minutes. The Reds won 4-0, with goals from Crouch and Hyypia and a late double from Kuyt. The latter would score seven in this competition, but only three in the league. The game was preceded by a moving tribute to the 11-year-old Rhys Jones, an Everton fan, who had been shot dead a week earlier.

With Liverpool top for the first time since 2002, there was talk of the title when they battered Derby County 6-0. With Gerrard still absent, and now Carragher missing, Hyypia wore the armband. A long-range Alonso free kick from out wide went straight in, with Kuyt distracting the keeper. A mesmerising dummy saw Babel add a second just before the break. The Reds cut loose in the second half. Mascherano's Alsatian-like pressing provided a goal for Torres. Alonso swept home the fourth from 20 yards after Benayoun was scythed down. Voronin and Torres completed the rout. Babel was continuing to catch the eye and was labelled 'the next Thierry Henry' by his international coach, Marco van Basten. But there was bad news for the Reds with the departure of assistant coach Pako Ayestaran, who had also been Benitez's number two at Valencia. Rumours had persisted for several weeks that they failed to see eye to eye on various issues.

Quite predictably, talk of winning the title was immediately followed by a draw at Portsmouth. A point was only secured courtesy of Reina saving Nwankwo Kanu's penalty – the fourth the Reds had conceded in seven games. Voronin hit the bar. Perhaps Liverpool could have done with Gerrard and Torres on the pitch, rather than on the bench. Perhaps the international break scuppered the side's momentum, with Arbeloa arriving in the nick of time and Mascherano returning too late to play. "My players travel more than Willy Fogg all the time, probably," Benitez told baffled journalists after the game.

The first Champions League group game was also drawn. A Porto side including Raul Meireles scored an eighth-minute penalty. Liverpool were so abject they could have been 3-0 down by then. At 34, Hyypia's lack of pace was exposed, but Kuyt headed past Nuno Espirito Santo, the future manager of Wolves. Pennant was sent off for a foul in the second half. Neither side managed to find a winner. Benitez was relieved to get a point. Two days after the Porto game, the club's television channel, LFCTV, was launched.

Two days after the news that Agger and Alonso would face lengthy spells on the sideline, Liverpool drew again, this time in a goalless league game with Steve Bruce's Birmingham at Anfield. Torres was benched and was badly missed, with the toothless Voronin and Kuyt in attack. Introduced after an hour, he nearly scored with an overhead kick. For the fourth time in five visits, Birmingham got a result at Anfield. Alonso would be back in the winter, but Agger was gone for the season. Both had metatarsal injuries.

Torres showed his worth again with a League Cup hat trick, despite the physical approach of the Reading defence. Goalkeeper Charles Itandje and defender Jack Hobbs made their debuts. Lucas and Leto also started. Gerrard was on the bench. Benayoun landed his first Liverpool goal with a fantastic run and finish. Reading equalised just before the half hour. Torres got his first, side-footing into the corner. Reading equalised again. Two more from the Spaniard in the final 20 minutes put the Reds into the fourth round. "He reminds me of Ian Rush," said Gerrard. But there was a growing frustration that Torres had started two cup matches and not the Premier League games, in which four points had been tossed away.

Benayoun popped up with a key goal just as it seemed the Reds were heading for a third successive Premier League 0-0. With just 15 minutes left at Wigan, with Torres having started, the Israeli playmaker took Pennant's pass and turned Titus Bramble inside out before finding the corner of Chris Kirkland's net from just inside the box. Having been top for the first fortnight of September, Liverpool ended it in fourth.

The first defeat of the season came in the 12th game. It was a major surprise as struggling Marseille, with a new manager, won 1-0 at Anfield. Bolo Zenden was in the Marseille team, as was Benoit Cheyrou, younger brother of Bruno. Djibril Cisse came off their bench for the last 20 minutes. The Reds were abysmal, particularly Sissoko and Leto. They were beaten by Mathieu Valbuena's exceptional 20-yarder with 13 minutes left. Benayoun missed an easy header. Torres hit the post in injury time. "That could be the worst performance of my time here," Benítez said.

More league points were tossed away when third-bottom Spurs left Anfield with a 2-2 draw. Voronin touched in a rebound from Gerrard's free kick on 12 minutes. Another Gerrard free kick came back off the post. Robbie Keane scored either side of the break to put his side ahead. Liverpool didn't play well, and it was left to Torres to rescue an injury-time point with a back-post header from Finnan's cross. In each of Benitez's four seasons to date, Liverpool had started badly in the league.

The form of Torres had been one of the few highpoints of an inconsistent and frustrating season, so it was wretched luck that he should be injured playing for Spain before the Goodison derby. Hyypia, who had been well below par against Spurs, scored an own goal towards the end of the first half. The Reds turned it around after the break with, according to the Blues, the help of referee Mark Clattenburg, who sent off two Everton players for professional fouls and awarded Liverpool two penalties. Those decisions were correct, but he chose not to award a late penalty against Carragher, which looked a 50-50 call. Gerrard won the first penalty when he was brought down by Tony Hibbert after running half the length of the pitch. Kuyt scored it. Benitez then surprised everybody by removing Gerrard and replacing him with Lucas. "We were playing with too much passion and we needed to keep the ball and pass the ball. Lucas can do this," was the manager's reasoning. Despite the inevitable criticism, it worked. Lucas's goalbound shot was saved on the line not by the goalkeeper, but by Phil Neville, who joined Hibbert in being red-carded. With the 90 minutes up, Kuyt dispatched the winner. Then came Carragher's challenge on Joleon Lescott, which went unpunished. As with Benitez's 'small club' comment the previous season, the Everton fume was never-ending.

The Champions League was turning into a nightmare as Liverpool lost 2-1 in Turkey to Besiktas. Torres was still missing. Hyypia scored another own goal when a shot hit his leg and beat Reina. Voronin missed a sitter. Gerrard and Hyypia could have scored. Instead, the Turks doubled their advantage in the last ten minutes with a superb goal on the counterattack. Gerrard got one back with a diving header from 16 yards. One point from nine meant that the bottom-placed Reds had to win their final three games to qualify from Group A.

Torres and Alonso were rushed back too soon for the visit of leaders Arsenal. Alonso's metatarsal hadn't healed properly, and he was substituted in the second half. He wouldn't be seen again until December. Torres's adductor injury saw him come off at half-time. In his 400th Liverpool game, Gerrard thundered in a seventh-minute free kick, but Arsenal were always the better side, and the inevitable equaliser came from Cesc Fabregas, who had earlier missed an open goal. Crouch impressed again off the bench, nearly scoring from 30 yards. His lack of game time this season had been mystifying, especially with Voronin playing so much. The Gunners were six points ahead of the sixth-placed Reds.

Robbie Fowler was given a hero's reception as he returned to Anfield with Cardiff in the League Cup. It would be the last time he faced the Reds. Nabil El Zhar's 25-yard blockbuster broke the deadlock. Darren Purse, who had scored against the Reds in the 2001 final, equalised before Benayoun set up Gerrard for the winner. Former Everton player Dave Jones, in charge of Cardiff, wasn't in the mood for a pint and a gloat. "You wouldn't understand how disappointed I am to lose here," he told assembled journalists. "Unless you have played football you wouldn't understand, and I hope you all have a shit journey home."

More league frustration followed at Blackburn where the Reds, with one up front, were impotent. As he had done in Athens, Gerrard played behind Kuyt, but it was a role in which he would only excel with Torres leading the line. There was little creativity, with Mascherano and Sissoko holding the midfield. The introduction of Crouch, once again, made Liverpool more of a threat. He had one effort cleared off the line. But he deserved more than 18 minutes. His lack of game time would prove to be an error, especially in 2008-09, when the only back-up to Torres was David N'Gog. Former Red Brad Friedel was man of the match. Two months after being top, Liverpool were seventh.

Suddenly, and unexpectedly, the Reds produced an avalanche of goals, racking up 21 in five games, starting with a Champions League record 8-0 win over Besiktas at Anfield. With the team still without Torres and Alonso, Crouch scored first. Benayoun scored the next three. Gerrard got in on the act. Babel scored two, including a sumptuous backheel and a complete fluke. He then hit the bar with an easy header. Crouch rounded off the evening's scoring with a header. It was the manager's 50th Champions League game in charge of Liverpool and Hyypia's 100th European game for the club.

Benitez fielded the same starting 11 for just the fifth time in 200 matches for the visit of Fulham. Crouch hit the bar. Benayoun and Voronin missed chances. Just as another goalless draw in the Premier League looked likely, Torres came off the bench to fire into the near post on 81 minutes from Reina's assist. Crouch won a penalty. Gerrard tucked it away. The Reds were up to fourth.

A lunchtime trip to St James' Park was negotiated with ease by the Reds. A stunning 35-yard free kick from Gerrard on 27 minutes didn't just beat Shay Given all ends up, it almost took the netting off the posts. It was particularly satisfying for Gerrard, who was abused by the home fans following England's failure to qualify for Euro 2008. Torres hit a post. A minute into the second half, a corner hit Kuyt on the knee and went in. In a dismal campaign for him, it would be his only league goal from open play all season. Babel made it 3-0 after a one-two with Gerrard to leave Sam Allardyce's job hanging by a thread. Lucas was outstanding. Torres spurned several chances. Despite the performance, Benitez's press conference a couple of days before the game was still the talking point. Having read an angry email from Tom Hicks earlier that morning, an irate Benitez answered every question with, "As always, I am focused on training and coaching my team." Benitez had instigated communication with the owners to ensure the club was ready for the January transfer window. Hicks wrote in capital letters that the manager should focus on coaching and training the team. "I was furious," Benitez wrote in his book. "The owners simply did not understand how we had to work if we wanted to catch Manchester United and Chelsea without matching their funds; they would not even listen when I was trying to save them, and the club, some money." Benitez had also heard the owners were trying to replace him with Jurgen Klinsmann. According to Rick Parry, the club had only sounded the German out in case Benitez left for Real Madrid, which he had hinted at more than once. Benitez, unusually, wore a tracksuit for the Newcastle game, with some claiming it was a protest at Hicks's use of the word 'coaching' rather than 'managing'. He claimed in his book he had forgotten to take his shoes to the northeast and only had trainers. That the manager's attire should now be the source of headlines showed how out of control things were at the club.

With the controversy still raging, 2,000 fans marched to the ground from a nearby pub to offer the manager their support before the crucial Champions League game with Porto. Rumour had it that defeat might have seen Benitez sacked, but the Reds won this penultimate group game 4-1. Torres headed Liverpool into the lead. Porto equalised. The game remained finely poised until the introduction of Kewell and Crouch. Torres got a brilliant second with 12 minutes left. The relief was palpable. Gerrard added a penalty. Crouch got the fourth. Liverpool still needed to win in Marseille.

The opening goal and a commanding performance from Hyypia helped Liverpool on their way to a 4-0 win over Bolton at Anfield. Other than Nicolas Anelka missing a wide-open goal, it was all Liverpool. Torres clipped the ball over the keeper just before the break. A Gerrard penalty after a foul on Crouch and a goal from Babel completed the rout. The Reds were still six points behind Arsenal, but if they won their game in hand, they would be two points clear of Chelsea in second.

Just as pressure on the manager eased off, he substituted Torres, Gerrard and Carragher in a 3-1 league defeat at Reading – the first domestic loss of the season. All hell broke loose. Benitez selected a strange line-up, which not only included Hobbs ahead of Hyypia, but a three-pronged attack of Torres, Voronin and Crouch, with Gerrard on the left. Reading led on 17 minutes after an incorrectly awarded penalty. Set up by Torres, Gerrard levelled up ten minutes later. The match came to life on the hour, when Kevin Doyle put the hosts ahead. Benitez immediately withdrew Torres for Kewell, to the disbelief of the travelling Kop. Gerrard hit the bar. James Harper soon made it 3-1. Gerrard saw his number go up, with Babel coming on. Crouch hit the post. Hyypia replaced Carragher. Even with the all-important match in France around the corner, Benitez's antics were strange.

Most, but not all, fans forgave him when the Reds swept past Marseille and into the last 16 of the Champions League. Liverpool could have ended the night in any position in Group A, but with a performance described by Benitez as "one of the best of my time at Liverpool," they topped the group with a 4-0 win. Gerrard, who had hit a rich vein of form over the last month, knocked in a rebound from his own penalty on four minutes. Torres quickly added a sensational second, after showing sublime footwork to get away from two defenders before side-footing into the corner. Kewell set up Kuyt to make it three just after the break. Babel got the fourth in injury time. After mustering a mere point from their first trio of group matches, Liverpool had scored 16 goals in the next three. It was the first time an English team had won in the intimidating Stade Velodrome. Sissoko was left out and told a radio station he would consider leaving in January. Gerrard returned home to discover he had become the latest player to be burgled while on match duties.

A significant off-field development came in a Marseille hotel room on the day of the game. Summoned by Gillett to his room, Parry and David Moores were asked to sign a whitewash procedure, which would allow the owners to transfer the debt they had incurred in buying Liverpool FC onto the club itself. They needed Parry and Moores to sign the document to confirm that the club could afford the repayments. They refused. After he calmed down, Gillett told them that mortgaging the club hadn't been the plan when they purchased the club, but that the credit crunch had drastically altered their finances and borrowing potential. It was for that reason the new stadium wasn't going to appear any time soon.

A second Premier League defeat came at home to Manchester United, who, for the second season in a row, had to do very little to leave Anfield with a 1-0 win. Kewell had a shot cleared off the line. Carlos Tevez got the only goal just before half-time from a well-worked corner routine. Babel was a whisker away from 20 yards. Liverpool threatened little else, despite their 19 goal attempts to the opposition's five. United became the first team since Everton in 1910 to keep four consecutive clean sheets in the league at Anfield.

Liverpool then found themselves out of the League Cup three days later, losing a quarter-final 2-0 at Chelsea. Itandje, Hobbs and Sissoko came into the side, and there was a welcome return for the much-missed Alonso. Chelsea, now managed by Avram Grant following the sacking of Mourinho in September, took the lead in the second half when Lampard's shot deflected in off Carragher. A minute later, Crouch lunged into John Obi Mikel and was sent off. Andriy Shevchenko got a late second. Benitez still hadn't seen his team score in seven matches at Stamford Bridge.

Respite came with a 4-1 Premier League home win over Portsmouth. Having collided with David James, Glen Johnson was still off the field receiving treatment when Benayoun's volley put the Reds a goal up. Sylvain Distin's own goal made it 2-0 in the 16th minute. Benjani pulled one back in the second half before Torres scored twice in the final quarter of the game. The Spaniard was in scintillating form, running Sol Campbell ragged all afternoon.

Another win came on Boxing Day, but it was less impressive. An exquisite goal by Torres put the Reds ahead at Derby, but they slackened off. Jay McEveley made it 1-1 with Derby's first home goal since September. Gerrard hit the bar, but just as the Reds faced the embarrassment of dropping points against the side marooned at the bottom of the table, the skipper scrambled in an injury-time winner. The three points were welcome, but the performance was miles off what was needed. Riise and Kuyt were having indifferent seasons. It was obvious that Voronin wasn't good enough. Babel was too inconsistent and often poor when starting. Benitez appeared to have little clue on who should play with Torres and which formation to play. For once, the manager showed his frustration on the touchline, when he squared up with Derby manager Paul Jewell, a former Liverpool reserve.

Kewell and Kuyt came in for Babel and Voronin as Liverpool drew 0-0 at Manchester City. Richard Dunne kept Torres quiet and cleared off the line from Kuyt. Didi Hamann protected the City defence superbly. At least Benitez had the January transfer window to look forward to. "We are getting close to some players," he said. At the end of the calendar year, Liverpool were fourth, ten points behind Arsenal with a game in hand.

The new year opened with four frustrating draws, with three of them in the Premier League, as Liverpool's faint title hopes crumbled away. The first was courtesy of a late equaliser from Wigan's Titus Bramble as Liverpool haemorrhaged more Premier League points. Torres fired the Reds into the lead from Finnan's pass, but the Reds couldn't put the game to bed and were punished by an adept finish from the defender, who had often been a figure of fun among Liverpool fans. It was an immensely frustrating result, especially coming at Anfield. Steve Bruce's impressive Anfield record was continuing – he was now managing Wigan.

Three years on from the classic 5-3 FA Cup tie in which Alonso had scored from his own half, the Reds travelled to Kenilworth Road again in the third round. This was a much more serene affair. Cash-strapped Luton had requested that

Liverpool not take their share of the gate receipts. The Reds declined, but the Hatters got their payday anyway when Riise's own goal cancelled out Crouch's opener.

For much of Liverpool's game at Middlesbrough, it looked like the Riverside hoodoo would strike again, as the Reds trailed to George Boateng's goal. But Torres conjured up a magnificent 25-yarder to earn a 1-1 draw. Crouch wasn't even a sub.

By now, Liverpool were in a far bigger mess off the field than on it. Two days after Boro, the Liverpool Echo ran an exclusive, with Hicks admitting that he and Gillett had indeed lined up Jurgen Klinsmann to replace Benitez. Klinsmann had joined the Hicks family for Thanksgiving in late November. Hicks said in the article it was only an insurance policy in case Benitez left, but Brian Reade later revealed that when Klinsmann had elected to go to Bayern Munich, an angry Hicks emailed Gillett and Parry, saying "Shame on us!" for missing out on the German. Unannounced, Foster Gillett left the club after this, getting on a plane and never returning. Before he left, he had been in negotiations to buy the rugby league club Wigan Warriors. They never heard from him again either.

Benitez sent out a strong side, albeit with Itandje in goal, for the replay against a Luton side that included former Red Don Hutchison. Unlike 1987, the Hatters managed to turn up and were beaten 5-0. Gerrard scored a hat trick with the third from 35 yards after persuading Benitez not to take him off. Babel had opened the scoring just before half-time. Hyypia scored the other goal for the Reds, who had 32 attempts on goal. The match was Carragher's 500th. He received a guard of honour as the teams came onto the pitch.

Just as they had done against Luton, home fans continued to protest against the owners when Aston Villa came to town. "Get out of our club!" and "Liverpool Football Club is in the wrong hands" were now the most popular chants on the Kop. An angry Riise wasn't even on the bench. Benayoun scored the only goal of the first half. Villa scored two from set pieces in three minutes midway through the second half, with Aurelio putting through his own goal for the second. Substitute Crouch rescued a point with a well-executed volley on the turn in the closing moments – his first league goal since the hat trick against Arsenal ten months earlier. He had only been on the pitch eight minutes. Martin Skrtel, a £6.5 million signing from Zenit St Petersburg, replaced Arbeloa in the 70th minute for his debut. Liverpool were now behind Everton in fifth, having drawn four league games in a row.

The protests at the Villa game, however impressive they were, would cut no ice with Hicks and Gillett in America. Realising that, it was at this point that supporters began to mobilise more effectively. Peter Hooton, vocalist with local band The Farm, contacted the Liverpool Supporters Network, a group of fans involved with fanzines and websites, to arrange a meeting and form a plan. Three hundred and fifty supporters packed into the back of The Sandon, the pub where Liverpool FC had been formed in 1892. From that, the Sons of Shankly was formed, soon to be renamed Spirit of Shankly. Karen Gill, Shankly's granddaughter, gave the name the family's blessing. A leaflet was produced which said: "An alliance of supporters and all major Liverpool fanzines and websites have come together to force the owners, the poisonous, dishonest Tom Hicks and George Gillett out of OUR club."

As for the finances, Gillett had been considering selling his shares to Sheikh Al Maktoum, but Hicks had the power of veto, and blocked it. Hicks was then approached by British businesswoman Amanda Staveley, working for Al Maktoum. She had initially spoken with Spirit of Shankly, a sign of how powerful they had become. They offered half a billion for the club. Hicks turned it down. He was still hoping for nearer a billion. Hicks would soon secure a £350 million loan from RBS and Wachovia, which included paying off the initial borrowing. It also included £60 million towards a new stadium. It was in Hicks' name only. The interest rate was over 7%. The club would now be paying £40 million a year in interest. It was another 12-month loan.

When Havant & Waterlooville led Liverpool 2-1 at Anfield in the fourth round of the cup, it was hard to imagine that this nightmare winter could get any worse. Richard Pacquette put the visitors, who were five divisions below Liverpool, ahead on nine minutes. Lucas equalised with a stunning 25-yard curler - his first goal for the club. Skrtel marked his full debut with an own goal and a terrible performance. It took the Reds until the 44th minute to restore parity, when Benayoun scored the first goal of a hat trick. His other goals helped the Reds lead 4-2 on the hour. Crouch scored a fifth in the last minute. Two days later, Sissoko joined Juventus for £8.2 million.

January ended with a 0-1 defeat at West Ham. Lucas and Torres missed chances. A Lucas Neill handball had prevented Hyypia from scoring. No penalty was forthcoming. Mark Noble scored an injury-time penalty after Carragher fouled Freddie Ljungberg. Liverpool were now seventh, 17 points behind United and Arsenal, albeit with a game in hand.

Liverpool eventually turned a corner in February but there was still one more terrible result on the horizon. The month started with a 3-0 home win over Sunderland, although it took the Reds the best part of an hour to break down a relegation-threatened side. The team selection was still mystifying. Lucas played left wing, despite Babel and Benayoun being on the bench. Carragher was at right back, with Finnan being on the bench. Alonso wasn't even a sub. Benitez was still fielding two strikers, and they both scored. Crouch got the all-important goal from Carragher's pinpoint cross. He also had a scissors kick saved and a header cleared off the line. From Crouch's flick-on, Torres added his 18th of the season. Gerrard converted a late penalty. It was the first league win since Boxing Day. Two thousand Kopites stayed behind to protest against Hicks and Gillett. The owners were no longer on speaking terms.

A 0-0 draw at Chelsea was neither the worst result nor performance, but it didn't really suit either side. It was a dull game but the first time the Reds had returned with something from a league game at Stamford Bridge since 2004. Torres missed out, having got injured again for Spain. Liverpool were locked in a four-way battle for fourth with Everton, Aston Villa and Manchester City, who had won impressively at Old Trafford, as Manchester marked the 50th anniversary of the Munich Air Disaster.

The nadir of this strange and frustrating season came at Anfield, when Barnsley humiliated Liverpool in the fifth round of the FA Cup. As usual in the competition, Itandje was in goal. Gerrard was benched. Torres was still injured. Other than that, it was a strong side. Alonso came back in. Crouch partnered Kuyt up front. The latter gave the Reds a 1-0 lead at the interval from Babel's pullback. Steve Foster headed the Tykes level. The visitors had an injury-time penalty appeal turned down, but they persisted and, with Alonso and Itandje at fault, won the game with a 20-yarder from Brian Howard, who beat the Cameroonian keeper at his near post. It was Itandje's last game for the club. He was last seen laughing and joking during the 20th anniversary service for Hillsborough at Anfield in 2009, for which he was disciplined by the club. He was later released. Gary Ablett, meanwhile, had led the Reds' second string to their league title, with skipper Stephen Darby lifting the shield at Anfield.

The turning point of the season, and indeed the next 18 months, came in the last 16 of the Champions League, as the Reds beat the Italian champions Inter Milan 2-0 in the first leg at Anfield. Having struggled for three and a half years to find the right players and balance on the wings and up front, Benitez plumped for a 4-2-3-1 formation, with Torres the focal point. Babel and Kuyt played wide. Mascherano and Lucas held the midfield, with Gerrard in between the lines, supporting Torres. That formation would ensure Liverpool would not only finish 2007-08 strongly, but that they would mount a genuine title challenge the following season. Benitez's game plan was for Torres to target the former Everton defender Marco Materazzi, the player Zinedine Zidane had infamously headbutted in the 2006 World Cup Final. Pressing high up the pitch and holding a high line at the back were also key for Benitez. Inter proved a tough nut to crack, but the 34-year-old Materazzi was dismissed after half an hour for two fouls on Torres. Inter brought on Patrick Vieira and kept things tight. Torres and Hyypia missed big chances, but Kuyt eventually broke the deadlock when his shot from the inside-left channel looped fortuitously into the Kop goal. It was a fantastic moment for a popular player whose form had long since deserted him. 1-0 would have satisfied many, but Gerrard doubled the lead with an inch-perfect diagonal drive from the right angle of the area. 2-0 was a great score, but older fans knew that taking a two-goal advantage to Inter could still be precarious.

That was the first of seven straight wins. The next came at home to Middlesbrough, when Torres, easily the best player on the pitch, displayed just how much he was enjoying the new formation. Two goals in as many first-half minutes put the Reds 2-1 up. His second was likened to his stunner at the Riverside. He scored his third on the hour. Stewart Downing pulled one back, but Liverpool were home and dry. Jeremie Aliadiere was sent off for trying to slap Mascherano. The big story of the day was Tom Hicks's son, Tom Jr., thinking

233

it was a good idea to go for a drink in The Sandon with his team of minders. A pint of lager was thrown at him as the locals chanted, "You lying bastard, get out of our pub!"

Alonso, often out of favour over the winter, came back into midfield for the trip to Bolton. It was a day Liverpool when would enjoy the rub of the green, as Jussi Jaaskelainen, the Wanderers keeper, scored a howler of an own goal early on when he tried to save Gerrard's shot, which was heading wide. Babel made it two in his first 90-minute league appearance. Aurelio scored a quite brilliant first goal for the club. Tamir Cohen, son of Reds legend Avi, pulled one back.

Torres scored his second Anfield treble in a row when he put West Ham to the sword, despite a stomach upset on the eve of the match. All three were clinical finishes. Gerrard scored the fourth with a stupendous strike from 25 yards – his 18th of the season. With ten games left, the Reds were back in fourth, ahead of Everton on goal difference.

Twelve years on from the Collymore 4-3, Kevin Keegan was Newcastle manager again when they came to Anfield on the second Saturday in March. It was the last of 16 occasions he would manage against the Reds. A couple of personnel may have changed from game to game, but the 4-2-3-1 formation was now serving Benitez well. It did take an outright fluke to open the scoring, when Jose Enrique's clearance hit Pennant on the shin and looped over the unfortunate Steve Harper. Torres made it two before half-time with a dummy so outrageous that it drew comparisons with Pele's in the 1970 World Cup. Gerrard added a third shortly after. These two were on fire, both individually and as a partnership.

A clinical piece of finishing by Torres at the San Siro got Liverpool into the last eight of the Champions League. Alonso made himself unavailable to attend the birth of his son, which angered Benitez. Their relationship was disintegrating. Materazzi's replacement, Nicolas Burdisso, was also sent off for two yellows on 55 minutes. Torres soon had his moment, taking Aurelio's pass, turning Cristian Chivu and firing into the corner. The Reds had beaten Inter 3-0 on aggregate.

Mascherano had now been signed on a permanent deal and scored his first goal at home to Reading. The southerners had taken an early lead, but the Argentine's 25-yard blockbuster in front of the Kop cancelled it out. A Torres header was the match-winner as he became the first Liverpool player to score 20 goals in a league season since Robbie Fowler in 1996.

Another game against Manchester United brought another defeat. Benitez's league record against them now stood at a pitiful five defeats and a draw in six matches. Mascherano, man of the match against Reading, was sent off for dissent in the first half at Old Trafford, with Benitez having to shepherd him away from the referee. The Reds were already one down to a cross that went in off Wes Brown's back. Goals by Ronaldo and Nani in the final ten minutes finished off an atrocious Liverpool side. With only eight goal attempts to United's 23, they had been outclassed.

The Reds were up against their other big rivals a week later when Everton came to Anfield in a match crucial to the top-four aspirations of both. An early Torres goal, after Alonso had pressed Yakubu was all it took to put Liverpool five points ahead of their nearest rivals. The margin may have just been one goal, but the Reds were clearly the better side. The goal was the team's 100th of the season. Reina's 100th game brough him clean sheet number 54, one more than Ray Clemence.

Liverpool had won more European Cups than the other seven sides in the quarter-finals. The draw pitted them against Arsenal, who had also won at the San Siro in the previous round, against AC Milan. A league game was sandwiched in between the two legs, so the sides would meet three times in seven days. At the Emirates, Emmanuel Adebayor headed in Robin van Persie's corner on 23 minutes. Kuyt soon equalised from close range. Late in the game, Kuyt escaped a penalty claim against him. And then, incredibly, an offside Nicklas Bendtner got in the way of Cesc Fabregas' goalbound shot on the Liverpool line. The game ended 1-1. Since the arrival of Skrtel, Carragher had played right back several times.

Benitez made numerous changes for the league match. It also ended 1-1. French midfielder Damien Plessis made his debut and played the full 90. Crouch earned a rare start and scored the Reds only goal from the edge of the box on 42 minutes. Bendtner equalised for the Gunners, with the Reds conceding from yet another set piece.

For the opening 20 minutes of the second leg, it looked like Arsenal's mesmerising football would secure their second Champions League semi-final in three seasons. Benitez had reverted to a 4-4-2, with Gerrard and Kuyt wide and Crouch joining Torres up front. But the Gunners would have been too good for any formation in those early stages. Abou Diaby finished off a superb move to put them 1-0 up. Anfield was stunned. "Where's your famous atmosphere?" gloated the Arsenal fans, from the seats where they had celebrated Michael Thomas's title winner 19 years earlier. Hyypia quietened them with a thumping header to score his third Champions League quarter-final goal. Liverpool had stemmed the tide, and several players grew into the game. Crouch nodded on Reina's clearance in the second half. Torres swivelled and drove the ball into Manuel Almunia's top corner on 69 minutes, sparking wild scenes of euphoria on the Kop. "That was the night that, in my mind, he took his place among the Anfield greats," said Benitez. Fifteen minutes later, after Gerrard's air shot, Theo Walcott countered at speed. With 40,000 fans urging anyone in red to "take him out", Alonso, Aurelio, Mascherano and Hyypia failed to get near him. He squared to Adebayor. 2-2. Arsenal were going through on away goals with just six minutes left to play. But, as with their title challenge, the Gunners imploded. From the kick-off, a long pass found Babel, who drove into the box and drew a penalty from the careless Kolo Toure. Anfield held its breath. Gerrard nervelessly drilled the ball home. Babel broke free in injury time to beat Almunia and make it 4-2. Anfield was rocking. It had witnessed yet another European classic. Torres called the night the greatest of his career. A third semi-final in four seasons with Chelsea loomed. This time the first leg would be at Anfield.

After Anfield fell silent to remember the 96, Liverpool disposed of Blackburn 3-1, with all the goals coming in the final half hour. The introduction of Benayoun, for Babel, was the catalyst for the goals. He won the ball, and Lucas played a one-two with Gerrard, who opened the scoring. The skipper, in his 300th league game, crossed for Torres to head in the second. The three subs combined for the third, with the Israeli and Riise teeing up Voronin, who scored from close range. Rovers pulled one back in injury time. Benitez's post-match comments largely concerned the owners. The club was still at war with itself. The day after the Hillsborough anniversary, Hicks tastelessly attacked Rick Parry in a Sky Sports News interview, urging him to step down. "Leadership – it's been a disaster," he said. "We've fallen so far behind other top clubs. The stadium should have been built three or four years ago. We have two sponsors, maybe three. We should have 12 or 15. We're not doing anything in Asia the way Man U is and Barcelona is. We have a tremendous number of fans in Asia, so we've got the top brand still in the world of football. We just don't know how to commercialise it and get the money from it that we can then use to buy great players. It all goes together. Rick needs to resign from Liverpool Football Club." But without Gillett's agreement, he couldn't fire him. He also spoke about buying Gillett out and offering Benitez a one-year contract extension. He and Benitez had now formed an unlikely alliance, perhaps based on common-enemy syndrome, although they still hated each other. The interview ended in the most cringeworthy fashion, with Hicks and his family, bedecked in Liverpool kits, watching the end of the Blackburn game. When it ended, Hicks declared, "Well, Everton won't like that."

Three days before the first leg of the Chelsea semi-final, the Reds went to Fulham. A year earlier, their heavily weakened team had been beaten by a Fulham team which avoided relegation by a point. Benitez wasn't so generous this time, although he did rest Gerrard and bench Carragher and Torres. Otherwise, it was a strong side, which returned with a 2-0 victory. Pennant and Crouch got the goals. Mascherano was outstanding on his return from suspension.

In a season not short of low points, the worst moment came in the third minute of stoppage time in the first leg of the Champions League semi-final with Chelsea. Having dominated the game, the Reds led 1-0 through Kuyt's close-range goal just before half-time. But they couldn't get another. Petr Cech made late saves from Gerrard and Torres. There didn't seem much danger from a late Chelsea attack when Salomon Kalou's cross headed the way of Riise, who was only on the field because Aurelio had been stretchered off. Instead of clearing with his weaker right foot, he tried to put the ball over the bar with a diving header. "I directed it into the top corner past a shocked Pepe Reina," Riise wrote in 2018. "The fans in the Kop stopped singing. It went completely quiet. I buried my face in the turf. God." A fan in the Main Stand turned to the directors' box and shouted, somewhat harshly, to Hicks, "Happy now, you fucking tosser? See what you've done?" A totally undeserved 1-1 was a great result for Chelsea. No Liverpool player had scored at Stamford Bridge since Bruno Cheyrou in January 2004. Someone was going to have to do that in eight days' time.

Nine changes were made for the trip to third-bottom Birmingham. The hosts, desperate for points, went 2-0 up. Crouch, with his last goal for the club, and Benayoun rescued a point for the Reds, whose best player was Pennant.

The Reds bowed out of the Champions League at Stamford Bridge, but they went down fighting. Didier Drogba, who had been awful in the first game, throwing himself to the turf at regular intervals, scored on 33 minutes. Fired up by Benitez labelling him a diver, he celebrated in front of the visitors' bench. Liverpool showed the resolve to be the next scorers. Their equaliser came on 64 minutes, when Benayoun cut in from the right and played a cute ball through to Torres, who steered it home. All square again. There were no more goals until extra time. Michael Essien had a goal disallowed, because Drogba, standing in front of Reina, was offside. The crucial moment came eight minutes into the added period. Hyypia, on as a first-half sub for the injured Skrtel, tripped Michael Ballack as he was heading out of the box. Lampard, playing despite the recent death of his mother, beat Reina from the spot. Still, one more goal would take the Reds through on away goals, but Benitez withdrew Torres, explaining later he was exhausted and had a hamstring concern. Drogba scored again. Hyypia was denied a penalty. Babel got one back with three minutes left, chancing his arm from 35 yards, but Liverpool had no more in the tank. Chelsea would play Manchester United in Moscow.

In the first of two meaningless league games, the Reds beat Manchester City 1-0 at Anfield. Emiliano Insua replaced Riise, who had been told by Benitez he would be released at the end of the season. Riise asked if he could play in the final two games. The manager refused. He didn't make the bench for either. Torres scored for the eighth home game in a row, equalling Roger Hunt's record from the Division Two days of 1961-62. Kuyt's header hit the bar. Liverpool missed a plethora of chances to extend the lead.

The season ended with a routine 2-0 win at Spurs. Voronin scored midway through the second half. Torres added another five minutes later, which was similar to his first goal for the club against Chelsea. The Spaniard had scored all but three of his 24 league goals at Anfield. An 18th clean sheet for Reina saw him win his third consecutive Golden Glove award. Liverpool finished in fourth on 76 points, 11 ahead of fifth-placed Everton and seven behind Arsenal in third. Manchester United were top with 87 and would go on to become Champions of Europe.

It was hard to know how to judge such a madcap season. The club was a mess. The squad had looked miles away from title-challenging standard over the winter, but the switch to 4-2-3-1 had invigorated the side and played to the strengths of both Gerrard and Torres. Further changes were needed, but with the captain in the number-ten role behind the sensational Spaniard, Benitez finally had a team that looked capable of scoring at will.

2008-09

"I'll give you £50 million Rafa, plus whatever we get in the draft."

O ther than Liverpool being in complete chaos, mortgaged to the hilt with owners everyone hated, one of the amazing things about their 2008-09 title challenge is that it was preceded by possibly Rafa Benitez's worst transfer window. It wasn't just the lack of quality possessed by incoming players like Philipp Degen and Andrea Dossena, but his attempt to finance the signings of Gareth Barry and Robbie Keane by selling Xabi Alonso showed an uncharacteristic lack of judgement, which led to the Spanish playmaker leaving a year later.

Neither Degen nor Dossena were up to scratch, which was particularly galling, as Dossena cost £7 million. Degen spent most of the year in the treatment room. Diego Cavalieri came in to replace Charles Itandje as the back-up goalkeeper. Other than Fernando Torres, Benitez had enjoyed little success signing wingers and strikers since 2004, and that pattern continued with the signings of Robbie Keane, David N'Gog and Albert Riera. Keane cost £19 million from Spurs and went back after half a season. It was a most puzzling signing, given the manager's switch to the 4-2-3-1 formation. Even as back-up for Torres, Keane wasn't good enough. Neither was N'Gog, a £1.5 million signing from Paris St Germain. Spanish winger Riera cost £8 million on the last day of August. He made a decent start, but his presence hindered the progress of Ryan Babel, whose Liverpool career would stall in its second season. The manager had hoped to sign Cardiff's 17-year-old midfielder Aaron Ramsay but was pipped at the post by Arsenal.

Benitez's decision to sell Alonso to fund Keane and Barry was catastrophic. It left supporters bewildered. Even putting Alonso to one side, it summed up just how incompetent Liverpool were in the world of business. Benitez had explicitly said he only wanted Keane if the club signed Barry, as Keane without Barry wouldn't fit into the system he had devised. But Rick Parry signed Keane first, as it was the easier deal to tie up, only for Barry to end up staying at Villa because Liverpool wouldn't match their demands. Co-owner George Gillett explained to Benitez that Barry was too old to justify the cost - even though he was younger and cheaper than Keane, aptly showing why the Spaniard was often so exasperated. Gillett would often say when asked about transfer funds by the manager, "I'll give you £50 million, Rafa, plus whatever we get in the draft." On another occasion, he replied to an email about potential transfers by saying he had discovered a new running machine that would improve Benitez's squad and he would happily send one over.

Juventus weren't willing to meet Benitez's £18 million demand for Alonso, which was good news for Liverpool fans in the short term. At a pre-season friendly with Lazio at Anfield, fans had cheered Alonso to the rafters. They also sang, "You can shove your Gareth Barry up your arse!"

Those who did leave the club in the summer of 2008 were John Arne Riise, Harry Kewell, Anthony Le Tallec, Peter Crouch, Danny Guthrie, Scott Carson and Steve Finnan. Sammy Lee replaced Pako Ayestaran as assistant to Benitez.

After an undefeated pre-season, the Reds had to contest another Champions League qualifier. They returned from Belgium with a 0-0 draw against an impressive Standard Liege side, which included Marouane Fellaini, who would very shortly sign for Everton. Reina kept goal. Alvaro Arbeloa and Dossena were the full backs. Jamie Carragher and the fit-again Daniel Agger were the centre halves. With Lucas Leiva and Javier Mascherano representing their nations in the Olympics and Steven Gerrard nursing a back injury, Alonso and Damien Plessis formed the central midfield. Yossi Benayoun and Dirk Kuyt were on the flanks. Keane joined Torres up front in a 4-4-2 formation. In the trickiest qualifier of Benitez's time at the club, Liege were easily the better side and spurned several chances, including an incorrectly awarded penalty, which Reina saved.

The Premier League campaign began at Sunderland's Stadium of Light. Liverpool wore a new grey away kit, just as Kenny Dalglish's last title winners had done. Hyypia and Gerrard came into the starting line-up. Agger and Alonso dropped out. The fans sang Alonso's name throughout the afternoon, and he set up the winner for Torres after replacing Plessis at half-time. Torres's low 20-yard finish was superb. The talented pair had been part of Spain's successful European Championship campaign, with Torres scoring the only goal of the final against Germany.

When Middlesbrough led 1-0 at Anfield going into the closing stages, it certainly didn't look like Liverpool would be mounting a title challenge. Carragher, of all people, equalised with five minutes left with the aid of a big deflection. And then in injury time, Gerrard won the match with a magnificent shot from the edge of the box, placed perfectly into the top corner. Liverpool were top.

Given the financial situation of the club, the second leg against Standard Liege was vital. Still without Mascherano and Lucas, Benitez kept the 4-4-2. Liverpool huffed and puffed, with little end product. The lack of width was alarming. Gerrard struggled through the match with a groin injury, which would sideline him for two matches. In the end, Kuyt's volley from Babel's pinpoint cross in the 118th minute settled the tie, in which Liege had been the better side.

Mascherano and Lucas went straight into the side to play at Villa. In what would become a familiar pattern in 2008-09, Torres picked up a hamstring strain and was replaced by debutant N'Gog after half an hour. The best chance fell to Keane on 73 minutes, but the struggling Irishman was muscled off the ball by Nigel Reo-Coker. Benitez was goaded all afternoon for his failed pursuit of Barry, who played superbly.

Before Liverpool's home game with Manchester United, Gillett asked a group of players which one Robbie Keane was. When the Irishman came forward, the co-owner declared, "Jeez, you're not very big for all that money we spent on you, are you?" An international break had given Gerrard and Torres the chance to recover for the visit of the champions. They both made the bench, although only Gerrard came on. Riera made an impressive debut. When Carlos Tevez struck in the third minute, it looked like Benitez's atrocious record against Manchester United would continue. Alonso's long-range drive was parried by Edwin van der Sar, but it hit Wes Brown and rebounded into the net. The Reds were excellent and looked more likely to find a winner. The big moment came in the 77th minute, when Mascherano dispossessed Ryan Giggs. Kuyt found Babel, who had been on the pitch for five minutes. His shot hit the turf and bounced into the roof of the net. One-time Liverpool target Nemanja Vidic was sent off in the last minute. Benitez had finally taken three points off Alex Ferguson. Mascherano was magnificent, as were many others. The Reds were second, United 13th.

Liverpool again came from behind to win by the same score in Marseille, in the first Champions League group game. Trailing to a Lorik Cana goal scored in the 23rd minute, Gerrard swept the ball spectacularly into the far top corner three minutes later. It was a sensational strike. Six minutes later, Babel won a penalty which the skipper dispatched after being ordered to retake. Benitez was delighted Babel had won the penalty by taking on the full back on the outside, feeling he cut inside too often.

If Liverpool had done the double over Stoke City in 2008-09, they would have won the Premier League title. They drew both matches 0-0. Gerrard had a second-minute free kick at Anfield disallowed for a contentious offside. Liverpool were otherwise insipid and short of ideas. Keane and Torres continued to look an unconvincing partnership. "There's no point beating United if we don't follow it up with another win," Benitez had written in his programme notes.

Crewe Alexandra were Liverpool's first opponents in the League Cup, giving Benitez an excuse to play the likes of Cavalieri, Emiliano Insua, Degen, Jermaine Pennant, Plessis, N'Gog and Nabil El Zhar. Agger blasted in a superb free kick for his first goal since the 2007 Champions League semi-final win over Chelsea. Crewe equalised from a corner. Lucas won the match with a second-half header from Pennant's cross. Tom Pope missed a sitter at the end, which would have forced extra-time. Degen had a couple of ribs broken on his debut, which summed up his Liverpool career.

Victory at Goodison Park was the first of five straight league wins for Benitez's men. Torres was the hero, scoring twice in three minutes in the second half. He had a hat-trick goal disallowed for a non-existent push. Keane supplied the cross for the first, which the Spaniard side-footed home. With the Blues still reeling, an unmarked Torres was able to pick his spot from 16 yards after Kuyt was tackled. Everton fans streamed out. Everton's Tim Cahill, who had earlier missed a sitter, was sent off.

PSV Eindhoven were seen off with relative ease in the Champions League. Kuyt scored first, after Torres' shot was saved. His European record continued to dwarf his Premiership exploits. Keane finally got off the mark for the club, side-footing in Torres' cross. Of all Liverpool strikers, only Peter Crouch, Arthur Rowley, Ian Rush and Michael Robinson had taken longer to net their first goal. Gerrard scored his 100th goal for the club, smashing in an indirect free kick from 30 yards. PSV pulled one back, but the Reds were comfortable winners in Benitez's 250th game in charge of the club.

As Liverpool mourned the death of club secretary Bryce Morrison, one of the most memorable wins of the season came on a Sunday afternoon as Liverpool won at Manchester City, who had just become the richest club in the world. Benitez went back to the 4-2-3-1 formation, with Mascherano and Alonso in midfield, Gerrard further forward, Riera and Kuyt wide and Torres up front. City were 2-0 up by half-time, thanks to goals from Stephen Ireland and Javier Garrido. But the imposters of the first half were replaced by the real Liverpool. Torres scored Liverpool's 1000th Premier League goal when he turned in Arbeloa's cross. The £36-million Robinho missed a glorious chance for City. Pablo Zabaleta was dismissed for a bad foul on Alonso. Torres equalised with a header from a corner. Liverpool were all over City now. Torres missed a sitter. Skrtel sustained a serious knee injury towards the end. Torres had an injury-time shot saved, but Kuyt was alert enough to gleefully ram home the rebound in front of Liverpool's jubilant fans. It was the Dutchman's first league goal for over ten months.

Joining Skrtel in the treatment room was Torres, who was injured again on international duty. Benitez selected Agger, Dossena and Pennant for the visit of Wigan. Egyptian Amr Zaki scored twice in the first half as they opened up a 2-1 lead. His first was a terrible error from Agger. His second was a tremendous scissor kick. Kuyt scored in between after wonderful play from the atoning Agger. He also hit the bar. Antonio Valencia was sent off for a foul on Alonso. Just as it looked as if time was running out, Riera scored his first for the club, drilling the ball into the bottom corner from 20 yards. The winner was scruffy, as Kuyt's shot hit the ground and reared up into the roof of the net on 85 minutes. The Kop were euphoric, sensing something special was brewing. After eight games, the Reds were behind only Chelsea on goal difference.

Keane scored again in Madrid as the Reds drew 1-1 with an Atletico team that included Luis Garcia and Florent Sinama-Pongolle. Keane, Benayoun and Babel missed chances to increase the lead. A penalty claim from Riera was ignored. Reina saved brilliantly from Simao Sabrosa, tipping his shot onto the post, but the one-time Reds target equalised on 83 minutes.

Former Chelsea defender Jason Cundy laughed at the idea that the Reds could win at Stamford Bridge, and with Torres absent, Liverpool fans may have agreed with him. But Liverpool leapfrogged the Londoners to go top with a 1-0 win when Alonso's unconvincing tenth-minute shot was deflected in by Jose Bosingwa. The Spaniard hit the foot of a post with a long-range free kick in the second half. Mascherano was in fine form, tailor-made for this sort of occasion. After 86 league games at Stamford Bridge, Chelsea, now managed by Luis Felipe Scolari, were finally beaten. Liverpool were three points clear of Chelsea and Hull City.

The Reds had been unable to deal with Stoke after beating Manchester United, so it was vital they disposed of Portsmouth at Anfield after the high of beating Chelsea. Gerrard's penalty on 75 minutes after a handball was the only goal. David James had earlier touched Kuyt's shot onto the post and saved from Benayoun in the second half. Torres was still missing.

Kuyt was on the scoresheet again at Tottenham, but it all went wrong for Liverpool in Harry Redknapp's first game in charge of Spurs. Kuyt took less than three minutes to fire in from a tight angle, but the Reds couldn't extend their lead, despite dominating the game. Darren Bent hit his own post. Gerrard hit the woodwork twice in the second half. Kuyt and Alonso missed easy chances. They were made to pay when Carragher scored an own goal on 69 minutes, before Roman Pavlyuchenko won the match in injury time. Redknapp looked embarrassed when shaking Benitez's hand and admitted they'd been lucky. Liverpool's first defeat of the season had come in the 17th match.

Another defeat looked likely when Atletico led 1-0 in the fourth Champions League group game. Future Red Maxi Rodriguez had scored seven minutes before the break. Torres was still missing. With time running out, Gerrard won a controversial penalty, which he converted with aplomb. The two sides were level at the top of the group with eight points from three matches. Marseille and PSV had three apiece.

Keane got his first league goals to help Liverpool beat West Brom. He clipped the ball over Scott Carson superbly for the first and rounded him for the second. Arbeloa added a late third, his only Liverpool goal. Torres was finally back, as a 72nd-minute substitute for Keane. "We have enough quality in the squad to be there for a long time," said Benitez of Liverpool's return to the top.

Tottenham beat Liverpool for the second time in 11 days when they won 4-2 in the League Cup. Benitez fielded a fringe team, although Torres played for the first 55 minutes. Spurs scored their goals in a 14-minute spell either side of half-time. Plessis scored his only Liverpool goal. Hyypia got the second. Stephen Darby made his Liverpool debut off the bench, the first of six appearances. In 2018, he was diagnosed with Motor Neurone Disease.

Kuyt's great form continued as he scored the Reds opener in a 2-0 win at Bolton. Having earlier hit the bar with a ferocious shot, he met Aurelio's cross with a powerful header. Torres replaced Keane for the last 30 minutes, during which time he hit a post, had a shot saved and twice set up chances for Gerrard. The skipper took the second of those to secure the points. Alonso played superbly. Keane was struggling and missed an open goal.

Liverpool's Achilles heel undid them in the next game, as they failed to beat

Fulham at Anfield. The away form was good enough to win the league, but although they would remain unbeaten at Anfield, there were too many draws, especially in November and December. Gerrard was injured. Keane missed a clear-cut chance, but Liverpool struggled against the Cottagers' low block. Alonso was named on the bench, with Lucas starting. The Kop sang his name ten minutes before half-time. He eventually replaced Mascherano after 64 minutes.

Benitez fielded one of his strongest line-ups for the home game with Marseille in the Champions League. The team was beginning to take shape now, with Arbeloa and Aurelio the full backs. Carragher and Agger were at centre back. Mascherano partnered Alonso in the middle, with Riera and Kuyt wide. Gerrard was back in the number-10 role behind Torres. Keane was becoming more and more acquainted with the substitutes' bench. Gerrard scored the only goal against the French side, heading in Alonso's magnificent cross. He was the top scorer in the competition. The game came three days before the tenth anniversary of his debut against Blackburn.

Chelsea's home defeat to Arsenal meant the Reds would return to the summit if they could get anything from a Monday night fixture at home to Gianfranco Zola's West Ham in early December. They did indeed go top, but another frustrating 0-0 draw saw parts of the crowd boo them. Torres missed out again – his injury record would be a major reason Liverpool would ultimately miss out on top spot. Hyypia headed over. Robert Green tipped over Benayoun's shot. The Hammers' Craig Bellamy hit a post from 25 yards. Before the game, the Kop had unveiled a mosaic in support of Michael Shields, who had remained imprisoned since the 2005 Champions League Final, wrongly accused of attempted murder. The Kop had produced a similar mosaic for him in 2005. His sentence was reduced from 15 years to ten after two appeals, and he was able to move to a British prison in 2006. After new evidence was considered, he received a royal pardon in September 2009 and was released.

For over an hour, it looked like the Reds were facing a third consecutive Premier League goalless draw but up stepped Alonso with a precise shot from 18 yards to break the deadlock at Paul Ince's Blackburn. Benayoun scored an excellent second with ten minutes left. Roque Santa Cruz got one back, but Gerrard secured a 3-1 win in the last minute with Paul Robinson out of his goal. Liverpool were a point clear of Chelsea after 16 games. Manchester United were six points adrift but had a game in hand.

The final European group game brought a 3-1 win in Eindhoven - the sixth time the sides had met since 2006. A weakened Reds overturned a 1-0 deficit with goals from Babel, Riera and N'Gog - his first for the club. Riera's was a stupendous strike from 35 yards. Jay Spearing and Martin Kelly debuted as subs. The Reds had topped their group for the fourth season in a row.

Another costly home draw came in the league against Hull. The Terriers stunned Anfield by taking an early 2-0 lead, the second of which was a Carragher own goal. Gerrard responded immediately and then got another to make level the game before the break. But having made a habit of overturning losing positions, Liverpool were unable to get a third in the remaining 58 minutes. Hyypia hit a post. Liverpool were missing Torres badly. Benitez preferred Babel, El Zhar and N'Gog to come off the bench rather than Keane.

Benitez missed the game at Arsenal with kidney stones. Sammy Lee took charge as the Spaniard kept in regular contact by phone. Mascherano also missed out with flu. Robin van Persie scored for Arsenal, but Keane responded in style. As was often the case in the 2000s, Arsenal fans yelled "Hoof!" as Agger cleared. Keane ran onto it, allowed the ball to bounce and hit a magnificent shot on the second bounce. The ball thudded into the roof of the net. Emmanuel Adebayor was dismissed for a raised foot in the second half, but the Reds couldn't take advantage. Agger missed with a long-ranger. El Zhar was wide with a late header. It ended 1-1. Despite eight dropped points since the fourth week of November, the Reds were top at Christmas. Chelsea had dropped nine in that time. Champions Manchester United were coming into the race.

With so many recent draws, it only took 25 minutes of scoreless football at home to Bolton on Boxing Day for Liverpool fans to start worrying. When Riera prodded in Gerrard's corner at the near post, all was well again. Two second-half goals in six minutes from Keane clinched the points. The second was a blistering counterattack as Reina rolled the ball to Alonso, who freed Benayoun down the right. Keane took his square pass and turned the ball home from just outside the six-yard box. Benitez was at the game, but Lee undertook the post-match media duties. Asked if the second half of the Reds' campaign could mirror the first, and if it would be enough for them to win the league, the former Reds midfielder quipped, "I can't answer that. With a face like mine, I don't look in the mirror."

Shay Given made several exceptional saves in the early stages as the Reds dominated Joe Kinnear's Newcastle on their own turf. Liverpool could have had four by the time Gerrard finally beat the Irishman. Hyypia's header from the skipper's corner doubled the lead. David Edgar made it 1-2 by half-time. Babel scrambled one in from a corner early in the second half. Freed by Lucas, Gerrard bore down on goal before clipping it over Given for number four. Alonso wrapped up the scoring with a penalty, won by N'Gog. If anything, the 5-1 score flattered Newcastle. "Gerrard was magnificent," said Kinnear. "That's the best individual performance I've seen in a long time." After the last game of 2008, the Reds topped the table, three points ahead of Chelsea after 20 games each. Manchester United were seven off the top, with two games in hand. Later that evening, Gerrard was arrested for a late-night fracas in Southport and spent 23 hours in custody, but was later found not guilty of affray in court.

The first game of the new year was an FA Cup tie at Preston, the first time the clubs had met since a Division Two fixture in 1962. The 5,000 travelling Reds sat in the Bill Shankly Stand. Benitez fielded a strong side, albeit with Cavalieri taking Reina's place. Riera scored a brilliant opener on 24, cutting back onto his left foot and arrowing the ball past Andy Lonergan, a future Red. They had a long wait for the second. Lucas's injury-time clearance set Gerrard free, and he unselfishly fed the ball to the returning Torres, on as a sub, to tap in.

Before the next game, away at Stoke, Benitez carried out his infamous 'facts' press conference. He was asked for his opinion on a comment Alex Ferguson had made about the team's respective fixture lists. "I was surprised by what has been said, but maybe they are nervous because we are at the top of the table," he said. "But I want to talk about facts. I want to be clear, I do not want to play mind games too early, although they seem to want to start." He went on to detail instances of Ferguson not being punished for improper conduct against officials, or refereeing decisions that benefited United, or fixture scheduling that favoured them. His words were quickly described as 'a rant', with the suggestion that he was cracking up in the face of Ferguson's mind games. What Benitez said was true but, with hindsight, poking a stick at a hornets' nest did the club no favours, especially when his players couldn't beat Stoke in the next game and United beat Chelsea 3-0 a day later. Gerrard recalled watching the press conference at home. "Rafa was sounding muddled and bitter and paranoid," he wrote in his 2015 book. "I wanted to jump behind the couch and cover my ears for Rafa's sake. He was humiliating himself and I have no idea what he was attempting to achieve."

The pre-Christmas draws had indeed been costly, but the Stoke game was the first of three more in January that saw United overtake the Reds and stay at the top, other than a couple of occasions when they had at least one game in hand. Gerrard hit a post in the closing stages. In his book he blamed Liverpool's loss of form on the departure of Benitez's assistant coach Pako Ayestaran. "We lost a lot when Rafa fell out with Pako in 2007," he wrote. "We all loved Pako's training and his methods. I always felt so fresh and fired-up when going out to play a match under Pako. He was also a great link to the manager."

The first of two Anfield derbies in a week came on a Monday night in the Premier League. By the time the game was played, United had won their games in hand to go a point clear. A late equaliser by Tim Cahill kept the Reds in second on goal difference, having played a game more. Torres, who had just come third behind Cristiano Ronaldo and Lionel Messi in the FIFA World Player of the Year award, was denied a clear penalty. In his 250th game as captain, Gerrard opened the scoring midway through the second half with a stunning low drive from 30 yards into the corner of the Kop goal. Instead of going for the killer goal, Liverpool tried to hold on, and Cahill's headed equaliser from a free kick stunned Anfield. United were clear favourites now for the title.

Six days later, in the fourth round of the FA Cup, there was another Anfield Derby, the tenth in a row Everton failed to win. Carragher's effort was just wide after some great footwork. Lescott headed in a corner at the other end – another set-piece concession for Benitez to mull over. The equaliser came in the second half after some magnificent skill from Torres. His impressive control of Gerrard's header was one thing. His sublime backheel that sent the skipper racing down the inside-left channel was quite another. The captain's low shot beat Tim Howard at the near post. Liverpool dominated possession but did little with it. They now had to go to Goodison for a replay.

Two more points were dropped at Wigan. Mascherano sent Benayoun in on goal. He rounded Mike Pollitt and scored from the tightest of angles. With seven minutes left, Wigan countered. Lucas carelessly conceded a penalty for tripping Jason Koumas. Mido beat Reina from the spot. To the disbelief of the away fans, Benitez immediately hooked Gerrard for Keane. Babel, described in the Echo as 'abysmal', played the full 90. Torres endured an evening to forget. Liverpool were now third. It had been a horrible month. "Liverpool are in grave danger of blowing their best chance of winning the league title since 1990," concluded the Liverpool Echo. It was Keane's last game for the club before he returned to White Hart Lane for £16 million. He had scored seven goals in his half season at the club. It had been a failed experiment.

Late goals by Torres in a 2-0 win over Chelsea was just what the doctor ordered. The euphoria that greeted the goals said much for the misery of the preceding month. Cech tipped over from Alonso and then parried Riera's shot. Frank Lampard was sent off on the hour for going studs-up on Alonso, who later hit the bar. Cech tipped Benayoun's shot around the post. Another piledriver from the Israeli went close. Something had to give. Aurelio's 89th-minute cross was met at the near post by Torres, whose glancing header gave him his first Anfield goal of the season. Cech tipped over from Gerrard. Deep into injury time, Benayoun dispossessed Ashley Cole and squared to Torres, who beat Cech. With 22 goal attempts to four, the Reds had been magnificent.

In an amazing cock-up, ITV managed to miss Everton's last-gasp winner against Liverpool in the cup replay. Gerrard went off injured. Lucas was sent off for two yellows. There were no goals in the 90. Two and a half minutes from penalties, ITV suddenly cut to a Tic Tac advert. When the coverage returned 31 seconds later, Everton's players were celebrating, and the nation had missed Dan Gosling's deflected goal.

A five-goal thriller at Tony Adams' Portsmouth, and another late winner lifted everybody's spirits. Benitez fielded a bizarre line-up, with three centre halves for the first time in the season – Carragher, Skrtel and Agger. Aurelio was in centre midfield, with Alonso on the bench alongside Torres. N'Gog was up front with Babel. Gerrard was absent. After a goalless hour, the game exploded into life. David Nugent put Pompey ahead against the run of play. Aurelio smashed in a 12-yard indirect free kick after David James had handled Peter Crouch's back pass. Hermann Hreidarsson restored Portsmouth's lead on 78, heading in a free kick. Kuyt equalised with six minutes left, beating James at his near post. And then in injury time, substitute Torres headed in Benayoun's cross to win the game 3-2.

Once again, it was back to earth with a bump. A Craig Bellamy shot deflected off Arbeloa to put Manchester City ahead at Anfield. Gerrard was still missing. Kuyt bundled in an equaliser with 12 minutes left. With the crowd at fever pitch,

Torres cushioned El Zhar's cross into the path of Benayoun, but his fierce 12-yard volley was too close to Shay Given. The Reds were now seven points behind United. They had lost just once in the Premier League, but ten draws was a depressing statistic. Rick Parry now realised his days were numbered. The day after the City game he reached a severance deal with the club and would stand down as chief executive at the end of the season. He later spoke of his regret in failing to win the title and deliver a new stadium.

"The final great cathedral of European football we conquered," was how Benitez described Liverpool's win against Real Madrid at the Bernabeu. What is often overlooked about the 2008-09 season is how remarkable it was that Liverpool competed so strongly in the Premier League and Champions League, given how the club was tearing itself apart behind the scenes. The continued ownership of Tom Hicks and George Gillett was causing chaos, and on the day of the Madrid first leg, rumours swept the football world that Benitez had left the club. He dined with the players, ignoring the constant stream of text messages asking if it was true. As ever, Liverpool were meticulously prepared for a big European game. Benitez was confident that if the Reds could contain Arjen Robben, then the main supply line to strikers Raul and Gonzalo Higuain would be cut. It worked. "Robben touched the ball only a couple of times in the game," said Riera. "That was because of Rafa's plan ... My job was to stop the pass from Sergio Ramos to Robben." Raul did get free once, but Reina saved. Iker Casillas did likewise from Torres at the other end. Alonso tried his luck from 60 yards. Casillas tipped it over. Torres limped off with an ankle injury. With eight minutes left, Benayoun, the smallest man in the box, headed in Aurelio's free kick. Gerrard came off the bench for the final couple of minutes as Liverpool held on to their priceless 1-0 win.

When the Reds lost 2-0 at the Riverside, the league was surely gone. A sixth European Cup was a much more realistic ambition. With Arbeloa injured and amid rumours that Carragher refused to play right back, Skrtel fulfilled the role. But he was dominated by Stewart Downing. The absence of Torres meant a start for El Zhar on the wing, with Kuyt up front. The Reds were awful and went behind to an own goal by Alonso, the second of his Liverpool career. Tuncay sealed the win on 63 minutes. Not for a moment did the Reds look like getting back into the game. Benitez withdrew Carragher and Gerrard as the game ebbed away. "How is it possible to go from beating Real Madrid in their own backyard to being all too easily overcome by Middlesbrough in theirs, all in the space of three days?" asked the Liverpool Echo.

A Tuesday night match at home to Sunderland gave the Reds a chance to collect a routine three points. Left back Insua played on the right. Winger Riera was at left back. A goalless first half set the nerves jangling, especially with Torres still missing, but N'Gog stabbed in Gerrard's header, and Benayoun made it 2-0 from a goalkeeping error as the Reds looked forward to hosting Real Madrid.

From the moment Torres took Gerrard's pass, spun away from the legendary

Italian defender Fabio Cannavaro and forced a low save from Casillas, it was clear that the Reds were on song in the home leg against Madrid. And so it proved. "The return leg was, I think, the finest European performance of my six years at Liverpool," said Benitez. "As we tore Madrid to shreds, we were almost perfect." Casillas tipped over Mascherano's dipping volley. Torres forced Pepe into an error, Kuyt squared the ball back and Liverpool were 1-0 up after 16 minutes. Torres was on fire. He soon embarrassed Sergio Ramos. His cross found Gerrard, who produced another great save from the world's best keeper. Such a blistering start showed up the Madrid arrogance. Their president, Vicente Boluda, had predicted a 'cascade' of goals - although he was ultimately proven correct. Marca, a Real-supporting newspaper, had said, "This is Anfield ... so what?" Gabriel Heinze, who could have been lining up for the Reds, conceded a penalty for handball, although it hit his shoulder. Gerrard nailed the penalty - all over, barring a collapse.

Babel swept down the left just after half-time, and his measured ball inside was turned into the roof of Casillas' net by the captain. Gerrard and Torres went close. Casillas was keeping the score in single figures. After such wintery discontent, those on the Kop couldn't believe their eyes, especially when Dossena tucked away Mascherano's cross to score his first Liverpool goal in the last minute. Raul tried to tap up Gerrard after the game, desperate for his side to rebuild. The skipper could bask in the glory of his team destroying the great Real Madrid, nine times winners of the game's most prestigious trophy, by four goals to nil; 5-0 on aggregate. "We had no more worlds to conquer," Benitez wrote of his European adventures.

On five occasions, Liverpool had dropped points after a European match. Nobody would have been surprised had it happened again at Old Trafford, with Manchester United ten points clear. Reina had a brainstorm in needlessly fouling Park Ji-Sung. Ronaldo knocked in the penalty. But the story soon diverted from the usual script. Torres embarrassed Vidic by beating him to a long ball. He drew van der Sar and found the corner of the net. Gerrard beat Evra and was fouled just inside the box on the stroke of half-time. Penalty. The skipper converted it with aplomb and kissed a TV camera in celebration. A one-goal lead is rarely comfortable at Old Trafford, so the Reds continued to pour forward. Gerrard got on the outside of Vidic. As it became clear he was going to bear down on goal, he was brought down. The Serb was sent off again. Aurelio dispatched the free kick magnificently. Among several late chances, Dossena, quite amazingly, latched onto Reina's long ball and lobbed it over a disbelieving van der Sar. He only scored twice for Liverpool – against Real Madrid and Manchester United. The champions' lead was down to seven points. "Rafa had set us up as if it was a European game," said Gerrard. "He totally outwitted Ferguson that day and, at his icy tactical best, he created a framework for Torres and me, with Mascherano, Lucas and Kuyt prompting all the way that afternoon, to destroy United."

A week later, it was whittled down to four, and the title race was alive again.

United lost 2-0 at Fulham. Wayne Rooney was sent off. The Reds took Aston Villa apart like a Duplo train set the following day. Kuyt slammed in a rebound on eight minutes. Reina saved superbly from John Carew and then got himself another assist when Riera smashed his clearance into the top corner. Gerrard scored the first of two penalties on 39 minutes when Riera was fouled. He calmly stroked in a free kick shortly after half-time, before completing his hat trick with another spot kick on 65 minutes. Friedel was harshly sent off for a professional foul on Torres, but it was later rescinded so he could play against Manchester United. Liverpool's 4-2-3-1 was clicking beautifully now. The system looked perfect. Everybody was playing their part.

The in-form Reds went to Fulham next where Dossena, Alonso, Torres and Dossena again hit the woodwork in a commanding first-half performance. The same intensity wasn't there in the second half, but with the game heading towards a 0-0 draw that would have ended Liverpool's title charge, Benayoun found himself with a yard of space in the penalty area and fired across Mark Schwarzer and into the corner of the net. It was the 94th minute. For a split second, Benitez, for once, celebrated joyously. "We're gonna win the league!" chanted the away fans. "That will be the most important goal of the season if we can win the title," said the manager. Twenty-four hours later, Villa led United 2-1 at Old Trafford. Ronaldo equalised with ten minutes left. Deep into injury time, Federico Macheda curled in the winning goal. United were still four points clear.

It took Torres six minutes to find the corner of Petr Cech's net in the first leg of the Champions League quarter-final at Anfield. Liverpool were flying. He could have had another after dispossessing Lampard. But the absence of Mascherano, suspended for one game, came back to bite as Chelsea settled into the game. The big defender Branislav Ivanovic headed in two corners to get his side a couple of priceless away goals. They were his first goals for the club. Didier Drogba added a third from Florent Malouda's cross. John Terry taunted the Kop at the final whistle, although he would be suspended from the second leg. For the first time in their nine Champions League games together since 2005, the away team had won. From Macheda to Ivanovic, in the space of four days, Liverpool's chances of winning one of the big trophies had been significantly diminished.

If they were down in the dumps, Liverpool didn't show it, as they hammered Blackburn 4-0. They were midway through a run of scoring 43 goals in their last 14 matches. After a tribute to the 96, which included former Red Stephen Warnock laying a wreath in front of the Kop, Torres scored one of the most spectacular goals of his career, lashing in a volley from the right side of the penalty area and over Paul Robinson. It was a carbon copy of Ian Rush's against Manchester United in the 1992-93 season, from almost the same blade of grass. The Spaniard then headed in a set piece at the near post, after Benitez had urged Alonso to send the free kick deeper. After the goal, Alonso asked the manager what he had been shouting. Benitez smiled and folded his arms, as if to say 'it doesn't matter now.' Astonishingly, he was later attacked for this gesture by Alex Ferguson as being 'beyond the pale.' Rovers manager Sam Allardyce joined in this ludicrous two-pronged attack, accusing Benitez of avoiding him after the game, which he said 'shows you the measure of the man.' He also admitted watching several replays of Benitez folding his arms, believing the Liverpool manager was arrogantly saying "Game over." Back in the real world, Agger made it three with a sensational strike from distance, before N'Gog headed a late fourth.

No one gave the Reds a prayer when they travelled to London for the second leg with Chelsea. Not only had they lost by a margin of two, but Chelsea had scored three away goals. Usual skippers Gerrard and Terry sat this one out. After 35 minutes, Liverpool were 2-0 up. They still needed one more, but they had made a game of it. Aurelio caught everybody by surprise as he took a free kick wide on the right. With everybody expecting a cross, he aimed for the near post from 35 yards and found the net. Nine minutes later, Alonso smashed a penalty past Cech after he had been impeded by Ivanovic. Gerrard celebrated in the stands. Chelsea fans booed their players off the pitch. Perhaps it did the trick. Within 12 minutes of the restart, they were level through Drogba and Alex. Reina had been badly at fault for the first. Alex's 30-yard free kick was unstoppable. Lampard put them 3-2 ahead. Back came Liverpool through Lucas and Kuyt. They were now 4-3 up on the night. One more would see them through on away goals. But it wasn't to be. This sensational evening was settled once and for all by Lampard, whose second goal made it 4-4, and 7-5 on aggregate. Chelsea lost in the semi-final to Barcelona.

One lone cry of "Justice!" was all it took. The day after the Chelsea game, Labour's Andy Burnham, the Secretary of State for Culture, Media and Sport, and an Everton fan, stood in front of the Kop to address the crowd at the 20th anniversary for Hillsborough. There were 30,000 present in Anfield. Some were confused why a member of a government that had failed the 96 should be talking at such an event. His speech was interrupted after less than a minute by a shout of "Justice!". The Kop bellowed "Justice for the 96!" All Burnham, a man with good intentions, could do was nod. He eventually finished his speech. He went back to the Prime Minister, Gordon Brown, and persuaded him to reopen an investigation into the causes of the disaster. The Hillsborough Independent Panel was set up to go through every piece of evidence relating to the disaster. The wheels of justice were finally in motion.

It's hard to guess what the odds of successive 4-4 draws would have been, but it happened again when the Reds hosted Arsenal in the league. Liverpool absolutely dominated, scoring four times from well over 20 shots. Arsenal scored four from five. All their goals, scored by the Russian Andrey Arshavin, began with Liverpool in possession. The Reds dominated the first half hour, but Arshavin grabbed his first. Torres headed in Kuyt's cross just after the break. Benayoun then scored a header whilst being kicked in the face. Arshavin scored two in four minutes to leave the Reds' title ambitions hanging by a thread. Torres equalised again. Arshavin scored in the last minute after supporting Theo

Walcott's breakaway. Benayoun hooked one in from close range deep into injury time. 4-4 again. Liverpool were top on goal difference, but the champions had two games in hand. They would need to lose two of their last seven.

A routine 3-1 win at Hull was just what Liverpool needed. Alonso's free kick hit the Hull wall on the stroke of half-time. The crowd mocked him, but he lashed the rebound into the net. It would be his final goal for the club. Hull's Caleb Folan was sent off for lashing out at Skrtel. In his 100th Premier League game, Kuyt made it 2-0 from close range. Geovanni got one back for the ten men, but the Dutchman wrapped up the points in the closing stages. As Reds fans headed back across the M62, Manchester United were 2-0 down in the late afternoon kick-off at home to Spurs. But Howard Webb gave a terrible penalty decision to United just before the hour, for which he later apologised. Ronaldo scored. Spurs collapsed. United won 5-2. Liverpool still had to claw back six points.

A fun-packed Sunday lunchtime fixture at home to Newcastle provided even more entertainment in this goal fest of a run Liverpool were on. The 3-0 score comprised only part of the story. On the verge of relegation, the Geordies were turning into a soap opera. The Kop sang "You should have stayed on the telly!" to their stand-in manager Alan Shearer. Joey Barton became the fourth player of the season to be red-carded for fouling Alonso. Michael Owen came on for the last ten minutes, to be reminded by the Kop that he should have signed for a big club. Out of Europe and with the chances of winning the league miniscule at best, the Reds were at least enjoying what was left of the season. Alonso hit the bar twice, but Benayoun, Kuyt and Lucas scored the goals, the latter's being the 200th by a Liverpool substitute. The first had been scored by Geoff Strong against West Ham in 1965.

The Reds went top again on goal difference when they won at West Ham on 9th May. But, again, United had two games in hand. In just the second minute, Gerrard rounded Robert Green and scored. Torres had had his shirt tugged. Gerrard's penalty was saved by Green, but he tucked away the rebound. At the other end, Carragher's air swing let in David di Michele, who rounded Reina, slipped and was wrongly booked for diving. Babel made it three after his header had been parried.

By the time Liverpool were next in action, United had beaten Manchester City and Wigan and had drawn with Arsenal to make sure of the title. Having seen United win the title 24 hours earlier, Reds fans and players may not have been in the best mood as they travelled to The Hawthorns. Carragher certainly wasn't, and had a spectacular argument with Arbeloa, reminiscent of Bruce Grobbelaar and Jim Beglin at Wembley in 1986. "Who do you think you are?" he screamed at the Spaniard after he tried to dribble out of defence. "Fucking Maradona?" Gerrard was gifted the opening goal by Shelton Martis. Kuyt made it two with a thunderous drive from the edge of the box. The result relegated West Brom.

LIVERPOOL F.C. THE PREMIER LEAGUE YEARS

In the last match of the season, Hyypia was given a rousing send-off to mark his final appearance for the club. The Finn was the subject of the latest Kop mosaic, and he was chaired around the pitch at the end by his teammates. Torres headed Liverpool into the lead from Kuyt's cross. It was his 50th for the club. In 84 appearances, he had reached the milestone quicker than Ian Rush, John Aldridge, Robbie Fowler or Michael Owen - without taking penalties. Alan Hutton's own goal doubled the lead as he diverted Kuyt's shot past Heurelho Gomes. An embarrassed-looking Robbie Keane pulled one back. Benayoun scored the final goal of the season on 81 minutes to make it 3-1. Hyypia was introduced moments later, with the departing Gerrard putting the armband on him. He so nearly scored with a header, but Gomes beat it out. Hyypia had been a magnificent player for the Reds, one of the best of the decade.

The 2008-09 team may have ended the season without silverware, but it was Liverpool's best Premier League side to date. Eighty-six points was the club's highest tally in the modern era until 2019. It was a record for the runners-up in a 38-game season. They amassed 43 points away from home, then a club record. They achieved some stunning results, most notably at Stamford Bridge, the Bernabeu and Old Trafford. It was the season when the manager's 4-2-3-1 formation really flourished. Why did they fall short? Manchester United's haul of 90 points would have been very difficult to overtake whatever the circumstances, but of the 13 games Liverpool failed to win, Torres missed five, including both defeats. Of the draws he played in, he broke down at Villa after half an hour and only played the last 30 as a sub at Stoke. Had he been able to stay fit, the Reds' points tally would have been well into the 90s.

The big question was whether Liverpool would challenge again, with the club seemingly in a permanent state of disarray. It was fast becoming apparent that Tom Hicks and George Gillette were now bigger enemies to Liverpool Football Club than Alex Ferguson and his team.

2009-10

"Blow me fuck face. Go to hell. I'm sick of you."

I f amassing 86 points but still coming second to Manchester United was tough for Liverpool fans, the following season was going to be painful for entirely different reasons. There would be no title challenge, as talk of Liverpool 'taking the final step' was as wide of the mark as it had been in 2002. They would lose 19 matches in all competitions. Luck deserted them as a beach ball lost Liverpool a league game and a volcanic ash cloud hampered preparations for a European semi-final. Disharmony and discontent coursed through the veins of the club, with the toxic owners still in situ.

Manager Rafa Benitez struggled to hold things together, having to break even or make a profit in each transfer window. But he wasn't blameless. He was starting to pay for his own errors, most notably his unsettling of Xabi Alonso a year earlier. "The pursuit of Gareth Barry took some time for me to accept and, in all honesty, it changed the course of my future," said Alonso. The playmaker departed in the summer of 2009 for £30 million and left a sizeable hole in midfield. Benitez himself would be gone at the end of the year, sacked by people who knew nothing about the game.

"For five years I had been manager of Liverpool Football Club," said Benitez as he looked back on what would prove to be his final pre-season. "By the start of my sixth, it was clear I had become something else entirely. I was suddenly supposed to be a bank manager." The Robbie Keane money from January hadn't been reinvested in the squad. After Benitez had missed out on Gareth Barry again, Alonso's replacement was the injured Roma midfielder Alberto Aquilani, who cost over £17 million. Benitez was confident he would show his class when fit, but he only completed one full match in the league. He had wanted David Silva but baulked at Valencia's price tag. With different owners, the money would have been there to sign the Spanish genius.

Alvaro Arbeloa departed for Real Madrid too. Liverpool received just £3.5 million, as he only had a year left on his contract. His replacement, Glen Johnson, an inferior full back, cost an eye-watering £17.5 million from Portsmouth. Liverpool could only afford that because Pompey still owed the Reds money for Peter Crouch. Benitez also wanted the Fiorentina striker Stevan Jovetic and either Matthew Upson or Sylvain Distin. He got none of them. There was only £2 million left in the kitty, so he plumped for Sotirios Kyrgiakos, who joined from AEK Athens. That the big Greek replaced the great Sami Hyypia spoke volumes for the state of the club. The Royal Bank of Scotland was bleeding the club dry, pocketing £110,000 per day, despite record low interest rates. Also heading out of the club were Jermaine Pennant, Sebastian Leto and Miki Roque.

Christian Purslow joined the club as managing director to renegotiate the £350 million loan with RBS. A finance man, who unwisely labelled himself the Fernando Torres of the business world, Purslow had been educated at Cambridge and Harvard. He supported Liverpool and was friends with the chief executive of Royal Bank of Scotland, Stephen Hester. When Tom Hicks and George Gillett refinanced, Hester insisted that Purslow joined the board. Purslow's remit was to run the club and either find a buyer or bring in new finance to pay down the debt. The Americans wanted £800 million for the club. Nobody was going to pay that. "Looking back, I still don't know what to think of Purslow," wrote Pepe Reina, "because I understand he was there to look for new owners, but ultimately he was making big football decisions that he was not qualified to make. Football-wise, he probably wasn't the right person to run a football club." Indeed, a year later, when Benitez was asked why the Reds had slipped down the table, his answer was "Christian Purslow". In the summer of 2009, Purslow gave the manager a limited transfer budget without informing him it included agents' fees and upgrades to current players' contracts. With Steven Gerrard and Fernando Torres two of the players signing new deals, it was little wonder Benitez only had money for Kyrgiakos by the end of the summer.

Liverpool had no Champions League qualifiers to negotiate for once, so the season began at White Hart Lane in the Premier League. Reina was in goal. Johnson and Emiliano Insua were the full backs. Jamie Carragher and Martin Skrtel were the centre halves, with Daniel Agger injured. Javier Mascherano and Lucas Leiva held the midfield, with Gerrard ahead of them. Ryan Babel and Dirk Kuyt played wide. Fernando Torres was up front. Liverpool's lack of depth was underlined by their choice of outfield substitutes. Only Yossi Benayoun was Premier League quality. The others were Andrea Dossena and Andriy Voronin, as well as the youthful Martin Kelly, Daniel Ayala and Jay Spearing. Eighteen-year-old Ayala replaced Skrtel, who had clashed heads with Carragher, who needed stitches. Robbie Keane spurned numerous chances before Benoit Assou-Ekotto scored just before half-time with a stunning 30-yarder. Johnson did well to win a penalty in the second half, which Gerrard converted. Three minutes later, Sebastien Bassong got in front of Carragher to head the winner. Benayoun replaced the wasteful Babel and immediately made Liverpool look more dangerous. He played in Voronin, who was fouled in the box, but the referee waved play on. Benitez got into trouble for suggesting the referee needed to borrow his glasses. "We deserved to lose by more than that," Reina wrote in his 2011 autobiography. "The mood wasn't right and the way we played was simply not good enough. There was a definite feeling that we were going nowhere and when that happens in the first game of the season, you should know that there is going to be trouble ahead."

Those hoping it was just a blip would have been buoyed by a 4-0 win over

Stoke, against whom Liverpool hadn't been able to score in 2008-09. Ayala made his full debut. Gerrard set up Torres to score after four minutes. Johnson made it two with an exquisite bicycle kick. Kuyt and N'Gog completed the rout late in the evening. Before the game, there had been another demonstration against the owners, organised by Spirit of Shankly.

It was clear there were problems as Aston Villa won 3-1 at Anfield in a Monday night fixture. It was the Reds' first Premier League home defeat since 2007. With Aquilani unavailable, Lucas had replaced Alonso in what was now an unbalanced midfield. He didn't have the Spaniard's range of passing and was too similar to Mascherano. "When Xabi left, everyone missed him," said Riera. "The base was gone, the first pass ... The mood changed." The Reds missed several chances before Lucas scored an own goal from a set piece, having initially given the free kick away. Just before the break, Villa's Curtis Davies made it two, profiting from terrible marking at a corner. Kuyt hit a post. Torres got one back on 72 minutes, but within three minutes, Gerrard stupidly conceded a penalty, which was tucked away by Ashley Young. A summit was called at Melwood to discuss the problems, as Carragher explained to the author Simon Hughes. "We had a meeting and most of the squad had their say," he said. "It reflected the bad feeling that had built up after Xabi Alonso left, because Xabi was a really popular character. I don't think Rafa ever really recovered from that meeting ... He rubbed too many people up the wrong way and it caught up with him in the end."

The meeting may have had a positive short-term effect as the Reds won six in a row, including four in the league. Benitez had criticised the senior players in the press, and it was certainly the case that Gerrard, Carragher and Mascherano were underperforming. The run started with a comeback at Bolton that was reminiscent of the season before. Kevin Davies put Bolton ahead. Johnson, who had started the season so well, equalised with a left-footed 20-yarder. Tamir Cohen restored Wanderers' lead after Davies had beaten Kyrgiakos to a long ball. Sean Davis was sent off for two bookings. Gerrard hit the bar. Torres equalised. Gerrard blasted the winner into the roof of the net on 83 minutes. "I held my hands up in the dressing room after the Aston Villa game and said I wasn't good enough," said the skipper.

Having beaten Manchester United, newly-promoted Burnley were hammered 4-0 at Anfield. Reina had caused a stir by stating before the game that a title challenge would be unrealistic. "It would be good if the owners made an effort economically," he said. He was one player who was prepared to publicly criticise Tom Hicks and George Gillett. Behind the scenes, he asked Gerrard and Carragher why they wouldn't do the same. They have both defended their stance in their autobiographies. Benayoun was the hero against Burnley with three goals. His first was a brilliant individual goal. Kuyt made it two, following in a rebound from Benayoun's shot. Gerrard presented Benayoun with a tap-in. The Israeli's third came from Voronin's pass. He now had a hat-trick in the league, the FA Cup and the Champions League. With an £80 million shirt sponsorship with Standard Chartered agreed and Michael Shields finally released, it had been a good week. Shields had been at the game.

The first Champions League game was thoroughly turgid, as the Reds squeezed past Hungarian side Debrecen 1-0 at home in Benitez's 300th game in charge of Liverpool. Kuyt scored the only goal on 45 minutes after Torres's shot had been parried. It was the club's 100th win in the competition.

An outstanding goal by Torres, similar to his first against Chelsea in 2007, got the Reds underway at Upton Park in a five-goal classic in mid-September. Zavon Hines' run ended with Carragher fouling him in the box. Alessandro Diamanti scored the penalty. Kuyt got a touch to Gerrard's header to make it 2-1. Three minutes later, on the stroke of half-time, Carlton Cole headed in a corner to level the scores. The only goal in the second half came on 72 minutes from Torres, who headed in Babel's inch-perfect cross. How Liverpool needed the Spaniard to remain fit. The defence was more of a worry, as it was the fourth time in six league games that two or more goals had been conceded.

There were starts for Diego Cavalieri, Kyrgiakos, Degen, Dossena, Spearing and N'Gog in the League Cup tie at League One leaders Leeds. Babel and Riera did little to help N'Gog but he scored the only goal in an unimpressive 1-0 win, turning well and firing into the corner. Degen and Dossena were poor, although Spearing did well.

Hull were another side who frustrated the Reds in 2008-09, but like Stoke, they were hammered on their next visit to Anfield. Torres scored on 12 minutes with a typically clinical piece of finishing. Geovanni equalised almost immediately when the Reds missed two opportunities to clear their lines. Torres fired the Reds ahead again before completing his hat trick two minutes into the second half. He had scored eight in seven league games. Gerrard was next to score, with an outrageous curler into the top corner from near the side of the pitch – or perhaps it was a cross that went straight in. Babel scored two late goals – the second a complete fluke as Riera's shot hit him on the heel and looped in. Liverpool had scored 22 goals in seven league games, their best total since 1895. They were just three points off the top.

And then the wheels fell off. Spectacularly so. Liverpool were missing Mascherano as they travelled to Florence, but a dreadful performance led to a 2-0 defeat which the team would fail to recover from. Aurelio partnered Lucas in midfield. The 19-year-old Stevan Jovetic, who Benitez had been so keen to recruit, scored both goals in the first half. He later won the league with Manchester City in a title race with the Reds. Insua was run ragged in the first half. Liverpool didn't lay a glove on Fiorentina after that. For the first time in 24 games, since Middlesbrough in February, the Reds couldn't manage a goal. A group exit from the Champions League was already on the cards.

A run of four league wins came to a sudden halt at Stamford Bridge as the Reds lost 2-0 to leaders Chelsea. Liverpool held out for an hour, with Mascherano back to his hustling best. Carragher and Skrtel looked commanding at the back. But Nicolas Anelka scored the opening goal after Johnson had been caught out of position. Florent Malouda got the second after Drogba had got the better of Insua and Carragher. Liverpool created little. After eight games, the Reds were six points behind Carlo Ancelotti's Chelsea.

If 2009-10 is synonymous with anything, it is the bright red beach ball at Sunderland. A young Liverpool fan threw it onto the pitch from behind Reina's goal just as the game was kicking off. It blew around for five minutes before deflecting Darren Bent's shot past the goalkeeper, leaving him wrong-footed. The goal should have been disallowed as, under law five of the game, the beach ball was an outside agent. Reina was livid, shouting at the linesman that he must have seen it. The official claimed the two balls hadn't collided. Liverpool still had 85 minutes to do something about it and failed. Skrtel had an awful game. With Gerrard and Torres absent with groin injuries, and Benitez operating a 3-5-2 formation, they offered little going forward. Babel missed a couple of chances. Jordan Henderson, a second-half substitute for the Black Cats, playing in his first match involving the Reds, came close to making it two. "The beach ball became the symbol of our season," said Reina.

When Lyon scored an injury-time winner at Anfield in the Champions League, the Reds' chances of qualification were severely dented. Benayoun put the Reds ahead five minutes before half-time, keeping his composure to find the corner. Aurelio should have headed in Kelly's cross before the break. But it all went wrong in the second half. Liverpool should have been out of sight when the French side, with future Red Aly Cissokho in defence, scrambled in a 72nd-minute equaliser. Searching for a winner, the Reds would have to rely on N'Gog or Voronin to provide it, with Gerrard having gone off injured and Benayoun puzzlingly withdrawn. But the goal came at the wrong end, as Cesar Delgado won the match with a far-post tap-in before a stunned Kop. For the first time since the spring of 1987, Liverpool had lost four on the bounce. The fans were still behind Benitez, who was under serious pressure again.

With suggestions from all and sundry that Liverpool needed a new manager, Benitez bought himself some respite with a magnificent 2-0 win over Manchester United. Taken in the same position from which he had scored so memorably at Old Trafford six months earlier, Aurelio's free kick was clawed away by Edwin van der Sar. Lucas dispossessed Paul Scholes and played in Kuyt, but he shot wide. Van der Sar saved Aurelio's header. Just as it seemed the Reds would regret their wastefulness, Benayoun found Torres with a beautifully measured through ball and the returning Spaniard outmuscled Rio Ferdinand and fired the ball into the roof of the Kop net. Benitez didn't celebrate, but the goal must have meant so much. Michael Owen came off United's bench and was barracked mercilessly. Antonio Valencia hit the bar. Carragher was booked for fouling Owen. There was still time for Nemanja Vidic's customary red card after he rugby tackled Kuyt on the halfway line. It was his third in a row against Liverpool. Mascherano followed him for going in on the goalkeeper. With home fans pleading for the whistle, Carragher clattered into Nani on the edge of the box. Lucas found Kuyt and received a magnificent return pass. The Brazilian then played in the marauding N'Gog who advanced on the Kop goal and slotted the ball into the corner. From 90 yards, Reina was the first to jump on him as the manic celebrations began.

Benitez chopped and changed for the League Cup tie at Arsenal. There was a long-awaited debut for Aquilani and also one for Nathan Eccleston. The highlight of the game was a sensational dipping volley by Insua, his first and only Liverpool goal. It was all the Reds could manage. Arsenal won 2-1 with goals from Fran Merida and Nicklas Bendtner. It would be the last time Benitez managed the Reds in a competition he so nearly triumphed in in 2005.

From the joy of beating Manchester United in the league came a calamity at Craven Cottage. In one of the lows of a wretched season, the Reds lost 3-1 to a side managed by Roy Hodgson and had two players sent off. Skrtel, Agger and Aurelio joined Gerrard and Johnson on the absentee list. Benayoun hit the bar. Fulham went ahead, but when Torres equalised brilliantly just before half-time, there was a confidence among the travelling fans that all would be well. But they were going to have to get used to some miserable times on the road. In a crazy 14-minute spell late in the game, Erik Nevland restored Fulhams's lead, Philipp Degen and Carragher were sent off and Clint Dempsey wrapped the game up. As well as that, Benitez withdrew Torres, Kuyt and Benayoun. Liverpool had lost six of their last seven games.

Lyon managed to score another injury-time goal against the Reds in the Champions League. This time it earned them a draw. Torres and Voronin spurned first-half chances. On 83 minutes, Babel put Liverpool ahead with a magnificent 25-yarder that flew into Hugo Lloris's top corner. But again, they let the lead slip when Lisandro Lopez fired past Reina. Babel, Agger and Kyrgiakos were at fault. With Gerrard still absent and Torres not fully fit, the Reds had acquitted themselves well, with Lucas in excellent form. But with two group games left, Liverpool were five points short of second place.

Torres was now injured, but Johnson returned to the side and was in magnificent form offensively, although the Reds could only draw 2-2 at home to Birmingham. The right back tricked his way into the box, and after N'Gog and stand-in skipper Kuyt had forced saves from Joe Hart, N'Gog volleyed home Riera's cross with aplomb. But despite playing so well, Liverpool found themselves 2-1 down at the break. Gerrard, on as sub, hit a post with a header. N'Gog then raced into the box and seemed to be brought down. A penalty was given, but replays showed the young Frenchman had dived. Gerrard sent the penalty past Hart for a 2-2 draw. The Reds had 25 shots to Birmingham's five. Gregory Vignal was a second-half substitute for Birmingham. Liverpool were seventh, 11 points off the top. Benitez still hadn't won on a Monday night at Anfield, nor had he beaten Birmingham in a league game.

Already with several injuries, Liverpool lost Agger and Babel within 20 minutes at home to moneybags Manchester City. It took 50 minutes for the first goal, and Skrtel got it, turning in Gerrard's free kick for his first for the club – he went on to have a decent record against City. But the scoring went the same way as the Birmingham game, with Emmanuel Adebayor and Stephen Ireland giving City a 2-1 lead. It lasted 72 seconds before Benayoun turned in N'Gog's low cross. In their last ten matches, Liverpool had only beaten Manchester United. They were now seventh.

Liverpool had to win against Debrecen at the Puskas Ferenc Stadium and hope that Lyon could get something from Fiorentina to remain alive in the Champions League after five matches. They did their part, thanks to a fourth-minute goal by N'Gog, but by the end of the night, they were consigned to Europa League football after Fiorentina won 1-0. The Reds squad gathered around a monitor and gasped as Lyon missed a late chance. Liverpool only had themselves to blame. That first half in Fiorentina and the late goals conceded against Lyon had cost them dearly. A crippling injury list and a lack of depth hadn't helped.

One of the few high points of the season was a 2-0 win at Goodison, although the performance was hardly impressive. Mascherano's 30-yarder hit Joseph Yobo and flew past Tim Howard for a rare piece of good fortune. Insua went close. Reina made a wonderful double save from Tim Cahill and Marouane Fellaini. Everton's Jo had two goals disallowed for offside. Kuyt decided the game with ten minutes left, turning in a rebound after Howard had saved from Riera. Mascherano and Carragher were at their best. Gerrard played but was only half fit. Torres was still injured. Aquilani had barely been seen since his League Cup cameo. Regularly a sub, he would either not play or get a few minutes at most.

Gerrard's 500th appearance for the club was a dull 0-0 at Blackburn in the first game of December. The Reds had barely tested Paul Robinson but came close to scoring when N'Gog turned Johnson's cross onto the bar and Kuyt's follow-up was blocked. The game was shown last on Match of the Day, a sign of how far Liverpool were falling.

Benitez fielded a League Cup-type side for the dead rubber against Fiorentina, the last game Liverpool would play in the Champions League for five seasons. Aquilani made his first start and, having played very well, he was given a rousing reception when he was withdrawn in the second half. Benayoun flicked in a wide free kick from Gerrard. Yet again, the Reds gave up a lead, when Martin Jorgensen equalised just after the hour, and Alberto Gilardino scored in injury time after Stephen Darby slipped. It summed up the six games Liverpool had played in the competition.

Torres returned to the side for the home game with Arsenal in mid-December, and a strong Liverpool side produced a cracking first-half, pressing Arsenal vigorously. Torres missed a chance after a scintillating counterattack. Gerrard was denied a penalty. Kuyt stabbed the Reds into a thoroughly deserved lead just before half-time. But they allowed Arsenal to come back at them. Johnson bundled a cross into his own net, and Andrey Arshavin scored his fifth Anfield goal of 2009 just before the hour. Liverpool had nothing left to give. Alonso watched the game from the Main Stand, probably disbelieving how much Liverpool were struggling without him.

LIVERPOOL F.C. **THE PREMIER LEAGUE YEARS**

With a Kop mosaic reading "Shanks the Legend", the club celebrated the 50th anniversary of the Scot's arrival at Anfield. The team responded with their first win in four games. N'Gog headed in Aurelio's cross after terrible goalkeeping by Chris Kirkland. On his 100th appearance for the club, Torres scored at the second attempt after going around Kirkland. He had scored 61 goals, more than Ian Rush and Robbie Fowler in their first century of matches for the club. Charles N'Zogbia got one back at the end for Wigan.

A Saturday lunchtime match at Fratton Park against bottom-placed Portsmouth was another embarrassing low in this nightmare season. There was a recall for Dossena. Nadir Belhadj cracked in a volley from a tight angle. Mascherano was dismissed in first-half injury time for a bad tackle which left him needing treatment. He would miss three matches. Frederic Piquionne made it two with ten minutes left. Insua was one of many poor performers. Benitez sarcastically called referee Lee Mason 'perfect' on numerous occasions in his press conference, but he and his players couldn't justifiably blame anyone else.

While most supporters still backed Benitez, there was a growing unrest. His recent promise of a top-four finish was looking tough to keep, and the pressure was building on the manager. "The media smelt blood and intensified their attacks on Benitez, pulling apart his transfer dealings and questioning his mental health," wrote Brian Reade. "When he offered a 'guarantee' of a top-four finish, obituaries were being written and filed away for May. Rafa didn't look great. He was white and gaunt through too much worry and too little sleep, he picked up infections and coughs and kept coming out in cold sweats. When friends told him how awful he looked, he'd invent stories about his daughters waking him up. The truth was Liverpool's decline was eating him up and as a result he would stay up all night devising ways of outflanking his growing army of enemies."

Aquilani started the Boxing Day clash with Wolves at Anfield and helped his side to a 2-0 win. The game was tight until Stephen Ward was sent off for a second bookable offence when he chopped down Lucas early in the second half. Gerrard scored with a towering header in his 200th game as captain. Benayoun doubled the lead when his shot was deflected into the roof of the net. Wolves were now owned by Steve Morgan, who had been so desperate to buy Liverpool from David Moores in 2004. He was in no doubt that Moores had erred badly in selling to Hicks and Gillett. "The fact is David Moores wanted what was best for David Moores, not the club," said Morgan. "He was entitled to do that but it's his decision that has led to the situation Liverpool are now in." But Morgan had still sold his shares to Hicks and Gillett. And as Wolves owner in 2013, he came under heavy fire for inviting Norman Bettison to a match as his guest. Bettison was reviled on Merseyside for his connections to the Hillsborough Disaster.

The Reds were finally enjoying some fortune after so much had gone against them. In a clash at Villa Park, so crucial to the top-four race, the hosts had been the better side, but it was still 0-0 going past the 90-minute mark. Then a tackle on Benayoun saw the ball fizz into the Villa area, straight to Torres, who drew Brad Friedel and clipped it past him, sparking scenes of euphoria in the away end. He became the quickest Liverpool player to reach 50 league goals. As well as Friedel, Villa fielded past and future Reds in Stephen Warnock, Stewart Downing and James Milner. Fourth-placed Spurs were on 37 points. City and Villa had 35. Liverpool were on 33. City had a game in hand.

The FA Cup took the Reds to the Madejski Stadium, where they drew 1-1 on the second day of the new decade. Benitez fielded a strong side. Struggling Championship side Reading went 1-0 up, exposing Liverpool's set-piece frailties. Gerrard equalised when Kuyt dummied his cross and it went straight in. Darby was the only young player selected, and he was most impressive. There was no other game until the replay 11 days later.

Another bizarre chapter of the Hicks-Gillett ownership was written in between the two games with Reading. Reds fan Steve Horner read an article by Dominic King on the Liverpool Echo website, entitled "Rafa Benitez should not have to manage Liverpool's debt." Angered by the current state of affairs, he forwarded it to Hicks, Gillett and Tom Hicks Jr. The latter replied immediately with the solitary word "Idiot". It was 3.30am his time. Horner asked for a more detailed response. Four minutes later, Hicks Jr sent the following response: "Blow me fuck face. Go to hell. I'm sick of you." Horner shared the exchange on 'The Liverpool Way' forum, and it escalated from there, gaining newspaper coverage. The episode concluded with Hicks Jr resigning as a director. Ten years later, he would be working for the Republican National Committee, helping Donald Trump to raise $1 billion to get reelected.

The next story in this sorry saga came a couple of days later, when Spirit of Shankly members Mick Carroll and Alan Kayll went to David Moores' house. They convinced his wife, via the intercom at the electric gates, to go and get him. They persuaded Moores they were genuine fans and not journalists, and that he should come out to talk to them. Moores had hitherto remained silent on the subject. "We're here because the club is on its knees and we think it's time you came out and said something," said Kayll. "You helped put us into this mess David, you've got to try to get us out of it." They did enough to secure a meeting between the three of them, Rick Parry and another SOS member, Kevin Sampson, who was friends with Moores. The upshot was Moores sending The Times a 3,000-word open letter to the owners, urging them to stand aside, although he didn't send it until the end of the season.

Benitez had suffered some embarrassing FA Cup defeats in his six years as Liverpool manager, against the likes of Burnley, Barnsley and Everton. Reading added their name to that list when they won 2-1 at Anfield. Ryan Bertrand scored Liverpool's only goal when he put through his own net after good work from Gerrard. But in stoppage time, Benayoun conceded a penalty, which was converted by Gylfi Sigurdsson. Ten minutes into extra time, Shane Long headed in at the Kop end from close range. Brian McDermott's side deserved their moment of glory. To complete a woeful night for the Reds, they lost Torres and Gerrard to injury. But Benitez was able to bring in the Argentine international winger Maxi Rodriguez on a free transfer from Atletico Madrid. The club also paid £500,000 for a 15-year-old Queens Park Rangers Academy winger called Raheem Sterling. Dossena and Voronin left the club.

Another late goal was conceded down at Stoke in the first league game of 2010. Benitez was criticised for picking a defensive line-up, but his options were limited, with Gerrard, Torres, Benayoun and Johnson injured. Aquilani was still not fit enough. Babel had tweeted, "Got some disappointing news ... The boss left me out the squad. No explanation." He was later disciplined. Just before the hour, Degen won a free kick, Aurelio crossed it in, and it was prodded in by Kyrgiakos. Maxi came on for his debut. Stoke mounted a barrage of corners and long throw-ins late in the game, and in injury time, Robert Huth equalised. There was still time for Liverpool to break at speed, but Kuyt headed Aurelio's cross against a post.

Fourth-placed Spurs, clear of Liverpool by four points, came to Anfield in a crucial game for Champions League qualification. It was a Wednesday night, and the home fans created a European-style atmosphere, even greeting the team bus on the final leg of its journey. Reina was overcome with emotion, telling Sammy Lee they had to win for the fans. Aquilani and Kuyt combined cleverly before the Dutchman fired into the corner from 20 yards inside six minutes. Riera headed Carragher's cross onto the bar. Kuyt, Kyrgiakos and N'Gog should have scored. After combining with Maxi, N'Gog won a penalty in the last minute, even though he'd lost control of the ball. Kuyt made no mistake after being asked to retake. The Reds were superb, with Carragher and Kyrgiakos leading by example. Degen had his best game for the club. Aquilani showed why the club had bought him. Kuyt was magnificent. Harry Redknapp called the Kop "the most amazing sight in football".

Maxi made his first start in a bore draw at Wolves. Torres was still missing, and the Reds were toothless. It was frustrating, having dismantled Spurs, but at least they had kept successive clean sheets.

Aquilani set up another goal for Kuyt at home to Bolton at the end of January, with a header back across goal that the Dutchman poked in. But the Italian midfielder was otherwise poor. With 20 minutes left, Insua's 20-yarder was going miles wide, but it struck Kevin Davies and flew past Jussi Jaaskelainen. In his fourth consecutive start, Kyrgiakos impressed again. Hicks attended the game, while Benitez reported that he was flattered to be linked with the manager's job at Juventus. He was still guaranteeing a top-four finish.

And the Reds duly hit fourth spot when they won the Anfield derby, the 11th in a row Everton failed to win. Carragher set the tone with a crunching tackle on Steven Pienaar inside ten seconds. Kyrgiakos was sent off on 34 minutes, leaving his teammates with a mountain to climb, especially as Everton had won four of their last five in the league. But instead of the match turning in their favour, the Blues froze, just as they had done when Gerrard was sent off in 2006.

Fellaini went off, the victim of the Greek's tackle, but he could have been sent off as well. Gerrard hit the bar with a free kick. Tim Cahill missed with a diving header. Ten minutes into the second half, Kuyt engineered half a yard of space in Everton's six-yard box and glanced Gerrard's corner into the Anfield Road net. Reina tipped over from Yakubu. Pienaar received a late red card to even up the numbers. Liverpool held on. Mascherano performed wonderfully, as did Gerrard, who had been well below his best all season. Liverpool were now a point clear of Tottenham, although Man City had games in hand.

Liverpool couldn't take anything from a midweek trip to Arsenal, in which Abou Diaby headed the only goal on 72 minutes. Carragher left the field with a groin injury. Babel hit the bar from 20 yards. The Reds were denied an injury-time penalty, when Fabregas, part of a defensive wall, stopped Gerrard's free kick with his arm above his head while standing on the 18-yard line. Liverpool still hadn't won at Arsenal since Titi Camara's goal in February 2000.

European competition started up again in February as the Reds entertained the Romanians Unirea Urziceni in the first leg of the last 32 of the Europa League, the new name for the UEFA Cup, which Liverpool had won in 1973, 1976 and 2001. Benitez fielded a strong team in a 4-2-3-1 formation. Carragher continued at right back, where he had played in recent weeks. The club did boast four specialist right backs in Johnson, Degen, Kelly and Darby, but they were injured, not of the right quality and too young respectively. Although a very different player, Aquilani was in the Alonso role, with Gerrard pushed forward to support N'Gog. Riera and Kuyt were the wide men. The Reds were again unimpressive and only won the game with an N'Gog goal on 81 minutes from Dani Pacheco's knock-down. Gerrard and Aurelio had gone close. A 1-0 score kept the tie in the balance.

Torres was back for the game at Eastlands as the Reds drew 0-0 with City, one of their rivals for fourth spot. He replaced Babel with 15 minutes left but couldn't light up a boring game. Skrtel failed to bury an easy header but did at least prevent Adebayor from scoring. He was one of the few to play well.

A year to the day after winning in the Bernabeu, Liverpool were playing in the Ghencea Stadium in Romania. Unirea levelled the aggregate score with a Bruno Fernandes header on 19 minutes. Mascherano scored a rare goal – a sumptuous 25-yarder, meaning Unirea needed two more. Babel killed the tie before half-time, poking past the keeper after the Romanians failed to clear. Gerrard made it 3-1 from Benayoun's approach play. It was his 33rd European goal, overtaking Alan Shearer's record for goals by an Englishman in Europe. Liverpool went through 4-1 on aggregate. But Skrtel broke a metatarsal and would be out for the season. Carragher also left the field injured.

It was always satisfying for Benitez to beat Sam Allardyce and that's what happened when the Reds saw off Blackburn 2-1 at the end of February in their 40th game of the season. Gerrard clipped the ball over Paul Robinson to make it 1-0. A Carragher handball led to Keith Andrews beating Reina from the spot. Just before half-time, Torres scored his first goal of 2010 to win the game from

Maxi's pass. Reina made a magnificent save in the second half to preserve the three points. But Aurelio would miss the rest of the campaign with an injured thigh.

A 1-0 defeat at Wigan left Liverpool a point behind top-four favourites Manchester City, who had two games in hand. Gerrard had another game to forget in what was becoming his worst season at the club. Torres hit a post. Hugo Rodallega scored the only goal on 35 minutes after Kuyt had conceded possession. Liverpool had no response. If anything, it was worse than the Fulham and Portsmouth displays, which could be partly blamed on red cards. Johnson made a welcome return as a second-half substitute for Lucas, much to Carragher's relief.

The Reds lost by the same score in Lille in the last 16 of the Europa League. Babel, Gerrard and Torres all forced fine first-half saves. Eden Hazard scored the only goal on 84 minutes when his wide free kick went straight in. Pierre-Emerick Aubameyang hit a post a minute later.

A 4-1 win over Portsmouth was Liverpool's sixth consecutive triumph at Anfield since the cup humiliation at the hands of Reading. Gerrard charged down a clearance from the Pompey goalkeeper Jamie Ashdown, allowing Maxi to square the ball to Torres for a simple finish on 26 minutes. Babel found the corner two minutes later from Torres's pass. And two minutes after that, Aquilani scored his first Liverpool goal, sweeping in with his left foot after Gerrard's dummy. It was vintage Liverpool. Gerrard and Torres were dovetailing beautifully again, with the Spaniard soon hitting the post. The second half was quieter. Babel hit the bar after wonderful approach play from Gerrard and Aquilani. Torres got his second from the Italian's pass. The Reds could have had several more, but Belhadj scored the final goal of the game. Portsmouth, now managed by Avram Grant, were still bottom.

Argentina manager Diego Maradona, who had praised Liverpool so much after Istanbul, was a guest of honour at Anfield as the Reds overturned their deficit against Lille. Benitez selected the same 11 as the first leg, and they set about their task quickly. Lucas dribbled into the area and won an early penalty, allowing Gerrard to level the aggregate score. Reina saved from Hazard, albeit with his head. Torres missed an easy chance from Kuyt's cross, but it was the Spaniard who broke the deadlock. Babel's long ball was misjudged by a defender, allowing Torres to bear down on goal and dink the ball over the keeper. Lille still needed just one to advance on away goals, but Torres put the game out of their reach in the last minute, turning in a rebound from Gerrard's shot. The Liverpool Echo were fulsome in their praise of the Spaniard, who had been linked with Chelsea. "In the wake of Chelsea's latest exit from the Champions League, it was perhaps inevitable that a story would emerge suggesting Roman Abramovich is prepared to dip into his reservoirs of cash in a bid to sign Torres this summer. Delve as much as you want, Roman. No matter how big the offer, no matter how much money you want to pay him, there is no way he would entertain playing at Stamford Bridge on a permanent basis."

A year on from beating Manchester United 4-1 at Old Trafford, much had changed for Liverpool. This time they started well but faded. Torres began a move and then headed Kuyt's cross into the net on five minutes. But Antonio Valencia cleverly won a penalty by waiting until he had crossed the 18-yard line before going down, with Mascherano tugging his arm. Reina saved Wayne Rooney's penalty, but he put away the rebound. Park Ji-Sung headed in the winner from Darren Fletcher's cross after an hour. Torres air-kicked with the goal at his mercy in the last few minutes, and as the ball came down, Benayoun headed it straight at Edwin van der Sar from six yards.

With his confidence soaring, Torres scored another early goal a week later, this time at home to Sunderland. Cutting in from the left wing, he unleashed a magnificent curling shot into the top corner of Craig Gordon's net. He then fired wide from Gerrard's square pass after a delightful move. Johnson fired in a deflected left-footer from outside the box. Torres hit a post and then put the rebound wide, but made up for it on the hour with a cute finish from Johnson's pass. An emphatic 3-0 was small payback for the beach ball, but it kept alive Liverpool's top-four hopes. Maxi and Agger enhanced their reputations with excellent displays. "When we play like this, we can beat anyone," Torres said. The problem with Liverpool in 2009-10 was that they were also capable of losing to anybody, especially if he wasn't fit.

The Reds lost their fourth away game on the bounce in Portugal, losing 2-1 to Benfica in the first leg of the Europa Cup quarter-final. Lady Luck again deserted them in spectacular fashion. Agger scored early with a goal reminiscent of his strike against Chelsea in the 2007 Champions League semi-final. Gerrard played a low free kick into the box, and this time the Dane backheeled it into the corner. They were the only European goals he had ever scored. Yet again, a 1-0 lead turned into a 1-2 loss. Babel was sent off for making the faintest of contacts with the face of Luisao. Oscar Cardozo scored two penalties. In between, Torres had a goal disallowed and missed a great chance supplied by Kuyt.

The critics had a field day when Benitez withdrew Torres for N'Gog on 65 minutes, with Liverpool desperate for a winner at Birmingham. He claimed his striker was exhausted. Earlier in the game, Maxi hit the bar from Torres's cross. Gerrard fired past Joe Hart just into the second half after turning Lee Bowyer inside out. Liam Ridgewell equalised after a cross evaded several defenders to find him unmarked at the back post. Liverpool desperately needed the three points to keep alive their Champions League hopes, but when Benitez substituted his in-form striker, the cameras captured a stunned look on the face of Gerrard, who turned away scratching his head. Torres was replaced by N'Gog, who missed a couple of chances. Insua tore a thigh muscle, which would curtail his season. Incredibly, in eight attempts, Benitez hadn't beaten Birmingham in the league. Liverpool were four points behind Manchester City, who had a game in hand.

A key development in the ownership saga came at the start of the following week, when Hicks and Gillett turned down an offer for the club from the New

York-based fund-management company Rhone Group. Their offer was £118 million for 40%, with the current owners retaining 30% each as sleeping partners. Rhone would commit £25 million for transfers in the summer. Turning it down proved to be a mistake, because RBS responded by calling in the outstanding loan, believing Hicks and Gillett weren't showing enough urgency to sell. They gave them one final six-month extension, with huge penalties if they defaulted. They would have until October 2010 to refinance or sell the club. The bank also insisted that a new chairman come in to oversee the sale. His name was Martin Broughton, the chair of British Airways and a Chelsea supporter. As with Purslow's appointment, Hicks didn't mind, believing he could manipulate both. He would come to regret that misjudgement.

From the frustration of St Andrews to a real Anfield high as the Reds moved into the Europa League semis in glorious fashion, hammering Benfica in the second leg. Kuyt levelled the aggregate score, heading in Gerrard's corner on 27 minutes. It was initially disallowed by a linesman, but he was overruled by the referee. 1-0 would be enough with the away-goals rule, but Liverpool wanted more. Seven minutes later, Gerrard fed the ball through to Lucas, who rounded the keeper in style and rolled the ball home. The Brazilian was playing in a more advanced role than usual. Thirteen minutes into the second half, the Reds counterattacked from a Benfica free kick. Mascherano found Benayoun. The Israeli switched play to the right. Kuyt sent in the perfect low ball to Torres, who turned the ball home before a jubilant Kop. With a low free kick, Cardozo got his third goal of the tie to set up a nerve-wracking final 20 minutes, because one more goal would be enough for the Portuguese. But any worries were abated on 82 minutes, when David Luiz lost the ball after a crunching tackle by Lucas in Liverpool's half. Mascherano played in Torres, who clipped the ball over the goalkeeper to set up a semi-final with his former club, Atletico Madrid.

Sadly, Torres wouldn't play again under Benitez. When he was withdrawn at Birmingham, an ice pack was applied to his right knee. He was magnificent against Benfica, but he was badly missed at home to Fulham. He was in Spain visiting a specialist. He needed surgery, and his season was over. Without him, they could only draw 0-0 with Roy Hodgson's side. The afternoon began with a tribute to the 96. Mark Schwarzer saved well from Mascherano and Babel, but he had little else to do. Hodgson's defensive tactics had paid off. With four games left, the Reds were four points behind City, who had a game in hand. It was nearly impossible from here.

A routine 3-0 win over West Ham was next. Benayoun touched in Gerrard's wide free kick with his chest. Before the half-hour mark, N'Gog made it two with an emphatic finish from Maxi's cross. The third went in off goalkeeper Robert Green after Kyrgiakos had hit a post.

It was somewhat emblematic of Liverpool's season that a volcanic ash cloud should hamper their trip to Madrid for the first leg of the Europa League semi-final. Numerous flights were cancelled over a period of days. The journey took 24 hours, starting at Runcorn train station and going via Paris and Bordeaux to the

Spanish capital. Benitez hosted his pre-match media conference in the train's buffet car. The Reds made a terrible start, as Kyrgiakos was caught out and Forlan fortuitously turned in a left-wing cross at the second attempt. Benayoun had a goal wrongly disallowed for offside. Liverpool created little else. Having turned around first-leg deficits against Lille and Benfica, they knew they could still reach the final.

A first Premier League away win of 2010 came in April as Burnley were hammered 4-0 at Turf Moor. All the goals came in the second half. The first three went down as assists by Aquilani, who now had six for the season. Gerrard scored from 20 yards with the aid of a deflection. He scored a brilliant goal from further out to make it two. The Italian midfielder played a wonderfully measured ball to Maxi, who scored his first for the club with a classy first-time finish. Babel finished off the rout in injury time after being played in by Lucas. It was the only time Aquilani played a full Premier League match. He was obviously a classy midfielder, but signing an injured player was a gamble that failed to pay off. The inability to replace Alonso was a major reason for Liverpool's decline.

The second leg against Atletico produced both an excellent Liverpool performance and an agonising exit from the competition. Benitez stuck with his 4-2-3-1. Mascherano played right back, with Johnson on the left. Gerrard played deeper than usual, with Aquilani pushed forward. Babel was the striker. Amid a raucous atmosphere, the Reds were on top from the off. Benayoun forced De Gea to save with his legs after a mere ten seconds. Agger had a header disallowed for offside. A minute before half-time, the outstanding Benayoun did well to get to the byline. His low cross was met by the in-form Aquilani, who swivelled and clinically found the bottom corner from 16 yards. He had his best game for the club and received a standing ovation when he was withdrawn in the last minute of normal time for El Zhar. Liverpool made a great start to extra time when Lucas chipped an exquisite ball over the defence to Benayoun, who drilled the ball left-footed inside De Gea's far post. They were 25 minutes away from meeting Fulham in the final in Hamburg. Anfield was buzzing. But Atletico needed just one goal to reach the final on away goals. And, sure enough, the worst happened. Having threatened little all night, Jose Antonio Reyes beat Johnson to a header and got into the box. He played it across to Forlan, who fired into the roof of the net at the Kop end from close range. Benitez sent on Degen and Pacheco, but it was to no avail. This patched-up team, shorn of so many players, had nothing left to give. It was the cruellest of defeats. Luck had deserted them throughout the tie. It was the first time the club had lost on away goals since the 1974-75 season when Ferencvaros knocked them out of the Cup Winners' Cup in Bob Paisley's first season.

The last two games were meaningless for Liverpool, but the title was on the line for Chelsea at Anfield. They were a point clear of Manchester United and had to win. Broughton, Liverpool's new chairman, stayed away, citing split loyalties. Mascherano was at right back again, with Agger on the left. With just over half an hour gone, Gerrard played a terrible back pass, which Drogba got to first. He rounded Reina and scored in front of the Kop. Maxi left the field injured. With Carragher barely able to walk, Lampard got in front of him to turn in Chelsea's second. The vice-captain was immediately substituted. The Reds slumped to their 19th defeat of the season.

The final game of this dreadful campaign ended 0-0 at Hull City, who had already been relegated. Aquilani and Gerrard hit the woodwork, but the game is best remembered for young left back Jack Robinson coming on as a late substitute and becoming Liverpool's youngest ever player at 16 years and 250 days. Liverpool staggered over the finishing line, in seventh place with just 63 points.

The majority of fans were still behind Benitez, but several former players had turned on him. A significant amount of the media had never been on his side. Broughton and Purslow weren't fans either, and so Benitez was sacked at the start of June by these men with no footballing expertise. Benitez had made mistakes over the last year, but with ownership and financial issues severely hampering the club, with injuries galore, and with Gerrard having his worst season in over a decade, it is hard to argue that much more could have been achieved. Had it not been for some extraordinary bad luck, he would have signed off with the Europa League. Many fans were devastated at his departure.

Even more important than the occupant of the manager's chair was the Hicks and Gillett debacle. Just before the end of the season, accounts had been published for Kop Football (Holdings) Ltd which showed record losses of £54.9 million, £40.1 million of which were interest payments. Outnumbered three to two on the board, Hicks and Gillett were now losing control. But there was still an abundance of dirty linen to be aired in public, with Broughton determined to sell the club by October 2010.

2010-11

The sacking of Rafa Benitez and the appointment of Roy Hodgson rank as two of the worst decisions Liverpool have ever taken. The Spaniard had just endured his only bad season in six, caused mainly by ownership issues and injuries, yet it was enough to see him sacked. Nothing on Hodgson's CV suggested he was suited to the role. He may have won a couple of Swedish titles with Halmstads, the first of 14 managerial positions he would hold in 28 years, but other than a spell at Inter Milan, which ended with fans pelting him with coins and lighters after a UEFA Cup Final defeat to Schalke, he had never managed a side approaching the higher echelons of European football. He had been sacked by Bristol City and Blackburn. Now on the back of getting Fulham to the UEFA Cup Final, he was appointed Liverpool manager, getting the job ahead of Manuel Pellegrini and Didier Deschamps. In fact, when Kenny Dalglish was asked to judge the shortlist, he told the board he could do a better job than any of them.

With the club up for sale, the directors believed it might be prudent to have a manager who wouldn't rock the boat, as Benitez often did. And with Danny Murphy convincing Steven Gerrard and Jamie Carragher of Hodgson's merits, the job was his. At 62, he became Liverpool's oldest manager at the time of appointment, beating Joe Fagan by 215 days. But he never stood a chance. The club was potentially just months from administration, and no one could work out quite how he'd got the job. It wasn't just the results that turned the fans against Hodgson. They were against him from the start. They knew the style of play would be agricultural at best. Two banks of four, long balls and a low block may have helped some of his teams overachieve, but this was never going to be accepted at a club that boasted five European Cups. On one infamous occasion, Daniel Agger brought the ball out of defence, only to have Hodgson bark at him, "Just fucking launch it!" This was against Northampton Town. His appointment smacked of a lowering of standards, a suggestion that maybe a season in mid-table was acceptable. Some in the media spoke of him 'steadying the ship'. He did no such thing. He was out of his depth from the moment he was employed.

Before Benitez was fired, he had signed midfielder Jonjo Shelvey from Charlton Athletic for £1.7 million and winger Milan Jovanovic from Standard Liege on a free. Hodgson, though, came very close to achieving a success rate of zero in the transfer market. Joe Cole, Danny Wilson, Christian Poulsen and Paul Konchesky were miles off the required standard, although back-up goalkeeper Brad Jones was no worse than some of his predecessors. Cole may have been free, but he signed a four-year contract worth £130,000 a week. It was Christian Purslow, the managing director, that wanted him. Portuguese central midfielder Raul Meireles was played out wide and only came good after Hodgson had gone. Hodgson also signed the talented young Spaniard Suso. His other signing, curiously, was Fabio Aurelio, who had been released by Benitez after another injury-plagued season. The Brazilian left back hadn't found a new club by the time Hodgson took over, so he went back to Liverpool.

Leaving the club were Yossi Benayoun, Albert Riera, Diego Cavalieri, Andriy Voronin and a smattering of young players. Emiliano Insua and Philipp Degen were loaned out, never to play for Liverpool again. Riera had been suspended during the previous season for having a training ground fight with the young winger Dani Pacheco. Javier Mascherano would play just one more game before forcing through a £17.25 million move to Barcelona. The young Hungarian striker Krisztian Nemeth, of whom huge things had been expected, moved to Olympiacos.

A seismic story in the latter part of the summer came via the front page of The Times on 5th August. Its story, headlined, 'China set to buy Liverpool', detailed how Kenneth Huang, a Hong Kong investment banker, along with China Investment Corporation, were determined to make Liverpool the biggest club in the Far East. They had the money to proceed, but during tricky negotiations, both parties lost patience. The club claimed there was still interest on the table from elsewhere, but none would prove to be serious bidders. Purslow and Martin Broughton remained determined to sell the club by October.

The first of Hodgson's 31 matches as Liverpool manager was against Rabotnicki of Macedonia in the first qualifying match of the Europa League. Hodgson fielded an inexperienced line-up with Diego Cavalieri in goal. Martin Kelly and Daniel Agger were the full backs. Martin Skrtel and Sotirios Kyrgiakos played centre back. Jay Spearing and Lucas Leiva were in central midfield. David Amoo and Jovanovic were on the wings. Alberto Aquilani was in the hole behind N'Gog. Stephen Darby, Nathan Eccleston and Lauri Dalla Valle came off the bench. Peter Gulacsi, Daniel Ayala, Shelvey and Thomas Ince weren't used. It was Dalla Valle's only game for the club and Darby's last. Gerrard, Carragher and Cole were left on Merseyside to continue their pre-season training. Fresh from winning the World Cup, Fernando Torres and Pepe Reina were still enjoying time off. With the team having failed to win any of the summer's friendlies, two goals by David N'Gog got Hodgson off the mark with a 2-0 win.

A stronger team won by the same score in the second leg. Set up by debutant Cole, N'Gog scored again with a close-range header. Gerrard added a penalty before half-time after the young Frenchman was fouled. Aquilani replaced Gerrard for his last Liverpool appearance before being loaned to Juventus, where he would play 32 Serie A matches. It was a shame Hodgson let the Italian go, because he'd started to find form in the second half of his debut season, and he was better than some of the options the new manager had. There were only 31,202 in attendance for Anfield's first competitive game of the new season. Another 2-0 win was hardly impressive. After all, Rabotniki had only just scraped past FC Mika of Armenia in the previous qualifier.

The opening Premier League game against Arsenal was full of incident. With more of the big names back on the teamsheet, Hodgson selected a 4-2-3-1. Liverpool's player of the season in 2009-10, Reina, was in goal behind a back four of Glen Johnson, Carragher, Skrtel and Agger, who was still filling in at left back. Gerrard was back in a conventional midfield role, alongside Mascherano. Kuyt and Jovanovic were on the wings. Cole played in the hole behind N'Gog. A goalless first half ended with Cole being sent off for the first time in his career after sliding into Laurent Koscielny. The second half started sensationally for the Reds as Mascherano played in N'Gog, who beat Manuel Almunia with a thunderous drive into the roof of the net. Reina made great saves from Theo Walcott and Tomas Rosicky as the pressure built, but Arsenal got their point in injury time, as Reina flapped at a cross, and as it came back off his right-hand post, he fumbled it into the net. Koscielny was sent off at the end for a second yellow card. Carragher and the departing Mascherano were Liverpool's best players. Some claimed a moral victory for the ten men, but Reina's own goal was a crushing disappointment. Arsenal had bid £20 million for him during the summer, but Liverpool refused to sell.

Turkish side Trabzonspor were at Anfield four days later for the first leg of a Europa League play-off – one stage away from the groups. It wasn't convincing, but the Reds won 1-0, with Babel taking Cole's pass and finding the corner of the net just before half-time. After Lucas was fouled, Cole missed a penalty seven minutes after the break. It was the first one he had attempted in his career. He now had a red card and a penalty miss in his first three games. His time at Liverpool didn't really improve. Poulsen made his debut in midfield and had a late goal disallowed.

Suggestions Hodgson had made a decent start were soon shot down as the Reds were humbled 3-0 at Manchester City. As Liverpool had got weaker since May 2009, City had gone from strength to strength, and the gulf in class was there for all to see. Mascherano refused to play and was soon off to Barcelona. Gareth Barry scored on 13 minutes and Micah Richards on 52. Both were set up by City debutant James Milner. Gerrard hit a post. Carlos Tevez fired in a penalty on 68 when Skrtel brought down Adam Johnson. If anything, the score flattered Liverpool. Skrtel and Agger were distinctly average at the back. Lucas couldn't get near Yaya Toure in midfield, where Mascherano's absence was sorely felt. Up front, Torres and N'Gog had nothing to feed upon.

In front of 91 travelling fans, Liverpool clinched a place in the group stage of the Europa League when they won 2-1 in Turkey. Trabzonspor scored on just four minutes after Kuyt lost the ball. The tie remained 1-1 on aggregate for most of the night. Defeat would have been humiliating, but a huge stroke of luck rescued Hodgson when Johnson's cross was turned into his own net by Remzi Giray Kacar with seven minutes left. Kuyt added another to make sure, following in a rebound from Pacheco's shot. Hodgson labelled it "another famous European night."

Torres made his first meaningful contribution of the season, firing in an impressive volley at home to West Brom, who had dominated the first-half possession. It was the only goal of the game and his 50th at Anfield. Albion's James Morrison was sent off for fouling the Spaniard. It was the club's 2000th league win, and it sent them all the way up to 13th in the table. Torres, meanwhile, would contribute little under Hodgson, later accused by Gerrard and Carragher of downing tools, knowing his future lay elsewhere. "I felt sorry for Roy Hodgson," Carragher told Simon Hughes in 2016. "He must have wanted to drop Torres in those first few months. Torres was playing so poorly and in training he couldn't get going. I remember watching Hodgson trying to butter Torres up and get the best out of him. I'd probably have grabbed Torres by the throat."

Liverpool's Birmingham hoodoo continued with a 0-0 draw at St Andrews. Meireles and Konchesky debuted. The latter would become synonymous with Hodgson's reign as one of the worst players to wear the red shirt. Reina made outstanding saves from Cameron Jerome and Craig Gardner. Liverpool barely had an attack of note. "It was good to come away unbeaten," said Hodgson.

The first European group game saw Reina captain the side against Steaua Bucharest, the 1986 European Cup winners. Cole got off the mark on just 27 seconds after a defensive howler sent him clean through. The Romanians equalised on 13 minutes when Liverpool were caught square. N'Gog converted a second-half penalty after Kyrgiakos was fouled at a corner. Lucas blasted in a superb 25-yarder before N'Gog added another in injury time. Hodgson became the first Liverpool manager to win his first five European games.

The day before the Reds' game at Old Trafford, an email campaign started by a fans' group called Kop Faithful saw the server of an American equity group crash by the Monday morning. It was the beginning of an astonishing, and ultimately successful, attempt to prevent Tom Hicks from refinancing his loan and keeping control of the club. It started with them emailing dozens of senior officials at the Royal Bank of Scotland, who, back in April, had given the owners six months to repay their loan. Hundreds of emails were received, leading to senior executive Rebecca Oliphant angrily taking out her frustrations on Kop Faithful's Mick Carroll when he phoned for her reaction. "I'm sick of it ... I haven't got time for things like this," she told him. Sensing they could then rattle cages on a much larger scale, the organisation planned to direct an email campaign at any bank linked with helping Hicks refinance. When the journalist Chris Bascombe told them he would be running an exclusive that Hicks had lined up the USA-based Blackstone Group, they put their plan into operation. If they lent him the money to pay off RBS, he would be in full control of the club again. Kop Faithful used online forums to persuade others to copy and paste their letter and send it to Blackstone. An incredible 14,000 emails were sent on the Saturday and Sunday. Blackstone pulled the plug on any possible deal. Days later another Liverpool fan, Paul Wilson, photographed Hicks and his son outside a different bank in New York. The photo went viral and another successful email campaign was directed at them. The story made the front page of the Wall Street Journal. Time was running out for Hicks.

By now the football was far less interesting, especially with hapless Hodgson at the helm. A Dimitar Berbatov hat trick consigned the Reds to their second defeat of the season in Manchester. A header from a corner and a stunning overhead kick put United 2-0 up but, from nowhere, Liverpool mounted a comeback. Johnny Evans fouled Torres in the box. Gerrard scored from 12 yards with 26 minutes still to play. Six minutes later, he beat Edwin van der Sar with a low free kick from 20 yards. But with six minutes left, the Bulgarian got above Carragher to head the winner. After the game, Alex Ferguson accused Torres of diving to win both set pieces, and even though it wasn't true, Hodgson didn't take the opportunity to defend his player in his post-match press conference. "Sir Alex is entitled to any opinion he wants to have, but I'm not going to come here and say I agree or disagree," he said.

Next came the match for which Hodgson's managership is best known – Northampton Town at Anfield in the League Cup. "They will be a formidable challenge," Hodgson predicted. In a weakened line-up, there were debuts for Jones in goal, Wilson, Shelvey and Thomas Ince. Kyrgiakos was named captain. Agger, who earlier in the week had said he wouldn't change his style to suit the manager's, played a wonderful ball, which dissected the defence. It was seized upon by Jovanovic in the inside-left channel, and he finished with aplomb on nine minutes. The fact Liverpool wouldn't score again for 97 minutes says a lot for how the evening panned out. Billy McKay equalised from a knock-down after Kyrgiakos was beaten to a header. Eight minutes into extra-time, Wilson, Scotland's Young Player of the Year in 2009-10, was beaten too easily, and Michael Jacobs turned the ball home after Martin Kelly had cleared off the line. With time ticking away, and Liverpool facing humiliation, Shelvey's corner was headed into the net by the in-form N'Gog. The game would be decided by penalties. Northampton went first and missed, but so did N'Gog, who fired wide. The next four penalties went in, with Shelvey and Agger scoring for the Reds. Northampton scored again to lead 3-2. Nathan Eccleston hit the bar, and Abdul Osman side-footed home to ensure Liverpool had lost for the first time to a team from the fourth tier. Just 22,577 were in attendance. After more protests against the owners, Hodgson remarked that fan demonstrations against the owners "do not help, but it is something I have had to live with since I came to the club." The majority of fans had already turned against him.

Thousands of Reds protested against the American owners before, during and after the home match with Sunderland. An incredible stroke of luck got Liverpool off the mark at home to Steve Bruce's Sunderland. In fact, it almost cancelled out the beach ball. The Black Cats were awarded a free kick in their own half. Michael Turner touched the ball to Simon Mignolet for him to take it.

The quick-witted Torres assumed the free kick had been taken. He bore down on goal, before squaring to Kuyt, who couldn't miss. Sunderland were livid. But Poulsen soon gave away a penalty for handball. Darren Bent beat Reina powerfully before scoring a second just after the break. Hodgson faced more embarrassment, until Torres crossed for Gerrard to head an equaliser. Eyebrows were raised as Gerrard ran past the Spaniard, avoiding him, before celebrating on his own, heightening rumours of a rift between the two. Gerrard accused him of "downing tools" in his book. Agger missed a gilt-edged chance in the last minute. "We deserved our point," said Hodgson. Gerrard and Carragher applauded the Kopites who had stayed behind to protest as the players did their warm down. The pair had previously stayed neutral in the club's civil war, to the consternation of many.

Torres looked leaden-footed in a 0-0 draw in the Netherlands against Utrecht, but it kept Liverpool on top of Group K. Lucas and Poulsen created little in midfield. Meireles was still out of position on the right. The Spaniard's form continued to be a major talking point. "My interest is in Liverpool Football Club, I don't spend every minute of my waking day on Fernando Torres," said the manager.

September had been appalling for Hodgson and the players. October started with defeat at home to Blackpool, but at least the month saw a change in ownership. Carragher played left back. Torres lasted ten minutes before a groin injury struck. Johnson conceded a penalty on 25 minutes, which Charlie Adam dispatched. On the stroke of half-time, Luke Varney made it two. "Dalglish! Dalglish! Dalglish!" chanted the Kop after 94 days of Hodgson. Kyrgiakos headed in Gerrard's free kick after 53 minutes. Cole went close to levelling the match, but it wasn't to be. Kyrgiakos ended the match up front. There was another post-match protest against the owners.

October was the month that the owners would have to repay their loan or face a £60 million penalty from RBS. The club faced going into administration, which would result in the loss of nine league points. They were already in the relegation zone, just two points ahead of bottom-place West Ham. On the day of the Blackpool humiliation, the new chairman Martin Broughton emailed the Americans to inform them he had two potential buyers. They were New England Sports Ventures, who owned the Boston Red Sox, and Peter Lim, a businessman from Singapore. A board meeting would take place in London two days later to consider the offers. The five board members were Hicks, Gillett, Broughton, Christian Purslow and Ian Ayre. Knowing they were outnumbered, the Americans tried to reconstitute the board, replacing Purslow and Ayre with another of Hicks's sons, Mack, and Lori Kay McCutcheon, who worked for Hicks. Even though this was filed with Companies House, Broughton refused to accept it was legal and went ahead with the meeting, in the absence of the owners.

Lim was offering £320 million compared to NESV's £300 million, but Broughton, Purslow and Ayre chose the latter, given their record of reviving the glory days at the Red Sox. The deal was announced on the Liverpool website on Wednesday 6th October. But the war wasn't over, because Hicks was now questioning the legitimacy of the board. A week later, at the Royal Courts of Justice in London, Mr Justice Floyd concluded that "in order to secure additional loans, [Hicks and Gillett] had released absolute control of the sale that they are now seeking to regain. When it became clear that it was proceeding on a basis unpalatable to them, they sought to renege on an agreement." Broughton was free to proceed with the sale to NESV. Hicks had one more stunt and obtained a restraining order from a Dallas court to prevent the club being sold. The matter went back to Floyd, who threw it out and accused them of "unconscionable conduct", having learned that the Texan court knew nothing of the High Court ruling. Back in Dallas, Hicks and Gillett were arguing in court that Broughton should be imprisoned for stealing their club. They had lost a fortune. Hicks was still threatening to sue for £1 billion, but nothing came of it. Purslow, meanwhile, stood down as managing director. He was unpopular with everyone – the former owners and the fans, while NESV would soon despair at many of the decisions taken on their watch. It is safe to say they inherited a mess.

The relief that Hicks and Gillett were finally gone was tempered by an abysmal defeat at Goodison that left Liverpool above only West Ham in the Premier League table, and that was on goal difference. New owner John Henry was in attendance. Hodgson managed to produce another zinger of a quote, suggesting that beating an Everton team that started the day level on points with Liverpool would have been 'Utopia'. "The way we played the game was as good as we have played all season," he said, in a mind-boggling state of denial. "I have no qualms with the performance whatsoever. I only hope fair-minded people will see it the same way. To get a result here would have been Utopia. But I can only analyse the performance. There is no point trying to analyse dreams." Contrary to those words, Liverpool were outplayed and outfought by Everton, who strolled to an easy 2-0 win. Kuyt, Agger and Johnson missed out after sustaining injuries on international duty. Carragher (at right back), Skrtel, Konchesky, Maxi, Lucas, Cole and Torres were all distinctly poor. Hodgson had made the worst start for a new Liverpool manager since George Patterson in 1928. It was the only time the Blues defeated the Reds in the 2010s. In the post-match press conference, the noise of Evertonians singing "Going down, going down!" led to Hodgson asking for the window to be shut.

Given the parlous state of affairs, a 0-0 draw in Napoli wasn't a bad result, especially with Gerrard, Torres and Meireles staying at home and Carragher substituted at the break. With seven changes, Hodgson selected a 4-2-3-1 formation, with Poulsen and Spearing solid in midfield and the impressive Shelvey in the number-10 position. Konchesky cleared one goalbound shot off the line. Other than that, Liverpool kept their shape well and deserved a point. They could have won, had Babel shown more conviction with a late chance. The Reds were two points clear after three group matches.

The fringe players showing the marquee players the right example in Italy was perhaps the pre-cursor of a mini revival, as Liverpool won their next four matches. The run started with a 2-1 home win over fellow strugglers Blackburn. All three goals came in six minutes early in the second half. Kyrgiakos headed in Gerrard's corner. Konchesky's clearance hit Carragher in the face for a bizarre own goal. Torres side-footed the winner on 53 minutes. Sam Allardyce was left bemoaning that Blackburn couldn't cope with Liverpool's aerial threat. Kyrgiakos and Lucas played particularly well.

Hodgson's solitary domestic success on the road came the following weekend at Bolton. It lifted his side out of the relegation zone, into 13th. The goal came in the 86th minute when Torres played a delightful backheel to Maxi, whose shot somehow went through Jussi Jaaskelainen. Torres had hitherto struggled to make an impression, as had Gerrard. Cole injured a hamstring. It was hardly a vintage performance, but the result was of far more importance. "Today was a famous victory, because we hadn't won more than once away in the whole of 2010," remarked Hodgson.

Benitez was now managing Inter Milan, and before a Champions League game with Spurs, he was asked to comment on Hodgson's criticisms of some of his signings. "I think that Mr Hodgson, he doesn't understand," he said. "Every single press conference is even worse than the last one. He's talking about things that he doesn't know. And some people cannot see a priest on a mountain of sugar. Maybe he hasn't been in Liverpool too long. We gave the fans their pride again. We fought for the fans, we fought for the club and we fought for our players. So maybe he cannot understand this. With £10m net spending, I left that squad with £300m value, 13 internationals. So, instead of talking about flips and flops, he has to concentrate on his job, try to do his best and not talk about the level of his players or the new players."

As the club welcomed Damien Comolli into the role of director of football strategy, Gerrard produced one of the finest performances ever by a Liverpool substitute. With the team trailing 1-0 at half-time to a Napoli team that included Andrea Dossena, Gerrard replaced Jovanovic and scored a hat trick between minutes 75 and 89 to secure a 3-1 win. The first came from a tackle on the goalkeeper. The second was an emphatic penalty after the returning Johnson was fouled. The third was a beautiful dink over the keeper, like his goal at Newcastle in December 2008. It was vintage Gerrard, but Liverpool fans hadn't seen enough of him in that form in the last 18 months. Comolli's job was to reverse Liverpool's transfer strategy, which had yielded so little in recent years.

The high watermark of Hodgson's time as Liverpool manager came three days later, when the table-topping champions Chelsea were humbled 2-0 at Anfield. An electric Torres got both the goals. His second was even better than his first for the club against the same opponents, as he took Meireles' pass on the left, ghosted inside Branislav Ivanovic and curled the ball wide of Petr Cech. Lucas, Meireles and Gerrard set the tone for the afternoon from midfield. Torres, for once, didn't stop running. Kuyt, on his comeback, forced a brilliant save from Cech. Reina made two magnificent saves. Nicolas Anelka hit the crossbar.

One of Chelsea's subs was a 21-year-old Daniel Sturridge. When Torres was struggling for goals at Stamford Bridge, Sturridge would be banging them in for fun at Anfield.

Torres scored again at Wigan after seven minutes, but the Reds were unable to come away with the win. Latching onto Gerrard's through ball, he controlled the ball superbly and finished from the edge of the box. But Liverpool couldn't find a second when they were on top and were punished by Hugo Rodallega on 54 minutes. Disappointingly, the Reds retreated after that, leaving Torres isolated. Hodgson replaced Kuyt with Poulsen, which showed his intentions. The Reds did manage one more attack, but Gerrard hit the bar from close range after a wonderful through ball from Maxi.

Hodgson was again forced to listen to Liverpool supporters chanting 'Dalglish!' as the Reds lost 2-0 to Stoke City. "Anaemic, weak and devoid of options," was the Liverpool Echo's assessment. The first was a classic Stoke goal, with Ricardo Fuller toe-poking past Reina after the mother of all goalmouth scrambles followed Rory Delap's long throw. Kenwyne Jones made it two in the last minute from Jermaine Pennant's pass. Lucas was sent off for a second yellow. "The fans can chant for whoever they want, and it will be up to the club to decide what they want to do," said Hodgson.

After the news that Gerrard would miss a month with a hamstring injury, the Reds produced a scintillating first-half display at home to bottom club West Ham. Johnson, formerly a Hammer, half-volleyed Liverpool ahead on 18 minutes in front of the Kop. Kuyt added a second from the spot after a handball nine minutes later. The third came from Maxi, who glanced in Konchesky's cross on 38 minutes. Johnson was man of the match just a week after stinging criticism from Hodgson, who said: "You would have to ask him 'Do you think you're playing at top form, and are you playing like the best right back in the country for your club?' If he says yes, obviously we will have to agree to differ. And if he says no, then you'd have to ask the question 'Why not?'"

A 2-1 defeat at Spurs was a Sunday afternoon to forget for Hodgson. Lucas and Meireles controlled the midfield in the first half. Skrtel scored just before the break. Torres missed two chances to make it 2-0. N'Gog was also off colour. Meireles cleared off the line from Gareth Bale. Jermaine Defoe put a penalty wide. Skrtel cancelled out his goal by slicing the ball past Reina on 65. Carragher dislocated a shoulder. Initial reports suggested he would be out for three months. Aaron Lennon scored an injury-time winner, firing past Reina after he raced past Konchesky to get to Peter Crouch's flick.

Back in Europe, a weakened side picked up a 1-1 draw in Bucharest. Aurelio, Wilson and Pacheco got rare starts, with Eccleston coming off the bench. Jovanovic headed in Babel's cross on 19 minutes. A terrible error by Reina saw Steaua equalise when he allowed Eder Bonfim's weak header to squirm through him. Despite fielding fringe players throughout the competition, the Reds had secured top spot with a game to spare.

Gerard Houllier made his first professional return to Anfield with Aston Villa, who were facing a fight to remain in the division. Houllier's popularity among Liverpool fans had diminished somewhat after a bizarre attack on Benitez when the Spaniard was relieved of his job. He told the Evening Standard: "One of the players sent me a message. He said, 'Boss, he hasn't beaten you.'" He also claimed credit for Benitez's Champions League win: "When I came into the changing room in Istanbul, some of the players said: 'Boss, it's your team'. Twelve out of 14 in Istanbul were players I had signed or developed," overlooking the fact he couldn't get past the quarter-finals of the UEFA Cup in his last two seasons with those same players. "I left Liverpool with a team in the Champions League," he continued. "But when you finish seventh with Torres and Gerrard..." With Torres missing the match to be at the birth of his son, Hodgson fielded a strike force of N'Gog and Babel, and within 16 minutes, they'd both scored. N'Gog did well to head in from close range. Babel finished clinically from Lucas's lofted pass. Maxi wrapped up a 3-0 win after exchanging passes with N'Gog. Reina wore the captain's armband and kept his 100th clean sheet in 198 appearances. Houllier initially received a lukewarm reception from the Kop, but they sang his name in the last minute, a gesture not yet afforded to Hodgson. The Frenchman, however, did upset the Villa fans by saying, "If I have got to lose 3-0, I would prefer it to be them, as I like Liverpool." Despite numerous protests by the Villa fans, he remained in his post until he was hospitalised in April. It was his last managerial role.

Another turgid performance was never far away under Hodgson. A 1-1 draw at Newcastle, where Alan Pardew was in charge for the first time, might not have been the worst of results, had the Reds been able to hang on to that, but late goals by Joey Barton and Andy Carroll saw the game end 3-1. A disbelieving Hodgson stood on the touchline and vigorously rubbed his face after Barton's goal. Carroll was involved in all three goals, including a sensational 25-yarder of his own in the last minute. He would soon be a Liverpool player, one of many in the modern era signed on the back of a decent performance against the Reds. Kuyt scored Liverpool's goal, with a mishit shot that was deflected into the corner. Torres was back but was miles off the pace.

Torres and Reina were initially selected by Hodgson for the final Europa League group game with Utrecht, but the club's new doctor, Peter Brukner, overruled him. Hodgson even issued an apology to fans expecting to see the Spaniards in action. Torres was an unused sub as the Reds drew 0-0. Eccleston made his first start but was out of his depth. With a terrible performance, Liverpool barely created anything all night. Jovanovic hit the bar from long range. Once again, Cole was a shadow of the player he had been at Chelsea.

On the day the sad news filtered through from Tel Aviv that Liverpool's former left back Avi Cohen had died after a motorcycle accident, the Reds lost 1-0 at Anfield to Wolves. They had started the day bottom of the league. Mick McCarthy's men took the lead on 56 minutes and had no trouble in holding onto it. "I think we were a bit unlucky to lose the game," said Hodgson. "0-0 would have been a reasonable result for us." Gerrard played his first match in six weeks. Hodgson played Kuyt on the left and Meireles on the right, the sort of baffling decisions that underpinned his time as manager. The Kop's chants of "Attack, attack, attack!" soon turned to "Hodgson for England!" - the first time his name had been chanted by Liverpool fans. Finally, there were more chants for Dalglish. "Ever since I came here the famous Anfield support has not really been there," Hodgson lamented. As Tony Barrett in The Times put it, "While Hodgson's supporters in the media have continued to fight his corner, those at the club have long since given up on him and the only question now is how long it will take for Liverpool's owners to follow suit." Liverpool had reached the turn of the year in 12th with 22 points, their lowest tally at that stage since the 1953-54 season, which culminated in relegation. They were 16 points behind leaders Manchester United.

The fat lady wasn't singing just yet, and Hodgson actually won his next game. Bolton were the visitors on New Year's Day and held a 1-0 lead with Kevin Davies scoring from a set piece just before the break. Torres volleyed Liverpool level, set up brilliantly by Gerrard. The winner came in the 90th minute, when Cole turned the ball in from a couple of inches to buy Hodgson more time. "We are all right behind the manager," said Cole. The players might have been, but the fans weren't, as 10,000 empty seats testified. Bolton were managed by Owen Coyle, who was being linked with the Liverpool job. Agger made his first appearance in over three months.

Hodgson was still one defeat from the sack, so when the Reds lost 3-1 in a Wednesday night fixture at Blackburn Rovers, he was done for. Blackburn, without eight players, scored first through Martin Olsson. Benjani scored two more to make it 3-0. This was humiliating. Gerrard pulled one back on 81 minutes. Five minutes later, he skied a penalty, which he'd won himself. Other than the skipper, only Lucas played well. It ended 3-1. Hodgson was finally put out of his misery a couple of days later. The 63-year-old had won just seven Premier League games out of 20. The new owners could never understand why he'd been appointed in the first place. He departed with a lower win percentage than any Liverpool manager of the last half-century. There was barely a Liverpool supporter who mourned his departure.

The supporters' joy that Hodgson had gone turned to absolute elation when it was announced that Kenny Dalglish would take over for the rest of the season. Dalglish's first spell as manager had ended on 22nd February 1991, when his shock resignation stunned the footballing world. It had followed a chaotic 4-4 draw in an FA Cup replay with Everton, in which haphazard Liverpool defending had cancelled out four magnificent goals. His resignation was put down to the everyday stress of managing a big club, but the most significant factor was that he hadn't recovered from Hillsborough. Just 38 at the time, Dalglish shouldered much of the grief, attending as many funerals as he could, including four in one day. It broke him. Three months after resigning, he wanted to go back, but it was too late. The board had turned to Graeme Souness. Dalglish went to Blackburn instead, got them promoted and won his fourth league title in 1995. He had an unsuccessful spell at Newcastle and a brief spell as caretaker manager of Celtic, where he won the League Cup. He returned to Anfield in 2009 in an ambassadorial role, which included working with the Academy. It had been a long time. Now he was back in the dugout.

From 100 yards away, Liverpool fans high up in Old Trafford's East Stand strained their eyes to see their hero emerge from the tunnel. There he was, in his trademark oversized manager's jacket. He raised his arms, with clenched fists. The roar wouldn't have been louder if Gerrard had scored a last-minute winner. Dalglish, now 59, was the manager of Liverpool Football Club again. It wouldn't quite make up for 1991, but here he was, managing Liverpool in the third round of the FA Cup against Manchester United. It took just 31 seconds for Old Trafford reality to bite. Howard Webb awarded United a questionable penalty after Agger's challenge on Berbatov. "He reacted like a feather in a wind tunnel," reported The Guardian. Ryan Giggs sent the penalty past Reina. 1-0 already. There was worse to come. Just past the half hour, Gerrard was sent off for fouling Michael Carrick. Babel was later disciplined for tweeting a picture of Webb in a Manchester United shirt. With Kelly and Lucas the most impressive performers, Dalglish's side dug in, and United couldn't extend their lead. Reina made an astonishing quadruple save. At the other end, Tomasz Kuszczak did well to keep out Aurelio's free kick. They may have lost, but with Dalglish in charge, with the defence looking much more robust already, and with Liverpool players passing the ball, rather than "just fucking launching it", there were reasons to smile again.

When Torres fired Liverpool into the lead at Blackpool inside three minutes, the new manager's honeymoon was well and truly alive. But it didn't last long. The Lancastrians quickly equalised, with Meireles and Agger at fault. With Charlie Adam at his most influential, they went on to win the game with DJ Campbell's header on 69 minutes. The Reds passed the ball nicely again, but there was little cutting edge. Liverpool were 13th, three points behind Blackpool, who had played a game fewer. Dalglish, by now, had brought in fellow Scot Steve Clarke as his assistant.

The new manager was still looking for his first win after a 2-2 draw in the Anfield derby, the 12th in a row Everton failed to win. Anfield gave Dalglish a raucous reception. Gerrard was still suspended, so Spearing made his first league start. The Reds were the better side for the most part. Torres hit a post. Tim Howard made two saves from Kuyt, after which Meireles hammered in the rebound to score his first goal for the club. But two Everton goals in six minutes at the start of the second half left Liverpool chasing the game. Howard came to the rescue when he needlessly fouled Maxi in the box, allowing Kuyt to equalise from the spot.

Dalglish's first win came at Molineux in a game that made headlines for the most unusual reasons. The team for his first success was Reina; Kelly, Agger, Skrtel, Johnson; Poulsen, Lucas; Kuyt, Meireles, Maxi; Torres. Now back in his best position, Meireles was outstanding, slamming in a magnificent volley to put the Reds 2-0 up midway through the second half. The first and third goals came from Torres – his last for the club. Meireles set up the first, with the assistant referee Sian Massey correct in keeping her flag down when, at first glance, he seemed to have strayed offside. Her appointment to the game led to a series of misogynistic, off-the-camera comments from Sky Sports' Richard Keys and Andy Gray, both of whom were subsequently fired by the broadcaster. Liverpool fans had little sympathy. Massey has gone on to enjoy an excellent career as a Premier League official and was appointed MBE in 2017.

Three more wins followed the Wolves success. Fulham at Anfield was first, although it needed a huge stroke of luck. After Torres had a goal ruled out for a very marginal offside, John Pantsil scored a freak own goal after the Spanish striker hit the post. Liverpool otherwise didn't threaten much, and the Cottagers twice came close to equalising. The Reds were now up to seventh.

In keeping with such a drama-filled season, Liverpool stole the headlines on the final day of the January transfer window. The Uruguayan forward Luis Suarez had already been signed from Ajax for £22.8 million. Babel went to Hoffenheim for £5.8 million. Konchesky was loaned to Nottingham Forest. And then, on the last day, in came Andy Carroll for a whopping £35 million, in what looked to be an enormous risk. He had only played half a season of top-flight football. He later admitted he had hoped he would fail the medical because he didn't want to leave Newcastle. Carroll had scored 26 goals in 2010 but would never again hit double figures in a calendar year. Then came a bigger bombshell. Torres would be joining Chelsea for a British transfer record of £50 million. Many fans were devastated, but Carragher took a different perspective, telling Sky Sports in his punditry days: "Torres's time was done. £50 million for Torres ... we couldn't believe it. I was shocked by the money they paid. I knew Torres wanted out since the summer. He hadn't had a great 18 months for us. His one good game had been against Chelsea at Anfield. We beat them 2-0, and he scored two. We knew Torres wasn't the same Torres of when he first came."

Suarez enjoyed a goalscoring debut against Stoke City, although he initially thought he hadn't even made the bench because he didn't understand Dalglish's pronunciation of his surname. He had only met his teammates once before he played alongside them. Gerrard was back in the side. Carragher was on the bench, although unused. Dalglish selected three centre backs – Skrtel, Kyrgiakos and Agger – to deal with Stoke's aerial threat. Meireles put the Reds ahead just after the break. Suarez replaced Aurelio on 63 minutes. A quarter of an hour later, he went around Asmir Begovic, and although his shot was unconvincing, it was deflected in via a post. It was the start of a great Liverpool career.

As luck would have it, Torres's first game for Chelsea was against Liverpool at Stamford Bridge. He had already spoken of his pleasure at now being at a 'top-level club', which hardly pacified the Liverpool fans. He suffered a nightmare afternoon. Liverpool's three centre halves gave him nothing, including the returning Carragher, who blocked a goalbound shot. Agger clattered into him in the first half, which brought a huge cheer from the away end. He was withdrawn on 66 minutes, mocked by the travelling Reds for never getting into the game. Three minutes later, Liverpool went ahead when the in-form Meireles turned the ball in at the back post. Earlier in the game, he'd hit the bar from two yards. The Reds held on with ease for a fantastic win. They even won without Suarez, who remained on the bench throughout. "It was a mistake by [Carlo] Ancelotti to play [Torres] in that game," said Carragher. "He'd just signed. It was against Liverpool. Our supporters were on his back. It was a big game. I didn't feel sorry for him, but to go into that game against his old club first game and getting lots of stick, I think it probably affected him for the rest of his time at Chelsea." As Carragher alludes, the Spaniard turned out to be an atrocious signing for Chelsea. Unfortunately, Carroll would be no better at Liverpool.

A run of four wins and four clean sheets came to an end with a frustrating 1-1 draw with bottom-three side Wigan. With Gerrard absent, Aurelio played in central midfield. Suarez impressed on his first start. Meireles continued his golden run when he volleyed the opening goal on 24 minutes – his fifth of the season, all since the managerial change. "[Dalglish] has given Raul a more advanced role and given him the belief to score goals," said Lucas. Suarez hit a post. But just like the away game under Hodgson, Liverpool failed to increase their lead and were punished by a second-half equaliser. Suarez hit the bar with a free kick. N'Gog and Jovanovic came on in the second half but only served to underline the lack of depth available to Dalglish. Carroll was still getting back to full fitness and was yet to make his debut. Two days later, Raheem Sterling scored five goals in a 9-0 win over Southend in the last 16 of the FA Youth Cup. The Reds would lose in the next round to Manchester United.

Dalglish's first European match as Liverpool manager was in the Czech Republic. His last European involvement with the Reds had been a player at the tragedy at Heysel in 1985. In came Wilson, Kyrgiakos and N'Gog for a 0-0 draw with Sparta Prague which put the Reds in the driving seat to make the last 16. Conor Coady made the bench, but wasn't used, while 16-year-old Raheem Sterling travelled with the party but missed out on the matchday squad. Suarez was ineligible. Aurelio came off injured, giving Cole his first chance under Dalglish. Sparta were playing their first competitive match since mid-December and finished the stronger side, but they couldn't beat the in-form Reina. Fifteen hundred Liverpool supporters made the journey, despite being charged £145 for a ticket.

Twenty years and two days after his 1991 resignation, Dalglish's side won the second leg 1-0 with a headed goal by Kuyt, from Meireles' corner, four minutes from time. An injured Johnson missed out. Kelly and Agger limped off. Kyrgiakos needed treatment on two occasions.

Gerrard was back for the trip to Upton Park. Defensive injuries meant a rare league start for Wilson. As he had done in the win at Chelsea, Dalglish elected to try a 3-5-2 formation, but it was to no avail, as the Reds were woeful in a 3-1 defeat to a team that had started the day bottom of the league. Scott Parker and Demba Ba opened up a 2-0 half-time advantage for the Hammers. It took 84 minutes for the Reds to get back into the game, when Johnson turned in Suarez's cross, but Carlton Cole scored again at the end. Kelly came off injured and would miss the rest of the season, which was a shame, as he was making an impression. The club's official magazine would name him their young player of the season.

The perfect way to bounce back was to beat table-topping Manchester United at Anfield two days after Dalglish's 60th birthday, and they did so in style. The Kop even sang 'Happy birthday, King Kenny'. Liverpool lost Aurelio to a first-half injury, but it didn't affect them. Kuyt hogged the headlines with a hat trick, but Suarez produced a magnificent performance, which underlined what sort of Liverpool career he was going to have. Stunning penalty-area trickery saw him beat Rafael da Silva, Michael Carrick and Wes Brown, before he nutmegged Edwin van ser Sar to allow Kuyt to slam the ball home from about an inch. Kuyt was immediately handed another easy goal, this time by Nani, who inexplicably headed Suarez's cross back to the Dutchman, just a few yards out. Nani then burst into tears when fouled by Carragher who, admittedly, could have been sent off. The Portuguese winger sprung from the turf and hopped to the referee, pointing to his leg. Then he went down again with his leg in the air. He was withdrawn at half-time by Ferguson, who was so angry that he refused to perform any post-match media duties. Kuyt completed his treble midway through the second half when van der Sar saved Suarez's free kick and he followed in the rebound. Carroll made his debut off the bench on 74 minutes and could have scored. Liverpool should have had at least a couple more but had to settle for a two-goal win when Javier Hernandez pulled one back at the end.

Unfortunately, Gerrard would miss both legs of the last-16 Europa League tie against Braga. A trip to Portugal saw a badly below-par Liverpool lose 1-0. The hosts scored an 18th-minute penalty after a careless foul by Kyrgiakos. Only the crossbar prevented the Reds from conceding another. Liverpool offered nothing in response in a performance that could not have contrasted more with the one that defeated United. "To come away only one goal behind was very fortunate," said Dalglish. "When you play as bad as that, you can only be happy when you have lost 1-0. Nobody can be pleased with their performance."

A 0-0 draw in the second leg was far from the famous European night Anfield is synonymous with. Carroll, who had been lively off the bench in Portugal, started the second leg with purpose. It was his full debut. His flick-on saw Cole force a good save. Carroll then headed the corner wide. Late in the game, Carroll's goalbound header hit Kuyt. Skrtel forced a save from close range. N'Gog failed to connect with Meireles' teasing free kick. Liverpool were out of the Europa League. The harsh reality was that when it came to the Europa League, Dalglish had been as negative as Hodgson had been. Four games against Sparta Prague and Braga had yielded just one goal. More alarmingly, and a sign of things to come, with Carroll up front, Liverpool were too quick to go long.

Back in the league, a wondergoal by Suarez helped Liverpool to an easy three points at the Stadium of Light. Spearing was fouled outside the box, but following advice from his linesman, the referee gave a penalty, which Kuyt converted. The game wasn't particularly entertaining, but it was lit up by the Uruguayan dribbling along the byline and hitting a swerving shot past Simon Mignolet and just inside the far post. John Mensah was sent off for a foul on Suarez. "Where's your famous beach ball now?" sang the travelling Kop. Speculation was mounting that Dalglish may be rewarded with a contract as permanent manager. Liverpool were sixth.

Hodgson enjoyed a very satisfying afternoon as West Brom's new manager when two Chris Brunt penalties gave them a 2-1 win over Liverpool. Skrtel headed a corner past Scott Carson, but with Johnson and Agger departing injured and Aurelio and Kelly absent, the Reds were vulnerable at the back. Carragher was out of sorts at right back. Peter Odemwingie ran Kyrgiakos ragged all afternoon. It was he that won both penalties, with the Greek at fault for both. Suarez was Liverpool's best, and came close to equalising, but Carroll had another poor game. In worse news, Gerrard would miss the rest of the season after picking up an infection following his recent groin operation. He had sustained the original injury doing a Cruyff turn at Melwood. The infection didn't just end this campaign for him, it meant he missed the start of the next one too. Agger would also miss the rest of the season, while Johnson would be absent for a month.

An unbeaten run of five games, in which Liverpool scored 17 goals, was the perfect way to respond. After a tribute to the 96 came a resounding 3-0 win over Manchester City, in which Jon Flanagan made his debut. Suarez hit a post. Carroll scored his first goals for the club, with a glorious 20-yarder and a brilliant header. Kuyt scored in between as the Reds took a 3-0 interval lead. There were no further goals, but it was one of the best performances of the season, against a team which had long since overtaken Liverpool. The Reds were now eight points behind City in fourth, with six games remaining. It remained a long shot, but the fact it was being talked about underlined the improvement Dalglish had made to Liverpool.

One of the funniest moments of the season was Dalglish telling Arsene Wenger to piss off after the Reds picked up a point at the Emirates. Yet again, two defenders had to leave the field – Aurelio and Carragher. The latter sustained a bad concussion, which led to a substantial portion of injury time. Teenager Jack Robinson replaced Aurelio and was impeccable, as was Flanagan at right back. Spearing was outstanding as he continued to deputise for Gerrard. But eight minutes into injury time, he conceded a penalty, which Robin van Persie dispatched. It looked like Liverpool would come away on the wrong end of a hard-luck story, having played so well, when Lucas was needlessly fouled by Emmanuel Eboue as he was moving away from goal. With 102 minutes on the clock, Kuyt equalised from the spot, and the referee blew for full time. Wenger, for some reason, believed his team had been hard done to and started ranting at his opposite number as he approached him for a handshake. Dalglish dismissed him with a wave of the hand and told him to piss off before walking away.

The last time Dalglish had managed Liverpool against Birmingham City, Gary Gillespie was an unlikely hat-trick scorer in a 5-0 win. It was the same score 25 years on, and this time the match ball went to Maxi, who had been an unused sub in the last three games. He scored after seven minutes, following up after Ben Foster spilled Spearing's shot. Kuyt got the next with a clever finish from 12 yards. Maxi got his second, volleying in Suarez's cross at the back post. His third came on 73 minutes when he side-footed home from six yards. Substitute Cole made it 5-0 with a deflected shot that squirmed through the keeper. He looked too embarrassed to celebrate. It was Liverpool's first league win over Birmingham in ten attempts. The Kop chanted Dalglish's name, desperate for him to be given the job on a permanent basis. Only Chelsea had taken more points than Liverpool since he took over.

Maxi was on target again, opening the scoring in a 3-0 home win over Newcastle. Kuyt maintained his excellent goalscoring run with a penalty after Suarez had been fouled. Suarez got the third from close range. Carroll remained on the bench for 70 minutes. He was again ineffective when he came on, but Newcastle were clearly missing him, and their fans sang, "You've let your city down."

Fulham were the next team to be hammered by Liverpool and, incredibly, there was another hat trick for Maxi, who scored after a mere 32 seconds. His next came in the seventh minute. Kuyt scored in his fifth consecutive league game on 16 minutes, after an awful error from Mark Schwarzer. Fulham pulled one back in the second half, but the Argentine's hat trick came with 20 minutes left as he rocketed a shot into the top corner. The outstanding Suarez quickly added the fifth from Shelvey's defence-splitting pass. The Uruguayan tormented Brede Hangeland all night. A late Steve Sidwell goal made it 5-2. Flanagan excelled again, this time at left back. Two five-goal hauls in three games was impressive going from Dalglish's men. Thirteen goals in three matches had been scored without Carroll being on the pitch for any of them. The game was also notable for Carragher moving ahead of Emlyn Hughes and Ray Clemence into second place in the list of Liverpool's all-time appearance makers with 666. During the season, he had also gone past Tommy Smith, Phil Neal and Ian Rush. Only Ian Callaghan with 857 was ahead of him.

Having moved within four points of fourth place, the Reds lost their last couple of games, without scoring a goal. Tottenham came to Anfield and won 2-0, with goals from Rafael van der Vaart and Luka Modric. The latter was a penalty after Flanagan and Steven Pienaar had come together outside the box. A start for Carroll coincided with the Reds failing to find the net, with his teammates resorting to long balls. He ballooned one easy headed chance into the stands. The game was something of an anti-climax for Liverpool fans, coming three days after Dalglish had been appointed permanent manager with a three-year deal.

The final game of a tumultuous season was a 1-0 defeat at Villa Park, which saw the Reds miss out on a place in the Europa League. Former Red Gary McAllister was in temporary charge of Villa, with Gerard Houllier on gardening leave. The only goal in a drab game was scored by Stewart Downing, who would soon be on Dalglish's radar. Liverpool finished sixth, ten points behind fourth-placed Arsenal and 22 behind Manchester United, who had now moved ahead of Liverpool by winning their 19th title.

Despite the many poor performances, Liverpool fans could at least go into the off-season knowing Hicks, Gillett and Hodgson had gone. The disappointment of losing Torres had been tempered by the arrival of the imperious Suarez. Dalglish's five months in charge had lifted everybody, but if the Reds were going to get back among the top teams, it was clear that the new manager would have to get his summer transfer dealings right.

2011-12

"Andy Carroll's drinking is out of control.
By 2.30 on Saturday, he'd sunk ten bitters!"

Towards the end of the 2010-11 season, Danny Murphy pointed out that Liverpool had strung impressive wins together when there was little to play for, including a whirlwind 5-2 win over his Fulham team. How would the Reds fare, he wondered, when the pressure was really on? Kenny Dalglish dismissed his surmising, as did most of the fans. But Murphy had a point. As much as the fans adored Dalglish, now was the time to deliver. His gross outlay on transfers would go past £100 million over the summer.

Dalglish had taken over on the back of 18 months of substandard football. Although he had signed Luis Suarez in January 2011, he also bought the misfiring Andy Carroll. He still had a decent goalkeeper in Pepe Reina. Problems had arisen at centre half, with Jamie Carragher, Martin Skrtel, Daniel Agger and Sotirios Kyrgiakos either getting old, injury prone or substandard. At right back, Glen Johnson missed too many games, although Martin Kelly and Jon Flanagan looked to have promising futures. On the left, Fabio Aurelio was surely heading for the exit. Danny Wilson hadn't cut the mustard. Jack Robinson had potential but was only 17. But they were all better than the execrable Paul Konchesky, who was now moving to Leicester City.

In midfield, Lucas Leiva had done well in the holding role. Young Jay Spearing was solid in the same position, when called upon. Christian Poulsen clearly wasn't good enough. Raul Meireles excelled when he was played centrally. Steven Gerrard had struggled with fitness and form since 2008-09 and would miss the start of the season with another injury.

Of the attacking players, Joe Cole and Milan Jovanovic were nowhere near Liverpool standard. Dirk Kuyt's work rate was immense, and he had improved his goalscoring record. David N'Gog had started promisingly but looked increasingly lightweight as the season wore on. Maxi was inconsistent, but his two hat tricks late in the season suggested there was plenty there for Dalglish to tap into.

Players that could be considered top-four standard in the summer of 2011 included Reina, Johnson, Carragher, Agger, Gerrard, Meireles, Kuyt, Suarez and possibly Maxi and Lucas, who had been voted Liverpool's player of the season in 2010-11. Dalglish needed to add four or five players of the same standard to that list. But he failed. He signed five players likely to play regularly: Sunderland's

Jordan Henderson for £16 million, Blackpool's Charlie Adam for £6.75 million, Aston Villa's Stewart Downing for £18.5 million, Newcastle's Jose Enrique for £6 million, while Manchester City's Craig Bellamy returned to Liverpool on a free. For £4.9 million, he also signed the Uruguayan defender Sebastian Coates, who would take Kyrgiakos's place as the fourth-choice centre half. The Brazilian Doni joined from Roma as a back-up goalkeeper. Henderson would become a club legend in time but endured a tough first season, often being played out of position on the right. Adam was inconsistent and not fit enough. Downing provided zero Premier League goals and zero assists in an awful debut season. Enrique started promisingly but faded. Bellamy did well but would be 33 by the end of the campaign.

Nobody had any quibbles with the senior players Dalglish shipped on – Konchesky, Jovanovic, Kyrgiakos, Poulsen, N'Gog, Philipp Degen and Emiliano Insua. But there was disappointment on the last day of August when Meireles handed in a transfer request and moved to Chelsea because of his desire to work with his compatriot Andre Villas-Boas, their latest manager. Youngsters Thomas Ince, Nabil El Zhar and Daniel Ayala also left. Cole and Dani Pacheco went out on loan. Alberto Aquilani, who scored the winner for Italy in a friendly with world champions Spain, went to AC Milan for the season, having spent the previous year on loan at Juventus. Sammy Lee was another who departed, having served on the coaching staff under Benitez, Hodgson and Dalglish. He was replaced by Kevin Keen, the former West Ham midfielder.

With no European football for Liverpool for the first time since the 1999-2000 season, their season began at home to Steve Bruce's Sunderland in the Premier League. Reina was in goal. Flanagan and Enrique were the full backs. Carragher captained the team, with Gerrard absent. Agger was the other centre half. Lucas and Adam made up the centre of midfield. Henderson was on the right, Downing on the left. Suarez, fresh from winning Copa America with Uruguay, partnered Carroll up front. None of Hodgson's signings started. Maxi failed to make the bench, having finished the previous season in such free-scoring form. Kuyt and Meireles came off the bench. Doni, Kelly, Robinson, Spearing and N'Gog weren't needed. The Reds created numerous first-half chances, but only had Suarez's 12th-minute header, from Adam's free kick, to show for their efforts. The Uruguayan had blazed a penalty into the Anfield Road end five minutes earlier. Downing hit the bar after a superb, slaloming run. Carroll had a goal disallowed. The Reds' intensity dropped after the break, and they were punished by Sebastian Larsson, who equalised on 57 minutes. Wes Brown had comfortably got the better of Carroll. Flanagan and Henderson struggled. Two points tossed away at home to one of the division's weaker sides contrasted sharply with champions Manchester United, who had won 18 and drawn one at Old Trafford the previous season.

Liverpool bounced back by winning at Arsenal for the first time since 2000. Kelly came in for Flanagan. Suarez, still recovering from his summer exploits, was benched. The Reds were easily the better side in a game which remained goalless for the most part. Reina was a mere spectator. Arsenal's debutant left back Emmanuel Frimpong was sent off on 70 minutes. A minute later, Suarez and Meireles were introduced by Dalglish for Carroll and Kuyt. The match was now Liverpool's for the taking. The two subs were prominent in an attack which ended with a bizarre own goal by Aaron Ramsey. Suarez then finished off Meireles's pass in injury time. A 2-0 win at Arsenal was a great result. Enrique won Sky's Man of the Match award. Lucas was also excellent, as he tended to be against the bigger sides.

With no European football, Dalglish fielded strong sides in the domestic cups and was rewarded with two Wembley finals and one trophy. A trip to Exeter in the second round of the League Cup saw starts for Wilson, Robinson and Spearing. Reina was captain. Suarez gave the Reds a 1-0 half-time lead. Maxi and Carroll scored in quick succession before the hour mark – the latter with a thunderous drive. Exeter scored a late penalty. The only dark cloud was Meireles dislocating a shoulder, in what would be his last Reds appearance. It was Dalglish's 200th win as Liverpool manager in 333 games, a record only bettered by the club's first manager, John McKenna.

Henderson and Adam got off the mark with the first and third Liverpool goals in a 3-1 home win over Bolton. Both were classy strikes from near the edge of the box. Skrtel headed the other goal after coming on as a first-half sub for the injured Kelly. Wanderers pulled one back at the end. Suarez was magnificent again, with the Telegraph describing him as "a sheer, unbridled terror." He and Kuyt again looked Liverpool's best attacking pair, with Carroll on the bench. Agger was another enjoying life under Dalglish. "The way he wants to play is pass and move, and with a high tempo," said the Dane, whose ability to bring the ball out of defence was almost unparalleled. Lucas had another fine match. After three matches, the Reds were top at the international break.

Not for the first time, Liverpool struggled after an extended break. Bellamy made his second debut for the club as Liverpool played Stoke off the Britannia Stadium. Somehow, they contrived to lose 1-0. Jonathan Walters scored a 21st-minute penalty, which had been wrongly awarded against Carragher. Wave after wave of Liverpool attacks were repelled one way or another, with defender Ryan Shawcross in commanding form. Suarez had a late penalty appeal turned down, leaving Dalglish incandescent. "The last thing I want to do is impinge on the club's reputation," he said. "I'll have to speak to the owners first. But we've had contentious decisions go against us in all four games."

An astonishing afternoon at White Hart Lane resulted in two red cards, a first-half injury for Agger and four goals conceded. Luka Modric made it 1-0 on seven minutes. Suarez had a goal disallowed. Agger departed, allowing Coates to make his debut. Adam was sent off for two bookings. The Reds kept the score at 1-0 for nearly 40 minutes but then Skrtel, at right back for the third game in a row, was sent off, for two fouls on Gareth Bale. The nine men conceded three further goals in the final quarter.

Bellamy made his first start and scored at Brighton and Hove Albion in the third round of the League Cup. His last Liverpool goal had been in the Nou Camp in 2007. There was no golf-swing celebration this time. Gerrard made his first appearance for six months as a 75th-minute substitute for Suarez. Kuyt soon made it 2-0, before Ashley Barnes dispatched an injury-time penalty conceded by Carragher.

Back in the league, a 2-1 win over Wolves at Anfield got things back on track. Suarez was impeccable again, brilliantly scoring the second after Roger Johnson had deflected Adam's long-ranger into his own net. Wolves pulled one back in the second half, but the Reds held on. Gerrard came on as a late sub again. Suarez's performances were in sharp contrast to those of Fernando Torres at Chelsea, who, a week earlier, had missed an open goal of Ronny Rosenthal proportions at Old Trafford. At half-time at Anfield, an announcement that he had been sent off against Swansea was greeted with huge cheers.

Carroll scored his first league goal of the season in a lunchtime kick off at Goodison, turning in Enrique's low cross. His goal came after 70 minutes of stalemate and 45 minutes after Everton's Jack Rodwell had been sent off. The otherwise excellent Kuyt, who replaced Henderson, had a penalty saved just before half-time – his first miss in nine attempts for the club. Adam and Kuyt hit the frame of the goal. Gerrard and Bellamy replacing a tired Adam and a badly below-par Downing just before the goal was a major turning point. Rumours circulating social media of Carroll's penchant for a few pints led to one wag's tweet going viral – 'Andy Carroll's drinking is out of control. By 2.30 on Saturday, he'd sunk ten bitters!' Suarez wrapped up a 2-0 win on 82 minutes, following a defensive mix-up. Objects were thrown at Liverpool players from the Gwladys Street stand. It was the manager's first return to Goodison with Liverpool since the infamous 4-4 draw in 1991, after which he had resigned two days later.

A real low moment in Liverpool's history occurred a fortnight later in the home game with Manchester United. The game ended 1-1, with Javier Hernandez cancelling out Gerrard's free kick. It was the skipper's first start. The Reds were the better side, with David de Gea having his usual blinder against Liverpool. After the game, United defender Patrice Evra told both the referee and the French TV channel Canal+ that he had been racially abused by Suarez. "I won't repeat what he said, but it was a racist word, and he said it more than ten times," he said. Suarez laid out his position in his 2014 autobiography. "The argument took place in Spanish," he wrote. "I did not use the word 'negro' the way it can be used in English. Negro can refer to anyone with dark hair as well as dark skin. I've been used to the word being used in Spanish in this way all my life. My wife sometimes called me 'Negro'. I'm not trying to pretend it was meant in a friendly way to Evra because clearly we were arguing. But nor was it ever meant as a racist slur." Liverpool backed their player and were confident he would be cleared, but the saga would dominate the entire season, and their handling of the episode damaged the club. Nine years later, Liverpool, under the same ownership, would eventually apologise to Evra.

With the Reds making decent progress in the league, a 1-1 draw at home to Norwich was somewhat frustrating. The pattern of the season of Liverpool dominating and the opposition keeper excelling continued, with John Ruddy in unbelievable form. Suarez had 11 shots of his own, out of the team's 29. Two of them hit the woodwork, along with one of Skrtel's. Bellamy scored on the stroke of half-time, but Grant Holt equalised on the hour. "As soon as our luck changes, we'll be alright," said Dalglish. But there were other issues - they had kept just two clean sheets in 11 games.

Suarez scored one of the goals of the season as Liverpool came back to win at Stoke in the League Cup. Kenwyne Jones scored just before the break. Suarez then collected the ball on the left wing, nutmegged a defender and curled the ball into the far corner from the right angle of the penalty area. Bellamy hit a post, but with five minutes left, Suarez headed in Henderson's cross to win the match. It was an excellent result at a bogey ground for Liverpool and proof that Suarez was one talented foreign player who could 'do it on a cold Wednesday night at Stoke.'

Gerrard had played the full 90 against United and Norwich, but sat out the League Cup game, which wasn't unexpected. The day before the next game, at West Brom, club physio Chris Morgan noticed an unusual swelling at the back of Gerrard's ankle as he walked behind him. Gerrard believes it saved his career. An infection had got into the ankle joint after Agger tackled him in training. As Liverpool were kicking off at the Hawthorns, he was going under the knife to fix the issue. "Chris explained the severity of my injury," Gerrard wrote. "If I had played against West Brom with an infected joint, it would almost certainly have been the last game of my career." A penalty from Adam got Liverpool on the way to three points. Reina captained the team, with Carragher also injured. A much-improved Carroll made it two just before the break, prodding the ball past the advancing Ben Foster from the edge of the box. Yet again, Suarez was Liverpool's best player. Gerrard would miss two months.

The last time Swansea had visited Anfield, Dalglish's class of 1990 had beaten them 8-0. This time the Welsh side, managed by Brendan Rodgers, earned a 0-0 draw, which left the Reds 12 points off the top. Carroll hit the bar. Other chances were squandered. Once more, the man of the match was the opposing keeper, Michel Vorm, although the result couldn't be blamed solely on that. Liverpool were way below their best.

The disappointment of failing to beat Swansea was followed, quite typically for this team, by a win at Chelsea as the Reds continued their excellent away form. Bellamy set up Maxi for the opener. Substitute Daniel Sturridge equalised for Chelsea ten minutes into the second half. Chelsea sent on Torres and Meireles with six minutes left, but Johnson won the game against his old club with a sublime goal three minutes from the end. He dribbled into the area from the right, turned Ashley Cole inside out and side-footed into the corner of Petr Cech's net.

The winless run at Anfield was extended to four games, although a 1-1 draw with leaders Manchester City wasn't a bad result. Vincent Kompany headed City into the lead from a corner. Within two minutes, Liverpool were level as Adam's strike from over 30 yards was deflected in by Joleon Lescott. It went down as an own goal. The Reds were the better side, but they couldn't find a winner. Joe Hart, always outstanding against Liverpool, made a magnificent save from Carroll in injury time. Lucas was Sky's Man of the Match. Future Reds James Milner, Mario Balotelli and Kolo Toure played for City, the latter two coming off the bench. Balotelli was sent off for two yellow cards in his 19-minute cameo.

Two days after the death of Wales manager Gary Speed, Liverpool won again at Stamford Bridge, this time 2-0 in the League Cup. Bellamy, a former teammate of Speed's, was devastated but insisted on playing and was the unanimous choice for man of the match. "I was determined to play against Chelsea," he wrote in his 2015 autobiography. "I had to play. I needed to play to help with my grief, to do something to try to escape what had happened. There was a minute's applause for Speedo before the game. I stood in the line with the rest of the Liverpool players. I felt okay. The Liverpool fans started singing his name. It was real to me then and I started crying. I'm a man's man. I'm not supposed to cry. I didn't like Chelsea fans. I didn't want to cry in front of them. But I couldn't help it. The Chelsea supporters didn't sing his name, but I don't expect that. They're not my cup of tea. They're not the type of fans I'd want to play for. 'I'm going to play fucking well tonight,' I thought. Jamie Carragher was great. He didn't say anything. He just gave me a little pat. When I wiped the tears away, I thought 'let's go'. And Chelsea couldn't get near me. It was one of the best games I have ever played. We won 2-0 and I set up both goals [for Maxi and Kelly]. The game was easy after the two days I had just had. It was a performance worthy of Speedo's memory. Kenny brought me off 10 minutes from the end and gave me the biggest hug when I got to the touchline, which is typical of him. Then I sat down on the bench, put a coat over my head and cried."

Lucas had sustained a knee-ligament injury in the Chelsea match and would miss the rest of the season. It was a significant blow, as he had been playing so well. Carragher also played but had to make do with a place on the bench in the league, with Agger and Skrtel now Dalglish's preferred pairing. A frustrating evening at Fulham saw the Reds lose to a late Clint Dempsey goal, shortly after Spearing had been sent off. He won the ball in a tackle but was adjudged to have jumped without control. Liverpool had been the better side. Henderson and Downing each hit an upright. Suarez had a goal wrongly disallowed for offside. Carroll, who had missed a penalty at Chelsea, endured another night to forget. Several other chances were spurned. But Reina couldn't hold a late shot from Danny Murphy, and Dempsey followed in. Suarez managed to court more controversy with a middle-finger gesture to the Fulham fans, for which he would later serve a one-game ban. The Reds were also in trouble with the FA for failing to "ensure its players conducted themselves in an orderly fashion" after Spearing was dismissed. A run of six consecutive away wins was over.

The last time Dalglish had managed Liverpool against Queens Park Rangers at Anfield, a 2-1 win had seen them secure the club's last league title. Twenty-one and a half years later, a 1-0 win was their first success at Anfield in two and a half months. Suarez scored the goal on 47 minutes, heading in Adam's pinpoint cross. Both scorer and creator had great games, as Liverpool again squandered several chances. QPR keeper Radek Cerny made three outstanding saves from Maxi alone, and another to deny Downing. Shaun Wright-Phillips hit his own bar from Bellamy's pullback.

Liverpool kept up their top-four challenge with an emphatic 2-0 win at Villa Park. Bellamy and Skrtel netted from a couple of corners in the first 15 minutes. Suarez went on to hit both post and crossbar, the latter from an exquisite chip. The Reds had hit the woodwork 17 times in 16 games, having scored just 20 goals. Downing was jeered by Villa fans throughout the afternoon.

Following the news that Suarez had been found guilty by the FA of racially abusing Evra, his teammates wore T-shirts to support him as they warmed up before their game at Wigan. It proved to be a catastrophic error of judgement. Nine years later, Carragher apologised to Evra when they worked together as pundits on Sky. A players' statement started: "Luis Suarez is our teammate and our friend and as a group of players we are shocked and angered that he has been found guilty by the FA." On the field, Liverpool started brightly but faded. Adam missed Liverpool's fourth penalty out of five in the 51st minute. Suarez was substituted on 87 minutes, with Wigan fans greeting his withdrawal like a goal of their own. His ban would begin after Boxing Day. He would serve nine games; eight for the Evra incident and one for his Craven Cottage misdemeanour.

Suarez's last game until February came at home to bottom-placed Blackburn the day after Christmas. It was widely reported Rovers' manager Steve Kean was on the verge of the sack, but Liverpool still couldn't beat them. Adam sliced a Blackburn corner into his own net on the stroke of half-time. Maxi headed in Skrtel's cross eight minutes into the second half. The returning Gerrard played the final 22 minutes. A dozen points had been dropped at home. The Daily Telegraph referred to Anfield as "a sanctuary for the Premier League's underprivileged all season."

The first game without Suarez ended in a 3-1 win at home to Newcastle, who were having a decent season under Alan Pardew. If they could negotiate his entire absence with such ease, all would be well. The Reds dominated the early stages, but Agger put the Geordies ahead with a 25th-minute own goal. Man of the match Bellamy soon made it 1-1 with a low drive into the corner of the Kop goal. The Welshman scored again with a deflected free kick midway through the second half. Carroll's header thudded into the Anfield Road-end crossbar. Gerrard, on as a sub for Adam, finally made the game safe with 12 minutes left, taking Henderson's lay-off and slotting past Tim Krul. At the turn of the year, Liverpool had been the better team in all but one of their 19 league games. But only 34 points accrued saw them lie in fifth, 11 points off the two Manchester clubs, who each had a game in hand.

The new year began with some sad news as the former Liverpool defender Gary Ablett lost his battle with non-Hodgkin's lymphoma. He was 46. He played for Liverpool between 1985 and 1992. His best performances came in the 1988-89 season, when he stood in for Alan Hansen at centre back. Ablett, who usually played at left back, moved to Everton, and also enjoyed a lengthy spell at Birmingham City. He later managed the Liverpool reserve team during Rafa Benitez's time at Anfield.

The new year got off to an awful start when the Reds lost 3-0 at Manchester City, who were coming off a surprising defeat at Sunderland. Downing fluffed his lines when Henderson played him in on eight minutes. Goals from Sergio Aguero and Yaya Toure had the Reds two down in 33 minutes. A second yellow card for Gareth Barry was a chink of light for Liverpool in the second half, but within a minute, James Milner made it three from the spot. Reina had an awful night. Skrtel, Adam, Kuyt and Carroll were no better. Hours earlier, the club announced they were dropping their appeal against Suarez's eight-match ban for the Evra episode. It was an embarrassing day all round.

After a moving tribute to Ablett, Liverpool's FA Cup run got underway with a 5-1 dismantling of Oldham on an ice-cold Friday night at Anfield. Robbie Simpson put the visitors ahead on 28 minutes. Bellamy, again man of the match, equalised immediately, diverting Shelvey's shot past Alex Cisak. Gerrard's penalty after a foul on Maxi gave the hosts an interval advantage. The Reds cut loose in the second half, with Shelvey and Downing bagging their first Liverpool goals. Carroll also scored with a sensational left-footed 20-yarder on his 23rd birthday. Sadly, the game was marred by an alleged racist incident involving Oldham's 20-year-old right back Tom Adeyemi and a Kopite of the same age. Believing he had been called "a black bastard" towards the end of the game, he looked understandably devastated and on the verge of tears. It took several minutes for several Oldham players and Gerrard to calm him down. The spectator was arrested, but an investigation saw numerous witnesses state that the offending word had been 'Manc' and not 'black'. The case was dropped.

Another excellent cup win came at Manchester City in the first leg of the League Cup semi-final. City may have been complacent after thrashing the Reds eight days earlier, but Liverpool were straight out of the traps, with Carroll, Gerrard and Agger forcing Joe Hart into early saves. The Dane was fouled in the box on 13 minutes, allowing Gerrard to beat Hart from the spot. City's influence on the game gradually increased, but they were unable to equalise, with Skrtel, in particular, defending doggedly. Dalglish saw the game out by reverting to a five-man defence, with substitute Carragher deployed as a holding midfielder. It was the first time City had failed to score at home all season.

Given the way the season had gone, no one was surprised when Liverpool failed to break down Stoke at Anfield three days later, especially with Dalglish picking three centre halves and Kuyt up front on his own. The in-form Bellamy played just the last 16 minutes. The Reds managed just one shot on target.

Several players were atrocious, most of all Downing. Kuyt still hadn't scored a league goal all season. Since the start of his ban, this was the game where Suarez's absence hurt the most. It was Liverpool's seventh home draw in the Premier League.

It got even worse in an early-evening Saturday kick-off at Bolton, scene of Roy Hodgson's only away win. Wanderers started the match in the relegation zone but were two up in half an hour. Bellamy pulled one back from Carroll's flick-on, but an early Bolton goal in the second half killed the match. The Reds offered little. Perhaps they had an eye on the City second leg, but with no European football, fatigue was no excuse. The only player to perform was Bellamy, with each of Dalglish's big-money summer signings struggling again. It was rare for Dalglish to publicly criticise his players, but he was irate afterwards. "They will not be here for much longer if that is the way they perform," he said. "We expect a much higher standard than that. It is all very well saying they might be distracted by a game on Wednesday, but every game is a massive game for us."

But this Jekyll and Hyde team made everybody forget about Stoke and Bolton when they knocked both Manchester teams out of the domestic cups in the space of four days. A 2-2 draw at home to City in the second leg of the semi-final was enough to book a place in the final with Cardiff City. In the biggest game of the season, Dalglish omitted Carragher and Carroll, playing a 4-2-3-1, with Henderson playing behind Bellamy up front. City welcomed back David Silva, who had missed the first leg, but were still without Vincent Kompany and the Toure brothers. Liverpool started well, only for Nigel de Jong to fire in a sensational opener from 25 yards. A controversial handball decision against Micah Richards, who tried to block Agger's shot, allowed Gerrard to equalise from the spot. As he celebrated, he taunted Hart, who had tried to put him off. Edin Dzeko put City ahead on the night, turning in a close-range cross. With the stage set for a hero to emerge, who else should it be than the in-form Bellamy, against his old club? In front of the Kop, he steered a loose ball into the corner of Hart's net from 16 yards after exchanging passes with Johnson. The Reds had 15 minutes to hold out, and with Reina making a late save from Adam Johnson, they managed it. The atmosphere was up there with some of the famous European nights under Rafa Benitez. The Reds were back at Wembley with Dalglish as manager for the first time since 1989.

Three days later, the other Mancunians were sent packing from Anfield, out of the FA Cup after a 2-1 defeat. Liverpool have scored precious few late goals against United down the years and have conceded more than their fair share. So it was particularly satisfying that Kuyt's winner, drilled emphatically past David de Gea, came in the 88th minute. Amid much bad feeling following the Suarez-Evra affair, United started brightly but went behind on 21 minutes when de Gea flapped at a corner, allowing Agger to head in. Ji-Sung Park equalised before the break. United rarely played expansively at Anfield in the second half of Ferguson's reign but were attack-minded for once, replacing the tiring Paul Scholes with striker Javier Hernandez. It backfired. Liverpool now had the extra man in midfield, and United's edge was lost. Just as the game appeared locked in stalemate, Reina's long clearance was flicked on by Carroll. Evra was caught flat-footed. Kuyt was clear down the inside-right channel and blasted the ball through de Gea to put Liverpool into the fifth round. Suarez's celebrations in the stands were caught by the TV cameras. He had one more game to sit out.

The pair of cup wins over the Manchester sides was to prove the season's high watermark – form-wise at least. The League Cup was still to be collected, but from hereon in, there would be more defeats than wins, as the season, and Dalglish's reign, unravelled in disappointing fashion. They did manage a comfortable midweek win at Wolves, however, which took them to fifth, despite Gerrard being rested. After a goalless first half, Carroll side-footed in Adam's low cross to mark the first anniversary of his arrival. It was his first league goal since October. Bellamy scored the second from 20 yards, although the keeper should have done better. Kuyt slid in the third from Adam's pass. It was his first Premier League goal of the season and his 50th in the competition for the club.

Suarez made his comeback off the bench in a 0-0 draw with Tottenham in an unusually physical encounter. There were few chances for either side. Indeed, one of the highlights of the evening was a cat getting onto the pitch and running the length of the field, leading the Kop, somewhat inevitably, to chant, "A cat! A cat! A cat, a cat, a cat!" Gareth Bale was a handful for the Liverpool defence, but they managed to contain him, with Skrtel in fine form. The one time he got free, with five minutes left, Reina denied him. The dream return was never on the cards for Suarez. He was lively, but the only real impression he made in his 24-minute cameo was on Scott Parker's stomach, with which his studs collided. Spurs were something of a bogey side for Dalglish in his second spell, despite a commendable record against the other top sides. Harry Redknapp's side had overtaken Liverpool long ago and were now firmly established in the top four. The Reds were seventh, four points behind fourth-placed Chelsea with 14 matches left.

Suarez being Suarez, there was always another controversy just around the corner. Perhaps, in hindsight, he should have missed the Saturday lunchtime trip to Old Trafford, with the club's reputation still on the line. He assured Lucas in the dressing room that he would shake Evra's hand before the game. Lucas passed that information on to Dalglish and Gerrard, and all seemed well. But the club's desire for a hassle-free day was scuppered when the handshake didn't happen. Evra grabbed at Suarez's arm in protest as he moved past him. Rio Ferdinand then refused to shake Suarez's hand. Match of the Day showed the incident three times. It was another public-relations gaffe. He did score a late goal, but Wayne Rooney had already netted twice for United. United found considerable joy in exposing Downing and Enrique on Liverpool's left. The latter had started the season well but was now badly short of form. Downing had barely had a decent game all season.

Liverpool faced Brighton again, this time at Anfield in the fifth round of the FA Cup. The Reds won a somewhat farcical match 6-1. It was originally reported that Albion had scored three own goals, but one of them was later credited to Gerrard. They also missed another penalty. Skrtel took five minutes to get the fun and games underway when he nodded in Gerrard's corner. Kazenga LuaLua, younger brother of Lomana, equalised with a 25-yard free kick. Liam Bridcutt scored the first own goal when a clearance hit him in the shin and flew into the net. Carroll made it 3-1 with a lovely finish from 12 yards. It was his sixth of the season, three of which had been against lower-division teams. Gerrard was fortunate to be credited with Liverpool's fourth, as his square pass from almost on the byline went in via Bridcutt's knee. The hapless Lewis Dunk then controlled Suarez's cross in the six-yard box, but as he lost control in trying to flick it up and smash it clear, it crossed the line for a laughable own goal. The Reds were then awarded a penalty, but with Kuyt due to take it, Dalglish signalled for Suarez to step up. He missed. He made amends with a goal of his own, heading in Carroll's knock-down from half a yard. To complete a strange afternoon, a large male streaker ran on and hugged Carragher.

Liverpool played their first game at the new Wembley on Sunday 26th February, when they landed their eighth League Cup after beating Cardiff City on penalties. It was hard to know what to make of the performance. They dominated the match but were taken to penalties and almost humiliated at the national stadium by a lower-division team. Still, as Gerrard lifted Liverpool's first piece of major silverware in six years, Dalglish was over the moon. It was the only domestic trophy he hadn't won him first time round, having lost to Arsenal in the 1987 final. He selected a 4-4-2: Reina; Johnson, Skrtel, Agger, Enrique; Henderson, Gerrard, Adam, Downing; Suarez, Carroll. The in-form Bellamy was surprisingly on the bench. Cardiff's Joe Mason opened the scoring on 19 minutes, sliding Kenny Miller's through ball between Reina's legs, with Enrique out of position. They barely got within 30 yards of Liverpool's goal for most of the rest of normal time. The Reds hammered away, missing chance after chance; the story of the season. Johnson hit the underside of the bar. Gerrard blazed the rebound over. Carroll failed to bury a header. Henderson was denied a penalty for handball. The Welsh side led 1-0 at the break.

Bellamy replaced Henderson just before the hour. Within a couple of minutes, Suarez hit a post and Skrtel turned in the rebound. The big defender nearly scored again with a volley. Tom Heaton saved well from Downing. Ben Turner missed a late header. Carragher replaced Agger. Extra time was needed. Heaton tipped Suarez's long-range shot around the post. From the corner, his header was cleared off the line. Carroll's header from yet another corner was just wide. Liverpool were dominating. Kuyt came on for Carroll and immediately made an impact, cracking the ball into the bottom corner from 18 yards after his cross ricocheted back to him. If anyone deserved to score a winner in a cup final, it was him. But it wasn't to be. First, he cleared a header off the line from a corner. When another came in, the ball was scrambled in by Turner on 118 minutes. Cardiff's fans went crazy. Their team had taken Liverpool to penalties at Wembley.

Gerrard went first and would surely score. Not so. His attempt was saved by Heaton. Scottish striker Kenny Miller hit a post. Adam sent his kick into orbit. Don Cowie scored. Kuyt finished emphatically. Rudy Gestede also hit a post. It was 1-1 after three kicks each. Downing, who had played excellently, beat Heaton. Peter Whittingham, who died in 2020, beat Reina. Johnson's penalty was superb, reminiscent of Carragher's in the same game 11 years earlier. Cardiff sub Anthony Gerrard, cousin of Steven, was next. He dragged his shot wide. Liverpool's captain consoled him as the rest of the squad celebrated wildly. Cardiff had missed three penalties without Reina saving one. Liverpool had got lucky. Several players played badly, most notably Henderson and Carroll, but they did enough to lift their first trophy in six years.

Liverpool's Champions League hopes were all but killed off when they lost at home to an Arsenal team which included Yossi Benayoun. Defeat left them ten points adrift of the fourth-placed Gunners. Had they won, they would have been within four, with a game in hand. Despite being without Gerrard, Liverpool could have been out of sight at half-time. Kuyt hit a post. Then he missed a penalty, won by Suarez. Next it was the Uruguayan's turn to hit the woodwork. The dam broke when Laurent Koscielny sliced Henderson's cross into his own net, but with Arsenal keeper Wojciech Szczesny in magnificent form, the Reds couldn't find the killer second. Robin van Persie headed the Gunners level just after the half hour. The Reds continued to dominate, but the winner wouldn't come. Kelly missed a sitter. Wenger introduced Alex Oxlade-Chamberlain for his first involvement in a Liverpool game. Then came the sucker punch. Two minutes into injury time, the Dutchman scored again, this time with an outstanding volley. It was a devastating blow for Dalglish. The master finisher had shown him where his team had been going wrong all season. He had scored seven goals from his last seven shots in the Premier League.

A third league defeat in a row came at Sunderland a week later. Nicklas Bendtner scored the only goal ten minutes into the second half. The Reds were unable to beat Simon Mignolet. For once, Suarez was particularly poor, as was Carroll off the bench. Spearing appeared to be fading as the season went on. The absence of Lucas was costing the Reds dearly.

The slump was reversed in the Anfield derby, the 13th in a row Everton failed to win. The Blues had recently beaten Manchester City, Chelsea and Tottenham, but Liverpool thrashed them, with Gerrard scoring all three goals in a virtuoso performance. It was his 400th league appearance and the 25th time a Liverpool player had scored a Premier League hat trick. It was the first treble in a Merseyside Derby since Ian Rush in the ScreenSport Super Cup Final in 1986. His first was a left-footed chip after Tim Howard had saved from Kelly. Suarez was superb, and it was he who set up the next two for Gerrard.

Back in the FA Cup, Stoke came to Anfield in the quarter-finals and were beaten 2-1. Suarez scored brilliantly midway through the first half, curling the ball past Thomas Sorensen from 20 yards after a one-two with Maxi. Peter Crouch headed in a corner within three minutes, with Dalglish complaining that Reina had been fouled. Downing scored the winner, exchanging passes with Gerrard before shooting into the bottom corner from just inside the box. Liverpool would play Everton in the semi-final at Wembley.

Coates scored one of the finest goals of the Premier League era at QPR, executing an astonishing scissors kick from near the edge of the box. Kuyt doubled the lead on 74 minutes after Suarez and Downing had gone close. It was his 71st and final goal for Liverpool. Surely Liverpool were home and dry against the team in 19th? Alas, no. They collapsed. Shaun Derry pulled one back. Former Red Djibril Cisse equalised. Jamie Mackie scored the winner right at the end after Enrique's error. Adam had been replaced at half-time with knee-ligament damage and would miss the rest of the season.

Raheem Sterling made his Liverpool debut aged 17 as a late substitute against Wigan. But there was nothing else to cheer, as the bottom side won 2-1 in the latest chapter of embarrassing results at Anfield. Flanagan was back in the side, after Kelly was injured at Loftus Road. The Reds fell behind to a penalty on 30 minutes after Skrtel kicked Victor Moses in the head. Gerrard crossed for Suarez to equalise. He was then booked for scoring with his arm before Wigan went ahead again just past the hour. Liverpool never looked like getting back into it. Sterling played the last four minutes and, according to Sunday Telegraph, "did more in that time than the rest of his team in The previous 86." "Credit to Liverpool," said Wigan manager Roberto Martinez, in the ultimate example of damning with faint praise. "They didn't just come to make up the numbers."

A third league defeat in a row at Newcastle was even more humiliating. Reina was sent off for headbutting James Perch. He left the field offering Perch a fight after the game. Papiss Cisse had earlier scored twice, and every touch of the ball by Carroll was barracked mercilessly by the home supporters. He was booked for diving when he could have stayed up and scored. He was substituted with ten minutes left, swore at Dalglish and stormed down the tunnel. When Reina was dismissed, Liverpool had already used all three subs. Dalglish came onto the pitch to help the reorganisation but was waved away by Gerrard. These were embarrassing scenes. Enrique went in goal. The only saving grace was that he didn't concede a goal in the remaining minutes. Liverpool were now looking likely to drop into mid-table. They were eighth, only just ahead of Sunderland, Fulham, Swansea, Norwich and Stoke. Enrique had left Newcastle saying they would never challenge for the top six. They were now sixth.

After Anfield fell silent for the 96, an unconvincing Doni made his debut in the home game with Aston Villa as Reina began a three-match ban, which would include the FA Cup semi-final with Everton. The Brazilian was picking the ball out of the net within ten minutes, after Chris Herd tucked away Barry Bannan's pullback. From then on it was Liverpool 2012 to a tee - over 20 shots; three against the woodwork, three penalty appeals turned down and the opposition keeper, Shay Given, in outstanding form. All they had to show for their domination was a Suarez equaliser on 81 minutes. Enrique and Downing were terrible. Speculation was mounting that there would be a new manager for next season. Liverpool's goal difference was only plus three after 32 matches.

An extraordinary midweek game at Blackburn probably turned out to be ideal preparation for the weekend's Wembley date with Everton. It may not have seemed so at the time, when Doni was sent off on 25 minutes, leaving Liverpool with a goalkeeping crisis at the worst time. Flanagan, whose uncle Bradley Orr was in the Blackburn side, was hooked for the Australian keeper Brad Jones. Jones's first task was to save a penalty from Yakubu. He poignantly looked skywards, gesturing towards his son, Luca, who had died five months earlier after a battle with leukaemia. The Reds were already 2-0 up at this stage, thanks to a brace from the rarely-used Maxi. But Yakubu did get on the scoresheet on 36 minutes, and when he added another from the spot just after the hour, it was suddenly 2-2. But the ten men rallied and won the game with Carroll's flying header deep into injury time. Such a late winner would have done wonders for morale ahead of the semi-final.

Damien Comolli lost his job as the club's director of football strategy a couple of days before the semi-final. The owners were unimpressed with the return on their transfer investments. He had been responsible for all the signings under Dalglish, from Suarez and Carroll to the £100 million summer splurge. He later claimed he was sacked because he had "wasted money" on Henderson. In time, there would be others following the Frenchman out of the door.

With two goalkeepers serving suspensions, Jones kept his place at Wembley. On the bench was Peter Gulacsi, who would go on to have a great career with Leipzig. Gerrard, Carragher and Suarez came back into the side. Carroll kept his place after his Ewood Park heroics. Enrique was dropped, with Agger in at left back. Dalglish persisted with Henderson and Downing on the wings, rather than Maxi and Bellamy. Everton were in form, having won three of their last four. Nikica Jelavic opened the scoring, profiting on a dreadful mix-up between Agger and Carragher. Liverpool created little in the first half, but just like in 1986, the Blues surrendered a 1-0 lead at the national stadium. The equaliser came from another error. Distin put nowhere near enough on his back pass. Suarez nipped in to steer the ball past Tim Howard. Carroll was a whisker wide from the edge of the box. Jones saved well from Jelavic. In the end, the winner came from the head of the £35 million man, when he steered Bellamy's free kick past Howard in the 88th minute. There was still time for Maxi to hit a post from close range. Dalglish's players had been far from impressive, but they were in the final, where they would play Chelsea. Suarez stood out for the Reds. Henderson and Downing struggled. It was a third Wembley win over Everton for Dalglish, whose side had won all three derbies in the 2011-12 season by an aggregate of 8-0. Boyhood Evertonian Carragher was relieved, not that Liverpool were in the final, but that Everton weren't. "Can you imagine the build-up to the cup final if Everton had beaten us?" he asked Simon Hughes. "A whole month of it in the Liverpool Echo and on the phone-ins; the reminders being there day in, day out; flags and scarves hanging out of car windows. Honest to god, it terrified me."

Reina returned to the side and assumed the captaincy for the visit of West Brom. For the second time since his sacking, Roy Hodgson got one over the

Reds as Peter Odemwingie scored the only goal of the game. In another display of profligacy, Liverpool created 27 chances and missed them all. Henderson and Kuyt struck the woodwork. Suarez, Maxi, Carroll and Spearing were all denied before Johnson's error resulted in West Brom's winner. It was the same old story for Dalglish.

Suarez rediscovered his touch at Carrow Road, where he scored a fabulous hat trick. His first was set up by Gerrard, and his finish was emphatic. For his second, he bore down on goal from the right wing and drilled his shot across John Ruddy and into the far corner. His third came in the final ten minutes, and it was worth waiting for. Positioned near halfway, towards the right, he looked up and sent a sublime chip over Ruddy. His bread-and-butter finishing was erratic, but his ability to score incredible goals was never in question.

The next team to embarrass Liverpool at Anfield was Fulham, who won 1-0 in a midweek clash at the beginning of May. The game was played on the day Roy Hodgson was appointed England manager and, incredibly, he had a part to play in the goal, despite the fact he was long gone from both clubs. Swedish winger Alex Kacaniklic attempted to score from John Arne Riise's cross, but Skrtel got the final touch and was credited with a fifth-minute own goal. Kacaniklic had been at the Liverpool academy and revealed in 2019 that he had accidentally been included as a makeweight in the deal Hodgson secured to bring Paul Konchesky to Liverpool from Fulham in 2010. Just before the deal went through, Hodgson phoned Kacaniklic to explain he had meant to sell another Alex, and that he could return to Liverpool. But the bemused Swede by now had his heart set on joining the Cottagers. With the FA Cup Final four days away, Dalglish selected fringe players like Doni, Aurelio, Coates, Kelly and Shelvey. Sterling was given another appearance off the bench, this time for 14 minutes. Liverpool had now dropped 30 points at home.

Dalglish's hopes of emulating Arsenal's 1993 team by winning both domestic cups in the same season were dashed at Wembley by Chelsea. For the club's 14th FA Cup Final, the manager selected a 4-5-1 formation: Reina; Johnson, Skrtel, Agger, Enrique; Bellamy, Gerrard, Spearing, Henderson, Downing; Suarez. It took the Reds an hour to get going, by which time they were two down to goals by Ramires and Didier Drogba. The first goal was easily preventable, but a weak hand from Reina couldn't stop it creeping into the near post. Chelsea enjoyed complete domination and could have led by more. Spearing endured a painful afternoon and was replaced by Carroll, with Liverpool switching to 4-4-2. When Carroll got one back on 64 minutes, turning John Terry and shooting high into Petr Cech's net, the game changed. Liverpool were now on top, with Chelsea clinging on. Eighteen minutes later, it appeared Carroll had equalised with a back-post header from Suarez's cross, but Cech's wonder save denied him. In truth, it would have been a travesty had Chelsea not won. They would go on to win the Champions League under their caretaker boss Roberto di Matteo. As Dalglish went up the Wembley steps, he was blanked by the club's owner John W Henry. It seemed certain his time as manager was coming to an end.

The sides met again three days later at Anfield and, typically, the Reds won the one that didn't matter. Dalglish brought Carragher, Maxi, Shelvey and Carroll into the side and was rewarded with a 4-1 win. A weakened Chelsea side gave starts to Daniel Sturridge and Fernando Torres. A burst of three goals in nine minutes started with a Michael Essien own goal from Suarez's pullback. Henderson was next, scoring his first since August when he finished calmly from the edge of the box after John Terry had slipped. Agger got in on the act, heading in Carroll's knockdown from a corner. Downing and Torres both hit the bar. Then, on the stroke of half-time, Downing hit the post with a penalty after Carroll had been fouled. He still hadn't scored in the league. Ramires pulled one back five minutes into the second half. Shelvey restored the three-goal cushion with a sensational half-volley from 30 yards, with Ross Turnbull out of position. Sterling and Kuyt came on with seven minutes left, the latter for his last Anfield appearance. Suarez chipped the goalkeeper from the touchline in injury time, but the whistle had already gone for a foul.

A truly frustrating season ended disappointingly, as the Reds lost 1-0 at Brendan Rodgers' Swansea on the day Manchester City won the title with the last kick of the season. Danny Graham scored the goal with four minutes left. Liverpool ended the season with 52 points in eighth place, a whopping 37 points off the top and 17 away from fourth.

Speculation in the weekend papers that Dalglish would be sacked turned out to be true when he was summoned to Boston to meet the owners within days of the final game. "Is it Kenny now or gaffer?" Carragher asked him as he boarded the plane. "It is Kenny now," came the reply. He had taken the club to two Wembley finals. On the other hand, he had won just six league games at Anfield in 2011-12. It was the third season in a row Liverpool had missed out on the top four. Three managers had been sacked in two years.

The club moved swiftly and appointed Brendan Rodgers as its new manager on 1st June.

2012-13

"Per aspera ad astra."

Brendan Rodgers attended his interview for the Liverpool manager's job armed with a 180-page dossier on how he would turn the team's fortunes around. It was called 'One Vision, One Club', and it went down a treat with the owners. He was young. He was in demand. He was fluent in management speak. He was relentlessly positive. Relegation had been expected of his Swansea side, but they played some exhilarating football, en route to finishing 11th. Liverpool owner John W Henry was convinced and appointed the 39-year-old Northern Irishman. He even allowed Rodgers to talk him out of appointing Louis van Gaal as sporting director. "I wanted to make sure I would be in charge of football matters," said the new manager.

Supporters weren't so sure. Not only was there anger at Kenny Dalglish being dragged all the way to Boston to be fired, there was also a feeling that Liverpool could do better than the Swansea manager, whose CV included being fired by Reading. It seemed a mediocre appointment, perhaps a reflection of where Liverpool were heading. It didn't go down as badly as sacking Rafa Benitez and appointing Roy Hodgson, but it was still a gamble. Liverpool's 20th manager told the fans, "[I will] leave no stone unturned in my quest. And that quest will be relentless."

It was a busy summer for players coming and going. Rodgers appeared to rate few of Dalglish's signings. Out went Charlie Adam and Craig Bellamy. He tried to send Jordan Henderson to Fulham, but the 22-year-old refused to go. He couldn't find a buyer for Andy Carroll, so he was loaned to West Ham. Also departing were Fabio Aurelio, David Amoo, Stephen Darby, Dirk Kuyt, Maxi Rodriguez, Alberto Aquilani and Nathan Eccleston. Jay Spearing was loaned to Bolton for the season. Just £13 million was raised in total. Goalkeeper Doni never played for the club again and left in January. He later revealed he had nearly died when his heart stopped for 25 seconds during a medical in the summer of 2012. A £20 million bid from Manchester City for Daniel Agger was rejected. Luis Suarez and Martin Skrtel committed their futures to the club.

The owners didn't want Carroll to depart until at least one forward came in. Rodgers briefed a local journalist that Carroll "wasn't a Liverpool centre forward," and wanted him gone, whether he was replaced or not. The board wanted Daniel Sturridge, but the club's director of communications Jen Chang privately briefed journalists that Rodgers was put off by the Chelsea striker's attitude.

Yet again, Liverpool's summer signings were far from impressive. Winger-cum-striker Fabio Borini joined from Roma for £10.4 million but wasn't even as good as Carroll. Midfielder Joe Allen cost £15 million from Swansea but failed to live up to promising early displays. The owners didn't think he was worth the money, but Rodgers talked them into it, christening him 'the Welsh Xavi'. "He is 5ft 6ins, but in terms of being a footballer he is 7ft 6ins," the manager explained. The £3 million signing Oussama Assaidi, from Dutch club Heerenveen, never looked like making it at Anfield. Later in the transfer window, Turkish midfielder Nuri Sahin joined on loan from Real Madrid, but despite three early goals, he wasn't up to it and returned in January.

If anything, the squad was weaker on paper at the end of the window than at the start. Many sympathised with the manager, which led to an exasperated Henry publishing an open letter, insisting money was available, but also acknowledging that "we are still in the process of reversing the errors of previous regimes. It will not happen overnight. It has been compounded by our own mistakes in a difficult first two years of ownership. It has been a harsh education, but, make no mistake, the club is healthier today than when we took over." He ended by saying, "We will deliver what every long-term supporter of Liverpool Football Club aches for." The manager was still new, but battle lines had been drawn. It was from this mess that the club's transfer committee was conceived.

Whomever was to blame, having only one recognised striker for the first half of the season meant Liverpool were likely to continue treading water. They were heavily linked with Fulham's Clint Dempsey on transfer deadline day, but, with Henderson refusing to leave, the American went to Spurs. An injury to Suarez would leave Liverpool in crisis. Things were so bad, they were linked with a move for free agent Michael Owen. He went to Stoke. Didier Drogba was another unlikely rumour. Rodgers was over-reliant on raw players like Raheem Sterling, Jonjo Shelvey and Suso. Short term, the club's approach to the transfer window prevented the team from getting back into the top four. Long term, 2012-13 proved to be something of a reset season, when the seeds of the incredible title challenge of 2014 were sewn.

Amid all this, the club released a cringeworthy fly-on-the-wall television series called 'Being: Liverpool', which followed players and management over the summer and in the early part of the season. Rodgers didn't come across well. Some of his quotes were compared to David Brent's most infamous lines, like "You train dogs; I like to educate players." He announced he had inserted the names of three players whom he felt would let the squad down in sealed envelopes. "Make sure you're not one of them," he told them on the eve of the Premier League opener. He explained he sometimes told the players, "Per aspera ad astra," Latin for "through adversity to the stars." He rounded on a bemused Sterling in training over a misunderstanding. He had a giant portrait of himself in his house. "We were brought up not with the silver spoon but the silver shovel," he said of his upbringing. His team talks were wooden and unconvincing. Surely it was unwise of the club to expose their new manager like this. Suarez, however, bought into Rodgers' philosophy, detailing in his book how the manager explained the team would play out from the back. "I listened and I was sold," wrote the Uruguayan. "It seemed so simple, but no one had walked me through it like that before."

Rodgers' first competitive game was in Belarus against Gomel in a Europa League qualifier. Brad Jones was between the posts. Glen Johnson and Jose Enrique were the full backs. Carragher captained the side on his 700th appearance, alongside Skrtel at centre back. Steven Gerrard, Spearing and Henderson were in midfield. Joe Cole and Stewart Downing were on the wings. Debutant Borini was up front. Lucas Leiva made a competitive return from a knee-ligament injury as a second-half sub for Henderson. Rodgers had urged his players to "do it for this guy here," in his pre-match talk, pointing at Lucas. Cole was back after a season on loan at Lille, but a hamstring injury on 14 minutes saw him replaced by Sterling, whom Rodgers would use on a regular basis. Martin Kelly was the other sub, replacing Johnson at half-time. Peter Gulacsi, Jack Robinson, Adam and Shelvey were unused. Downing cracked in a beauty from 20 yards midway through the second half. Gomel missed several chances to equalise.

The second leg was more comfortable, thanks to goals from Borini, Gerrard and Johnson. Suarez made the first two. Johnson finished clinically from outside the box for the third. Pepe Reina was back in goal.

After Sterling, Lucas and Carroll scored in a 3-1 friendly win over Bayer Leverkusen at Anfield, the Premier League began at the Hawthorns, where Allen made his debut. Rodgers' rather muddled team talk was captured by 'Being: Liverpool'. "Everyone together, nice and tight," he started. "Okay. Listen, today's the start of a long, hard journey for us. Okay. And I've never ever once said in the time here that it's going to be easy. If it was easy, it wouldn't be worth doing. Okay. The thing to remember before we start this campaign is one thing: you can only trust yourselves, no one else. You can trust the supporters because they're the best. And you trust your family at home. And that three group, that is why we're here and why we're doing it. Okay. So let's make sure we go and perform. Okay. We concentrate on our performance and we'll win the games. Okay. Good luck. Let's enjoy, and let's get the three points." West Brom won 3-0. The Reds conceded two penalties and had Agger sent off. The players did well for 44 minutes, but Zoltan Gera fired in spectacularly just before the break. Rodgers reassured his players at half-time that the game was still winnable, and they should still move the ball. But the second half was gruesome. Agger was dismissed after an hour for a professional foul on Shane Long, whose tame penalty was saved by Reina. Skrtel was soon penalised for a foul on Long. Odemwingie slammed in the penalty. Romelu Lukaku scored the third. Suarez was Liverpool's best player but missed several chances. Borini was one of many to struggle. Albion were managed by Steve Clarke, who found out he had been sacked by Liverpool in the summer "from a girl in human resources." He didn't gloat. It was a chastening start for Rodgers, but one manager in Liverpool's history had endured a worse league start – Bill Shankly, who lost 4-0 to Cardiff in December 1959.

A trip to Edinburgh saw Liverpool play Hearts in the first leg of a Europa League play-off, the last hurdle before the group stage. There were starts for Jack Robinson, Sterling and Shelvey. Young striker Adam Morgan, prolific at academy level, made his debut as a last-minute sub. The Reds had to rely on an Andy Webster own goal on 78 minutes. Borini hit the post in the first half but was otherwise ineffective. Sterling was Liverpool's best player on his first start for the club. Henderson made his 50th Liverpool appearance, but it was an unhappy one, with Rodgers telling him before the game that he wanted to swap him for Fulham's Dempsey. According to The Athletic, "Henderson went back to his room, shed some tears, rang his dad, and vowed to stay and fight and prove Rodgers wrong."

The visit of champions Manchester City was a major test. Rodgers told his players the season started here, and they responded well. Allen passed the ball with stunning accuracy. Sterling played the full 90, attracting plenty of praise. Coates started ahead of Carragher. Henderson and Downing were unused subs. Lucas strained a thigh muscle and was withdrawn after five minutes, so soon after his comeback. He wouldn't feature again until December. Ten minutes before half-time, Skrtel rose magnificently to head in Gerrard's corner, with Coates blocking off the defender Kolo Toure. Yaya Toure equalised on 63 after Reina missed a cross and Kelly miscontrolled at the back post. Suarez bent a superb free kick around the wall, into the corner of Joe Hart's net a couple of minutes later. But with ten minutes to go, Skrtel, unusually playing at left-sided centre half, played a backpass straight to Carlos Tevez, who rounded Reina and equalised. Rodgers defended the Slovak after the game and gave an idea of his footballing philosophy in the process. "The easy thing is to get a player to smash the ball upfield and then the opposition have the ball and they're on the attack again," he said. "There's no blame on Martin. For us to dominate games, we need to have players who have courage on the ball."

The second leg against Hearts was as dull as the first. Morgan made his first start and had a goal disallowed. Downing was now at left back. Henderson struggled again. Hearts took the lead when Reina fumbled David Templeton's shot over the line. Just as extra time seemed likely, Suarez muscled his way down the inside left and beat Jamie MacDonald from a tight angle. He lifted his jersey to reveal a T-shirt, which said, "Be strong Lucas."

Having played so well against City, Rodgers was hoping to gain his first league win against Arsenal at Anfield two days into September. Sahin made his debut. Sterling kept his place and hit a post, one of the few chances Liverpool created, despite the commendable efforts of Allen. Goals in each half from Lukas Podolski and Santi Cazorla handed the Gunners a 2-0 win – the latter after another Reina error. When Shelvey missed a late chance, Arsenal fans sang, "Andy Carroll, he would have scored that!" The Reds were in the relegation zone.

After 23 years of campaigning for the truth, the Hillsborough Independent Panel reported its findings on 12th September 2012. The report demonstrated that 41 of the 96 victims 'had the potential to survive'; emergency services made 'strenuous attempts' to pass the blame onto the supporters; 116 out of 164 police statements were 'amended to remove or alter comments unfavourable to South Yorkshire Police'; police carried out blood-alcohol tests on children and other victims, and also searched the police national computer for criminal records to 'impugn their reputations'; and that Sheffield Hallam's Conservative MP Irvine Patnick - whose 1994 knighthood remains a shameful stain on the nation - and the South Yorkshire Police had conspired with a Sheffield-based news agency to spread the lies. Tory Prime Minister David Cameron, whose party had done so much to facilitate the cover-up, told the House of Commons he was 'profoundly sorry' for the 'double injustice' of the disaster. Sheffield Wednesday and SYP chief constable David Crompton also apologised. It was a momentous day and a vindication of those who had campaigned for the truth, in the face of those who chose to believe the lies.

Rodgers was still without a Premier League win after a trip to Sunderland, although at least Suarez earned him a point. Steven Fletcher's opener followed sloppy defending by Johnson. Gerrard and Johnson hit the woodwork. Sterling's trickery on the right wing allowed him to find Suarez, who finished at the second attempt. Simon Mignolet's excellent save from Shelvey denied Liverpool a winner. Borini had another poor game.

The first Europa League group game was a goal fest in Bern. There were debuts for right back Andre Wisdom, Assaidi and Spanish playmaker Suso, whose loan move to Burnley on the final day of the transfer window had collapsed. Brad Jones and Dani Pacheco were also included. A comical own goal from Young Boys' Juhani Ojala gave Liverpool the lead. Raphael Nuzzolo equalised, with Enrique badly at fault. The outstanding Wisdom restored the lead with a thumping header. Ojala then scored at the right end. Gonzalo Zarate gave his side the lead. Coates headed an equaliser, which Borini tried to divert but missed his kick. Shelvey turned in Henderson's pass and then made it 5-3 from the edge of the box.

The home game with Manchester United was preceded by a moving tribute to the 96 after the findings of the Hillsborough Independent Panel. A mosaic in the Lower Centenary read 'Justice'. One on the Kop said 'The Truth'. In the first minute of the second half, Gerrard chested down Johnson's pass and fired left-footed into the corner from 12 yards, before pointing skywards to remember his cousin Jon-Paul Gilhooley who, at ten, was the youngest of the 96. But with Shelvey having been sent off on 39 minutes, in an incident that could have seen United's Johnny Evans dismissed too, the Reds couldn't hold on. Rafael da Silva equalised. Suarez saw a penalty appeal rejected. Robin van Persie scored the winner from the spot with nine minutes left after Johnson fouled Antonio Valencia. Kelly ruptured his anterior cruciate ligament. His season was done. The Reds were 18th after five games.

At 16 years and six days, Jerome Sinclair became the youngest player in Liverpool's history as they began their defence of the League Cup with a 2-1 win at West Brom. There was a start for the 18-year-old striker Samed Yesil, signed on transfer deadline day. Jones dropped a cross, and Gabriel Tamas scored on three minutes. Sahin levelled when his long-range shot was fumbled by Ben Foster. The Turkish international got his second with eight minutes left from Assaidi's low cross.

The first league win finally came at Carrow Road. Suarez scored after barely a minute, the first of another hat trick at Norwich. He soon spurned a clear-cut chance, but with the home fans still taunting him, he immediately won the ball back and bent a lovely shot into the corner with the outside of his right boot. He then set up Sahin to make it three from close range. Suarez's third was a sumptuous curler into the bottom corner just before the hour. Steve Morison pulled one back after Reina fumbled. By his own admission, the Spaniard had been below his best in 2011-12 and had made an awful start to the new campaign. Gerrard's shot was then diverted into his own net by Leon Barnett. Grant Holt got a late goal for Norwich after a slip by Skrtel. It ended 5-2. Liverpool started with three teenagers - Wisdom, Suso and Sterling. The average age of the side was under 25.

Another fringe side was fielded in the Europa League, but they lost 3-2 at home to Udinese. Shelvey headed in Downing's cross for a 1-0 half-time lead. But three goals in the first 24 minutes of the second half, including an own goal from Coates, gave the Reds too much to do. Suarez, on as a sub, curled in a magnificent free kick, but there would be no equaliser.

Having finally won a league game, a 0-0 draw at home to Stoke was a disappointment. The Reds struggled to deal with Stoke's physicality, although Suarez, Sterling and Skrtel all hit the frame of the goal in the second half. Kenny Dalglish's woodwork hoodoo hadn't gone with him. Cole made his first league appearance since May 2011. Stoke fielded Charlie Adam and Peter Crouch, but Michael Owen missed out with injury. Liverpool were 14th heading into an international break, during which time Borini fractured a metatarsal. He wouldn't play again until January.

Sterling scored his first Reds goal in a 1-0 home win over Reading, finding the corner of Alex McCarthy's goal from Suarez's pass. Despite his recent goals, Sahin struggled against both Stoke and Reading, failing to complete either match. Jones kept goal, with Reina struggling with a back injury. He wouldn't be back for six matches.

Anzhi Makhachkala were the next visitors to Anfield. Rodgers picked a stronger-than-usual side, including Suarez, for this competition. The Reds were far from convincing, winning 1-0 with a screamer from the out-of-favour Downing. All four of his Liverpool goals had come in cups. Johnson was withdrawn at half-time, injured. Samuel Eto'o played up front for the Russians but failed to justify his £330,000 weekly wage. The Reds were two points clear after three group games.

David Moyes stirred the pot in the build-up to the Goodison derby by suggesting Suarez was a diver. He was correct but had to suffer the twin indignities of Suarez celebrating a goal by diving in front of the Everton bench and his captain, Phil Neville, getting booked for a laughably bad piece of simulation. An own goal from Leighton Baines, caused by Suarez, gave Liverpool the lead, which the Uruguayan soon doubled. Within minutes, Leon Osman got one back after a weak punch by Jones. Steven Naismith equalised on 35 minutes. Sahin and Suso were replaced at the break. There were no more goals, but the game remained gripping until the end. Everton were the better side, but Suarez had a late goal wrongly disallowed for offside from Coates' header.

Rodgers reverted to his squad players for the visit of his former side Swansea in the League Cup. The decision backfired, as their defence of the competition ended with a 3-1 defeat. Chico Flores headed the only goal of the first half, which prompted the manager to make another double switch at the break, introducing Suarez and Gerrard for Yesil and the abysmal Cole. Gerrard hit a post from 25 yards, but it was the Welsh side, managed by Michael Laudrup, who scored next, through Nathan Dyer. Suarez glanced in Gerrard's cross, but Jonathan de Guzman put Liverpool out of their misery in the last minute.

Suarez scored one of the goals of the decade in Liverpool's 1-1 home draw with Newcastle - Gerrard's 600th game for the club. Trailing to a Yohan Cabaye stunner, Suarez controlled Enrique's 50-yard pass on his left shoulder and took it around Tim Krul as it bounced, before rolling it into the empty net. It was an astonishing piece of skill. Sterling and Shelvey spurned late chances. Enrique, Suso and Sahin struggled. Suarez was easily Liverpool's best player again. The club's inability to sign another striker in August had brought out the best in him.

Conor Coady made his Reds debut in the Europa League game at Anzhi. He did well in midfield, but the fringe players weren't up to it again. The 6ft 8in Lacina Traore scored the only goal, leaving Coates in his wake and dinking the ball over Jones. He missed other chances to increase the lead. Cole could have equalised but shot straight at the keeper.

It was no surprise that it was Suarez who scored Liverpool's equaliser at Chelsea on Remembrance Sunday, but the identity of the creator was a different matter. Carragher, a bit-part player by now, flicked on Suso's corner, and Suarez headed in from close range. The scorer ran to the corner flag, turned and looked devastated when he noticed none of his teammates had followed him. They had all gone to congratulate Carragher. He was part of a new three-at-the-back system, along with Wisdom and Agger. John Terry had headed the title-chasers into a first-half lead before succumbing to injury. It was a decent result for the Reds, for whom Enrique was outstanding at left wing back, as was Jones in goal. Allen and Sahin were particularly poor. Henderson was an unused sub. After refusing to go to Fulham, he was going to have to win back his place.

An embarrassing episode concluded in the week after the Chelsea game, when the club's director of communications, Jen Chang, left the club after being accused of threatening a supporter. Sean Cummins had created a spoof blogger called Duncan Jenkins, a 'perspiring journalist' who was desperate to become part of the 'footballing paternity'. Jenkins proved to be quite adept at beating journalists to Liverpool scoops like the signings of Borini and Sahin and revealing the starting line-up every week before it was made official. Chang hired people to find out who was behind the Jenkins blog and Twitter account, and when the two met, he told Cummins that Roma had increased Borini's price by £300,000 when Jenkins revealed Liverpool's interest in him. Cummins claimed it was a lucky guess, based on Neil Jones at the Liverpool Echo saying he knew Rodgers liked Borini. According to Cummins, Chang threatened to ban him and his friend from Anfield for life and suggested that "crazy" Liverpool fans would put "dog shit through your letterbox" and that the newspapers would "ruin your dad's online business." The club apologised after Cummins wrote about his version of the meeting. Chang departed three weeks later.

Reina was back in goal for a 3-0 win over Wigan. After a goalless first half, Suarez got the first two, set up by Sterling and Enrique, both of whom figured prominently in the game. Suarez had scored or created 12 of Liverpool's 17 Premier League goals and was the competition's top scorer with ten. Enrique scored his first for the club, tapping in a rebound from Sterling's shot. Roberto Martinez, who had been heavily linked to the Liverpool job in the summer, accused Suarez of stamping on his midfielder David Jones. Suso had been replaced by Henderson after 36 minutes in a tactical switch, allowing the Reds to press higher. "We want to create and get on the front foot," said Rodgers. "In the second half, the pressure was outstanding."

A late equaliser by Young Boys at Anfield meant that Europa League qualification would go down to the last group game in Udinese. Downing was at left back again. Wisdom came off with a knee injury, replaced by Gerrard. Henderson went to right back. Cole played a neat one-two with Suso and then put a goal on a plate for Shelvey, the false 9. Raul Bobadilla equalised. With 18 minutes left, Cole finished well from Gerrard's pass. It was his best Liverpool performance. But Elsad Zverotic made it 2-2 on 88 minutes with a clinical finish. Young Boys fans received a standing ovation from the home crowd for unfurling a banner which read "In Memory of Hillsborough."

A fourth frustrating result in a row against Swansea since their 2011 promotion was a 0-0 draw at the Liberty Stadium. The impressive Johnson twice went close. Sterling hit the bar. Enrique had a goal disallowed for a borderline offside. Sterling and Suarez made a hash of a late opportunity. Henderson was handed his first league start of the season but failed to justify it. It was Downing's second, and he fared little better at left back. Gerrard struggled too. After 13 games, Liverpool were 11th with 16 points, 14 away from the leaders Manchester United. They hadn't been in the top half all season.

A freak own goal by Gareth Bale was all Liverpool could muster at White Hart Lane, where they had now lost six in a row. The Welshman was otherwise outstanding. He beat four defenders and crossed for Aaron Lennon to make it 1-0. Henderson missed an open goal and then deflected Bale's 25-yard free kick past Reina - all this in 16 minutes. Gerrard had a penalty appeal turned down. A Suarez attempt was kicked off the line. The Reds eventually got back into the game on 72 minutes when Gerrard headed goalward. Lennon poleaxed Bale as he cleared it, and the ball rebounded into the net. Suarez volleyed a late chance over the bar.

A Southampton team including Nathaniel Clyne, Adam Lallana and Rickie Lambert visited Anfield on the first day of December. Before the game, the Reds had made their joint worst start in Premier League history. After a 1-0 win, Rodgers was talking up a top-four finish. The manager had now abandoned his three centre-back system, with Carragher and Wisdom back on the bench. Shelvey's shot thudded off a post. Just before half-time, a wonderful, curling free kick by Suarez hit the bar. From the rebound, Johnson's cross found Agger, who headed into the top corner. Suarez was later booked for trying to score with his hand again. Southampton's closest effort on goal was a 40-yard volley from Lambert. Johnson was man of the match again.

A goal from Henderson was enough for Liverpool to top their Europa League Group as they downed Udinese 1-0. His shot from a corner beat former Reds keeper Daniele Padelli. Sahin lasted just 12 minutes after sustaining a bloodied nose. Carragher replaced Agger and captained the side in the absence of Gerrard, who had a bug. Suso, Suarez and Henderson missed chances to extend the lead. A draw would have eliminated Liverpool, but Udinese offered little threat until the last kick of the game, when Antonio Di Natale fired over after Henderson had lost the ball. 'Phew Dinese!' was the Mirror's headline.

Suarez was suspended for the trip to Upton Park where, remarkably, Liverpool managed to score three goals without him. Each was scored by a former Hammer. Man of the match Johnson arrowed a piledriver into the top corner of Jussi Jaaskelainen's net. Enrique departed injured on 27 minutes, replaced by Cole. Allen handled, and Mark Noble equalised from the spot. Gerrard headed an own goal, but Liverpool turned things around in the second half. Sterling forced a formidable save from Jaaskelainen. Cole ran onto Sterling's through ball and fired brilliantly into the corner on 76 minutes. It was the first time in the league the Reds had scored in the last 15 minutes. Three minutes later, Shelvey got to Henderson's cross at the near post, and the ball looped over the stranded keeper for the winning goal. It was initially credited as a James Collins own goal, but the goal belonged to Shelvey, who had been a West Ham junior. Now in tenth, the Reds were finally in the top half of the table.

Three wins in eight days had been a great start to December, but the run came to a shuddering halt at home to Aston Villa. Christian Benteke was unplayable, scoring twice and setting up another for substitute Andreas Weimann with a clever backheel. The Reds trailed 3-0 after 51 minutes. Gerrard scored a late goal, diverting Johnson's shot past Brad Guzan. The injured Kelly, meanwhile, had turned down a contract offer of £35,000 a week, feeling that as an England international he was worth more. His solitary cap had come in 2012 against Norway, when he played for two minutes, giving him the record of the shortest

England career ever, by that point. Sterling was another trying to negotiate a new contract, understandably wanting an improvement on his £2,500 per-week deal. He eventually agreed to £35,000 a week.

Having been told he could leave in January, Downing produced his best Liverpool performance, his first league goal and his first league assist in the 4-0 home win over Fulham. Playing on the right wing, he dominated John Arne Riise. "Being told I could go was a kick up the arse," he said. A thumping volley from Skrtel gave the Reds an eighth-minute lead. A clever reverse pass from Downing enabled Gerrard to double the lead on 36 minutes. Seven minutes after the break, the £20 million winger cut inside Riise and drove the ball inside the near post before putting a finger to his lips in front of the Kop. Suarez made it four in injury time, turning in Enrique's cutback. He had equalled his 2011-12 tally before Christmas.

Inconsistency struck again when Liverpool were beaten 3-1 at Stoke on Boxing Day. Ryan Shawcross fouled Suarez in the box in under a minute. Gerrard sent Asmir Begovic the wrong way from the spot. But within ten minutes, Stoke were 2-1 up after a barrage of long balls. Agger and Skrtel were at fault for Jonathan Walters' equaliser. Kenwyne Jones was left unmarked at a corner and headed past Reina. Suarez hit a post early in the second half. Walters made it 3-1 on 49 minutes.

The final game of the calendar year was a stroll in the park at Loftus Road, as the Reds went 3-0 up in 28 minutes. Suarez scored with a wonderful individual goal after Liverpool dominated for the first ten minutes. He soon had another, smashing a rebound high into the net. Agger headed the third from Gerrard's cross. Harry Redknapp's QPR, marooned at the foot of the table, were abysmal, but managed to stem the tide. Rodgers missed the match with a stomach virus, so Colin Pascoe was in charge. As 2012 ended, the Reds were ninth, 21 points behind leaders Manchester United.

Another comfortable win came at home to Sunderland on the second day of January. Suarez lofted a pass for Sterling to lob Simon Mignolet. Suarez then stayed on his feet when fouled and beat the Belgian. Seven minutes after the break, the Uruguayan made it 3-0 from Gerrard's inch-perfect 40-yard pass.

Now the transfer window was open, Rodgers could finally sign a striker. He chose well, bringing Daniel Sturridge to the club for £12 million from Chelsea, whose interim manager was Rafa Benitez. Sturridge described Liverpool as 'humungous' and got off to an impressive start by scoring on his debut at non-league Mansfield in the FA Cup. It took him just seven minutes – nine quicker than it had taken Suarez on his debut – as he ran onto Shelvey's through ball and slotted past Alan Marriott. "Daniel was about to become the best partner I'd had in my career," wrote Suarez in 2014. The scorer was replaced in the second half by Suarez, who, for the third time in the season, attempted to score with his hand. This time he was successful. Just before the hour, he took Downing's pass, and as the ball reared up, he knocked it past Marriott with his right hand before making sure as it crossed the line. Matt Green got one back on 79 minutes. Mansfield would have earned a replay but for Jones making a full-stretch save from the same player. As Sturridge came in, leaving the club were Cole, who went to West Ham on a free transfer, and Sahin, who returned to Real Madrid. The latter blamed his lack of success on Rodgers playing him out of position.

Sturridge also scored on his league debut, coming off the bench to score at Old Trafford. Unfortunately, the Reds were 2-0 down to goals from Robin van Persie and an offside Nemanja Vidic. A half-time switch to 4-4-2 saw a marked improvement, and the new boy's moment came on 57 minutes when he gobbled up a rebound after David de Gea parried Gerrard's 20-yarder. Sturridge had three more attempts but failed to hit the target. Another sub was Borini, returning from injury. He volleyed wide from 20 yards. United were relieved to hear the final whistle. Allen had been a standout player in the home fixture with United but was now struggling badly for form. The Reds were in eighth, having taken just three points – all draws – against the top five.

Sturridge emulated the great Ray Kennedy by scoring in his first three Liverpool games in a 5-0 drubbing of Norwich. The team may have been lacking consistency, but this was the fourth thumping league win in less than a month. Reina missed out with a nose injury. A 20-yard half-volley by Henderson and a calm finish from Suarez following Sturridge's impudent dummy established a 2-0 lead. Sturridge tapped in Downing's cross just before the hour. Gerrard smashed a 25-yarder into the bottom corner. Ryan Bennett turned Sterling's shot into his own net.

With Liverpool moving up the table and with Sturridge on board, they were looking a shrewd bet to win the FA Cup. Unfortunately, an abject performance at Oldham, whom they had thrashed a year earlier, put paid to such hopes. Rodgers fielded a mix of established and fringe players, which he later regretted, and saw his side lose 3-2. Matt Smith gave Oldham an early 1-0 lead. Suarez, wearing the captain's armband for the first time, equalised after running from inside his own half. Smith scored again on the stroke of half-time after a howler from Jones in the Liverpool goal. Oldham made it 3-1 three minutes into the second half when Reece Wabara headed in. Liverpool could only get one back, when Allen scored his first for the club with a deflected 20-yard volley. Gerrard struck the underside of the bar in the last minute. Oldham had taken just one point from eight games in League One, but they still had too much for Liverpool. The Echo called it a 'dog's dinner of a performance'.

Oldham was the first of five matches without a win, although the Reds were impressive many in their next outing. With Suarez on the left of a 4-2-3-1, Liverpool went two up in a midweek match at the Emirates with goals by Suarez and Henderson. It should have been more, given Arsenal's shambolic defending, but the Gunners hit back through Olivier Giroud and Theo Walcott to grab a 2-2 draw.

It was the same score at the Etihad Stadium four days later. Edin Dzeko scored for City. Sturridge drilled an emphatic equaliser from 20 yards. Gerrard put the Reds ahead with an even more spectacular goal on 73 minutes. Sergio Aguero soon made it 2-2. Rodgers still hadn't beaten any of the sides above Liverpool: Manchester United, City, Chelsea, Spurs, Everton and Arsenal.

West Brom completed a league double over Liverpool when they won a Monday night fixture at Anfield. Sturridge missed out with a thigh strain. His replacement, Shelvey, had an early goal disallowed. Ben Foster saved a 77th-minute Gerrard penalty. The Albion goals, scored by Gareth McAuley and Romelu Lukaku, came in the last ten minutes. It was their first win since Boxing Day and their third in a row over the Reds in the league. But there was a silver lining for Liverpool fans, as Philippe Coutinho made his debut as a late sub. The 20-year-old had signed from Inter Milan for a bargain £8.5 million.

Liverpool endured a miserable Valentine's Night in Russia when they were beaten in the first leg of their last-32 tie against Zenit St Petersburg. Suarez missed several chances in a game that was goalless for 70 minutes, but goals from Hulk and Sergei Semak in two minutes left the Reds with a huge task at Anfield. It was the 20th time Liverpool had conceded two or more in the season.

After such a tough week, a much-needed win came against Swansea. The game was a week before the Swans played Bradford in the League Cup Final at Wembley. Liverpool won 5-0. Swansea boss Michael Laudrup admitted it could have been ten. Gerrard's 34th-minute penalty, following a foul on Suarez, was the only goal of the first half. It took Coutinho just 16 seconds of the second half to score his first goal for the club from Suarez's pass. Coutinho's final Liverpool goal would also come in a 5-0 home win over Swansea, nearly five years later. Enrique finished a lovely move involving Suarez and Sturridge. The outstanding Uruguayan then scored his 23rd of the season with a fine individual effort. Gerrard allowed Sturridge to round off the scoring with an emphatic penalty after a handball. The Reds had 35 shots on goal in all in a truly dominant performance. Borini sustained a shoulder injury which would sideline him until the end of April. Swansea went on to win the League Cup Final by the same margin.

The second leg against Zenit resulted in European exit for the Reds, but they did salvage some pride. The Kop responded to Rodgers' rallying call, producing a raucous atmosphere. Allen and Henderson came in for the ineligible Sturridge, and Coutinho and performed well. From Carragher's error, Hulk scored again to put his side three up on aggregate. The away goal meant Liverpool needed four. Suarez drilled a low free kick into the Anfield Road goal. Allen added another just before half-time. When Suarez scored another superb free kick just before the hour, the Reds were one goal away. But it wouldn't come. Gerrard had a shot tipped over. Shelvey hit the side netting. Agger headed wide. The aggregate score was 3-3, with Zenit going through on away goals.

Downing headed his second Premier League goal for the club at Wigan from Coutinho's inch-perfect cross, but it was Suarez who stole the show with a hat trick in a 4-0 win. He had now scored 28 goals during the season. He and

Coutinho already looked on the same wavelength, and they combined for the first of Suarez's trio. He then scored with another free kick before half-time, with the aid of a deflection and the post. His hat trick was completed on 49 minutes when he shot through Ali Al-Habsi's legs after Johnson's mazy run. Suarez was delighted with the signing of the Brazilian. "Philippe was incredible," he wrote in 2014. "He changed us completely. He's the one that gave us faith in having the ball because his technical ability is so good … We were all hugely impressed with him from day one."

Liverpool's hopes of making the top four were slim at best, so victory over Tottenham was imperative when the two sides met at Anfield on 10th March. It turned out to be Liverpool's only win of the season against one of the six sides that would finish above them. The game was a thriller, although how Spurs left empty-handed was a mystery. Suarez's 50th goal for the club made it 1-0 from a move which included a Coutinho backheel and a clever through ball from Enrique. Coutinho had a penalty appeal turned down. Gareth Bale created the equaliser, with Jan Vertonghen heading past Jones. The Belgian defender scored again when Bale's free kick wasn't cleared. With Spurs well on top, Johnson diverted Gylfi Sigurdsson's shot onto a post. But Andre Villas-Boas' side collapsed. Kyle Walker's terrible back pass allowed Downing to beat Hugo Lloris and make it 2-2. Benoit Assou-Ekotto then felled Suarez in the box and, with eight minutes remaining, Gerrard scored the winner from the spot. The captain was enjoying a much-improved season, playing every second of the league campaign so far, compared to 35.4% of minutes in 2011-12 and 54.6% of 2010-11.

Top-four hopes were all but over when the Reds surrendered meekly at Southampton a week later. Goals by Morgan Schneiderlin and Rickie Lambert had the Saints two up in 33 minutes. Coutinho scored just before the break, but Jay Rodriguez wrapped up the points with ten minutes left after dribbling through the defence. They should have won by more, with Adam Lallana pulling many of the strings. Allen had a dreadful game and was replaced by Lucas at half-time. Downing offered little. The defence was all at sea. Skrtel played a part in all three goals conceded. Carragher's absence with a shin injury was sorely felt. Without him, they looked soft-centred. He would be retiring at the end of the season. Suarez, Gerrard and Sturridge were way below their best.

An international break gave Rodgers a chance to regroup. Reina and Carragher were fit again for the trip to Villa Park. Lucas and Henderson were recalled. Christian Benteke scored his 18th of the season to maintain his great record against Liverpool. It took less than three minutes of the second half for Henderson to restore parity after a stunning pass from Coutinho. Johnson hit a post from outside the box. Just past the hour, Suarez was brought down, allowing Gerrard to win the match from 12 yards. The skipper later produced an outstanding clearance as it seemed Benteke had equalised. Reina gave him a kiss.

Three draws on the bounce meant that improving on seventh place was going to be unlikely. The Reds failed to break down West Ham at Anfield on the first Sunday in April. Lucas cleared a Hammers' shot off the line, and Sturridge had a goal chalked off. Agger was Liverpool's best player and made a crucial block from Carlton Cole. West Ham's James Tomkins kept Suarez quiet. Assaidi came on for the last 20 minutes but continued to look out of his depth.

Liverpool were also unable to find a way through the Reading defence at the Madejski Stadium. Alex McCarthy had an inspired game, making repeated saves from Suarez, Gerrard, Sturridge and Coutinho. When he was finally beaten, Suarez had a header cleared off the line.

A minute's applause for the Kop's 'Iron Lady', Anne Williams, who had campaigned so fervently for justice for her son Kevin, one of the 96 unlawfully killed at Hillsborough, preceded the home match with Chelsea. She had died after a long battle with cancer. The game ended up producing the biggest talking point of the season. Suarez had enjoyed a magnificent campaign and, apart from the occasional dive and handball, it had been relatively free of controversy. Then he bit Branislav Ivanovic. There was no provocation. The incident was missed by officials, but Suarez was subsequently banned for ten games, two more than he'd served for the Patrice Evra episode. The incident dominated the headlines, with The Times' 'Liverpool shamed by Suarez' the most succinct. As an Ajax player in October 2010, he had bitten the PSV Eindhoven midfielder Otman Bakkal and was banned for seven games. He tweeted: "I'm sad for what happened this afternoon, I apologize Ivanovic and all football world for my inexcusable behaviour. I'm so sorry about it!!" The media demanded Liverpool sack him. Had he not committed the crime, he would have still hogged the headlines, because he was the outstanding player in a breathless game. Oscar headed in Juan Mata's corner to open the scoring. Liverpool were outplayed in the first half, but the introduction of Sturridge for Coutinho at the break turned things in their favour. Fired up against his former club, Sturridge hit a post from 25 yards. Then, on 52 minutes, Carragher lofted a pass down the right wing for Downing. He flicked it back to Suarez, who curled a delicious first-time cross for Sturridge to score from close range. Chelsea, managed by Rafa Benitez and with Fernando Torres starting the match, hit back when Suarez handled a corner and Eden Hazard converted the penalty. And then Suarez bit the Chelsea defender. He still had the final word. In the seventh minute of injury time, Suarez headed Sturridge's cross past Cech. As word of his misdemeanour filtered around the ground, those in the stands wondered if they would ever see him in red again.

Amid the negative headlines, Liverpool played with a weight lifted from their shoulders when they went to St James' Park without Suarez at the end of April. Sturridge led the line. Downing and Coutinho played wide. Gerrard, Lucas and Henderson made up a three-man centre midfield. Agger sprung the offside trap to head in on three minutes. Coutinho sent Sturridge racing through and as Rob Elliot advanced, he calmly squared the ball to Henderson for a tap-in. Sturridge scored twice in the first 15 minutes of the second half, turning in an exquisite pass from Coutinho before Henderson returned the compliment with a similar pass. Even Borini scored, toe-poking in Downing's pass for his first Premier League goal on his comeback. Henderson got the sixth with a wide free kick that went straight in. Coutinho might not have scored, but he played superbly. Gerrard came off after 72 minutes, so for the first time in the season he failed to complete a full game. It was Newcastle's heaviest home defeat since construction of the Tyne Bridge had begun in 1925.

A third goalless draw in five matches came in an instantly forgettable Anfield derby, the 14th in a row Everton failed to win. Sylvain Distin had a second-half header disallowed. The Frenchman also cleared off the line from Gerrard. Phil Jagielka made crucial blocks from Coutinho and Sturridge. The Blues were now five points ahead of the Reds with two games remaining.

A clinical treble by Sturridge saw the Reds collect three points at Fulham as Gerrard missed his first game of the season. The Uruguayan finished brilliantly from Wisdom's long ball for the first, twisting and turning in the area before unleashing a rocket into the top of the net to cancel out Dimitar Berbatov's opener. In the second half, he took Coutinho's pass to side-foot past Mark Schwarzer, moments after Fulham felt they should have had a penalty. With five minutes left, Coutinho provided another assist with a wonderful 40-yard pass, which Sturridge casually flicked over the onrushing Schwarzer for his first Liverpool hat trick.

With Gerrard absent again, Carragher captained the side on his 737th and final appearance for the club against QPR. The Bootle boy had made his debut in 1996 and here he was, still marshalling the Liverpool defence. He had been out of favour for much of his last two seasons but earned his recall after Skrtel's horror show at Southampton. The Kop displayed a mosaic of cards reading 'JC23' as he walked onto the field with his children. Jordon Ibe made his debut, and Coutinho scored the only goal against the bottom-placed side with a thunderous shot from 30 yards. But the moment of the match was Carragher's, as his glorious 35-yarder thundered into the frame of the Kop goal. What an exit that would have been. In five years of Champions League runs under Rafa Benitez, Carragher came up against the world's best forwards time after time. None of them got the better of him. Never fully appreciated outside Liverpool, he retired as one of the club's great defenders and will be forever remembered for his heroic defending, despite being riddled with cramp on that incredible night in Istanbul.

With 61 points, Liverpool finished the 2012-13 season in seventh place, behind Everton for the second year in a row. They were a dozen points off fourth-placed Arsenal and 28 behind Manchester United, who were crowned champions for the 20th time. There were reasons to be optimistic, and not just because Alex Ferguson had finally retired. Coutinho and Sturridge had proven to be inspired signings. Had they played in the first half of the season instead of Borini and Suso, the Reds would have accrued many more points. Liverpool didn't look like a side in need of a major overhaul, assuming, of course, they could keep hold of Suarez.

2013-14

"This was a perfect illustration of two teams moving in opposite directions. Liverpool free-flowing, wonderfully exciting and ever more ambitious under Brendan Rodgers; United abject, turgid and increasingly forlorn under David Moyes."

So near, yet so far.

The Premier League title was finally within Liverpool's grasp with just three matches of the 2013-14 season left. William Hill priced them at 2-11 to become champions for the first time since 1990. And then Steven Gerrard slipped.

Few expected Liverpool to challenge for the title in the summer of 2013. They had just finished seventh and started the new campaign at odds of 33-1. But towards the end of April, they were in pole position after winning 11 on the spin, a run which included defeats of Arsenal, Manchester United, Tottenham and the eventual champions Manchester City. Prompted by Luis Suarez, who was even better than he had been in Brendan Rodgers' first season, the Reds scored 101 league goals. But, most damningly, they also conceded 50 - far too many for a team hoping to be crowned champions.

Just like in 2008-09, Liverpool challenged for the title despite an uninspiring summer transfer window, but, like Rafa Benitez five years earlier, Rodgers was profiting from his earlier groundwork. He'd balanced the side, turfed out the underachievers, and built a team that played to Suarez's strengths. Daniel Sturridge and Philippe Coutinho had immediately improved the team when they signed in January 2013. There was young Raheem Sterling, who was fast becoming a world-class footballer. Steven Gerrard could still open up a defence with an exquisite pass. Jordan Henderson was maturing into a high-class, all-round midfielder. The defence was far from perfect, but Rodgers looked to have enough firepower to compensate. He also looked ready for business himself after losing three stones and having his teeth whitened in the off-season.

After the shambolic summer of 2012, Liverpool now had a transfer committee, which was responsible for scouting and analysing potential recruits. It comprised Rodgers, the head of recruitment David Fallows, chief scout Barry Hunter, head of performance Michael Edwards and chief executive Ian Ayre. Together they undertook the roles traditionally carried out by a director of football. But their summer deals weren't the best. Spanish duo Luis Alberto and Iago Aspas signed for a combined £14 million. "Straightaway, as soon as I saw them in the dressing-room, I knew they weren't going to make it in the

Premier League," Gerrard wrote in 2015. "They had the bodies of little boys." Simon Mignolet replaced Pepe Reina in goal but would always be an accident in waiting. Reina's form had dipped in the last three seasons, but he was still far superior to the Belgian. Kolo Toure was past his best at 32 when he joined on a free transfer. Mamadou Sakho and Tiago Ilori made it a trio of new centre backs. Valencia left back Aly Cissokho and Chelsea winger Victor Moses signed on loan. The capture of Sakho excited fans the most. The France international cost £15 million from Paris St Germain. But they missed out on Diego Costa and Henrikh Mkhitaryan, who would later end up at Chelsea and Manchester United respectively.

As well as Reina, the list of departures included goalkeeper Peter Gulacsi, Andy Carroll, whose move to West Ham was made permanent for £15 million, Danny Wilson, Jonjo Shelvey, Jay Spearing, Stewart Downing, Dani Pacheco and Adam Morgan. The combined loss on Carroll and Downing was a mind-boggling £34 million.

The name on everybody's lips during the summer was that of Suarez, who was four games into a ten-match ban for biting Branislav Ivanovic. He decided his future lay away from Anfield, and the issue dominated the off-season. He accused Rodgers of reneging on a promise to let him leave, so he was dispatched to train alone. Desperate to play in the Champions League, the 26-year-old wanted to go to Arsenal. His preference was a European club so he could escape the English media, but only the Gunners showed an interest. They believed the Uruguayan had a clause in his deal, allowing him to be sold for an offer of over £40 million, prompting them to publicly bid that amount plus one pound. Liverpool owner John W Henry memorably tweeted, "What do you think they're smoking over there at Emirates?" Gerrard persuaded Suarez to stay, pointing out that if he had another productive season, he would attract bigger clubs than Arsenal. It did the trick. Suarez announced he would stay.

The season got underway with a lunchtime kick-off against Stoke City, in the first Premier League match to be televised by BT Sports. Mignolet looked ill at ease, and his kicking was erratic, but he emerged the hero, saving a late penalty. Glen Johnson and Jose Enrique were the full backs. Toure and Daniel Agger was the first centre-half pairing of the post-Carragher era. Lucas Leiva, Gerrard and Henderson made up a three-man centre midfield. Aspas and Coutinho played behind the lone striker Sturridge. Sterling was the only substitute to see action, replacing Aspas. Brad Jones, Alberto, Joe Allen, Fabio Borini, Jordon Ibe and Andre Wisdom were unused. Liverpool were dominant, and only a man-of-the-match performance from Asmir Begovic kept the margin of victory to one. Toure hit the underside of the bar. After having a goal disallowed, Sturridge got the winner with a low drive into the corner from 20 yards, eight minutes before half-time. Henderson hit a post, but Liverpool couldn't find a second. The big moment came with a minute to go, when Jon Walters lined up his 12-yard kick after Agger handballed. Mignolet saved to his right before springing up to deny

Kenwyne Jones on the rebound. His teammates mobbed him. Sturridge and Coutinho were Liverpool's best players. "These are the wins that galvanise you," said Rodgers. "They are better than 4-0s and 5-0s at times."

The same line-up accounted for Aston Villa on their own ground. Sturridge got the winner again, this time after 21 minutes, rounding Brad Guzan before flicking the ball into the roof of the net with the outside of his left foot. It was Liverpool's only attempt on target and the 100th goal of Rodgers' reign. Cissokho came off the bench for his debut. Christian Benteke was a handful, but the Reds managed to keep a clean sheet, with Mignolet making several saves to protect the points.

Notts County came to Anfield in the League Cup and played their part in a thriller. There were run outs for Wisdom, Alberto, Allen and Ibe. Cissokho lasted just nine minutes. By then, Liverpool were one up after Sterling had beaten a couple of defenders and scored from just inside the box. Sturridge added another with an emphatic finish, although County forced extra time with two second-half goals. Sturridge gave Liverpool the lead again on 105 minutes. Henderson nutmegged the last defender and side-footed home five minutes later. The Reds won 4-2, but with Allen and Toure also suffering injuries and Alberto having gone off, they finished with ten men.

Sturridge had racked up the goals since his January transfer, but his captain was concerned about his mental fragility. Ahead of the home game with Manchester United, the striker had a troublesome thigh. Gerrard believed that if he didn't cajole him into playing, Sturridge might sit the game out. He wrote in 2015: "Daniel is one of those people you have to boost sometimes with a 'C'mon you're our main man. We need you so just go for it.' You never needed to say that to Luis … Luis and Daniel had different mentalities." After his captain's encouragement, Sturridge agreed and in the fourth minute, he flicked Agger's header past David de Gea for his third winning goal in three league games. Mignolet made another crucial late save, this time from Robin van Persie. Skrtel and Lucas were exceptional. The Reds were the only side with a 100% record. "I headed towards the international break feeling happier and more hopeful than I had for a long time," Gerrard wrote. "Manchester United were in trouble; and Liverpool were back where we belonged."

Sakho and Moses made their debuts at Swansea as the Reds dropped points for the first time. Jonjo Shelvey, having only just left Liverpool, put the Swans a goal up after just 87 seconds before gifting an equaliser to Sturridge almost immediately. Shelvey then conceded possession to Moses, who scored with a neat shot from the edge of the box to give Liverpool an interval lead. Wisdom missed a chance to secure the points. Coutinho injured a shoulder on 55 minutes, after which the Reds lost some intensity. Ten minutes later, Swansea made it 2-2, with Shelvey setting up Michu. Shelvey had scored one goal and assisted the other three, two of them for the opposition. There was still time for him to get booked. Coutinho needed shoulder surgery and would sit out six games.

LIVERPOOL F.C. THE PREMIER LEAGUE YEARS

The only defeat during Suarez's ban came in the last game, as the Reds lost 1-0 at home to Southampton. Rodgers picked Toure and Sakho as full backs, despite Enrique, Kelly and Wisdom being on the bench. Dejan Lovren scored the winner, heading in Adam Lallana's corner on 53 minutes. "Criminal," said Rodgers of his side conceding from a corner with four centre halves on the pitch. Liverpool were second rate all afternoon and could have no complaints at the result, however costly it would prove to be.

Suarez returned to action at Old Trafford in the League Cup. Rodgers fielded just three centre halves this time – Toure, Skrtel and Sakho. Henderson and Enrique filled the wing-back roles. Javier Hernandez scored the only goal in the first minute of the second half. Again, the goal came from a corner. The Reds dominated, creating chance after chance, but were unable to equalise. Suarez hit the bar with a late free kick. Suarez and Rodgers were barely on speaking terms until they buried the hatchet in October.

Rodgers maintained the wing-back system for the trip to Sunderland, where Suarez marked his Premier League return with a couple of goals. Skrtel had a goal disallowed. Sturridge accidentally scored with his arm from Gerrard's corner just before the half hour. Suarez made it two, touching in Sturridge's low pass. Sunderland pulled one back early in the second half, but Sturridge set up Suarez to make it 3-1. Henderson made his 100th Liverpool appearance.

An exemplary first half against Crystal Palace at Anfield saw Liverpool race into a 3-0 lead. Sterling was selected at right wing back, with Henderson dominating the midfield. Suarez slipped but still manage to score from a sedentary position. Sturridge hammered the ball into the bottom corner for number two. Gerrard added a penalty to become the first Liverpool player to score in 15 consecutive league seasons. Moses fluffed a gilt-edged opportunity. Dwight Gayle glanced one in for Palace in the second half. Sturridge hit a post. Talk of a title challenge was beginning to spread.

The new system remained in place for Liverpool's away game with Newcastle. This time the wing backs were Johnson and Cissokho. Twice Liverpool went behind, twice they drew level. Man of the match Gerrard converted another penalty for his 100th Premier League goal after Mapou Yanga-Mbiwa was sent off for fouling Suarez. But even with a numerical advantage, the Reds fell behind again, conceding yet another goal from a set piece. The Reds looked more dangerous after switching to a back four, and Suarez set up a diving header for Sturridge to make it 2-2. Suarez skimmed the bar and had a free kick saved. It was a far cry from April, when Liverpool had won 6-0.

Suarez was at his imperious best for the visit of West Brom, scoring his fourth Liverpool hat trick inside an hour. He nutmegged a defender for his first and then scored with an astonishing header from the edge of the box; shades of Steve Nicol at Highbury in 1987. He glanced in Gerrard's free kick for his third. Sturridge almost snapped the Kop crossbar. Suarez's overhead kick was brilliantly saved by Boaz Myhill. James Morrison hammered a penalty past Mignolet. Sturridge added a world-class fourth, chipping the keeper from outside the box. With 14 goals between then, the front two were the most prolific pairing in European football, one ahead of the Hoffenheim pair, Roberto Firmino and Anthony Modeste. After nine games, the Reds were second behind Arsenal.

The top two met at the Emirates in a Saturday evening kick-off in early November. An injury to Johnson saw a rare start for Flanagan as the manager persisted with three centre backs. Liverpool barely threatened and were beaten 2-0 with a goal in each half. Rodgers withdrew Flanagan and the appalling Cissokho for Coutinho and Moses, switching to 4-2-3-1, but it made no difference. Toure, Skrtel and Sakho were pulled all over the pitch by Arsenal. Coutinho looked promising on his return from injury. It was a sobering result. It seemed it would be Arsenal, not Liverpool, challenging for the title.

A home game with Fulham was the ideal opportunity to get back to winning ways. With four at the back again, the Reds produced another scintillating first half, leading 3-0 at the break. Fernando Amorebieta scored a clumsy own goal. Skrtel then headed in Gerrard's corner, the first of seven league goals he would score during the season. Maarten Stekelenburg tipped over Coutinho's dipping volley. Suarez made it three, turning in Henderson's through ball, and scored his second nine minutes after the break. Gerrard got a hat trick of assists. He, Lucas and Henderson bossed the midfield. The latter's Liverpool career was finally moving in the right direction.

A six-goal Goodison derby saw Liverpool drop two more points. The set-piece Achilles hurt Liverpool again. Other than that, Allen was the main culprit, with a glaring miss in the second half. Coutinho scored first, stabbing in a loose ball from a corner. Kevin Mirallas equalised after Liverpool couldn't defend a free kick. It was 1-1 before eight minutes had been played. Suarez made it 2-1 with a fabulous free kick. Ross Barkley was booked for a dive. Mirallas could have been sent off for going in studs up on Suarez. Suarez laid a gilt-edged chance on a plate for Allen from 12 yards, but he couldn't hit the target. Romelu Lukaku side-footed another equaliser from 12 yards. The same player headed the Blues into the lead from a corner. Sturridge glanced in an 86th-minute leveller from Gerrard's cross to take a share of the points. He had made the best goalscoring start to a season since John Aldridge in 1987-88. Flanagan and Suarez did their bit, but Lucas stood out the most.

Rodgers declared that the difference in the mentality of his players in his 16 months in charge was like comparing night and day. He may have been right but, unfortunately, Liverpool fell to pieces in their next game, as Steve Bruce's Hull City beat them for the first time ever. In a diabolical performance, they lost 3-1. Sturridge was absent and expected to miss six weeks. Jake Livermore's shot ballooned up off Skrtel and beat Mignolet for the opener. Gerrard responded with a perfectly placed 20-yard free kick, but the Reds were unable to build on it. Moses missed from close range. David Meyler made it 2-1. Suarez was inches away with a long-range free kick. Skrtel's nightmare of a game was complete when he headed a late own goal. Johnson, Sterling and Moses also had afternoons to forget. Alberto contributed little off the bench. The Daily Post summed it up succinctly: "Embarrassing. Humiliating. Poor. Alarming. Or just plain awful. Take your pick." The Reds were now fourth, having won only one of their last four games.

Suarez led the revival with a world-class display in a 5-1 hiding of Norwich. After a frustrating 15 minutes, in which he could do nothing right, he unleashed an unbelievable dipping volley from 35 yards. His second was comparatively mundane as he fired into the roof of the net from close range. His hat trick came on 35 minutes, when he lobbed the ball over a defender and smashed it into the corner from 20 yards on the half-volley, becoming the first Liverpool player to score three hat tricks against the same club. Goal number four came in the second half, as he executed the perfect free kick from 25 yards. Bradley Johnson got one back. Gerrard nearly scored a goal more astonishing than any of Suarez's when he pirouetted and flicked Coutinho's lofted pass onto a post. Sterling wrapped up the scoring from Suarez's pass in the final moments." I think he's getting so close to the main two, Ronaldo and Messi," Gerrard said of Suarez.

The Reds won comfortably again when Sam Allardyce's West Ham were in town three days later. A Guy Demel own goal put the Reds ahead. Sakho turned in Gerrard's free kick for his first goal for the club. Skrtel scored another own goal to set up a nervy final quarter. But Suarez scored twice in the final ten minutes to wrap up a 4-1 win. In between his goals, Kevin Nolan was sent off for going in studs up on Henderson's calf. The score flattered Liverpool somewhat, but Suarez was developing a habit of giving scorelines a flattering look. "Rarely has the Barclays Premier League witnessed a reign of terror like this one," the Telegraph said of the 26-year-old's scintillating form. Coutinho was also at the top of his game, but Gerrard injured a hamstring and would have Christmas off.

One of the best wins of the season came at White Hart Lane, where Liverpool had lost their last six games. This time they hammered Tottenham 5-0, and Spurs boss Andre Villas-Boas was sacked the next day. Suarez captained the side in Gerrard's absence and opened the scoring from Henderson's pass. Henderson, who played magnificently, doubled the lead after he and Suarez had shots saved. Sakho hit the post. Skrtel blazed the rebound over the bar. Paulinho was sent off just after the hour for fouling Suarez. Flanagan then produced one of the moments of the season when he crashed a half-volley in off the bar. Suarez lobbed Hugo Lloris for his 17th goal in 11 Premier League games. He'd scored two more than Spurs had all season, and he hadn't played in the first five games. He then set up Sterling, who completed the rout in the last minute. Arsenal's lead was down to two points.

There were two more for Suarez in the 3-1 defeat of Cardiff in the last game before Christmas. The first was a precise 20-yard volley; the second a delicious curler, set outside the far post, which nestled in the bottom corner. In between, he set up a goal for Sterling when he could have scored himself. Coutinho and Flanagan also went close. Cardiff got a goal back from a second-half set piece.

"We were excellent until Suarez showed why he is just about the best player in the world right now," said Cardiff's manager, Malky Mackay. Suarez had hit ten goals in December alone. Liverpool were top at Christmas.

The final month of the year had brought four wins from five, with 18 goals rattled in. Suarez was on fire. But it ended in frustrating defeats at Manchester City and Chelsea, which saw the Reds slip from top to fifth in just a couple of days. Liverpool did themselves credit at City but were beaten 2-1 in a crucial six-pointer. Cissokho came in for the injured Flanagan and endured a tough night. Another left back, the 19-year-old Australian Brad Smith, was named on the bench for the first time. An awful offside decision against Sterling on 19 minutes probably cost Liverpool a goal, although it should be noted that Joe Hart heard the whistle and made no attempt to save his shot. Five minutes later, Coutinho found the net from a tight angle after Sterling had gone past Hart. After Skrtel blocked Yaya Toure's shot, Vincent Kompany nodded in the corner, beating the Slovak to the ball. Coutinho should have restored the lead after a beautiful touch by Suarez, but his weak shot was saved by Hart. Alvaro Negredo put City 2-1 up in first-half injury time, with Mignolet at fault. The visitors were excellent after the break, but Johnson and Sterling squandered great chances. Suarez was denied a late penalty when Joleon Lescott seemed to want to swap shirts early. Liverpool had been undone by a goalkeeping error, a linesman's decision and an inability to convert second-half chances. Rodgers, meanwhile, called the performance of the officials 'horrendous' and questioned the integrity of referee Lee Mason, pointing out his Greater Manchester connections. He was fined £8,000.

It was the same story at Jose Mourinho's Chelsea three days later, although Liverpool didn't play as well. Samuel Eto'o should have been sent off for a horror challenge on Henderson in the fourth minute. From the free kick, Skrtel bundled in a loose ball to make it 1-0. Mignolet saved brilliantly from Frank Lampard, but Eden Hazard levelled on 17 minutes. Eto'o scored the winner ten minutes before half-time. Mignolet could have done better with both goals. Sakho hit the bar early in the second half. Having been such a handful for the City defenders, Suarez was ineffective, but he was tripped off the ball by Eto'o in the box and denied a clear penalty. Mignolet went forward for a set piece deep into injury time, but there was to be no late equaliser. Smith was introduced after an hour for Allen, in a puzzling substitution. Perhaps Rodgers was trying to demonstrate the squad's lack of depth ahead of the opening of the transfer window. Sixteen-year-old midfielder Jordan Rossiter was another sub, although unused. At the turn of the year, the Reds were fifth, half a dozen points behind Arsenal. City, Chelsea and Everton made up the top four.

If Liverpool were going to challenge for the title, beating Hull on New Year's Day was imperative. Aspas earned a rare start. Gerrard made his comeback as a second-half sub. Agger headed in Coutinho's corner to give the Reds a half-time lead. Suarez made it two with another sensational free kick from 25 yards on 50 minutes. It was his 20th league goal of the season, and he'd hit the milestone quicker than anyone in Premier League history. Henderson was outstanding again.

Aspas scored his only Liverpool goal in the FA Cup against Oldham. It was the third year in a row the sides had met in the early rounds of the competition. Jones, Kelly and Alberto played. Ilori and 17-year-old midfielder Cameron Brannagan were unused subs. Alberto and Moses were withdrawn at the break for Lucas and Coutinho, with Rodgers fearing another embarrassing result against Oldham. Eventually, Aspas opened the scoring in the ninth minute of the second half. James Tarkowski scored an own goal on 82 minutes to make it 2-0. The impressive Sterling had a hand in both goals. Rodgers' son, Anton, played the final seven minutes as an Oldham substitute.

At the sixth attempt, Liverpool finally won a Premier League game at the Britannia Stadium, when an eight-goal thriller ended with a goalscoring return for Sturridge. Stoke's Ryan Shawcross scored a fifth-minute own goal, diverting Cissokho's 20-yarder past Jack Butland. Suarez made it two, but goals from former Reds Peter Crouch and Charlie Adam tied the scores before the break. Gerrard converted a penalty after Sterling was fouled. Suarez scored again. Jonathan Walters pulled one back. It was 4-3 with five minutes left. Sturridge wrapped up the points, firing in from a tight angle with three minutes left.

Rodgers fielded an attacking line-up for the visit of Aston Villa. He experimented with Gerrard as the holding midfielder, at the expense of Lucas. Coutinho and Sterling played behind Sturridge and Suarez. But Villa's counterattacking game exposed the flaws in the plan, and they went 2-0 up thanks to goals from Andreas Weimann and man of the match Christian Benteke. Mignolet, Skrtel, Toure, Cissokho, Gerrard and Coutinho all struggled. Sturridge finished an exquisite move involving Suarez and Henderson on the stroke of half-time. Half-time sub Lucas stiffened the midfield and balanced the side. Suarez soon won a penalty, amid accusations of a dive. Gerrard levelled the scores from 12 yards. But the Reds couldn't find a winner. Lucas, having only been on for 20 minutes, was subbed himself with injury, making way for Allen. Rodgers admitted he got his selections wrong. "Across the board, we were not very good," he said. "Myself included." Liverpool, meanwhile, were heavily linked with a move for the Basel winger Mohamed Salah, although Rodgers wasn't keen on him. He eventually went to Chelsea.

Gerrard sustained a lacerated penis during Liverpool's 2-0 win in the FA Cup at Bournemouth on the last weekend of January. "I tried to close down a winger to block his cross but felt a stinging in my privates," he wrote. "I thought, 'Shit - that doesn't feel right!' The gash looked pretty bad, right across the middle. There was plenty of blood. I needed four stitches and the lads were absolutely pissing themselves." The goals came from Moses and Sturridge, who later hit the bar.

The captain's stitched-up genitalia didn't keep him out of the Anfield derby, the 15th in a row Everton failed to win. "Are you Moyesy in disguise?" the Kop sang to Roberto Martinez as the Blues fell to a 4-0 hammering. Gerrard was the midfield anchor. Coutinho played centrally. Sturridge was on the left. Suarez was pelted with coins as he took a corner in front of the away fans and Gerrard planted his inch-perfect delivery into Tim Howard's top corner after 21 minutes. Gareth Barry and Romelu Lukaku collided, which led to the latter being led off. Sturridge put the game to bed, scoring twice in 120 glorious seconds. Toure set up the second, floating a measured pass towards Sturridge, who allowed the ball to bounce over his left shoulder before expertly lifting the ball over the onrushing Howard. It was a truly remarkable strike, as he hit the ball with his back to goal, without looking up at either the goal or the keeper. The players celebrated by lining up for an imaginary photo in front of the devastated Everton supporters. Suarez made it 4-0 early in the second half, winning possession and sprinting from halfway before side-footing into the corner. Sturridge fluffed a chance to complete his hat trick by blazing a penalty over the bar before the hour. It affected Liverpool, who created little thereafter. The Reds had scored twice by pressing and transitioning quickly, a tactic which was quickly taking off across Europe. "When you look at the stats of the modern game, I'm big on controlling domination of the ball," said Rodgers, "but against Everton we were able to dominate without the ball. Tactically, where we are compared to when I arrived 18 months ago, it is very, very pleasing." The Reds were fourth, six points behind Arsenal.

Liverpool may have been racking up the goals, but they were still inconsistent, as they showed in a frustrating 1-1 draw at West Brom. Sturridge scored his 18th of the season. Gerrard was on top form, but the Reds were unable to find the killer goal. Halfway through the second half, Toure gave the ball away and was ruthlessly punished by Victor Anichebe. Two days earlier, Liverpool missed out on the signing of Ukrainian winger Yevhen Konoplyanka.

Arsenal were eight points clear of the Reds when they came to Anfield for a Saturday lunchtime fixture on 8th February. They were obliterated by one of the best starts Liverpool have ever made to a match. Skrtel volleyed in Gerrard's free kick within a minute. The Slovak then headed in Gerrard's corner on eight minutes - the 23rd goal of the season from a set piece. Suarez hit the post with a stunning 25-yard volley on the turn. You had to see it to believe it. Toure missed an open goal from the rebound. Henderson robbed Mesut Ozil on halfway, and the ensuing counterattack ended with Sterling making it three. "This was football of brutal purity and pace," wrote Gerrard. Coutinho sent Sturridge through on goal, and he slotted past Wojciech Szczesny. All this was inside the opening 20 minutes. "Poetry in motion," sang the Kop, who could barely believe what they were witnessing. With a minute left of the half, the fans gave the players a standing ovation. Had there been a better first half in Liverpool's history? Sterling grabbed another on 52 minutes to make it 5-0, and then they eased off. Mikel Arteta pulled one back from the spot. It ended 5-1. The performance announced to everybody that Liverpool were going for the title and not just the top four. "We have absolutely demolished a top team from start to finish," said

Gerrard. Arteta said Arsene Wenger was angrier than he had ever seen him at half-time. Four of their players were awarded three out of ten by The Times. Alex Oxlade-Chamberlain, who won the penalty, was their best with six. Coutinho and Sterling, who received nines, were turning into fabulous players.

Inconsistency almost cost Liverpool again, but this time Gerrard's injury-time penalty gave the Reds three barely-deserved points at Fulham. Toure sliced a comical own goal past Mignolet. Then he accidentally flattened the referee Phil Dowd. Sturridge equalised courtesy of one of the best assists in living memory from Gerrard, who pounced on a loose ball in the centre circle and, first time, sent it spinning 30 yards into the striker's path with the outside of his right boot. Sturridge controlled it and scored with a low shot via the post. Suarez hit the woodwork. Kieran Richardson re-established Fulham's lead after a mishap between Skrtel and Flanagan. Coutinho made it 2-2 on 72 minutes with a precise low shot from the edge of the box. Young winger Joao Carlos Teixeira made his debut as a sub in the closing stages. And then, with the 90 minutes up, Sturridge won a penalty, which Gerrard converted. It was the only crucial late goal Liverpool would score all season.

Eight days after their massacre at Anfield, Arsenal gained some sort of revenge by knocking Liverpool out of the FA Cup in the fifth round. Man of the match Oxlade-Chamberlain and Lukas Podolski had the Gunners two up by the 47th minute. Gerrard converted a penalty after a challenge on Suarez, who was denied another by Howard Webb after a foul by Oxlade-Chamberlain. Sturridge was aiming to become the first player in the club's history to score in nine consecutive appearances but spurned three chances. The Gunners went on to win the cup, but their league form tailed off.

Liverpool had a dozen league games remaining, starting with Swansea at home. They edged another goal fest 4-3 after Swansea had come back from 2-0 and 3-2. Sterling slalomed through the Swansea midfield and played Sturridge in on goal with the outside of his right foot. He went around Michel Vorm and opened the scoring on three minutes. Henderson doubled the lead with a stunning shot from the edge of the box. Jonjo Shelvey got the Swans on the board. Skrtel scored his third own goal of the season. The unmarked Sturridge headed Liverpool back into the lead on 36 minutes. Skrtel conceded a penalty, which Wilfried Bony converted, to make it 3-3 after the break. Henderson scored the winner at the second attempt with 16 minutes left. Gerrard hit a post from distance. If Liverpool games were going to be like this during the run-in, it would be a hell of a ride for the fans.

The Reds were put under pressure at Southampton, and even after Suarez slid the ball into the corner for his first goal in six games on 16 minutes, it was never comfortable. Adam Lallana could have had a penalty after a challenge by Flanagan. He also hit a post. Mignolet had an excellent game. Sterling replaced Coutinho on 57 minutes and scored within 60 seconds. After Suarez was fouled, Gerrard planted a late penalty past Artur Boruc to make it 3-0. Suarez now topped the goalscoring chart with 24 and had the most Premier League assists with ten. Liverpool were second, four points behind leaders Chelsea. They were two points ahead of Man City, who had two games in hand. Both sides had still to visit Anfield. "We're gonna win the league!" sang the Liverpool fans. Gerrard, too, was upbeat about their chances. "We're in it," he said. "Man City and Chelsea are still favourites, but they know we're a big threat because we've got no Europe, and we can be fresh every game."

The juggernaut rolled on to Old Trafford, where Liverpool took Manchester United apart. They won 3-0. It should have been six. "This was a perfect illustration of two teams moving in opposite directions," reported The Times. "Liverpool free-flowing, wonderfully exciting and ever more ambitious under Brendan Rodgers; United abject, turgid and increasingly forlorn under David Moyes." Having spent years accusing Scousers of living in the past, United fans spent the entire game singing about their 20 titles. With Alex Ferguson gone, they didn't look like winning another any time soon. Rafael da Silva, who had just been booked, handled in the box. Gerrard beat David de Gea from the spot and didn't celebrate. Mignolet denied Wayne Rooney. Twenty-five seconds into the second half, Phil Jones brought down Allen, and Gerrard helped himself to another penalty. He looked happier this time. Incredibly, the skipper was given a third spot kick when Vidic lunged in on Sturridge. The Serb received his fourth red card against Liverpool. Gerrard, whose first game at Anfield as a young fan was when Jan Molby hit a hat trick of penalties against Coventry City in 1986, spurned the opportunity to match the Dane's achievement when he hit de Gea's right-hand post. The keeper saved magnificently from Suarez, who soon made amends by beating the offside trap to make it 3-0. He cried as he celebrated.

A crazy game at Cardiff looked more like a five-a-side match than the Premier League. There were nine goals this time, and although Liverpool picked up another three points, their defence was clearly a cause for concern. Since Gerrard had moved into the deep-midfield role, the Reds had been more porous. Jordon Mutch scored first for Cardiff, who were now playing in red on the whim of owner Vincent Tan. Henderson released Johnson down the right with a glorious pass, and the right back put a goal on a plate for Suarez. Frazier Campbell restored the hosts' lead. Skrtel scored either side of half-time from Coutinho assists, the first a volley from a cross and the second a header from a corner. Suarez slotted home Sturridge's backheel and then returned the compliment for the striker to make it 5-2. Mutch got one back. Suarez scored the ninth goal of the game when he latched onto Skrtel's clearance, ignored the supporting Sterling and beat David Marshall to make it 6-3. It was his sixth hat trick for the Reds. Cardiff, managed by one-time Liverpool supporter Ole Gunnar Solskjaer, were heading for the Championship.

Gerrard proved he could still take a mean free kick, against a stubborn Sunderland side in Liverpool's first home game in over a month. With no clear-cut chances created in 38 minutes, and with plenty of anxious faces in the stands, Gerrard lined up a central free kick, 20 yards out, and steered the ball into the top corner. Just into the second half, former Red Andrea Dossena naively showed Sturridge onto his left foot, and he curled in his 20th league goal. Cattermole and Sturridge each hit the bar before Ki Sung-yueng headed one in from a corner. John O'Shea could have snatched a draw but let Liverpool off the hook. The Reds stayed second, a point behind Chelsea. They were two ahead of Manchester City, but had played two games more. City were the title favourites.

Without playing, Liverpool enjoyed a very satisfying last Saturday in March when leaders Chelsea lost 1-0 at Crystal Palace and Manchester City were held 1-1 at Arsenal. The Reds then went top with a 4-0 home win over Spurs the next day. Younes Kaboul scored an own goal after 100 seconds. Suarez finished emphatically on 25 minutes after a defensive error. Hugo Lloris tipped Suarez's header onto the bar. Coutinho hit the bottom corner with deadly accuracy from 20 yards to make it three after clever approach play from Flanagan, who was still filling the left-back position with aplomb. Lloris saved an impudent backheel from Sturridge. Somewhat fortuitously, a wide free kick from Henderson went straight in with 15 minutes left. The Reds were top for the first time since Boxing Day. It was 50 years to the day that a brace of goals from Ian St John against Tottenham had taken the Reds top, en route to the 1964 title.

According to Gerrard, Sam Allardyce's West Ham tried every trick in the book to derail Liverpool's title bid on the first Sunday in April. "We knew what to expect and we got a bit more than we expected — a hot dressing room, a dry pitch and the bus had to park a mile away," he said. "I think they tried everything to upset us. It was a good test of our character. We needed to prove that we're capable of fighting for this title and we did that terrifically well. They were throwing 70-yard balls into our penalty box from every different angle." Liverpool's goals in a 2-1 win were both penalties by Gerrard, slotted past Adrian with typical accuracy. He had now scored eight penalties from nine attempts during the 14-match unbeaten run that had propelled the Reds to the summit of the Premier League. Andy Carroll, seemingly with a point to prove, was exceptional for West Ham, better than he ever was for Liverpool. He set up the Hammers' equaliser for Guy Demel on half-time, although he did elbow Mignolet in the process. Carroll also hit the bar when the score was 1-1. Suarez hit the crossbar twice, both with audacious attempts on goal from wide positions. The Reds hadn't looked comfortable for much of the game, but when Rodgers withdrew Coutinho and brought on Lucas, reverting to a midfield diamond, they looked a more balanced side. Flanagan won the deciding penalty with 19 minutes to play, and Liverpool were able to hang onto their lead.

The visit of Manchester City was billed as a title decider. City were four points behind Liverpool with two games in hand. The Reds needed three points to take over as title favourites. Sterling played centrally, as Rodgers sought to capitalise on Yaya Toure being out of position when Liverpool countered. His superb performance belied his teenage years. The Reds started brightly, storming into a two-goal lead inside 26 minutes. Sterling sent Joe Hart and Vincent Kompany into a different postcode with one swivel of the hips, before rolling the ball into the Kop net. Sturridge side-footed Sterling's teasing cross wide. Toure departed injured, replaced by Javi Garcia, but City were more balanced without him. Hart saved spectacularly from Gerrard, before Skrtel escaped the clutches of Kompany to make it 2-0 with a glancing header from Gerrard's corner. Anfield erupted, in stark contrast to the 25th-anniversary tribute to the 96 which had preceded the game. It was end to end for the rest of the half. Sterling was inches away from being handed a tap-in, firstly by Suarez and then Sturridge. Sakho's foul on Edin Dzeko in the box went unnoticed. One after the other, Sterling and Flanagan cleared off the line from a City corner. A heavy touch from Sturridge spoiled a promising counterattack. Mignolet did well to deny Fernandinho. 2-0 to the Reds at half-time.

City's next substitute, James Milner, gave them width and turned the game. Within minutes of replacing Jesus Navas, he set up a goal for David Silva after Flanagan had switched off. City could have scored twice more before Johnson deflected Silva's pass into his own net to make it 2-2. Just over an hour had elapsed. Sturridge was withdrawn for Allen as Liverpool looked to stem the blue tide. But they still saw plenty of promising possession, and Suarez was denied a penalty after being manhandled by Kompany. Sergio Aguero, returning from injury, replaced Dzeko, with City now favourites to win the game and the title. When Skrtel sold himself, City looked certain to score, but David Silva couldn't get enough on Aguero's low cross in front of an anxious Kop. The crucial goal came in the 78th minute, and to the relief of the home fans, it was at the Anfield Road end of the ground. Kompany, who had picked up an injury in training 24 hours earlier, miskicked a clearance, and Coutinho pounced to rifle the ball into the bottom corner from 18 yards. It was a truly clinical finish. Henderson was sent off in injury time, Liverpool's first red card since Jonjo Shelvey against Manchester United in 2012. Crucially, he would be suspended for three games. Skrtel escaped a late penalty shout for inexplicably punching a cross clear. Lucas replaced the man of the match Sterling. Gerrard avoided a tenth booking of the season, which would have seen him banned for the next two games. The final whistle signalled Liverpool's tenth league win in a row. Gerrard was in tears as he gathered the players around him at the end, amid the Anfield cacophony, urging them to keep focused. Sky cameras picked up the words, "This does not slip!" as he urged his teammates to remember the title wasn't won yet. The Reds were now seven clear of City, who still had those two games in hand.

By the time Liverpool played again, Sunderland had done them two huge favours. They drew 2-2 in midweek against a City team which looked like the wind had been knocked out of their sails. Three days later, the Black Cats won 2-1 at Chelsea, with Liverpool players celebrating in the foyer of their Norwich hotel as their former teammate Fabio Borini scored a late penalty. So, a 3-2 win over the Canaries on the Sunday put daylight between Liverpool and their rivals. Sturridge was injured, but Sterling scored a fabulous opener, arrowing in an unstoppable shot from 25 yards on four minutes. Seven minutes later, he set up the second for Suarez, who became the first Liverpool player to score 30 league goals in a season since Ian Rush in 1986-87. The Reds were flying, but the defensive problems showed up again when Mignolet failed to deal with a cross, and Gary Hooper turned the ball in. Sterling made it 3-1 with a fortunate deflection. The 19-year-old had enjoyed a terrific second half of the season, benefiting from the club's inability to get the Konoplyanka deal over the line. Robert Snodgrass narrowed the deficit again. Liverpool held on grimly for the last 13 minutes and managed to win 3-2. The points were vital, but they couldn't keep defending like this. Something had to change. The Reds had scored just three goals in their first four Premier League matches but had rattled in an astonishing 93 in the next 31. There were just three games left, two of which were at home. Liverpool needed seven points to win their first league title in 24 years.

And then came the day it all went wrong - Sunday, 27th April 2014. Chelsea arrived at Anfield in between the two legs of a European Cup semi-final with Atletico Madrid that they would eventually lose. Mourinho seemed to care more about hurting Liverpool. They slowed the game down. They wasted time. They parked the bus. They frustrated the Reds, who showed there wasn't much of a Plan B when it really mattered. Gerrard had spent all week receiving treatment for a lower-spine injury and was taking diazepam, Voltarol and ibuprofen. A cortisone injection was administered 24 hours before kick-off. "I sensed an overconfidence in Brendan's team talks," Gerrard wrote in 2015. "He thought we could go out and attack Chelsea – just as we had done against Manchester City and Norwich. We played into Mourinho's hands. I feared it then, and I know it now. We should have gone into the game with a much more compact formation ... But, at the same time, it was not my place to knock on Brendan's door and discuss tactics with him. He would have been entitled, if I had done so, to tell me to piss off." Even before the infamous slip, Liverpool had looked one-dimensional and unable to breach Chelsea's rigid defensive lines. Gerrard's fears were coming true. The absence of the suspended Henderson was instrumental in Liverpool failing to set any sort of tempo. The moment of horror came in the third minute of first-half injury time. He was positioned in between the centre backs as Sakho squared the ball to him. The pass rolled under his right boot. He turned to get to the loose ball before Demba Ba. He slipped. The striker, who was signed during Rafa Benitez's brief tenure at Stamford Bridge, was clean through on goal at the Kop end of the stadium. He strode forward and placed his shot between the legs of Mignolet and into the net. It was a devastating moment.

"In the dressing-room, I was a wreck," Gerrard recalled. "I sat on the wooden bench, in my usual space in the corner, unable to say a word. I caught sight of my reflection in the mirror opposite my seat. I looked ashen and shell-shocked." Given how the first half had gone, few were confident Liverpool would win the game from here, although a draw would keep them as title favourites. Mark Schwarzer saved from Allen. Sturridge, fit again after a hamstring injury, was introduced but looked off the pace. The Reds created little. Desperate to make amends, Gerrard tried his luck from distance on a few occasions. Mignolet prevented Andre Schurrle from scoring. Tomas Kalas, who played only a handful of Chelsea games in nine years, had Suarez, the newly crowned footballer of the year, in his pocket. Aspas replaced Flanagan and produced one of the worst corners anyone had ever seen. And then in injury time, substitute Fernando Torres, once adored by the Kop, streaked clear from his own half. He drew Mignolet and put an open goal on a plate for Willian. Full time. "'You'll Never Walk Alone' rang around Anfield," remembered Gerrard. "I just wanted to be swallowed up by the ground. I wanted to disappear down a dark hole." An hour later, he was crying in his mate's car. He quickly arranged a trip to Monaco to get away from Liverpool. City won at Crystal Palace later in the day. The title was back in their hands, and their run-in didn't look difficult.

Liverpool had two small hopes left. The first was that Everton could stop City winning at Goodison the following Saturday, two days before Liverpool went to Palace. The second was, assuming both sides won their remaining fixtures, that the Reds could win their games by eight goals more than City won theirs – very unlikely, especially as City had an extra game to play. Everton went 1-0 up and were getting stuck in, but with most of their supporters cheering on City, they fell to a 3-2 defeat. After 36 games, Liverpool and City were on 80 points apiece, but City's goal difference was superior by nine. And so the Reds went to Selhurst Park dreaming of racking up a rugby score. Suarez played with illness, which didn't help. Sakho missed a sitter from a corner. Allen headed in another corner on 18 minutes. Mignolet saved wonderfully from Mile Jedinak. There were no more first-half goals. Julian Speroni tipped Sturridge's curler onto his right-hand post. Two goal in two minutes, an own goal from Damien Delaney and one from Suarez, briefly fired hopes of a big score. Liverpool's goal difference was now +53, compared to City's +59. It was still very unlikely they could overtake them, especially with City having an extra fixture to play. And then everything caved in. Delaney scored with a deflection off Johnson's back on 79 minutes. Dwight Gayle made it 2-3 on 81. Hopes of winning the league on goal difference had gone. And then Gayle scored again with two minutes left to complete a humiliating collapse. Moses missed his kick with the goal gaping right at the end. Suarez covered his face with his shirt to hide the tears as Gerrard, Toure and Johnson guided him off the field. On Sky Sports, Jamie Carragher berated his former teammates for defending too deeply. They needed a leader, he said, to keep the line high. Perhaps he could have been that leader. Had he retired a year later, he could have gone out on the ultimate high. Hopes of winning the league now rested on Aston Villa or West Ham winning at City, or both of them getting a draw. Suarez was inconsolable. Liverpool knew they had blown it.

It was 0-0 for an hour when City entertained Villa in midweek, but they found a way through and went on to win 4-0. The final-day games kicked off simultaneously. It was the first time that a Liverpool Premier League title challenge was alive on the last day. Suarez had an incredible free-kick goal from the touchline disallowed, having taken it too quickly. Newcastle went one up through Skrtel's fourth own goal of the season, a record for a Liverpool player. It was also the 50th goal shipped in by the Reds, more than 11th-placed Crystal Palace – the real reason they didn't win the league. City took the lead against the Hammers just before the break. Then they made it two just after. The title was theirs. Liverpool salvaged some pride when Agger and Sturridge scored from Gerrard free kicks. Newcastle ended up with nine men, with Shola Ameobi and Paul Dummett dismissed. The Reds won 2-1 and ended up in second place with 84 points from 38 matches, two points behind Manchester City. They also scored 101 goals, a club record, although City also bettered that by one.

The Premier League trophy may not have been Anfield-bound, but the memories of an incredible season would last forever. Two questions lingered over the summer. Would Suarez hang around to lead another challenge? And how long would it take the club to recover from missing out on the title in such a gut-wrenching manner?

2014-15

"Caged animals don't last very long on a football field."

The unfortunate truth for Brendan Rodgers was that when Steven Gerrard slipped against Chelsea, it was the beginning of the end for him as Liverpool's manager. He did sign a new contract in May 2014 as a reward for taking Liverpool so close, but to have glory snatched away in such agonising circumstances ripped the heart out of the club. He never recovered. Nor did Gerrard, whom Father Time was rapidly hunting down in any case. Luis Suarez left. Daniel Sturridge couldn't stay fit. And none of the new signings were able to compensate.

Jordan Henderson, Raheem Sterling and Philippe Coutinho were still around, so if Rodgers could improve the defence, logic dictated that anything should be possible. But how strong Liverpool were on paper wasn't so relevant anymore. Morale had sunk. It would take Liverpool's players and fans a couple of years to recover from missing out on the title. Unfairly or not, Rodgers quickly became a diminished figure.

That said, there were no suggestions Rodgers should have been sacked in the summer of 2014, and rightly so. But he was steering a slowly sinking ship from that point, and the season would prove very difficult for all concerned. He got his recruitment wrong again. He lurched desperately from one formation to another. There were square pegs in round holes all season. His relationship with Sterling collapsed. Midway through the campaign, Gerrard announced he would leave in May. The team was always fighting a losing battle to get into the top four. They were awful in Europe. The games with Manchester United were nightmares. The FA Cup semi-final was humiliating. The last day of the season was even worse.

The big news over the summer was the departure of Suarez to Barcelona for £65 million, but not before one last controversy. He bit the Italian defender Giorgio Chiellini during the World Cup. It was the third time in four years he had attacked a player in such a way. He had signed a new contract in December 2013, but from the moment he attacked Chiellini, it was clear that this Machiavellian genius would no longer be wearing the red of Liverpool.

The big question was whether Rodgers and the transfer committee would invest the money wisely. They also had a bit more to spend from the sales of Conor Coady, Pepe Reina, Martin Kelly, Jack Robinson and Daniel Agger. Aly Cissokho also left after his loan deal expired. In came the Southampton trio Rickie Lambert for £4.5 million, Adam Lallana for £25 million and Dejan Lovren for £20 million. The young German midfielder Emre Can cost £9.75 million from Bayer Leverkusen. Benfica winger Lazar Markovic set the club back £19.8 million. Nearly £10 million was spent on Lille's Divock Origi, but he would be stay on loan with the French club for another year. Full back Javier Manquillo joined on loan from Atletico Madrid. Worst of all, in came Mario Balotelli from AC Milan for £16 million.

Lallana, Can, Lovren and Origi would go on to flourish for spells under Jurgen Klopp, but Markovic and Balotelli are two of the worst buys Liverpool have ever made. When Rodgers told Gerrard he was signing Balotelli, the captain's reaction was "Uh-oh." Rodgers labelled Lovren the natural replacement for Jamie Carragher, but the Croat endured an abysmal debut season. The summer could have been rescued by the signing of Barcelona's Alexis Sanchez, but Arsene Wenger got there first. Gerrard texted Bayern Munich's Toni Kroos, hoping to entice him to Anfield, but he chose to join Real Madrid. Rodgers had also wanted Karim Benzema, Edison Cavani, Radamel Falcao or Loic Remy. Remy was the only one of the quartet to want to sign, but a problem was detected during his medical and the Reds called the deal off. An angry Remy went to Chelsea instead and won a league title.

William Hill priced the Reds at 12-1 to win the Premier League, but they were miserly odds. Perhaps they were influenced by a 4-0 friendly win over Klopp's Borussia Dortmund at Anfield, in which Sturridge, Lovren, Coutinho and Henderson scored. An opening-day win over Southampton was a welcome result, but the performance was a far cry from the joys of 2013-14. Rodgers fielded a 4-2-3-1 formation, with Simon Mignolet in goal, Manquillo and Glen Johnson the full backs, Martin Skrtel and Lovren at centre back, Gerrard and Lucas Leiva holding the midfield, and Henderson, Coutinho and Sterling behind Sturridge. Joe Allen and Lambert came on for Lucas and Coutinho, while Brad Jones, Kolo Toure, Mamadou Sakho, Can and Jordon Ibe weren't used. Sterling grabbed the first goal of the new campaign from Henderson's through ball. Future Red Nathaniel Clyne equalised at the Kop end, but Sturridge grabbed the winner on 79 minutes. It was his 36th goal in 50 Liverpool games. Mignolet made a world-class save in the dying moments, tipping Morgan Schneiderlin's close-range half-volley onto the underside of the bar. Shane Long headed the rebound wide. Lovren impressed, but Sterling was widely adjudged to be the best player.

An early-season trip to Eastlands was hardly ideal, and to prove the point, Manchester City were 3-0 up on 70 minutes. Stevan Jovetic, a one-time Liverpool target, scored twice for the champions. Sergio Aguero got the third 23 seconds after coming onto the pitch. City exploited the yawning gap between debutant Moreno and Lovren. The Reds did get a late goal when Joe Hart's save from a Rickie Lambert header rebounded into the net off Pablo Zabaleta. Markovic and Can made their debuts from the bench.

Hopes were raised when the Reds won 3-0 at White Hart Lane. Balotelli made his debut in one pink boot and one turquoise. He missed a chance after three minutes, but Sterling was soon turning in Henderson's low cross at the back post to complete a scintillating counterattack. With Hugo Lloris stranded, Balotelli had an open goal from 35 yards, but his shot was hopelessly mishit. Rodgers smiled; the fans winced in the realisation that the world's best striker had been replaced by a court jester. Gerrard converted a penalty after Allen was fouled. Moreno finished the scoring with a mesmerising run from his own half, before hammering the ball past Lloris. It was reminiscent of John Arne Riise's goal at Goodison in September 2001. Rodgers explained how the narrow 4-2-3-1 formation of Spurs was never going to outnumber his midfield diamond.

Aston Villa came to Anfield and delivered a crushing early-season blow, just as they had in September 2009. Sturridge was now absent with a thigh strain, sustained on England duty, with Rodgers blaming it on Roy Hodgson's decision to deny the striker a much-needed rest day. He was initially ruled out for three weeks but wouldn't be seen again until the new year after injuring a hamstring in training. Sterling was benched. Lallana made his debut. Balotelli was totally out of his depth as the lone striker. Gabriel Agbonlahor scrambled in an early goal from a corner. He then spent the game man-marking Gerrard, denying him the time to spread the play as he had done so effectively in 2013-14. Other than Coutinho hitting a post late in the game, the Reds had no answer, even with Aly Cissokho in the Villa defence. Fabio Borini, back from a loan spell at Sunderland, came on as a late sub. The Times gave every Liverpool player a five-out-of-ten rating, apart from Henderson, who got a six.

The first Champions League game since 2009 was very nearly an embarrassment. Ludogorets Razgrad from Bulgaria were holding them 0-0 at Anfield before Balotelli opened his Liverpool account on 82 minutes. Relief poured from the stands, but Daniel Abalo Paulos rounded Mignolet and equalised in the 90th minute. There was still time. The visitors' keeper miscontrolled the ball and then brought down Manquillo. Gerrard, the only survivor from Liverpool's last Champions League match, dispatched the penalty.

Back in the league, West Ham's Winston Reid and Diafra Sakho each scored with a header inside the first seven minutes, exposing a pathetic Liverpool defence at will. Sterling quietened the Upton Park crowd when he smashed a 20-yarder past Adrian to give the team a club record of scoring in 17 consecutive top-flight away matches. But the Hammers wrapped up the points with just a couple of minutes left as Morgan Amalfitano toe-poked past a static Mignolet. Again, only one player avoided a five in The Times, and that was Sterling with a seven. Man of the match Stewart Downing stuck close to Gerrard, as Agbonlahor had done seven days earlier. It was a tactic the skipper would have to get used to. To make things worse, he no longer had Suarez and Sturridge making runs for him. The static Balotelli wasn't so easy to find.

The third round of the League Cup at home to Middlesbrough brought some respite courtesy of a 27-goal penalty shootout. The Reds selected a smattering of fringe players, including 17-year-old midfielder Jordan Rossiter, who marked his debut with a tenth-minute goal from over 30 yards. Adam Reach equalised for Boro, who then had the better chances to win the game in normal time. Suso looked to have decided it in extra time, only for Toure to concede a penalty in the 120th minute. Patrick Bamford sent Mignolet the wrong way. After five penalties each in the shootout, it was 4-4, with Mignolet saving Boro's first and Sterling missing Liverpool's fourth. Balotelli, Lucas, Lallana and Suso each scored twice. Debutant Jordan Williams, Toure, Sakho, Manquillo, Jose Enrique and Mignolet also scored. Boro's Albert Adomah missed the 30th penalty to give Liverpool a 14-13 victory. In other news, the club had been given permission to rebuild the Main Stand, which would increase the capacity by 8,500 to 54,000. It would be ready for the 2016-17 season.

Just as it seemed Gerrard had won the Anfield Derby, the 16th in a row Everton failed to win, Phil Jagielka popped up in injury time with the goal of a lifetime, hammering it into the roof of the Kop net from 20 yards. Markovic was surprisingly selected ahead of Coutinho and played poorly. Balotelli hit the bar, among his ten efforts on goal. Sterling was denied a blatant penalty. "It was practically a save," Rodgers said of Gareth Barry blocking Sterling's shot. "Short of grabbing the ball with both hands, it could hardly have been more obvious." Gerrard hoped his free kick would silence the growing number of critics after an indifferent start to the season. "People take it too far and say that, 'He's 34 and he can't run, and he's finished'. I can still compete with the best players around." After six games, Liverpool were 12th with just seven points.

Liverpool's first trip to the continent ended in a 1-0 defeat to Basel at the St Jakob Stadium, where the Reds had exited the competition in 2002-03. Gerrard believed Liverpool were overconfident and far too open. Rodgers was raging at half-time, exempting only Gerrard from his criticism. The goal came on 52 minutes from another set piece, as Skrtel headed a corner towards his own goal. Mignolet saved but could only parry to Marco Streller. "If we'd had Suarez and Sturridge up front, with Sterling behind them, we would have dismantled Basel and most teams in Europe," Gerrard wrote. "But we only had Sterling of those three – and Balotelli was playing up front on his own ... If I'd been in charge, I would have said, 'We have to do this differently tonight.'"

The Reds moved up to sixth with a 2-1 home win over West Brom. Lallana's first Liverpool goal came on the stroke of half-time as he fired into the corner after a one-two with Henderson. Saido Berahino equalised from the spot after Lovren was incorrectly penalised. Henderson won the game five minutes later, side-footing Sterling's short pass into the corner from 15 yards. Gerrard was one of the best players, finishing the game in the number-10 role, linking nicely with Balotelli.

A crazy game at Loftus Road saw the Reds pick up another three points. The game was 0-0 for over an hour but then exploded into life. Shortly after Balotelli missed an open goal, Richard Dunne scored his tenth Premier League own goal from Johnson's cross. QPR, the division's worst team, equalised on 87 minutes

337

through Eduardo Vargas. Then they threw too many men forward for a last-minute corner and were punished by a ruthless counterattack, which ended with substitute Coutinho driving the ball into the bottom corner. Incredibly, Gerrard, who had struggled in an advanced role, scored his third Liverpool own goal to make it 2-2 two minutes into injury time. And then, even more incredibly, there was still time for a winner. Lovren cleared a free kick. The outstanding Sterling, against his first club, ran onto Coutinho's pass, and his square ball intended for Balotelli was knocked into his own net by Steven Caulker in the 95th minute. QPR may have been unlucky to score two own goals, but those old enough to remember the 1986 Milk Cup semi-final may have sported a wry smile.

A horrible run of results followed as the Reds were about to lose five of their next eight, starting with holders Real Madrid at Anfield in the Champions League. Alvaro Arbeloa was still in the Madrid line-up after transferring between the clubs in 2009. Liverpool played well for 22 minutes before Cristiano Ronaldo put his side ahead with a clinical finish. Karim Benzema got the next two. Coutinho hit the post from 25 yards. Balotelli angered fans by swapping his shirt with Pepe at half-time, with Liverpool 3-0 down. He was immediately replaced by Lallana. Sterling moved to false 9. The Reds improved, but there were no more goals.

The Reds missed a bucketload of chances in a goalless stalemate at home to Hull, whose third-choice keeper Eldin Jakupovic was superb. He made top-class saves in quick succession from Sterling, Coutinho and Balotelli. Coutinho had again been relegated to the bench but was the biggest threat when he replaced the anonymous Lallana. Balotelli missed a sitter at the end. This was the seventh time a team managed by Steve Bruce had left Anfield with at least a point, although he did raise eyebrows when he compared Balotelli to Eric Cantona.

Late goals by Balotelli and Lovren against Swansea ensured League Cup progress against Swansea. Rodgers fielded a 4-2-3-1 formation, with Coutinho tucked in behind Lambert. Trailing to a Marvin Emnes goal, Liverpool eventually found an equaliser on 86 minutes when substitute Balotelli turned in Borini's cross. Federico Fernandez was sent off in the second minute of injury time for scything down Coutinho. From the free kick, Lovren nodded in his first Reds goal in front of the Kop. Gerrard's contract was up at the end of the season, and he caused a stir when he said: "I will play beyond this season. We will have to wait and see if that's at Liverpool or somewhere else. That's Liverpool's decision."

Defeat at Newcastle was yet another disappointment. Ayoze Perez scored the only goal midway through the second half. It was the fourth league defeat in ten games. "We have lost goals," said Rodgers. "We scored 101 last year, but take away nearly 80 per cent of that [the absence of Suarez and Sturridge] and it can become difficult, alongside the introduction of lots of new players. It is not rocket science."

Many sympathised with Rodgers' plight, but public opinion began to change when he named his starting line-up for the Champions League match at the Bernabeu. The team was: Mignolet; Manquillo, Skrtel (captain), Toure, Moreno; Lucas, Can; Allen, Lallana, Markovic; Borini. What was overlooked amid the avalanche of criticism was that the fringe players played far better than anyone expected, and better than the strongest line-up had done at Anfield. They did lose, but only 1-0, and were the first team since August to stop Cristiano Ronaldo scoring. Toure and Lucas were imperious. Karim Benzema scored the only goal midway through the first half, after which Liverpool grew into the game. Madrid looked flat, and when Rodgers sent on Gerrard, Coutinho and Sterling, the Reds were more than hopeful of grabbing an equaliser. Alas, it didn't materialise. Gerrard was incandescent, writing in his book: "How could I go on playing for Liverpool another year if these were the kind of empty nights that awaited me? It did feel like Brendan had surrendered even before kick-off."

If players had been saved for the forthcoming match with Chelsea, it didn't work. Can gave the Reds a ninth-minute lead with a 25-yarder that deflected in off Gary Cahill, who soon equalised from a set piece. Diego Costa, a one-time Liverpool target, scored the winner halfway through the second half, with the Reds opened up far too easily. Lovren had another stinker. Gerrard, Can and Allen were totally outplayed by Jose Mourinho's midfielders, in particular Nemanja Matic. Chelsea were four points clear at the top. Southampton were in second, 11 clear of Liverpool, and clearly not missing Lallana, Lambert and Lovren.

The mental scars from losing the 2014 title meant it was no surprise that Liverpool should play so badly at Selhurst Park, scene of that infamous collapse in April. Lambert scored his first Liverpool goal inside two minutes from a delightful pass by Lallana, but the Reds were taken apart after that, conceding goals to Dwight Gayle, Joe Ledley and Mile Jedinak. Liverpool were now 12th, having made their worst start since 1992. "Can we play you every week?" gloated the home fans. Rodgers admitted he was "not so arrogant" as to assume his job was safe. Jamie Carragher concluded that they had "no leadership on the pitch," despite his mate Gerrard being out there.

Liverpool did stem the run of defeats, but a 2-2 draw in Bulgaria against Ludogorets was still a bad result. Victory at home to Basel in the last game would put them in the last 16, but conceding a late goal to a set piece summed up the season. Gerrard played in an advanced role behind Lambert, with Lucas anchoring the midfield. They fell behind to a third-minute goal, with Mignolet at fault, but it was quickly cancelled out by Lambert's header. Henderson made it 2-1 before half-time. Lambert and Sterling missed chances, and Liverpool paid the price when Georgi Terziev headed in a corner with Johnson hopelessly out of position.

As a miserable November drew to a close, the first win of the month came courtesy of a late Johnson header against Stoke. Rodgers caused a stir by benching Gerrard. He came on for Lucas with 15 minutes left. Lambert rose highest to meet Henderson's cross. The ball rebounded off the bar and Johnson dived in bravely to head home in front of the Kop. Mignolet was instructed not to play out from the back. The full backs were told not to overlap, despite Johnson being in the six-yard box when it mattered most. It might not have been pretty, but Liverpool had their first three points in nearly six weeks.

Another win came at bottom side Leicester three days later. An own goal by the struggling Mignolet put Leicester ahead. Lallana lashed an equaliser into the near post. Nine minutes into the second half, man of the match Gerrard side-footed a loose ball into the corner to make it 2-1. Wes Morgan was sent off for wrestling Lambert to the floor. Henderson sealed the points when he turned Sterling's backheel into an unguarded net. The Foxes were two points from safety. Who could have foreseen that within 18 months they would be champions of England?

A goalless bore draw at home to Sunderland halted the brief winning run. Gerrard was benched, saved for the do-or-die game with Basel, and only played the final quarter. Coutinho was hauled off again for Markovic. Lallana didn't get into the game, although Sterling impressed. Lambert was isolated up front. But Toure excelled again, having been reinvigorated since his Bernabeu recall.

Ten years after the glorious win over Olympiacos, a calamitous evening against Basel saw this wretched season fall to new depths. Trailing to a Fabian Frei goal at half-time after an abysmal first-half performance, Rodgers made a double substitution, withdrawing Enrique and Lambert for Moreno and Markovic, leaving Coutinho on the bench. Markovic was then red-carded on the hour for a swinging arm, although it was only the very tips of his fingers that came accidentally into contact with Behrang Safari's face. Gerrard fired in a superb free kick with ten minutes remaining. Urged on by the Anfield crowd, the Reds were unable to bag a winner. They were unlucky with the sending-off decision, but the inescapable truth was that this Liverpool side weren't good enough to progress. The manager's frustrating lack of faith in Coutinho was also holding the team back. Without Suarez and Sturridge and with Gerrard on the wane, they had found their level – mid-table mediocrity and a place in the Europa League.

As they nursed their wounds, the last thing the Reds needed was a trip to Old Trafford. United had problems of their own, in their second post-Ferguson season, but after a dismal start to Louis van Gaal's managership, they were now in the top four. Rodgers fielded a new wing back system, with Henderson on the right and Johnson in one of the centre-back positions. He also dropped the erratic Mignolet after 93 consecutive league starts, a decision which had been coming, but many wondered whether it was right to pitch Brad Jones into a game like this. In total contrast, David de Gea was in unbeatable form for United, making numerous saves from Sterling, including one early in the game from which United immediately countered and scored, with Wayne Rooney firing past the flat-footed Jones. Those 30 seconds summed up the match. An offside Juan Mata headed in the second. Sterling missed a clear-cut chance early in the second half. De Gea pushed Balotelli's shot onto the bar, one of three saves he made from the Italian. United then countered after Toure lost the ball, and Van

Persie made it 3-0, with Jones miles out of position. Only nine months earlier, Liverpool had won by the same score at Old Trafford.

League Cup progress continued at Dean Court a week before Christmas. Rodgers fielded a bizarre line-up of centre backs, midfielders and wingers, shoehorned into another 3-4-2-1 formation. But perhaps the new style had its merits as, having created several chances at Old Trafford, Liverpool rattled in three goals at Bournemouth. A fantastic cross from Markovic allowed Henderson to set up makeshift striker Sterling for a close-range header. Markovic scored his first for the club after Coutinho's shot had been parried. Sterling got another, taking Lallana's pass, turning the last defender inside out and firing past the keeper. Dan Gosling got one back for the Championship high-fliers and later hit a post, but the Reds were in the last four, where they would play Chelsea. It was a welcome result for Rodgers, who had to deny reports of dressing-room disharmony at the club.

The result was the start of a ten-match unbeaten run, which eased the pressure on the manager. The hero in a thrilling 2-2 draw at Anfield with Arsenal was Skrtel, who needed several minutes of attention after being trodden on by Olivier Giroud. He soldiered on with his head bandaged up and thundered in a 97th-minute header to rescue a point. The majestic Coutinho had earlier given Liverpool the lead, but Mathieu Debuchy quickly equalised. Giroud put Arsenal ahead before Skrtel's injury. Lucas, Coutinho, Gerrard and Borini all went close before the latter was dismissed for two needless bookings. Then came Skrtel's moment of glory from Lallana's corner. With Sturridge due back in January and with the new system eliciting an obvious improvement, Rodgers waxed lyrical about Liverpool's top-four chances.

A Boxing Day trip to Burnley saw the end of Jones's time between the posts, as he came off with a thigh injury after 16 minutes. He was replaced by Mignolet. Henderson and Markovic were the wing backs. Coutinho and Lallana played behind Sterling. Young Sheyi Ojo was an unused sub. Still in the false-9 role, Sterling got the only goal just after the hour mark, running onto Coutinho's through ball, rounding Tom Heaton and rolling the ball home. The Reds were hardly impressive, but it was another result for the new formation.

The final game of a tumultuous calendar year was a routine home win over Swansea, who had once been such a bogey team for the Reds. With Gerrard benched again, Henderson was captain. Moreno scored a rare goal from Henderson's cross. Having played so well, the Reds deservedly doubled the lead on 51 minutes with a truly bizarre goal, as Lukasz Fabianski's clearance was charged down by Lallana and the ball looped into the Kop net. Gylfi Sigurdsson immediately halved the deficit. Sterling hit a post. Lallana got his second, taking the ball away from two defenders and firing home. Jonjo Shelvey then continued his run of erratic performances against his old club by glancing in an own goal from Henderson's corner to make it 4-1. At the turn of the year, Liverpool were eighth, 18 points behind leaders Chelsea, but only five behind Southampton in fourth.

Leicester City were still bottom when they came to Anfield on New Year's Day. When Gerrard converted two penalties inside 40 minutes, another routine win seemed certain. His second was the club's 100th successful Premier League penalty. Lallana succumbed to a thigh injury. By the hour mark, David Nugent and Jeffrey Schlupp had tied the game up. Riyad Mahrez's free kick cannoned back off an upright. Liverpool barely threatened a winner. The big news came later in the day, when Gerrard announced he would leave at the end of the season to play in the MLS with LA Galaxy. The club had offered him a one-year incentive-based contract with a 40% cut in basic pay. The month would also see Oussama Assaidi and Suso leave for pastures new.

The BBC televised Liverpool's banana skin of an FA Cup tie at AFC Wimbledon, who were 12th in League Two. There were lots of reminders about the 1988 final, but this time the Crazy Gang didn't quite have enough to beat the Culture Club. With much of the focus on Gerrard, it was he who scored both goals in a 2-1 win, playing number 10 behind Lambert. His first was a header from Manquillo's right-wing cross, but Liverpool fan Adebayo Akinfenwa brought the house down by scrambling in a 36th-minute corner. Gerrard cleared one off the line in the second half before firing in a free kick just after the hour to win the game. He was denied a hat trick in stoppage time by a goal-line clearance. The final would be on his 35th birthday. Lifting the cup at Wembley would be the perfect way to sign off.

Some of Liverpool's more misguided signings down the years have got at least one game in which they were half decent - Nigel Clough against Manchester United, Bruno Cheyrou against Newcastle, Alberto Aquilani against Atletico Madrid and Andy Carroll against Manchester City. Now it was Lazar Markovic's turn against Sunderland. In the ninth minute of the game at the Stadium of Light, the right wing back grabbed the only goal of the game, prodding the ball between the legs of Costel Pantilimon. It was his first Premier League goal. He then should have had a penalty before he hit the crossbar with an incredible volley which looked more like a kung-fu kick. It was easily his best Liverpool performance. Sunderland's Liam Bridcutt was sent off for two yellows. Adam Johnson hit the bar. The score remained 1-0. Coutinho played well again. Gerrard had come off at the break with a tight hamstring. Sterling was enjoying a mid-season break in Jamaica. Balotelli played the last 23 minutes and called Sunderland, "the fucking coldest city I've ever fucking played in." Italian champions Juventus were surprisingly linked with him.

After the rare luxury of seven days in between games, three more points were picked up at Aston Villa. Henderson crossed superbly for Borini to make it 1-0. The Italian hit the post in the second half. Mignolet saved from Benteke. His form would be a real plus in the second half of the season. Lambert made the game safe from the edge of the box before being mobbed by the travelling supporters. The back three of Can, Skrtel and Sakho were outstanding, as was Coutinho.

A wonderful individual goal from man of the match Sterling was the highlight of a 1-1 draw at home to Chelsea in the first leg of the League Cup semi-final. It was their 20th cup meeting since 2004. Gerrard struck a fierce 25-yarder which Thibaut Courtois tipped over. Eden Hazard sent a penalty past Mignolet on 18 minutes, after he had been fouled by Can. The Reds had seven shots to Chelsea's one, but still trailed at the break. Sterling's moment came on the hour. He took Henderson's pass in midfield, turned past one defender, surged into the area and drilled the ball into the corner of the Kop goal. Gerrard hit a post. Courtois parried a stinger from Coutinho. Skrtel failed to convert a free header. Courtois made a double save from Henderson and Sterling. Then he handled outside the box but got away with it. He also tipped Lallana's shot around the post. Liverpool had dominated the runaway leaders.

The fourth round of the FA Cup brought Bolton to Anfield in a Saturday-evening kick-off. News had just filtered through that Chelsea and Manchester City had lost to lower-division clubs. Rodgers selected a strong team against the Championship side, but Liverpool failed to break them down. That was largely down to a man-of-the-match performance from Stoke's Hungarian keeper, a certain Adam Bogdan, who made great saves from Henderson, Sterling, Coutinho, Borini and Lucas. Bolton fielded an experienced forward pair of Emile Heskey and Eidur Gudjohnsen, but they also drew a blank.

The second leg at Chelsea came too soon for Sturridge. Can was still one of the three centre halves. Markovic and Moreno were the wing backs. Lucas partnered Henderson in the middle, with Gerrard and Coutinho in advanced roles behind Sterling. Lucas and Henderson were magnificent as Liverpool held firm, taking the game into extra time. They also threatened going forward, with Coutinho having a blinder. Costa, having had an infamous stare-off with Henderson in the first leg, stamped on Can's ankle after 12 minutes, right in front of the fourth official, but wasn't red-carded. He also left stud marks on Skrtel. Courtois saved from Moreno and Coutinho. Mignolet made a couple of saves from Costa. The introduction of the ineffective Balotelli on 70 minutes saw a rejig which cost Liverpool some of their fluency. The Reds had done well to force extra time, but after 94 minutes Branislav Ivanovic was left unmarked at a free kick and headed Chelsea into the final. Henderson missed a gilt-edged chance to force penalties. In a difficult season, these two performances against the champions-elect are often forgotten, but the Reds were outstanding and were only denied by the brilliance of Chelsea's goalkeeper.

After five months of injury, Sturridge marked his return by scoring 12 minutes after replacing Markovic to seal a 2-0 home win over West Ham. Coutinho set up both goals, firstly for Sterling on 51 minutes and then Sturridge with ten to go. The latter's was a lovely near-post finish past Adrian from a tight angle. Teenage sub Jordon Ibe almost added a third. Liverpool had been competitive over the last six weeks in Sturridge's absence. If he could stay fit, there was every hope they could get back into the top four.

Just when it looked like the Reds would be embarrassed at Bolton in the FA

Cup replay, Sterling and Coutinho scored in the last five minutes. Bogdan was injured, and his place was taken by another future Reds keeper, Andy Lonergan. After missing West Ham, Gerrard returned for his 700th Liverpool match. Sterling hit a post in the first half. The game was goalless for nearly an hour when Skrtel tripped Zach Clough. Gudjohnsen sent Mignolet the wrong way. Liverpool poured forward. Neil Danns was sent off for two yellows. Sturridge came on. Henderson's shot was deflected onto a post. Lonergan tipped Can's piledriver onto the bar. Eventually, the dam broke when Can floated a pass over the defence and Sterling turned it in from seven yards. There were still four minutes left. Coutinho didn't need any longer. Collecting the ball 25 yards out, he made space for himself and unleashed a magnificent high, curling shot that went in off the bar.

A 0-0 at Goodison was an irritating result which left Liverpool five points behind fourth-placed Manchester United at the end of the weekend. The game never got going. Lucas was withdrawn early with a thigh injury. Coutinho injured a knee. Sturridge played another 34 minutes. Man of the match Ibe, in his first derby, hit a post. Mignolet saved Everton's first shot on target, from Seamus Coleman, with three minutes left. It was the eighth goalless draw between the sides since the formation of the Premier League, more than any other fixture. Liverpool's top scorers in the league were Sterling and Gerrard, with five each. At the same stage of 2013-14, Suarez had 23 and Sturridge 14.

Balotelli's first league goal saw Liverpool edge a thrilling midweek home game with top-four rivals Spurs. Sturridge, back in the 11, set up the opener for Markovic, but Harry Kane equalised, with Liverpool opened up too easily. Lloris saved from Ibe. Sturridge's crafty backheel cannoned off an upright. Gerrard made it 2-1 with a 53rd-minute penalty after Sturridge's mazy run was ended illegally. He was now level with Robbie Fowler on 183 Liverpool goals, only behind Ian Rush, Roger Hunt, Gordon Hodgson and Billy Liddell. Moussa Dembele equalised after Mignolet saved Christian Eriksen's free kick. Gerrard was withdrawn for Lovren. The skipper would be sidelined for nearly five weeks with a hamstring injury. Can went into midfield. Substitute Balotelli's big moment came when he turned in Lallana's driven cross from three yards. He didn't even celebrate. Liverpool held on for the last seven minutes to move within a point of Spurs and just three away from Arsenal in fourth. There were 13 games left. They were timing their run nicely.

After two nightmares at Selhurst Park in under a year, it was no surprise that the Reds went 1-0 down to Crystal Palace in the fifth round of the FA Cup. Skrtel failed to head away a high ball, Mignolet parried Dwight Gayle's header and Frazier Campbell tapped in the rebound. Mignolet was otherwise excellent. Julian Speroni saved from Lallana and Henderson. Coutinho had a shot blocked. Sturridge was tripped, but no penalty was forthcoming. The dominant Reds eventually equalised four minutes into the second half, when Sturridge buried Henderson's lofted pass. Soon, they were in front when Balotelli's free kick was spilled by Speroni and Lallana gleefully knocked in the rebound.

The last time Besiktas had come to Anfield, they had lost 8-0 in the 2007-08 Champions League. They did better this time, in the last 32 of the Europa League. Ibe, still doing well at right wing back, won the spot kick which Balotelli scored after arguing with Henderson over who should take it. Earlier on, Demba Ba went clean through at the Kop end, but this time Mignolet denied him, having failed to do so a year earlier. Moreno hit a wondrous shot from over 35 yards, but it was tipped over. Liverpool dominated possession, had ten more shots and deserved the win. But was it enough to take to Turkey?

A 2-0 win at St Mary's on the last Sunday in February was an impressive result, given Southampton were third. Just as the home fans were starting their boring repertoire of Lovren songs, Coutinho silenced them with an incredible 20-yard shot which thundered in off the crossbar. Southampton, with Sadio Mane coming on in the second half, pushed for an equaliser. The Saints had three penalty appeals turned down before Sterling made it 2-0. It was far from convincing, it wasn't particularly entertaining, and in Lovren, Markovic and sometimes Lallana, the Reds had players who were still struggling, but they were keeping clean sheets and winning matches.

Liverpool hadn't had to contend with many low points in 2015, but going out of Europe to Besiktas was a huge disappointment. It was the club's third defeat in 15 penalty shootouts. Tolgay Arslan scored a stunning left-footer from the edge of the area. Demba Ba hit the crossbar in the 90th minute. It ended 1-0. The first nine penalties were converted, with Lambert, Lallana, Can and Allen scoring. Then Lovren blazed his kick over the bar. Rodgers had won over many doubters since December, but leaving out Coutinho and Henderson was a mistake. Balotelli made his first start since 8th November. Skrtel was captain. Can was poor, even though he was playing in his preferred central-midfield position. Toure was poor. Allen tailed off badly after half-time. Sterling, Ibe and Sturridge were on the periphery of the game.

Redemption for the players and the manager came in a 2-1 defeat of Manchester City on the first day of March. The recalled Coutinho and Henderson scored identical goals that three Joe Harts wouldn't have saved. Either would have been a worthy Goal of the Month winner. It was a costly result for City in their ultimately doomed pursuit of Chelsea at the top and a very handy one for Liverpool in the race for fourth. Henderson's wonderstrike came on 11 minutes, as he fired the ball into the top corner with unerring accuracy. Edin Dzeko slid Sergio Aguero's clever reverse pass past Mignolet 14 minutes later. Coutinho's winner came from a wider angle and didn't go as high as Henderson's, but it was just as good. The Brazilian's ethereal brilliance was becoming the highlight of the season. The Reds held out for the last 15 minutes and were thoroughly deserving of the points. Coutinho and Lallana were unplayable. Allen excelled in the middle. Can looked adept in defence again. Moreno and Lovren were still the weak links. The Reds were the only unbeaten team in the Premier League in 2015.

Having played in seven consecutive midweeks, Liverpool beat bottom-three

345

side Burnley, with Henderson producing a goal and an assist in a 2-0 win. It still hadn't been confirmed he would take over the captaincy from Gerrard, but he was doing his chances no harm. Sturridge pressed Burnley keeper Tom Heaton into action after just 24 seconds. Henderson headed over from a corner and then had a shot tipped around the post. Then, after Coutinho's shot was blocked, he slammed in the rebound from the edge of the box. Coutinho's curler was just wide. Sturridge missed a one-on-one with Heaton. Mignolet saved from Ashley Barnes at the other end. Just after the break, Sturridge headed in Henderson's cross to secure the points. Can, Allen, Henderson and Sterling were the best players.

Championship club Blackburn came to Anfield in the quarter-finals of the FA Cup and forced a replay. Rovers stymied the Reds, with Markovic, Coutinho, Sturridge and Lallana below their best. Sterling was now at wing back. Skrtel fell awkwardly on his head and back after two minutes and was stretchered off after eight minutes of treatment, replaced by Toure. Lallana and Sturridge were denied penalties. Mignolet saved from Alex Baptiste. The replay was a month away.

After the luxury of eight days without a game, the Reds consolidated their bid for fourth with a 1-0 win at Swansea. Gerrard returned to the bench after a month's absence. Rodgers was livid with the players at half-time. Pointing at Gerrard, he said: "One of the hardest decisions I've had to make is to not put him straight back into the team. One of the best players in the fucking world and I've kept him out because you've been playing well ... How fucking wrong was I? Does he have to go and put his cape back on and save us again?" Rodgers switched to a diamond formation. Gerrard replaced Moreno on 64 minutes. Within moments, Henderson scored the winner, although it was an outright fluke. Sturridge flicked Skrtel's pass into his path. Jordi Amat came across with a sliding tackle, but the ball cannoned off Henderson, hit the ground and looped over the helpless Lukasz Fabianski. Allen was man of the match against his old club. Liverpool hadn't conceded an away goal in the league since December.

Having collected 32 points from a possible 36, the Reds could now leapfrog Manchester United by beating them in a Sunday lunchtime fixture at Anfield. The question all week was 'Would Gerrard start?' The manager texted him on Wednesday night: "You've trained so well the last couple of days. Can we have a chat? Come to my office in the morning before training." Gerrard was delighted, assuming he would start, but Rodgers told him he would be on the bench again. "A sudden lump formed in my throat," he wrote in his 2015 book. "I looked at Brendan and, in that mad moment, I had a split-second decision to make. Do I have a go at him? I went the other way. I went the right way. I decided to stay professional." Gerrard still hadn't calmed down by the morning of the game and told his psychiatrist, Steve Peters, that he felt like a caged animal. "Steve wishes now that he had made me stay with him and calmed me down," Gerrard wrote, "because caged animals don't last very long on a football field."

Both sides were in form. United had just dismantled Spurs, their third league win in a row. Liverpool's unbeaten Premier League run stretched over three months. Having trailed United by ten points in December, they had cut the gap to two prior to kick-off. The journalist Tony Evans later recalled the build-up to the game in The Independent: "Brendan Rodgers held court. This was not the uplifting Red spring of the previous year when Rodgers' side had come close to winning the title, but the team had not lost since before Christmas. The manager felt positive. He does positivity brilliantly. The audience were journalists. Although the meeting was off the record and he could not be quoted directly, what the Liverpool manager said made great copy. He talked about long, sleepless nights when he weighed up complex tactical issues and how he arrived at a 'eureka' moment and changed his principles to get the best out of his squad. He talked about his CORE philosophy – Commitment, Ownership, Responsibilities, Excellence – and explained how to apply each point. And he discussed players, articulating how he had improved Emre Can and Jordan Henderson while detailing why Mario Balotelli was doomed to failure on Merseyside." The resultant articles were published on the weekend of the United match.

And then it all went wrong. In a season-defining game, Juan Mata put United ahead on 14 minutes as they dominated the first half. And then came the moment everyone remembers. Having replaced Lallana at the break, Gerrard lasted 38 seconds for stamping on Ander Herrera. Up went Martin Atkinson's red card. "What have you just done?" Gerrard muttered to himself. "Are you fucking stupid?" Anfield was stunned. Mata scored again with a jaw-dropping scissor kick. Three months of progress had been undone in an hour. Sturridge got one back, running onto Coutinho's pass and firing past David de Gea. Can wasn't on his game and conceded a penalty in injury time, although Mignolet saved from Wayne Rooney. Gerrard apologised after the game, taking full responsibility for the defeat. The result represented more than three points lost. It killed Liverpool's momentum, and the season plunged into a tailspin. "In truth, that 13-game run was arguably one of the most underwhelming unbeaten stretches in Premier League history," continued Evans. "There were plenty of other debatable issues around Liverpool at the time, too. It was a club on the edge, and it took a remarkable lack of perception of the problems for Rodgers to choose that moment to project such a rosy image of his managership."

With Gerrard banned, Henderson kept the captaincy for the trip to Arsenal. Sturridge, the injured Lallana and the suspended Skrtel made way for Markovic, Lucas and Toure. Worst of all, it was now becoming clearer that Sterling was agitating for a transfer. An interview he did with the BBC, when he tried to explain his position, projected him in an unflattering light, and it precipitated the start of the fans turning against him. Rodgers blamed "outside influences," but Sterling could hardly have been happy with being used as a winger, striker, number-10 and wing back in under a season. He was Liverpool's best player in this game. For 37 minutes the game was goalless. By half-time, it was 3-0 to Arsenal after Hector Bellerin, Mesut Ozil and Alexis Sanchez scored. Liverpool had caved in, with Toure and Moreno the biggest culprits in an appalling defensive performance. Lucas and Allen weren't much better in front of them. Rodgers' latest baffling selections included Henderson at right wing back and Markovic playing behind Sterling, who was up front on his own, with Sturridge on the bench. There was no quality among the other substitutes, so none came on. Sterling won a penalty, which Henderson converted. Olivier Giroud made it 4-1 in injury time after Can got a second yellow - the fourth sending-off of the season. Within 180 minutes, the Reds had gone from being the form team in the Premier League to having to sift through the wreckage of a hugely disappointing campaign. Monday's Mirror told of a dressing-room bust-up. Journalist Jim Boardman reported that "a couple of senior LFC players tore strips off the boss after he'd 'had a go' at Kolo."

The cup replay at Ewood saw Liverpool move into the semis with a 1-0 win. After two cataclysmic results, Rodgers dispensed with three at the back, reverting to a 4-3-3. Sturridge came back into the side but sustained a hip injury in the closing stages which would sideline him until September. Sakho pulled a hamstring and was replaced by Toure. The Reds had little cutting edge against a weakened Blackburn and had to rely on Coutinho's magic again. He stayed wide after taking a corner, ran onto Henderson's pass, and found the far corner from a tight angle. Sturridge missed a promising chance. Allen was denied a penalty. Mignolet saved from his opposite number Simon Eastwood after an injury-time corner. The sleep-deprived Henderson put in a commanding display – he had become a dad again overnight. The Reds had struggled against three lower-division teams but were in the semi-finals, where they would play Aston Villa at Wembley.

After a minute's silence for the 96, a routine 2-0 win at home to Newcastle kept the Reds in fifth, four points behind Manchester City with six games left. Sterling was still in the news, and not just because he still hadn't signed a new contract. He was pictured smoking a shisha pipe one day and then inhaling laughing gas, or 'deadly nitrous oxide' as the Mirror put it, the next. He was the matchwinner against the Magpies, controlling Henderson's deep cross, evading two defenders and bending his shot into the corner. With Sterling and Coutinho running the show, Liverpool dominated. Allen doubled the lead when a corner wasn't cleared. Moussa Sissoko received a late red card for a horrific tackle on Lucas, who had held Liverpool's midfield superbly. There were still concerns at the back, where Can and Lovren looked unconvincing. The referee missed Lovren's foul on Ayoze Perez in the box. Newcastle did have chances, but Mignolet excelled again. Earlier in the day, Gerrard had played in an Under-18s match against Shrewsbury Town at Melwood to help improve his match fitness ahead of the semi-final. He handed the captain's armband to Trent Alexander-Arnold. "It was my way of telling Trent that I believed he could make it for Liverpool one day," said Gerrard.

The United game may have exposed Liverpool's mediocrity and ignited a calamitous end-of-season slump, but the FA Cup semi-final against Aston Villa was the real nadir of the campaign. Rodgers reverted to 3-4-2-1, with Can, Skrtel and Lovren at the back. Markovic and Moreno were the wing backs. Henderson and Allen were in the middle. Gerrard and Coutinho filled the number-10 roles, behind Sterling. Sturridge, Sakho, Lallana, Lucas and Ibe were unavailable. Allen blasted a chance over the bar. Mignolet tipped over Charles N'Zogbia's long-ranger. Lovren stopped Christian Benteke going clean through. Sterling had a penalty appeal turned down. Villa had started brightly, forcing Rodgers to switch to a flat back four, a decision which soon paid off. Coutinho took Sterling's pass, sprinted past a couple of flat-footed defenders and slotted the ball into the corner to continue his impressive cup form. The lead lasted just minutes. Can, now at right back, was caught out of position. Man of the match Fabian Delph, who had wanted to join Liverpool at the start of the season, got into the box, and Benteke side-footed past Mignolet from the edge of the box. It was the Belgian's fifth goal in six games against his future club.

Balotelli replaced the ineffective Markovic at the break, but Villa were soon ahead when Delph cut inside Lovren and Can and beat Mignolet. Moreno's last-ditch tackle prevented a third. Johnson replaced Allen, pushing Can into midfield, his third position of the game. He didn't play well in any of them. Gerrard had a header cleared off the line. Balotelli had an equaliser wrongly disallowed for offside. In injury time, the Italian headed Henderson's cross over the bar. And then Lovren ballooned a long-ranger hopelessly high and wide. It summed up not just Liverpool's day, but their season too. Only Coutinho, Mignolet and possibly Sterling deserved to escape severe criticism. Liverpool had been humiliated in the national stadium. The manager's job was hanging by a thread.

There were six league games left. Top-four hopes were bleak. The only realistic aim was to send Gerrard out on some sort of a high, although a 0-0 at West Brom wasn't the best start. Rodgers unveiled yet another formation, this time 4-1-4-1. Lovren was the best defender, but Can struggled at right back again. Coutinho was the most effective going forward and had a shot saved by Boaz Myhill. Ibe hit a bar after a one-two with Balotelli. Clearly desperate for strikers, Rodgers played down reports the club were interested in Memphis Depay. He would sign for Manchester United in the summer.

The Steve Bruce hoodoo continued at the Kingston Communications Stadium, where Hull beat the Reds 1-0 in the last game of April. Over 1,000 Liverpool fans stayed away in protest at ticket prices. The players didn't turn up either. Rodgers tried a 4-3-3, with Ibe and Sterling either side of Balotelli, but nothing the manager did was working. Gerrard was rested. Can was still at full back, with Hull exploiting him all afternoon. Their goal came from a corner. From the second ball, Skrtel and Lovren pushed up, but Balotelli, of all people, played Michael Dawson onside, and he scored the game's only goal. The Echo's man of the match was Allen, aptly describing him as "the best of a bad bunch." Rodgers' position was fast becoming untenable, especially with the manager of Borussia Dortmund, Jurgen Klopp, signalling his intentions to seek pastures new.

The final victory of the season came courtesy of a late Gerrard winner at the Kop end against QPR. He led the team out, carrying a bouquet of white lilies for Rio Ferdinand, whose wife had just passed away. Joey Barton accepted them on his teammate's behalf. A plane flew overhead with a banner reading, 'Rodgers out, Rafa in'. "In my dark mood, I briefly wondered if Rafa had put someone up to the stunt," said Gerrard. His winning goal was the nearest he was going to get to a Roy of the Rovers moment in this miserable run-in. The visitors made the better start, but Coutinho curled Lambert's pass into Robert Green's top corner to give the Reds a half-time lead. Skrtel, Lallana, Sterling, Gerrard and Lovren missed chances to double the lead. They were punished when Leroy Fer volleyed in Joey Barton's corner on 73 minutes. Nedum Onuoha gave Liverpool a lifeline when he brought down Skrtel, but Gerrard's last penalty for Liverpool was saved by Green. He had scored 47 of his 57 attempts, finishing five ahead of Jan Molby. Onuoha departed after a second yellow. There was still time for Gerrard to redeem himself, and he beat Barton to power home Coutinho's corner on 87 minutes. He kissed the badge before his teammates swamped him. Gerrard was now one ahead of Robbie Fowler as Liverpool's fifth-highest scorer of all time. Sterling was below par and was barracked by the Kop for pulling out of a tackle. "Hasn't had a good game since he started telling everyone he might be too good for Liverpool," wrote John Gibbons on The Anfield Wrap website.

The skipper scored another header on a trip to the new champions. The Reds formed a guard of honour for Chelsea's players, and after another slow start, John Terry scored from a fifth-minute corner. Johnson, Coutinho and Sterling all went close before Gerrard headed in Henderson's free kick on the stroke of half-time. It was his first goal at Stamford Bridge. Jerome Sinclair replaced the ineffective Lambert for his Premier League debut. There were no further goals. Liverpool's best player, Coutinho, was denied by Thibaut Courtois' fine save in the closing minutes. Fourth was gone, barring two Liverpool wins, two Manchester United defeats and a goal-difference swing of miraculous proportions.

The last two games were an utter embarrassment. Crystal Palace overturned another 1-0 deficit to win 3-1 on Gerrard's last Anfield appearance. The skipper walked onto the field accompanied by his daughters, with the crowd displaying mosaics that read 'Captain' and 'SG8'. A banner on the Kop read: "The best there is, the best there was and the best there ever will be." In response to the incident at the QPR game, another plane carried the message "In Rodgers we trust." Lallana scored first, punishing Martin Kelly's wayward pass. When the skipper skied a free kick, fans on the Kop chanted, "What the fucking hell was that?" Jason Puncheon equalised just before the break. Wilfried Zaha and Glenn Murray scored in the second half – the latter with a rebound from Mignolet's penalty save. The Reds were abject. Only Mignolet, Gerrard, Lallana and Coutinho scored higher than five out of ten in The Times. Sterling had another shocker in what would be his final Liverpool appearance.

And then came the biggest humiliation of them all. In Steven Gerrard's 710th and last game for Liverpool Football Club, on the day before the tenth anniversary of Istanbul, they were 5-0 down at half-time to a team managed by Mark Hughes. Rodgers unveiled yet another formation, with Gerrard getting forward to support the front men Lallana and Coutinho. Sterling was dropped to the bench after his agent said he wouldn't stay at Liverpool for £900,000 a week. Biram Diouf got the first two for Stoke. Scouser Jonathan Walters made it three. Even Charlie Adam got in on the act. Steven N'Zonzi scored just before the break. Still at right back, Can had a nightmare, and apologised to his teammates at half-time. He and Moreno were hooked at the break for Ibe and Toure. Gerrard went clean through on 70 minutes and scored his 186th and final Liverpool goal. Peter Crouch made it 6-1 near the end. It usurped the 5-1 shellacking at Coventry in 1992 as Liverpool's biggest Premier League loss.

The Reds finished in sixth on 62 points, down 22 from a year ago. They were 25 points behind Chelsea and eight away from Manchester United in fourth. They had regressed to the levels of 2010-2013. Supporters waited for Rodgers to be fired in the aftermath of the shambles at Stoke, but he limped on into pre-season and beyond. Meanwhile, a certain German manager was treating himself to an extended break after seven years at Dortmund. He would be ready to work again in the autumn ...

2015-16

"We have to change from doubters to believers. Now!"

Brendan Rodgers' last summer transfer window was probably his best, although that wasn't saying much. He picked up Roberto Firmino, Joe Gomez and James Milner, all of whom would be integral parts of Jurgen Klopp's title-winning team of 2020. The Northern Irishman wasn't keen on Firmino, who was a target of the transfer committee. He wanted Christian Benteke, so the club signed both. But if Rodgers didn't rate Firmino, his successor certainly did. "Nobody asked me about [Firmino], but he was a player I thought was one of the best in the Bundesliga," Klopp would later reveal.

As well as Firmino (£29 million from Hoffenheim), Gomez (£6 million from Charlton Athletic), Milner (free from Manchester City) and Benteke (£32.5 million from Aston Villa), the Reds signed Burnley's Danny Ings for £8 million, Southampton's Nathaniel Clyne for £12.5 million and Bolton goalkeeper Adam Bogdan on a free. Another newcomer was Divock Origi, who had been signed a year earlier. The Belgian forward had remained on loan at Lille in 2014-15 and endured a terrible year, arriving at Anfield with little confidence.

The summer included the 30th anniversary of the Heysel Stadium disaster and the naming of Jordan Henderson as the new captain. But the big story was the conclusion of the Raheem Sterling saga. After long agitating for a move, he went to Manchester City for £49 million. Glen Johnson, Brad Jones, Rickie Lambert and Fabio Borini also moved on. Iago Aspas and Sebastian Coates left permanently after previous loan deals. Mario Balotelli and Lazar Markovic had also played their last Liverpool matches, heading to AC Milan and Fenerbahce on loan. Javier Manquillo, who had been on loan from Atletico Madrid, went to Marseille. £70 million was raised in sales, although QPR were entitled to a hefty chunk of the Sterling fee. Assistant coaches Colin Pascoe and Mike Marsh were replaced by Sean O'Driscoll, Pepijn Lijnders and Gary McAllister.

The biggest change would come in October, when Rodgers was fired after a draw at Goodison and swiftly replaced by Klopp. It is unclear whether Liverpool had lined up the German over the summer. Klopp had left Borussia Dortmund in May, with suggestions he wanted a sabbatical of several months. If Liverpool had eyed him up at the end of 2014-15, they might have known they couldn't get him until after the season started, and they would need Rodgers to remain in situ. Or perhaps it was all a coincidence.

Liverpool began the season at odds of 28-1 to win the title, which was unsurprising given how far they'd fallen in a year. There were few top-class players in the squad after the exits of Gerrard and Sterling. Simon Mignolet had been one of the best performers from January to May 2015, but there were much better keepers out there than him. Mamadou Sakho was another who had recovered after an initial struggle. Martin Skrtel, as ever, was a mixed bag, as was Kolo Toure. Dejan Lovren and Alberto Moreno had endured tough debut seasons.

In midfield, Henderson had enjoyed another distinguished season. Joe Allen was the classic bellwether player, often shining when Liverpool were on top but not when the side was struggling. Emre Can had played mainly at the back but was a midfielder of great promise. Lucas Leiva was a dependable midfield anchor, but not in the class of Javier Mascherano. Adam Lallana was another who'd struggled in his first season. Jordon Ibe looked promising at wing back in the first couple of months after his January recall from Derby but had tailed off. Talk of him being as good as Sterling proved to be nonsense. Philippe Coutinho, on the other hand, was looking every inch a world-class footballer.

The only striker to remain from 2014-15 was Daniel Sturridge, who was continuing to struggle with fitness issues. He had played just 19 of the 58 games and even failed to nail down a regular place in the team in March and April. He was due to miss the first portion of the new season. At least a couple of the new forwards would need to bed in quickly for Liverpool to be competitive. A shot at the top four was more realistic than a title challenge. The points tallies of the previous six seasons had averaged just 63. The wonderful 2013-14 campaign was very much the outlier.

Rodgers wasn't dealt the kindest hand when the fixtures for 2015-16 were released. The first seven away games included the five clubs which had just finished above Liverpool, a Merseyside Derby and, first up, a return to Stoke, where they had just been humiliated 6-1. To Rodgers' credit, they won that opener at the Britannia 1-0. He selected a 4-1-4-1 formation: Mignolet; Clyne, Skrtel, Lovren, Gomez; Henderson; Ibe, Milner, Coutinho, Lallana; Benteke. Firmino and Can came off the bench. Bogdan, Toure, Moreno, Origi and Ings were unused. Liverpool were understandably cautious after May's embarrassment, but Lovren's defending was assured. Gomez, out of position at left back, didn't give Jonathan Walters an inch. Liverpool, however, fell into the trap of lumping it long to Benteke, as they used to with Heskey, Crouch and Carroll. Mignolet's kicking was a worry. But just as the game was petering out, Coutinho thumped in a screamer from 25 yards.

The Reds followed that up with a dreary home win over Bournemouth. Benteke marked his home debut with his first goal, turning in Henderson's cross at the back post. He later hit the crossbar, and Lallana fired the rebound over. It was promising that the Belgian had got off the mark quickly, but many were unconvinced. He would prove over time to be inconsistent and injury prone. He didn't press, and he was a poor passer. Henderson, who had earlier hit the bar, sustained a heel injury. When he eventually recovered, he broke a metatarsal in training. He wouldn't play again for Rodgers.

Liverpool won plaudits at Arsenal but not the game. Lucas replaced Henderson. Firmino made his first start at the expense of Ibe. Can came in for Lallana. Milner wore the armband in his third game, and his performance did justice to the role. The game was wide open, and the Reds were only denied victory by the quality of Petr Cech. In a one-sided first half, Coutinho hit the bar and then the post. Benteke somehow passed up an open goal. Milner and Coutinho could have scored. Mignolet made a couple of big saves after the break. Gomez was a shining light at left back, after a slightly shaky game against Bournemouth. Clyne continued to impress. "This was the night that proved there is real substance to Liverpool's revival," concluded the Echo.

Then came the day everything crumbled. In one painful Saturday afternoon, West Ham came to Anfield and strolled to a 3-0 victory. Gomez was run ragged. He was a teenage centre half playing left back in his introduction to the rat-a-tat world of the Premier League, so it was hardly surprising. Manuel Lanzini scored on three minutes after Skrtel failed to clear a cross. Firmino hit a post with a stunning 25-yarder. Mark Noble took advantage of Lovren's error to make it two. Can was hooked at the break for Moreno. Coutinho was sent off for a second yellow. Noble followed him later in the second half for a foul on debutant Ings. Diafra Sakho put the cherry on the Hammers' cake right at the end. Darren Randolph had one save to make all afternoon – a hit and hope from Lovren. Benteke was hopelessly isolated. There was no way back from this for Rodgers. The goodwill built up in the first three games had evaporated. His exit was just a matter of time.

On he limped to Old Trafford, where Benteke scored one of the most spectacular goals the ground had ever seen, but it counted for nothing. Just as in December, the Reds were embarrassed at the home of their biggest enemy. Ings replaced the suspended Coutinho. Lucas, Milner and Can struggled to exert any foothold in midfield. Benteke was isolated and outnumbered again. Somehow Liverpool made it to half-time intact, but soon found themselves behind to a Daley Blind goal after falling asleep at a free kick. The Reds stirred briefly. Skrtel's header was cleared off the line. Firmino failed to convert the easy rebound. He was soon replaced by Ibe. Gomez conceded a rash penalty, which Ander Herrera converted. Origi made his debut off the bench for Ings. Benteke scored an acrobatic overhead kick with seven minutes remaining, but Anthony Martial turned Skrtel inside out before firing into the corner to make it 3-1. Liverpool had scored just three goals in seven and a half hours of football. The new strikers hadn't caught the eye. Like a forlorn chancellor of the exchequer, Rodgers had spent the last 18 months revising his forecasts downwards as his team had gone from title challengers to top-four contenders to the shambles they now were.

The Europa League campaign began in the south of France with a 1-1 draw against Bordeaux. In a three-at-the-back system, in came Kolo Toure and Jordan Rossiter, while there were debuts off the bench for Pedro Chirivella and Cameron Brannagan. It was a brave selection, considering the pressure the manager was under. Sakho wore the armband. Coutinho hit a post from 25 yards. Mignolet made a key save just after the hour. Seconds later, Lallana put Liverpool ahead, cleverly nutmegging a defender and sliding the ball home. Ings nearly made it two, but Jussie Ferreira Vieira equalised with nine minutes left. Sakho, Rossiter and Coutinho were the standout players. Origi and Ibe struggled.

Beating newly-promoted Norwich at home was vital, but the Reds could only manage a draw. Sturridge returned, playing for an hour. After an insipid first half, Ings replaced the injured Benteke at half-time. He opened the scoring almost immediately, chesting down Moreno's pass and beating John Ruddy. But Mignolet's weak punch was punished by Russell Martin, who made it 1-1. It was the 18th time in 20 matches the Reds had failed to score more than one goal. They were 13th, already seven points off the top.

Carlisle United were next at Anfield in the League Cup. Surely the Reds would beat the Cumbrian minnows. They did, but they needed penalties, despite fielding a strong side. Bogdan made a memorable debut, saving three penalties in the shootout. Liverpool's best player, Ings, scored from Lallana's cross. The Reds failed to add to their tally, despite a mammoth 47 shots and 19 corners over two hours. The visitors levelled when Bastien Hery set up Derek Asamoah, with Lovren embarrassed. Firmino suffered a back injury. Played on the left, he had struggled so far in England. Coutinho came on in the second half. Lovren injured an ankle in the last minute of extra time. Milner took the first penalty and scored. Bogdan saved Danny Grainger's. Can scored a Panenka. Gary Dicker got Carlisle on the board. Lallana, Luke Joyce and Coutinho were all denied. Alexander McQueen made it 2-2 after four each. Ings scored straight down the middle and then Bogdan made the match-winning save from Hery. The Reds were through, but Carlisle took the plaudits. Liverpool were going from bad to worse.

The first victory of a miserable six weeks came at home to Aston Villa towards the end of September. It was Rodgers' last win as Liverpool boss. For the fourth game in a row, he played three centre halves. After 65 seconds, Milner, in a more attacking role, emphatically fired in his debut goal from 20 yards. Just before the hour, Sturridge played a one-two with Milner and volleyed the return exquisitely into the Kop goal. Rudy Gestede pulled one back seven minutes later, but Sturridge scored again within 60 seconds after a one-two with Coutinho. Gestede powered in a towering header. Sturridge couldn't take a late chance for his hat trick after another one-two.

October began with the Europa League visit of Sion, who had lost 6-3 at Anfield in 1996. Events were more mundane this time. Lallana scored early from Origi's pullback. Ebenezer Assifuah made it 1-1. Ings was denied by the linesman's flag. Toure hit the top of the bar with an overhead kick. Origi went clean through, but Andris Vanins denied him.

Rumours swept through Merseyside that the Goodison Derby on Sunday 4th October would be Rodgers' last match in charge of Liverpool. And so it proved. He selected the same line-up as the Villa game and saw Ings head Liverpool ahead on 41 minutes. Romelu Lukaku made it 1-1 before the break when Can failed to clear. There were no further goals, thanks largely to positive displays from Mignolet and Sakho. Clyne, Milner, Coutinho and Sturridge were off form. Of 11 matches so far, three had been won, with two defeats and six draws. The Reds were tenth in the league, six points adrift of leaders Manchester City after eight games. The 42-year-old defended his reign in the post-match press conference but warned of a lengthy rebuilding job, "whether that is with me or someone else in the job."

Rodgers was summoned to meet Ian Ayre at Melwood a couple of hours after the Everton game, where he was informed he was no longer the Liverpool manager. When it was announced on Sky Sports, Thierry Henry clutched Jamie Carragher's leg in shock. "Aimless, broken display showed why time was up for Rodgers," was the headline in The Times. Given the number of formations Rodgers had tried since August 2014, it was no surprise that the newspaper also reported that, "Liverpool played without any form of coherence, any sort of plan ... They seemed to be deployed in some sort of 4-0-6, vast green spaces opening up where the midfield once stood." But no matter what shortcomings had been exposed in his last 15 months, Rodgers would always be associated with that white-knuckle ride of a 2013-14 season.

The newspapers immediately linked Klopp and Carlo Ancelotti with the job. Bournemouth's Eddie Howe was also on Liverpool's shortlist. The club indicated they would use the international break to ponder the choice but just four days later, the 48-year-old German penned a three-year deal to be the new manager of Liverpool Football Club. He would prove to be in a different stratosphere to his predecessor.

Klopp had managed Mainz 05 between 2001 and 2008, taking them into the Bundesliga in 2004. After two mid-season finishes, they were relegated in 2007. Having failed to get them straight back up, Klopp resigned and moved to Borussia Dortmund, where he won the Bundesliga in 2011 and 2012. He guided them to the Champions League final in 2013, where they lost 2-1 to Bayern Munich. After consecutive second-place finishes, Klopp's final season at the Westfalenstadion saw them struggle at the foot of the Bundesliga during the first half of the season, before a recovery led to a finish of seventh.

The club parted ways with the Head of Performance Glen Driscoll and Head of Opposition Analysis Chris Davies. Gary McAllister moved from the coaching team to an ambassadorial role. Development coach Pepijn Lijnders, goalkeeper coach John Achterberg, academy director Alex Inglethorpe, head physio Chris Morgan and first-team doctor Andy Massey remained in their posts. They would be joined by Zeljko Buvac and Peter Krawietz, Klopp's assistant and analyst at Dortmund. The transfer committee would also remain in place.

At his unveiling, Klopp referred to himself as the 'Normal One', a nod to Jose Mourinho's narcissism. That phrase made the headlines, but more noteworthy was a plea to the supporters on LFCTV: "We have to change from doubters to believers. Now!" Before he had taken charge of a game, Ings and Gomez sustained long-term cruciate injuries.

LIVERPOOL F.C. **THE PREMIER LEAGUE YEARS**

Klopp's first game as Liverpool manager was on 17 October at Tottenham, where a German flag in the away end read 'Mein Held' – My Hero. His first line-up, in a 4-3-2-1 formation, was: Mignolet; Clyne, Sakho, Skrtel, Moreno; Lucas, Can, Milner; Coutinho, Lallana; Origi. Allen and Ibe were late substitutes. Bogdan, Toure, Connor Randall, Joao Carlos Teixeira and Jerome Sinclair weren't called upon, although the latter was stripped and ready to come on when the final whistle went. With Klopp imposing on the squad a laser-like focus on gegenpressing, they harassed the Spurs defence from the off. Firmino, Sturridge, Benteke and Ings were injured, so Origi started and hit the crossbar from close range from a corner that had been forced by enthusiastic pressing. Mignolet, Sakho and Lucas were standout players. The new manager also praised Lallana's work rate. The Reds were far better than they had been at Goodison, but they could only manage another draw. It was Liverpool's first clean sheet in nine games. "We don't have to sprinkle magical dust on them," Klopp said of his players. "They know how to play. We just have to create a situation where it is possible to do this." Graeme Souness remained the last Liverpool manager to win his first league match in sole charge.

Forty-five minutes before his first home game, Klopp walked onto the Anfield turf with the Beatles' 'She Loves You' playing over the public address system. He had dampened expectations by saying, "I hope that no one is waiting for 3-0 after four minutes and is disappointed." It was another tough European night for the Reds, who went behind to Rubin Kazan, but the visitors were reduced to ten men on 35 minutes when right back Oleg Kuzmin was dismissed for two bookings. From the free kick, Can scored Liverpool's first goal under Klopp from Origi's header. Klopp ran from his technical area and punched the air with delight. The Reds created numerous second-half chances, with Coutinho and Can unable to convert the best of them.

The Reds were back at Anfield three days later against Southampton on the dreaded Thursday-Sunday cycle. After a tight and tense 76 minutes, Benteke's towering header sent Milner's cross into the Kop goal. Klopp celebrated wildly again. The Reds couldn't hold on and were punished by Sadio Mane's equaliser with four minutes left after a free kick wasn't dealt with. The future Red was sent off in injury time for fouling Firmino and Moreno, but it was too late for the Reds to capitalise. Virgil van Dijk was also in the Saints team and was typically imposing at set pieces. After three games, Klopp was still awaiting his first win. The Reds had drawn eight of their last nine, with seven of them finishing 1-1. In five of the last six games, 135 Liverpool attempts on goal had yielded just four goals. Little was clicking in the final third. Coutinho and Origi were struggling.

Klopp's first win came in the League Cup at home to Bournemouth, with Clyne scoring the only goal of the game. With Randall making his debut at right back, Clyne was shifted to the left. There were also starts for Bogdan, Ibe, Brannagan and Teixeira. Only Clyne and Origi kept their place from Sunday. Firmino started and looked the part. The goal came on 17 minutes, when Adam Smith cleared Teixeira's impudent backheel off the line, but Clyne scored his first Liverpool goal from the rebound. Lucas and Teixeira went close to a second.

357

A significant turning point for Klopp was the match at champions Chelsea. They were having a nightmare season, and Jose Mourinho's job was reportedly hanging by a thread. Liverpool's 3-1 win left Chelsea in 15th, just four points above the relegation zone. Significantly, it was the first time Klopp used Firmino in the false-9 role, and it was the first time he used his favoured 4-3-3 formation. Chelsea took the lead on four minutes when Ramires headed in Cesar Azpilicueta's cross, with Moreno at fault. Unable to get his head around Klopp's tactics, BT Sport co-commentator Trevor Francis suggested that Liverpool bring Benteke on immediately. But the Reds assumed control of the game, with Lallana (twice) and Lucas going close. Then, in first-half injury time, Coutinho bent a delicious shot from outside the box beyond Asmir Begovic. The Brazilian put the Reds 2-1 up in the second half, and with Chelsea's spirit completely broken, Benteke wrapped up the points with eight minutes left. Regardless of Chelsea's woes, it was a stellar win. Firmino and Coutinho were outstanding.

A trip to Russia brought Liverpool their first European win of the season as they downed Rubin Kazan 1-0. Man of the match Ibe, still only 19, scored his first goal for the club seven minutes into the second half after a one-two with Firmino. Milner had earlier hit the bar. He was withdrawn on the hour and was struggling to find any form. Klopp now had three wins and three draws.

The German's first defeat came at home to Crystal Palace, who had now beaten Liverpool in three consecutive league games. Gerrard was in the crowd for the first time since his move to Los Angeles. Lucas was captain, with Henderson and Milner unavailable. Ibe's form earned him another start, and he linked well with Clyne on the right. Yannick Bolasie put the Eagles ahead after Can's error. The Reds were conceding so many goals from basic defensive lapses. Sakho, easily the team's best defender of the season, departed with a knee injury. Lallana set up an equaliser for Coutinho just before half-time. Coutinho remained a threat, while the Clyne-Ibe combination on the right looked promising again. Firmino replaced Can midway through the second half as the Reds pushed for a winner, but with Lucas the only out-and-out midfielder, Liverpool were susceptible to a Palace counterpunch. And sure enough, Scott Dann popped up with the winner with eight minutes remaining, snapping up a rebound after Mignolet's parry. Moreno, Can and Benteke were awful. Mignolet's distribution was horrific. Liverpool fans streamed out, leaving Klopp bemused. "I felt pretty alone at this moment," he said. His team were eighth after nine games, going into another international break.

Klopp reverted to his Stamford Bridge tactics as Liverpool travelled to leaders Manchester City. In recent games, he had started Benteke in a 4-2-3-1, but benched the Belgian forward in favour of Firmino playing false 9 in a 4-3-3. It worked again, as they were 3-0 up in just over half an hour of scintillating pressing and one-touch transitioning. Coutinho won the ball from Bacary Sagna and found Firmino, whose pullback was diverted into his own net by Eliaquim Mangala. One became two when Coutinho turned in Firmino's low cross. Then Firmino opened his account, finishing a scintillating move which included a sumptuous backheel by Can – what a contrast to the defensive way that Rodgers had used the German. Liverpool were ripping City apart, and Firmino was twice a whisker away from a fourth. Sergio Aguero got one back at the end of the half, but Skrtel, who had played superbly, put the game beyond doubt with a fierce volley on the turn. The Brazilian forwards earned the plaudits, but Can, Milner, Lucas and Lallana were all on song. City's back four and two central midfielders were all rated three or four out of ten by The Times, having been pressed into the ground. Despite his touchline celebrations, Klopp remained guarded after the game. "The top four? It's only okay that you ask me this if you ask it after we lose as well."

Bordeaux took a 33rd-minute lead at Anfield from an indirect free kick inside the box in the fifth Europa League game, but the Reds were ahead by the break. A foul on Benteke saw Milner score from 12 yards. And the big Belgian hammered in the winner from the edge of the box in the last minute of the half. Toure put in a commanding display. Firmino struggled, seemingly only able to shine without Benteke. Already qualified, Liverpool needed a point at Sion to win the group.

After a minute's silence for 1965 Wembley hero Gerry Byrne, Klopp earned his first Premier League win at Anfield against struggling Swansea. Kyle Bartley hit his own post in trying to stop Ibe's mazy run. Milner scored the only goal from the spot on 62 minutes after a handball. Henderson and Sturridge made welcome returns as second-half substitutes. Moreno, Milner and Can were impressive, but a howling gale resulted in a forgettable game. They were now in sixth, just six points behind Manchester City and Leicester.

Another tough-looking away assignment brought another emphatic win as Liverpool slaughtered Southampton in the fifth round of the League Cup. When Sadio Mane headed a 39th-second goal, things looked far from rosy, but something clicked, and Liverpool ran riot against a defence that boasted future Reds Steven Caulker and Virgil van Dijk. Sturridge equalised clinically from Allen's long ball. The Welshman had an excellent game. Sturridge then latched onto Can's beautifully lofted pass to make it 2-1. Origi scored his first Liverpool goal on the stroke of half-time, touching in Moreno's 20-yard drive. The Belgian got his second with a thunderous drive that went in off the bar. Ibe made it 5-1 from Moreno's cross. Origi headed in Brad Smith's cross to complete his hat trick.

Liverpool came up against another future Red at bottom-three side Newcastle, and he proved to be the match winner. After nearly 70 minutes of goalless action, Gini Wijnaldum beat Lovren, and his cross shot was diverted into the roof of the net by Skrtel. The in-form Moreno scored a magnificent volley from Milner's pass, a la Marco Van Basten, but it was wrongly ruled offside. Man of the match Wijnaldum made it 2-0 in the 93rd minute, calmly lifting the ball over Mignolet. Ibe played well again, but Clyne, Lucas, Benteke and Firmino were particularly poor – the latter two again incompatible.

The Reds topped their Europa League group with a 0-0 draw at Basel.

359

Henderson started, as did Toure and Smith. The Australian left back was exceptional. Origi was just wide with a 30-yarder. Little else of note happened.

Liverpool's Anfield struggles continued against West Bromwich Albion 12 days before Christmas. Henderson swept in Lallana's header, but Craig Dawson equalised when Mignolet got nowhere near a corner. It was 12 months to the day that Rodgers had dropped him at Old Trafford. The old weaknesses were still there, and no other Premier League player had made more mistakes that led to goals than Mignolet in the past three seasons. He was beaten again, only for Jonas Olsson's header to be ruled out. Lovren was carried off after a challenge by Craig Gardner. With 17 minutes left, West Brom scored from another corner, when Olsson glanced the ball in. Lallana went clean through but couldn't beat Boaz Myhill. This time the crowd stayed put and were rewarded when Origi's 25-yarder was deflected past Myhill in the 95th minute. After the game, Klopp, who had spent the game arguing with Tony Pulis, insisted the players salute the Kop. They lined up, hand in hand. Klopp was mocked by fans of other clubs on social media for celebrating a draw against West Brom, but he had successfully made his point about the Anfield support. They wouldn't give up on his team again.

Next up was one of the low points of the season as the Reds crashed 3-0 at Vicarage Road. Bogdan, deputising for the injured Mignolet, dropped an early corner, allowing Nathan Ake to score. Liverpool were soon two down when Odion Ighalo muscled Skrtel off the ball and scored. An unmarked Ighalo got his second with five minutes left to complete a miserable afternoon. Only Henderson emerged with any credit.

Surprise leaders Leicester City came to Anfield on Boxing Day and lost their unbeaten record to this Jekyll-and-Hyde Liverpool outfit. Lallana hit the side netting. Kasper Schmeichel saved from Can and Origi, who soon sustained the 22nd injury of Klopp's 11 weeks in charge. He needed knee surgery. Some put that down to the training methods of the manager, who, in turn, blamed it on fixture congestion. Just past the hour, Benteke put away Firmino's cross from 12 yards. The same player fluffed a sitter in injury time after Schmeichel had gone up for a corner. The Reds had won their 4,000th top-flight game.

Liverpool ended a tumultuous year with another 1-0 win. This time it was at relegation-threatened Sunderland. Vito Mannone tipped a thunderbolt from Firmino onto his right-hand post. Benteke helped himself to another winner, latching on to Lallana's clever touch 23 seconds into the second half. He later botched another injury-time sitter. Lovren defended resolutely. Can and Lucas also stood out. At the halfway point, Liverpool were in seventh, nine points behind Arsenal and Leicester.

The new year began with an appalling performance at Upton Park. Michail Antonio scored after ten minutes, courtesy of a lightning-quick counter. Manuel Lanzini hit a post. Benteke went close. Can hit the crossbar. Liverpool were finished off by Andy Carroll's towering header in the early stages of the second half. The Reds were struggling for goals, having scored just 22 in 20 league games.

The first leg of the League Cup semi-final took Liverpool to Stoke, where they won 1-0. Coutinho and Lovren succumbed to first-half hamstring injuries. Ibe, one of the replacements, scored the winner seven minutes before the break. Milner released Lallana down the right. He pulled it back to Allen, and the Welshman cleverly found Ibe, who couldn't fail to score. Toure, who tended to feature in the cups, was Liverpool's man of the match. Skipper Lucas wasn't far behind. Stoke created little. Considering Liverpool's injury problems, it was a commendable result.

Having complained so much about the winter fixture pile-up, it was no surprise that Klopp chose to field an inexperienced team at Exeter in the third round of the FA Cup. He was already without 13 injured players. Tiago Ilori, Ryan Kent, Kevin Stewart, Sheyi Ojo and Joe Maguire made their Liverpool debuts – the latter two from the bench. There were also starts for Bogdan, Jose Enrique, Smith, Randall, Brannagan, Teixeira and Sinclair, with Benteke captaining the team. It was Enrique's first involvement in nearly a year, and he played out of position at centre half. Tom Nichols opened the scoring on nine minutes for Exeter, who were 76 league places below their illustrious opponents. Sinclair equalised within three minutes, side-footing into the corner after a defensive mistake. On the stroke of half-time, Lee Holmes scored direct from a corner with Bogdan at fault. Smith made it 2-2 when he fired in a rebound after Ojo's cross had only been partially cleared. Brannagan was the pick of the kids. Teixeira and Kent also played well, in stark contrast to Bogdan and Enrique.

A Wednesday night game under the Anfield lights against leaders Arsenal turned out to be a classic. On nine minutes, Petr Cech saved from Can, but Firmino fired in the rebound. Aaron Ramsay equalised five minutes later, beating Mignolet at his near post. The Brazilian scored his second by curling in a beauty from 20 yards, but Olivier Giroud made it 2-2 from a poorly defended corner – all this inside 25 breathless minutes. Firmino grazed the bar. Giroud put the Gunners 3-2 up on 55 minutes. Mignolet, who had just been offered a five-year contract, had another shocker. The Reds' injury crisis had seen a loan move for Steven Caulker, and he made his debut as a late replacement for Lallana, using his huge frame up front. In the driving snow, Allen rescued a point from Benteke's knock-down in injury time. Klopp's celebration was as joyous as that of any Kopite. It was the fourth crucial injury-time goal Liverpool had scored against the Gunners at the Kop end since 2003. Firmino was man of the match. Can and Henderson pushed him close. As well as Caulker, Klopp also picked up the Serbian midfielder Marko Grujic and the Polish goalkeeper Kamil Grabara in the January sales for £5.1 million and £250,000 respectively. Grujic was loaned back to Red Star Belgrade for the rest of the season.

Manchester United were next in town, and they completed another smash-and-grab at Anfield. Benteke was on the bench again – Klopp clearly didn't rate him. Toure, Lucas, Can and Firmino were exceptional, but too many were below par. David de Gea kept out Lallana's header. Firmino put the rebound wide. Henderson dragged his shot wide. De Gea twice saved from Can. Grimly holding on for a point one minute, United then forced a corner. Mignolet failed to take charge. Marouane Fellaini beat Henderson, Toure and Sakho to the header. It crashed off the bar. Wayne Rooney, with United's only shot on target, fired in the rebound. Caulker was sent on up front but to no avail. Firmino spurned a promising opening, as United held on to their 1-0 lead.

Klopp gave the kids another run out in the replay with Exeter. Enrique was captain. Jon Flanagan came on for his first appearance in 619 days. Allen scored first from Smith's cutback. Ibe hit the underside of the bar. The second took a long time to come, but it was worth the wait, as Ojo's curler found the top corner from the right angle of the penalty area. Teixeira wrapped up a 3-0 win. Allen and Ibe were the best players, with Smith, Stewart and Teixeira not far behind.

The craziest game of the season came at Carrow Road as Liverpool edged a nine-goal thriller in injury time. Milner set up Firmino for the opener on 18 minutes, but Norwich, whose chairman was the recent Shadow Chancellor Ed Balls, went into the break 2-1 up after Dieumerci Mbokani's backheel and Steven Naismith's drilled shot. Wes Hoolahan made it 3-1 from the spot after Moreno's senseless foul. Henderson quickly got one back after Firmino's dummy. Lallana replaced Ibe. The Brazilian got his second to make it 3-3 midway through the second half. Milner made it 4-3 with 16 minutes left, capitalising on Russell Martin's woeful backpass. Benteke came on for the ineffective Henderson. The Canaries lumped a long ball forward in injury time, and Sebastien Bassong, the centre half, smashed in a sensational equaliser from 20 yards. Just as it looked like two more points would be tossed away, Can fired in a cross, Caulker, sent on as a striker for the third game in a row, had a shot. After some head tennis, it fell to Lallana, whose first league goal in eight months made it 5-4. Klopp sprinted onto the pitch. His players swarmed all over him, and Benteke broke his glasses in the celebrations. When he had calmed down, he acknowledged his team's problems at the back. "I was an under-average player but if I could do something, it was defend set plays," he said. "It's not that difficult."

The Reds' 14th penalty-shootout success out of 17 saw them advance to the League Cup Final, where they would play Manchester City at Wembley. It was barely deserved, as Stoke won 1-0 after extra time, with numerous Liverpool players playing abysmally. Mignolet made a couple of great saves. Lucas and Sakho played well, as did Benteke as a substitute. But that was about it. Flanagan was handed a start, but his passing was all over the place. The Stoke goal came on the stroke of half-time, as Marko Arnautovic turned in Bojan Krkic's cross in front of the Kop to make it 1-1 on aggregate. Firmino hit a post in the second half, as did Marco van Ginkel in extra time. Stoke went first in the shootout, with Jon Walters scoring. Lallana made it 1-1. Mignolet saved from Peter Crouch. Can hit the post. Glenn Whelan, Benteke, Ibrahim Afellay, Firmino, Xherdan Shaqiri, Milner, van Ginkel and Lucas all scored to force sudden death. Mignolet saved brilliantly from Marc Muniesa. Allen had the responsibility of sending Liverpool to Wembley, and he found the top corner with conviction.

The ninth fixture of a crazy January came in the fourth round of the FA Cup at home to West Ham. Klopp again rested several first-teamers. Brannagan's 25-yarder was tipped around the post by Darren Randolph, who also saved from Teixeira. It ended 0-0. Clyne and Brannagan were the pick of the bunch. The month ended with Liverpool refusing to pay the huge asking price for Shakhtar Donetsk striker Alex Teixeira, who instead went to the Chinese Super League.

Leicester City remained three points clear of Manchester City at the top of the Premier League when they beat Liverpool 2-0 at home. Lallana partnered Firmino in what appeared to be a 4-4-2, but it didn't work. Mignolet denied from Riyad Mahrez in the first half but could do nothing with Jamie Vardy's stunning 30-yarder on the hour mark. Eleven minutes later, the same player made it 2-0. Liverpool hadn't scored in five hours. The Foxes, managed by Claudio Ranieri, priced at 5,000-1 at the beginning of the season, would go on to win the league in one of English football's most incredible stories.

All season, the new Main Stand was being built behind the existing structure. It was due to be opened in September. When the club announced that some tickets would cost £77, it was decided that fans would stage a walk-out in the 77th minute of the next home match with Sunderland by way of protest. Black flags were flown on the Kop. The fans chanted, "You greedy bastards, enough is enough!" The Reds were 2-0 up when the walkout began, but then, in front of a half-empty stadium, they conceded two late goals. Nevertheless, the point had been made to the owners, who performed a swift U-turn. Klopp was absent, hospitalised after having his appendix removed. Lovren lasted 12 minutes before injury struck. The lively Allen felt his hamstring go and was replaced by Ibe at the break. It took Liverpool nearly an hour to break through, when Milner's inch-perfect cross set up a headed goal for Firmino. Ten minutes later, Lallana doubled the lead from Firmino's pass after the Brazilian's pressing had regained the ball. After a difficult four months, Firmino was now showing what he could do, and he was Liverpool's best player again. But in the last ten minutes, Simon Mignolet allowed Adam Johnson's unconvincing free kick to beat him. It was the last game the winger would play before his imprisonment for sexual offences involving minors. With Sakho turned too easily, Jermain Defoe equalised for Sam Allardyce's team in the 89th minute. "Liverpool suffer humiliating defeat – by their own fans," reported The Times. Defoe was very generous to the protesting fans, saying, "What can you say about the fans here? I've never played for this club, but the fans are fantastic."

Coutinho made a goalscoring return to action in the cup replay at Upton Park, but the Reds lost 2-1. Klopp was also back. Michail Antonio scored just before the interval for the Hammers. Having earlier hit a post, Coutinho threaded a low free kick through the wall three minutes into the second half. Sturridge returned after a two-month lay-off and looked sharp, but in the last minute of extra time, Liverpool's hopes of emulating the 2001 treble were ended by Angelo Ogbonna's towering header. It was a credible performance and they didn't deserve to lose. Lucas was commanding at centre back. Stewart held the midfield superbly. Pedro Chirivella and Flanagan also caught the eye.

After five games without a win, Liverpool annihilated Aston Villa on their own ground. Even Toure scored. It was that sort of afternoon. Sturridge headed the opener. Milner's wide free kick went straight in. The fantastic Can made it three from 20 yards just before the hour. The returning Origi scored a minute after coming on. Clyne made it five with his first league goal, and Toure sparked scenes of joy when he headed his first Liverpool goal on 71 minutes. The Reds had scored four in 13 minutes. Villa, who had been such a bogey team in the last ten years, were heading for the drop.

A trip to Germany to play Augsburg in the last 32 of the Europa League was Liverpool's 24th fixture in just under 13 weeks – an introduction to English football that Klopp will never forget. Finally, after this game, there would be seven days until the next outing. A goalless draw in the WWK Arena made Liverpool clear favourites to progress. Ragnar Klavan, the vastly experienced Estonian, was in the Augsburg side. The struggling Sturridge missed Liverpool's best chance from Milner's cross. Ji Dong-Won hit the post for the hosts.

Milner's fifth-minute penalty, which followed a needless handball, settled the tie seven days later in a 6pm kick-off at Anfield. Sturridge blew a great opportunity to seal the tie. The failure to get another meant a nervy ending, and a 90th-minute free kick from Kostas Stafylidis went just wide. Liverpool would play Manchester United in the last 16.

The 2016 League Cup Final was Liverpool's first visit to the national stadium in four years. The opponents were Manchester City. It was the first time the clubs had met in a major final. The team was: Mignolet; Clyne, Lucas, Sakho, Moreno; Henderson, Can, Milner; Coutinho, Firmino, Sturridge. Faced with Sergio Aguero, Lucas was dominant at the back. But Liverpool's defensive problems increased when Sakho departed injured on 25 minutes, replaced by Toure. Mignolet saved from Aguero in the first half but made a hash of Fernandinho's shot from a tight angle, and it squirmed into the net. John W Henry looked furious. But Mignolet made up for it as City couldn't put the game to bed. Moreno was lucky not to concede a penalty and be sent off. With seven minutes left, Lallana hit the post, and Coutinho tucked away the rebound. It was the only positive from the front three all afternoon. Mignolet saved brilliantly from Aguero again in extra time. Willy Caballero saved Origi's header from point-blank range in the second period. For the third time in the competition, Liverpool faced penalties. Can's nerveless Panenka fooled Caballero. Fernandinho hit the post. Caballero saved from Lucas. Mignolet got a hand to Jesus Navas' penalty but couldn't keep it out. Coutinho's weak effort was saved. Aguero scored. Caballero made his third save, this time from Lallana. Yaya Toure found the corner to win the cup for City.

And just as in 2012, Liverpool thrashed their Wembley conquerors three days later in a league game at Anfield. With rumours of a clear-out in the summer, the players responded tremendously, pressing City like Alsatians. Lovren returned. Flanagan was promoted from the bench. Both played their part in a superb defensive performance. Hart couldn't keep out a 20-yarder hit into the bottom corner by the imperious Lallana. Milner made it two from Firmino's pass. On his first return to L4, Raheem Sterling was barracked mercilessly by the crowd. He was withdrawn at the break, having been outplayed by Flanagan. He hadn't got much change out of Clyne at Wembley, either. Early in the second half, Firmino side-footed Lallana's pass beyond Joe Hart. Allen was close to a fourth with a dipping volley. Liverpool were eighth, 16 points behind Leicester with a game in hand. Defeat had probably ended City's title chances.

When a lethargic Liverpool were a goal down and a man down at Selhurst Park, the Crystal Palace jinx looked likely to strike again. Henderson, Milner and Lallana had laboured. But Klopp responded to the dismissal of Milner by withdrawing Flanagan for Coutinho. The Reds looked a different team and went forward without inhibition. Alex McCarthy's comical faux pas allowed Firmino to equalise. And then, deep in injury time, Benteke was clipped in the box and calmly rolled in the winning goal from the spot. It was Liverpool's first Premier League win at Selhurst since 1997. Mignolet, Lovren, Can and Coutinho excelled.

Liverpool and Manchester United met in European competition for the first time, and amid a typically rousing atmosphere, the Reds won the first leg on home soil 2-0. It should have been a lot more, but David de Gea made several spectacular saves. United's Marcus Rashford wasted a chance in the opening minute. It was their only threat. Memphis Depay tripped Clyne in the box on 20 minutes. Sturridge's emphatic penalty made it 1-0. De Gea somehow saved from Coutinho. Then he blocked Sturridge's shot from close range. United's only first-half tactic had been pumping long balls in the vague direction of Marouane Fellaini. They were better after the break, but it was still Liverpool creating the chances. Klopp sent on Allen for Sturridge. The Welshman was superb. De Gea tipped over Coutinho's dipping volley in the second half. A ferocious shot from Clyne was turned away. Henderson missed a great chance. Firmino, who vied for man-of-the-match honours with Lallana, poked in a second on 73 minutes to give the score some reality. Sakho also played well, with Joey Barton tweeting that he was, "the most unorthodox, efficient, unbalanced, effective defender on the Planet. Watching him is similar to viewing a clown spin plates. You are just waiting for them to smash on the floor. Yet, somehow he keeps it going."

Liverpool's FA Cup exit gave them the weekend off to prepare for the second leg. Milner replaced the injured Moreno. Firmino played behind Sturridge in a 4-4-1-1 formation. Allen was back on the bench. Mignolet's reflexes were tested when he pushed away Jesse Lingard's header. De Gea kept out Coutinho's low drive. Clyne brought down Anthony Martial, who sent Mignolet the wrong way from the spot on 32 minutes. Sturridge hit the bar with an audacious free kick from wide. And then came the moment that killed the tie. Coutinho, who had started slowly, was released down the left in the last minute of the half. He stood up the young right back Guillermo Varela, waltzed around him and then lifted the ball over de Gea from close range with sangfroid aplenty. The away goal meant United needed three. They didn't come close to getting one, as Klopp's men took the sting out of the game. Fellaini should have been sent off for elbowing Lovren. Coutinho almost got his second. By that time, Old Trafford was half empty. Sakho produced one of his best performances in a Liverpool shirt. Lovren was just as good. Four United fans were subsequently imprisoned for violent behaviour.

Plenty had been seen of Dr Jekyll in a most encouraging month, but with this Liverpool side, there was always a chance Mr Hyde would put in an unwelcome appearance. The Reds were 2-0 up and coasting at Southampton. Then they capitulated. With Henderson benched and Milner suspended, Flanagan was a surprising choice as captain, soon after signing a three-year extension. Firmino was absent with a hamstring concern. Coutinho scored magnificently from nearly 30 yards. On a rapid counter, Origi set up Sturridge for the second on 22 minutes. Allen spurned a one-on-one. It could have been four- or five-nil at the break, but the game was changed by two half-time substitutes - Skrtel and a certain Sadio Mane. Skrtel's clumsy challenge on Graziano Pelle saw a penalty awarded, but Mignolet saved from Mane. The Senegalese made amends by halving the deficit with an unstoppable shot across Mignolet. Substitute Benteke was sent clear by Lallana but dragged his shot wide. Pelle equalised from the edge of the box with seven minutes left. Feeling the pressure, Mignolet sliced a clearance. The Saints launched another attack, and Mane hammered the ball into the corner to score his fourth goal of the season against the Reds. Cliché or not, it had been the archetypal game of two halves.

There was a fortnight to get things right before the visit of title-chasing Spurs at the beginning of an eight-match April. Coutinho made it 1-0 after a one-two with Sturridge. Kane turned Lovren and fired across Mignolet into the corner. Lovren and Coutinho were the best players again. Sakho was all over the place – according to 'The Anfield Wrap', he "lost a 50-50 with himself". Can wasn't at the races. Neither side could force a winner, meaning Tottenham had won just four league matches at Anfield since 1912. The Reds were ninth, 21 points behind Leicester and nine points off the top four with a game in hand.

Europa League progress clearly wasn't going to be done the easy way as, having seen off Manchester United, Liverpool were paired with Borussia Dortmund, Klopp's last club. The Reds were excellent in Germany, much better than they had been against Augsburg, and led at half-time through the impressive Origi. Roman Weidenfeller prevented the Belgian from making it two. A languid Henderson retired with a knee injury at half-time, replaced by Allen. The skipper would barely be seen again in the campaign. Former Red Nuri Sahin came on for Dortmund. Mats Hummels headed the equaliser from a Marco Reus cross early in the second half. Origi and Coutinho came close to a winner. It ended 1-1. Lovren, Sakho, Can and Origi were instrumental in an impressive result for the Reds.

Klopp fielded Skrtel, Stewart and Ojo for the visit of Stoke, choosing to rest Sakho, Lovren, Coutinho and Lallana ahead of the second leg. Moreno made it 1-0 with a 20-yard stunner. Bojan Krkic glanced in Xherdan Shaqiri's inswinger to score Stoke's first league goal at Anfield since 1983. Sturridge restored

Liverpool's lead from Ojo's wonderful cross before a classy second-half brace from the in-form Origi, on as a sub, made it 4-1. Klopp singled out Sturridge for post-match praise. Along with Moreno, Allen and Origi, he was in top form.

The second leg against Borussia Dortmund was hugely anticipated. Could Klopp get the better of his successor Thomas Tuchel? Would the Kop outshine the Yellow Wall? Could Liverpool defeat a genuinely top team when it mattered? Klopp had rested a few for Stoke, but Dortmund had made eight changes for their 2-2 draw with Schalke. After a silence and a mosaic for the 96, Henrikh Mkhitaryan cancelled out Liverpool's away goal in the fifth minute. Pierre-Emerick Aubameyang quickly made it two. Suddenly, Liverpool needed three. The Reds got to half-time with no further damage done.

Klopp told the players to "create a moment you can tell your grandchildren about." And they did just that. Three minutes later, Can played a couple of one-twos and then freed Origi with a perfectly weighted pass. The Belgian calmly slid the ball past Weidenfeller. But Reus seemed to put the tie to bed when he curled the ball into Mignolet's bottom corner. The Reds needed three goals in 33 minutes to reach the semi-finals. Allen and Sturridge provided fresh legs, replacing Lallana and Firmino, Liverpool's best pressers. But Coutinho was still out there, and after a one-two with Milner he bent the ball perfectly into the corner from the edge of the 'D'. Twelve minutes remained when Coutinho's badly-hit corner somehow found its way into the six-yard box, and Sakho stooped to head his first goal in nearly two and a half years. Klopp celebrated provocatively in front of the Dortmund bench. The crowd was getting louder. Lucas came on for Can. In the first of four added minutes, Milner played a free kick down the line to Sturridge. He mis-controlled. Then he showed his composure to thread a lovely ball into Milner in the inside-right channel. The number seven sent over the most inviting cross to the back post. Lovren jumped from the six-yard line and powered his header goalward. The net bulged. The roof almost came off the Kop. It was 4-3. Ilkay Gundogan lined up a free kick, and with the last kick of the game, he sent it half a yard wide. Liverpool were in the semi-finals of a European competition for the first time in eight years. It may not have been the Champions League, but this logic-defying evening signalled that Liverpool were back as a major European force.

A trip to Dean Court was somewhat anti-climactic after Dortmund. Klopp took the chance to rest several regulars. In came Danny Ward for his debut. Toure, Smith, Randall, Ibe, Stewart and Ojo also started. Four minutes before half-time, Sturridge's backheel was parried by Artur Boruc, and Firmino turned the ball home. Sturridge headed in Ibe's free kick. He hit the post twice in the second half. He then tried to lob Boruc from his own half. Bournemouth did get one back.

Next up was the Anfield Derby, the 17th in a row Everton failed to win. It was a procession. Liverpool destroyed their neighbours with a performance of magisterial proportions, especially after the break. The game was open for 20 minutes, with both sides getting forward. Lallana went clean through after five minutes. He chose not to give Firmino a tap-in, and his shot was saved by Joel Robles. Sakho's tackle prevented Romelu Lukaku pulling the trigger. Liverpool began to take control as the half went on, and Origi headed in Milner's deep cross at the back post. It was his fifth goal in five games. Milner put another on a plate for Sakho just before the break. It was a deserved lead, but how Liverpool only scored two in a one-sided second half remains a mystery. Funes Mori badly injured Origi's ankle with a vicious and cowardly stamp and then gestured towards the badge on his shirt when dismissed. It was the 21st red card in a Premier League derby, and Everton's 14th. Sturridge replaced Origi, and within eight minutes, he was played in by Lucas and found the corner of the net. Coutinho made it four with a brilliant low drive from just outside the box. The shots continued to rain in, but there were no more goals. The Reds had 41 attempts to the Blues' three, with 15 on target to none. They should have won by more.

Sakho was named man of the match in several newspapers, but then came the bombshell that he had taken a drug test after the second leg of the Europa League tie at Old Trafford and had tested positive for a banned substance. Liverpool agreed to stand him down from first-team selection while an investigation was carried out. His season was over. He also missed out on playing for France in the European Championships. It later transpired that he had only taken a fat-burning pill which wasn't on the banned-substance list – it was UEFA's error to suggest it was. His mistake was not telling the club he had taken it, and that was the beginning of the end of his relationship with Klopp.

Rafa Benitez was back at Anfield, for the second time since his 2010 exit, with Newcastle towards the end of April. He had just taken over from Steve McClaren and was immediately in the teeth of a relegation fight. Sturridge turned on the edge of the box and found the corner after 76 seconds. From virtually the same blade of grass, Lallana made it 2-0 with an exquisite curler into the top corner. It was Liverpool's 14th goal from outside the box – the most in the Premier League. Man of the match Moreno set up both goals, but when Mignolet missed a cross, Papiss Cisse got one back. Jack Colback made it 2-2 midway through the second half, with Mignolet wrongfooted. Liverpool's top-four hopes were all but gone.

Finally, after a two-year inquest into Hillsborough, a jury in Warrington returned their verdict that the 96 had been unlawfully killed and that the supporters were completely blame free. The news came 11 days after the 27th anniversary. How could it have taken so many years for the lies to be corrected? The real truth was now known. The pursuit would now be for accountability. "They didn't expect this fight," wrote Karl Coppack on 'The Anfield Wrap' website. "They didn't expect this level of emotional stamina nor did they expect the families to get off the canvas time and again. But they did. The police and media hurled accusation at grief to reduce their fight to nothing and they still came back. They expected that fight to die. It did not." As for how the police and the government got away with their lies, Tony Barrett used the same website to blame the media. "If there is a more damning indictment of my industry, I cannot think of one," he wrote. "With obvious honourable exceptions – the peerless Brian Reade and David Conn in particular – journalists in this country failed the Hillsborough families."

The Europa League semi-final took Liverpool to Spain, where they would play Villarreal in the first leg. Sturridge was on the bench, despite his recent form. Coutinho and Lallana played either side of Firmino. Allen failed to convert an early chance. Lucas went close. At the other end, Clyne and Moreno were struggling against Denis Suarez and Jonathan Dos Santos, the Villarreal wingers. At half-time, Ibe replaced Coutinho, who was ill. Cedric Bakambu hit a post. Firmino also hit the woodwork. The game was even. In the closing stages, Mignolet saved from Bakambu. Moreno broke away from the resulting corner, but his shot was wayward. The only goal came two minutes into injury time. With Moreno out of position, Suarez got down the right and set up Adrian Lopez for the only goal of the game. Liverpool had come so close to an excellent result. Allen and Lovren were the best players.

The fringe players got another go at Swansea, but this time they were comfortably beaten. Liverpool only had six substitutes after Randall was sent home with a virus. Andre Ayew headed in a corner. Jack Cork made it 2-0 before half-time. Benteke nodded in Ojo's corner just after the hour, but Ayew soon squeezed in his second. Smith was sent off for two yellow cards. Ward was probably Liverpool's best player, despite conceding three.

The sheer magnificence of the Dortmund win meant the second leg of the Villarreal semi isn't remembered how it should be. The Reds set about the Spaniards and beat them comfortably. Sturridge was selected to start, supported by Coutinho, Firmino and Lallana in a 4-2-3-1. There were no other surprises. Liverpool started with intent, although Mignolet was required to make a crucial save. The breakthrough came quickly. Alphonse Areola missed Clyne's low cross. Firmino sent it back into the six-yard box where Bruno Soriano turned it into the Kop goal. It was 1-1 on aggregate – but if they conceded, the Reds would need two more. There were no more goals in the half. At half-time, the travelling fans held aloft a yellow flag adorned with '96', for which Liverpool's fans showed their appreciation.

The score remained unchanged for nearly an hour, until Sturridge took Firmino's pass and knocked it past the keeper and into the net via the post. Toure made some telling interceptions. Firmino's trickery on the left wing took the breath away. Moreno's shot was off target. Victor Ruiz collected a second yellow card for fouling Lallana. There were hearts in mouths when Denis Suarez went down in the box after Moreno seemed to push him. No penalty. Lallana settled the tie from close range, turning the ball past Areola after Sturridge scuffed his shot. Klopp withdrew Sturridge and Firmino, who took the acclaim of the crowd for their virtuoso performances. Toure, Lovren, Can, Lallana and Milner were also exceptional in a fantastic team performance. The Reds were in their fourth final in this competition, where they would play Sevilla in Basel. They had won their previous three finals in 1973, 1976 and 2001.

There were three meaningless league matches to play before the final, starting with Watford at Anfield, although some at the club may have had eyes on seventh place, which would mean qualification for the Europa League should they lose to Sevilla. Allen turned in Benteke's knockdown for the first. Mignolet saved superbly from Troy Deeney. Firmino scored from the edge of the box for 2-0.

The final home game of the season saw the visit of Guus Hiddink's Chelsea, who had recovered after sacking Mourinho. Liverpool started brightly in Klopp's 50th game as manager, but Eden Hazard scored a stupendous goal at the Kop end. Mignolet kept Liverpool in the game with numerous saves. Just as the Reds looked like coming up empty, Benteke scored his tenth of the season in injury time from Ojo's cross.

The Premier League season was wrapped up with a 1-1 draw at The Hawthorns. Ings and Henderson made comebacks from injury in the 64th minute, although it was unlikely either would play against Sevilla. Salomon Rondon beat Bogdan at his near post in the 13th minute. Ibe scored a quite brilliant goal, as he ran from his own half, bore down on goal, cut inside and fired past the keeper. Liverpool finished in eighth, six points from Manchester City in fourth and 21 behind champions Leicester City. They conceded a whopping 50 goals, scoring just 63 in the process.

The 2016 Europa League decider was Liverpool's 12th European final. Klopp fielded the following side in a 4-2-3-1 formation: Mignolet; Clyne, Toure, Lovren, Moreno; Milner, Can; Lallana, Firmino, Coutinho; Sturridge. Having beaten La Liga's fourth best team, Villarreal, in the semi-final, the Reds were favourites to beat Sevilla, who had just finished seventh, although they had won the Europa League two years in a row. Liverpool started nervously but soon settled. Can's shot from 25 yards was pushed away by David Soria. Sturridge's 11th-minute header from Clyne's cross was hooked off the line. Firmino should have had a penalty when Daniel Carrico handballed. And then in the 35th minute, Sturridge scored one of Liverpool's finest European goals, taking Coutinho's pass and curling the ball into the far corner with the outside of his left foot, before doing his trademark dance in celebration. Lovren's header was disallowed a couple of minutes later because Sturridge tried to get a touch from an offside position. Liverpool were on top and looked like getting a second. Clyne's cross flashed across goal. Another penalty appeal for handball was turned down, leaving Sturridge enraged. Sevilla held out. Liverpool should have been further ahead. Lallana and skipper Milner had been exceptional.

And then they wilted when it mattered most. With the beautiful old trophy and a Champions League place up for grabs, the Reds collapsed. An awful defensive header by Moreno allowed Sevilla in down their right. He was then nutmegged, and Kevin Gameiro turned in the equaliser. The goal knocked the stuffing out of Liverpool. Toure made a crucial goal-saving tackle. Mignolet saved at point blank from Gameiro. The dam would soon break. A clinical finish from Coke made it 2-1. Sevilla were rampant. Origi replaced Firmino, but within a minute, the same player made it 3-1 with Moreno out of position. "Sign a fucking left back," tweeted Jamie Carragher, although he later deleted it. In truth, the Spaniard hadn't been too bad since Klopp's arrival, but few were surprised when the mistakes came. Klopp threw on Allen for Lallana and Benteke for Toure, Liverpool's best player, but to no avail. The midfield had been overrun. With so many injuries and having played 63 fixtures, Liverpool had hit the wall. Can was in tears at the end. Liverpool's performance summed up their season – fabulous in spells, indescribably bad at other times. But as he moved into his first pre-season as Liverpool manager, Klopp would have known he had an abundance of potential to tap into.

2016-17

"It's unbelievable how Liverpool move, how they stand, how they work together. It's like a symphony."

The disappointment of losing the Europa League Final was quickly forgotten for one simple reason - Jurgen Klopp was the manager of Liverpool Football Club. Despite finishing eighth, losing two cup finals and not qualifying for Europe, it was abundantly clear that the Reds would be going places under the gregarious German.

As in the previous summer, three players were signed who would go on to become European Cup and Premier League winners – Sadio Mane, Joel Matip and Gini Wijnaldum. Mane, who had scored four times in three games for Southampton against Liverpool, cost £30 million. Cameroonian centre back Matip came on a Bosman from the Bundesliga side Schalke. Wijnaldum cost £25 million from relegated Newcastle. He was a versatile midfielder, particularly adept at getting forward, as Liverpool had discovered in December. Klopp and the transfer committee seemed to be on the same wavelength, more so than Brendan Rodgers had been.

Klopp also signed the goalkeepers Loris Karius (£4.75 million from Mainz) and Alex Manninger (on a free). The 100-cap veteran of Estonian football, Ragnar Klavan, who had played for Augsburg against the Reds, also joined. But to the disappointment of many, in light of Alberto Moreno's performance in Basel, there was no new left back, despite links with the German Jonas Hector. James Milner would fill the role for much of the 2016-17 campaign. Other reported targets like Mario Gotze, Piotr Zielinski, Ben Chilwell and Marc-Andre ter Stegen didn't sign. World champion Gotze would have joined if Liverpool had qualified for the Champions League. It would prove to be his loss.

Out went a lengthy list of players headed by Christian Benteke, for whom Liverpool received £32 million from Crystal Palace. Sergi Canos went to Norwich for £4.5 million. Fenerbahce paid £5.5 million for Martin Skrtel. Bournemouth paid an astonishing £21 million for Jordon Ibe and Brad Smith. Joe Allen went to Stoke for £13 million. Luis Alberto signed for Lazio for £6 million. Tiago Ilori would head to Reading in January for £3.75 million. In total, over 20 players left the club, including Jose Enrique, Kolo Toure, Jordan Rossiter, Joao Carlos Teixeira, Jerome Sinclair, Samed Yesil and Mario Balotelli on free transfers. Jon Flanagan was loaned to Burnley. Mamadou Sakho was being frozen out. Having been exonerated at the end of the season over the failed drug test, he then irritated Klopp on a pre-season of America with poor timekeeping and other disciplinary issues. He was sent home early and banished from the first team. He would eventually be loaned to Crystal Palace in January. In all, the club raised over £80 million without losing a player that would have featured regularly. The days of Liverpool being walked all over in the transfer market appeared over.

The erection of Anfield's new Main Stand meant the first three games of Liverpool's 125th season would be away from home, as the final touches were applied. Older fans remembered that the first three matches of the great 1987-88 campaign had also been on the road after a sewer on the Kop had collapsed. To excite the omen-believers further, both seasons began with a trip to Arsenal. On this occasion, the Reds were tremendous, building up a 4-1 lead with some breathtaking football before hanging on grimly to win a chaotic game 4-3. It was reminiscent of 2013-14, when defensive vulnerability was compensated by world-class firepower at the other end. Wearing a natty black away kit, the opening-day team was: Simon Mignolet; Nathaniel Clyne, Dejan Lovren, Klavan, Moreno; Jordan Henderson, Wijnaldum, Adam Lallana; Philippe Coutinho, Roberto Firmino, Mane. Emre Can, Divock Origi and Kevin Stewart came off the bench. Manninger, Matip, Trent Alexander-Arnold and Marko Grujic weren't used. James Milner had been injured in a 4-0 pre-season win over Barcelona at Wembley. Karius, Joe Gomez and Daniel Sturridge were also crocked.

For the second time in four seasons, Mignolet saved an opening-day penalty, this time from Theo Walcott in the 29th minute after a rash tackle by Moreno. Walcott made amends by scoring two minutes later, capitalising on Moreno being out of position. It was deserved on the balance of play, but in the dying embers of the half, Coutinho curled a sensational free kick into the top corner of Petr Cech's net from 25 yards. What a player the young Brazilian was turning into. He kissed his wrist, Suarez-style. The goal didn't just cancel out 45 minutes of Arsenal outplaying Liverpool, but it broke the Gunners, who shipped in three goals in the first 18 minutes of the second half. Liverpool's narrow front three exploited Calum Chambers and Rob Holding, Arsenal's inexperienced centre halves. Lallana made it 2-1, chesting Wijnaldum's pass and firing through Cech's legs. Clyne set up Coutinho to complete a scintillating passage of passing. Cech denied Coutinho a hat trick. Hector Bellerin's tackle stopped Lallana knocking in the rebound. And then Mane scored the sort of debut goal that wouldn't have looked out of place in a Boys' Own annual. He went down the right, beat two defenders by cutting inside and unleashed the perfect curler into the top corner. He ran to the manager and jumped on his back in celebration. Liverpool were 4-1 up and running rings around Arsenal, but it took a minute for the sobering reality of the Reds' defensive issues to hit home. Alex Oxlade-Chamberlain beat Clyne, Lallana and Henderson and fired a deflected shot past Mignolet. On came Can for Coutinho. Eleven minutes later, Chambers glanced in a wide free kick. 4-3. Fifteen minutes left. Reds fans were left watching through the cracks in their fingers. The final whistle brought palpable relief. One down, 37 to go.

Then came the sort of expectation-lowering early-season defeat that Liverpool had experienced too many times down the years. They were often at the hands of Aston Villa. It had been West Ham a year earlier. This one was at newly-promoted Burnley. Maybe it was a claret-and-blue thing. In a fluorescent lime green kit, Liverpool had 81% of the possession, 12 corners and 26 shots. They lost 2-0. Burnley's 19% of possession was the lowest recorded by a winning side since Opta had started producing such statistics in 2003. This was the game that should have been at Anfield but was switched. Sturridge came in for the injured Mane. Milner replaced Moreno. Clyne gave the ball away, and Sam Vokes scored in the second minute. Liverpool never looked like equalising and were reduced to potshots from distance. Andre Gray made it two before half-time, with Klavan at fault. The second half was painful. Grujic debuted as a late sub and forced a save from Tom Heaton. Numerous players were dire: Klavan, Milner, Henderson, Sturridge and Firmino. Liverpool couldn't have been sent crashing down to earth more abruptly.

The League Cup took Liverpool to Burton Albion, who were managed by Nigel Clough. Despite a game at Spurs four days later, Klopp fielded his strongest side, including debutant Matip, and was rewarded with a 5-0 win, with goals from Origi, Firmino, Tom Naylor (an own goal) and a late brace from Sturridge. Mane provided a couple of assists in his second game for the club. Origi limped off late in the game to leave Liverpool with ten men.

Back in the league, the Reds drew 1-1 at White Hart Lane. They were the better side before the break, and when Erik Lamela fouled Firmino, Milner gave them a deserved lead from the spot. Matip, looking comfortable on his first league start, hit the bar in the second half. Mane had a goal disallowed for offside. He was clearly going to be some player. Mignolet saved impressively from Toby Alderweireld but was beaten when Danny Rose fired home Eric Dier's cross. Liverpool were denied a late penalty for handball against Alderweireld.

The new £115 million Main Stand was in use for the first time as Liverpool welcomed the champions Leicester City to Anfield on 10th September. The crowd of 53,075 was the largest at Anfield since May 1977, when 55,675 had attended a match against West Ham. The Liverpool Echo concluded, "One man who undoubtedly has the talent to make that leap if he stays around is Firmino." They weren't wrong. The Brazilian was magnificent. Lovren had a head injury, so Lucas played alongside Matip. With Sakho out of favour, Toure gone and no new left back, the Reds had little depth at the back. Sturridge earned another start. After a slightly nervy start, the Reds took the lead after 12 minutes, when Firmino took Milner's cross away from Robert Huth and beat Kasper Schmeichel. The second was exquisite, as Sturridge's backheel put a goal on a plate for Mane. But Lucas's lapse gave Vardy an easy goal. The 29-year-old, who five times in the last six seasons had been the Premier League's top tackler, didn't let it affect him and finished the game strongly. Lallana crashed in a superb third in front of the Kop. Mignolet saved from Vardy. Henderson blazed into the Kop. The skipper was otherwise exceptional and had a hand in the fourth when he released Mane, who went past Schmeichel 40 yards from goal and squared to Firmino to make it 4-1. The atmosphere was noticeably improved, and there was a hope that would continue to be the case with the new stand. The Anfield Wrap's Ben Johnson described the old Main Stand as "a collective drain on the atmosphere and the team."

When Liverpool won a Friday night fixture at Chelsea, there was a genuine belief that Klopp's men could challenge for the title. With Firmino injured, Sturridge led the line in a 4-2-3-1, with Lallana at number 10 and Mane and Coutinho wide. The four of them interchanged so effectively. Lovren volleyed the Reds into the lead in the 17th minute after Chelsea left four men unmarked at the back post. Later in the half, Henderson, who hadn't scored in 24 games, went for goal, somewhat ambitiously from over 25 yards. As the ball carved its passage through the air, that split second of realisation that it was going to beat Thibaut Courtois and fly into the top corner was a wonderful feeling. Liverpool were two up at Stamford Bridge. Chelsea, now managed by Antonio Conte, got one back on the hour through Diego Costa. Origi, on for Sturridge, had a point-blank header saved by Courtois. Lucas replaced Coutinho to strengthen the midfield. Stewart made his fourth league appearance of the season, all of them as a late sub. Clyne kept Eden Hazard quiet. Lovren, Lallana and Henderson were excellent. Lucas conceded his customary late free kick, but Cesc Fabregas hit the wall. Liverpool had held out for a win that was a significant statement of intent.

The next stop on the League Cup journey was Derby, in a game that saw debuts for Karius, who had broken a hand in pre-season, and the talented young winger Ovie Ejaria. There was a first start for Grujic and some valuable minutes for the returning Danny Ings. An almost full-strength 11 won the game 3-0, with the goals by Klavan, Coutinho and Origi. Ings came on for the last 27 minutes. Ejaria, also recovering from injury, played for 13.

Back in the league, the Reds thrashed Hull City 5-1 with a masterclass in gegenpressing. Goals by Lallana, Milner (penalty) and Mane made it 3-0 at the break. Ahmed Elmohamady had been sent off for his part in the penalty incident. David Meyler pulled one back. Coutinho immediately restored the three-goal cushion with a stunning 25-yarder. Another penalty from Milner, after Sturridge was fouled, wrapped up a great afternoon. Each of the scorers enjoyed exceptional games, as did Matip and Henderson. The result improved Klopp's mood, after Sakho had sent a Snapchat message at 3:05am airing his frustrations at not being considered for selection.

On the first day of October, Liverpool showed in South Wales that they weren't going to pick up points just by thrashing teams. Their character would be just as important. Having gone 1-0 down to an early goal by Swansea's Leroy Fer, they were struggling. Borja Baston had failed with two headed opportunities. Karius looked nervous with crosses and hadn't made a save of any real note since he came into the team. Lallana departed midway through the first half, replaced by Sturridge. The Reds created little before the break, with Wijnaldum and Milner struggling. Then they woke up. "Big credit to the manager," reflected Milner. "He was angry [at half-time] but he kept most of it in, said the right things, and got us going." A rejuvenated Henderson lobbed the ball back into the box for Firmino to head the equaliser on 54 minutes. With the full-time whistle six minutes away, the Brazilian was fouled in the box by Angel Rangel. Milner chipped the penalty down the middle for the three points. It was the final game of Klopp's first 12 months as Liverpool manager.

Manchester United had been negative enough under Louis van Gaal, but now Jose Mourinho was in charge, it was no surprise they parked the bus and played for a 0-0 at Anfield. Unfortunately, they were successful, courtesy of David de Gea having his customary blinder against Liverpool, denying Coutinho and Can. Liverpool improved after a dull first half, especially when the returning Lallana replaced the ineffective Sturridge. Antonio Valencia made a crucial tackle on Firmino when it looked like he was clean through. Henderson, Can and Mane also failed to make an impression. United pressed the Liverpool fullbacks, restricting their ability to bomb forward. An anxious crowd didn't help.

Liverpool dominated their home fixture with West Brom, having 21 shots to six. They took a deserved 2-0 lead into the break, but the concession of another set-piece goal late in the game resulted in another nervy finish. The goals were superb. For the first, Coutinho dummied, Firmino crossed and Mane found the corner of Ben Foster's net. Mane then found Coutinho, who feigned to shoot, cut inside and made it 2-0. Several chances were spurned before Gareth McAuley got one back with ten minutes left from a corner. West Brom couldn't force an equaliser.

Trent Alexander-Arnold made his Liverpool debut in the fourth round of the League Cup at home to a second-string Tottenham at Anfield. Having played strong teams against Burton and Derby, Klopp fielded a weaker side this time, with Klavan, Stewart, Grujic and Ejaria also starting. A lively Sturridge got the opener inside ten minutes. Origi forced a brilliant save from 25 yards. Sturridge doubled the lead midway through the second half. Spurs converted a late penalty after a foul by Lucas. Sturridge hit the bar. Ings spurned a late chance. He picked up another injury and would miss the rest of the season, which was devastating news for such a popular member of the squad. According to The Guardian, Alexander-Arnold "impressed with his awareness, strength and athleticism." He played for 67 minutes before being replaced by Clyne.

Both centre backs scored in a 4-2 win at Selhurst Park. Can opened the scoring from Moreno's pass. James McArthur levelled after a catastrophic error by Lovren. The Croat made amends by heading Liverpool back into the lead from Coutinho's corner, only for McArthur to equalise again. Matip, who kept Christian Benteke quiet all game, made it 3-2 just before half-time from another corner by the Brazilian. The clincher came from Firmino, as he latched onto Henderson's through ball and clipped the ball over Steve Mandanda. He peeled his shirt off in celebration before the ball had even crossed the line.

The run continued with a 6-1 dismantling of in-form Watford. Mane headed

Coutinho's cross inside the far post with incredible agility. It was virtually identical to Luis Garcia's magical header against Anderlecht in 2006. Coutinho hammered in a low shot from 20 yards. When Can headed in Lallana's cross, the Reds were three up at the break. Firmino tapped in the fourth. Mane made it five. The Hornets pulled one back to deny Liverpool their second clean sheet in 11 games. Sturridge hit the bar twice after replacing the excellent Lallana. Wijnaldum put the cherry on the cake in injury time, following up after Costel Pantilimon parried Sturridge's shot. For the first time since May 2014, the Reds were clear at the top of the Premier League, having scored 30 times in 11 matches.

After an international break, Liverpool's second goalless draw of the season came at St Mary's, where they couldn't break down a Southampton defence that included Virgil van Dijk. Fraser Forster denied Mane. Charlie Austin headed wide for the Saints. Forster kept out Firmino's shot. Clyne headed a late chance wide. Southampton midfielder Pierre-Emile Hojbjerg rated Liverpool better than Bayern Munich and Manchester City. "It's unbelievable how they move, how they stand, how they work together," he said. "It's like a symphony." Can struggled to get into the game. The standout players of the afternoon were Matip and Van Dijk, with whom Liverpool were linked after the game.

It took Liverpool 75 minutes to break down stubborn Sunderland at Anfield in the last week of November, in a game perhaps best remembered for Karius putting a goal kick straight out of play for a Sunderland corner. It was Origi who made the breakthrough. He received the ball on the left wing, shifted it onto his right foot and aimed a shot just inside the far post that Jordan Pickford couldn't do anything about. Sunderland manager David Moyes called it a fluke, but had he done his homework, he would have seen Origi score an identical goal against Stoke in April. Mane, who came alive late in the game, won an injury-time penalty, which Milner converted. But Coutinho injured an ankle and would sit out nine matches. Liverpool were now second, a point behind Chelsea, who would stay top for the rest of the campaign.

Leeds United came to Anfield in the fifth round of the League Cup. Liverpool Echo man of the match Alexander-Arnold collected the first of many assists. But it was 17-year-old Ben Woodburn who stole the show by becoming the club's youngest goalscorer. Leeds' Kemar Roofe and Wijnaldum struck woodwork. Origi then broke the deadlock, this time on 76 minutes, as he finished Alexander-Arnold's tantalising cross. Welshman Woodburn crashed the clincher into the roof of the net five minutes later. His beaming smile showed how much it meant. He was 98 days younger than Michael Owen had been when he scored against Wimbledon in 1997. Lucas captained the Reds on an emotional night, as the players stood in silent tribute to remember the victims of the Chapecoense plane crash, which had claimed the lives of 71 of the 77 passengers on board. The Brazilian club lost all but three of its players in the tragedy.

A hideous collapse at Bournemouth in early December saw the Reds lose 4-3, after they had been 3-1 up with 15 minutes to go. Matip's absence was telling

377

and they continued to miss Coutinho. Some of the defending was comical. The madcap afternoon began with quickfire goals from Mane and Origi halfway through the first half. The score remained 2-0 until the 56th minute, when Callum Wilson converted a penalty after a foul by Milner. Can replied with a thumping 20-yarder. Then came the mayhem. Klopp had described Bournemouth as "a little village always fighting back, like Asterix and Obelix," and so it proved, as goals from Ryan Fraser and Steve Cook made it 3-3. Just when it appeared the sides would share the spoils, a howler from Karius allowed Nathan Ake to score the winner in the 94th minute. The German keeper hadn't looked convincing in his ten games, but this was his first genuine clanger. Lucas and Lovren struggled at the back. The defeat was a hammer blow to Liverpool's title chances and the beginning of another difficult winter for Klopp. They were now in third, four points from the top.

Another seesaw game came at home to West Ham. Lallana scored on the turn from Mane's cross in the fifth minute. But the Hammers were soon ahead. Dimitri Payet's free kick penetrated Karius's weak attempt at a save. Michail Antonio made it 2-1, profiting from some abysmal defending from Lovren, who soon departed injured. His replacement Klavan looked much more assured. Three minutes into the second half, Origi tapped in the equaliser after a mistake by Darren Randolph. Wijnaldum (twice), Origi and Henderson went close but there were no more goals. Having not shone for some time, Firmino was poor again. The absence of Coutinho was continuing to hurt.

A winning run of four matches began at Middlesbrough. Mignolet was back in goal and kept his 50th clean sheet for the club. Lallana's thumping header from Clyne's cross gave Liverpool the lead on the half hour. Mane hit a post. Origi doubled the lead on the hour, poking home a square pass by Lallana, who capped a tremendous personal performance with the third. Alexander-Arnold replaced Origi in the last minute to make his league debut.

One of the best moments of the season came six days before Christmas, when Mane scored a 94th-minute winner at Goodison. The Blues made a strong start, but neither side had a shot on target in the first half. With Matip still absent, Klavan was Liverpool's best player. Klopp urged his players to be more direct in the second half. Everton faded, although Liverpool failed to take advantage until the very end. Ross Barkley should have been sent off for an appalling challenge on Henderson but escaped with a yellow. Joel Robles saved brilliantly from Firmino. Sturridge, so far enjoying a mixed season, came on with ten minutes to go, having recovered from a recent calf injury, and it was he who went across the edge of the box before shooting against the post. The ball rebounded perfectly for Mane to fire in the only goal of the game. The players leapt upon one another amid red smoke emanating from the nearby away fans. It was the team's first 1-0 win in the Premier League in 2016. It was also Liverpool's third injury-time winner at Goodison in the Premier League era.

Stoke City went 1-0 up at Anfield when Mignolet failed to keep out Jon Walters' header. The Reds then clicked into gear. Peter Crouch cleared off the line from Firmino. Lallana scored his seventh of the season from a tight angle. A minute before the break, Firmino made it 2-1 with a shot that struck both posts. Giannelli Imbula's own goal from Origi's cross made it 3-1. And then Ryan Shawcross's awful back pass put Sturridge away, and he rounded Lee Grant to make it four, 56 seconds after coming on for Origi. Lallana was prominent again. Milner and Henderson weren't far behind.

Pep Guardiola managed Manchester City against Liverpool for the first time on New Year's Eve. Wijnaldum scored the Reds' 87th goal of the calendar year, which equalled the tally of 1985 as the best in the modern era. The Dutchman headed in Lallana's cross in the eighth minute. It was the playmaker's seventh assist of the season. It was the only goal of a usually high-scoring fixture. Liverpool had just five attempts, the lowest of the Klopp era by the summer of 2020. Mignolet pulled off some world-class saves. Milner won his battle with Raheem Sterling. As well as Wijnaldum, Can also stood out, but Henderson suffered a heel injury. The result saw the Reds emerge as Chelsea's biggest threat. They ended the year in second, on 43 points, half a dozen behind the leaders. They were four ahead of City in third. Fourteen points out of 18 had been taken from Arsenal, Spurs, Chelsea, Manchester United, Everton and City.

Four wins on the bounce was a satisfying way to end 2016, but the first month of 2017 was a nightmare. Nine games would bring just one win and none in the league. The first match was at the Stadium of Light, less than 48 hours after the City game. With Matip, Henderson and Coutinho unavailable, it would be Mane's last game before he departed for the African Cup of Nations. His four-week absence would prove costly. Milner only lasted half the game. Sturridge picked up another injury but not before his wonderfully opportunistic header gave Liverpool the lead. Jermain Defoe soon equalised from the spot for bottom-three Sunderland after Klavan and Wijnaldum impeded the progress of Didier Ndong. Liverpool were comfortably the better side, and the departing Mane scored at the back post from a corner but, again, the Reds conceded a penalty soon after scoring, this time in bizarre fashion, as Mane was penalised for handball in a defensive wall. Defoe scored his second to earn a point for Sunderland. Liverpool only had themselves to blame, with Klavan, Can and Wijnaldum off-colour. Two days later, Chelsea's run of 13 straight league wins was ended with a 2-0 defeat at Spurs. They were still five points clear of the Reds.

The third round of the FA Cup saw Plymouth Argyle come to Anfield for their first meeting since Alan A'Court, Ian St John and Roger Hunt had scored in a 3-2 win in 1962. In a side largely made up of fringe players, Joe Gomez made a welcome return after 465 days battling injury, lining up at centre back alongside skipper Lucas. With an average age of less than 22, it was the youngest-ever side fielded by Liverpool. The game was goalless, with substitutes Sturridge, Lallana and Firmino unable to engineer a breakthrough. Plymouth defended resolutely, as did Stewart, whose perfectly-timed tackle on Craig Tanner prevented an embarrassing result. Origi had a first-half goal disallowed. Sturridge twice went close.

If the senior players were saved for the first leg of the League Cup semi-final at struggling Southampton, it didn't work. The Reds were dire, lucky to lose by just one goal. Klavan's miskick allowed Nathan Redmond to score on 20 minutes. Karius made several saves to keep Liverpool in the tie. Lovren cleared Redmond's chip off the line. Coutinho made his first appearance for seven weeks off the bench. Can struggled again, as did Klavan, Wijnaldum and Firmino. One piece of good news earlier in the day was Coutinho signing a five-year deal with no buyout clause.

Alexander-Arnold made an impressive first league start at Old Trafford in a much-improved performance. "Are you ready?" Klopp had asked him three hours before kick-off. The manager later told how the teenager's face had dropped when he realised what he meant. Clyne had an abdominal injury, and his teenage replacement produced a performance reminiscent of Rob Jones on the same ground in 1991. The Reds weren't just without Mane due to the African Cup of Nations, but also Matip. Although he had retired from the Cameroon team, they argued he should sit out his club football for the duration of the tournament. Henderson was back. Paul Pogba handled Milner's corner, and the Yorkshireman beat David de Gea from the spot. It was Liverpool's sixth Premier League penalty at Old Trafford – more than any other team. Pogba was having an awful game and should have been penalised at another corner for wrestling Henderson. Mignolet kept out a fierce free kick from Zlatan Ibrahimovic, one of several outstanding saves. De Gea stopped Firmino doubling the lead after some clever approach play by the substitute Coutinho. Jose Mourinho sent on Marouane Fellaini as a target man, and it worked. His 84th-minute header came back off the bar, and Ibrahimovic nodded in the equaliser. Wijnaldum was sent through in injury time by Can, but he fluffed his lines. Chelsea were now seven points clear, with Spurs leapfrogging Liverpool into second.

The only win of the month came at Home Park in the FA Cup replay against Plymouth. This time, Klopp fielded the second-youngest side in Liverpool's history, but it was 30-year-old Lucas who was the unlikely matchwinner, heading in Coutinho's corner. Debutant Harry Wilson replaced Coutinho. Origi had a weak penalty saved in the closing moments, but it didn't affect the outcome. Most of the young players, especially Alexander-Arnold, did themselves proud again, although Stewart was struggling for form.

Liverpool were now about to enter a phase which would almost ruin the season. A spell of five defeats in seven was a major test for the manager and saw the team drop out of the top four. The run started with a 3-2 defeat at home to relegation battlers Swansea. Matip was still unable to play. Coutinho started. After a goalless first half, Fernando Llorente scored twice in seven minutes. Firmino responded with a double of his own, the second of which was a stunning finish as he chested down Wijnaldum's cross and smashed a half-volley into the corner on the turn. There were 20 minutes for the Reds to bag a winner, but within five minutes they were behind again. Klavan presented the ball to Gylfi Sigurdsson, and his finish beat Mignolet. Clyne, Lovren, Klavan, Can and Henderson were all abject. The Times pinned the first home defeat for a year on "the lack of strength in depth, the flimsy rearguard, and poor game management," also blaming the club's inability to bring in fresh faces during the January window. Klopp had wanted a wide player but was unable to bring in Christian Pulisic, Julian Brandt or Julian Draxler.

Liverpool were about to exit both domestic cups with abject displays at Anfield. First came Southampton in the second leg of the League Cup semi-final. Saints' Skipper Jose Fonte had just been sold. Virgil van Dijk was absent with a knee injury, having recently been appointed club captain. Even without him to get past, the Reds looked impotent. Matip made his first start since 11th December after his Cameroon impasse was broken. Mane was still with Senegal. They would eventually lose in the quarter-finals. Back at Anfield, Klopp's programme notes said, "We punch back and we punch back hard." But they didn't. Fraser Forster fumbled Can's piledriver on 53 minutes and scrambled it away as it was crossing the line. Sturridge blazed a close-range volley over the bar. Two hopeful penalty appeals were turned down. Milner's injury-time corner was cleared. Saints broke downfield, and Shane Long gave his side a 2-0 aggregate win. Confidence and energy levels were on the floor.

Wolves were next, in the fourth round of the FA Cup. Klopp selected Randall, Ejaria and Woodburn in another inexperienced team. Richard Stearman headed in Helder Costa's free kick on just 53 seconds to set the tone for a painful afternoon. After a scintillating counterattack, man of the match Costa then played in Andreas Weimann, who rounded Karius to make it two. Liverpool could only muster one themselves, with Origi turning in Sturridge's header. Despite 79% of the possession and 20 shots, the Reds lost 2-1. Klopp was enduring another miserable English winter. The Anfield Wrap's Andy Heaton gave Gomez a two out of ten, pointing out he had the "kind of game that can finish off a Liverpool career … His head had clearly gone." Randall, Klavan, Moreno, Lucas, Wijnaldum and Origi got four or less. "I am responsible for this performance because I thought this line-up was ready for this game," said Klopp. "All I can say – sorry." For the fifth season in a row, the Reds would end up trophyless.

Liverpool had just three days to lick their wounds before runaway leaders Chelsea visited L4 on the last day of January. The returning Mane was named sub. How he had been missed during this wretched month. The Reds started brightly, but David Luiz hammered in a free kick with Mignolet caught off guard. Firmino skied an opportunity. Former Red Victor Moses hit a post. And then Henderson, whose performance led by example, crossed to Milner, who headed back across for Wijnaldum to level the score and ensure Liverpool didn't lose four consecutive games for the first time since December 1923. Klopp's men surged forward for the winner, buoyed by the 75th-minute introduction of Mane, but within minutes, the ball was sitting on Liverpool's penalty spot after Diego Costa reacted theatrically to minimal contact from Matip. Costa, the ultimate pantomime villain, saw his spot kick saved by Mignolet. Firmino missed a late header as an enthralling encounter ended 1-1. Liverpool had done themselves credit, but their title ambitions were long gone. January's nine games had brought one win, four draws and four defeats.

There was still more pain to come. The Reds were woeful at Hull, conceding a goal towards the end of each half. The first was another set-piece shambles. The second was a breakaway. Only Mane possessed any spark. Hull fielded a young Scotsman at left back by the name of Andy Robertson, who could have been penalised for a handball when Firmino's shot struck his arm. But he got the better of Mane and produced a performance Klopp would remember. Coutinho fluffed a great chance. The Times gave every player a five. Mignolet, Milner and Can were lucky to get that. Lallana, previously having such a good season, was in a rut. It was the club's worst start to a calendar year since 1954.

Having failed to beat several teams in the bottom half of the league, including four teams fighting relegation, it wasn't entirely a surprise that Liverpool should play so well at home to Tottenham. The Reds benefited from the rarity of seven days between fixtures. They blitzed Spurs, with Mane scoring twice by the 18th minute. He raced onto Wijnaldum's pass for number one, set himself and blasted past Hugo Lloris. For the second, Lallana's shot was parried by Lloris, as was Firmino's, but Mane hammered the rebound high into the net. Klopp was in raptures. Mane should have a had a third before the break but slid the ball wide. Matip and Coutinho spurned second-half chances. Lucas was at the back again and marked Harry Kane with contemptuous ease. Firmino was at his best. The Reds closed the gap on Spurs in second to one point.

But still the inconsistency wasn't out of the system. Facing a relegation battle, champions Leicester had just sacked 2016 miracle worker Claudio Ranieri. Craig Shakespeare had taken over, and the new manager bounce would hurt a lifeless Liverpool. A foot injury would keep Henderson out not just of this game, but for the rest of the campaign. His absence left a hole in the Reds' midfield at Leicester, especially in an abysmal first half. Wijnaldum surrendered possession in midfield. The ball was instantly sent forward for Jamie Vardy, who slotted past Mignolet for Leicester's first league goal of 2017. Several attempts to clear a long throw were hashed, and Danny Drinkwater fired in a 20-yarder. Vardy got in between Lucas and Can to head in the third on the hour. Having had Kane in his pocket, Lucas struggled all night with Vardy. Coutinho, one of the only players to put in a half-decent performance, pulled one back from the edge of the box. The Reds were in fifth, having lost two of their three matches in February. The month also saw Steven Gerrard return to the club as coach of the Under-18s.

Spring would be much a happier time for the Reds. Arsenal came to Anfield and befell the same fate as Spurs. A quick start saw Firmino finish at the back post from Mane's cross. The Senegalese made it two five minutes before the break, when he was left unmarked and drilled the ball past Petr Cech for a deserved 2-0 lead at the break. Danny Welbeck got one back when he clipped the ball over Mignolet. But Arsenal couldn't find an equaliser, and in injury time, Wijnaldum finished off a Lallana-instigated counterattack, tucking Origi's cross into the bottom corner from 12 yards. Lallana, Mane and Firmino were the standouts in a tremendous team performance. The Reds were still unbeaten against the top six.

Bearing in mind Liverpool's abject record against the less glamorous sides in the division, Burnley would probably prove stiffer opposition than Spurs and Arsenal. And so it proved. With Clyne caught napping, Ashley Barnes scored the Lancastrians' first goal at Anfield since 1975, on seven minutes as they sought to do the double over Liverpool. They had picked up just two points on their travels all season. "How shit must you be, we're winning away!" mocked their fans. It took the Reds a long time to get going, but Wijnaldum's equaliser on half-time was timely. They started the second half with a spring in their step, and the inconsistent Can drilled home a 30-yard winner just after the hour. Mane was excellent. Woodburn impressed for the last third, having replaced the anodyne Coutinho, who had done little right since returning from injury. It wasn't pretty, but Liverpool walked off with three vital points in their pursuit of a Champions League place.

Manchester City hosted Liverpool in a crazy game where the quality didn't quite match the entertainment. The casual viewer would have no idea of the extent to which the two sides were about to dominate the next three years. Lallana produced one of the worst bloopers in front of goal in years, not quite of Ronny Rosenthal proportions, but not far off, as the Reds hunted a late winner. Both sides had 13 attempts on goal. Can, playing the holding role in a 4-3-3, was magnificent, as were Wijnaldum and Mane. Mane, Firmino and Lallana were denied by Willy Caballero. Raheem Sterling and Fernandinho failed to convert a teasing cross by David Silva. Klopp couldn't watch as Milner, booed by the City fans all afternoon, opened the scoring from the spot six minutes into the second half when Firmino was fouled. He still hadn't failed with a penalty for Liverpool. Sergio Aguero got in front of Klavan to prod home Kevin De Bruyne's cross. Both teams searched for the winner. De Bruyne hit a post. In the last five minutes, Lallana played Firmino in down the inside left and when the Brazilian returned the ball, Lallana was four yards out with just the keeper to beat. He completely missed his kick. It was a costly error, as Liverpool failed to overtake City. They stayed fourth, four points ahead of Manchester United, who had two games in hand going into the international break.

On 22nd March 2017, former player, coach and caretaker manager Ronnie Moran died at the age of 83. Serving the club for 49 years, he worked with Shankly, Paisley, Fagan and Dalglish, all the way through to 1998 when he finally stepped down. "He should be remembered as a great local boy who achieved all he could in football with his team," said Ian St John, a former teammate. Moran, also known as 'Bugsy', played 379 games for the club between 1952 and 1964. He stepped in as caretaker manager when Kenny Dalglish resigned in February 1991 and when Graeme Souness required heart surgery towards the end of the 1992 season. One of his proudest moments would have been leading Liverpool out at Wembley when they beat Sunderland in the FA Cup Final.

When the international break was over, the Reds had nine games to cement a top-four spot. The run started with the Anfield Derby on April Fools' Day, the 18th in a row Everton failed to win. After a tribute to Moran, which included a Kop mosaic that read 'Bugsy', the Reds produced a terrific performance. On eight minutes, Mane found the bottom corner with a precise finish after a one-two with Firmino. Matthew Pennington scored an equaliser against the run of play from another badly defended corner. Coutinho then produced one of the most memorable derby moments when he collected the ball 40 yards from goal, motored forward, evaded a challenge, got into the box, shifted the ball onto his right foot and curled a delicious shot into the top corner of Joel Robles' goal. The punishment kept coming, as substitute Origi sealed the points on the hour, smashing home a 20-yarder. Klopp thumped his chest in celebration. Lucas was imperious in his final derby. Lovren dominated Romelu Lukaku. The attacking players dovetailed beautifully, although Mane injured a knee, which would sideline him for the season. He would later be crowned the club's player of the season. Given how the Reds had collapsed without him in January, it was a major concern. After his appalling challenge on Henderson in December, Ross Barkley's victim this time was Lovren. Again, there was no red card. Klopp went berserk on the touchline.

The first game without Mane veered off script, even though Liverpool scored twice at home to Bournemouth. Henderson and Lallana were also unavailable, with Matip only fit enough for the bench. As usual with the game closest to 15th April, there was a tribute to the victims of Hillsborough. Following the verdict of unlawful killings, the minute's silence was replaced with applause. The Reds were woeful, defended disgracefully and ran out of legs in the final 20 minutes. It took seven minutes for Benik Afobe to score the Cherries first goal at Anfield since 1968, from Wijnaldum's error. Coutinho levelled things up just before the break, and his goal was greeted on the Kop by Kenny Dalglish's trademark beaming grin and applause. He sat on the famous stand for the first half as part of a documentary. The goal saw Coutinho draw level with Juninho as the highest-scoring Brazilian in the Premier League with 29. From Wijnaldum's cross, Origi made it 2-1 on 59 minutes. As well as the goalscorers, Clyne was superb on his 26th birthday and hit the bar. But as the Reds were heading for a fourth win in five games, Joshua King punished some Keystone Cops defending. That it came from a long throw was little surprise. The Reds, meanwhile, were banned from signing academy players from English clubs for two years after being found guilty of tapping up an 11-year-old Stoke City player.

Bobby Firmino was shirtless. It could only mean two things. One, a booking. Two, he'd just scored a jaw-dropping winner at Stoke in a game Liverpool had looked destined to lose. Looking to freshen things up for a thoroughly fatigued squad, Klopp picked a bizarre team in a 3-5-1-1 formation: Mignolet; Lovren, Matip, Klavan; Alexander-Arnold, Can, Wijnaldum, Milner, Clyne; Woodburn; Origi. They played like strangers. Xherdan Shaqiri set up Jon Walters for the opener a minute before half-time. Defeat would have left Liverpool as outsiders for a top-four spot. Klopp brought on Coutinho and Firmino for Alexander-Arnold and Woodburn. The teenage pair hadn't been the worst players. That mantle could be shared by Lovren, Klavan, Clyne and Wijnaldum. The team was livelier after the break, culminating in 126 seconds of pure ecstasy. Coutinho rammed the equaliser into the corner of the net from near the penalty spot. Wijnaldum's long ball then released Firmino. It bounced high. He was 25 yards from goal. Lee Grant was hastily retreating. The Brazilian genius let it come down onto the half-volley before smashing it over Grant's head with enough dip for it to come down into the top corner, sparking pandemonium in the away end. Off came the shirt. It was hard to think of a more celebrated goal all season. Wijnaldum hugged Klopp. But there was still a 2-1 lead to defend – not exactly Liverpool's forte. Marko Arnautovic laid a sitter on a plate for Saido Berahino six yards out with Mignolet, who had made a string of fantastic saves, rooted to his line. It was hardly as important, but the Belgian's stunning save was reminiscent of Dudek's from Shevchenko in Istanbul. The points were Liverpool's. With half-a-dozen games to go, the Reds were third.

The Reds needed to keep winning, no matter what the score, and so a 1-0 win at Tony Pulis's West Brom was enough. Positioned on the edge of the box, Lucas flicked on Milner's free kick, and the unmarked Firmino headed past Ben Foster just before half-time. Mignolet was excellent again and saved a one-on-one from Matt Phillips. Milner skied a volley. Origi had a header disallowed. With Foster out of his goal, injury-time substitute Moreno was miles off the target. The midfield triumvirate of Lucas, Wijnaldum and Can were highly effective. Firmino was the best player. His two winning goals in eight days had earned four extra points. It was the first time in eight games that Tony Pulis had lost a home game against Liverpool. Klopp's relationship with Pulis and Burnley's Sean Dyche had a similar dynamic to that of Benitez and Sam Allardyce, so recent wins over both was no mean feat, especially with such an embarrassing record against the lower sides.

Talking of Allardyce, his Crystal Palace team, with Christian Benteke up front, came to Anfield determined to derail their top-four charge. Klopp's bench comprised Grujic, Moreno and four teenagers, including the 17-year-old Rhian Brewster. Coutinho fired in a supreme free kick from 25 yards. But three minutes before the break, a fired-up Benteke scored his first, beating Mignolet after a cross wasn't cut out. Then, with 16 minutes left, a corner came all the way through, and he stooped to head the winner. When Benteke was substituted on 88 minutes, the Kop begrudgingly afforded him a generous reception. It was his seventh goal against the Reds in eight matches for Villa and Palace. Liverpool could have no complaints with the outcome. Several players, including Lovren, Matip, Firmino and Origi, hadn't done themselves justice. At the time of writing, more than three years later, it remained Liverpool's last Premier League home defeat.

Heading into May, the top four was still in Liverpool's hands. The next game was at Watford, where Can scored with a laws-of-physics-defying volley. Coutinho departed with a dead leg. His replacement, the returning Lallana, hit the bar with a first-time, dipping volley from way out. A couple of minutes later, in first-half injury time, Lucas lofted a ball into the box from midfield. Can considered heading it, before instinct took over, and he executed a picture-book scissor kick from 16 yards, which curled away from Heurelho Gomes and into the top corner of his net. He wouldn't have scored a goal like that in his dreams, let alone with Champions League football at stake. He'd had an up-and-down season, capable of brilliance and anonymity in Liverpool's engine room. He was about to enter the final year of his contract, with no obvious intent to sign a new one. But all that mattered at Vicarage Road on the first day of May was his phenomenal goal and what it meant for the season. Liverpool held on, although Mignolet had to make a couple of second-half saves, and Sebastian Prodl hit the bar. The Reds were third, three points clear of City, who had a game in hand. Liverpool's goal difference was superior by one. More crucially, they led United, who had one game in hand, by four, and were nine ahead of Arsenal, who had two extra matches to play.

After the announcement that the Centenary Stand would be named after Kenny Dalglish, Liverpool drew 0-0 at home to Southampton. The same result against the same club on the same date in 2000 had been extremely costly, as Gerard Houllier's Reds had collapsed on the final strait and fell short of Champions League qualification. This time, the irritation was exacerbated by Milner missing his first Liverpool penalty, on 66 minutes. The Reds had barely threatened before they were awarded the penalty for handball against Jack Stephens. Fraser Forster sprang low to his right and kept it out with a one-handed save. Far too many players were off their game, including Coutinho. They hadn't scored against Southampton in four attempts in 2016-17. In six matches managing Lyon and now Southampton against Liverpool, Claude Puel still hadn't lost. Klopp stated that Liverpool had been affected by the dry pitch. At least both Manchester sides lost over the weekend, so Liverpool were still in charge of their own destiny.

A significant tactical change was responsible for a trip to West Ham being much easier than anticipated. Klopp fielded a 4-4-2 diamond, with Lucas sacrificed and Sturridge and Origi up front. Lallana played at the tip. Coutinho was in one of the deeper midfield roles and had a blinder, scoring twice and creating another. The Hammers started strongly, but in a game Liverpool had to win, they gradually exerted their authority. Matip's header thudded against the crossbar. Sturridge struck the side-netting. Ten minutes before the interval, Coutinho received the ball inside his own half. He looked up and slid an inch-perfect ball through to Sturridge. The striker allowed it to roll on before beating Adrian and sliding it home. Andre Ayew should have equalised. His miss from a corner defied belief. Coutinho's double came inside four minutes around the hour mark. After Wijnaldum's volley cannoned off the crossbar, Coutinho picked up possession 25 yards out, weaved his way through a couple of tackles and found the corner from the edge of the box. Two became three when Liverpool broke from a West Ham corner. They escaped a penalty shout against Wijnaldum for both handball and a foul – it could have been either. Within seconds, Coutinho was firing past Adrian. Origi hit the bar but did get the fourth to seal a comprehensive win. Coutinho was everybody's man of the match. Lovren, Can, Lallana and Sturridge weren't far behind.

Going into the final day of the season, Liverpool were fourth, two points behind Manchester City, and a point ahead of Arsenal. Manchester United were out of the picture. The Reds had to beat Middlesbrough, as Everton would inevitably roll over at Arsenal. Fit-again Firmino replaced Origi as Klopp kept his diamond. Wearing their 2017-18 kit, Liverpool started nervously and were repelled by their already-relegated opponents for 45 minutes. Clyne fired wide. Boro were denied a penalty after a Lovren foul. Coutinho (twice) and Can went close. Sturridge was a yard wide. Klopp urged on the crowd. Arsenal were already 2-0 up. And then, in first-half injury time, not long after Boro fans had burst into a chorus of "Champions League, you're having a laugh," Wijnaldum broke into the Kop penalty area, chose not to square it to Sturridge and smashed the ball inside the near post. It was a vital goal. Coutinho scored another 25-yard free kick six minutes into the second half. It was all but done. Lallana finished a counterattack to score Liverpool's third in 11 minutes of play. Lucas replaced his compatriot Firmino for his final appearance for the Reds before the final whistle signalled the team's return to the Champions League.

The Reds finished fourth, two points behind Manchester City and one ahead of Arsenal. Qualifying for the 2017-18 Champions League would prove to be the start of something very special for Jurgen Klopp's Liverpool.

2017-18

*"We got Salah. A-ha Mane, Mane. And Bobby Fir-mi-nooo.
But we sold Coutinho."*

For the third successive summer, a trio of players came to Anfield that would become regulars in a European Cup and Premier League-winning team. Having snared Joe Gomez, James Milner and Roberto Firmino in 2015, and Sadio Mane, Joel Matip and Gini Wijnaldum 12 months later, Jurgen Klopp signed Mo Salah, Andy Robertson and Alex Oxlade-Chamberlain before the summer transfer window closed. He also persuaded RB Leipzig to part with the much-sought after Naby Keita, although the Guinean midfielder wouldn't arrive for another year. Virgil van Dijk was the cherry on the cake when he signed in January.

Salah had doubts about signing because Mane was playing so well on the right, but Klopp assured him the Senegalese would switch flanks. There were question marks over the £43.9 million Egyptian, too. He had failed at Chelsea, where Jose Mourinho didn't rate him. Journalist Mina Rzouki wasn't a fan either, telling 5 Live, "I'm not convinced of his footballing IQ. I do think he's a player that tends to run forward and then look second, which irritates me somewhat. He is, for me, another Juan Cuadrado. You see him sometimes under pressure, he just looks like he doesn't know where to go or how to make an intelligent move." She could not have been more wrong. Salah found the net on his debut at Watford and couldn't stop scoring. A footballer of cathartic brilliance, his debut season was a dream, as he rattled in 44 goals in 52 games, breaking records galore.

Robertson, 23, cost £8 million from Hull. He would have to wait until the winter before usurping Alberto Moreno as Klopp's first-choice left back. From then on, he was magnificent. Oxlade-Chamberlain was a surprising signing at the end of the transfer window, but Klopp knew he would struggle to hold on to Philippe Coutinho and planned the Brazilian's succession in advance. On Sky, Gary Neville and Thierry Henry were scathing of Oxlade-Chamberlain. Neville questioned why "everyone was eulogising over him." Henry said, "I still don't know what he's good at." Perhaps Henry had his answer when Oxlade-Chamberlain fired in a 25-yard missile to put Liverpool 2-0 up against Manchester City in the Champions League quarter-final. The £35-million 24-year-old did need time to settle in but would become a crucial cog in Liverpool's midfield during the spring, before injury struck. The other new boy was Chelsea's 19-year-old forward Dominic Solanke. He had just helped England win the Under-20 World Cup, collecting the Golden Ball as the tournament's best player.

Nevertheless, going into the season, the overriding feeling was one of disappointment, and not just because there would be a year's wait for Keita. Liverpool had wanted Van Dijk but, having been caught talking to him without Southampton's permission, the Reds apologised and ended their interest in the Dutchman. They would have to wait half the season to get their man and would head into the new season with the same goalkeeper and centre backs. Realistically, that meant no shot at the title.

On their way out of Anfield were Andre Wisdom, Lucas Leiva, Kevin Stewart and Mamadou Sakho for a combined £44 million. For the second year in a row, Liverpool raised significant funds by selling fringe players. Jack Dunn, Alex Manninger and Ryan Fulton left on free transfers. At the end of August, Divock Origi left for a season-long loan at Wolfsburg. In hindsight, this was probably an error by Klopp, as Solanke struggled in front of goal. One player who was keen to leave was Coutinho, although Liverpool managed to prevent him from joining Barcelona until January, when they would receive a whopping fee. But he angered fans by not playing until the August transfer window closed, citing a back injury.

The new season began at Watford, a day after Coutinho had submitted a transfer request. The Reds tossed away two points after conceding twice from corners. The opening-day line-up was: Simon Mignolet; Trent Alexander-Arnold, Dejan Lovren, Matip, Robertson; Wijnaldum, Jordan Henderson, Emre Can; Salah, Firmino, Mane. Origi, Milner and Gomez came on late in the game, while Loris Karius, Ragnar Klavan, Marko Grujic and Solanke were unused. Adam Lallana (hamstring) and Nathaniel Clyne (back) would be absent long-term. It took eight minutes for the Reds to be breached, when Stefano Okaka headed in Watford's first corner. Mane equalised after an exquisite touch from Can. Abdoulaye Doucoure capitalised on more abysmal defending to restore the Hornets' lead. Firmino made it 2-2 with an emphatic penalty after Salah was felled by the keeper. Two minutes later, Firmino latched on to Lovren's high, bouncing ball and lifted it over Gomes. It was drifting wide, but Salah applied the finishing touch. The front three were combining beautifully. Matip glanced Alexander-Arnold's corner onto the crossbar as the Reds looked to put the game to bed. But they couldn't. Wijnaldum made a hash of clearing a corner in the dying seconds. Mignolet touched Richarlison's shot onto the bar, and even though Miguel Britos, who bundled in the rebound, was offside, Liverpool only had themselves to blame. They dominated the second half but drew 3-3.

Having finished fourth, Liverpool had to enter the third qualifying round of the Champions League. Instead of being drawn against some of the easy beats of the past, they drew Hoffenheim, whose manager was the 30-year-old Julian Nagelsmann. Up stepped a couple of unlikely heroes in Mignolet and Alexander-Arnold as the Reds won the first leg 2-1. The Belgian saved an unconvincing 12th-minute penalty from Andrej Kramaric after a foul by Lovren. The 18-year-old full back then put Liverpool ahead, curling in a 27-yard free kick. Milner's cross was diverted into his own net by Havard Nordtveit for the second, but a late goal by Mark Uth kept the tie alive. Solanke made his debut as a late sub, with Klopp now favouring him to Origi.

The manager reshaped the defence for the visit of Crystal Palace. Gomez made his first league start since September 2015, at right back. On the other side was debutant Robertson, who had a fine game, whipping in several tantalising crosses. Matip and Klavan were between them. Sturridge came in for his first start of the season, replacing Salah, but he was off the pace. Palace frustrated Liverpool until the 73rd minute, when Solanke's pressing allowed Mane to latch onto a loose ball to score the game's only goal. The Reds, meanwhile, had turned down a third bid from Barcelona for Coutinho, worth £82 million plus £36 million in add-ons. Barca had just received £198 million for Neymar, and Liverpool knew more could be squeezed out of them.

Liverpool blew Hoffenheim away in the second leg, racing into a 3-0 lead after 21 minutes to progress to the group stage. Mane's backheel freed Can, whose deflected shot beat Oliver Baumann. Firmino's cutback was hit against the post by Wijnaldum. Salah tapped in the rebound. The next goal was a thing of beauty. Firmino's exquisite touch found Wijnaldum. The Dutchman's Gerrard-like pass sent Mane racing away. His backheel released Firmino, who dinked over a cross that was turned in by Can. It was 5-1 on aggregate. But the back door was still open, and Uth scored his second of the tie before half-time. Henderson laid the fourth on a plate for Firmino, who had been exceptional in both legs against his old club. Hoffenheim pulled another back, but the Reds were through 6-3 on aggregate.

Not for the first or last time under Klopp, Arsenal at home proved to be easier than anticipated. Firmino got in between the centre halves to nod in a cross from the excellent Gomez. Mane scored a tremendous goal, cutting in from the left and curling the ball inside the far post. Arsenal lined up a corner on 56 minutes. Matip headed clear. Hector Bellerin lost the ball under pressure from Salah, who bore down on the Kop goal and put the game beyond the Gunners. Twitter user @thesmigger very amusingly added the Benny Hill tune to footage of the goal filmed from the tunnel, which showed the Egyptian sprinting through the centre circle with a swarm of players trying in vain to keep up with him. Salah's cross then allowed Sturridge to head his first of the season. Liverpool were majestic and hadn't missed Coutinho one bit, racking up 14 goals in five games. The front three were playing like a dream. Playing his final game for Arsenal was Oxlade-Chamberlain, four days before his move north.

With the window closed, Coutinho was obliged to return to the squad. His mysterious back injury had cleared up sufficiently for him to score for Brazil in the international break. He rejoined training on 5th September, four days before the trip to Manchester City. Many seemed prepared to forgive and forget. He didn't play at the Etihad and was probably glad he didn't, as Liverpool were routed 5-0. The reason for the thrashing was the first-half dismissal of Mane, August's Premier League Player of the Month, who led with a high foot on the

City keeper Ederson. Although an accident, it was deemed dangerous play. By then, the Reds were already a goal down through Sergio Aguero. Gabriel Jesus nodded in Kevin De Bruyne's cross. Still groggy, Ederson was withdrawn at the break for Claudio Bravo. Klopp substituted the threatening Salah for Oxlade-Chamberlain, who had raised a pre-match smile by telling an interviewer, "We beat Arsenal 4-0 last week. Hopefully we can carry on that momentum." Liverpool remained positive, but City found it easy to counter. Jesus scored another, and Leroy Sane bagged a late double to complete the rout. A man down or not, Liverpool defended abysmally, with Klavan the biggest culprit.

Coutinho returned to the matchday squad for the opening Champions League group match at home to Sevilla, for whom Wissam Ben Yedder scored an early goal. Back came Liverpool to lead at half-time through Firmino and Salah. Firmino hit a post with a penalty after Mane was fouled, and the Reds were punished when Joaquin Correa equalised with 18 minutes left. Coutinho replaced Can on 76 minutes to a generous reception from the crowd. Sevilla nearly grabbed a winner before Gomez was sent off in injury time for a second booking.

Liverpool celebrated the 125th anniversary of their first match when they had beaten Rotherham Town 7-1 in a friendly on 1st September 1892. This time the opposition was a tad more robust, as Burnley took home a point in the first game of Mane's suspension. Coutinho operated behind a front three of Salah, Sturridge and Firmino. A long ball undid Liverpool on 27 minutes when Scott Arfield fired home from the edge of the box. Salah equalised from Can's long pass, giving the Reds an hour to find a winner. Alexander-Arnold came close in the second half. Solanke hit the bar from two yards. Despite enjoying 71% of possession, Liverpool had to settle for a frustrating 1-1 draw.

The League Cup took Liverpool to Leicester, where they were beaten 2-0. Danny Ward, Jon Flanagan, Grujic and Solanke started, and there was even a place on the bench for the long-forgotten Lazar Markovic, although he didn't feature. The Reds dominated the first half, but it was the usual story of vulnerability at one end and profligacy at the other, as they failed to score and were duly punished by second-half goals from Shinji Okazaki and Islam Slimani. Flanagan, Grujic and Oxlade-Chamberlain laboured badly. A video mocking the latter's performance, watched over 2.5 million times, circulated on Twitter.

Klopp and his players returned to the King Power Stadium four days later and collected three points with a 3-2 win. Can hit the bar. Salah couldn't finish the rebound, but he soon headed the opener from Coutinho's cross. The Brazilian doubled with lead with a sublime free kick. Okazaki got one back on the stroke of half-time. Man of the match Henderson scored his first goal in a year, finishing off a swift counter to make it 3-1. Jamie Vardy got one back on 69 minutes, but when he was handed the chance to equalise from the spot, Mignolet denied him.

The Reds went to Russia for their second Champions League game and drew 1-1 with Spartak Moscow. Finding themselves a goal behind, with Karius beaten too easily from a free kick, Liverpool levelled on the half hour through their best player Coutinho, after a one-two with Mane. Numerous opportunities to win the game were spurned, with Salah, Firmino and Sturridge the main guilty parties.

It was the same old story in a 1-1 draw at Rafa Benitez's Newcastle. Wijnaldum hit the post, from which there was a heart-stopping goalmouth scramble, with Lovren and Mane somehow missing the target. Coutinho, yet again the star player, scored from distance. Six minutes later, inconclusive defending handed Joselu a lucky equaliser. There were some promising openings for the Reds, along with lengthy periods of horribly disjointed football.

Mane would sit out five games with a hamstring injury, starting with Manchester United at home. Liverpool missed him, as Jose Mourinho's United thwarted the Reds again. David de Gea saved with his feet from Matip, with Salah putting the rebound wide. Can blazed over at the Kop end in the second half. Liverpool created little else.

Having struggled in front of goal from the start of September, the Reds won 7-0 in Slovenia – their largest away win in European football. Maribor were the victims. Salah presented Firmino with a fourth-minute tap-in. Coutinho volleyed Milner's cross into the corner. Salah got two before the break. Firmino glanced in Coutinho's free kick. Oxlade-Chamberlain strolled through the defence for the sixth. Alexander-Arnold rounded off the scoring in the last minute from 20 yards.

Liverpool had one more depth to sink to in this frustrating autumn. It came in front of a Premier League record crowd of 80,827 at Wembley, where Tottenham were now playing their home games. Lovren had such a torrid opening half hour that he was substituted. The failure to get the Van Dijk deal over the line in the summer had seen the Reds haemorrhage goals. For the first goal, Lovren didn't even try to head clear, and Harry Kane rounded Mignolet and scored. The Croat's misjudgement of a goalkeeper's clearance then released Kane, who slipped it to Son for the second. Salah got one back with a scuffed finish from Henderson's through ball. Lovren was hooked soon after, but Liverpool didn't improve. Dele Alli made it 3-1. Mignolet spilled a free kick, which allowed Kane to make it 4-1. It was a chastening afternoon for the Reds, who were now 12 points behind Manchester City. Twenty-four goals had been conceded in 15 matches. But it would be their last defeat for three months.

Huddersfield were the first side to face Liverpool in that unbeaten run of 18 matches. The Yorkshire side were managed by David Wagner, Klopp's best man and reserve-team manager in his days at Dortmund. Klopp had wanted him to coach the Under-23s at Liverpool, but he chose Huddersfield. The absent Coutinho would miss three games with a thigh injury. Salah, whose last-gasp penalty had just taken Egypt to the World Cup, had a spot kick saved by Jonas Lossl towards the end of a frustrating first half, after Firmino was pulled over in the box. Henderson clipped the post with the rebound. Sturridge broke the deadlock on 50 minutes, calmly lifting the ball over Lossl. Firmino headed in a corner from man of the match Milner. Wijnaldum thumped in the third. "I'm officially happy," beamed Klopp.

Maribor came to Anfield on the first day of November and were probably content to concede just three. Salah flicked in the first on 49 minutes from Alexander-Arnold's superb cross. Milner then fluffed Liverpool's fifth penalty in seven, but Can and Sturridge ensured it wouldn't matter. The only blot was a first-half muscle injury suffered by Wijnaldum.

Six months after scoring four goals at West Ham, Liverpool repeated the dose with a full-throttle performance. Mignolet was captain. The first goal came from a Hammers corner as Salah and the returning Mane led a stunning breakaway, with the Egyptian calmly slotting past Joe Hart. Matip scored from close range after a scramble from a corner. Manuel Lanzini got one back in the second half, but as the Hammers' fans were still celebrating, Firmino played in Oxlade-Chamberlain, who scored his first league goal for Liverpool. Salah, the game's leading light, arrowed one into the bottom corner on 75 minutes to complete a satisfying win.

Southampton had kept four clean sheets against Liverpool in 2016-17 but were beaten 3-0 at Anfield after an international break. Matip's thigh strain meant a quick return for Lovren, who played well. Salah was on fire, scoring his 13th and 14th goals of the season in 18 games. The first was a lovely curler from outside the box; the second came from Coutinho's clever through ball. No player had topped 14 since Luis Suarez left. Coutinho wrapped up a 3-0 win. The 'Fab Four', as the media had christened Coutinho, Salah, Firmino and Mane, were head and shoulders above every other player. Van Dijk spoke later of how much he wanted to play at Anfield regularly.

Just as things were looking up, the Reds blew a 3-0 lead in Spain against Sevilla. Qualification would now go down to matchday six. Firmino scored in the second minute, and Mane made it two - both from corners. Firmino got the third on the half hour after Mane's shot was blocked. In the second half, Wissam Ben Yedder sent a header and a penalty past Karius. Guido Pizarro equalised in injury time from a corner. It was akin to the Europa League Final collapse, and Moreno was just as bad as he had been then. The Anfield Wrap's Ben Johnson described him as "quite possibly the stupidest player I have ever seen play for Liverpool."

Champions Chelsea, now in third, came to Anfield in late November. Firmino and Mane were benched. With 25 minutes left, Salah scored at the Kop end after Oxlade-Chamberlain's touch. Late on, Willian then chipped Mignolet to equalise, although it was probably a cross. Lallana made his first appearance of the season as an 89th-minute substitute.

A wintry midweek trip to Stoke resulted in a routine 3-0 win. Klopp played a 4-4-2, with Solanke partnering Firmino. Solanke threaded a clever ball to Mane, who lifted it over Lee Grant. Mignolet was lucky to escape a red card for rushing out of his box and fouling Mame Biram Diouf. Joe Allen failed to convert Peter Crouch's knock-down. Salah, a late sub, kept up his scintillating form with two more goals, the first of which was a crunching volley.

Klopp selected an experimental line-up against Brighton in early December. Can, Lovren and Wijnaldum made up a makeshift back three with Matip, Gomez and Klavan absent. Can hadn't played at the back since the days of Brendan Rodgers. Wijnaldum had never played there. Can headed in Coutinho's free kick. Within a minute, Firmino finished off a lightning counterattack, when he turned in Coutinho's cross at the back post. Three minutes after the restart, Mignolet made a stunning save from Glenn Murray. Fourteen seconds later, the ball was in the Brighton net, after Firmino took Salah's pass and finished off another scintillating counter. Half the team celebrated with Firmino, the rest with the goalkeeper. Murray converted a penalty after a foul by Can. In the last few minutes, man of the match Coutinho fired in a low free kick, and Lewis Dunk repeated his 2012 own goal against the Reds to make it 5-1.

The return of Klavan and Gomez for the visit of Spartak Moscow eased Klopp's defensive predicament, but it was the players at the other end of the field that grabbed the headlines as Liverpool won 7-0 again. Henderson, Milner and Mignolet were on the bench, so Coutinho captained the side and helped himself to a hat trick. His first was an early penalty after Salah was pulled down. The Brazilian got another after an inviting pass from Firmino, who then stabbed in the third. Mane scored a venomous volley from Milner's cross. Coutinho completed his treble with the aid of a deflection. Mane turned in Sturridge's pass. Salah fired high into the Kop goal for the seventh. The Reds finished top of the group, having scored 23 goals, beating their previous best of 18 in 2007-08.

Next up was the Anfield Derby, the 19th in a row Everton failed to win. The Reds dominated in the driving snow and led through a wonderful individual effort by Salah, which won him FIFA's Puskas Award for the most aesthetically pleasing goal of the calendar year. Receiving the ball on the right wing, he muscled past two defenders and, using Ashley Williams as a shield, bent the ball past Jordan Pickford into the top corner. Mane then blew a three-on-one by dragging the ball wide. Salah missed an easy header. Everton, now managed by Sam Allardyce, with Sammy Lee his assistant, broke on 76 minutes and were awarded a mystifying penalty after Lovren and Dominic Calvert-Lewin came together. Wayne Rooney scored. Coutinho and Firmino came off the bench as Liverpool searched for a winner, but having been much the better side, the Reds failed to create anything. Despite having 23 shots to Everton's three, it ended 1-1. Klopp was criticised for resting his Brazilians, but given how costly his first two winters had been, his desire to rotate was understandable. One positive was the performance of Gomez, who was magnificent at right back.

The 'Fab Four' started at home to West Brom three days later, but the Reds were held to a frustrating goalless draw, leaving them fifth. Firmino's shot flashed just wide. Hal Robson-Kanu hit the bar from 25 yards. Substitute Solanke had a second-half goal disallowed for handball and another effort cleared off the line. He still hadn't scored for the Reds. Mane struggled the most against the Baggies' low block. Karius made his second league appearance in 12 months, with Mignolet nursing an ankle problem. Alexander-Arnold was Liverpool's best player.

A year on from their collapse at Dean Court, the Reds continued their away form with a 4-0 win over mid-table Bournemouth. Having earlier hit a post, Coutinho made mugs out of a couple of defenders and fired inside the near post. Lovren scored with a diving header. Jermaine Defoe hit a post. Salah produced another classy individual goal. Firmino glanced in Coutinho's cross to make it four on 66 minutes.

Just as it seemed Liverpool's defensive problems were a thing of the past, they conceded three goals in five minutes at Arsenal. The Reds were in control at 2-0, after Coutinho's cute header looped over Petr Cech and Salah's 20-yarder was deflected into the corner. But with Henderson substituted with an early hamstring injury – replaced by the impressive Milner – Arsenal stormed back. Gomez was at fault for Alexis Sanchez's headed goal, which came a minute after Salah had scored. Mignolet made a hash of Granit Xhaka's 25-yarder. Mesut Ozil made it 3-2. But Firmino rescued a point from the edge of the box. It wasn't just Liverpool's defence under the microscope. The midfield was often outplayed, with Henderson, Wijnaldum and Can all inconsistent. Another player out of form was Mane, with Ian Wright putting his blip down to jealousy of Salah. The Reds were fourth on Christmas Day.

Boxing Day saw the Reds thrash bottom-placed Swansea at Anfield. Coutinho's first goal for the club had come in a 5-0 win over the Swans, but when he put the side 1-0 up with a stupendous 25-yard curler on his 200th appearance, few realised it would be his last. It was the 250th goal of Klopp's management, in 128 games. Coutinho set up Firmino for the second, before man of the match Alexander-Arnold smashed the third into the top corner of the Kop goal. Firmino got his second from Salah's square pass, before being taken off. Oxlade-Chamberlain completed the 5-0 rout with a delicate lob.

The announcement that Virgil van Dijk would soon be a Red came the next day, with the club tweeting a picture of him holding a Liverpool shirt in front of his Christmas tree. The 26-year-old would join on New Year's Day. Southampton had excluded him from their last three matchday squads, amid worrying speculation he may be on the verge of moving to Manchester City. The fee was £75 million. It was believed it may have been £50 million had the transfer taken place in the summer – but the Dutch colossus would be worth every penny.

Van Dijk had barely taken his seat in the Main Stand for the final game of 2017 when Matip gave the ball away. A quick transition ended with Leicester's Jamie Vardy turning the ball home in the third minute. Liverpool had been making mistakes like that all season. Karius was now the first-choice keeper. Klopp's last defensive selection before Van Dijk could play was Gomez-Matip-Lovren-Robertson. The latter had now made the left-back spot his own. Salah fired wide and was then thwarted by Harry Maguire's sliding tackle. Mane had a goal disallowed for offside. The dam finally broke on 49 minutes. Mane's backheel found the Egyptian, who turned inside a defender and fired past Kasper Schmeichel. Mane had another goal chalked off. Salah brought the house down with the winner on 76 minutes, as he collected Milner's flick, rolled his man and found the bottom corner from 14 yards. The Reds ended the year in fourth place on 41 points after 21 games, 18 behind unbeaten leaders Manchester City.

The big news from Burnley on New Year's Day was the absence of Coutinho. Nike, sponsor of both Barcelona and the player, had announced his transfer to the Nou Camp before swiftly deleting it, but the deal was announced within days. Liverpool rinsed the Catalonians for £142 million, which included £36 million of add-ons. And with Salah in the form of his life, they didn't need to sign a replacement. Sturridge was also on his way out, albeit temporarily, as he was loaned to West Brom for the rest of the season. Klopp rotated again, with Mane the only member of the 'Fab Four' to play at Turf Moor, and he opened the scoring on the hour with a turn and volley that was reminiscent of Jimmy Case's goal in the 1977 FA Cup Final. With three minutes remaining, the Reds failed to deal with a cross, and the unmarked Johann Berg Gudmundsson equalised. Enter Klavan. Oxlade-Chamberlain hoisted a free kick into the box. Lovren headed it down, and the Estonian bundled in a 94th-minute winner. "That was one of my favourite moments of the year," said Klopp.

Van Dijk made his debut in the third round of the FA Cup, which just happened to be an Anfield Derby, the 20th in a row Everton failed to win. On the BBC, Danny Murphy predicted the Dutchman would bag the winner and, sure enough, he rose at the Kop end to head in Oxlade-Chamberlain's 84th-minute corner, much to the almost-exaggerated dismay of Everton assistant Sammy Lee. Van Dijk was the 93rd Liverpool player to score on his debut, joining the likes of Billy Liddell, Roger Hunt, Kevin Keegan, Ray Kennedy and Robbie Fowler, as well as Mane and Salah. Milner had put the Reds ahead from the spot after a foul on Lallana. Just like the recent league game, an Everton equaliser came from nowhere, as Gylfi Sigurdsson beat Karius from the edge of the box. Although they hadn't been near their best, the Reds responded positively to Everton's equaliser this time, and Van Dijk's winner was thoroughly deserved. But there was sad news to follow, with the death of legendary goalkeeper Tommy Lawrence, who died at the age of 77. He had helped the Reds win their first FA Cup in 1965.

A tight hamstring kept Van Dijk out of the home match against Manchester City. Lovren was the latest player to wear the armband. During the week, Kevin Murphy, 'Cork's biggest Liverpool fan', released his irritatingly catchy ditty to the tune of The Archies 1969 hit 'Sugar, Sugar'. It went: "We got Salah. A-ha Mane, Mane. And Bobby Fir-mi-nooo. But we sold Coutinho." It was never going to be adopted by the Kop, but it went viral, and at the end of Sky's broadcast of Liverpool's jaw-dropping 4-3 win, they showed the goals scored by the remaining trio to the original tune. The scorers grabbed the headlines, but Robertson and Wijnaldum produced their best Liverpool performances to date. After a driving run from midfield, Oxlade-Chamberlain lanced the early tension with a low drive from the edge of the box that nestled in the corner of Ederson's net. Klopp's patience in his new midfielder had paid off. He was looking more impressive by the week. But defensive flaws proved costly once more when Gomez was beaten to a cross-field pass by Leroy Sane. The German beat Matip and Gomez again, before beating Karius at his near post. 1-1 at half-time.

LIVERPOOL F.C. THE PREMIER LEAGUE YEARS

The game exploded into life around the hour, as the Reds dynamited the leaders' unbeaten record in nine breathtaking minutes. Oxlade-Chamberlain released Firmino down the inside left, and Liverpool's number 9 lifted the ball over Ederson for a goal remarkably similar to Robbie Fowler's second at Old Trafford in 1995. Mane hit the post a minute later. Within another 60 seconds, the Senegalese larruped the ball into the top corner after Salah had dispossessed the City defence. The next came from the Egyptian king himself. The majesty of his 35-yard chip for the fourth goal, with Ederson out of his goal, further enraptured an already-disbelieving crowd. It was a devastating period of nine minutes which perfectly summed up Klopp's Liverpool. It also showed the runaway leaders from whom their biggest challenge would soon come. City got back two scruffy goals, but the Reds deservedly held on. The performance bore out the optimism of Murphy's lyrics. Liverpool wouldn't just be okay in their post-Coutinho world. They would thrive without him.

After the Lord Mayor's show came defeat at bottom side Swansea, less than a month after Liverpool had beaten them 5-0. It was the Reds' first loss in 19 matches. Nothing went right. With Lovren injured, Can became the sixth captain of the campaign. Van Dijk made his first league start, and his poor header led to centre back Alfie Mawson scoring the only goal on 40 minutes. Firmino hit a post at the end. Lallana couldn't put away the easy rebound. This dreadful performance elicited memories of the 1-0 defeat at Coventry in 1996, after the glorious 4-3 that had preceded it. Gomez, Can and Mane were among many to be below par.

Liverpool's first brush with VAR came in the FA Cup fourth round at home to second-bottom West Brom, and two big first-half decisions were overturned in their favour. Firmino chipped Ben Foster in the fifth minute, but a rapid brace from Jay Rodriguez put the visitors ahead. Craig Dawson thought he had headed a third, but a foul on Mignolet by Gareth Barry was detected by VAR, and it was disallowed. It looked harsh. Then Salah keeled over in the box, and VAR showed that he had been grabbed by Jake Livermore. Firmino hit the bar from the spot. On the stroke of half-time, Matip touched in Dawson's cross-shot. The Reds were 3-1 down. Henderson made his comeback after missing six matches as a 65th-minute sub for Mane. Liverpool plugged away for much of the second half without reward, until Salah stroked in a loose ball with 12 minutes left. Van Dijk's glancing header was saved by Foster. The Reds were out, beaten at home for the first time in nine months.

Henderson started the league game at Huddersfield. Van Dijk dropped down to the bench. Man of the match Can scored first with a deflected 25-yarder. Firmino made it two in first-half injury time. After dummying to pass, he squeezed the ball past the keeper from the tightest of angles. Salah's penalty following a foul on Can rounded off the scoring.

Spurs came to Anfield on the first Sunday in February and played their part in a classic. Salah scored early, and Liverpool were comfortable for the most part. But Victor Wanyama came off the bench to lash in a stunning equaliser. Spurs were awarded a penalty, but Karius saved from Harry Kane in the 87th minute. Four minutes later, Salah, the best player on the field, scored a belting goal, wriggling his way through the defence before firing into the roof of the net. It seemed sure to be the winner, but there was still time for Spurs to launch a late attack. A long throw came in, and the linesman spotted Van Dijk inadvertently kick Erik Lamela's standing leg. This time Karius was beaten by Kane, and a thrilling game ended 2-2. Klopp sarcastically applauded the officials, but the decision was correct.

Five former Southampton players were in the Liverpool squad that went down to St Mary's stadium. Van Dijk received the most ire from the home fans, but he was flawless. Matip replaced Lovren as the auditions to partner the Dutchman continued. Henderson was rested. Firmino turned in Salah's pass for an early opener. Then the Egyptian made it 2-0 after a mesmeric backheel by the Brazilian.

After something of a mid-season blip, Mane's return to form couldn't have been better timed. Liverpool travelled to the Estadio do Dragao on Valentine's Day for a seemingly tricky game with Porto in the first match of the Champions League knockout phase. They won 5-0. Wijnaldum found Mane on the left, and his relatively tame shot was spilled over the line by Jose Sa. Moments later, Milner smashed the post from distance. The rebound fell to Salah, who flicked over the keeper and then into the net. Eight minutes into the second half, the breaking Salah found Firmino, who drew a save from Sa, but Mane turned in the rebound. Firmino made it four from Milner's square pass. Mane smashed in his third in the 85th minute from 20 yards. Klopp had recently said, "We can't possibly compete with Manchester City, so we have to do it a different way." But the City-like performances were becoming more common. In the stands, 'Allez, Allez, Allez' was heard for the first time. It would become synonymous with Liverpool's exhilarating journey to Kiev.

The front three were on the scoresheet again as the Reds disposed of David Moyes's West Ham. Can headed the team's 100th goal of the campaign from Salah's corner. Salah found the bottom corner for his 31st of the season, equalling Luis Suarez's tally from 2013-14. Firmino made it three after an error from his future teammate Adrian. Antonio got one back. Mane hit the post, but soon turned in Robertson's cross to finish a flowing move. Karius looked assured again and made a vital save from Marko Arnautovic at 0-0. In eight games since the departure of Coutinho, the Reds had rattled in 22 goals. Moyes had still never won at Anfield.

Next up was Newcastle, another team hovering just above the relegation zone, on a bitterly cold night at Anfield. Salah side-footed home Oxlade-Chamberlain's pass. Firmino played in Mane for the second and he finished with aplomb. Oxlade-Chamberlain was outstanding, with the Telegraph praising his "jet-heeled forward runs from midfield, intelligent passes, and the chutzpah to beat an opponent with a piece of skill." For the first time in six matches as opposition manager with Valencia, Chelsea and Newcastle, Rafa Benitez was on the losing side against Liverpool.

With a 5-0 first-leg lead, the return match with Porto threatened to be the non-event of the season. Klopp rested Van Dijk, Alexander-Arnold, Robertson, Oxlade-Chamberlain and Salah. Porto's only ambition was to avoid any further damage. Mane hit a post. Substitute Ings was denied by a great save from the veteran Iker Casillas.

For once, Jose Mourinho's tactics against Liverpool didn't only involve parking a bus, when Manchester United hosted Liverpool on 10th March. He exploited weaknesses in the defence, knowing that the right-sided duo of Alexander-Arnold and Lovren could be fallible. Lovren was drawn out of position by David de Gea's long clearance and was beaten to the ball by Romelu Lukaku, whose flick-on isolated Alexander-Arnold against Marcus Rashford. The young striker beat the full back with ease before firing past Karius. Then another long ball saw Lukaku beat Lovren, and Rashford made it 2-0. The Reds struggled against United's banks of four, with the Echo noting that "if United's backline had dropped any deeper, they would have been sat in the East Stand." Eric Bailly scored a 66th-minute own goal from Mane's low cross, but the Reds were beaten.

Liverpool bounced back in a blizzard against Watford. Gomez and Matip replaced Alexander-Arnold and Lovren, but it was Salah who stole the show with four goals. He skipped past Miguel Britos for the opener and slid the ball past the keeper. He turned in Robertson's superb cross for his second, just before half-time. Six playing minutes later, his low cross from the right was flicked home deftly by Firmino. Salah's hat-trick goal saw him thread the ball through a crowd of players into the bottom corner as he was losing his balance. With five minutes left, he bagged his 36th goal in 41 games, hammering in a rebound after Ings's shot had been parried by Orestis Karnezis. When his teammates signed the match ball for Salah, Henderson's message was simply, "Well done superstar." The only blot was a back injury sustained in the first half by Can, who would miss 11 games.

Liverpool collected another three points ahead of the Champions League first leg with Manchester City. Klopp opted not to rest his big guns against Crystal Palace, and they overturned an early deficit to win 2-1. Wilfried Zaha was causing havoc, and after Karius clattered into him, Luka Milivojevic converted the penalty. Mane was denied a penalty and booked for diving. He then had a goal disallowed for offside. Four minutes into the second half, his luck changed as he turned in Milner's driven cross. Christian Benteke spurned a couple of sitters. Mane somehow escaped a second yellow when he picked the ball up in the belief he had been fouled. He was soon substituted. A switch to a three centre-back system in the last 20 minutes gave them more rhythm. With six minutes remaining, Firmino left Robertson's low cross and Salah, now a centre forward, controlled it and drove the ball into the bottom corner. City, meanwhile, made short work of Everton at Goodison, winning 3-1. Footage later emerged of their manager Pep Guardiola telling one of his coaches after the game that Liverpool's front three "scare me".

The first leg of the Champions League quarter-final against City would take its place as a truly momentous Anfield occasion. 'Allez, Allez, Allez' was sung on an endless loop from about two hours before kick-off as the streets around Anfield filled up. Red smoke and a cacophony of jeers greeted the City team bus, not to mention a few stray bottles. The hostility rattled one of the City officials, as footage from inside the bus would later indicate. Perhaps it affected some of their players, too. A hamstring injury had ended Matip's season, so Lovren came into the 11. With Gomez and Klavan also injured, young Conor Masterson took his place on the bench as back-up centre half. Oxlade-Chamberlain came in for Wijnaldum, who dropped to the bench. Liverpool were down to the bare bones in crucial areas - their other outfield subs were Clyne, Moreno, Ings and Solanke, compared to nearly £200 million of talent on City's bench in Danilo, Stones, Sterling, Delph, Bernardo and Zinchenko. Alexander-Arnold had recently been roasted by Marcus Rashford and Wilfried Zaha. How would he fare against Leroy Sane? And what about Lovren, up against a team that had scored 124 goals? Few could see anything other than City progressing to the semi-final.

Everything that encapsulates what is good about Jurgen Klopp's Liverpool was on display in a magnificent first half. Among many City errors, they dropped Sterling for Ilkay Gundogan – "a feather in the Anfield storm," according to The Times - and they turned Liverpool around, so they attacked the Kop in the first half – a big mistake against a team who were clearly going to go hell for leather from minute one. "Just like United, you live in the past," crowed the travelling fans, but they were about to witness Liverpool's current team blowing their heroes off the park. City actually started positively and forced an 11th-minute corner but, within seconds, Salah was planting the ball into Ederson's net after a scintillating counter. Lift-off. There was no chance the Reds would sit on a 1-0 lead. With the decibels off the chart, Milner flew into a tackle. The ball came to Oxlade-Chamberlain, who controlled it and struck a 25-yard thunderbolt into the corner of the net. The clock had only just ticked past 30 minutes when Salah delivered a tantalising cross for Mane to nod in the third. Liverpool were over the horizon and well into footballing utopia, after one of the greatest half hours of football anyone could remember. Salah had stand-in left back Aymeric Laporte on toast. Mane was giving Kyle Walker nightmares. Freed by not having to mark Sterling, Robertson bombed forward at will. Henderson, Milner and Oxlade-Chamberlain won the midfield battle convincingly. Van Dijk should have made it four at the end of the first half, but his glancing header went inches wide. Television cameras captured City's damaged bus being driven away at half time. Their Champions League hopes were going with it.

The second half was very different. Salah lasted only seven minutes before a groin problem saw him replaced by Wijnaldum. Moreno and Solanke also came on. The Reds took the sting out of the tie, preserving their lead with ease. A late booking for Henderson ruled him out of the second leg. Among at least half a dozen candidates for man of the match, Alexander-Arnold probably edged it, with a performance that belied his years as he disdainfully snuffed out the threat of Sane. City didn't even have a shot on target. They had a mountain to climb now.

In between the two legs, Clyne, Klavan, Wijnaldum, Ings and Solanke came into the side for a Goodison derby. A dull game ended goalless. Theo Walcott got little change from makeshift left back Klavan. Wijnaldum did well in the holding-midfield position in preparation for the return match with City. Solanke missed a couple of chances. Karius denied Yannick Bolasie. Dominic Calvert-Lewin should have scored at the end but fluffed his lines. It was the first derby without a booking since 1992.

Klopp's only change at the Etihad was Wijnaldum replacing Henderson. Everyone knew it was vital that Liverpool didn't concede early, but Van Dijk lost the ball, and Gabriel Jesus finished a lightning-quick transition. Klopp had warned his players to expect a 'thunderstorm' and, sure enough, Liverpool were clinging on for dear life. Bernardo Silva hit the post with a 20-yard scorcher. Leroy Sane's goal was incorrectly ruled out for offside, but City had blown themselves out after 40 minutes. The half ended with Oxlade-Chamberlain missing a sitter from a rapid counterattack. It was a shot across City's bow. The second half would be different. Mane surged into the box ten minutes into the half, and Salah settled the tie when he took the ball past Ederson and calmly lifted it over the covering Nicolas Otamendi. Guardiola, banished to the stands for abusing the officials at half-time, was ashen-faced. City needed four in 34 minutes. With 13 minutes left, Firmino dispossessed Otamendi and made the aggregate score 5-1 by rolling the ball into the far corner. Among numerous stunning performances, those of Lovren and Oxlade-Chamberlain stood out.

After a minute's applause to remember the victims of Hillsborough 29 years earlier, Liverpool beat Bournemouth 3-0, with the front three each helping themselves to a goal. Mane slammed in a rebound after Asmir Begovic had parried his header. Salah bagged his 40th goal in all competitions with an exquisite looping header from Alexander-Arnold's deep cross. Firmino scored his 25th of the season in injury time.

With a Champions League semi-final with Roma three days away, Klopp rested Alexander-Arnold, Robertson, Lovren, Oxlade-Chamberlain and Firmino for the trip to bottom-placed West Brom. Ings scored his first goal under Klopp in the fourth minute from close range. He had suffered a cruciate ligament rupture in the German's first week as manager, causing him to spend 210 days on the sideline. In October 2016, he needed knee surgery, which put him out for a further 288 days. Salah made it two, lifting a ball from Oxlade-Chamberlain over Ben Foster. With little over ten minutes left, Jake Livermore bundled one in for West Brom, and Salomon Rondon headed in an 89th-minute equaliser. Liverpool were eight points clear of fifth-place Chelsea, who had a game in hand and who still had to host the Reds.

Quite unbelievably, Liverpool were 5-0 up after 70 minutes of the Champions League semi-final first leg against Roma. Klopp's men were better even than they had been against City. The only negative was a knee injury sustained by the in-form Oxlade-Chamberlain, who would now be absent for a year. For 36 minutes, Liverpool had been the better side but had failed to score. Then Henderson dispossessed Dzeko in midfield. Firmino found Salah just inside the area, on the right. He shifted it onto his left foot and unleashed an unstoppable curling shot which beat Alisson Becker all ends up. Salah, who had recently collected the PFA Player of the Year award, didn't celebrate against his former club, but his teammates mobbed him, particularly a fired-up Henderson. In first-half injury time, Firmino poked through a perfectly weighted ball, and Salah lifted it over Alisson. For a split second it seemed not to have enough pace, but it beat the last defender and crossed the line. Still not smiling, he calmly put his hand through his hair as Anfield went berserk.

Ten minutes into the second half, the Egyptian was released into oceans of space down the right. He unselfishly squared to Mane, who made it three. Firmino tapped in Salah's low cross and then headed in Milner's corner. Five goals in 34 minutes of football heaven. Salah went off. He and Firmino now had 11 each in a European campaign, breaking Dean Saunders' record of nine from the 1991-92 UEFA Cup. But these goals weren't against the likes of Kuusysi Lahti and Swarowski Tirol. But there was a sobering conclusion to the game. Dzeko finally got free and slotted past Karius. Four minutes later, Milner was adjudged to have blocked a shot with his arm. Diego Perotti put the penalty into the top corner. A 3-0 home win would be enough for the Italians to reach the final. But the worst news of the night was the pre-match attack of Liverpool supporter Sean Cox by cowardly Roma fans. He lay in a coma for several weeks and only returned home in March 2020. When the Reds won the league title three months after that, chief executive Peter Moore tweeted, "One man in Ireland is loving every moment of this...thinking of you this evening Sean. You'll Never, Ever, Walk Alone."

There was a yellow shirt hanging among the red in the home dressing room before the match before Stoke. It belonged to St Peters Gaelic Football Club, of whom Sean Cox was a member. With an eye on the second leg in the Eternal City, Klopp stood down Lovren, Robertson, Milner and Mane and was frustrated by another league draw, with Chelsea breathing down Liverpool's necks. Alexander-Arnold played in midfield, with Gomez at right back. The latter struggled. Salah, who had also been crowned the Football Writers' Player of the Year, was sent clean through by Henderson but amazed everybody by clipping the ball wide of Jack Butland's goal. Ings thundered in a close-range volley, but he was offside. A blatant penalty was turned down when Erik Pieters handled Wijnaldum's late cross. The Reds had been awarded one penalty at home in the league all season. Despite having 72% of possession, Liverpool didn't have a goal in them. They were six points clear of Chelsea, who had a game in hand. They also had to visit Stamford Bridge, but their goal difference was superior to Chelsea's by 17. The best news of the week was Firmino agreeing to a new five-year deal.

Liverpool travelled to the Stadio Olimpico, scene of their 1977 and 1984 European Cup triumphs, with a three-goal lead, but would have been mindful of the previous round, when Roma had overturned a 4-1 deficit against Barcelona, winning the second leg 3-0 to go through on away goals. In his 11th game in the competition, Alexander-Arnold, still a teenager, had now made more European Cup appearances than Everton. The Reds were in for another crazy game. When Mane, Liverpool's best player on the night, scored on nine minutes, Roma needed four. But Milner scored a bizarre own goal six minutes later as Lovren's clearance hit him and flew into the bottom corner. Wijnaldum headed the Reds back into the lead on the night with his first away goal for the club. What a time to get it. Roma hadn't conceded a home goal in the competition but had just shipped in two in 26 minutes in front of the Curva Sud.

Seven minutes into the second half, Dzeko turned in a rebound after Karius parried a shot from Stephan El Shaarawy. With four minutes left, the aggregate score was 7-4 to Liverpool but Radja Nainggolan then fired a 25-yarder in off the post. Roma got another in injury time when the same player converted a penalty, which was harshly given against Klavan for handball. The game kicked off again, and the referee immediately blew for full time. The Reds were in their eighth European Cup Final, where they would play Real Madrid in Kiev. As the players celebrated, they held up a banner which read, "Sean Cox – You'll Never Walk Alone."

The top four was still in the balance when Liverpool went to Chelsea, who were mourning the recent death of Ray Wilkins. A win would secure a Champions League spot for the Reds. A draw would also suffice, barring a goal-difference swing of miraculous proportions. So when Chelsea beat Liverpool 1-0, courtesy of a first-half goal from Olivier Giroud, Champions League qualification would go down to the final day for the second year in a row. Two crucial matches lay ahead for the fatigued players – a top-four decider and a Champions League Final.

After a week in which Salah won the club's Player of the Year award, the Reds entertained Brighton in their final league game. Henderson was back, and Solanke started as Klopp switched to a 4-2-3-1. The young striker set up the opener for Salah, whose low finish saw him break the Premier League record for the most goals in a 38-game season, with 32. He was later presented with the Golden Boot by Kenny Dalglish for his season's work. Lovren, who had a superb game, got the second five minutes before half-time, heading in Robertson's cross. Solanke finally broke his duck, hammering Salah's pass in off the bar eight minutes into the second half. By this time, Chelsea were three down at Newcastle. The top four was in the bag. Mane, Salah and Firmino were substituted for Lallana, Woodburn and Ings with an eye on Kiev. Robertson also scored his first goal for the club with five minutes left. It was the 14th game of the season Liverpool had scored four or more goals and the perfect send-off ahead of the Champions League Final in 13 days' time. The Reds finished fourth on 75 points, five ahead of Chelsea. But they were 25 points off top spot, with Manchester City waltzing to the title in unprecedented fashion, finishing on 100 points.

Saturday 26th May 2018 saw Liverpool take on Real Madrid in Kiev's Olympic Stadium. Fans spent the afternoon in Shevchenko Park, booming out 'Allez, Allez, Allez' and other classics from the Anfield hymnbook. The side chosen by Klopp was: Karius; Alexander-Arnold, Lovren, Van Dijk, Robertson; Henderson, Milner, Wijnaldum; Salah, Firmino, Mane. Lallana and the returning Can came off the bench, with Mignolet, Clyne, Klavan, Moreno and Solanke unused.

Liverpool started brightly. Karius was quick off his line to make an important punch. Firmino nearly got Mane in on goal. Alexander-Arnold was a whisker away from a loose ball coming his way with only the keeper to beat. Firmino had an opportunity to shoot from point-blank range but failed to adjust his feet. Klopp applauded the Reds start. He would have been delighted with the press, which was causing Madrid problems. Cristiano Ronaldo blazed over the bar from a tight angle. Firmino tried to play Mane in with a header but put too much on it. Ramos then blocked Firmino's shot, and Keylor Navas saved the rebound from Alexander-Arnold. After 24 minutes, Liverpool were the better side but hadn't created a genuine gilt-edged chance. And then it happened. In the 25th minute, Salah chased a throw-in halfway inside the Madrid half. Ramos pursued him, grabbed his right arm and pulled him down as they ran side by side. Salah fell on his left shoulder under the weight of the Spaniard. It was dislocated. He left the field in tears, having initially tried to continue. It was no accident. Ramos had identified Liverpool's best player and had taken him out with a manoeuvre that belonged in a wrestling ring. It was the cruellest of endings to Salah's debut season. Lallana replaced him, having played just 17 minutes since the end of March. He went to the left, with Mane moving to the right, but he was off the pace. Klopp could have used Solanke, who had looked the part against Brighton. More ideal replacements would have been Origi, had he not been loaned to Wolfsburg for the season, or Ings, had he been named on the bench. Madrid also lost a player, with the injured right back Dani Carvajal making way for Nacho. Karius saved brilliantly from Ronaldo, with Benzema turning in the rebound, but it was disallowed for offside. The goalkeeper had had little to do, but was reliable when needed. Nacho hit the side netting, and Benzema was just wide from distance, but Karius had them both covered. The half ended goalless. Worryingly, Liverpool hadn't had an attack since the Salah incident, and they weren't pressing as high up the pitch.

The second half of the Champions League Final couldn't really have been any worse. The only consolation was, unlike losing the title in 2014, it didn't precipitate a long-term collapse in the team's fortunes. It simply proved to be a mere blip on the journey to the stunning successes that followed in 2019 and 2020. Everybody recovered from the disappointment, apart from Karius, whose career fell apart in a devastating 32 minutes. A couple of minutes into the half, Isco hit the bar after Lallana conceded possession. A minute later, Ramos elbowed Karius in the face in an off-the-ball incident. Nobody knew at the time, but he was concussed. Three minutes later, he casually rolled the ball out. Benzema stuck out a leg, and the ball trickled into the corner of the net.

It was an extraordinary piece of ill fortune, as Salah's injury had been. But the Reds showed the resolve to bounce back quickly and were behind for just four minutes. Raphael Varane saved a goal by glancing Milner's dangerous cross behind for a corner, with Firmino waiting to pounce. Milner sent in a corner to the back post. Lovren headed it goalward, and Mane's outstretched foot got to the ball and poked it past Navas. Thirty thousand fans watching the game on big screens at Anfield erupted with joy. The character Liverpool had shown in recovering from two such grievous blows was phenomenal. With 25 minutes left, the final was locked at 1-1.

The next turning point came with the introduction of the Welshman Gareth Bale, who replaced Isco just past the hour. Having equalised, Liverpool would see little of the ball during the next passage of play. On the field for little more than two minutes, Bale executed an outrageous scissor kick from 14 yards, sending the ball past Karius and into the top corner. It was as good a goal as any in a European final. Madrid manager Zinedine Zidane celebrated a goal even better than his famous volley in the 2002 final.

Robertson nearly got Mane in on goal with a great ball, but Ramos cut it out. Then the Senegalese hit the post from 20 yards. It was one of Liverpool's last threatening moments. Robertson prevented Ronaldo from pulling the trigger with the goal at his mercy. Desperate for a goal, the Reds struggled to lay a glove on Madrid. There was little on the bench for Klopp, who was about to lose his fifth successive final. Karius made a routine save from Benzema. Mane was booked for a foul on Ramos. With seven minutes left, Can replaced Milner for his first appearance since mid-March. It was his last for the club. Almost immediately, Karius made another horrendous error. Bale cut in from the right and launched a hit and hope from 35 yards. His shot was struck nicely, although straight at Karius. But with his head scrambled, the goalkeeper spilled it. In it went. 3-1. In the stands, his partner and mother wept. They were comforted by Ulla Klopp. Lovren denied Bale a hat trick with a sensational tackle. Van Dijk intercepted, with Ronaldo ready to pounce. Each of the defenders had played well. The final action was as bizarre as anything that had preceded it, as a pitch invader tried to get to Ronaldo, as he was lining up a shot. The stewards dragged the perpetrator away, and the final whistle went. Real Madrid had won their third European Cup in a row and their 13th overall. Karius fell to the turf, crying. Madrid players went to console him, noticeably before any of his teammates did. He went to the Liverpool fans, with his arms up, apologising. Like Can, he had just played his last competitive game for the club, but for very different reasons. The hedonistic joyride of the road to Kiev had ended with the wheels falling off.

Spirits were raised the next morning when a video emerged of the manager partying into the small hours with his baseball cap back to front. The disappointment of 90 crazy minutes could be put to one side, because there was a bigger picture to examine. The season's tally of 135 goals had been bettered only once in 126 years. Liverpool under Jurgen Klopp weren't just going places. They were standing on the verge of greatness.

2018-19

"We've conquered all of Europe!"

oris Karius's horror show in Kiev was the hottest topic of the summer. Surely Liverpool would be signing a new goalkeeper, but as the new campaign approached, there was no sign of it happening. The German's performance against Tranmere Rovers in a pre-season friendly showed that he hadn't even started the process of recovering from the Champions League Final. The idea of Simon Mignolet becoming first choice again hardly lightened the mood, either. Klopp was considering young Danny Ward as his first choice for the new season. And then, out of the blue, Roma reduced their £75 million price tag for Alisson Becker. It had originally been £90 million. Liverpool were now interested. Even though the 25-year-old Brazilian had conceded seven goals in the Champions League semi-final against the Reds, he was vastly better than anything Klopp had at his disposal. The Reds got him for £65 million and received £12.5 million from Leicester for Ward. Karius would soon be on his way to Besiktas on loan. Mignolet stayed to be Alisson's understudy.

By the summer of 2018, it was abundantly clear that Klopp had improved Liverpool's defence beyond recognition. Trent Alexander-Arnold and Andy Robertson had enjoyed breakthrough seasons and had plenty of time to develop further, with Nathaniel Clyne and Alberto Moreno having to take a backseat. Everybody could see the quality of Virgil van Dijk, who was now the world's best defender. With him at the back, the Reds would challenge for the biggest of prizes. Dejan Lovren had enjoyed an excellent second half to the season, culminating in a commanding performance in Kiev, but he aggravated a pelvis injury at the World Cup, where he had helped Croatia reach the final. He would miss seven games. Joel Matip and Joe Gomez were competing for the spot next to Van Dijk. Both would have magnificent seasons. Ragnar Klavan left for Cagliari for £2 million.

The midfield had been down to the bare bones by the end of the season, with Jordan Henderson, Gini Wijnaldum and James Milner the last three standing. None had played particularly well in Kiev. Emre Can was heading to Juventus on a Bosman. Adam Lallana had endured a stop-start season. Alex Oxlade-Chamberlain was still on the long-term injured list. New blood was needed, and a few days after Kiev, Liverpool announced the £40 million capture of Monaco's Fabinho, a Brazilian holding midfielder. Naby Keita was on his way from Leipzig, having been signed a year earlier for £52.75 million. And there was nearly another newcomer when Lyon's highly-rated attacking midfielder Nabil Fekir went as far as posing in a Liverpool shirt with everything agreed, but the club didn't like the results of his medical, and the deal collapsed.

Mo Salah, Roberto Firmino and Sadio Mane made up what was arguably the best attacking trio in world football. Salah won his race to play in the World Cup after Sergio Ramos had dislocated his shoulder in Kiev, but he wasn't right, and Egypt exited at the group stage. But strength in depth still needed to be addressed. Dominic Solanke hadn't cut the mustard and was snapped up by Bournemouth for £19 million. Danny Ings was still in the initial stages of recovering from two long-term injuries. In came Stoke winger Xherdan Shaqiri for what seemed like a bargain £13.75 million. He immediately endeared himself to the fans with a spectacular overhead kick in a 4-1 pre-season friendly win against Manchester United. Daniel Sturridge and Divock Origi returned from loan spells at West Brom and Wolfsburg. Origi's confidence was shattered after an awful season in the Bundesliga. Few thought he had a future at the club, but he would soon be writing himself into Anfield folklore.

Ahead of the 2018-19 season, bookies rated Liverpool as 4-1 second-favourites to lift the Premier League trophy. The odds were more a reflection of Manchester City's brilliance in 2017-18 than anything else, and while the bookies correctly predicted that the trophy would remain at the Etihad, the Reds would play their part in a thrilling title race. Happily, Liverpool would recover from losing out to City by a solitary point in 195, as they went on to lift their sixth European Cup in Madrid.

Track one of Jurgen Klopp's eagerly awaited fourth album was a beauty, as Liverpool thrashed West Ham 4-0 at Anfield on the first Sunday of the season. The manger named the following side: Alisson; Alexander-Arnold, Gomez, Van Dijk, Robertson; Wijnaldum, Milner, Keita; Salah, Firmino, Mane. Off the bench came Henderson, Shaqiri and Sturridge, with Karius, Clyne, Fabinho and Lallana unused. The Reds dominated West Ham. Salah scored the first goal of the season, turning in Robertson's left-wing cross following an important contribution from debutant Keita. Mane turned in Milner's cutback in first-half injury time. He had matched John Barnes in scoring in three successive season-openers and added another just into the second half. Sturridge had only been on a minute when he scored from close range to make it 4-0. The forwards were as sharp as ever, and their performances were equalled by Robertson, Milner and Keita.

Crystal Palace away on a Monday night still invoked nightmares from 2014, but this time the Reds eased to a 2-0 win. Palace's Andros Townsend hit the bar with a 25-yard screamer. Mamadou Sakho fouled Salah in the box. Milner coolly put away the penalty. Alisson kept out Luka Milivojevic's free kick. Aaron Wan-Bissaka was sent off for a professional foul on Salah. Mane broke away deep into injury time, rounded Wayne Hennessy and wrapped up the points. Van Dijk and Gomez were immense at the back. Keita looked extremely promising.

Next up was Brighton. The Reds were unconvincing. Klopp picked the same side again, and they eked out a 1-0 win. Alexander-Arnold hit the bar with a free kick. Salah scored the only goal midway through the half, slotting Firmino's pass into the bottom corner. Hearts were in mouths when Alisson flicked the ball over Anthony Knockaert, who was closing him down. It wasn't his first piece of showboating of the season. Brighton squandered a couple of big chances to equalise. Earlier in the day, Manchester City drew at Wolves.

Alisson finally conceded a goal in his fourth game, at Leicester, and it was a horrendous error. Fortunately, Liverpool were already 2-0 up. Henderson made his first start of the season. Mane took Robertson's pass and poked the ball past Kasper Schmeichel. Firmino headed the second from Milner's corner. Halfway through the second half, Alisson attempted a Cruyff turn on Kelechi Iheanacho, lost the ball and was helpless as Rachid Ghezzal turned it home. "I am angry that I made a mistake that put the team in a difficult situation," he said later. The Reds held on, with Gomez leading by example. Liverpool had 54 throw-ins against Leicester and had raised eyebrows with their recent employment of the Danish throw-in coach, Thomas Gronnemark. Such a job title was widely ridiculed, but there was more to his job than teaching players to throw the ball. In 2017-18, Liverpool had retained possession just 45.4 per cent of the time when they had a throw-in under pressure. That was the third lowest in the league. During 2018-19, it would go up to 68.4, which ranked them at number one. Under Gronnemark's tutelage, the Reds would score more goals from moves beginning with a throw. They would also lay pressing traps from opposition throw-ins. His appointment proved to be a masterstroke.

Liverpool made it five from five with a 2-1 win over Spurs in the sunshine at Wembley, where they had been humiliated the previous October. Firmino flicked in Milner's cross, but Mane was offside. Michel Vorm saved from Salah and Mane but missed a corner later in the half, and Wijnaldum headed the opener. Firmino made it two from close range early in the second half after Jan Vertonghen had hit his own post. Liverpool should have been out of sight by the time Erik Lamela pulled a goal back in injury time. Then the Reds got lucky, as Mane could have conceded a penalty for a challenge on Son Heung-min. Liverpool had been vastly superior but were clinging on at the end.

Firmino had sustained an eye injury in London, and dropped to the bench for the opening Champions League match at home to Paris St Germain, whose weaponry included Neymar, Edinson Cavani, Kylian Mbappe and Angel Di Maria. Sturridge replaced the Brazilian and headed Robertson's cross past Alphonse Areola on the half hour. Milner soon made it two from the spot after Wijnaldum was tripped. But the French side found a way back with goals from Thomas Meunier and Mbappe. Salah had given the ball away before the equaliser and was substituted. Klopp threw on Fabinho for his debut. Firmino, the first sub to come on, drilled the winner into the bottom corner two minutes into injury time. Anfield erupted but, intriguingly, an angry-looking Salah threw a water bottle to the ground. Earlier in the day came the sad news that former Red Stephen Darby, now at Bolton Wanderers, was retiring from football at the age of 29 after being diagnosed with Motor Neurone Disease.

Shaqiri was handed a first start at home to Southampton and had a strange afternoon. His shot led to a tenth-minute own goal by Wesley Hoedt. Matip headed in Alexander-Arnold's corner to make it two. In first-half injury time, Shaqiri's almost-perfect free kick hit the underside of the bar, bounced down and was bundled over the line by Salah, who had earlier fluffed a couple of chances. The team was cheered off, with Shaqiri taking most of the plaudits. But Liverpool had been susceptible to the Southampton counter and were perhaps lucky to be 3-0 up. Klopp withdrew the Swiss winger at the break, switching from 4-2-3-1 to 4-3-3. The second half was goalless.

Fabinho earned a first start in the League Cup game at home to Chelsea, along with Mignolet, Clyne, Moreno, Lovren, Matip and Shaqiri. Sturridge, who had earlier missed a sitter, executed a pearler of a scissor kick on the hour, after Keita's shot had been parried. But Emerson Palmieri equalised. Sturridge hit the bar with a long-range, left-footed curler. With five minutes to go, Eden Hazard scored a remarkable individual goal, dribbling into the box from the right, beating Moreno all ends up and unleashing a rocket past Mignolet.

Salah had endured a mixed season so far. He had scored three goals, but he looked anxious, and some easy chances had gone begging. He would shine again soon, but he was off-colour once more at Stamford Bridge as Liverpool's perfect league record came to an end. Another who wasn't having everything his own way was Keita, who was now on the bench. Hazard scored again after the Reds were opened up by the Chelsea midfield. Kepa Arrizabalaga saved from Mane. Alisson did likewise from Hazard. Shaqiri blew a great chance to equalise. Just as it seemed time was running out, Sturridge, who had been on the field for three minutes, unleashed a curling, dipping 25-yarder which found the top corner in the 89th minute.

A trip to Italy saw the Reds lose 1-0 to Carlo Ancelotti's Napoli, with Lorenzo Insigne scoring in the last minute. A back injury saw Keita depart on a stretcher after 18 minutes. He'd started terribly in any case and was replaced by Henderson. Napoli were the better side, with Insigne going close, Jose Callejon having a shot cleared off the line by Gomez and Dries Mertens hitting the bar. The pressure told right at the death, when Insigne slid home a low cross after Van Dijk had been pulled out of position. Alexander-Arnold, Milner and Wijnaldum, as well as Keita, all had an evening to forget.

Liverpool's disjointed form continued with a 0-0 draw at home to Manchester City in the Premier League – their fourth game in a row without a win. Riyad Mahrez fluffed a late penalty in front of the City supporters. Klopp dropped Alexander-Arnold, moving Gomez to right back and bringing in Lovren. The Croat produced his usual mixed bag of a performance. He could have conceded a first-half penalty with an error followed by a foul, but later atoned with a Beckenbauerian tackle on Gabriel Jesus to end a dangerous counterattack. Milner came off on the half hour, replaced by the fit-again Keita. Each team had a few half chances, with Salah spurning Liverpool's best. With four minutes left, Van Dijk fouled Leroy Sane, but Mahrez sent his penalty high into the Anfield

Road stand. His team still hadn't won at Anfield since 2003. The Reds' defenders and midfielders all did their jobs, but the attacking trio were a shadow of their usual selves. Guardiola had successfully stifled them but, in doing so, blunted his own team's threat.

After an international break, Liverpool won their first game in five with an underwhelming performance at Huddersfield. Milner's hamstring had recovered in just ten days. Lallana and Sturridge made their first league starts for nearly a year, with Shaqiri playing central midfield in a 4-3-3 formation. Mane was injured. Firmino was benched. David Wagner's team were still winless and conceded the winner to a rare moment of class, as Gomez and Shaqiri combined cleverly to set up Salah's 50th goal in English football. Jonathan Hogg hit a post from 25 yards, Alex Pritchard had a goal disallowed, and other chances went astray, as the home side came close to embarrassing Liverpool.

There was nothing missing from the performance at home to Red Star Belgrade, as the Serbians were spanked 4-0. Klopp switched to 4-2-3-1, which would become a regular feature over the coming months. Fabinho and Wijnaldum played as holding midfielders – known as a 'Double Six'. Firmino got the opener from Robertson's low cross. Salah made it two after Shaqiri's clever touch. He got another from the spot six minutes into the second half after Mane was fouled. It was the Egyptian's 50th goal for the club in a club-record 65 appearances. The previous holder of the record, Albert Stubbins, had needed 77 games. With Salah substituted, Mane took the next penalty, but Milan Borjan tipped it onto the bar. The Senegalese, who played with a broken thumb in a protective cast, did make it 4-0 from Sturridge's pass. Shaqiri stood out again, while fans got their first real glimpses of the brilliance of Fabinho. Klopp had been patient as the Brazilian learned the intricacies of the English game from the sidelines and on the training ground.

The Reds scored another four in their next home game, which was against Neil Warnock's Cardiff. Salah scored the only goal of a first half in which Liverpool enjoyed 86% of the possession as they completed 412 passes to Cardiff's 35. The highlight of the half was a prostrate Firmino preventing a corner with a backheeled nutmeg on a bemused forward. The Welsh side cracked in the final quarter of the game, conceding goals to Mane, Shaqiri and Mane again. The Swiss's finish was calm as he turned inside the last defender and slotted the ball into the corner. In his last four games, he had assisted three goals, created six chances and now had his first goal. But Cardiff did grab one themselves through Callum Paterson as they became the first opposition team since February to score in the league at Anfield.

Klopp reverted to 4-3-3 as the Reds drew 1-1 at in-form Arsenal. With Fabinho struggling – thankfully that proved to be a one-off – Liverpool struggled for an hour, with Arsenal's Lucas Torreira bossing the midfield. Alexander-Arnold also had a difficult afternoon. Nonetheless, Mane had a goal wrongly disallowed, and Van Dijk missed an easy chance and then his header kissed a post. Klopp stiffened the midfield by dropping Wijnaldum back alongside Fabinho and was rewarded when Milner fired in his first goal from open play for over two and a half years. Van Dijk had a header tipped over the bar, but the Reds were punished when Alexandre Lacazette curled in the equaliser.

However bad the Reds were for the first hour at the Emirates, they were far worse in Belgrade, as they lost 2-0 to Red Star. A Wijnaldum-Milner-Lallana midfield was found wanting, both defensively and offensively. Alexander-Arnold was poor again and was replaced at the break by Gomez. On a rare start, Sturridge was hooked at the same time, for Firmino. The 1991 European champions scored their goals in the 22nd and 29th minutes - the first from a corner and the second after a mistake by Milner. A Robertson cross was deflected onto the bar in the second half. Salah also hit a post. The night ended with Van Dijk up front. Only a fortnight earlier, Liverpool had beaten Red Star 4-0.

Exactly 100 years to the day of the Great War ending, Fulham gave Liverpool a couple of early scares at Anfield, but seconds after a disallowed goal, Salah broke away to make it 1-0. Man of the match Shaqiri doubled the lead in the second half with a beautifully cushioned side-footed volley from Robertson's cross - the Scotsman's fifth assist of the season. Henderson returned as a sub for Wijnaldum after sitting out four games with injury.

After an international break, the Reds hammered Watford 3-0 at Vicarage Road. Henderson partnered Wijnaldum in the middle of a 4-2-3-1. Shaqiri started on the right, with Firmino behind Salah. Mane set up Salah for the crucial opener after three-quarters of the game had elapsed. Alexander-Arnold curled in a stunning free kick a week after scoring for England. Henderson stupidly got himself sent off for a couple of bookings, which meant he would be pencilled out of the forthcoming encounter with Everton. Firmino nodded in the third after Ben Foster had parried Mane's shot.

The Reds lost their third Champions League away match, with a lethargic performance in the French capital. Klopp had demanded "big balls football," but Henderson, Milner and Wijnaldum were outplayed in midfield. At the Parc des Princes, the stadium where Bob Paisley's men had won the competition in 1981, Juan Bernat put PSG ahead, after Van Dijk failed to clear. Marco Verratti was lucky not to be dismissed after a crude challenge on Gomez. Neymar made it two after a quick counter. Gomez, playing right back, could have done better with both goals. Milner converted a penalty just before the break, after Angel Di Maria fouled Mane. Liverpool barely tested Gianluigi Buffon in the second half. Their hopes of qualifying for the last 16 would depend on them beating Napoli at Anfield in December.

Just as it seemed Liverpool would pay the price for another insipid performance, up popped the long-forgotten Divock Origi, with one of the funniest goals ever scored, to win the Anfield Derby, the 21st in a row Everton failed to win. The teams matched each other for much of the afternoon. Mane blazed a promising opening into the Anfield Road stand. Alisson saved Theo Walcott's close-range header. Gomez miraculously cleared off the line after the ball had ricocheted back off the prostrate winger. Jordan Pickford saved well from Shaqiri. Alisson denied Walcott again. Origi replaced Firmino with six minutes left. He caused Everton problems on the right, running at defenders and winning a couple of corners, although he could only hit the crossbar from close range. Another derby was petering out – another in which the Blues had frustrated the Reds.

And then came the most astonishing moment. Six minutes into injury time, Alexander-Arnold pumped a long diagonal ball into the Everton box. Yerry Mina headed clear. Van Dijk attempted a match-winning volley from 20 yards. He skied it horribly and turned his back on it, cursing himself. Liverpool would now be four points behind Manchester City. An Everton fan threw a blue flare onto the pitch to celebrate another great derby draw. Everton started to plan the DVD release. The ball was still in the air. Down it came. A befuddled Pickford panicked. He got a hand to it but didn't have the reach to push it over the bar. The ball hit the top of the crossbar and came down perfectly for Origi to head into the empty goal. Anfield went crazy. Klopp ran onto the pitch to hug Alisson. There was as much laughter as cheering in the stands. The goal kept Liverpool within two points off the top. A Manchester City fan on Twitter observed that the Reds were like wasps at a picnic. They weren't going to go away.

Origi's moment of glory proved to be a turning point in the season. Eleven wins from 14 represented a promising start to the season, but something wasn't right. As the defence had improved out of sight, Liverpool were less of a threat at the other end. Klopp couldn't get his midfield right. Keita was now stranded on the bench. Fabinho had taken three months to settle in. Salah was scoring but didn't look like the player that had taken his debut season by storm. But Liverpool were about to enjoy a dream December, as a lot of those issues were resolved. Klopp sent out a strange-looking line-up at Burnley three days after the derby. In came Moreno, Matip, Keita, Milner, Sturridge and Origi. With Liverpool 1-0 down on the hour, it looked like being a costly decision. Gomez had broken his leg in the first half. His season was as good as over. Jack Cork scored Burnley's goal from a corner, but Milner fired in the crucial equaliser from 20 yards. On came Salah and Firmino. Van Dijk immediately set up a goal for the Brazilian. On his first league start for three months, the superb Keita went close a couple of times. Alisson made a crucial save in the last minute. Then he threw the ball to Sturridge on the right. He found Salah. The Egyptian hooked it to Shaqiri, who sealed the points. "Questions keep being asked of this Liverpool team and they keep coming up with the answers," mused James Pearce in the Liverpool Echo.

A Saturday lunchtime date on the south coast resulted in a 4-0 win for the Reds. Milner played right back on his 500th Premier League appearance. Salah played up front, with Firmino behind him. Shaqiri and Keita filled the wide roles in a 4-2-3-1. Matip came in for Gomez and would fill the role with aplomb for the rest of the season. Bournemouth were rightly upset at the opener when an offside Salah gobbled up the rebound from Firmino's shot. But the Cherries fell apart, with Salah grabbing a hat trick. He got his second a couple of minutes after half-time after breaking away and firing into the corner. Robertson's cross was turned into his own net by Steve Cook. The Egyptian King sealed his treble by going round the keeper, beating him again and then slotting past a couple of statuesque defenders on the line. The Ramos hangover was gone. He was back to his best. Liverpool went top. When City lost 2-0 at Chelsea the next day, Liverpool were a point clear after 16 games.

Qualification to the last 16 of the Champions League was cemented after a 1-0 win over Napoli at Anfield. Salah rolled Kalidou Koulibaly 12 minutes before the break and put the ball between the legs of David Ospina. He missed a couple of chances in the second half. Henderson and Alexander-Arnold tried their luck from distance, but Ospina foiled them. Mane should have scored on two occasions. Despite Salah's goal, Alisson emerged as the hero, making a stunning, point-blank save from Arkadiusz Milik that kept Liverpool in the competition. Mane should have scored, but the final whistle sparked celebrations on the pitch and in the stands. Alisson's save would turn out to be as important as Steven Gerrard's screamer against Olympiacos 15 years earlier.

After the simultaneous joy and relief of getting past Napoli came the satisfaction of beating Manchester United and ending Jose Mourinho's unhappy time as their manager. Instead of defending for their lives, United attempted to play a bit of football, but playing their way out of defence invited the Liverpool press. After incessant pressure, man of the match Fabinho opened the United defence with a beautifully chipped pass to Mane, who beat David de Gea to make it 1-0. Lovren failed to convert a great chance, but completely against the run of play, Alisson spilled a low cross and handed Jesse Lingard the equaliser. In the second half, De Gea saved from Firmino. Just as it seemed Liverpool were running out of ideas, on came Shaqiri. Mane tied Matteo Darmian up in knots on the left, and his low ball was hammered home by the Swiss substitute. Eight minutes later, he got another, with a deflected left-footed shot from the edge of the box. The 3-1 score flattered United. Every Liverpool outfield player had at least one attempt on goal. "Don't sack Mourinho," chanted the Kop. But United did.

Liverpool confirmed they would be top at Christmas with an excellent 2-0 win at Molineux on a rainy Friday night. Former Red Conor Coady captained Wolves, who boasted an impressive record against the bigger clubs. Milner played right back again. Henderson made his 300th appearance for the Reds. Fabinho set up a well-worked opener for Salah on 18 minutes. Van Dijk, the game's best player, scored his first league goal for the club, steering in Salah's cross. Liverpool's lead increased to four points when City were surprisingly beaten 3-2 at home by Roy Hodgson's Crystal Palace the next day. The Reds had 48 points from 18 matches, having kept 11 clean sheets.

Rafa Benitez brought his Newcastle side to Anfield on Boxing Day, and they were hammered 4-0. Lovren half-volleyed a wonderful opener. Salah won a penalty two minutes into the second half, which he converted himself. Shaqiri tapped in a low ball from the returning Alexander-Arnold. News that Manchester City were 3-2 down at Leicester spread quickly through the stands. Fabinho got off the mark for Liverpool, heading in a corner from close range to seal the 100th win of Klopp's reign. City hadn't found an equaliser at the King Power. The Reds were in dreamland - seven points clear of the Champions and six clear of Spurs, who were now in second.

The annual Anfield stroll against Arsenal was next. The Gunners did take an early lead through Ainsley Maitland-Niles, the first time in 364 days that Liverpool were behind in a league game at home. Within five minutes, Firmino had scored twice. The first was an outright fluke. The second followed a slaloming run through Arsenal's threadbare defence. They were his first home league goals of the season. Mane made it 3-1 from Salah's clever touch. There was still time for Salah to make it four from the spot after Sokratis fouled him. Salah let Firmino complete his hat trick when another penalty was awarded following a push on Lovren. The Brazilian caught the eye, but so did Wijnaldum. Spurs lost to Wolves so, at the turn of the year, Liverpool led the way by seven points from Manchester City.

After eight wins from eight in December, January began with disappointment, as City beat Liverpool at the Etihad to cut the gap at the top to four points. Klopp surprisingly left out the much-improved Fabinho in favour of Milner. The game was described as a free hit for Liverpool but, in reality, defeat would re-energise City. There was little wrong with Liverpool's performance, but nothing went their way. The Reds went within a whisker of scoring first, when Mane hit a post. They were even closer when John Stones smashed the rebound into Ederson, but with the ball 11 millimetres from crossing the line, he hooked it clear. Even the clearance went through Salah's legs on the line. Vincent Kompany somehow stayed on the field after a late challenge on Salah when he was the last man. But City struck first when Sergio Aguero turned Lovren and fired into the roof of the net. Fabinho replaced Milner 12 minutes into the second half. The Reds immediately improved and scored a sumptuous equaliser seven minutes later. After an exquisite passing sequence, Liverpool's best player, Robertson, found Firmino, whose diving header made it 1-1. Robertson's performance was all the more impressive as he had been up all night at the birth of his second child. But parity didn't last long. Leroy Sane was released down the left. His shot across Alisson hit one post and then the other before going in. City held out to win this crucial six-pointer by two goals to one. A chance for Liverpool to open a ten-point lead had gone.

Klopp caused a stir by sending a weakened team to Wolves in the third round of the FA Cup. His selection was: Mignolet; Rafael Camacho, Lovren, Fabinho, Moreno; Milner, Keita, Curtis Jones; Shaqiri, Sturridge, Origi. Youngsters Caoimhin Kelleher, Ki-Jana Hoever and Isaac Christie-Davies were among the subs. An abject first-half performance wasn't helped by Lovren departing early with a hamstring injury, replaced by debutant Hoever. The 16-year-old Dutchman came on at centre half alongside the out-of-position Fabinho. Both excelled.

Camacho and Jones were also playing their first senior matches. Milner made the mistake which led to Raul Jimenez scoring. Origi equalised from the edge of the box on 51 minutes, but the Reds were sent packing from the competition after a wondergoal by Ruben Neves, who found the corner with a bouncing shot from over 30 yards. Shaqiri's curling free kick was brilliantly tipped onto the post by John Ruddy. The young players did themselves proud, especially Hoever, but Sturridge, Keita and Moreno struggled. The media hammered Klopp for his selection, but with the Reds chasing the Premier League title and another European Cup, it was entirely understandable.

With Lovren joining Gomez on the injured list, and the returning Matip only fit enough for the bench, Fabinho continued at centre half in the league at Brighton. He looked a natural at the back again, this time alongside the imperious Van Dijk. Liverpool won the game with a 50th-minute penalty by Salah, after he had been fouled. Wijnaldum and Salah went close to adding a second.

The club honoured the 100th anniversary of Bob Paisley's birth before the home game with Crystal Palace. Having scored three at the Etihad, the Londoners repeated the feat, but Liverpool scored four and picked up another invaluable win. Andros Townsend scored the only goal of the first half. Salah equalised almost as soon as the second half began, with a clever finish after Van Dijk's deflected shot fell perfectly for him. Firmino made it 2-1 with a low drive into the corner. James Tomkins headed an equaliser. Salah restored the lead after a howler from Julian Speroni. Makeshift right back Milner was sent off for a couple of rash challenges. Mane made it four deep into injury time with a clinical low finish. There was still time for Palace to get another back through Max Meyer. The Reds were grateful to Camacho for a late challenge on Wilfried Zaha, as Palace sought an equaliser with seconds of stoppage time left. Fabinho looked the part again, although he did sustain a minor hamstring injury. Keita still looked a shadow of the player that had ripped up the Bundesliga with Leipzig. In his defence, his continued selection on the left of a 4-2-3-1 was doing him no favours.

By the time Liverpool played their next game, at home to Leicester, Manchester City had been beaten 2-1 at Rafa Benitez's Newcastle. The Kop sang the Spaniard's name. A win over the Foxes would send the Reds seven points clear, but they drew 1-1. Henderson was the latest right back, with Clyne now loaned out to Bournemouth. On a snow-covered pitch, Mane slid the ball into the corner for a third-minute opener after a 29-pass build-up. All seemed well. Kasper Schmeichel saved from Firmino. Harry Maguire should have been red-carded for a professional foul on Mane. The centre half then equalised after a free kick wasn't cleared in first-half injury time. Liverpool played with no rhythm in the second half, and it was the 2016 champions who came closest to winning. However, Keita was denied a stonewall penalty and the perpetrator, Ricardo Pereira, should have received a second yellow card. The Reds had pulled a further point away from Manchester City, but it felt like an opportunity squandered. They were five points clear with 14 matches remaining.

Another midweek fixture ended in another 1-1 draw as momentum began to swing City's way. This time it was at West Ham, where Milner played right back and wore the armband in the absence of Henderson. Many fans on social media reacted badly to the inclusion of Lallana, but he was excellent. Mane put Liverpool ahead, despite Milner being offside from Lallana's clever flick. Again, the Reds couldn't hold on, and within six minutes, a clever free kick exposed their high line, and Antonio fired into the corner. A leaden-footed Liverpool rarely threatened a winner until the end, when Keita's chip found Origi, who fluffed his lines. Keita was poor again and so were Salah and Firmino. The latter was struggling for form.

After just two wins in six, Liverpool gained a much-needed win at home to Bournemouth, despite a bug sweeping through the camp. Wijnaldum maintained his outstanding recent form. Again, it was Mane who put the Reds 1-0 up, when he headed in Milner's cross. Wijnaldum made it two with a precise lob over the stranded Artur Boruc. Three minutes into the second half, Keita bent a wonderful pass into the path of Firmino. The Brazilian backheeled to Salah, who fired into the corner for a beautiful goal. Several more chances went awry. Firmino was much more effective in his usual number-9 role. Alexander-Arnold made his return from injury off the bench. He had been missed.

Van Dijk was suspended for the first leg of the Champions League last 16 at home to Bayern Munich, meaning Matip was partnered by Fabinho at the back. Bayern failed to take advantage, with Henderson's commanding performance in the holding role a major reason. Alisson prevented a Matip own goal with a point-blank save. Salah failed to hit the target a couple of times. Matip steered Firmino's pullback wide. It ended 0-0. Advantage Bayern.

With Manchester United players dropping like flies in the first half, it looked certain that Liverpool would take advantage and pick up three vital points at Old Trafford towards the end of February. Ander Herrera, Juan Mata and Jesse Lingard all left the field, as did Firmino. Marcus Rashford also picked up a knock but carried on. As the game wore on, Liverpool became more subdued and created little. Firmino's absence was more telling than that of the United trio, as his replacement, Sturridge, was well off the pace. Milner, again at right back, Salah and Mane were also ineffective. The Reds had no bite in midfield, and the final ball was too often astray, with Klopp electing to keep Keita and Alexander-Arnold on the bench. The draw did put Liverpool top, but their lead had been whittled down to a point.

A 5-0 midweek hammering of Watford at Anfield lifted spirits, although, at the same time, City sneaked past West Ham 1-0. Playing through the middle, Mane scored two early goals, the second of which was an impudent backheel. Origi cut inside to score number three. Alisson saved fabulously from Andre Gray. Van Dijk bagged a couple of late headers. Alexander-Arnold set up three of the goals. Liverpool were back on track.

Or so they thought. There was still room for another agonising draw, at Goodison of all places, which put City into the title-race driving seat for the first time since

December 7th. Jordan Pickford saved twice from Salah. Michael Keane denied him in the second half with a perfectly-timed tackle. Fabinho was presented with a clear sight of goal, but his touch let him down. As at Old Trafford, Liverpool lost control the longer the game went on. Salah was poor again. Keita was an unused sub again, in a game that was crying out for him. Everton supporters were euphoric at the final whistle. "You're gonna win fuck all!" they sang. With nine games left, City had 71 points to Liverpool's 70, and a goal difference that was seven better. If both sides won their remaining games, City would win the league by 98 points to 97. Surely the Reds couldn't be that unlucky?

For the second time in the season, Burnley led Liverpool 1-0. Ashley Westwood scored straight from a corner in the sixth minute, but Liverpool dominated thereafter. Firmino tapped in Salah's low cross. Mane curled in the second to make it 2-1 at the break. Firmino scored after Salah had been tackled in the box. Mane hit the bar from close range. Peter Crouch was a late Burnley sub. Johann Berg Gudmundsson got one back in stoppage time. There was still time for Mane to go around Tom Heaton and roll in his 50th goal for the club to make it 4-2. Van Dijk was at his commanding best, as he had been all season.

Ray Kennedy had been the hero the last time Bayern Munich and Liverpool had met in a knockout tie. His goal in the Olympic Stadium in 1981 sent Liverpool to Paris, where they beat Real Madrid in the final. Howard Gayle's 61-minute cameo is just as fondly remembered. Mane and Fabinho played the Kennedy and Gayle roles this time as the Reds swatted away the German champions to move stylishly into the quarter-finals. Henderson was restored alongside Milner and Wijnaldum, but lasted just 13 minutes before injury saw him replaced by Fabinho. An error by Firmino gave Thiago Alcantara an opportunity from 20 yards, but he sent it over the bar. The big moment came on 26 minutes, when Mane got on the end of Van Dijk's inch-perfect long pass, controlled it, turned away from Manuel Neuer with his back from goal and then chipped the covering defenders. But within 13 minutes Matip turned Serge Gnabry's low cross into his own goal.

It was 1-1 at the break. That would be enough for Liverpool, but they didn't settle for it. The game-breaking moment came with little over 20 minutes left. Milner sent in a corner from the right, and Van Dijk rose above everybody on the six-yard box to head firmly down into the corner of the net. The Dutchman had got the better of Robert Lewandowski all night and had now scored the key goal. Bayern needed two. Salah should have played in Mane but took the selfish option. But he did send over an 84th-minute cross which Mane emphatically buried. The Reds were through to the last eight with a 3-1 win, which was as much a statement of intent as a turning point in their season.

For a few horrible minutes, it seemed that Ryan Babel had almost ended Liverpool's title bid. With his hair dyed bright red, the 32-year-old capitalised on a defensive mix-up to score an equaliser for Fulham in the 74th minute of their home game with the Reds. Mane had earlier put Liverpool 1-0 up, slotting in Firmino's cutback for his 11th goal in 11 games. But they couldn't get a second and the Cottagers, who were almost certain to be relegated, started to exert some pressure of their own. Milner mishit a clearance. Van Dijk headed weakly back to a hesitant Alisson, and amid the confusion, Babel, who had recently signed for Fulham eight years after Kenny Dalglish had let him go, nipped in to make it 1-1. But this team knew how to win without being on their game. Mane was manhandled by Fulham keeper Sergio Rico, and Milner side-footed the penalty down the middle to earn his side three crucial points.

Another league game, another nail-biting 90 minutes, another late winner - Liverpool weren't going to do this the easy way. With City still winning, the Reds simply had to beat Spurs at Anfield on the last day of March. All was well when Firmino headed home an inch-perfect Robertson cross in the 16th minute. Alexander-Arnold hit the post direct from a corner. Kane, briefly out of Van Dijk's pocket, took a quick free kick just inside the Liverpool half. Liverpool were caught napping. Kieran Trippier found Christian Eriksen, and when the ball was moved on to Lucas Moura, he made it 1-1 with 20 minutes left. The Reds could even have lost the game, but Moussa Sissoko blazed a great chance over the bar. Right at the end, Salah's relatively tame header wasn't held by Hugo Lloris. It ricocheted off Toby Alderweireld and rolled slowly over the line as Anfield exploded in a moment of pure euphoria. Klopp's post-match fist pumps raised the volume even higher.

Liverpool needed to demonstrate even more resolve at Southampton. Shane Long bagged an early goal, but Keita headed his first goal for the club ten minutes before half-time. Henderson and Milner came off the bench on the hour, replacing Wijnaldum and Alexander-Arnold. They stiffened Liverpool up, but with ten minutes to go, the score remained 1-1. Liverpool cleared a Southampton corner. Salah collected the ball just shy of the centre circle. He powered forward, straight down the middle of the pitch. This was his ninth game without a goal. He had Firmino to his left. He moved slightly in that direction to open up the angle and, from the edge of the box, his shot found the bottom corner of Angus Gunn's net. Sometimes accused of greed, he was justified in going alone this time. It was a goal of gargantuan importance. To pilfer a cliché, Henderson put the cherry on the cake with four minutes left, when he steamed onto Firmino's square pass to score his first goal of the season. The Reds had overcome another tricky hurdle to win 3-1.

A year after beating them 5-0, Liverpool would play Porto again in the Champions League. The first leg of the quarter-final came at Anfield as the Reds built a 2-0 advantage to take to Portugal. The fit-again Gomez was named sub, although not called upon. The two-time European champions could have had a second-minute lead, but Moussa Marega fired wide at the Kop end. But before the five-minute mark, Keita, now beginning to look the part, scored with a deflected shot from the edge of the box. Salah pulled a one-on-one just wide. Man of the match Firmino tapped in Alexander-Arnold's low pass to make it 2-0. Alisson made a crucial save from Marega. Alexander-Arnold escaped a VAR check for handball. The Malian Marega missed another big chance. Firmino failed to make it three from Henderson's cross. The captain put in a dominant performance. Mane had a second-half goal disallowed for offside.

LIVERPOOL F.C. THE PREMIER LEAGUE YEARS

The home game with Chelsea was played the day before the 30th anniversary of the Hillsborough Disaster, and those inside Anfield paid fitting tribute to both the 96 and to the 'Anfield Iron' Tommy Smith, who had died at the age of 74 two days earlier. Chelsea boasted an impressive recent record at Anfield, and it was goalless at the break. But Liverpool exploded into life in a devastating three-minute spell early in the second half. Henderson lifted the perfect cross to the back post for Mane to head the opener in front of a jubilant Kop. With the stadium bouncing, Salah then scored the goal of the season. He trapped Van Dijk's long pass, cut in from the right and unleashed an Exocet into the top corner of Kepa Arrizabalaga's goal. The Egyptian celebrated with a yoga pose in stark contrast to the mayhem around him. It ended 2-0.

The return leg in the Estadio da Dragao was a breeze, as Liverpool strolled to a 4-1 win (6-1 on aggregate). Keita, Henderson and Firmino were benched. From Salah's low cross, Mane beat Iker Casillas for the opener, which was awarded after a VAR check for offside. Porto needed four goals but, with Matip in splendid form, they had no chance. Salah made it two on 65, finishing off a lightning counterattack. Gomez made his comeback, replacing Alexander-Arnold. Eder Militao nodded in a corner, but Liverpool responded with headed goals from Firmino and Van Dijk. At the same time, Manchester City, who had been favourites to win the competition, were knocked out by Spurs. The Reds would play Barcelona in a mouth-watering semi-final. Tottenham were pitted against Ajax.

Liverpool's next game was at Cardiff City, a club still in mourning for the Argentinian Emiliano Sala, who had died in January in a light-aircraft accident without playing a game for them. It took the Reds nearly an hour to break through. Firmino skied an early chance. Neil Etheridge and Alisson made spectacular saves from Salah and Oumar Niasse. The key moment came on 57 minutes, when Alexander-Arnold sent over a low corner which Wijnaldum smashed into the corner of the net from 12 yards. The players planned the set piece at half-time. Henderson scooped a big chance over the bar. Sean Morrison missed an open goal. Then the defender wrestled Salah to the ground in the box. Milner converted the penalty and celebrated by clutching his back and hobbling like an old man – a nod to his status in the squad. Cardiff, managed by Neil 'Colin' Warnock, were heading to the Championship. Liverpool had now amassed their highest Premier League points tally and still had three games left. But City were a point clear again after winning their game in hand against Manchester United.

The young Reds won the FA Youth Cup for the first time since 2007, beating Manchester City on penalties. They had seen off Portsmouth, Accrington Stanley, Wigan, Bury and Watford along the way, with skipper Paul Glatzel scoring eight times. Played at City's Academy Stadium, Nabil Touaizi put City ahead, but an 86th-minute equaliser from Bobby Duncan, his fifth of the competition, took the game to an extra half hour, during which time there were no more goals. Neco Williams, Elijah Dixon-Bonner, Abdi Sharif, Jack Bearne and Glatzel scored the Liverpool penalties. Cole Palmer's miss for City proved decisive. Unfortunately for Glatzel and Duncan, their fortunes would soon take a turn for the worse. Duncan, a cousin of Steven Gerrard, had signed from City in the summer of 2018 for £200,000 and scored 32 goals in an encouraging debut season at Liverpool. He moved to Fiorentina for £1.8 million four months after the Youth Cup success, when his agent accused Liverpool of "mentally bullying" him. Liverpool denied the allegations, and Duncan didn't last long in Italy. Glatzel, meanwhile, went on to sustain a serious knee injury in pre-season against Tranmere, and sat out the whole of the 2019-20 season.

Twenty-four hours later, it took Keita 15 seconds to open the scoring against already-relegated Huddersfield. Under pressure from the Guinean, Jon Gorenc Stankovic passed it straight to Salah, who found Keita, who threaded the ball into the bottom corner. Huddersfield had a strong 20 minutes before Mane headed in Robertson's cross. Salah made it three in first-half injury time when he lobbed Alexander-Arnold's lofted pass over Jonas Lossl. Van Dijk went down early in the second half, sparking panic in the stands, but he continued. Mane scored another header from Henderson's cross. The biggest cheer of the night was reserved for Oxlade-Chamberlain, who replaced Wijnaldum for his first appearance of the season, a year and two days after sustaining his cruciate-ligament injury against Roma. He very nearly scored but was denied by Lossl's legs. Mane hit the post with another header. Robertson set up the fifth for Salah. Two days later, hopes were raised when City were being held at Burnley, but Sergio Aguero scored the only goal on the hour.

If ever a result failed to represent a performance, it was at the Nou Camp in the first leg of Liverpool's semi-final against a Barcelona team which included Luis Suarez and Philippe Coutinho. Matip made a crucial third-minute interception from Ivan Rakitic. Mane was bundled over in the box by Gerard Pique, but nothing was given. Robertson made a vital tackle on Messi. The Reds broke away, but Salah was unable to put Mane clean through. Keita had started superbly but was withdrawn with an adductor injury and replaced by Henderson. The Guinean's season was over just as he was hitting his best form. With Van Dijk at fault, Suarez stole a yard to turn Jordi Alba's cross past Alisson. Fabinho saved a goal with a brilliant tackle in the six-yard box. Mane should have equalised but lifted his shot over the bar. Milner angered Messi by barging him over the sideline. The hosts led 1-0 at the break. Firmino, whose muscle injury had left him fit enough only for the bench, had been sorely missed. Wijnaldum started in the false-9 role and would later ask the Brazilian how on earth he coped with such a demanding role.

Liverpool were scintillating for the first 25 minutes of the second half. Marc-Andre ter Stegen made spectacular saves from Milner and Salah. Van Dijk released Salah down the right with a long pass, but when the ball went into the middle, Milner's shot was too close to the keeper. Barcelona broke away in the 74th minute, Suarez hit the crossbar and Messi bundled in the rebound. Liverpool were so unlucky to be two down. Suddenly it was three. Fabinho fouled the Argentine genius just over 30 yards from goal. Messi stole a couple of yards with the free kick, and then curled the perfect dead ball into the top corner. Suarez ran past Robertson, taunting him. That wouldn't be forgotten. Firmino had a shot cleared off the line with seven minutes remaining. Salah inexplicably hit the easy rebound against the post. Nothing was going right. In fact, the only bit of luck Liverpool enjoyed came when Ousmane Dembele spurned an absolute sitter with the last kick of the game. Klopp and his players were stunned. It was never a 3-0 game. Matip, Milner and Salah had been outstanding, but Gomez, who had replaced Alexander-Arnold, struggled on his first start in five months. The final was exactly a month away, and it looked certain that Liverpool wouldn't be in it.

The stomach-churning rollercoaster ride of the title race continued at St James' Park, where Liverpool fans were treated – perhaps subjected is a better word – to a five-goal nail-biter. With Firmino still not right, Sturridge took over the number-9 duties from Wijnaldum, who reverted to midfield, replacing Milner. Alexander-Arnold came in for Gomez. There had been suggestions that Rafa Benitez might make life easy for Liverpool for old times' sake, but that certainly wasn't the case, as Newcastle did everything they could to derail the Reds. Mane was kicked in the head by former Red Javier Manquillo, but neither penalty nor red card was forthcoming. Van Dijk was left unmarked and headed in Alexander-Arnold's corner in the 13th minute. Klopp attributed the goal to the work of his analysts. Newcastle were soon level, and Alexander-Arnold was lucky not to be sent off when he cleared off the line with his arm. Christian Atsu slammed home the rebound and saved Alexander-Arnold's bacon in the process. A goal was a better outcome for Liverpool than a red card and a penalty. The young right back soon bagged another assist when Salah diverted his cross into the bottom corner with a beautifully cushioned volley.

It was 2-1 at half-time, but the lead didn't last for much longer. After Sturridge skied a promising chance, Salomon Rondon fired home when Liverpool failed to clear a corner. The Reds were desperate for a winner. In the final quarter of the game, Shaqiri, Origi and Milner replaced Wijnaldum, the injured Salah and Lovren. Liverpool failed to create a clear-cut chance, but with four minutes to go they were awarded a free kick on the right. Van Dijk went forward and insisted that the left-footed Shaqiri take it, and his inswinger was glanced into the net by Origi. Klopp's men saw out a lengthy period of injury time to win 3-2. If Liverpool were going to win this league, it would be down to sheer bloody-mindedness as much as anything else. The character they were showing was exceptional.

As the squad left the North East, there were more questions than answers. Would Salah be fit to face Barcelona at Anfield? Could the players recover from such physical and mental exertion when Messi and his teammates had been given the weekend off? And could Brendan Rodgers' Leicester City do Liverpool an almighty favour against City two days later? Sadly, the answer to the latter was no. Leicester held out for 70 minutes before City's departing skipper Vincent Kompany scored the goal of his life to give them a priceless 1-0 win. City's former striker Kelechi Iheanacho missed a great chance for the Foxes in injury time. If City won at Brighton on the final day, they would retain the title. If they dropped points and Liverpool beat Wolves, the Reds would win the league for the first time in 29 years. But before that, there was the not-so-small matter of the Champions League semi-final second leg.

The crazy events at Anfield on Tuesday 7th May 2019 will live long in the memories of those lucky enough to be there. Despite the disappointment of the first-leg score and of Kompany's goal, the Liverpool fans set about creating a frenzied bear pit of an atmosphere. Their heroes got themselves back into the tie with an early goal and then stunned the Spanish champions with three more in the second half. It was Istanbul and then some. The atmosphere was compared to Internazionale, St Etienne and Chelsea. And to further the delight of the home fans, Coutinho's pathetic performance saw him subbed after an hour, while a snarling Suarez, hoist by his own petard, cut a lonely, frustrated and impotent figure. Not only did the result put Liverpool into their ninth European Cup Final, it also gave this magnificent team the belief that they were at least the equal of any team on the planet. It bridged the gap between hopes and dreams and cold, hard silverware – something the Reds had failed to do all too often in the past 30 years. The record-breaking Premier League title win of 2020 had its roots in this most incredible of nights.

Klopp had to select a team shorn of two of its magnificent attacking triumvirate. Salah's head knock at Newcastle ruled him out. Firmino was still injured. The manager decided that Sturridge wasn't up to the rigours of such an occasion and decided instead to field Origi and Shaqiri alongside Mane in the front three. It was Shaqiri's first start in four months. Milner was selected in midfield with Fabinho and Henderson, to the disappointment of the benched Wijnaldum. In fact, the day before the game, Liverpool trained with just 14 outfield players fit, as Van Dijk, Lallana and Oxlade-Chamberlain also had various fitness issues. In his pre-match press conference, Klopp had said: "Two of the world's best strikers are not available, and we have to score four goals to go through in 90 minutes. As long as we have 11 players on the pitch, we will try for 90 minutes to celebrate the Champions League campaign to give it a proper finish. That's the plan. If we can do it, wonderful. If we can't do it, let's fail in the most beautiful way." And Klopp would have known that Barcelona had been involved in some madcap Champions League ties in the last couple of years. In 2017, they'd overturned a 4-0 first-leg deficit against Paris St Germain by winning 6-1 in Spain with two injury-time goals. Twelve months later, they'd capitulated in Rome, losing 3-0, having won the home leg 4-1. Anything was possible.

Liverpool needed a quick start. Robertson shoved Messi in the head after he had been tackled by Fabinho. It was symbolic of the sort of night the world's best player would endure and of the fact that Liverpool would be no respecters of reputation. Then came the requisite early goal after six and a half minutes. Matip played it long. Jordi Alba's misplaced header presented Mane with the ball on the right. With defenders out of position, he squared it to Henderson, who surged into the box. A ricochet went his way. He was in on goal. Ter Stegen parried. Origi turned in the rebound. 1-0. With an accompanying picture of

Suarez, Barcelona tweeted: "We score, Liverpool need FIVE – and we're going to get at least one… agreed?" The sheer arrogance of it defied belief. Fabinho was wrongly booked for a perfect tackle on Suarez. Alisson tipped Messi's shot over the bar. Then he thwarted Coutinho after a quick break and made a crucial save from Alba in first-half injury time. The Reds led 1-0, still two goals shy of drawing level. Henderson had picked up a knee injury, and spent half-time on an exercise bike so it didn't seize up.

Liverpool were about to produce the dream 45 minutes. Robertson had gone off at the break, kicked out of the game by Suarez, who seemed to have discovered new levels of gamesmanship in the last five years. On came Wijnaldum. With more of a licence to attack than usual, he would make the difference. Milner went to left back and played like Robertson. Ter Stegen saved Van Dijk's improvised flick from a corner. Alisson made yet another save, this time from Suarez. Eight minutes into the half, Alexander-Arnold conceded possession with a wayward header. He won it straight back from Alba. He powered to the line, and his cross was turned into the net by Wijnaldum from near the penalty spot. The goalkeeper should have done better. The Dutchman grabbed the ball from Ter Stegen to get the game restarted as quickly as possible. He may as well have said, "You can have it back in a minute," because in the blink of an eye, Liverpool's number five was rising like a salmon to head Shaqiri's cross into the top corner. The roof nearly came off the Kop. Unbelievably, it was 3-3 on aggregate and there were still 35 minutes of the 90 left.

The dynamic of the away-goal rule made the tie even more interesting. If Barca could find a goal, Liverpool would need two more. Coutinho was hauled off, amid jeers and catcalls from the entire crowd. The humiliation of the £142 million man couldn't have been greater. Alisson saved from Messi, although his near-post effort was never going to beat the Brazilian. And then came one of Anfield's most glorious moments. Alexander-Arnold placed the ball in the quadrant for a corner he had won himself. Origi kicked a second ball off the pitch. The right back was walking away to let Shaqiri take the kick. Then he spotted something. He quickly sent in a low cross. The goalkeeper and defence weren't set. Some, including Ter Stegen, weren't even looking. Origi swivelled and swept the ball into the top corner of the Spion Kop goal. Anfield went ballistic. An away goal would still have eliminated Liverpool, but Barcelona didn't threaten. They had succumbed to the power of Anfield. They had nothing left to give. The final whistle elicited scenes of joy.

It was almost impossible to pick a man of the match. Alisson had made so many saves. Matip even outshone Van Dijk. The full backs were sensational. Fabinho protected the defence with so much authority. Wijnaldum, the unlikely hero, collapsed to the turf. A beaming Salah came onto the pitch in a black T-shirt, which read 'Never give up.' Milner was crying. The ubiquitous Henderson lay on the ground in agony. This most wonderful of captains slowly rose to his feet, barely able to walk, and lifted both arms in the air. 'Allez, Allez, Allez' filled the night air and then 'You'll Never Walk Alone', as the squad and the staff lined up, arm in arm, in front of the Kop. What they had done was extraordinary. "These boys are fucking mentality giants," said Klopp. Liverpool would play Tottenham Hotspur in the final on June 1st in Madrid.

There were two matches left of this whirlwind season. In 180 minutes of football, Liverpool could be champions of England or Europe. Or both. Or neither. Wolves came to Anfield on the final day of the season, with Manchester City playing at Brighton simultaneously. The champions had squeezed home by one-goal margins in three of their last four matches, so perhaps they would struggle on the south coast. Salah had recovered and took Shaqiri's place, meaning Tuesday's hero Origi also started. Mane turned in Alexander-Arnold's cross at 3.18pm to put Liverpool ahead. At 3.27pm, false information swept around Anfield that Brighton had taken the lead. They hadn't. "But they have now! Holy Hell!" reported The Guardian one minute later, when Glenn Murray headed in a corner. It felt like Anfield might spontaneously combust. Those who still didn't know the first one was a hoax thought the latest cheer meant Brighton were 2-0 up. Liverpool fans prayed that Brighton could protect their lead until half-time at least. They couldn't. All Murray's goal did was relieve City of their inhibitions. Sergio Aguero equalised just over a minute later. Aymeric Laporte made it 2-1 at 3.39pm. Brighton and Wolves both came close to scoring just before the respective half-time whistles.

There was an air of acceptance during the break at Anfield that maybe it wasn't going to be Liverpool's day. And so it proved. City scored twice more before Mane made it 2-0 to Liverpool, glancing in a cross by man of the match Alexander-Arnold. The Reds finished a point behind Manchester City with 97, easily the biggest total for a team finishing second. City had been phenomenal in holding Liverpool at bay, winning their last 14 matches. Alisson collected the Golden Glove for 21 clean sheets. Salah, Mane and Arsenal's Pierre-Emerick Aubameyang shared the Golden Boot with 22 goals apiece. Alexander-Arnold ended up with 12 league assists, a record for a defender and one ahead of Robertson. Van Dijk had already collected the PFA Footballer of the Year award. Partners and children accompanied the players on an emotional lap of honour. "We've conquered all of Europe," the crowd sang, already with an eye on the next game.

Madrid's Metropolitano Stadium was the setting for Liverpool's latest Champions League Final, against Tottenham Hotspur, who had finished 26 points behind the Reds. It was their fourth since 2005. The city's Felipe II Square rocked to the sound of various Anfield songs, as over 50,000 Reds soaked up the early afternoon sun. Thoughts soon turned to the game, which kicked off at 9pm, local time. There was no escaping the fact that Liverpool had to win. Another defeat in a major final could have left Klopp wounded and damaged morale in the squad. The step from nearly men to winners had to be taken, and this was the day to do it.

With Firmino deemed fit again, there were no surprises in Klopp's line-up, which was: Alisson; Alexander-Arnold, Matip, Van Dijk, Robertson; Fabinho, Henderson, Wijnaldum; Salah, Firmino, Mane. For once, there were

424

more players on the bench than the pitch, with the clubs permitted to name a dozen substitutes, an increase of five in a year. Liverpool's 12 subs were: Mignolet, Caoimhin Kelleher, Gomez, Moreno, Lovren, Milner, Lallana, Oxlade-Chamberlain, Shaqiri, Sturridge and Rhian Brewster.

The 2019 Champions League Final was defined by its early goal. With not even a minute on the clock, Mane was found by Henderson on the left. He lifted the ball, and it struck the arm of Moussa Sissoko. Twenty-one seconds had elapsed. Referee Damir Skomina pointed to the spot. VAR confirmed the decision. Salah's penalty wasn't convincing, and Hugo Lloris came close to saving it. But he didn't, and Liverpool led 1-0. From that point, the final essentially became a battle between Tottenham's playmakers, Christian Eriksen, Dele Alli and Son Heung-min, and Liverpool's midfielders, Fabinho, Henderson and Wijnaldum. With the latter two having recent experience of the holding role, it was second nature for them to play deeper and neuter Spurs' creativity, leaving Harry Kane with no service. The result was that, while the Londoners had more possession, they were unable to prise Liverpool open, and their shots tended to be from distance. The Reds created little either, but protecting the lead was their priority. Their passing had no rhythm, and the team looked disjointed with the ball. Alexander-Arnold and Robertson had hopeful cracks from distance, but that was about it in the first half. They got to the break with their 1-0 lead intact.

With Liverpool's midfield so deep, Firmino was isolated. He didn't look entirely fit, either, but he'd put in a great shift. After 58 minutes, he was substituted for Origi. Milner replaced Wijnaldum and went within a whisker of making it two. Spurs had more shots than Liverpool, by 16 to 14, with eight on target to three. Many of them were late in the game, and none were particularly threatening. The fabulous Alisson caught a curler from Alli, beat out Son's 25-yarder and saved the follow-up from Lucas Moura. He then tipped a wide free kick from Eriksen around the post. Spurs had nothing left to give, and Origi put them out of their misery in the 87th minute, when he took Matip's pass following a corner, controlled it and fizzed a low, left-footed shot into the bottom corner of the Tottenham net. 2-0. After five minutes of injury time, the European Cup was Liverpool's again.

The subs and the coaching staff raced onto the pitch. Steven Gerrard, manager of Glasgow Rangers, beamed with pride in the stands. He was no longer the last Liverpool captain to win the European Cup. Spurs players lay heartbroken on the turf as those in red celebrated. Henderson shared tearful hugs with Klopp and his father, Brian, who had recently overcome a battle with throat cancer. The trophy was engraved with the name of its new winner, and Henderson lifted it into the air with his teammates behind him. It was the 13th time an English team had won it. Six of those triumphs had been Liverpool's.

With an average age of just over 26 and a manager planning to stick around, it felt like this could be the start of an era laden with trophies for this set of players. The world was their oyster and there was one particular prize in their sights...

2019-20

"Prepare for a party when this bullshit virus is over!"

A t last!
Liverpool Football Club. Champions of England again.
In season 2019-20, Jurgen Norbert Klopp and his players took the Premier League by storm, producing the most stunning sequence of results from August to March, when the season was suspended because of the coronavirus pandemic. At that point, they had amassed a quite unbelievable tally of 82 points from a possible 87. After 29 matches, they were 25 points clear of Manchester City.

The Reds were 13-5 second favourites behind City to win the Premier League at the season kick-off. There were numerous reasons given by the experts for predicting Liverpool would fall short again. So many of the players, most notably Mane, barely had a pre-season, because a lengthy international programme began so soon after the Champions League Final. No new senior players were bought. Many believed that coming so close in 2019 would be too hard for Liverpool to take, and that they would fall away as they had done in similar circumstances in 2002-03, 2009-10 and 2014-15. And, as everyone knew, City boasted a world-class squad, stuffed full of matchwinners.

The reality was different, of course, and as the new season approached, Liverpool were on the verge of creating history. Unlike 2002, 2009 and 2014, they had ended the 2019 season on a high, by winning the Champions League. No first-teamer had departed, unlike Xabi Alonso and Luis Suarez after the title challenges of 2009 and 2014. The last three months of 2018-19 had demonstrated that this team could handle the most intense pressure and fixture pile-ups. If they could beat Barcelona 4-0 without Mo Salah and Roberto Firmino, they could do anything. And perhaps Manchester City had peaked. In choosing not to sign a replacement for their departing skipper, Vincent Kompany, they were certainly taking a risk.

Klopp, it could be argued, was taking the same gamble, because there was little transfer activity at Anfield. Daniel Sturridge left on a free, having struggled for fitness since his wonderful 2013-14 campaign. Alberto Moreno also moved on. While gifted going forward, Moreno had a congenital inability to defend and all too often went into malfunction mode. Connor Randall and Adam Bogdan also departed on frees. Young Rafa Camacho joined Sporting Lisbon for £7 million. Having been at Southampton on loan during 2018-19, Danny Ings moved there on a permanent basis for £20 million and would enjoy a stellar campaign. Simon

Mignolet headed back to Belgium with Club Brugge for £8.2 million. Ryan Kent made a permanent move to play for Steven Gerrard's Rangers for £7.5 million.

In came the young Dutch defender Sepp van den Berg from PEC Zwolle for £4.4 million. Fulham starlet Harvey Elliott signed for a fee yet to be determined by a tribunal, at the time of writing. Back-up goalkeepers Adrian and Andy Lonergan also arrived on free transfers. Some bemoaned the lack of at least one marquee signing. Others could see that this set of players were just hitting their peak, and that trophies would continue to be won.

In comparing the City and Liverpool squads in the summer of 2019, it wouldn't have been unreasonable to suggest that Liverpool had a more able goalkeeper, easily the better full backs, more consistent and dominant centre halves, better defensive-midfield options and a more prolific and explosive attacking trident. Even so, there seemed to be a collective belief among the footballing fraternity that no matter what Liverpool did, the team from the Etihad were still better. The gradual realisation through the autumn and early winter of 2019 that perhaps that wasn't the case was a joy to behold. Klopp and his players hadn't just overtaken City by then. They had blown them out of the water.

The new campaign began on 4th August 2019 at Wembley, with the Community Shield against the champions, Manchester City. The team was: Alisson; Alexander-Arnold, Gomez, Van Dijk, Robertson; Fabinho, Henderson, Wijnaldum, Salah, Firmino, Origi. The subs who saw action were Matip, Keita, Shaqiri, Lallana and Oxlade-Chamberlain. Mignolet and Lovren were unused. Leroy Sane and Salah fired early chances wide. Sane's afternoon would soon be over, as he departed with a serious knee injury which ruled him out for the majority of the season. Raheem Sterling got the first goal in the 12th minute, turning in a low cross. Alisson should have saved it. Liverpool were excellent for most of the game, with Salah squandering several chances. Van Dijk hit the underside of the bar. Salah hit a post. Sterling went clean through but fell over. Liverpool eventually equalised on 77, when Van Dijk's lofted cross was headed in by Matip. Salah looked to have won it in injury time, but Kyle Walker made an astonishing goal-line clearance. The game went to penalties. City scored all of theirs. Shaqiri, Lallana, Oxlade-Chamberlain and Salah were successful, but Wijnaldum failed with Liverpool's second, and City lifted the Shield.

The league season began on a Friday night, with a 4-1 win over newly-promoted Norwich City. The starting line-up was unchanged. Mane was among the substitutes now his African Cup of Nations campaign was over. He'd barely had a rest all summer. Within ten seconds, the Kop was singing 'Champions of Europe'. Just as in 1984, the Canaries supplied Liverpool's first goal of the season. Back then, it was a Steve Bruce own goal. This time, Grant Hanley sliced Origi's low cross past Tim Krul. Salah made it two after a lovely pass from Firmino. Van Dijk headed in Salah's corner. The unmarked Origi nodded in Alexander-Arnold's deep cross for the fourth – all by the 42nd minute. But a couple of minutes earlier, Alisson had injured a calf muscle taking a goal kick and had to be replaced by Liverpool's new back-up goalkeeper, Adrian. Mignolet, who had just left the club, would have been cursing his luck, as Alisson would be out for some time. Krul tipped Henderson's shot onto the bar in the second half. Somehow, Firmino failed to score from a couple of yards and, incredibly, wouldn't score an Anfield goal in the league until the final home game. Norwich played well, and deservedly pulled a goal back through Teemu Pukki just after the hour. Mane replaced Origi with 16 minutes left and, for the first time, failed to score in Liverpool's Premier League opener.

Alisson would miss 11 matches. It was a cruel blow. Whether he was the world's best goalkeeper or not was debateable. He was probably in the top three. For Liverpool fans with long memories, he was in a different stratosphere to many of his predecessors. To sit on the Kop and not panic when the opposition had a corner, like when David James, Sander Westerveld or Loris Karius had been in goal, was a relief. To have complete faith in a Reds keeper was a great feeling, which the defence probably felt more than the fans. Adrian had big boots to fill, but he was about to make the perfect start.

For the second time in 11 days, Liverpool faced a penalty shootout, this time in the European Super Cup in Istanbul against Chelsea. Matip, Milner, Oxlade-Chamberlain and Mane started, while there were places on an 11-man bench for a trio of highly-rated Academy graduates – Ki-Jana Hoever, Harvey Elliott and Rhian Brewster, although none would be used. Chelsea's Pedro hit the crossbar. Adrian denied Mateo Kovacic. Olivier Giroud then took Pedro's slide-rule pass and slotted it past Adrian in the 36th minute. N'Golo Kante was running the show. A couple of minutes later, Christian Pulisic thought he had made it two on his full debut, but he was offside. The Reds trailed at the break, but the introduction of the imperious Firmino was the turning point. It took Mane just a couple of minutes to level the game when he tapped in the Brazilian's clever touch. Kepa Arrizabalaga somehow tipped Van Dijk's close-range shot onto the bar, having just made a low save from Salah. Chelsea had another goal disallowed when Mason Mount was caught offside by Liverpool's high line. Extra time beckoned.

Mane turned in Firmino's pullback after 95 minutes to make it 2-1, as the clock struck midnight in Istanbul. Adrian saved well from Tammy Abraham, but he was soon adjudged to have fouled the striker by referee Stephanie Frappart, with VAR choosing not to overrule her. It was a tough call, and Jorginho calmly rolled in the penalty. Abraham was inches away from a winner, before Adrian saved from Mount. Penalties. The first nine penalties went in, with Firmino, Fabinho, Origi, Alexander-Arnold and Salah scoring for the Reds. At 43 minutes past midnight, Abraham tried to force sudden-death, but Adrian saved with his feet. Liverpool had won their fourth Super Cup. Klopp and his players ran to the Spanish keeper, before Henderson lifted the Super Cup after his now-trademark shuffle.

Klopp had little more than 48 hours to prepare his players for a game at Southampton. Adrian had sustained an injured ankle after a Liverpool fan had jumped on him in celebration in Turkey, but he was passed fit to make his first league start for the club. Matip kept his place at the heart of the defence, with Gomez not having started the season well. The Reds were outplayed for 45 minutes and were grateful to the Spaniard for keeping their goal intact, before Mane scored a sizzling opener in first-half injury-time. The goal broke the Saints' resolve, and Firmino appeared to have put the game to bed from the edge of the box with 20 minutes left. Robertson was close to making it three after Mane's backheel. The Senegalese was on fire, unperturbed by his lack of a pre-season. Oxlade-Chamberlain and Firmino were also in exceptional form. But Adrian gave the ball straight to former Red Danny Ings, who pulled one back with seven minutes left. Ings then fluffed a gilt-edged opportunity to equalise right at the death - a huge let-off for Liverpool. In terms of pattern of scoring, goalscorers, a howler from the keeper and Liverpool clinging on for dear life, the game was identical to the one at Leicester 12 months earlier. But there was good news later in the day from Manchester, as City were held at home by Spurs.

A blistering 17 minutes of football either side of half-time saw the Reds rack up three goals at home to Arsenal. Pierre-Emerick Aubameyang and Nicolas Pepe, with whom Liverpool had been linked over the summer, should have scored, before man of the match Matip powered in a header from Alexander-Arnold's corner. Liverpool led 1-0 at the break. David Luiz stupidly clutched Salah's shirt, allowing the Egyptian to double the lead from the spot. And then, quite magnificently, he beat Luiz near the halfway line, ran down the right, cut inside and shot across Bernd Leno and into the corner. This was a genius at the peak of his powers. The Reds had dominated, but Lucas Torreira pulled back a late goal. In five league games at home to Arsenal under Klopp, the Reds had scored 18 times.

Liverpool's first clean sheet of the season came at Turf Moor, as Burnley were beaten 3-0. Salah's left-footed curler hit a post, before the Reds took the lead with an outright fluke, as Alexander-Arnold's cross from deep deflected off the back of Chris Wood's shoulder and looped over Nick Pope. It was an own goal. Four minutes later, Firmino intercepted Ben Mee's stray pass and drove forward, before releasing Mane at just the right time. He slid the ball past Pope into the corner. Firmino got the third with a sweet strike into the corner from the edge of the box. The game ended strangely, with Mane angry with Salah for not passing to him. Klopp withdrew Mane, who vented his frustrations on the bench. With the help of Wijnaldum, the pair sorted out their differences in the changing room. Liverpool had broken a club record by winning their 13th top-flight match in a row.

Rafa Benitez had left Newcastle for the Chinese Super League during the summer. Now managed by Steve Bruce, the Magpies took an early lead at Anfield in mid-September but were beaten 3-1. With Firmino and Henderson rested, Liverpool started poorly, and Jetro Willems arrowed a shot into the top corner in the seventh minute. Matip was denied a penalty after being wrestled to the ground at a corner. Mane equalised with a lovely side-footer into the top corner, before making it 2-1 five minutes before the break. Wijnaldum and Robertson came close to scoring in the second half, before Liverpool wrapped up the game with a stunning third, as Salah took Firmino's backheel, motored past a couple of static defenders and beat Martin Dubravka. "Liverpool's front three are as good as you can get," admitted Bruce. After a slow start to the season, Robertson played tremendously. For the first time since Jim Beglin had broken a leg at Goodison in 1987, Liverpool had a world-class left back. A couple of hours later, Norwich made it a perfect afternoon for the Reds when they beat Manchester City.

The first defeat of the season came in the Champions League at Carlo Ancelotti's Napoli, where the Reds had also lost a year earlier. On that occasion, they had got what they deserved. This time, they were unlucky. Adrian made an early double save from Fabian Ruiz. Mane was denied by Alex Meret. Mario Rui as good as prevented a goal by cutting out Milner's low cross to Salah. Firmino's header went inches wide, with Meret stranded. Adrian, who along with Fabinho was Liverpool's best player, saved superbly from Dries Mertens a couple of minutes into the second half. Mane blew a two-on-one with an overhit pass to Salah. Meret saved tremendously from Salah. Callejon was then lucky to be awarded a penalty after a challenge from Robertson. Adrian got a hand to Mertens' penalty, but in it crept. Fernando Llorente, who had been a Tottenham substitute in Madrid, made it 2-0 in the second minute of injury time, following Van Dijk's error.

A crucial Premier League win was gained at Stamford Bridge as the Reds maintained their 100-percent start. Salah rolled a 14th-minute free kick along the edge of the box to open up the angle, and Alexander-Arnold curled it with unerring accuracy into the top corner of Kepa Arrizabalaga's goal. Adrian denied Tammy Abraham. Cesar Azpilicueta thought he had equalised, but Mason Mount was ruled to be offside in the build-up by VAR. Firmino soon made it two, heading in Robertson's cross on the half hour. The Brazilian was denied another by the keeper in the second half, before N'Golo Kante scored a marvellous goal from the edge of the box after a mazy dribble, but the Reds held on for three valuable points, with Matip and Fabinho in great form again. A day earlier, Manchester City had beaten Watford 8-0, but Liverpool were still five points clear.

Keita made his first appearance since the Nou Camp in May in the League Cup at MK Dons. Caoimhin Kelleher, Elliott, Brewster, Herbie Kane and Van den Berg made their Liverpool debuts - the latter two came off the bench. There were also starts for Hoever and Curtis Jones. On the day he became Liverpool's youngest starter at 16 years and 174 days, Elliott hit the bar in each half in a performance of great promise. Milner made it 1-0 from distance, although goalkeeper Stuart Moore should have kept it out. The Dons hit the post in the second half, before Hoever headed in Milner's left-wing cross on his first start for the club. Oxlade-Chamberlain hit a post with a low drive from 30 yards.

Liverpool enjoyed some luck at Bramall Lane when Wijnaldum's weak shot in the 70th minute squirmed under the body of Dean Henderson and trickled over the line. It was the only goal of the game. Mane mishit his shot after a perfect long pass from man of the match Van Dijk. Then he hit a post. He was denied a clear penalty in the second half. So much for VAR. Adrian touched Oliver Norwood's long-ranger around the post. Origi replaced Henderson as the Reds switched to a bold 4-2-4 formation. Wijnaldum's shot was a volley from the edge of the box, and it was Liverpool's first attempt on target. Henderson, on loan from Manchester United, had an otherwise excellent season for the Blades, but made a schoolboy error in letting the Dutchman's daisy cutter slip through his fingers. Salah squandered a late chance to make it two. Liam Clarke should have equalised at the other end.

Anfield got its first glimpse of Takumi Minamino, when Red Bull Salzburg came to Anfield in the Champions League. All seemed well for the Reds when they led 3-0 after 36 minutes, but the Japanese star helped inspire a magnificent comeback which so nearly earned the Austrians a result. Minamino's third-minute shot from 20 yards flashed just wide. Mane soon scored against his old club, when he took a return pass from Firmino and slid it past Cican Stankovic. Robertson made it two, starting a move in his own half before bombing forward and turning Alexander-Arnold's low cross into the net. Salah got the third, after Stankovic made a hash of Firmino's header. But Hwang Hee-chan quickly pulled one back, turning Van Dijk and firing emphatically into the corner. The Reds led 3-1 at the break. Minamino's big moment came ten minutes into the second half, when he volleyed Hwang's cross past Adrian. Klopp grinned on the touchline. Perhaps he knew something. And Anfield was stunned when Minamino crossed for substitute Erling Haaland to equalise. Gomez and Van Dijk weren't having a comfortable evening. Liverpool still had one more gear to hit, and Salah won the game, latching onto Firmino's header and steering the ball home in front of the Kop. It had been a crazy night.

The 2-1 win at home to third-placed Leicester City proved to be a key stepping stone en route to the title. Brendan Rodgers' players looked set to earn a point, when the Reds were awarded a 95th-minute penalty. Milner had earlier sent an inviting cross from Alexander-Arnold high into the Kop. Firmino was next to waste an inch-perfect cross from the young right back. Milner made amends by playing a sumptuous ball down the left that was too good for Jonny Evans. Mane ran on to it and beat Kasper Schmeichel. An inability to get a second meant that James Maddison's goal in the 80th minute could have been very costly. Salah's ankle was injured by Hamza Choudhury, who was lucky to stay on the field. But Liverpool's mental fortitude surfaced again. With Schmeichel drawn out of his goal, all Mane had to do was find Lallana a couple of yards away for the winner, but he was fouled by Marc Albrighton, and Milner beat the Danish keeper from the spot. A day later, Manchester City lost at home to Wolves. Liverpool's pristine record after eight matches meant they were eight points clear.

Despite having a two-week international break to recover, Salah wasn't fit to play against 14th-placed Manchester United at Old Trafford. Origi took his place. The Reds weren't at their best but were unlucky to trail to Marcus Rashford's goal ten minutes before half-time, after Origi had been fouled. United countered quickly, and Rashford beat the returning Alisson to score. But although it was clearly a foul, VAR deemed it not serious enough to overturn. Mane thought he had equalised, but VAR ruled it out, as the ball had accidentally brushed his arm in the build-up. According to a new rule, it was the correct decision to disallow it. Liverpool grew into the game, and after switching to 4-2-4 again, they equalised on 85 minutes, when Lallana touched in Robertson's low cross. It was his first goal since May 2017 and his last for the club. Oxlade-Chamberlain was inches away from finding the bottom corner in the dying embers of the game. The Reds had shown character to gain a point, but they had been poor - Alexander-Arnold, Henderson, Fabinho and Firmino in particular. Liverpool's run of consecutive Premier League wins had been halted at 17. United were now two points clear of the relegation zone.

A 4-1 win in Genk three days later saw Oxlade-Chamberlain score one of Liverpool's best goals of the season. It took him two minutes to score his first, when he took Fabinho's pass and sent a low shot into the corner from 25 yards. Alisson made a key save from Paul Onuachu minutes later. Firmino played Mane in on goal with a stunning round-the-corner backheel, but the goalkeeper came to the rescue of his team. Mbwana Samatta had a header disallowed by VAR for offside. Oxlade-Chamberlain's second came 12 minutes into the second half when, positioned in the 'D', he flicked Firmino's pass with the outside of the toe of his right boot and sent it spinning into the net via the underside of the bar. The third goal was a classic example of Liverpool laying a pressing trap from an opposition throw-in. They left an easy option for the taker of the throw, who was ten metres short of halfway. As soon as the ball was released, Wijnaldum charged towards the recipient, Onuachu, and pinched the ball. The front three then combined for Mane to lift the ball over the sprawling keeper. Nine seconds elapsed between the Genk throw-in and the goal. Salah scored the fourth after a glorious turn on the edge of the box. Genk got one back through Stephen Odey, after Lovren lost the ball in the right-back area.

Another one-goal win in the Premier League came at home to Spurs, whose fortunes had plummeted since the Champions League Final, to the extent that Mauricio Pochettino was now on borrowed time. But the visitors did take the lead inside 47 seconds. Henderson was dispossessed in midfield, Moussa Sissoko carried it forward, Son Heung-min's shot hit the bar after a huge deflection off Lovren's head and Harry Kane stooped to head home the rebound in front of a disbelieving Kop. Based on intense pressing, Liverpool dominated the rest of the game, despite 89 minutes of Spurs time-wasting. Paulo Gazzaniga was alert enough to make a double save from Salah and Firmino. The Argentine then kept out a piledriver from Alexander-Arnold. Son should have doubled the lead when he rounded Alisson, but he could only hit the bar. Gary Neville, these days a supporter of whomever Liverpool were playing, groaned in the commentary box. He knew what was about to come from the champions-elect. Henderson, with his left foot, found the corner of the Kop net after a lofted ball from man of the match Fabinho. The Reds had 38 minutes to find a winner. They managed it in 23. Mane was fouled by Serge Aurier, and Salah blasted home the winner from 12 yards. It was another victory for Liverpool's endless reserves of persistence and character.

The latest home game with Arsenal brought about another five goals, although in different circumstances from usual. It was in the League Cup, so both teams fielded several young players. And the Gunners managed to score five themselves as the teams produced the highest-scoring match in the history of the competition, before the Reds progressed on penalties. Young Welsh right back Neco Williams made his debut. He was joined in the starting line-up by Kelleher, Van den Berg, Elliott and Brewster. Oxlade-Chamberlain was released by Williams. He crossed from the right and Shkodran Mustafi got to the ball before Brewster to score an early own goal. The Gunners responded to lead 3-1 through Lucas Torreira, Mesut Ozil and Gabriel Martinelli. Milner pulled a goal back with a penalty just before half-time, after Elliott was fouled. Arsenal led 3-2 at the break. Milner then played a terrible back pass, and Ainsley Maitland-Niles made it 4-2 on 54 minutes. Back came Liverpool. Oxlade-Chamberlain hammered in a fabulous 25-yarder. Origi turned and blasted in from 20 yards. The Gunners scored a long-ranger of their own when Joe Willock beat Kelleher from over 25 yards. And then, in the 90th minute, the impressive Williams crossed for Origi to make it 5-5 with an overhead kick. Milner, Lallana, Brewster and Origi were successful in the shootout. Kelleher's save from Dani Ceballos meant that it was down to Curtis Jones to win the game, and the local boy planted his penalty into the bottom corner, via the inside of the post. The Reds would go to Villa Park for the quarter-final. The only problem was that they were also due to be in Qatar, playing in the Club World Cup.

Liverpool would go on to win the Premier League by such a convincing margin that there was never a that-was-when-we-won-it moment. The closest may have been at the start of November, when they travelled to Villa Park and Manchester City hosted Southampton simultaneously. The Premier League's top two both found themselves 1-0 down at half-time. Both came back to win 2-1. But the manner of Liverpool's win energised their campaign further and must have hurt City. James Ward-Prowse put the Saints ahead at the Etihad on 13 minutes. Very soon, Trezeguet scored for Villa, with Liverpool's high line at a wide free kick failing to catch him offside. Firmino had a goal controversially ruled out by VAR when his armpit was deemed to be offside, even though the line drawn on the screen appeared to be wonky. In the second half, Mane's close-range header was kept out spectacularly by Tom Heaton. Lallana, who had started in the holding role instead of the rested Fabinho, was denied a penalty when his shot was charged down by the hands of Bjorn Engels. City, meanwhile, had gone 2-1 up. The Reds were still behind, and if they couldn't get a goal, City would have the chance to come to Anfield and go top on goal difference. Enter Mane. His deep cross was headed in at the back post by Robertson in the 87th minute. The Scotsman grabbed the ball and sprinted to the centre circle. As City fans left for home, Liverpool were still plugging away, searching for a winner. Deep into injury time, Alexander-Arnold's free kick was deflected behind for a corner. He took the kick himself, and Mane's glancing header bounced once before nestling in the corner of the net. Klopp celebrated with Lallana on the bench. The Reds were still six points clear. They could increase it to nine by beating City in the next league game.

Genk came to Anfield and put up an admirable fight before going down 2-1. Wijnaldum stabbed home the opener, after the visitors couldn't clear Milner's cross. Gaetan Coucke made a double save from Keita. Salah flashed a shot wide. But the Belgians equalised through Mbwana Samatta's towering header. They could have taken the lead soon after. But Oxlade-Chamberlain, playing up front, came to the rescue with his third goal in two games against Genk, when he turned and fired into the bottom corner of the Kop goal. Alisson's late save from Bryan Heynen ensured the lead remained intact. Nine points from 12 meant a home win over Napoli on matchday five would ensure progress to the last 16.

For much of the Villa game, journalists would have been sharpening their pencils, preparing to criticise Klopp for resting Fabinho. The manager had taken the decision because the Brazilian was a booking away from missing the City game. It turned out to be a masterstroke, because the midfielder was at his imperious best as Liverpool beat the champions 3-1. The visitors had to make do without their goalkeeper, Ederson, with Claudio Bravo coming into the side. Surprisingly, they kicked off as favourites to win the match. City had an early penalty appeal for handball against Alexander-Arnold turned down. At the speed of light, Liverpool surged upfield, and Fabinho thumped in a glorious sixth-minute goal from 25 yards. VAR had the onerous task of deciding whether to give City a penalty or to award a goal to Liverpool. They went with the latter. City did have the better of the play in the first 13 minutes, but they were two down by that point. Alexander-Arnold played a cross-field ball to die for to Robertson on the other flank. The Scottish captain elected not to release Mane, instead crossing to Salah, who had been poor in recent weeks. But after one bounce, he headed Liverpool's second goal into the corner of the Anfield Road net. The Reds had only been out of their own half a couple of times and were 2-0 up, but despite City cursing their ill fortune, they had allowed themselves to be countered twice in a game of such importance.

Six minutes into the second half, Mane headed in a cross by Henderson, who wasn't fully fit, to make it 3-0. Liverpool's midfield had dominated City's. Bernardo Silva got one back. Raheem Sterling wanted a handball against Alexander-Arnold, but the referee's refusal to point to the spot prompted Pep Guardiola to lose his rag, Basil Fawlty style, waving two fingers in the air. Sterling lost his temper with Gomez late in the game and still hadn't forgiven him when they met up on England duty the next day. He was turfed out of Gareth

Southgate's squad for confronting the Liverpool defender. Liverpool were nine points clear of City, who were now fourth behind Chelsea and Leicester. Despite creating plenty of chances, they looked a shadow of the side that had amassed 198 points in the last two seasons. Nothing went right for Sergio Aguero, who still hadn't scored at Anfield. City had won this fixture once in 38 years. The result felt symbolic of the power shift between the two clubs.

Another late winner was needed at Selhurst Park as the Reds won 2-1. Palace's Jordan Ayew spurned an early chance. VAR disallowed a Palace goal for Ayew's needless foul on Lovren as a free kick was crossed in. More VAR conspiracies were floated on social media. Liverpool didn't have a shot on target in the first half, but Mane scored for the fifth game in a row against Palace, in the 49th minute. His unconvincing finish went in off both posts. Firmino went clean though but failed to score. Christian Benteke was a whisker away with a scissor kick. Wilfried Zaha equalised with eight minutes left when he fired across Alisson into the corner. But the Reds went straight up the other end, and Firmino ended a run of nine games without a goal, with a side-footed finish from close range after the hosts couldn't clear Alexander-Arnold's corner.

The Reds were unable to progress to the Champions League last 16 when they could only draw at home to Napoli. Dries Mertens gave the Neapolitans the lead on 21 minutes, after a foul on Van Dijk went unpunished. Kalidou Koulibaly cleared off the line from Firmino. In-form Lovren, who had played well against City and Palace, headed an equaliser halfway through the second half, but the Reds were unable to find a winner. It was another performance riddled with imperfections, but the Reds would qualify for the last 16 with a draw in Austria. Even worse than the inability to win was an ankle-ligament injury sustained by Fabinho. With the winter period crammed full of important fixtures, Liverpool would be without their world-class holding midfielder for 13 matches. There was worse news a day later when David Duckenfield was found not guilty of gross negligence manslaughter of those unlawfully killed at Hillsborough.

For the seventh time, the Reds won a Premier League match 2-1, this time at home to Brighton. After Jonjo Shelvey had scored a sensational late equaliser for Newcastle in the lunchtime fixture against Manchester City, Van Dijk twice headed in crosses from Alexander-Arnold as his team took a firm grip on the game. All was well until the 77th minute, when Alisson was sent off for handling the ball outside the box. Fortunately, Klopp still had a substitution up his sleeve, so Adrian replaced Oxlade-Chamberlain. To make matters worse, Lewis Dunk beat the Spaniard from the free kick. The Reds had to endure a nervy final ten minutes, but they saw the clock down. They were now 11 points clear but were about to face a hectic nine-match programme in December.

For the second season in a row, Klopp used a midweek fixture in early December to field an experimental line-up. It had worked against Burnley 12 months earlier. This time he did it in the Anfield Derby, the 22nd in a row Everton failed to win. The match was televised on Amazon Prime. Adrian replaced the suspended Alisson. Klopp also drafted in Milner, Lallana, Shaqiri and Origi.

Among the substitutes were Henderson, Firmino and Salah. Origi had been the hero 367 days earlier, and this time he scored twice, including the opener, when he latched onto Mane's perfect through ball, rounded Jordan Pickford and rolled it home. Alexander-Arnold swept a stunning pass over to Mane, who took it on and set up the second for Shaqiri. Michael Keane got one back against the run of play. Lovren's long pass released Origi, and the Belgian brought it down with contemptuous ease, and lifted it over Pickford. Only Robbie Fowler and Steven Gerrard had scored more Premier League goals against the Blues than the Belgian. The long ball was becoming an effective weapon in Liverpool's armoury. Mane side-footed Alexander-Arnold's pass into the bottom corner from the edge of the box to cap a stunning individual performance in the first half. Richarlison got Everton's second just before the interval - the sixth goal in a chaotic half. Firmino embarrassed Mason Holgate, got to the byline and set up Wijnaldum right at the end to make it 5-2. It was reminiscent of John Barnes and Peter Beardsley combining in the famous 5-0 rout of Nottingham Forest in 1988. This team was now at least as good as that one. Everton manager Marco Silva was sacked the next day. Klopp had achieved 100 league wins at Liverpool in 159 matches, quicker than any of his predecessors.

A 3-0 win at struggling Bournemouth maintained Liverpool's unstoppable charge. The opener came from another long ball, this time from Henderson to Oxlade-Chamberlain, who finished first time. With a hamstring concern, Lovren was taken off for Alexander-Arnold. Gomez moved into the middle. It may have been bad luck for the Croat, but Gomez would seize his chance and remain first choice for the season. Man of the match Keita, making his first league start since April, scored the second when he took a return ball from Salah and flicked it past Aaron Ramsdale for his first goal of the season. The scorers were the 15th and 16th players to register a league goal for Liverpool in this record-breaking campaign. The Guinean then set up the Egyptian, who rolled the final goal into the corner of the net. The pair were dovetailing beautifully. Salah looked back to his best after a recent dip in form. Later in the day, City lost the Manchester derby at home to United. Fourteen points clear of the champions, Liverpool were running away with the title.

The required result was attained in Austria, as the Reds beat Salzburg 2-0 to progress in the Champions League. Keita and Salah shone again, scoring both goals just before the hour. Van Dijk was everyone's man of the match, with another colossal display. Takumi Minamino was involved in an early scramble in front of Alisson when he or Hwang Hee-chan could have scored. Minamino then set up teenager Erling Haaland, but Alisson saved. Keita played Salah in on goal, but he dragged it horribly wide. The two combined again in first-half injury time, but Cican Stankovic denied Keita. The Egyptian blazed over at the start of the second half when played in by Keita once more. Salah was then denied when going around the keeper. Haaland hit the side-netting. Finally, the Reds took the lead when Keita headed in Mane's cross with the goalkeeper out of the picture. Then Salah, previously so wasteful, took the ball around Stankovic way out on the right and squeezed the ball home from the tightest of angles. Mane scooped a late chance over the bar. It mattered not. The holders were in the last 16, where they would face Atletico Madrid.

The home game with bottom side Watford was the last before the departure for Qatar. Nigel Pearson had just taken over as Watford's manager, and they played well, but a couple of Salah goals were the difference. Running on to Mane's pass, he cut across Kiko Femenia and bent the ball inside Ben Foster's far post. At the other end, Ismaila Sarr totally missed his kick from point-blank range. Mane buried Shaqiri's cross, but VAR spotted a marginal offside. In the last minute, Origi's shot was heading wide, but Salah flicked it past Foster for his second goal. The Reds flew out of the UK ten points clear of Leicester and 14 ahead of Manchester City. They would be top on Christmas Day. Eight of the last eleven festive leaders had gone on to win the Premier League. On the three occasions it hadn't happened, Liverpool had been the team to fall short.

With the senior players and some of the best kids watching from their Doha hotel 4,000 miles away, the youngest team in Liverpool's history took to the field for the quarter-final of the League Cup at Aston Villa. Neil Critchley, the Under-23s manager, was in charge for the night. There were a club-record eight debutants – Isaac Christie-Davies, Luis Longstaff, Morgan Boyes, Tony Gallacher, Thomas Hill, Jack Bearne, Leighton Clarkson and James Norris, with the latter three coming off the bench. Elliott nearly scored early in the game, but his shot was palmed away by Orjan Nyland. At the other end, Conor Hourihane scored slightly fortuitously from a wide free kick. The second was even luckier, when a Villa cross hit Boyes and looped over Kelleher. They had started so well but were two down in 17 minutes. Jonathan Kodjia scored two more before the break as Villa threatened to overwhelm the teenagers. The Reds competed strongly for the second half but conceded a fifth to Wesley at the end. Elliott and Hoever were Liverpool's most notable performers.

The Reds joined the FIFA Club World Cup at the semi-final stage and faced the Mexicans Club de Futbol Monterrey at the Khalifa International Stadium, a week before Christmas. Henderson played centre back, in the absence of Van Dijk (who was ill), Matip, Lovren and Fabinho, and did a decent job. Firmino and Mane were benched. Salah played a superb through ball to Keita, who scored his third goal in three appearances on 12 minutes, but Rogelio Funes Mori, twin brother of the former Everton player, made it 1-1 almost immediately. Alisson made a couple of key saves in the first half. Firmino replaced Origi on 85 minutes. The Brazilian had scored one goal in his last 16 appearances, but he turned in Alexander-Arnold's perfectly-placed low cross in the last minute. Alisson, Keita and Salah were the best players.

Brazilian champions Flamengo, conquerors of Bob Paisley's Liverpool in the 1981 final, were waiting for them in the final and, for the first time in four attempts, the Reds were crowned champions of the world. The team was: Alisson; Alexander-Arnold, Gomez, Van Dijk, Robertson; Henderson, Oxlade-Chamberlain, Keita; Salah, Firmino, Mane. A 12-man bench included Hoever and

Elliott, who had flown over for the final after playing so well at Villa. Firmino skied an early opportunity. He hit a post in the second half, and the ball ran along the line and went wide of the other post. It defied the laws of physics. Alisson saved brilliantly from Gabriel Barbosa. Diego Alves tipped over Henderson's piledriver. Mane was awarded a penalty right at the end of the 90, but it was overturned. The goal that confirmed Liverpool's status as world champions came nine minutes into extra time and, unsurprisingly, it came from Firmino. Henderson released Mane with a precise long pass. Up against Rafinha, the last defender, he held the ball up before playing Firmino into the clear. Liverpool's number 9 cut inside the covering Rodrigo Caio and turned the ball home. Substitute Lincoln missed a late chance to force penalties. The outstanding Henderson lifted his third trophy in a little under seven months.

Those hoping that Liverpool would begin to wobble at the top of the Premier League would have been banking on them struggling at second-placed Leicester on Boxing Day, five days after the Flamengo match. After all, a 4,000-mile trip wasn't ideal preparation. Instead, the Reds produced their best performance of the season as they blew Brendan Rodgers' Foxes away. Wijnaldum replaced Oxlade-Chamberlain, who had suffered an ankle knock in the second half of the decider in Qatar. Mane somehow fluffed a first-minute chance, but the in-form Firmino headed Liverpool into a 31st-minute lead from Alexander-Arnold's cross. It was still 1-0 when Leicester caused them some problems just after the hour, but Liverpool cut loose, producing a scintillating final 20 minutes. Substitute Milner made it 2-0 from the spot with his first touch after Caglar Soyuncu handled Alexander-Arnold's corner. Firmino controlled another cross by Alexander-Arnold and casually placed the ball into the top corner with Kasper Schmeichel hopelessly wrong-footed. And then came the goal of the night, as the magnificent Alexander-Arnold did his finest impression of Carlos Alberto's iconic goal in the 1970 World Cup Final. From Mane's pass, he hammered a diagonal shot with his laces into Schmeichel's bottom corner from 20 yards. The game precipitated an alarming collapse in Leicester's form, and they went on to collect just 23 points in their last 19 games as they slipped out of the Champions League places. As for the Reds, they were purring. It looked like nobody could stop them.

The final game of a momentous 2019 came at home to Wolves. The Reds were rescued by two VAR decisions, although both were correct. Salah turned Alexander-Arnold's cross just over the bar. Mane put a promising chance wide. With three minutes of the half left, Van Dijk's long ball was touched onto Mane by Lallana, and the Senegalese turned it inside Rui Patricio's near post. It was initially disallowed for handball by Lallana, but VAR disagreed and awarded the goal. Pedro Neto thought he'd equalised on the stroke of half-time, but it was chalked off for an offside in the build-up. The decisions were correct, but they spurred Wolves into raising their game. They were the better team in the second half, but Liverpool managed to keep them at bay to end the year on 55 points from a possible 57, 13 clear of Leicester with a game in hand. Only the most calamitous collapse could deny them now.

As Liverpool entered the 2020s, they couldn't have been in better shape. Klopp had moulded a wonderful side that was breaking records galore. The other teams were miles behind. Talk of Liverpool blowing the title was no longer taken seriously. But there was bad news before Liverpool kicked off against Sheffield United on 2nd January, when Keita hobbled out of the warm-up with a groin strain. The Guinean was finally beginning to look like the midfielder Liverpool had snared from RB Leipzig, but now he would miss five matches and presumably wouldn't go straight back into the starting side. Milner replaced him. After three and a half minutes, George Baldock slipped, allowing Robertson to roam free down the left, and his low cross was turned in to the net by Salah. Dean Henderson made one of the saves of the season, when he tipped over from Salah. He soon denied him again, and the Egyptian then hit the post when he clipped a lofted pass into the area that everybody missed. Mane made it two on 64 minutes when he exchanged passes with Salah. Henderson parried his shot, but Mane hammered the rebound into the roof of the net from a couple of yards. Elliott made his Premier League debut in injury time at the age of 16. Henderson was magnificent again in the holding role. Some had panicked when Fabinho got injured, but the skipper ensured he hadn't been missed. Liverpool had now gone 12 months without losing a league game. Twenty-four hours earlier, Klopp had completed the signing of Salzburg's Takumi Minamino, who had been so impressive against the Reds in both Champions League matches. He cost £7.25 million and would join the squad immediately.

Many expected Klopp to rest some stars for the FA Cup third round, which just happened to be an Anfield Derby, the 23rd in a row Everton failed to win. But no one expected him to go nuclear. To the disbelief of all and sundry, his team selection was Adrian; Williams, Gomez, Nathaniel Phillips, Milner; Lallana, Jones, Chirivella; Elliott, Minamino, Origi. Incredibly, they won. Liverpool were clinging on in the first 30 minutes, as Everton, now managed by Carlo Ancelotti, forced Adrian into a string of saves. And they lost their skipper, Milner, to a hamstring injury in the ninth minute. He was replaced at left back by debutant Yasser Larouci. The Algerian teenager took his place in the defence next to Phillips, who had been recalled from a loan spell at Bundesliga 2 side Stuttgart just for this match. Lallana assumed the armband. Having failed to score when they were on top, Everton wilted. They were under enormous pressure to end their miserable winless streak at Anfield, especially as they were up against a team of fringe players. As they deteriorated, Liverpool grew, and Jones produced one of the great derby moments in the 71st minute, when he took Origi's pass on the edge of the box and curled a magnificent right-footed shot into the top corner of Pickford's net. Anfield exploded. Everton were humiliated. In the remaining 20 minutes, they didn't threaten an equaliser. The standout players were Adrian, Williams, Chirivella, Lallana, Jones and Larouci. "I loved it," said Klopp. "I loved each second of this game." Bill Shankly's quip that the best two teams on Merseyside were Liverpool and Liverpool's reserves was true again. Liverpool hadn't lost to Everton at Anfield in over 20 years.

The second league match of 2020 saw the Reds travel to Tottenham's new ground for the first time. As they were now managed by Jose Mourinho, Liverpool fans expected another masterclass in bus parking, especially as the Portuguese had recently said as a Sky Sports pundit it was the only way to stop Klopp's team. Tottenham did indeed stick rigidly to a typical Mourinho template, but Liverpool created plenty of chances and won the game with a beautiful piece of skill from Firmino, who beat debutant Japhet Tanganga prior to slamming the ball past Paulo Gazzaniga. The Reds failed to add to the goal, but near the hour mark they produced a breathtaking ten-second move involving Alexander-Arnold, Wijnaldum, Firmino, Henderson, Salah and Mane, which sliced Spurs open before Mane's pass was cut out en route to Firmino. Liverpool had now beaten Spurs at White Hart Lane, Wembley and Tottenham Hotspur Stadium and could now boast a win at more away grounds in the Premier League era than any other club. Since 1992, they had only failed to win at Nottingham Forest's City Ground and Blackpool's Bloomfield Road.

The 2-0 win over Manchester United, a day after City conceded a late equaliser at home to Crystal Palace, was another huge step towards the Holy Grail. Liverpool were now 16 points clear with a game in hand. Indeed, Salah's injury-time clincher was the most celebrated goal of the season. United made a decent fist of denying the Liverpool full backs too much space, but their three centre backs were pulled all over the place by Mane, Firmino and Salah. Henderson and Wijnaldum were magnificent again as the Reds dominated the midfield. Klopp's men should have had a hatful. Goals by Firmino and Wijnaldum were disallowed, while Mane and Salah squandered several gilt-edged chances. Henderson hit a post from 20 yards, via David de Gea's fingertips. At half-time, they only had Van Dijk's bullet header from Alexander-Arnold's corner to show for their efforts. Somehow, it was only 1-0 as the end of the match was in sight. United sent in a few crosses as the crowd began to worry. Alisson took a routine catch. Fifty-thousand Reds urged him to hold on to the ball and waste time. He didn't. He saw the unmarked Salah near halfway. His long punt sent the Egyptian free. Having never scored against Manchester United, Salah held off Daniel James, bore down on De Gea and slipped the ball into the net. Off came his shirt. Alisson was first to congratulate him. The euphoria was off the charts, as Anfield trembled to the words, "We're gonna win the league," sung for the first time in the season. It was only three points, but it was the sweetest of victories.

No other team would have beaten in-form Wolverhampton Wanderers twice in a matter of weeks, but a gritty 2-1 win was earned at Molineux. Henderson nodded home Alexander-Arnold's early corner, but an inability to score a second and an injury to Mane, replaced by Minamino, kept Wolves in the contest. Salah spurned chances either side of half-time and was soon punished as the outstanding Adama Traore crossed for Raul Jimenez to head past Alisson. Wolves controlled the next 15 minutes. Gomez made a great block. Alisson denied Traore and Jimenez. Things evened up in the final 20 minutes, and one sensed Wolves had missed the boat. Sure enough, it was the Reds who converted one of their chances. Alexander-Arnold's throw-in was missed by Coady and found Salah, who kept the ball brilliantly from three defenders. Henderson found Firmino, who cut across Conor Coady and fired magnificently into Rui Patricio's top corner. It was the Reds' 12th goal of the season from a throw-in. Thomas Gronnemark was earning his corn. The Reds held on to record a win that perfectly epitomised the character of Klopp's Liverpool. Gomez, Henderson and Wijnaldum were the pick of the bunch.

A team similar to the one against Everton threw away a 2-0 lead at Shrewsbury in the fourth round of the FA Cup. Jones again scored the first goal after a slide-rule pass by the impressive Chirivella. A comical own goal just seconds after the break from Donald Love doubled the advantage. But the Reds eased up, not helped by poor performances from Lovren, Matip and Fabinho, all of whom were making their first starts after injury. Midway through the half, Larouci conceded a penalty, although his foul on Laurent had taken place outside the box. There was no VAR to overturn it. Cummings slotted past the otherwise outstanding Adrian. Ten minutes later, Cummings controlled a long ball, beat Lovren and calmly finished past the Spanish keeper. Substitute Salah missed a late headed chance. Klopp later ruffled some feathers by saying he would not be present at the replay, nor would any senior players, citing a letter from the FA in April which promised a winter break.

Liverpool broke a record set by Preston North End in 1889 when they won 2-0 at West Ham. They had now beaten every other team in the league, and they were the quickest to achieve the feat, having done it by January, compared to Preston's February. David Moyes' Hammers were relentlessly negative, playing a rigid 5-4-1 formation. The Reds didn't need to progress from second gear. Origi won a penalty on 34 minutes, which Salah converted to make it 14 successful spot kicks on the bounce for the team, going back to the autumn of 2018. The club record of 21 had been set between 1986 and 1988, courtesy of John Wark, Jan Molby, John Aldridge and Peter Beardsley. Oxlade-Chamberlain ran onto Salah's exquisite pass seven minutes into the second half to make it 2-0. West Ham, only above the drop zone on goal difference, still offered nothing, and Liverpool were able to ease up.

Two days before the home game with Southampton, the club unveiled a statue of Bob Paisley carrying a battered and bruised Emlyn Hughes off the field in 1968, made from one of the most iconic Liverpool photographs ever taken. Fans flocked to have their picture taken with it before their heroes opened up a 22-point lead, a Premier League record, with a 4-0 win over Southampton. The first half was turgid fare, although Van Dijk nearly scored with a backheel, and Firmino was denied a stonewall penalty. Liverpool were in sizzling form after the break. Oxlade-Chamberlain scored from 20 yards early in the second half, straight after a Southampton penalty appeal. Salah had an effort disallowed for offside, after a scintillating move which had started with Alisson on his own goal line. It would have been one of the goals of the season. Henderson was set up by Firmino to make it two. Salah added two more and almost set up a maiden goal for Minamino, who fired a clear-cut chance into the Kop. Each of the scorers played magnificently, as did Firmino, who produced a hat trick of assists.

Klopp was true to his word, staying away from the Shrewsbury replay, leaving Critchley in charge, with none of the senior players involved. The youngest team in the club's history included debutants Adam Lewis, Liam Millar and Jake Cain, with Joe Hardy and Elijah Dixon-Bonner also making their first appearances from the bench. At 19 years and five days, Curtis Jones became the club's youngest captain. The shirt numbers ranged from 46 (Lewis) to 93 (unused substitute James Norris). The Reds had used 69 players in their last 13 FA Cup matches. Incredibly, the team of kids kept the dream alive, as an own goal from former Manchester United defender Ro-Shaun Williams, shortly after Shrewsbury had a goal correctly disallowed by VAR for offside, put the Reds into the fifth round. Sam Ricketts, the Shrewsbury manager, even had the nerve to complain about VAR, conveniently forgetting his side wouldn't have earned the replay had the technology been in place in the first game. The performances of Jones and Neco Williams were astonishing. Kelleher was outstanding in goal, not bad for someone who was an outfield player until he was 12. Leighton Clarkson, signed by the club at the age of seven, got a hero's reception when he was withdrawn in the last minute. Van den Berg and Hoever were unbeatable at the back. Critchley had done an outstanding job, although he would soon be leaving the club and heading to Blackpool.

After the mid-season break, Klopp took his players to the team in last place, Norwich City. The Canaries had beaten Manchester City earlier in the season, but they hadn't beaten the Reds since the Kop's last stand in 1994. Their fans unfurled a huge banner celebrating Justin Fashanu's goal of the season against the Reds in 1980. Liverpool started brightly, with Firmino showing some wonderful touches, but it was Norwich who came closest to scoring in the first half when Lukas Rupp got clear of Liverpool's high line, moved the ball wide of Alisson, shaping to go around him. Instead he passed it to Teemu Pukki, on his left shoulder, but out came a big arm from the Brazilian, and he diverted the ball to safety. Pushing Alexander-Arnold further forward and relying less on the long ball in the second half, the Reds were more effective, but it wasn't until Mane and Fabinho were introduced on the hour that the game turned in their favour. The Brazilian balanced the midfield, allowing Henderson to push forward. Mane created several openings on the left, but the final ball from his teammates was still lacking. In the end, it was he who won the game on 80 minutes, coolly controlling Henderson's 30-yard lofted pass with his right foot, then turning and firing into the bottom corner with his left. There didn't seem to be the room between Tim Krul's hand and the post. But there was, and Liverpool were running away with the title.

The Reds returned to the scene of their sixth European Cup win in mid-February but were beaten 1-0 in the first leg of the first knockout stage. Atletico Madrid's

Saul Niguez scored after four minutes when the Reds failed to clear a corner. The Spaniards went on to deliver a masterclass in both low-block defending and play acting. Even so, Liverpool would have fancied their chances of a result had so many players not been way below their best. Salah spurned three chances. Alexander-Arnold's delivery ranged from average to awful. Fabinho's passing was awry. Firmino wasn't in the game. Nor was Mane before he was withdrawn at the break. His replacement, Origi, had a second half to forget. To cap a disappointing night, Henderson tweaked a hamstring late in the game.

Mane got another late winner against a bottom-three side, scoring the final goal in a 3-2 thriller at home to West Ham. When Wijnaldum headed in Alexander-Arnold's fabulous cross after nine minutes, a routine win seemed inevitable. But Issa Diop glanced in a corner three minutes later. The goal took the wind out of Liverpool's sails, and they threatened little for the rest of the half, other than Van Dijk hitting the bar from a corner. Substitute Pablo Fornals stunned Anfield by sweeping West Ham into a 2-1 lead nine minutes into the second half. Klopp withdrew the ineffective Keita, sending on Oxlade-Chamberlain, who immediately upped the tempo, although Salah was having a frustrating evening. When he was unmarked from 14 yards, his shot trickled towards Fabianski. But the Pole let it squirm under his body, and Liverpool were level with 22 minutes left. An abundance of corners led to nothing, while the Hammers continued to look for a winner at the other end. With just under ten minutes left, Gomez's shot was deflected into the path of Alexander-Arnold in the inside-right channel. He lifted the ball over the advancing keeper, allowing Mane to side-foot home from a couple of yards. The same two players combined again, but VAR correctly adjudged the Senegalese to be offside. West Ham had late chances, but Alisson blocked Jarrod Bowen's dink when he was clean through, and Wijnaldum deflected Mark Noble's shot wide. The Reds had won, but again it was far from convincing. For the third game in a row, they had dominated possession but played poorly. Half of Liverpool's wins so far had been by one goal. After 27 games, they were on 79 points from a possible 81, needing four more wins to clinch the title.

Liverpool's unbeaten Premier League record was ripped up by Watford, where they were hammered 3-0. The injured Gomez and Keita were replaced by Lovren and Oxlade-Chamberlain. Several players were below par in a goalless first half. Salah hitting the side-netting was their only shot. The second half was even worse. A rapid double from Ismaila Sarr gave Liverpool a mountain to climb. Lallana brightened things up off the bench and hit the post with a 20-yard volley. But an atrocious back pass from Alexander-Arnold left Alisson out of position, and Troy Deeney curled the ball into the empty net. It could have been four had Sarr not shot wide when he went clean through. Henderson and Gomez were badly missed. No one was quite sure why Lovren was selected ahead of Matip. Van Dijk had his worst game in a Liverpool shirt. After several unconvincing performances, perhaps a Premier League defeat was in the offing, but nobody would have predicted one in this manner.

A third defeat in four matches came at Stamford Bridge in the fifth round of the FA Cup. The kids had enjoyed a glorious run, seeing off Everton and Shrewsbury, but Klopp fielded a more experienced team, which included Van Dijk, Fabinho and Mane. Adrian kept his place, but 30 seconds after making a great save from Willian, he fumbled a shot from the same player into the corner of the net. The Reds created several chances to get level, including an astonishing triple save from Kepa Arrizabalaga. Liverpool didn't get going in the second half, and when Ross Barkley made it 2-0, they had no answer, despite the introduction of Firmino, Milner and Salah. Williams had another outstanding game at right back. Jones played well and was unlucky to be subbed. But Fabinho continued his struggle to rediscover his pre-injury form.

Liverpool won a record 22nd consecutive home league match when they beat Bournemouth in the last league match played before the season was suspended. The previous record had been held by Bill Shankly's side in 1972. The visitors took an early lead when Callum Wilson tapped in at the back post, but it should have been disallowed for a blatant push on Gomez in the build-up. Firmino missed a great chance to equalise, but the Reds were soon on terms when Salah collected a loose pass from Mane and fired into the bottom corner from near the edge of the box. Later in the first half, Van Dijk slid a ball through to Mane with the Bournemouth defence all at sea. He took a touch and fired in the winner. Mane hit a post with a stunning 25-yarder. Struggling for form, Firmino missed another sitter at the end. The points were actually secured at the other end by Milner, standing in for Robertson at left back, when he made an acrobatic goal-line clearance. City lost to Manchester United the next day to leave Liverpool just two wins away from their Holy Grail.

The second leg of the Champions League tie against Atletico went ahead despite mounting concerns over coronavirus. Amid another raucous European atmosphere at Anfield, the Reds dominated for 95 minutes but still managed to exit the competition. The key to Liverpool's performance was the inclusion of Oxlade-Chamberlain, at the expense of Fabinho, with the returning Henderson playing the anchor role. Oxlade-Chamberlain caused the Spaniards numerous problems, particularly wide on the right, where Alexander-Arnold was also at his best. From Oxlade Chamberlain's cross on 43 minutes, Wijnaldum headed the opening goal past Jan Oblak. Liverpool could have had a hatful in the second half but failed to build on their lead. Robertson, on his 26th birthday, hit the bar. Mane nearly scored at the end with a spectacular scissor kick. In the third minute of extra time, Firmino scored his first Anfield goal of the season, side-footing in the rebound after he had headed Wijnaldum's cross onto the post. Atletico had barely had an attack, but within minutes, Adrian's poor kick led to a goal by substitute Marcos Llorente. The same player made it 2-2 on the night, finishing a speedy counterattack at the end of the first period. And then right at the end of the 120 minutes, he set up a goal for Alvaro Morata. The Spaniards won 4-2 on aggregate.

Two days later the season was suspended, initially until the start of April, because of the pandemic. It was the diagnosis of the Arsenal boss Mikel Arteta that led to the decision. Chelsea's Callum Hudson-Odoi had also tested positive. West Ham director Karren Brady immediately leapt on the chance to claim the season should be expunged, with her club only out of the relegation zone on goal difference. Fans of Liverpool's rivals salivated at the prospect of coronavirus costing the Reds the title, which Klopp later admitted to being worried about. Project Restart was eventually successful, and the season would recommence on Wednesday 17th June, with Aston Villa hosting Sheffield United and Manchester City entertaining Arsenal. The Reds would be in action four days later.

After a 6-0 friendly win over Blackburn at Anfield, Liverpool's first competitive game after the enforced break was at Goodison, as it had been in 1989. And the result was 0-0, as it had been 31 years earlier. Liverpool's players got changed in a car park portacabin. Five substitutes were now permitted, and Klopp made them all by the 73rd minute, which probably stifled his team's flow. There were drinks breaks midway through each half. As with all clubs, Liverpool's shirts carried logos for the NHS and the 'Black Lives Matter' movement, which had come to prominence since the murder of George Floyd by a policeman in America.

Klopp's first starting line-up in 106 days saw six changes from the Atletico match. It was Alisson; Alexander-Arnold, Matip, Van Dijk, Milner; Fabinho, Henderson, Keita; Minamino, Firmino, Mane. The Reds dominated possession but failed to create anything of note. The final ball was lacking, with Alexander-Arnold noticeably below his best. A hamstring concern for Milner saw him replaced at left back by Gomez just before the break. Oxlade-Chamberlain replaced Minamino at half-time. Origi and Wijnaldum came on for Firmino and the outstanding Keita just before the second-half drinks break. Lovren then replaced the injured Matip. The changes seemed to stymie Liverpool's flow. Everton grew into the game, successfully exploiting Lovren's weaknesses, and missed a flurry of chances with ten minutes left. Alisson parried Dominic Calvert-Lewin's backheel. Tom Davies hit the post with the follow-up under pressure from Gomez. From the corner, Calvert-Lewin headed a great chance wide. Then Richarlison was denied by Alisson after rolling Lovren, but he should have picked out the unmarked Alex Iwobi for an open goal. Everton had created more in three minutes than either side had done in the entire game. Fabinho's injury-time free kick was tipped over by Jordan Pickford. The spoils were shared. Everton had now gone 22 derbies without a win.

Next up was Crystal Palace on the Wednesday, two days after City had beaten Burnley. Five more points – either gained by Liverpool or dropped by City – were required. The Reds produced a counter-pressing masterclass and created more in the first ten minutes than they had in 90 at Goodison. Wijnaldum and Henderson missed early chances. Firmino and Mane looked sharp. Alexander-

445

Arnold opened the scoring seconds before the mid-half drinks break with a sumptuous 25-yard free kick after Van Dijk had been fouled. It was totally deserved, and the Reds kept turning the screw. Henderson hit a post. Salah then scored the team's 100th goal of the campaign when he chested Fabinho's beautifully lofted pass and fired low into the net. Roy Hodgson's Palace, who lost Wilfried Zaha to injury in the opening stages, had offered nothing. Ten minutes after the restart, man of the match Fabinho cracked in a beauty from 32 yards. He had struggled for several weeks after his return from injury, culminating in his exclusion from the team against Atletico, but had done well at Goodison and was outstanding against Palace. The first substitution didn't come until the 63rd minute, when Henderson was replaced by Oxlade-Chamberlain, and Liverpool had more rhythm without regular interchanges. Mane slotted home the fourth after Salah's magnificent diagonal pass set him free. Williams made his Premier League debut, replacing Alexander-Arnold, and Minamino came on for Firmino. Keita and Elliott replaced Mane and Robertson. Welsh full back Williams was very impressive and came close to scoring on a couple of occasions. Salah was inches away from setting up Minamino for a tap-in. Klopp spoke of his delight at four players pressing a single opponent in the last few minutes. Liverpool's domination was total, with Palace failing to register a single touch in the Reds' penalty area in the entire game. If City failed to win at Chelsea 24 hours later, the Reds would be champions.

After 30 years and 58 days, 1151 league matches, 1957 goals, eight managers and 240 players, Liverpool's status as champions was confirmed on 25th June 2020 when Manchester City lost 2-1 at Stamford Bridge. Footage emerged of the players celebrating Chelsea's winning goal – a penalty by one-time Liverpool target Willian after Fernandinho had been sent off for handball. Klopp phoned his family with ten seconds left and left the phone on a table for them to listen to the celebrations. Crowds flocked to Anfield with flags, scarves, songs and pyrotechnics, turning the night sky red, although they were criticised for not adhering to social-distancing policies. Klopp, wearing a playing shirt, was interviewed at the team hotel and, clearly struggling to keep his emotions in check, ended the interview before breaking down. He was later filmed at the club party, dancing in that same red shirt, with speedos and his cap back to front. The title was wrapped up with seven games remaining, adding two to the record. Sixteen different scorers in a title-winning campaign was another record. Liverpool were simultaneously champions of England, champions of Europe and champions of the world.

Manchester City manager Pep Guardiola and their players afforded Liverpool the traditional guard of honour seven days later. In the first couple of minutes, Salah forced an instinctive save from Ederson. Firmino's follow-up effort was weak. Robertson made a crucial interception to prevent Phil Foden going clear. Mane failed to bury a header after a quick counterattack. The long ball from Alexander-Arnold to Mane was causing City problems. Salah hit the post from the edge of the box. Mane miscontrolled the rebound. Gomez conceded a penalty for holding Raheem Sterling, and Kevin De Bruyne made it 1-0 in the 25th minute. Sterling soon made it two after cutting inside Gomez and slotting past Alisson. Foden was next to score with Robertson out of position. The Scotsman had had a poor half. The Reds went into the break 3-0 down.

Gomez was withdrawn for Oxlade-Chamberlain, with Fabinho moving back into defence. City continued to cut Liverpool open. Gabriel Jesus and Sterling went close. Van Dijk cleared off the line from Foden. From Henderson's pass, Mane suddenly found himself eight yards out with no one near him but inexplicably failed to control the ball with just the keeper to beat. "Mane does his best impression of a Sunday league player," read the minute-by-minute update on the Sky Sports app. Firmino missed another big chance. Liverpool had created just as much as City, but their finishing was dire. Keita and Origi replaced Wijnaldum and Firmino. Oxlade-Chamberlain scored an own goal in trying to prevent Sterling from scoring. Williams was brought on for Alexander-Arnold. Minamino was the final sub, coming on for Mane. Riyad Mahrez thought he had made it 5-0, beating Alisson at his near post deep into injury time, but VAR spotted a handball in the build-up. The Reds had gone five away games without scoring for the first time since 1992. On the strength of one result, City overtook the Reds as favourites to win the 2020-21 Premier League title.

Third-bottom Aston Villa also gave Liverpool a guard of honour when they came to Anfield, as would every opponent for the rest of the season. Under normal circumstances, Anfield would have been bouncing, with the crowd welcoming home the champions for the first time. But it wasn't to be. Klopp brought in Keita, Oxlade-Chamberlain and Origi for Henderson, Wijnaldum and Firmino. Origi started in the middle and then moved to the left. Little of interest happened in the first half, with Liverpool legend Pepe Reina barely tested in the Villa goal. Alisson made a couple of key saves early in the second. Just before the hour, at which point the Reds had had just one attempt on target, the trio that had been left out came on for Fabinho, Oxlade-Chamberlain and Origi. Mane broke the deadlock by turning Keita's low cross onto the underside of the bar and over the line from 12 yards. Reina tipped Firmino's shot around the post. Jones, having just signed a new five-year deal, replaced Keita and fired a wild shot into the supporter-less Kop. But he soon became the team's 17th Premier League scorer of the season when he fired Salah's knock-down into the corner to make it 2-0. Williams made his third consecutive appearance in injury time, replacing Robertson. Liverpool had now won all 25 Premier League games in which they had taken the lead, and they had won all 17 games at Anfield.

The Reds' next assignment was a midweek fixture at Brighton, where Manchester City had sewn up the title a year earlier. Williams started at left back, with Robertson on the bench. Keita made an impressive start and dispossessed Dale Stephens deep in Brighton's half. He squared it to Salah, who side-footed into the corner as the clock hit five minutes. It was Liverpool's first away goal in six games. Two minutes later, Adam Webster coughed up possession. Keita found Firmino, who sent Salah away. The Egyptian laid it off to Henderson, who curled his shot from 20 yards into the bottom corner. It could not have been more Gerrard-like in its execution. Sadly, it would be the skipper's last game of the season, as he later departed with a knee injury. Albion came back into the game, working a few half-chances. Leandro Trossard pulled one back with a clinical finish on the stroke of half-time. Salah wrapped up the game with 14 minutes left, glancing Robertson's corner in at the near post. He was presented with a hat-trick chance in injury time but headed over. The highlight of the game was a backpedalling Van Dijk, going up for an aerial duel, heading it to himself and calmly bringing the ball away.

Williams and Jones started in the home game with Burnley. Nick Pope, who was vying with Alisson for the Golden Glove award, saved brilliantly from Salah, who was three behind Jamie Vardy in the race for the Golden Boot. Jones had a shot deflected wide. Robertson then quite superbly scored his second header of the season from Fabinho's lofted pass. With the last touch of the half, Pope tipped over magnificently from Mane. Still without a home league goal, Firmino hit a post at the Kop end early in the second half. Alexander-Arnold and Keita were introduced during the second drinks break, for Williams and Jones. Both had done well. Jay Rodriguez equalised straight after the resumption, drilling the ball into the corner from the edge of the box. Burnley hit the bar in the closing moments. Salah missed a great chance in injury time, and the game ended 1-1. Liverpool's chance of becoming the first team since 1892 to win every home game had gone, after they had won their first 17.

In the week when Manchester City won their appeal against their two-season ban from European competition, Liverpool made the trip to the Emirates to take on Arsenal. Despite an excellent home record against the Gunners, Klopp had only beaten them away from home once, and he failed to improve on that record. An early clearance from the Arsenal goalkeeper Emiliano Martinez hit Firmino, and the ball rebounded onto the outside of the post. The Brazilian soon released Robertson down the left, and Mane turned in his pullback. It was the 160th goal in Premier League matches between the two sides – a record for any fixture. It was soon followed by another when Van Dijk played a terrible pass, and Alexandre Lacazette nipped in to round Alisson and equalise. Another cataclysmic error, this time from Alisson, handed Reiss Nelson a goal which gave Arsenal the lead before the break. It was reminiscent of the Keystone Cops defending of Klopp's early days at the club. Keita and Minamino replaced Oxlade-Chamberlain and Firmino. Shaqiri was next off the bench for his first appearance since January. He and Origi replaced Wijnaldum and Salah. Mane went in on goal from the left but slid his shot wide under pressure from Ainsley Maitland-Niles. Alexander-Arnold went within a whisker of equalising. Shaqiri put the ball in the net right at the end, but the whistle had already gone for a foul. Hopes of 100 points for the season had gone.

Liverpool would finally get their hands on the Premier League trophy on Wednesday 22nd July, but first the Reds had to overcome Frank Lampard's Chelsea, who were battling for a place in the top four. There was little in the first

20 minutes, but just before the drinks break, Keita's howitzer flew into the top corner of Kepa Arrizabalaga's net. The Guinean had been one of Liverpool's best players since the resumption of the season but often found himself excluded from the starting 11 or being taken off. Still without an Anfield goal in the league, Firmino chose to square to Mane than shoot, but it was blocked. Wijnaldum got free from a corner but could only head straight at the goalkeeper. Mason Mount had a goal disallowed for offside. Alexander-Arnold, already a megastar at 21, curled in a phenomenal free kick from nearly 30 yards. The dubious awarding of the free kick led to a memorable spat between Lampard and the Liverpool bench. It was the full back's second such goal of the season against Chelsea. Robertson's corner was handled, but before the penalty could be awarded, Wijnaldum smashed it into the roof of the net. Olivier Giroud bundled one in after Alisson had saved from Willian.

It was 3-1 at half-time, and none of Liverpool's front three had scored. Salah should have put that right early in the second half but screwed his shot horribly wide. Firmino's big moment finally arrived when he nodded Alexander-Arnold's cross into the Kop goal. It was the young Scouser's 25th Premier League assist in the last two seasons, more than City's Kevin de Bruyne. After a mazy run, Christian Pulisic set up a goal for Tammy Abraham on the hour. Keita and Wijnaldum made way for Milner and Jones, with the latter now qualifying for a medal, as it was his fifth league appearance. After Van Dijk and Gomez collided, Pulisic chested down Callum Hudson-Odoi's cross and hit the top corner to make it 4-3. Oxlade-Chamberlain replaced Salah and soon became the third Liverpool midfielder to score when he turned in Robertson's low cross after a thrilling counterattack. Mane and Firmino were replaced by Origi and Minamino, meaning no farewell Anfield appearance for Lallana. An entertaining game ended 5-3.

Sir Kenny Dalglish had been chosen to present the Premier League trophy to Jordan Henderson on a podium that had been erected at the front of the Kop. Dalglish had managed the Reds to titles in 1986, 1988 and 1990, and had also won the league with Blackburn Rovers five years later. In his second spell as Liverpool manager, he had signed Henderson from Sunderland. The 21-year-old struggled on the right for much of the 2011-12 season, and when Brendan Rodgers took over from Dalglish, he decided to let Henderson go. The midfielder refused, and the rest is history. He was magnificent in Rodgers' last two seasons and took over the captaincy from Steven Gerrard in 2015. He occasionally struggled with fitness and form in Klopp's first couple of seasons, but as the players evolved into the champion team they would become, Henderson emerged as one of the Premier League's best midfielders and one of the club's finest captains.

The stadium lights were switched off. Dalglish, in his red Liverpool mask, emerged with the trophy. Klopp, wearing a playing shirt and with a scarf tied around his right bicep, was first onto the podium, punching the air and hugging Dalglish. He was joined by his staff and players like Kelleher, Lonergan and

Elliott, who didn't qualify for a medal. Alisson was the first of the senior players to climb the steps and receive his medal. Firmino wore red John Lennon glasses. Wijnaldum, also in shades, took a selfie in front of the trophy. Salah had sprayed his hair red in the 30 minutes since the game had ended. It was Minamino's second league title of the season - he triumphed with Red Bull Salzburg in Austria before signing for Liverpool. Then it was the turn of the injured Henderson. He limped up the steps, hugged his former manager, collected his medal, picked up the trophy, faced his teammates and performed his customary shuffle. Turned around with a beaming smile, he hoisted the Premier League trophy into the air. Liverpool were champions again and, poignantly, the trophy was lifted with them on 96 points. The only negative was the lack of fans in the stadium to see it happening, but as Klopp later remarked, "Prepare for a party when this bullshit virus is over!"

A couple of days before the final game of the season, it was announced that Lovren would be joining Zenit St Petersburg for £10.9 million. Lallana would be moving to Brighton and signed off with an emotional interview on LFCTV. But the big news was confirmation that Henderson had won the Football Writers' Player of the Year award, a thoroughly deserved award for a tremendous season.

Liverpool's final game of the season, at Newcastle, saw Klopp rest several stars. His side was Alisson; Williams, Gomez, Van Dijk, Robertson; Wijnaldum, Keita, Milner; Oxlade-Chamberlain, Origi, Minamino. After 26 seconds, Liverpool conceded the fastest goal in their Premier League history, when Dwight Gayle latched on to a quick free kick from former Red Jonjo Shelvey and beat Alisson. The goal stood after a lengthy VAR check for offside. Minamino, yet to score for the Reds, forced a lovely save from Martin Dubravka with a fierce shot heading for the top corner. On the day Van Dijk became Liverpool's first player of the modern era to play in every league match for two seasons, his looping header from Oxlade-Chamberlain's cross made it 1-1 at half-time.

As Firmino, Mane and Salah were ready to come on, Origi let fly with a magnificent curling shot from the outside the box, which put the Reds 2-1 up just before the hour. It was his first goal in 23 games. The assist came from Robertson. For the second season in a row, the Scotsman would finish one behind his fellow full back, Alexander-Arnold, in the assists' column. It was 13-12 this season. It had been 12-11 in the previous season. Their numbers defied belief. They were called full backs, but they played higher up the pitch than most wing backs and had provided more assists than any of their teammates for two seasons in a row. The big three did soon come on, replacing Origi, Minamino and Oxlade-Chamberlain. Salah hit a post with his first touch, as he aimed to become the first Liverpool player since Roger Hunt to score 20 league goals in three consecutive seasons. Williams and Keita were substituted for Alexander-Arnold and Jones. Mane curled an exquisite third, cutting in from the left and beating Dubravka from 20 yards. The full-time whistle sounded. What a season it had been. Liverpool had won the league with 99 points, finishing 18 ahead of Manchester City and 33 ahead of Manchester United and Chelsea in third and fourth. However good the players had been though, this stunning achievement was down to one man more than any other.

What Jurgen Klopp had done in nearly five years at Liverpool was barely believable. To recap, the first Liverpool team he had fielded, in 2015, was: Mignolet; Clyne, Sakho, Skrtel, Moreno; Lucas, Can, Milner; Coutinho, Lallana; Origi. Subs: Bogdan, Toure, Randall, Allen, Ibe, Teixeira, Sinclair. He'd had a fraction of the money spent by the two Manchester clubs, in terms of net spend, yet he had assembled a team that would become champions of England, Europe and the world. He worked with players and improved them. He kept faith in those, like Henderson, who were often criticised. He had quickly fostered a tremendous team spirit and culture. He experimented with various formations before settling on one that few teams could get to grips with. He gave new signings time to bed in. He rarely bought a bad player. He had taken the players' strength and fitness levels beyond any reasonable expectation. He gave academy players their chance. He sold fringe players for huge amounts. He had created "mentality monsters". In short, he had got everything right. Liverpool and Jurgen Klopp were the perfect fit.